Their Bloody Lies
& Persecution

of

DAVID CAMM

Part I

Gary M. Dunn
Retired FBI Agent

the Peppertree Press
www.peppertreepublishing.com

Edited by Cathy Murphy

Cover design and graphics by Hannah Ter Vree.

ISBN: 978-1-61493-851-4
Library of Congress Number: 2022914581
Printed September 2022

This Book is Dedicated to
Jill, Kim, and Brad

**TO THE ONLY ONE
WHO REALLY KNOWS ME:
ALWAYS & FOREVER, GINNY**

*Loving Thanks To
Jessica & J.R.*

TABLE OF CONTENTS

PROLOGUE
The Dark Side

During my law enforcement career, I wore a badge, packed a gun, and arrested bad guys. Then, after I retired from the FBI, I worked relentlessly to free a man already convicted of cold-bloodedly murdering his pretty and intelligent wife, precocious seven-year old son, and full-of-life little five-year old daughter whom he had also molested. I did it all because I lost my moral compass and abandoned any principles of justice I once had. In short, I went to the Dark Side.

At least that's the description of me as painted by some in Indiana law enforcement circles, including former friends and associates. It makes for a simple and compact explanation of why I, after 27 years of service, retired as a Special Agent from the Federal Bureau of Investigation and went to work in 2004 for a defense attorney who represented the most notoriously bad—and by bad, I mean abhorrent—person in the entire state of Indiana. Those who had any knowledge of the case agreed that David Camm, convicted two years before, had cold-bloodedly executed his wife and two small children.

Making it even worse, at least according to the Floyd County, Indiana, prosecutor who convicted Camm, the former Indiana State Police (ISP) trooper had slaughtered his family for three rancid reasons: to cash in over $600,000 in life insurance proceeds; to freely pursue a wild, sex-filled single lifestyle; and, worst of all, to hide the fact he had molested his precious little girl.

After listening to two months of damning testimony, a jury convicted Camm of the murders in 2002, and he was sentenced to 195 years in prison by an outraged judge. Two years later, in August 2004, citizens in the Louisville Metropolitan area, as well as throughout Indiana and the nation, were appalled when the Indiana Court of Appeals reversed all three murder convictions.

Anyone who knew anything of me and my background was shocked when they learned of my involvement in the case. And they had a right to be, as I'd been a devoted law enforcement officer who worked well and closely with men and women of all law enforcement departments and agencies. More than a few had become very good friends as well as confidants with whom I had celebrated arrests, courtroom victories, and justice being served. We'd shared a profound belief that we were not only professionally but personally working for the people we served, and that was especially true for victims of violent crimes and their families.

After learning of the aggressive work I was doing for Camm, some of those former colleagues, including ISP detectives and troopers, had shunned me, complaining to others I had become a traitor to our once-shared cause of seeking justice: "Dunner's gone to the Dark Side."[1]

The ISP was a department I knew well and regarded highly. I had an 18-year, very productive history with "Indiana's Finest," as they were known, including being intimately involved with them in many cases over the years, including a three-year whodunit investigation of the kidnapping of a mentally-disabled Indiana woman whose tortured and sexually-abused body was discovered in Illinois. Because of the successful outcome of that case, including the arrests of five men and women, the convictions of all, and life sentences for the three men, I'd been humbled to be awarded an honorary rank of ISP Lieutenant Colonel. That accolade had meant a lot to me but not nearly as much as my friendship with every detective and most of the troopers and staff in the Bloomington, Indiana, ISP Post.

When I began to school myself on the ISP's investigation of David Camm, conducted by the ISP Sellersburg Post,[2] what I read, saw, and then later experienced was nothing remotely like I had previously experienced with Indiana's Finest.

Camm's arrest, I discovered, was based upon false deductions, distorted allegations and totally inaccurate conclusions. Charges against him occurred well before routine leads had been covered; before many witnesses had been identified or much less interviewed; prior to any forensic evidence being scrutinized, at least by any bona fide expert; and prior to any of that evidence being tested in any laboratory or compared to any database.

The fallacious narrative of the lead detective and the county prosecutor, who had assumed control of the investigation, was contained in a probable cause affidavit charging David Camm with murder and was pushed—and pushed hard—by the prosecutor to a public desperately seeking answers to the horrific murders. That prosecutor, facing a difficult re-election, even later claimed independent and respected witnesses were liars; liars, that is, because they contradicted his official narrative.

That same first prosecutor, in his zeal to convict Camm, also violated the standards as set forth in a well-quoted U.S. Supreme Court ruling.[3] Prosecutors, the Court had written, "may strike hard blows (but are) not at liberty to strike foul ones." Furthermore, prosecutors were in a "very definite sense *the servant of the law*, the twofold aim of which is that *guilt shall not*

---

[1] My FBI nickname was Dunner.

[2] The ISP Sellersburg Post is located nine miles north of Louisville, Kentucky.

[3] Berger v. United States, 1935.

escape or innocence suffer…[4] Sadly, a guilty man did escape punishment, and an innocent one did suffer due to the foul blows struck by that first prosecutor and others with an eventual cost of over \$5 million to the taxpayers of Floyd County.

Over those same 13 years, several judges made critical, very questionable, and/or wrong decisions, not surprisingly almost always in favor of the prosecution, as the State of Indiana was intransigent in keeping David Camm behind bars.

The horrific murders of Kim, Brad, and Jill Camm were beyond tragic. The noxious prosecutions and false incarcerations of David Camm, however, were atrocious yet preventable. I can speak to all of this since I know this case very well, having spent nine years of my life immersed in it. I know of the leaders who spearheaded the deplorable efforts, their many bogus allegations, the unraveling of their official stories and theories, the horrendous deals made with jailhouse informants/liars, and of lost or undocumented parts of their investigations.

Indeed, and as we're sadly learning more and more in the United States, someone convicted of a crime doesn't always mean 1) the agency which investigated the crime conducted a fair, thorough, and impartial investigation without any preconceived conclusions or biases; 2) "forensic experts" are really experts who rely on the principles of science; 3) prosecutors played fair and/or by the rules; and 4) the rulings of judges follow the law and the facts.

Those four failings, however, paled in comparison to the handling of the real killer, who had only been discovered through the relentless efforts of those defending Camm. Once identified, that callous and hardcore murderer, who had remained hidden for over four years, was first treated by the authorities not as the perpetrator, but as a victim.

Even though I was able to secure a confession from that violent, Satan-worshipping, psychopathic murderer of three innocents, his confession and admissions were also ignored by the "fresh eyes" investigative team who then, unbelievably, helped him escape the death penalty in exchange for an impossible and thoroughly mendacious story implicating Camm.

By any decent measure, when it came to the case of David Camm, the justice system in Indiana was perverted. That pernicious defilement, however, was staunchly opposed as several stalwarts never folded under the State's enormous pressure. Under the most difficult of times, David exhibited an incredible will to survive and overcome; his defense teams brought honor and integrity to the legal profession; and David's family and friends, and

---

[4] Emphasis mine.

in particular his uncle, Sam Lockhart, never wavered, even under withering personal and financial pressure.

While this is a damning story in so many ways, it is also an inspiring tale of righteous and steadfast individuals who came together and tenaciously fought for—and finally achieved—justice for an innocent man and his slain family.

My thoughts and views are mine and mine alone, not only based upon my extensive involvement in this case but also on my career of investigating innumerable crimes, interviewing thousands of witnesses, interrogating and arresting hundreds of suspects, writing dozens of affidavits, executing uncountable search warrants, seizing and scrutinizing evidence of every kind and type, and testifying in many grand juries and in federal and state courtrooms throughout the United States. My opinions, assessments, and deductions, therefore, come from the standpoint of a very knowledgeable, experienced, and successful criminal investigator.

I am not an attorney, though, and my story is not predicated upon explaining legalities or arguing law. I will occasionally provide quotes from trial testimonies, legal briefs, rulings, and appellate opinions. For me to attempt to quantify and fully describe the utterly outstanding defenses of David by his three legal teams of Mike McDaniel, Debbie McDaniel, and Patrick Biggs; Kitty Liell and Stacy Uliana; and Stacy, Rick Kammen, and Mary Spears, all of whom were/are highly skilled and dedicated attorneys and litigators, would be a huge disservice to all of them.

Because the David Camm case was one of the most lengthy, expensive, and hotly contested criminal cases ever in the State of Indiana, the events cannot be presented in a compressed or truncated manner. That is especially so since the misleading and outright false narratives were presented to and consumed by the public, not only for the 13 years of criminal investigations and trials, but for nine more years when David sought compensation for the long years he was falsely convicted and wrongfully imprisoned in Indiana's toughest prisons.

Indeed, history demands an accurate, in-depth, and exhaustive re-telling of this case. Murder trials—and in David's case there were three—don't simply appear. They are the result of careful planning, strategizing, and organizing, each designed to sell a jury, and—equally as important—the public, a careful narrative designed to convict David both in and out of court.

As such, I believe it mandatory that the public, which has been given many false stories, know of the intimate details of how the Indiana criminal justice system functioned in Dave's case. Because it occurred over such a lengthy period of time and involved the unrelenting efforts of numerous investigators, prosecutors, and courts, this is but the first of two parts, which begins with my involvement just after Dave's first three murder convictions were reversed.

Part I is laser-focused on the first investigation conducted initially by the ISP and then seized and controlled by a prosecutor hell-bent on getting a conviction. It also examines the testimony of the 11 alibi witnesses who were with Dave at the time of the murders, but whose testimonies were trumped by two self-proclaimed bloodstain experts and crime scene reconstructionists.

Also examined are the second ISP investigation and their "fresh eyes" facts, under the control of a former ISP officer/prosecutor, the usage of prison informants who made a living by informing on and testifying against others, the real killer and the surreal way the investigators groomed him, and the identity and handling of his probable accomplice, all of which led up to Dave's second trial.

After one particularly bruising legal battle, Keith Henderson, the second of three prosecutors, told the assembled press, "I think at the end, when the case is concluded, that the public [should] know what we know."[5]

I couldn't agree more. This is what really happened.

---

[5] *Prosecutor Keith Henderson Speaks Out on Camm Trial*, WDRB-TV, February 15, 2012.

SECTION I
"Everybody Knows"

CHAPTER 1

"He's Innocent!"

After I retired from the FBI in 2003, I spent 18 months teaching at the college level.[6] I soon found I missed the freedom of being my own boss, the adventure of chasing leads, and conducting my own investigations. In the summer of 2004, I resigned from academia with the intent of becoming involved only in civil investigations, as I didn't want to find myself on the other side of a criminal case from my law enforcement friends.

> "I CAN'T IMAGINE THE STATE OF INDIANA CONVICTED A MAN OF MURDER WHEN HE HAD 11 ALIBI WITNESSES."

Soon after I notified the local bar of my availability, I was contacted by Katherine Liell, a criminal defense attorney in Bloomington. She quickly got to the point. A client of hers had been criminally charged with voter fraud but, in actuality, was a victim of a political vendetta. Or at least that's what she claimed.

"Sure," I thought, "there are lots of innocent people everywhere." Rather than verbalize those sarcastic words, though, I agreed to meet with her. After all, I was in the process of getting my name out to civil attorneys and thought, if nothing else, she might refer other lawyers to me on cases that I would take.

The next morning I met with Liell. She was in her early 40's, very blond and equally as brash. "Call me, Kitty" were her first words, and then she began her spiel. Her client, Richard Benton,[7] had for many years been very active as a county chairman of a political party in a mostly rural county in southwestern Indiana, 80 miles and a time zone away from Bloomington.[8] He had been accused of stealing absentee ballots, but Kitty claimed that Benton

---

[6] I was the first Program Chairman of the Criminal Justice Department at Ivy Tech Community College in Bloomington, Indiana.

[7] This is a pseudonym; I will at other times not identify other witnesses and individuals.

[8] Indiana, at one time or another, has had three separate time zones.

hadn't stolen anyone's vote and had only been a messenger who had delivered absentee ballot *applications*.

I was somewhat intrigued by her claim, and, since the charges were white collar and not violent in nature, and the case didn't involve any law enforcement friends of mine, I thought for a moment, overcame my initial hesitancy, and told her I'd take the case. Our understanding was I'd just follow the evidence wherever it took me. "If it cuts for Richard," I said, "that's great, but if it doesn't, it doesn't. It is what it is, Kitty." She readily agreed.

The next day, I knocked on Benton's door, greeting him with "Hello, Richard, I'm your private investigator, Gary Dunn." That was weird, because for 27 years, exhibiting my credentials and badge and announcing my name had often brought surprise, uneasiness, and occasional hostility. As a private investigator, though, I certainly didn't have the power or clout I'd once had. I would be reminded of that many times throughout the next few years.

I wanted to get as many details from Richard as possible and certainly to compare to the stories of others. Corroboration was always imperative in cases, of course. "If someone lies," as we used to deadpan in the FBI, "that might be a clue."

After spending hours with Richard, reviewing the local newspaper on the library microfiche, and interviewing my first round of individuals, I realized the local political climate was brutal.[9]

It was apparent to me the prosecutor had been attempting to gain a legal edge, as well as score political points, by trying the case against Benton in the press so close to the general election. Even if, however, the criminal charges had been politically driven, it didn't cause me to accept automatically Benton's strong and repeated assertion that he was innocent.

In the next few weeks, I interviewed over 30 people, including officials from both political parties who had been involved in some degree of election capacity as well as all of the alleged "victims."

The interview results were beyond troubling, as those people either totally refuted their witness statements or were elderly, mentally challenged in some capacity, or both. It was easy to understand how they could have gotten confused or swayed and, in the process, signed witness statements, the contents of which they later either didn't remember or else contradicted.

None of the many election officials I interviewed from either party knew

---

[9] Very telling was that Benton hadn't been notified or provided copies of the charges against him until after the county prosecutor had given his press conference. At that event, the prosecutor had handed out copies, among other documents, of *witness statements* to the local newspapers and television stations. I'd never before seen or heard of any prosecutor giving out witness statements at a media event.

of any irregularities nor had they filed any type of complaint against Richard or anyone else. In fact, all said the proper protocols had been diligently followed. Amazingly, though, *most of the people involved in that process*, and particularly those whose duties dealt with absentee ballots, *hadn't been interviewed by the investigators* sent by the State's Attorney General investigators who had secured the statements from the "victims."

In fact, one of those election officials I interviewed had been paid a visit at home by the county prosecutor, not for the purpose of gaining any insights into the election process, but rather for evangelizing for his church. After his religious outreach, the prosecutor made an ominous comment about Benton, promising, "We're going to get him."

I also learned the prosecutor had conspicuously posted, in the public entrance to his office in the courthouse, these words: "When will this madness end?" Those same words had been uttered by Benton to others in the same courthouse housing the prosecutor's office. After what I had already seen, I wasn't surprised by his unprofessionalism, but the fact the prosecutor was publicly engaging in such conduct was stunning.

Even more astonishing, though, was the fact the prosecutor had personally taken part in the original "examination" of the suspect ballots. Because he was now a witness, he couldn't be an impartial prosecutor.[10]

At the conclusion of my investigation, I found not one person who had any solid personal knowledge of any wrongdoing, nor any documentation or evidence from any reputable source, to support the charges against Benton. The victims' recollections didn't jibe with their previous statements, but they did coincide with plenty of rumor and speculation, which was fueled, in my view, by rank politics and/or personal animosity towards Richard.

Additionally, it was clear the prosecutor couldn't continue to be involved in the case. He was obviously no longer an independent arbiter of justice, as he had publicly opined about Benton's guilt, had disseminated witness testimony to the press and public, and was himself a material witness.

During my investigation, I constantly kept Kitty up-to-date with written reports, suggested subpoenas, gave her copies of my taped interviews, and shared what I planned for my future investigations. During one of our calls, she asked if we could meet the next morning to discuss a special prosecutor motion she was going to file. She then added there was another case she wanted to run by me.

---

[10] Equally as shocking, a photographer/reporter had also been in attendance at the initial examination of those suspect ballots. It was apparent to me the discovery of the "tampered" ballots and the ensuing investigation been orchestrated for the press.

"Great," I thought after hanging up, "maybe another fun and easy investigation."

The Pitch

The next day, I met with Kitty, telling her I had two more interviews to conduct in order to wrap up my end of the Benton case. She then produced her motion, which called for a special prosecutor to replace the county prosecutor due to "immature [and] unprofessional [conduct]" coupled with a "complete disregard for [his] own professional duty…" The evidence was overwhelming; Kitty was confident the judge would have to comply with the request.

After I finished reading the motion, I told Kitty it was spot on. She responded not with what I expected but by excitedly telling me that she had another case that was much worse.

"What are you talking about?" was my quick question.

She told me her client's name was David Camm, the former Indiana State trooper convicted of three murders, and then exclaimed, "Dunner, he's innocent!" She explained she and her young associate, Stacy Uliana, had gotten Camm's guilty convictions overturned on appeal, and they were going to defend him if the murder charges were re-filed.

"Whoa, Kitty, this is the guy from Floyd County, right?"

She said he was.

Defense Attorney Kitty Liell who with co-counsel Stacy Uliana successfully argued and secured the reversal of David Camm's three murder convictions. The two attorneys then became the two trial attorneys in Camm's second trial in 2006.

"I was born and raised in New Albany.[11] I know a little about that guy," I said. "He was a former Indiana State Police trooper who said he had found

---

[11] New Albany is the largest city and also the county seat of Floyd County, on the north side of the Ohio River and directly across the river from Louisville, Kentucky.

his wife and two kids in their garage after he returned home from playing basketball, claiming he had found them shot to death, right?"

Kitty said that was true.

"And his wife and kids had just left the boy's swimming practice," I said, "around 7:00 p.m. at the Hazelwood pool." That had stuck in my mind because that's where I'd swum competitively for years. "Anyway, his wife was found dead on the garage floor, and his kids were dead, in the back seat of the family car, which was parked next to their mother's body?"

"Right, again," said Kitty.

"And he claimed he took his son out of the car, saying he thought he might still be alive and gave him CPR, but that was actually a ruse."

"No!" she exclaimed, and continued saying that Camm's wife and daughter were shot in the head and clearly dead.

"His son was shot in his chest, but Dave thought he might possibly be alive, and he pulled him from the backseat of the car. It turned out the little boy was dead, too, but it wasn't a ruse. Dave was desperately trying to save his son's life," she said.

I essentially ignored Kitty. "But in actuality, he was a serial adulterer who was due to make a load of money off of his wife's life insurance." Kitty tried to interject, but I wouldn't let her. "Not only that," I said, "but he molested his daughter."

Kitty was becoming exasperated with me and attempted to stop me from talking, but I ignored her. "Two years ago, I was involved in a bunch of federal drug searches in Floyd County and was teamed with Sean Clemons."[12]

Kitty said she absolutely knew of Clemons.

I continued, "He was the ISP lead detective on the Camm case, and he was adamant Camm was guilty, Kitty. Obviously, the evidence against him also convinced 12 members of a jury."

Kitty was quick to correct me, saying that I didn't know the whole story, and what I did know wasn't accurate. She also claimed the jury in Camm's case had been tainted by women telling their stories about his affairs with them. Despite the perception in the press, Camm had been very protective of his kids and, despite his affairs, he'd loved his wife.

She continued, saying that a new prosecutor was deciding whether to re-file charges and then said if charges were refiled, they would need me as Camm's defense investigator.

---

[12] It wasn't uncommon for agents, limited in number in the State of Indiana, to be assigned on a temporary basis to assist other agents throughout the state, particularly during large-scale arrests or searches. On many occasions, the FBI would be assisted by and/or assist other agencies in mass-scale collaborative searches and/or arrests.

Before I could respond, a slight, attractive, late 20's black-haired female walked past the open door of the conference room with a file clutched to her side. Kitty yelled at her associate, Stacy Uliana, "Stacy! Come and meet Dunner."

Stacy Uliana, co-counsel with Kitty Liell on the successful murder convictions appeal of David Camm and second chair of Camm's second trial in 2006.

Stacy, I was told, had collaborated with Kitty for well over a year working on the appeal for Camm. Indiana is quite conservative, legally and otherwise, and it was a profound shock, in August 2004, to the legal and law enforcement community, as well as everyday people, when the three murder convictions had been reversed by the Indiana Court of Appeals. Kitty didn't mince words, though, as she proudly proclaimed that she and Stacy "had kicked the State's ass."

Stacy, I would find, wasn't nearly as brash as Kitty but was equally as bright. She said the court transcripts were replete with testimony that shouldn't have been allowed. Further, there wasn't any evidence whatsoever connecting Camm to the murders, other than the opinions of two purported bloodstain experts. They'd claimed blood on a small section of Camm's T-shirt was blowback from a gunshot wound; in actuality, Stacy claimed, it had been caused by contact with the bloody hair from his daughter, Jill. That latter deduction, she asserted, had come from two very respected forensic scientists who specialized in bloodstain interpretation.

Stacy summed up her off-the-cuff argument: "David Camm is innocent, for sure, but he was also denied a fair trial. The Indiana Court of Appeals did the right thing when they reversed the convictions."[13]

Kitty took the baton, saying the original prosecutor, Stanley Faith, had been allowed by the very prosecution-friendly judge, Richard Striegel, to go

---

[13] I'd find out later that Stacy's low-key yet factual demeanor was but a thin veneer for her intense and aggressive advocacy for Camm.

into intricate and very lurid details of the extramarital affairs—consensual, she emphasized—that Camm had engaged in with several women. The jury had been so disgusted and thus prejudiced, she contended, the appellate court ruled the testimony had eliminated any chance of a fair trial for Camm.

Now on a roll, Kitty continued with her narrative. Camm, she said, had been represented by Michael McDaniel, a long-time Southern Indiana defense attorney. "Mike and I were on the Board of Directors of the Indiana Public Defender's Council," she began, adding, "Before Dave's trial, Mike would fill us in on the State's poor investigation. More importantly, he was passionate about Dave's innocence. After the verdicts, he was crushed."[14]

It was obvious Kitty held McDaniel in high esteem. "He and Pat Biggs[15] did all they could do, but they and Dave didn't have a chance," as she added the judge had ruled against the defense on practically every critical issue.

Surprisingly, however, Kitty then said that Faith, the Floyd County Prosecutor for 16 years, had been defeated for re-election only a few months after obtaining the convictions. The new prosecutor was a former ISP trooper, Keith Henderson. Whether or not Camm would again face murder charges would be Henderson's decision; his decision, that is, if the Indiana Supreme Court chose not to overturn the lower court's ruling.

There was a small glimmer of hope, Kitty opined, that Henderson wouldn't pursue another trial. Since the case against Camm was largely based on using the affairs to taint Camm's character, there was a possibility, albeit a small one, that Henderson would drop the case.

Continuing, Kitty said there was also unknown male DNA found on a sweatshirt at the crime scene, which needed to be run through the national DNA database and which might identify the real murderer. She was hopeful the results would exonerate Camm and force prosecutors to drop the charges.

Returning to her sales pitch, Kitty said that both she and Stacy had agreed to be David's trial attorneys if Henderson pursued the case. And, she added, after I joined them, "We'll make a great team."

"There's no way," I thought, but I did respond diplomatically: "My first inclination is to say no." It was one thing to be involved in a voter fraud case, quite another to be involved in a case defending a man who had already been convicted of the murders of his wife and two children. Not only that, but his convictions had been overturned, most thought, on a technicality. Added to all

---

[14] I knew of the suspender-wearing McDaniel through law enforcement friends. He had, they said, a well-deserved reputation as a funny story-teller who was also an excellent and shrewd litigator. Mike, as he was known to all cops, treated them with deference and was fair and courteous. They were also leery of him as a wily, experienced, and well-prepared defense attorney.

[15] Pat Biggs was the long-time Floyd County Public Defender who retired in 2022.

of that, New Albany was my hometown, and that had been reason enough for me not to even think about touching the case.

I tried to excuse myself politely, telling Kitty, "I'll think about it." I began to leave, intending to join two cop friends for the ribeye sandwich lunch special at the nearby Bloomington American Legion.

Kitty ignored my movement, though, as she then claimed the probable cause affidavit, which had caused Camm's arrest, was chock full of falsehoods, further stating that the State didn't even have the probable cause to arrest him, an assertion I told her I found difficult to believe.

But then she unleashed her grand finale, saying as bad as all of that was, there had been 11 alibi witnesses who'd been with David when his family had been murdered. "Eleven. Alibi. Witnesses!" she'd repeated.

"Huh?" I incredulously responded, "Are you serious? You can't be serious!"

Kitty was now standing and practically preaching from her pulpit, when she proclaimed that Camm, in fact, had 11 eyewitnesses, all of them honest people, who'd been playing or watching basketball with him when his family had been murdered. That meant, she continued, not only was he innocent and "we" would be working to free him, but "we" would also be attempting to find the real killer of his family who was still at large.

"Well, *WE* ain't involved in the case, Kitty," I quickly retorted. "I can't imagine the State of Indiana convicted a man of murder when he had 11 alibi witnesses. And really? The real killer is still on the loose? That's light-years beyond my imagination."

Claiming it would be the "weirdest" case I would ever encounter was another good lure, but I didn't want to hear anything else. As I hurried out the door, I told Kitty it was too premature for me to make a decision.

CHAPTER 2

The Stunning Appellate Decision

Driving to lunch, I thought back four years, to the fall of 2000, when the Camm murders had occurred, when I'd been totally immersed in the investigation of a missing college coed who had been presumed kidnapped and murdered.[16] As such, I was ignorant of many details in the Camm case.

What I did know, though, had come from an occasional newspaper article and from a visit to New Albany, also the hometown of my wife, Ginny. In mid-2002, as we were having lunch there with two old friends, they'd left no doubt.

> "THE JURY MIGHT HAVE FOUND CAMM NOT GUILTY OF MURDERING HIS WIFE AND TWO CHILDREN IF….."

"Everybody knows David Camm is a rotten son-of-a-bitch who murdered his family because he tried to hide the fact that he molested his little girl."

Those conclusions had been etched in stone. "He was lucky," our friends had continued, "to have received a 195-year prison sentence rather than the death penalty."

Later in 2002, I'd been educated even more when I'd helped conduct several drug-related search warrants. As I had told Kitty, I had been paired with Sean Clemons, and within minutes of meeting him, he had let me know he was the lead detective on the Camm case. Not only had he been totally convinced of Camm's guilt, but he'd been quite pleased his former colleague was serving three murder sentences.

Kitty and Stacy's oral arguments to me in their office, however, made it impossible for me not to further acquaint myself with the case, at least to some additional degree, even if I decided not to get involved. After lunch, when I arrived home, I first spent several minutes playing with Petey, our loyal Labrador who knew, of course, that each and every day was meant especially for her. I then walked to my office and was soon online, reading and making

---

[16] After I retired in 2003, her body had been found in a rural area in a nearby county by two hunters. Three years later a man had been arrested, based upon a veiled confession his grandmother had finally revealed to police. John Myers had been convicted in 2006, but in 2019, a federal district court granted habeas relief, which the U.S. 7th Circuit soon overturned. In 2021, the U.S. Supreme Court refused to review the 7th Circuit's ruling. Myers is still incarcerated.

notes from the Indiana Court of Appeals opinion that had reversed David Camm's convictions.

The Court had provided some background on the case, noting that evidence supporting the arrest of Camm had been based, "in part," on blood on his shirt. According to the State's forensic expert, the shirt had contained "high velocity impact spatter[17] resulting from a gunshot." The blood had later been determined as originating from Jill Camm. That expert's opinion was also the "key physical evidence" that had led to David Camm's three convictions.

The blood opinion had only been "part" of the evidence that caused his arrest, yet it was the "key physical evidence" resulting in his convictions. Did that mean some of the initial evidence wasn't accurate and/or had been excluded? Was that what Kitty was referring to when she claimed there wasn't enough probable cause to arrest Camm?

Also, while I certainly didn't know the State's blood experts and knew very little of bloodstain interpretation, I knew both prosecution and defense experts testified as to their *opinions*. Opinions, by their very nature, are not precise. If they were, then all experts would agree all of the time. Even medical examiners, who had many years of post-graduate medical training, occasionally differed as to their findings.

The Court had even called the blood testimony "the Battle of the Experts" with the State experts claiming the blood on Camm's shirt was blowback and the defense experts claiming it had been caused by simple contact with a bloody victim. Those were two hardcore, diametrically opposed opinions and not mere nuance. Two questions had again arisen: 1) who were the experts and what was their expertise, and, equally if not more important, 2) what made one expert more credible than the other?

The Court had focused the lion's share of their opinion, though, on the affairs. Defense attorney Mike McDaniel had tried to prevent such testimony, including those from women with whom Camm had only flirted. There was, McDaniel had argued vociferously, no relevance between the affairs and murders. The judge had denied his motion, though, and a string of women, no doubt quite reluctant and very embarrassed, had testified as to their relationships with Camm.

The key question, therefore, before the Court of Appeals was quite clear: had the prosecutor instructed those women to testify because Camm's infidelities and flirting were "proof of motive [or] intent..." or rather had he made them testify because they would show the jury he was simply a person of bad character? According to the Indiana Rules of Evidence, if the

---

[17] High Velocity Impact Spatter is often shortened to HVIS.

testimony were merely to "…prove the character…," then such testimony should have been deemed inadmissible.

Incredibly, in defending the convictions before the court, the Indiana Attorney General had argued "the Defendant did have a defect in his character [which allowed] him to engage in these acts. He did not act as a proper husband and father." The Court had seized upon that admission as a "…virtual concession that the evidence of Camm's extramarital sexual escapades was introduced to establish that he was a person of poor character who was more likely to commit murder because of that character."

The Court had continued, "This is precisely what [the Rules of Evidence] and volumes of case law prohibit." They'd finally concluded that "the State's portrayal of Camm as an immoral, self-centered individual of poor character because of his philandering was central to its case."

I was further amazed that the court had addressed the issue as to whether the testimony of the women, even though irrelevant, had been prejudicial and influential to the jury. It absolutely had been, they'd concluded, further adding, "…we are left with the definite possibility that *the jury might have found Camm not guilty of murdering his wife and two children*[18] if it had not been exposed to a substantial amount of improperly admitted and unfairly prejudicial evidence…" That last assessment wasn't something I'd expected, but I then thought not guilty doesn't necessarily equate to innocent.

The Court then focused on the assertion that Jill had been molested. It first observed the medical examiner had opined that trauma to her "genital region [was] consistent with either molestation or a straddle fall." The State had argued "Camm was likely the culprit and that he murdered Jill and the rest of the family, either to escape detection [of the molestation] or after a confrontation with Kim…"

There was a significant problem, however, inasmuch as there had been absolutely no evidence presented at trial to link Camm to Jill's genital trauma. The Court had warned any future court to weigh carefully any possible testimony about Jill's injuries with the probative value of "any evidence that Camm molested Jill." Translation: if the State is going to claim Camm molested his daughter, then a link with that genital trauma and Camm must be proven; i.e. you have to present real evidence and not just make an inflammatory accusation.

That conclusion, I thought, didn't make any difference to most people in Floyd County, where "everybody knew" that Camm had molested his daughter and were equally convinced that the reversal of his convictions was a "technicality."

---

[18] Emphasis mine.

And then Kitty's incredible assertion of Camm's having 11 alibi witnesses at the time of the murders was indelibly etched into my mind. The Court had, in fact, recognized that 11 "witnesses with varying degrees of familiarity with Camm testified that he was playing basketball at a church at the time his wife and children most likely were murdered" and that they had all agreed he "was there the entire time" and "did not leave the gym."

The Court hadn't been finished, though, as it further noted, and in the process, answered one of my first scribbled questions: "the improper admission of evidence [Camm's affairs] *may have consciously or subconsciously influenced which expert or experts the jury chose to believe*[19] and the weight it assigned to the testimony of Camm's alibi witnesses." Translation: once you slime a defendant, it's really easy to believe anything else about him, even if he had 11 alibi witnesses who were with him, miles away from the crime scene, when the murders occurred.

And then the Court had addressed other issues of which I knew nothing:

- The State had claimed in their opening argument Camm made a phone call from his house at 7:19 p.m. That would have refuted the alibi witnesses' testimony that he was at the gym … "[but the time] was … incorrect … [it was a telephone company] software [billing] error … [and] was instead made at 6:19 p.m.";

- A gunshot residue witness had said that a few gunshot residue (GSR) particles found on Camm's clothing didn't necessarily equate to his being present when the murder weapon was fired;

- There was "unexplained evidence," which had unknown DNA, in the form of a sweatshirt bearing the name of "BACKBONE" found near Brad; and

- Both Kim and Brad's clothing also had DNA that hadn't been identified.

In summary, the Court had found the following: 1) there'd been no relevance or motive between Camm's infidelities and the murders; 2) the trial judge had allowed the prosecutor to get away with destroying Camm's character; 3) the prejudice of painting Camm as a "defective" person had overwhelmed and tainted the jury; 4) there'd been no definitive evidence that proved Jill had been molested; 5) likewise, no evidence had been presented that her father had caused the injuries; 6) regardless, the prosecutor had been allowed by the compliant judge to introduce those unproven claims; 7) the State had presented evidence in the form of a phone call, which purportedly refuted

---

[19] Emphasis mine.

the 11 alibi witnesses; 8) amazingly, the prosecutor's phone evidence hadn't been accurate; 9) still, those 11 alibi witness who'd accounted for Camm's whereabouts during the murders apparently hadn't swayed the jury; 10) there'd been possible evidence of a person, possibly named "BACKBONE," who'd been present at the crime scene and had possibly committed the crimes; and, finally, 11) "BACKBONE" had obviously never been identified and/or eliminated as a suspect.

The Court, at least in my assessment, had also gone out of its way to educate the future prosecutor and judge as to the misconduct of the State and the facilitation of such by the judge. "Beware," they'd been saying, "and make sure you follow the rules and allow only actual evidence."

The most significant questions of all, though, were the obvious deductions from the Court of Appeals accepting that Camm's alibi witnesses had been telling the truth. If so, then how in the world had he killed his family? How could the man be in two places at one time? Why the hell had there even been a trial? Or better yet, why would a second trial even be considered? Certain that I must have missed something, I read the opinion once more, trying to find the missing element to convince me not to get involved. After I finished my second reading, I realized what I had originally deemed unbelievable was, in fact, unthinkable: the State of Indiana had more than likely prosecuted and convicted an innocent man.

CHAPTER 3

"I'll Probably Be Sorry"

In mid-November 2004, a few days after I had read the Court of Appeals decision, the Indiana Supreme Court officially refused to review that lower court's ruling. Kitty was quick to file a motion demanding that Camm be released from custody.

Shortly thereafter, I interviewed the final two witnesses in the voter fraud case and then spent some time with Richard Benton. I told Richard that I was convinced the witnesses we had found and interviewed, as well as other supporting evidence, had completely exonerated

> "I'VE GOT TO SEE FOR MYSELF HOW A GUY GETS CONVICTED OF THREE MURDERS WHEN HE HAS 11 ALIBI WITNESSES."

him. I further said that I was convinced he had been targeted by a prosecutor solely for political purposes. Richard knew he was innocent, of course, and Kitty had already told him of our findings, but it was important that I tell him the same thing. He was, in my view, a victim of nothing less than dirty politics.[20]

After I left Richard, and while driving back to Bloomington, my cell phone rang. It continued ringing as I pulled off to the side of the road and parked under an overcast, dingy sky and next to an abandoned and equally dingy stripper pit.[21] "Yeah, Kitty, what's up?"

She said that she was in New Albany and that Prosecutor Keith Henderson had just refiled murder charges against David Camm. She ended with "We need you."

"Kitty, I told you, I wasn't making any promises."

Kitty kept repeating that Camm was innocent, then telling me that Camm's uncle, Sam Lockhart, was with her and that she'd just left Camm, who had been transferred to the Floyd County Jail from the State Prison. They both, she emphasized, would tell me David was innocent. Finally, she pleaded, "Please...*please.*"

---

[20] Due to our investigative results and Kitty's motions, the County Prosecutor was eventually replaced, a special prosecutor was appointed, and several more months elapsed before that special prosecutor finally dropped all the charges against Richard.

[21] Prior to reclamation laws, surface coal mining—strip mining—in southwestern Indiana left pits that filled with water.

I didn't answer for a moment but finally conceded. "Okay. I'll agree to listen some more, but I'm not guaranteeing anything. Okay?"

Kitty's answer was again to reassure me that David was truly innocent and further that the team would be seeking justice for him and his family. After hanging up, I continued to just sit, my mind as somber as the day, as I thought first about the very damning Court of Appeals opinion. I then thought of the consequences I would likely face. My consequences, though, didn't include spending the rest of my life in prison.

After arriving home, I went immediately to my office and queried the internet, quickly finding the story about Henderson's charging Camm. It was the lead story on all of the Louisville television stations as well as in all of the local newspapers, as Henderson had proclaimed he was going to vigorously and aggressively attempt to secure another conviction. He then claimed the investigation had uncovered important new evidence in the form of a confidential informant to whom Camm had confessed.

"Great," I thought. "They've got new evidence, evidence which Kitty conveniently didn't bother to mention." I kept thinking of my career as an FBI agent. I wasn't some schlep for the defense. Yes, on occasion, when defense attorneys had thought parts of my investigations could help their clients, I had become a defense witness. Testifying for the defense, particularly since it was honest and accurate, had obviously never been an issue, but it also hadn't equated to being a proactive member of their team.

Recalling, though, what I had originally told Kitty about Benton's case, that I'd follow the evidence wherever it led, I tried to convince myself that if I did join the defense team, I'd only be doing what I had always done. It had always come down to the story the evidence was telling and not who was telling the story or any narrative someone wanted to hear.

But I kept returning to the long-held mindset that I'd shared with my other compadres about many defense attorneys. I couldn't get the fact out of my mind that some of my friends would think I had sold out. I kept asking myself my true motivation. Did I miss investigations so much that I would do anything to get back into the game? Was I just deluding myself?

And then, waffling again, I thought of teaching my introductory criminal justice course just a few months prior. Standing in front of 25 students, I'd righteously preached that our Constitution demanded that every accused person receive a staunch defense, not only because they deserved such, but also to make the system itself accountable and trustworthy. While I was a firm believer in fundamental fairness and due process, it didn't make my decision any easier.

I finished reading another article, which included comments by Stan Faith, wherein he'd offered his opinion on the extra-marital affairs: "They [the women with whom Camm had affairs] were brought to testify to show his motive. It's the same as in the [Scott] Peterson case,[22] to get rid of his family to pursue his habits."[23]

Very conveniently for Faith, Scott Peterson had just been convicted of killing his pregnant wife and unborn son. Faith was obviously a man who knew how to get his name into print and, even more so, inflame the public by linking Camm with a murderer all of America despised.

A few days passed, and finally Kitty called and said she and Henderson had agreed to a change of venue. The only question was to which county it would be moved. Kitty wanted either Marion County, located in Indianapolis, or Lake County, in extreme northwest Indiana near Chicago, but Henderson wouldn't agree to either one. She then asked me about Warrick County, located in southwest Indiana, bordering the Ohio River and adjacent to Vanderburgh County, home of Evansville, the largest city in the southern half of the state.

I told Kitty I knew little about Warrick County or its county seat, Boonville, where the courts were located. Regardless of which county would be chosen, the fact many in the jury pool would know of the case was a given. And most people, in spite of what they'll tell you under oath, automatically believe a person's guilty of a crime, even if they've only been *charged* with a crime. Finding a county free of any preconceived notions about Camm's guilt would be impossible. The best hope was to find 12 jurors who would actually listen to testimony and weigh evidence before they came to a conclusion.

An equally important key to finding the correct county, of course, was to secure a judge who would be fair and impartial to the defense and defendant as well as to the prosecution. One needed only to read the appellate decision on Camm to find a judge who had overwhelmingly—and wrongly—ruled on behalf of the prosecution. Nonetheless, I told Kitty I was ignorant of Warrick County and any of their judges.

Days passed and then, a day before Thanksgiving, Kitty reached out and said that she and Henderson had agreed to Warrick County and, further, that Robert Aylsworth, Judge of Superior Court 2, would be presiding. "Let's meet next week," she said, and then asked, "have you made up your mind? I told her I was still not committing. "You know you *have* to do this, Dunner" was Kitty's reply.

The day before the meeting, I reread the appellate decision and also digested several online stories about the case. Other than having briefly worked with Sean Clemons, I didn't know any of those involved, but one name struck me

---

[22] Laci Peterson, Scott's wife, was reported missing by him on Christmas Eve of 2002; four months later, parts of her and her unborn child were found in San Francisco Bay. Scott Peterson was convicted and sentenced to death, but the sentence was overturned in 2020.
[23] Amany, Ali, Camm Decision Expected Tomorrow, *The Tribune*, November 14, 2004.

as vaguely familiar: Sam Lockhart. Lockhart was often quoted in the stories as a spokesman on behalf of his nephew, David Camm, and Lockhart was vehement, to say the least, in defending his sister's son.

As I was reading another story, it finally dawned on me how I knew of Lockhart. Checking an online source to be sure, I confirmed that we had both attended New Albany High School. Additionally, he and I and were members of the athletic club, but it ended there: since he was two years older than me, we didn't share any common friends, and I had never interacted with him.

On Tuesday, I arrived early at Kitty's office. She wasn't yet in, but Carrie Stremming and Jennifer True, the firm's two paralegals, were in their office and very welcoming. Carrie, an especially positive and always smiling young lady, primarily worked for Kitty's husband, Michael McNeill, a patent attorney. Jenn, on the other hand, a lifelong friend of Kitty's, worked mostly for Kitty and Stacy on criminal defense and appellate cases. I had interacted with each on a limited basis on the Benton case and would soon realize they were as efficient, energized, and professional as Kitty and Stacy.

Jenn took me into the conference room, where, on the large oval table, rested six large banker boxes. She told me that I could explore whatever I wanted and that Kitty would be in the office momentarily. She pointed me to the coffee pot down the hallway; I thanked her, walked the few steps, got myself a cup, returned to the boxes, and began shuffling through them.

One large, brown expandable folder caught my eye: **SAM LOCKHART**. Inside were several documents, including ISP reports and his trial transcript. As I was thumbing through the stack of papers, Kitty entered the room, enthusiastically shouted, "Good morning!" and, after looking at the folder, made a declarative statement that Sam Lockhart was one of the finest persons she'd ever met.

"Tell me why," I said.

"Because," she said, "he is a man of incredible honesty and principle." She then proceeded to give me a brief history of his background and involvement in Camm's case. Sam was a hard-working guy who had built his one-man foundation repair and water-proofing business into two companies, United Dynamics Incorporated (UDI) and Perma Dry Incorporated (PDI),[24] now employing over 40 people, with one of them his nephew, David Camm.

Sam, I was further told, was positive his nephew hadn't killed his family since he was one of the 11 people with him at the time of the murders. His belief in David's innocence was so strong that Sam, as well as the entire family, had sacrificed much—and not just in terms of the money they had

---

[24] Ironically, PDI was also the name I had chosen for my PI business, i.e., Professionally Dunn Investigations (PDI).

spent for Camm's original trial and appeal. Kitty—very correctly, as I would learn—then summarized Sam's commitment by telling me that he not only wouldn't stop, but couldn't stop, seeking justice, not only for David but for Kim and the kids.

"Okay," I responded, "I don't need to know any more about Sam."

"Well, I want you to meet Sam," was Kitty's quick rejoinder, adding that once I did, I'd be convinced of David's innocence and want to be on the team.

I responded that I had already made up my mind and then added, "I'll probably be sorry that I said yes."

Kitty let out a "Whoopie!"

I quickly dampened some of her enthusiasm when I said I still wasn't 100 percent convinced of Camm's innocence. Yes, I said, he *might* be innocent, and yeah, he *possibly* is or maybe even *probably* is, but then added, "I'll just do the same thing I did with the Benton case, letting the evidence speak for itself. And I'll tell Sam Lockhart the exact same thing."

"I shouldn't ask," Kitty began, "but why did you say yes?"

"Richard Benton's case greased the skids, and I figure you possibly knew that might happen, but the appellate decision really suckered me in," I said. "They said Camm might not have been found guilty were it not for the introduction of the affairs. That, and I've got to see for myself how a guy gets convicted of three murders when he has 11 alibi witnesses. And, if David Camm is actually innocent, there is at least one murderer running around free, possibly for the past four years. Maybe we can find whoever is responsible. Anyway, those are my reasons."

Kitty nodded but also smiled. She then got serious and began to fill me in on some other things, noting that the new investigators, as the original investigators, were ISP detectives. She gave me a copy of the new probable cause affidavit, which, she said, was almost as bad as the original affidavit. "Yeah, okay," I responded, "I'll want to review that, but first I'm going to go through the original affidavit and see what they had to originally charge Camm. I want to track their evidence from the beginning."

"I also want to meet with Sam Lockhart and arrange to get into the house," I said. Kitty previously had told me that wouldn't be a problem since a friend of a family member had purchased the home. "But wait until I go through the two probable cause affidavits and some other stuff first," I added. Kitty said once she heard from me, she'd call Sam, and we'd all meet in Bloomington, as she also needed to speak with him.

Kitty next told me that she hadn't gotten any court authority to pay me for my work.[25] "Not a problem," I said. "I'll let you handle that with the judge." I then loaded the six boxes of reports in my car. Within 30 minutes, I was in front of my computer keyboard, monitor and scanner, having opened the first Camm sub-file, entitled *Probable Cause Affidavits.*

It would take me several weeks to go through all six boxes and to scan appropriate documents, but I wanted my initial focus to be on 1) the allegations in the original probable cause affidavit and, if possible, the strength of the evidence; 2) the individual stories of the basketball players; 3) Camm's own story or stories of what happened that night; 4) the most recent affidavit sworn to by Henderson's investigators, dubbed by him to be "fresh eyes," and 5) a meeting with Sam Lockhart, during which we could walk through and absorb the crime scene and the church gym.

---

[25] Kitty and Stacy were being paid by Sam Lockhart, the Lockhart family, and the Camm family. My billings would go through the Floyd County Public Defender's office and be paid by Floyd County, subject to the approval of the judge.

CHAPTER 4
The Basis Of Camm's Arrest

Probable Cause (PC) affidavits are needed to satisfy a mandatory requirement of the Fourth Amendment of the U.S. Constitution that a seizure of a person—an arrest—would be accomplished only upon the presentation of facts that establish probable cause.

The key question is, of course, "What is probable cause?" Generally, that somewhat imprecise legal requirement is considered

> "THE TEE SHIRT WORN BY DAVID R. CAMM…HAD HIGH VELOCITY BLOOD MIST WHICH OCCURS IN THE PRESENCE OF GUNSHOT AT THE TIME OF THE SHOOTING."

to mean the totality of the presented facts to cause a reasonable person—a judge—to believe a crime had been committed by a specific individual. Probable cause is well below the legal standard of proof beyond a reasonable doubt, the standard required to convict a person of a crime.

In my career, I had authored many affidavits, asking federal or local judges to issue search warrants and arrest warrants. Some were as short as two pages in length. The longest criminal affidavit of mine was 81 pages, carefully reviewed and scrutinized by U.S. Department of Justice (DOJ) attorneys as well as FBI officials, which asked a federal judge to issue a court order allowing the FBI to monitor and record telephone calls in a racketeering case. Assimilating probable cause for that took several months to achieve.

Every assertion of fact I made in each and every sworn document was corroborated by witness statements, records, and/or other evidence, all of which were easily found in the investigative case file. I wasn't about to risk my integrity or my career by claiming something not supported by facts or thoroughly documented. Sworn affidavits weren't for guessing or speculating.

Camm's Arrest Affidavit

After a few moments of searching, I found the file containing the two-page affidavit authorizing the arrest of David Camm. Authored and signed by ISP Detective Sean Clemons, it began with the expected paragraph, which asserted a crime had been committed and read as follows:

I am a Detective with the Indiana State Police.

1. On the 28th day of September, 2000, I was called to David R.

Camm's residence at 7534 Lockhart Road, Georgetown, Floyd County, Indiana, where I found three people who had been shot: Kimberly Camm; Bradley Camm, age 7, Jill Camm, age 5.

2. *The following evidence has been processed from the crime scene at the above-mentioned address:*

   a. *The crime scene was manipulated by use of a high Ph [sic] cleaning substance.*[26]

   b. *The tee shirt worn by David R. Camm on the above-mentioned date had high velocity blood mist, which occurs in the presence of gunshot at the time of the shooting.*

   c. *The cleaning substance was thrown over the back deck of the above-mentioned house, also leaving a trail from the garage area, along with a transfer of blood on the house.*

   d. *A witness said that between 9:15 p.m. and 9:30 p.m. she heard three distinct sounds that can be interpreted as gunshots.*

   e. *Jill Camm, age 5, had a recent tear in the vaginal area consistent with sexual intercourse.*

   f. *There is a wet mop in a bucket in the utility room of the house at the above-mentioned address with the strong odor of bleach.*

   g. *Witnesses playing basketball with David R. Camm said that he left the game on or around 9:00 p.m., and David R. Camm told them he was headed to his house, the above-mentioned crime scene.*

   h. *There was a flow of blood from the garage that is inconsistent with the viscosity of blood and was aided in its flow by the presence of water and cleaning substance.*

   i. *Kimberly Camm and Jill Camm were killed by gunshot wounds to the head from a certain .380 caliber firearm.*

   j. *Bradley Camm was shot in the chest which exited in Bradley's back eventually killing Bradley Camm.*

3. *The above-mentioned information was gleaned from statements or reports made to me by Tracy Corey-Handy, M.D., Dora*[27] *Hunsaker, M.D., all pathologists, Robert Stites crime scene re-constructionist.*

---

[26] Ph should read pH. A high pH solution, or one of 12+, could be bleach or another cleaning substance.

[27] Dr. Hunsaker's first name is Donna, not Dora as written.

4. I make these statements not as complete recital of all facts, but to establish probable cause.

5. All of which gives me probable cause to believe that David R. Camm has committed Murder, in Floyd County, State of Indiana.

(Signature of Sean Clemons)
ISP 5751

Subscribed and sworn to before me this 1st Day of October, 2000.

(Signature of Stanley O. Faith)
Prosecuting Attorney
52nd Judicial Circuit

The corresponding warrant authorizing the arrest of Camm was signed, on October 1, 2000, by Judge Richard Striegel, the same judge who later presided over Camm's two-month trial and who sentenced him to 195 years for the three murders.

The booking mugshot of David R. Camm on October 1, 2000

Breaking Down the Allegations

After reading the affidavit twice, I began to de-construct the allegations, making numerous notes, not just on the claims that had been made, but also on what I saw as missing. I concentrated on several areas, from which numerous thoughts and questions sprung:[28]

- The *cause of death*:

---

[28] Italics are mine.

◊ Kim, Brad, and Jill had all been shot to death, and the murderer had been close to his victims.

- The *murder weapon*:
  ◊ A .380 is a semi-automatic weapon; ejected shell casings had probably been found at the scene;
  ◊ If the shell casings had been in good shape, a manufacturer of the gun had probably been identified;
  ◊ If the murder weapon had been found, it would have been so noted by Clemons, and certainly any gun linked to Camm would have been alleged.
  ◊ Had the gun been found later?

- *Who was the witness* who'd heard the *interpreted gunshots*?
  ◊ What had the witness actually said?
  ◊ Why had Clemons used the term interpreted? In my career, I'd never seen any affidavit that used that term.

- The *time the murders occurred*, according to Clemons, had been *after Camm left the basketball game*, "around 9:00 p.m." and when someone had heard the sounds, which were interpreted by Clemons as gunshots, or after 9:15 p.m.
  ◊ That certainly didn't comport with the finding from the appellate decision: Faith had claimed the murders had occurred after 7:19 p.m., which had been disproven.
  ◊ How had Faith and Clemons moved the time of the murders from after 9:15 p.m. and after the ball games when the basketball players apparently weren't important, to during the games, which then made the basketball players alibi witnesses?
  ◊ Equally as important, how had such a major mistake been made?

- The *forensic evidence involving blood:*
  ◊ That dynamite piece of evidence had come from "crime scene reconstructionist" Rob Stites, who most critically claimed that blood on Camm's T-shirt had *"high velocity blood mist."*
    - High velocity equated to blood blowback from a victim's gunshot wound, further meaning Camm had to have been present and in close proximity of the victim.

- The victim had been Jill, but how much blood? Where on the shirt?
- Perhaps most critically, who was Stites and what were his qualifications?

- The *"crime scene was manipulated"* by a *cleaning substance, which had also added to a blood flow.*
  ◊ How, specifically, had the crime scene been manipulated?
  ◊ What had been the purpose of adding a cleaning substance?
  ◊ There were no references to laboratory reports, so the deductions of manipulation and cleaning substance had been deductions by Stites.

- *Molestation had been a motive:*
  ◊ The assertion was that "Jill Camm, age 5, had *a recent tear in the vaginal area consistent with sexual intercourse."*
  ◊ By very strong inference, it was her father who had molested his daughter.
  ◊ The appeals court found there had been no evidence presented that Camm had molested his daughter, so how did the ISP conclude that he had?

It was inescapable that Clemons and Faith had relied on inference and one man's interpretations as the foundation of their affidavit. Viewing it in its totality, the entire affidavit, I thought, was skinny. Very skinny.

Autopsies

I found the autopsy reports to see if the deductions by the medical examiners had supported the affidavit. All three autopsies had occurred the day after the murders, on Friday, September 29, 2000, at the Kentucky Medical Examiner's office in Louisville,[29] and had been conducted by Tracy Corey-Handy, M.D., and Donna Hunsaker, M.D.

Kim and Jill had each suffered one fatal head shot, Jill from a close distance and Kim from an intermediate distance. Each had caused massive trauma and a huge loss of blood. Brad's lethal gunshot wound, from intermediate range, had entered his left side, severed his spinal cord and exited at his right shoulder blade. He, too, had died of massive blood loss.

---

[29] Floyd County contracted with them to conduct autopsies; the State of Indiana had, and still has, no state medical examiner's office.

Dr. Corey-Handy had observed stippling on Brad's face, which meant he'd been shot from such a distance that powder from the nearby gun had landed on him, causing pinprick burns.[30] That also meant that he had been looking at the muzzle of the gun when he was shot. I had to stop and pause. The little guy had probably seen his mother and sister shot and had then known he was going to be killed. The horror of that was inescapable.

For all three victims, death had occurred quickly, although it was possible Brad may have survived for a few minutes.

As for Jill having been molested, the autopsy reflected she had suffered "non-specific…blunt trauma of the external genitalia (hymen intact)." The autopsy didn't reflect any injury whatsoever to the "vagina area" as had been alleged by Clemons, nor was there any evidence or comment of any "sexual intercourse" as he had claimed. Rather, the terminology used by Doctor Corey-Handy equated to a conclusion that Jill may or may not have been molested; the specific cause of her injuries was unknown.

The appellate decision noted the trauma to Jill's genital region was "consistent with either molestation or a straddle fall," which had probably come from Doctor Corey-Handy's trial testimony. Still, it reinforced the possibility Jill had injured herself and offered the possibility of other means of injury.

All in all, something was way out of kilter. If the ISP had good evidence that 1) Jill had been molested and that 2) Camm had been the perpetrator, they would have detailed such explosive evidence in the affidavit—e.g., assertions from the Camm family physician, another family member or friend, and/or a teacher. It also meant that Kim must have known or at least suspected her daughter was being abused. The fact they hadn't alleged anything from any source was a huge red flag.

Yet another question arose. Camm was a veteran law enforcement officer, but anyone with a modicum of common sense would know murder victims are autopsied. Injuries from molestation, and any other prior injuries for that matter, would certainly have been discovered by a pathologist. The molestation motive of the ISP, therefore, meant Camm had killed his daughter in order to hide a secret that he knew wouldn't remain a secret after a pathologist had scrutinized every part of her body. That wasn't logical.

Although I intended to focus next on the time of the murders, information in Kim's autopsy report wouldn't allow it, for it was both very telling and even

---

[30] The tissue around gunshot entrance wounds may be accompanied with soot deposits and/or powder (burned and unburned) and often appearing as small dots. The presence or absence of such deposits aids in determining the distance of the gun from the gunshot wound.

more chilling. Dr. Hunsaker's external examination of Kim's body revealed she had suffered a total of 22 abrasions, contusions, and bruises found on her chin, neck, left lower face, elbows, knees, the top of both feet, especially her left foot, and several toes.

Additionally, Kim's right index fingernail had been torn and the fingertip bloodied, indicating she had probably broken it as she fought and possibly scratched her assailant. The injuries also indicated she had been grabbed or struck in some manner, with the chin injury possibly consistent with an uppercut from a fist. Photographs taken during the autopsy confirmed all of those injuries.

Kim's Foot Injuries

As I was looking at a photograph of the top of Kim's left foot, my wife, Ginny, walked in my office and asked, "Are you going to eat dinner?" I apologized and said I had lost track of the time. She then asked, "What's that you're looking at?"

"Nothing you want to see," I responded and immediately knew that wouldn't fly. And then continued, "It's a photo from Kim Camm's autopsy. You can see the obvious bruising and torn skin on the top of her left foot and on two toes."

Ginny came closer to my desk, looked at the photo for a few moments and then said, "Somebody was really angry about her feet."

"What do you mean?" I asked. "Whoever did it was trying to control her and obviously stomped on her foot."

"Maybe," Ginny responded, adding, "but her toenail polish is chipped on three toes and missing on the other two and it's obvious she hadn't had a pedicure in a long time. Somebody didn't like what they saw and was really pissed off."

"Come on," I said, "you're telling me somebody stomped on her feet because her toenails weren't pretty?"

"I'm just telling you that first, she probably was a working mother since she didn't have the time to maintain her toenail polish, and second, it's possible someone was directing their anger at her feet."

Her explanation, at least to me, was implausible. It was quite apparent Kim's assailant had really stomped hard, particularly on her left foot, possibly with a hard-sole shoe or boot. Could the motive, which I thought had been control, have been another reason?

"Go ahead and eat," I said. "I'll grab something later." Ginny left my office, and I returned to the autopsy and photographs. Kim's elbow and knee injuries were possibly caused, I thought, by first having been tackled or grabbed and thrown down and then having struck the concrete garage floor. Other injuries were consistent with having been struck, probably by a fist.

Regardless of how they occurred, it was abundantly clear that Kim had been viciously physically assaulted and that she had fought in a desperate attempt to save her life and the lives of her children. If she had been totally compliant, she wouldn't have suffered any injuries. It was also clear her wounds had to have been sustained repeatedly and possibly over several minutes. Another deduction was her tenacious fight would probably have caused at least some scratches, cuts, or other injuries to her attacker.

Had Camm had any such injuries? I wanted to know immediately, as I then searched for the ISP report that dealt with his first sit-down interview and events that occurred at that time. The interview had been conducted by two of Camm's former fellow ISP officers, Acting District Investigative Commander (ADIC) Mickey Neal and Detective Darrell Gibson, shortly after midnight on Friday, September 29, at the ISP Sellersburg Post, or about three hours after Camm claimed he had found his dead family.

I quickly reviewed the interview and found that Camm had provided his T-shirt, shorts, socks, and shoes to the detectives. At the same time, they had visually examined his entire body but had found no abrasions, bruises, cuts, or scratches on him—none whatsoever.[31] That didn't seem plausible, given the nature and extent of Kim's injuries.

Returning to the autopsy of Kim, I saw where the bottom of her feet had "fine particular black to gray matter and adherent blades of dried grass." That obviously meant she had been barefoot when killed.

Crime Scene Photos

I again deviated from my original plan and quickly found the crime scene photographs. Kim was pictured lying on the floor with a massive pool of dark red blood blood surrounding her head. She'd been clad in a blue sweater, but her white pants had been off, bunched near her bloody head and sprawling hair. She'd worn only black panties from the waist down and no socks or shoes. Her bare feet had been just barely under the car.

Kim's brown shoes, in fact, had been sitting very neatly, side-by-side, on the top of her black Ford Bronco on the passenger side. What the hell did that mean? Why would she or her assailant have put her shoes on top of her car, particularly in an aligned manner? That neatness indicated they had been placed there before all hell had begun to break loose, further indicating that Kim had been compliant with the attacker's initial commands.

---

[31] The protocol for most investigative agencies would be to photograph a suspect's body, but the ISP had failed to do so with Camm.

Gary M. Dunn

Kim's brown shoes had been neatly placed side-by-side on the top of her Ford Bronco.

Also, in the same photograph, Kim's blue sweater had contained a massive number of hair strands. Did such an inordinate amount of hair lend credence to the possibility, as she had fought and flailed, her hair had been grabbed by her assailant in an effort to control her?

In the same photograph of Kim was Brad, fully clothed in athletic gear, lying on the floor, essentially parallel to the car with his head towards the rear. His arms were outstretched, and his right foot appeared to touch his mother's left hand, which was at her waist. His right hand was within two or three inches of the trail of blood from his mother's head. Other than a small amount of a rust-colored splotch on his face, there was no obvious sign of blood on him. The lack of noticeable blood was explainable, for his gunshot wound had been to his torso, which had been covered by a long-sleeve sweatshirt.

As for Jill, I thumbed through the crime scene photos until I found some of her, dressed in typical little-girl clothes, including sandals. She was slumped over and bent towards the center of the back seat, with her seatbelt still stretched across her little body and blood on her forehead, right cheek, and left hand, which was folded into her lap.

What the photos made clear was Jill had obviously been shot when she'd been sitting upright since there had been a hole through the seat behind where her head would have been. That hole had extended through the seat and followed a downward path to a hole in the cargo bay carpet.

Supporting the fact Jill's head had changed location, from when she'd been shot until the photos had been taken, a rivulet of blood was flowing from behind her right ear and directly into the corner of the right side of her mouth, indicating the blood had followed the law of gravity. That was important for two reasons: 1) the flow of blood had to have occurred after her head had changed positions; otherwise, the blood would have flowed horizontally when she was upright, which, of course, was impossible, and 2) it also meant the blood had still been liquid enough to flow well after she had been shot, when the position of her body had changed.

The key question, at the moment, however, and from looking at that photograph was, specifically, just how had blood blowback from Jill's head wound found itself on Camm's T-shirt, particularly since she had been sitting upright when shot, and whoever shot her had probably been on the right side and outside of the car? Could blood have flown outside the car and landed on the left side of Camm's shirt? That didn't seem likely.

I found another photograph of the empty rear seat behind the driver's seat. Blood was visibly present on the left edge of the seat and on top of the interior left rear wheel well. It had to have been the location Brad was shot.

Clemons' affidavit, however, said nothing about where each of the three bodies had been found and, in fact, he'd never specifically identified the garage as having been the location of the murders.

The basic facts, as to the victims, at least as I understood them at that moment, based upon the photos and my limited knowledge of the case were as follows: 1) Jill had been summarily assassinated, shot through the head, while she'd been strapped helplessly in the back seat of the family car; 2) sometime after Jill was shot, her head and upper torso had tilted over and to her left; 3) Kim, possibly the victim of a sexual assault or attempted assault, had apparently been forced to partially disrobe but then had fought tenaciously and fallen where she had been shot; and 4) the position of Brad on the floor and the blood in the left rear seat confirmed he had been removed from the Bronco and placed on the floor.

Brad's wound hadn't been a head wound and, unlike his mother and sister, a very limited amount of blood had been visibly present. It was understandable how Camm might have thought his son, unlike Kim or Jill, possibly had a chance to live and took him from the car to try to resuscitate him.

As for Kim's lack of clothing and her almost two dozen injuries, the affidavit didn't mention them, only offering the comment that she had been killed due to a fatal gunshot to the head. There was also no mention of her being partially clothed or of her shoes placed on the car, which meant that the ISP couldn't explain those facts. Certainly, if they had pointed toward Camm, they would have tried to link them to him.

As far as any sexual assault of Kim, Dr. Corey-Handy had found no forensic evidence. That didn't mean, of course, that a sexual assault hadn't occurred, and no visible evidence had been left—i.e. that the perpetrator had used a prophylactic, that she had been forced to perform oral sex, or that a sexual assault wasn't consummated.

I then pondered the question if Camm had, in fact, committed the murders, then why had he removed Kim's pants, shoes, and socks? Why would he have done that? And what had he, or anyone for that matter, wanted to accomplish by placing the shoes on top of the car? And in a neat manner?

One crime scene photo was particularly graphic with Kim's head being surrounded by a massive pool of blood from which a trail ran towards the open garage door and which changed colors in the process. There was also a very distinct linear pattern, a pooling of the dark red color and then the yellowish-clear fluid color, but there was no depiction of what object or obstruction had caused the damming.

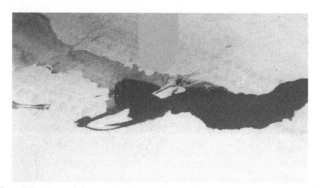

Blood and fluid trail from Kimberly Camm's head wound, her head to the right in this picture. Something apparently had been sitting on the floor causing the damming of the blood. The blocked area in the top middle of the picture covers the outstretched arm of Bradley.

The Blood Experts & Crime Scene Reconstructionists

Stites, the crime scene reconstructionist/expert in blood dynamics, referred to the trail as being "inconsistent with the viscosity of blood and was aided in its flow by the presence of water and cleaning substance."

I began a search for lab reports and found one where, weeks after the murders, scrapings from the fluid had finally been analyzed for cleaning substance. There'd been nothing found. That revelation didn't bode well for the supposed expertise of Stites. I had a good idea, from visiting other crime scenes, of what caused the color change but wanted to verify my suspicion.

A query of the internet revealed the answer. In a pooling of blood and over time, red blood cells separate naturally from the liquid plasma, causing a distinct change in colors. That separation is a natural phenomenon that doesn't need the assistance of any added liquid.

Finding the report of McDaniel's blood experts, Barton Epstein and Terry Laber, I read where they confirmed that blood-serum separation was a natural phenomenon. There was now no escaping the stark conclusion that the ISP's blood expert, Robert Stites, didn't know all that much about blood.

Stites had further implied a wet mop found in a laundry room had been used in the cleanup. Mops, though, are normally found in such places, and a wet mop in a utility room certainly wasn't unusual. While there had been no direct mention in the affidavit of blood having been found on the mop, it had nonetheless been implied.

I searched for any lab analysis of residue and/or scrapings from the mop. That report was also damning: no blood had been found, meaning yet another of Stites' inferences/deductions hadn't been supported.

And it got worse. A lab report had determined the deck and railing spots were dated and not fresh.[32]

The guy who was the expert "crime scene reconstructionist" had been totally wrong on three of his critical allegations. It was now making sense as to why the Court of Appeals had noted more physical evidence had been alleged in the probable cause affidavit than had been presented at trial. In reality, it's supposed to be the other way: as the investigation lengthens, the forensic evidence becomes greater and stronger.

Another aspect of the allegation of manipulation and cleanup bothered me. There'd been no explanation or suggestion as to how any such half-assed cleanup would have benefited the murderer. For the sake of argument, I thought, accept the premise the murderer had added a cleaning agent to the blood flow. What had been the purpose, and how had that "manipulation" assisted the murderer? It was as though Stites had thought the mere *assertion* of a manipulation, in and of itself, was conclusive and incriminating.

Since Stites had been woefully wrong about his claims of a solution added to the blood flow and a cleanup of the crime scene with the mop, then his credibility when it came to assessing blood mist on Camm's T-shirt was in serious jeopardy. That credibility, I reminded myself, had already been challenged with Stacy's comment that the two experts Mike McDaniel had retained had also discounted Stites' assertion of blood blowback.

It was time to educate myself on just who Robert Stites was and how he got to be such an influential aspect of a triple homicide investigation.

I discovered Stites hadn't been the person Stanley Faith had wanted, for it was Faith who had told the ISP, within hours of the murders, that he'd wanted bloodstain expert, Rodney Englert, to receive explicit and complete access to the crime scene and every bit of evidence.

It was Faith who had reached out for Englert's assistance, but Englert had apologized and said he was indisposed, teaching a class on bloodstain interpretation. Not to worry, though, for Englert had told Faith he'd send his

---

[32] Camm had a part-time business of pressure washing; I later learned that he had cleaned the deck several months before the murders and those spots had remained.

protégé, Rob Stites, who would pinch hit for him. Okay, so now who was Rod Englert?

Englert, I learned, had testified for Faith in two previous cases, including one wherein the victim's body had never been found. Faith had secured a murder conviction in that case, and Englert therefore was a known and obviously trusted commodity of Faith's.

Not only did Faith trust Englert, a retired Multnomah, Oregon, Deputy Sheriff, but other prosecutors throughout the country had used him in their investigations, almost always murder cases. A quick search of the internet also revealed Englert, dba Englert Forensic Consultants, had previously served as the President of both the International Association of Bloodstain Pattern Analysts and Association of Crime Scene Reconstructionists. The man was a forensic expert in many areas, he had claimed, but particularly in the analysis of bloodstains and reconstruction of crime scenes. It was in those two forensic fields that he also specialized in teaching, especially to law enforcement officers.[33]

Okay, if Englert was such an expert and outstanding teacher, then how had his own protégé struck out on all of his reconstruction claims? Why had his opinion on the bloodstains been disputed by McDaniel's experts?

The two defense experts used by McDaniel, I learned, were or had been career forensic scientists at the Minnesota Bureau of Criminal Apprehension (BCA) Laboratory. Barton Epstein, a graduate in Criminalistics at the University of California, Berkeley, had 32 years of expertise in microscopy, serology, and blood spatter interpretation. He had retired two years before the murders as the Assistant Director of the Laboratory.

Terry Labor, an associate of Epstein's, had also been a forensics expert for decades and was a partner of Epstein's in their private forensics consulting service. Although precluded by their employment from consulting or testifying in any civil or criminal case with jurisdiction in Minnesota, they nonetheless had worked on many criminal cases outside Minnesota for prosecutors as well as defense attorneys.

Epstein had directed an experiment using human blood, taken from himself and others, in the Camm garage under similar circumstances as what had occurred during the murder—e.g., time of day, temperature, and humidity had nearly been the same. The collected blood, spilled on the concrete floor, had assisted him in determining the time needed for the serum to separate from the blood cells had been over an hour.

The two forensic scientists also reached another conclusion after spending several days and numerous experiments searching for the source of blood

---

[33] He later wrote a book, *Blood Secrets*, in 2010.

on Camm's lower T-shirt. The eight tiny dots of supposed high-velocity mist, which were on the hem and lower left front of Camm's shirt, had been consistent with transfer and not blowback.

But what kind of transfer had caused those tiny dots of blood? Their experiments corroborated Camm's story, as he, in an attempt to resuscitate Brad, had entered the back seat, between the front bucket seats, placed his left knee to the right of Jill's body, causing a depression in the middle of the seat, which in turn had caused her upper body and head to roll over with the loose ends of her blood-tipped hair making light contact with the lower left shirttail hanging off the body of Camm.

The two forensic experts had directly contradicted Stites and Englert. Why, then, hadn't the jury believed them over Stites, who had been proven wrong in deduction after deduction? Why had the jury believed his mentor, Englert?[34]

As I was cogitating on those questions, I recalled, from the cobwebs of my mind, the words of one scientist: "Science is the belief in the ignorance of the experts."[35] That, I thought, couldn't have been more spot-on with the four Camm "blood experts." The only problem, of course, was that two of the "experts" weren't in the same league as the other two, for they couldn't have been right. The only question for the jury was to have chosen which "experts" to believe, and they had picked Stites and Englert.

Still, I wanted to know more, and in order to acquaint myself with the basics of bloodstain analysis, I did my own preliminary research. There were, most agreed, several basic aspects involved in *interpreting* bloodstains, as an analyst first had to consider the 1) size, 2) shape, 3) distribution, 4) number and 5) pattern of the stains, and then had to examine the 6) surface on which the stains had landed.[36]

The biggest variable of all, of course, was that bloodstains were *interpreted*—interpreting what bloodstains meant was subjective, and in this case, apparently very subjective.

I returned to the crime scene photographs and reached yet another undeniable deduction. The murderer, probably after shooting and killing Kim, had then looked directly at and shot a totally helpless, terrified, and probably screaming little girl in the head and then murdered her equally terrified

---

[34] While both Epstein and Laber conducted joint experiments and came to the same conclusions, it was only Laber who testified in the first trial.

[35] Richard Feynman, physicist and Nobel Prize winner.

[36] Those are but the essential aspects of interpreting bloodstains. Obviously, a crime scene can have multiple areas which are blood spattered or have blood pooling, as did the Camm crime scene, and each can be interpreted independently and/or in conjunction with the other areas. The big question, of course, is whose interpretation is correct?

brother who'd certainly looking straight at him. The one pulling the trigger, be he David Camm or someone else, had been one stone-cold, remorseless, evil son-of-a-bitch.

BACKBONE Sweatshirt & Murder Weapon

And who could the murderer have been if not Camm? While searching among the hundreds of photographs and reports, I also found a picture of a gray, long-sleeved, extra-large, sweatshirt with the same name referenced in the appeals decision. In the inside rear collar of that garment were block black letters that spelled BACKBONE.

What did the sweatshirt mean? There, of course, had been no mention of it in the affidavit, so lacking an explanation, it, too, had been ignored by Clemons, who had apparently not attempted to link it to Camm.[37] Could it have possibly belonged to the real perpetrator? Could someone have left behind such a monumental clue? Had no one followed up on BACKBONE?

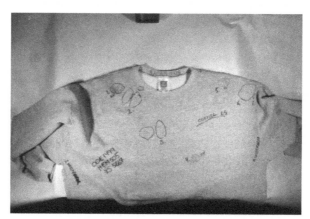

The gray BACKBONE sweatshirt that had been
underneath Brad on the garage floor.

Obviously, we'd pursue BACKBONE. The fact such a person existed was pretty conclusive, but who was the person with such a name?

I stayed with the original PC affidavit and searched for the lab report on the manufacturer of the .380, which was the murder weapon. An ISP firearms expert, several days after the murders, had deduced the three spent cartridges found at the scene had been fired from a Lorcin .380 semi-automatic handgun.

---

[37] Only later did the ISP find a neighbor who claimed to have seen a gray sweatshirt in the detached garage, albeit there had been no one who had claimed to have seen the BACKBONE sweatshirt, per se.

A Lorcin, after a quick internet check, verified my vague recollection that it was a poorly made, very cheap, and undependable "Saturday Night Special" kind of weapon. Would Camm, a trained police officer, have relied on such a junk weapon?

My questions were being answered, but two other answers needed to be found: 1) which of the basketball players, purportedly alibi witnesses, said Camm left the games around 9:00 p.m. and 2) how did Clemons come to "interpret" three sounds as gunshots?

CHAPTER 5
Alibi Witnesses

The initial Camm investigation contained many disparate ISP reports by over 40 troopers and detectives but had no overall indexing of subject matter or identity of witnesses. Neither was there a table of contents or cogent administration of over 1,000 pages of investigative and laboratory reports. The crime scene and autopsy photographs had also been co-mingled without any indexing, and all the reports had been on paper, eliminating any possibility of an electronic search.

Additionally, individual reports occasionally read like a chronology of the daily log of a detective/trooper—i.e., in the morning, he/she had attended mandatory breathalyzer refresher training; in the early afternoon, he/she had conducted a background interview on a prospective trooper; and later he/she had contacted a possible Camm murder witness.

While it was accurate the ISP had been well behind times in terms of records management, it was also true that such poor administration was somewhat beneficial for the prosecutors. The defense would spend, and ultimately

> **DAVID CAMM COULDN'T SIMULTANEOUSLY BE PLAYING BASKETBALL IN THE GYM AND KILLING HIS FAMILY IN THE GARAGE.**

waste, many hours trying to find germane interviews and references to events or whatever issue was being searched. It took me several days to assimilate the following information:

The basketball games had taken place every Thursday evening at the newly-built Georgetown Community Church (GCC) Family Life Center, which contained classrooms, a kitchen, elevated running/walking track, and a full-court gym. The arrival and departure times for the games had normally been 7:00 p.m. and 9:00 p.m. with a varied number of men showing up, ranging in age from late teens to 55 years of age, the oldest person being Sam Lockhart. The week prior to the murders only eight people, rather than the desired ten, had shown up, and the men couldn't play their preferred five-on-five full-court games.

Access to the locked gym had been gained through Jeff Lockhart, the son of the church's pastor, Leland Lockhart, who was a brother to Sam. The church gym was located about three-and-a-half miles from the Camm residence with the driving time being around five minutes, more or less, depending on the traffic and weather.

Those round-ballers, at least according to the ISP Regional Investigative Commander (RIC) Lieutenant James Biddle, were supposed to have been interviewed the night of the murders. However, with the exception of Sam Lockhart and his son, Phillip, who had raced to the crime scene where they were later first interviewed, none of the other players had been contacted until *two days after the murders*. That was an astounding revelation, for not timely interviewing witnesses who were with a murder suspect prior to his finding his family murdered is considered a major breach in investigative protocol.

In fact, when they were interviewed, the ball players had been contacted by detective Todd Prewitt, who'd been called to Sellersburg from the Seymour ISP Post on Saturday, September 30. Once there, he had sat for several hours until he'd been directed by ADIC Neal to interview the ball players.

Amazingly, though, Prewitt had been told by Neal just to *telephonically interview* the men. That order didn't make sense from a logistical point of view because everyone lived within thirty minutes of the post. It also didn't make sense from an investigative aspect because as seasoned a detective as Neal should have known personal interviews allowed a detective to gauge verbal and non-verbal reactions to questions, which might have been critical in formulating other questions and judging credibility.

The fact the ball players had been treated in such an off-handed way strongly suggested the ISP didn't think they were important witnesses two days after the murders. Still, Prewitt had followed his orders and done as he'd been instructed to do by Neal.

According to Prewitt's later account, the purpose of his interviews "... was to talk to these people *as soon as possible*[38] so they could get the freshest recollection of the events on the guys that David Camm had played basketball with." Among the questions posed to the players were 1) what time did David Camm arrive, 2) what time did he leave, 3) what was he wearing, 4) what kind of vehicle was he driving, 5) did he personally own hand guns, 6) did he have any personal or family problems, and 7) did anyone ever threaten him.

Nine ball players were contacted over the phone, including Phillip Lockhart, with Prewitt's apparently not knowing he had already been interviewed twice by other detectives. That meant the ISP investigators most likely hadn't communicated among themselves, not a good practice in an investigation with dozens of investigators conducting interviews. Regardless, according to those present, Camm had been at the gym at 7:00 p.m. or within a minute or so of that time.

---

[38] Emphasis mine.

Prewitt's efforts had yielded other results: a total of 11 guys had showed up, with the last one being Sam Lockhart, around 7:15-7:20 p.m. Prior to Sam's arriving, there had already been ten players present; thus, they had already begun to play their desired five-on-five full-court games. David Camm had been among those ten.

The five-on-five games had lasted for around two hours with three guys leaving prior to or right at 9:00 p.m., leaving eight players, along with Camm, who had agreed to play another game. After that four-on-four game, the recollections of all, in addition to Camm's own, had been consistent: he had left the gym sometime between 9:15 and 9:30 p.m.

As I finished reading Prewitt's last report, I was totally flabbergasted. Clemons' sworn assertion in the arrest affidavit claimed Camm had left the gym around 9:00 p.m. That was flat-out not true. Prewitt had very accurately secured the information on Camm's true departure time a day prior to Clemons' affidavit. *No one said he left at 9:00 p.m.—not a single player!* The most elementary aspect of Clemons' timeline had been off by at least 15 minutes, if not more. At best, it meant that Clemons had been woefully ignorant of Prewitt's information, confirming there'd been no coordination or dissemination of critical information; at worst, well, at worst it meant Clemons had willfully distorted his own sworn affidavit.

Reading further, but not in any interview with the ball players, I found the door to the entrance of the gym had also contained a security alarm. Jeff Lockhart had been entrusted with the key and alarm code, and it had been he who'd unlocked the door to the gym and disengaged the alarm. After the last game, he'd engaged the same alarm just prior to locking the same door. On each occasion, both entering and leaving the gym, David Camm had been present, his presence witnessed by several other players.

It had taken several days after Camm's arrest for the ISP to even get those alarm records. They had finally done so—but only after learning Camm's uncle, Nelson Lockhart, a retired police officer, had previously asked the alarm company for those records.[39]

Amazingly, what those records reflected was the alarm had been disengaged at 6:59 p.m. and re-engaged at 9:22 p.m. *9:22 p.m.!* I couldn't believe it. Clemons' alleged time of Camm's departure had been off by 22 minutes!

Further corroborating that departure time were the cellular phone records of some of the players who had called their wives or girlfriends, as records of those calls verified they had been made within a minute or two after 9:22 p.m.

The stories provided by Camm and the other ball players, as independently verified, were very consistent with one another and completely refuted

---

[39] Nelson Lockhart arranged to have the alarm system installed in the church building.

Clemons' timeline allegation. It was unimaginable a homicide investigator could get such an easily provable and critical fact completely wrong. It was an egregious error, but it also enabled their manufactured timeline to fit with Camm's killing his family after he'd left the gym.

Additionally, the distance from the gym to Camm's house took four to five minutes to drive, further meaning Camm had arrived home around 9:26–9:27 p.m. Two or three minutes later, at 9:29 p.m., he had made the frantic call to the ISP Post.

The deductions from those known times, at least according to the allegations in Clemons' affidavit, had been that within two or three minutes of arriving home, Camm had completed all the following:

- Ambushed his family;
- Forced Kim to disrobe;
- Placed her shoes neatly on top of the car;
- Engaged in a life and death struggle with Kim;
- Inflicted 22 wounds on her;
- Emerged from the struggle with his wife unscathed;
- Methodically shot and killed his wife, daughter Jill, and son Brad;
- Removed his son from the car to engage in the ruse of CPR;
- Retrieved a mop, bucket, and cleaning solution from the middle of the house;
- Cleaned and manipulated the blood flow for an unstated purpose;
- Toted, spilled, and then tossed the cleaning solution off the back deck;
- Returned the mop and bucket to the middle of the house;
- Called the ISP Post screaming for help; and
- Somewhere during those few minutes, managed to hide or destroy the murder weapon.

The times alleged by Clemons also meant that the blood-serum separation in Kim's blood flow had to have occurred by 9:42 p.m. when the first ISP units arrived at the scene and noticed the distinct color change. The separation, therefore, had to have occurred within 17-18 minutes. If the timeline were accurate, not only had Camm achieved superman status in accomplishing all those events, but he had also been able to overcome nature—e.g., he had enabled the natural phenomena of blood-serum separation to have occurred within mere minutes rather than an hour or so needed at every other crime scene.

Such events, which would have enabled Camm to murder his family as alleged by Clemons and Stan Faith, were not only beyond improbable but impossible. Totally impossible. Why hadn't someone within the ISP or Faith's office realized that prior to Camm's arrest? I had to take a break from my office as I walked outside in the crisp autumn air, asking just what the hell had happened to cause the demise of common sense.

Interpreted Gunshots

After several minutes, I began the search for the mystery witness who supposedly had heard the three "interpreted" gunshots that had killed Kim, Brad, and Jill. In one of Clemons' own reports, I was surprised to discover the witness was Debbie Ter Vree. Debbie was one of Camm's aunts and the youngest Lockhart daughter who lived in the house in the woods just north of the Camm residence as she, her husband Bob, and eight-year-old daughter Hannah shared the common driveway with the Camm family.

Aerial photo of the Camm residence taken by me in 2005. The blacktop driveway leads into the woods (lower left) to the residence of the Ter Vree family; across the gravel road was the home of Camm's grandfather.

On the morning after the murders, Ter Vree, still in shock, had walked down her driveway, spoken with Clemons, whom she had known for several years, and asked him if he could come to their house. Hannah had been experiencing nightmares, her mother had explained, and perhaps a comforting word from a police officer she knew might help alleviate some fears. Hannah, not only related to Brad and Jill, had also been best friends with each, and had been devastated when told of their deaths.

During their walk to her house, Ter Vree had mentioned to Clemons that she had put Hannah to bed around 9:00 p.m. the night before, and several minutes later she'd heard some sounds. Debbie, when later interviewed on tape by Clemons, had described those sounds as "…thump, thump, thump or bang, bang, bang. And I thought my husband was knocking with his fist on the…computer desk or whatever…" She told Clemons she'd walked to the computer room and asked Bob if he'd been making the noises, and he told her he hadn't.

Debbie was married to a former police officer and was herself a former emergency responder. One had to think she knew the sound of gunshots and would have told Clemons if that's what she heard. During her taped interview, she had never mentioned or implied the noises she'd heard could have been shots. Ter Vree, in fact, had been completely unaware of Clemons' "interpretation" of the sounds she'd heard until several days after Camm's arrest. When finally told Clemons had distorted her story to support the arrest of her nephew, Ter Vree had been livid.

I was dumbfounded. If Clemons had wanted to know the cause of the three sounds, why hadn't he simply asked Ter Vree: "Those sounds, could they have been gunshots?"

To determine what Ter Vree had heard, though, I pored through the ISP reports. Shortly after ISP trooper Josh Banet had arrived on the scene at 9:42 p.m., Camm, restrained from going into the garage by his uncle Nelson, had begun to scream in an unintelligible manner. He then, as witnessed by several people, had viciously struck the tailgate of his truck with his balled fist. Then, he had fallen to the ground, in a fetal position, and had begun shrieking, "WHY MY KIDS? WHY MY KIDS?" and "THIS CAN'T BE HAPPENING!"

As others had attempted to get Camm off the ground, Banet had stopped them, telling them to let Camm get it out.[40]

Knowing that Clemons had "interpreted" the strikes to the tailgate as gunshots, I was equally sure that Camm's screams had been "interpreted" by some as Camm *acting* as a grief-stricken husband and father.

Other questions arose, as I was mystified as to how ADIC Mickey Neal and RIC James Biddle, supervisors who each presumably had been aware of the details of the ongoing investigation, would or could have allowed Clemons to swear to inaccuracies or even if they had seen the affidavit.

Prosecutor Stan Faith, of course, had also signed the affidavit. Had he been duped by Clemons? Even if he had been confused or deceived, intentionally or otherwise by Clemons, Faith obviously wasn't a stupid man. In the days after Camm was arrested, it had to have been obvious to him, or anyone who

---

[40] One neighbor witness had been interviewed by an investigator of Faith's the day after the murders. After he'd heard sirens, he had then heard a piercing, hysterical scream and three loud bangs, as though someone were hitting a door.

knew the details of the case, the affidavit he and Clemons had presented to the judge had not only been inaccurate but hadn't contained the probable cause needed to arrest Camm.

Timeline On Day Of Murders

Okay, if the murders hadn't occurred after 9:15 p.m., what time had they happened? Strangely, there was nothing I could find in any report where a time or range of times was articulated. Was that oversight or intentional? Regardless, piecing together several reports revealed Kim and the kids had a very busy day, particularly after school. After Brad's grandmother had taken him for his allergy shot around 4:00 p.m., Kim had taken Jill to her dance class, which had lasted from 4:30 p.m. to 5:30 p.m.

Next, after a quick visit to Kim's parents' home, the three had been off to Brad's swim practice from 6:00 p.m. to 7:00 p.m. All those activities had taken place in New Albany, between ten and 12 miles from their home, meaning they'd arrived home well after 7:00 p.m. and certainly after Camm had already been playing basketball.

In another report, a neighbor interviewed within hours of the murders told of having just sat down to watch a 7:30 p.m. television program when he'd seen Kim's black Bronco pulling into Lockhart Road, a few hundred feet from the Camm house. That tightened the time frame and begged the question of the likelihood of kids and Kim still having been alive in the Bronco and garage, almost two hours after they arrived home.

Back-timing the separated blood meant Kim had been shot at least an hour or so before Camm had found her, or around 8:27 p.m. at the latest.

All of this information meant Faith and Clemons had to have recognized their deduction of 9:15 p.m. wasn't remotely accurate, and knowing Camm couldn't simultaneously be playing basketball in the gym and killing his family in the garage, Clemons and Faith had to realize they were faced with a huge conundrum. That meant, I thought, only three courses of possible action: 1) acknowledge they didn't have enough evidence to charge or arrest Camm, thus admitting they screwed up big-time and in the process, face a severe backlash from the public; 2) also admit someone else, still at large, was the murderer, and face even larger repercussions; or 3) keep silent about their humongous error, admitting no error whatsoever, while they silently changed their theory on when and how Camm had committed the murders.

CHAPTER 6

Changing The Time Of The Murders

Prosecutor Stan Faith was in an untenable situation. Faced with incontrovertible evidence and thus knowing the time he and Clemons had claimed Camm had killed his family had been egregiously wrong, he knew something needed to be done. His only solution? He had to claim David Camm slaughtered his family, not *after* the basketball games, but *during* the games because, after all, that was the only possible time frame of their murders.

That improbable, if not impossible, feat could only be managed if those 11 ball players, now alibi witnesses, were attacked. David Camm, though, hadn't made them his

> "CAN YOU SAY THAT FOR CERTAIN? THAT HE DIDN'T LEAVE THE GYM?"
>
> "YEAH, SAY THAT FOR SURE!"

alibi witnesses, by anything he had said or done, but by the events themselves.

To achieve his goal, Faith needed help, but instead of calling on lead detective Sean Clemons and the ISP, he had his own investigators conduct new interviews of the basketball players. Those investigators were all politically-appointed, of course, and owed their jobs to Faith.

Beginning on October 23, 2000, or almost four weeks after the murders, prosecutor investigators Jacque Vaught, Tony Toran, and Emily Fessel, among others,[41] began their own interviews of the now very problematic witnesses.[42]

Vaught and Toran began their interview of Jeff Lockhart, Camm's cousin, with a challenging question. Vaught asked, "Did you, did you have your eyes on him the whole time, I mean, did you ever see him leave?" Jeff responded that he hadn't seen Camm leave the gym, but rather had seen him playing; then talking with Tom Jolly, a church member who was sitting on the sideline, or else stretching on the sideline, and then playing again.

Vaught pressed harder. "But you don't feel like he could have left anytime, you wouldn't have noticed?"

The response was direct: "I mean, I, there's no way he would have had time to go all the way home and do that and then come back."

I took a few minutes to research Tom Jolly. Where had this guy come from? It turned out that Jolly, a church elder, had been working on his nearby

---

[41] Apparently only one of Faith's investigators had law enforcement experience.

[42] The transcripts of their statements contained the ISP case number, but the ISP, we were later told, had never received a copy of those transcripts.

horse farm when forced to stop at dusk. As one who championed the building of the church gym, and as a former athlete but too old to play, he had driven the short distance to the church gym to watch the pickup games.

Jolly, who hadn't been interviewed before Camm had been arrested, had arrived at the gym after 8:00 p.m. and sat in a chair at the south end of the gym, near the basket, and watched the end of a five-on-five game, which included Camm as a player. Within a short time, the game had concluded, and Camm had walked over to Jolly and begun speaking with him, asking him about his two sons, one of whom was a good friend.

The two had spoken for several minutes as the next game commenced, with Sam Lockhart taking Camm's place among the ten players. While talking with Jolly, Camm had occasionally exchanged barbs with several of the other players. As the game neared its end, he'd begun stretching and running to loosen up for his return to the next game, which had begun close to 8:30 p.m.

Returning to the interviews of Faith's people, Fessel, in her interview with Martin Dickey, had maintained the same approach as had Vaught: "But you, do you know if you saw Dave the entire time he wasn't playing? Can you say that for certain? That he didn't leave the gym?"

Martin's answer surely wasn't the one desired by Faith. "That he didn't leave the gym? Yeah…say that for sure!"

Martin Dickey had recalled Camm's sitting on the sideline the one game he sat out, speaking with someone, but he hadn't known the man's identity.

The interview of Scott Schrank, however, had been tweaked a little by Vaught. "Have you ever known him to, to sit out games before?" Schrank had responded that was the only time, in four or five nights of playing, he had seen Camm sit out. That must have been good news for Faith, for the obvious conclusion was Camm, during previous game nights, hadn't sat out because he wasn't going to kill his family those nights. Vaught, however, hadn't brought up Tom Jolly's name to Shrank or asked any questions about Schrank seeing Camm off the court.

All of the other players had verified Camm had been playing basketball throughout the evening; that he had sat out one game; that he had been on the sidelines speaking with Jolly; and that after three of the guys left, the eight remaining guys had played from around 9:00 p.m. to the time the alarm had been engaged.

The faulty time Clemons and Faith had initially claimed the murders occurred wasn't the least of their problems, as another unexplained issue had been addressed. Vaught claimed to Jeff Lockhart that two of the players "believe they saw [Camm] with a gray…sweatshirt…Were you one of those…?" In fact, no ball player had claimed to have seen him wear a sweatshirt, and Vaught's assertion had been a fabrication.

The sweatshirt line had continued with the same insinuation to Jeremy Little by Fessel. "So you didn't inform [the police] that he had a sweatshirt on at all?"

Fessel had also questioned Martin Dickey, "Do you remember telling the police that David had on a gray sweatshirt?" And another player, Mark Werncke, hadn't been immune from Fessel's very leading question: "…you don't remember telling the police that he had a gray sweatshirt on?"

No one took the bait, as all had said Camm had only been wearing a T-shirt, either white or gray in color, and that everyone had come to play in the clothes in which they were dressed. Clearly, Faith's investigators had been trying to connect Camm with the BACKBONE sweatshirt, but no one had seen him with a sweatshirt or jacket, and no one had known of any nickname of Camm's other than Dave or Davy.

The basketball players hadn't played the game Faith needed, and it wasn't a shock when he later claimed in a video interview that "everybody [basketball players] out there [church gymnasium] is either mistaken or lying."[43]

We'd soon interview all the players and Tom Jolly and make our own judgements as to their credibility and honesty.

---

[43]   The Alibi: Disturbing the Peace, *"48 Hours Investigates,"* October 11, 2002, CBS Television Network.

CHAPTER 7
Camm's First Stories

Still weighing heavily on my mind was the personality of the individual who had pulled the trigger. The fact a woman had been murdered during a violent attack, possibly motivated by sex, unfortunately isn't uncommon in the United States. After all, violent murders are daily occurrences, especially in many large cities. The intentional, cold-blooded execution of two very innocent children isn't the norm or routine anywhere, however.

The evidence suggested Kim had been cooperative, at least in the beginning, until she had viciously fought her attacker. Something must have caused that sea change.

> **"THIS JUST AIN'T HAPPENING. I MEAN, SOMEBODY DIDN'T REALLY MURDER MY WIFE AND TWO KIDS."**

Had she believed death was imminent, and she had no other choice? Had her kids been threatened? Had she, Brad, or Jill recognized the attacker? Whatever the reason or reasons, all had not only been victims but witnesses. The conclusions as to why the kids had been killed were either 1) dead witnesses, particularly those who recognize their attacker, don't testify; and/or 2) the killer flew into an uncontrollable rage.

Cold-bloodedly assassinating two little kids takes a special kind of personality, one without a conscience or a sense of guilt. During my lengthy FBI career, I had interviewed and/or interrogated numerous individuals who were totally devoid, in my assessment, of any conscience and never honestly expressed remorse for their acts. On the contrary, they routinely painted themselves as innocent or even as victims while lying repeatedly about not only their crimes but themselves.

Prolific liars didn't necessarily make credible liars as their multiple stories often conflicted with their previous claims. All were manipulators who thought they were charming; most considered themselves smarter than others, including any law enforcement officer; most lived off the efforts of others; parts of their crimes were impulsive in nature; and, for some, when their charm and guile didn't get them what they wanted, they resorted to physicality and violence.

In short, they preyed on their victims who were almost always weaker in some degree: physically, mentally, or emotionally. Remember the hyena targets not the strongest or fastest in the herd but rather the small, weak, and/or wounded. The hyena in the Camm case either found a way, through guile and lying, into being allowed in Kim's car, or else sprung from the darkness in the garage.

The term often utilized in today's world for that kind of creature is one who has an Anti-Social Personality Disorder. Terms in the past included sociopath and/or psychopath. I don't argue with any of the terms, as I'm not a psychologist diagnosing those people in order to receive any kind of treatment, other than from the criminal justice system, which, of course, is where many ultimately find themselves.

Anyway, and in that regard, I wanted to know more about David Camm the person. If he had literally looked into the eyes of his daughter and son and then pulled the trigger ending each of their lives, he would have had to, in my assessment, exhibit some traits that foretold, in some manner, his impending acts of violence. The first place to begin such a search was to inform myself of the first stories he told the ISP and others of what happened that evening and ultimately to find what kind of life he had led for the months and years leading to the murders.

Was David consistent with his stories? Did he lie and/or make any claims that were later used to impeach his credibility? Conversely, and equally as important, did his story dovetail with known facts and the recollections of others, particularly the basketball players?

The ISP Call

I began by listening to the first words spoken by Camm to anyone about the murders. At 9:29 p.m., from the kitchen of his house, where he supposedly had run in a panic, he had called the ISP Sellersburg Post. His one minute and 21 second taped call had been answered by a female radio dispatcher. Camm had immediately identified himself and loudly told her he needed to speak with "Post Command."[44] When she had told him that Post Command was on another phone, he had screamed, "RIGHT NOW, LET ME TALK TO POST COMMAND!"

There were a few seconds of interminable background music before Post Command trooper Andrew Lee had inquisitively said, "Dave?"

Camm had screamed again, "GET EVERYBODY OUT HERE TO MY HOUSE NOW! MY WIFE AND MY KIDS ARE DEAD! GET EVERYBODY OUT HERE TO MY HOUSE!"

Lee, reacting quickly, had alerted on-duty troopers, via the ISP radio, to "GO TO DAVE CAMM'S HOUSE NOW!" Camm had again screamed

---

[44] Post Command is the ISP trooper in administrative charge of the Post during the evening and early morning hours.

for him to get everyone out to his house, with Lee trying to reassure him, "Everything's gonna be okay, alright, we're gonna get…"

Camm had literally shrieked, "EVERYTHING'S NOT OKAY! GET EVERYBODY OUT HERE NOW!" His next few words were indecipherable, even though I listened several times. Lee, responding in a measured and professional voice, had then asked Camm if he knew what had happened.

Camm's next response, in a voice several octaves higher than before, was, many had claimed, a voice and a man out of control with grief. "No, they're dead…I just got home from playing basketball…*oh, my God, what am I gonna do*?" Others, after hearing those same words, had claimed Camm was indeed a psychopath and a poor actor trying to hide the fact he was the murderer.

Anyone, I thought, hearing his words, at least for the first time, had to have been unnerved.

And then, Camm had continued, in an almost subdued plea, "Andrew, get everybody out here, please…" Lee had responded by trying to get Camm to speak with the radio dispatcher, but Camm hadn't responded to that suggestion or Lee's question if he needed an ambulance. Rather than respond, Camm had yelled, "I GOTTA GO ACROSS THE STREET, I GOTTA GET SOME HELP!" and then, as Lee had attempted to get his attention, "GET EVERYBODY OUT HERE! I GOTTA GO!"

I re-played the call several times, trying to listen from the viewpoint of one who thought Camm was the cold-blooded, unconscionable murderer or another who thought him to be the consummate victim. The bottom line was that whatever side I took prior to listening, the tape, I knew, wasn't going to be any smoking gun but rather viewed and explained in the manner of those convinced one way or the other. Still, I thought, if Camm had killed his family, he was one helluva actor.

Next Contacts

The next person Camm had screamed at was his uncle, Nelson Lockhart, who was across Lockhart Road.[45] Nelson had been on the phone, speaking with his brother, Sam, when their nephew, after slamming down his phone in his own house, had run across the road and into the side door of his widowed 92-year-old grandfather's house.[46]

Nelson, although a 35-year police officer, had said he had at first been stunned when his nephew yelled that his family had been killed. The retired

---

[45] Nelson had been chipping golf balls in his father's front yard when Camm came home earlier that evening, about 5:30 p.m., and the two of them had spoken for a few minutes.

[46] One of Amos' nine children had been spending each night with their increasingly feeble father.

officer had recovered enough to tell Sam that something bad had happened at Dave's house and quickly hung up the phone. He had then run barefoot out the door and across the dewy grass and gravel road after his nephew.

Once he had turned the corner of the garage and seen the carnage, Nelson had been shocked into utter disbelief. He'd thought he remembered seeing Camm attempt to give Brad CPR at the same time he was told by his nephew to check on Jill in the car. Nelson had thought—he couldn't remember for sure, he said—that he next went into the driver's door and through that door reached into the back seat. He had gently touched Jill's arm, shaking it a bit and asked, "Jilly?" She had been unresponsive and cold to the touch, and Nelson had known she was dead. As he came around the car and looked into the eyes of Brad and Kim, he had recognized they were also dead.

I stopped for a few moments as two thoughts popped into my mind, and both dealt with the fact that Nelson Lockhart was a 35-year police veteran. First, Camm had certainly known of his uncle's background and further that he was staying the night across the road. Would he have taken a chance of firing three shots in the garage, not knowing if his uncle might hear those shots? Secondly, Nelson had probably seen dozens of death scenes, yet he, too, was stunned and shocked before he finally engaged into what he called his "police mode."

Nelson, regaining that sense of police reality, had told his nephew all three were dead, and they had to get out of the garage, for it was a "crime scene." Camm hadn't wanted to leave but was forced to do so by Nelson, who had begun to console him outside the garage and who was, in Nelson's words, "beyond distraught."

The next conversations Camm had occurred a few minutes later, as Sam Lockhart and his son, Phillip, arrived.[47] Both had recalled they were initially speechless and in shock. Sam had been told by Nelson that it was Kim on the floor of the garage, causing him to be momentarily confused. Sam's eldest child was also named Kim, and shock waves went through his mind before it registered the body was that of David's wife. He also had tried to enter the garage but was grabbed by his brother, who told him it was a crime scene, and no one could enter.

While the four of them had stood outside the garage, "helpless" as they later described themselves, Camm had begun to get angry with himself, saying he shouldn't have played basketball that night. The others had tried to console him, but he broke away from their embraces.

---

[47] Both had been playing basketball with Camm a few minutes earlier. Sam, after Nelson's call, raced to his garage and was met by Phillip, returning home in his own truck. The two got into Sam's car and began the frantic dash to Camm's house, reaching speeds of over 100 mph.

Soon, the first of many ISP marked units and other police and emergency vehicles had arrived. Included among them had been Sean Clemons, who had worked with Camm for several years at the Sellersburg Post. The ISP reports noted the time as 9:42 p.m.[48]

Kim's Bronco had been parked in the left bay with Camm's white pickup truck parked in front of the right bay of their garage. The doorway in the background is to the breezeway, which leads to the side door of the house and kitchen.

Minutes later, Clemons had begun to ask Camm some questions. His old friend had told him that after he arrived home from playing basketball, he had turned into his driveway and used the remote to open the right side of his two-bay garage. He had then seen a body lying on the floor, adjacent to the right side of Kim's black Bronco, which was parked in the left bay.[49]

Camm said he'd stopped his truck, jumped out, run to the body, and bent over it, finally recognizing it as Kim, whom he knew was dead. He'd then jumped up, looked into the Bronco, had seen Jill in the back seat, and recognized that she, too, was also dead.

Dave had next seen Brad slumped over the back seat, behind the driver's seat, as though he had been trying to escape. Camm said he had gotten into the front seat and then climbed into the back seat, squirmed through the two front bucket seats, clutched Brad, turned around, and removed his son from the Bronco via the front passenger door.

Camm also said he wanted Clemons to be aware of what he had done to the degree he could remember with any clarity. He told Clemons he knew,

---

[48] Clemons, who had recently been promoted to detective, drew his weapon and helped clear the house with other troopers to determine if the perpetrator(s) were still present and/or other victims inside. There was no one in the house. Back in the garage, they also confirmed all three victims were dead.

[49] Clemons report is his recollection of David's story and wasn't taped. As such, it reads as an emotionless narrative of what Camm saw and did.

from his own police training, that whenever anyone entered a crime scene, evidence would be disturbed or altered in some way.

After removing Brad, Camm told Clemons he had placed his son on the garage floor and begun CPR, thinking his young son may have had a chance to survive. The CPR, though, wasn't working. He had next run through the garage, onto the breezeway, and into the house. There, in the kitchen, he called the ISP Post.

After the call, Camm said he'd run across the road to get his uncle Nelson, screaming his family had been murdered. Nelson, he said, had run after him, back to the garage.

Camm had then told Clemons he'd take care of whoever it was who killed his family. That was the first time, I noted, he had exhibited any kind of anger, other than at himself, for not being present to save his family. As with the call to the ISP Post, I was sure his words would be interpreted as genuine rage or false outrage, depending on what belief one had in regards to his guilt or innocence.

Also interacting with Camm in those first few minutes was trooper Josh Banet. He had asked if Camm had any idea as to who might have been responsible. Camm had apparently thought for a few moments before he answered. Three years earlier, he'd said, while still a trooper, he had been informed a neighbor had an outstanding arrest warrant for marijuana possession. Camm hadn't liked arresting a neighbor, even one whose name he hadn't known. Regardless, the guy had been very angry when told he was being arrested. Banet had made a note to secure the man's name from the ISP files.

Among the dozens of other officers and first responders was a close friend and former fellow trooper of Camm's, Shelly Romero.[50] She had immediately gone to him, describing Camm as very agitated, waving his hands and pacing. Camm had kept saying, "Somebody's killed my fucking family." Romero had finally grabbed his arm in an effort to calm him. She had asked him several questions. Where had he been? "Playing basketball." Where had his family been? "At swim practice." That had prompted another response: "I should have gone with them." Again, actual or fake remorse?

In response to another question, he had said he didn't know why Kim's shoes were on top of the car. As for the killer, he had thought the murders could have been committed for revenge for something he may have done as a cop. Romero, per her report, had said all of the officers "were all trying to think of a major case he had made where somebody may have just gotten out

---

[50] In addition to the ISP, several other agencies had responded with literally dozens of officers, paramedics, coroners, and others, including prosecutor Stan Faith, his deputy prosecutors and several investigators.

of jail..." Romero had opined it could also have been someone still "stewing over" something small, such as a warning ticket. The bottom line was no one, including Camm, had known of the reason or had strongly suspected anyone.

Throughout the remainder of the evening, Romero had either stayed with Camm or ensured someone—friend, family or ISP officer—was with him at all times.

Clemons had then asked Camm if he could give a more detailed interview at the ISP Post. He had initially refused, saying he didn't want to leave his wife and kids still alone in the garage. They were alone because officers were waiting for a search warrant, which was normal protocol, even though Camm had given his permission for the search to begin.

After repeated pleas to leave, however, Camm had finally relented and after midnight was driven from his house to New Albany by two Floyd County Sheriff's deputies, Russ Wyatt and Dale Slaughter, who had been at a night firearms training session. Slaughter, a good friend of David's, had then picked up his own vehicle in New Albany and taken Camm the remaining way to the Sellersburg ISP Post. During the 15-minute ride, his old friend had apparently said little, if anything.

First Taped Interview

At the Post, Camm had been met by detectives Michael "Mickey" Neal and Darrell Gibson, both good friends of his. Neal, the acting DIC, had been shift partners with Camm for several years. I couldn't help but think how utterly incongruous the situation was for Neal; he was interviewing the guy whom he had depended upon for backup yet who might have killed his wife and children. That had to have been a bizarre feeling.

Camm, who suffered from migraine headaches, had said he needed his migraine meds, but they were in his house. Another trooper, though, Sean Hannon, was in the Post and phoned Camm's family doctor to explain the need. A prescription had been ordered, later to be picked up by Camm's brother and sister, Donnie and Julie.

Camm had been taken into an interview room, but there was no video, as the machine was inoperable. The audio of the interview, at least the one I heard, wasn't of good quality. I listened to the tape as I also read the transcript.

Told he could stop the interview at any time, Camm nevertheless had told his two friends to interview him in detail, saying that any little thing might help them determine who'd been responsible. He had told them, as he had Clemons at the scene, that he wanted them to "do it right."

When asked by Neal to do so, Camm had given a rundown of the day in chronological fashion, how he thought the day would have gone and where his family would have been. Kim, he had said, had handled practically everything when it came to their kids but had help from her mother. Their schedule after school had included Brad's allergy shot, Jill's dance class, and Brad's swim practice. Kim would not have gotten home until after swim practice ended at 7:00 p.m. Camm noted he'd been home until shortly before that same time when he'd left for the basketball games. In fact, his wife and kids would probably not have been home until around 7:30 p.m.

Even though the games normally ended at 9:00 p.m., Camm said they had played a little longer, and at the time, he'd thought to himself, "Man, I'm gonna be in trouble" because he needed, he'd said, to help with the kids' baths and homework.

Continuing, he'd told of pulling in his driveway, raising his garage door, and seeing a body come into view. Camm said he'd first thought it was Jill because he thought Kim's pants, lying next to her, were Jill's dance outfit. He'd also thought that Jill had possibly slipped and hit her head, but when he'd gotten out of his truck, run to and finally recognized Kim, he'd thought, "This ain't good."

And then, after seeing Kim dead, Camm had thought immediately of his two kids, thinking, "BRAD AND JILL…BRAD AND JILL…WHERE ARE THEY???"

He had then turned around, Camm said, and looked into the car. Jill had been sitting upright in her seat, although her head had been tilted forward. Brad had been draped over the back of the bench seat, looking as though he were trying to get away. Camm had then scrambled, he'd said, into the Bronco, through the two front seats and grabbed his son whom, he thought, felt warm. He had then pulled him from the Bronco, laid him on the floor, and performed CPR.

As I listened and read, there were times Camm had sounded measured and deliberate, as when he gave his thoughts as to the times certain events occurred. At other times, he had seemed confused, as with not recalling if he had first run into the house to call the ISP or performed CPR. And on other occasions, his words had sounded as though he could have been in shock, specifically when he ironically said his family would have had a "pretty normal" and "routine" day. Yeah, I thought, a normal and routine day, except they got murdered at the end of it.

The reason why he had called the ISP Post, rather than 9-1-1, Camm had explained, was because he hadn't wanted some "stupid dingy dispatcher" to answer, implying that he wanted to call the ISP Post, staffed by people he knew. Would that be normal? Not to call 9-1-1 but a ten-digit number? Probably not if Joe Public had found his family murdered but a former ISP trooper? The answer, once again I thought, probably depended upon one's belief of his guilt or innocence.

Gibson had asked Camm if his house was usually locked. His answer was somewhat surprising. There were two doors on the breeze way, he had said, one to the garage and one that led into the kitchen, and both had usually been unlocked.

After telling the two detectives of Kim's work schedule, one she had been able to manage in accordance with the needs of Brad and Jill, Camm had suddenly and emotionally exclaimed, "I should have gone to swim practice." Had that truly been a spontaneous utterance of a man who was feeling guilt over not preventing the murder of his family? Or had it been contrived? Again, the answer lay in the ear of the beholder.

Camm had then thought out loud that maybe someone had been waiting for Kim and the kids. He said that maybe "it was somebody after me…how else can you explain it?'

When Gibson had pressed him if any suspects came to his mind, Camm told him what he had earlier told Banet about the neighbor who had gotten very angry after Camm had arrested him. As he drove to jail to book that neighbor, Camm had asked him if he was going to do something to him or if he was going to "come over and shoot my dog or anything like that…?"

The neighbor, however, had responded that he "wouldn't do anything like that."

Camm had then recalled two other people, names unknown by him, who should be interviewed. A neighbor, living through the woods and north of them several hundred feet, had only recently been released after serving a lengthy prison sentence for dealing drugs. That person lived with his aged father, a former bar owner, who, a year earlier, had accidentally started a large brush fire that almost had gotten out of control.[51] Camm had gone to the neighbor's house, driving his ISP marked unit, and had spoken with each of those men.

When asked as to the seating arrangements in the two-door Bronco, Camm had said Brad usually sat behind Kim, and Jill sat on the other side of the rear passenger seat. He had added the front passenger's seat was broken and had to be held forward in order for anyone in the back to get out that side. The kids would have waited, he said, until Kim came around the car, opened the passenger door, and pulled the broken seat forward.

In an obvious reference to Kim's shoes being on top of the Bronco, Gibson had asked if she had ever taken them off while driving. "No," was the response, but Camm had said he also noticed the location of the shoes. As for her clothes, Camm hadn't remembered what clothes Kim was wearing

---

[51] Living in-between that neighbor and the Camm house was the Ter Vree home, situated deep in the woods.

and said she wouldn't have come home prior to going to swim practice. She therefore had probably been wearing the same clothes as when she had left the house in the morning.

In the very short time he'd been in the kitchen, calling the ISP Post, Camm had recalled seeing the envelope containing his paycheck and the bottle containing his prescription migraine headache medication sitting on the kitchen counter. "Was it strange," I asked, "that Camm could recall those two items yet was confused about the sequence of giving his son CPR vis-à-vis calling the ISP Post?"

Camm had continued that there wasn't anything of "extreme value" in the house, but Kim did have a pair of $2,500 diamond earrings that he had given her for a Christmas gift. His wife, he had said, didn't often wear them, and they would probably be on her dresser in their bedroom.[52]

The detectives had then asked Camm if he had bought his ISP-issued handguns when he left the department. "No," he had responded, telling them he had no need for a handgun. He'd added, though, that he did have a lot of accumulated ammunition from his ten years with the ISP, which was in the basement along with some shoulder weapons.

For the first time, Camm had recalled a Schwan's delivery man had been at the house prior to his leaving for basketball. He even remembered the exact price of the two frozen-food items he bought, $17.85. The salesman, he said, had been at the house around 6:30 p.m. or quarter till seven, and he came every other week.

Camm didn't flash money, he'd said, and the only time he had gotten cash was at an ATM a few days prior. The family's financial condition, he had continued, was very good.

Referring to the fact Kim's pants and shoes were off and she was only wearing her panties, Camm had said the murders didn't make any sense to him, unless "somebody was just…gonna rape her."

If Kim had, in fact, been the intended victim, Camm had then asked the obvious question of why his kids had been killed. That question, of course, was a big one. Why were two small, physically non-threatening children, safely contained in the backseat of a vehicle, murdered? About the only answer, I again thought, was they hadn't been non-threatening, particularly if they could have described or even recognized the attacker.

I returned to the paused audio recording. Neal had asked Camm with whom he had been playing basketball. He knew most of them, he had responded,

---

[52] Most burglars steal items of value, but weird stuff is occasionally stolen—e.g., early in my FBI career we arrested a prolific burglar of homes and cars who had a stash of over 400 stolen lighters, souvenirs of his "accomplishments."

identifying his cousins Phillip and Jeff; his uncle, Sam Lockhart; and the Dickey brothers. Of the others, he'd said, "I don't know who they are."

Neal had quickly moved past the basketball players, not going into any other details. "Okay, that's fine. Uh, your wife hasn't ever spoken about anything as far as any problems at work…co-workers…boss?" Camm had responded that Kim hadn't told him anything about any issues, including anyone flirting with or stalking her or any other problems.

As for any suspicious phone calls or suspicious cars that had driven along the private dead-end Lockhart Road, no, he had said, he wasn't aware of any. And no, Kim wasn't having any affair, Camm had emphasized.

Camm had suddenly remembered the Schwan's man left his house about five minutes before he had left for basketball and that it was a couple of minutes before 7:00 p.m. when he had arrived at the church gym.

The exact position of Jill in the back seat wasn't clear in his mind, and Camm had said he also didn't know if her seatbelt was on or off. Brad, however, didn't have on his seatbelt, and Camm had said his position, with his body over the back seat, indicated he was clearly trying to get away.

For the second time, Camm had begun crying. "The kids saw things and they were probably screaming and trying to get away…and I wasn't there and I wasn't there…how long did they lay there and bleed…and how long did they hurt…those are the things I just don't know if I can live with."

Camm had then become angry, asking what kind of God had let a human being do what they did. He had told Neal and Gibson that he'd probably end up in hell if he killed himself, but he didn't know if he could live without his wife and his "awesome kids."

I once more stopped the tape. Anger and grief were two well-established responses exhibited by a surviving loved one, but not for those who'd made up their minds Dave was only acting.

Hitting the play button, I listened as Gibson had asked his former colleague if he thought his past affairs could have anything to do with the attack on his family. No, according to Camm, there was no one who was jealous or anyone in his opinion who would have killed his wife and kids over any affair he'd ever had.

I paused again. During my law enforcement career, I knew of men and some women who had engaged in affairs, including with co-workers. Some were good investigators; some weren't. Some were good parents and spouses, but a few weren't. The point I made to myself was having affairs, or not having any for that matter, didn't totally define a person. Not only that, but certainly none of the men or women I knew who had engaged in affairs had ever killed their spouse or children.

Gibson had then told Camm, "Right now, we don't have a whole helluva lot to go on." He'd then reassured his friend, though, they were looking at "every angle and every aspect," and they had the manpower and the people to do what they needed to do.

Reacting to Gibson's comment, Camm had emphasized that all his neighbors should be interviewed, and the two detectives readily agreed; all cops are fully aware that conducting a thorough neighborhood investigation is Investigations 101.

Neal, meanwhile, had shifted gears as he told Camm, "I want to clear you as much as I can" so "no one can point a finger at you." It was then he'd asked for his old partner's clothes, to which Camm had willingly agreed, telling them the clothes he had on were the ones he had when he found his family.

Camm had quickly replied, "Do whatever you need to do."

Gibson had echoed Neal's comments about clearing Camm, but then he'd said something odd about getting the clothes, at least to my way of thinking: "This don't have anything to do with *our*[53] investigation or anything." That begged the question, of course, if taking Camm's clothes hadn't pertained to the ISP's investigation, then to whose investigation had it pertained?

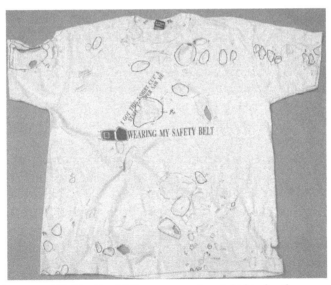

The multi-stained T-shirt David Camm wore the night his family was murdered, depicted after it had been subjected to many tests and cuttings at the ISP Laboratory.

After providing his clothes, Camm had then allowed the two detectives to examine his body for any scratches, abrasions, or injuries. They'd found none. Once again, it would be highly unusual for the one who had engaged

---

[53] Emphasis mine.

Kim in a life-and-death struggle not to have at least one scratch or bruise. The two detectives had then given Camm another pair of pants, socks, and shirt, which had been retrieved from his home.

Gibson had then cautioned Camm, "People will make up stuff," including spreading gossip saying Camm was the one responsible for the murders. The detective had added if he were in the same position, he'd have a hard time maintaining control of himself.

If he'd indeed been the surviving loving husband and father, Camm had then entered the state of denial. "This just ain't happening. I mean, somebody didn't really murder my wife and two kids. I mean, I live on a private road, you know, nobody bothers me, we don't have any problems, somebody doesn't just pick out my house and go kill my wife and kids. I mean this just, this just didn't happen."

Plodding onward, Neal had said that somewhere there was a common thread, and they were going to find it. The two detectives had then asked the obligatory questions about drugs and alcohol and other possible vices. Their former comrade had said he never took any bribes, had gambled a little money at a nearby casino on the Ohio River, drank one beer a week, and didn't do drugs. He'd added the last time he smoked marijuana was when he was 19.

The interview had been interrupted when Julie, Camm's sister, had arrived with his migraine meds, which were then provided to him.

While Gibson was getting contact information from Camm's sister, Neal had asked how much money Kim would have had on her. $20 or $30 at the most had been the response. Kim had also worn a watch, which he'd bought her a couple years ago, and earrings and rings on most days.

Camm had then offered the fact the light bulbs in the garage were burned out and, further, Rusty, the family dog, slept in the basement but liked to be outside. The mention of Rusty had caused Camm to recall his dog's coming to his uncle Nelson and him as they stood outside the garage. She'd wanted to play so they had put her in the nearby detached garage, only for her to get out through another door and run back to them again. The second time they'd made sure every door was shut.

Rusty, Camm had said, would bark at a stranger, but she'd quickly make up to anybody. I got the impression Camm had wanted to talk about his dog rather than anything related to the murders. Again, was that denial? An emotional defense mechanism? An effort to divert any further questions from ones he didn't want to answer? Ear of the beholder.

In addition to sister Julie, Camm's older brother Donnie had been waiting for him in the nearby Squad Room when the interview terminated around 2:30 a.m. The questioning had lasted about two hours.

It would have been much better had I been looking at a video of Camm rather than just listening to him on audio tape because, yes, one's behavior, particularly during a stressful interview, can be telling. There's a huge caveat to that, as one has to be very careful of which comes first, one's unbiased analysis of the behavior or one's pre-conceived conclusion that supports the purported analysis.

I'd been around more than a few police officers who'd claimed they could analyze a person's behavior and determine guilt, or for that matter, even determine innocence, based upon their "behavior analysis" ability. The truth was cops had biases, too, and often weren't all that good in judging a person's behavior.

After spending several hours listening to, reading, and studying Camm's primary interview, I wanted to know what, if anything, he had lied about. Catching a suspect in a lie, particularly a substantive one, could be a dynamite piece of evidence. If, therefore, he had given the two detectives any reasons to disbelieve him and/or made any false exculpatory statements,[54] those would have been highlighted in Clemons' affidavit. None were, of course. Nonetheless, I was anxious to see what later evidence, if any, would contradict any part of Camm's story. If he were a cold, calculating and remorseless psychopath, he'd most likely also be a pathological liar as those folks just couldn't help themselves. It was who they were.

---

[54] A false exculpatory statement is one made or claimed by a suspect that tends to eliminate involvement but isn't true and that can be refuted by other evidence. For example, an armed robbery suspect might claim, "I've never even touched a gun," yet a photograph is discovered of him previously shooting one.

CHAPTER 8
The "Fresh Eyes" Affidavit

I turned my attention to the amended affidavit, used to justify the most recent arrest of Camm, which had been filed in Floyd County Superior Court on November 16, 2004. The affiant was Gary Gilbert, who had stated that he'd been an officer with the ISP for 25 years and a detective for 16 years; he had been assigned the Camm case three weeks after the appeals court had overturned Camm's convictions. His investigation had been deemed as "fresh eyes" by prosecutor Keith Henderson.

Following normal protocol, Gilbert had asserted the incontrovertible facts of the case: "…on September 28, 2000, Camm reported to the Indiana State Police at Sellersburg that he had returned home and found his wife, Kimberly Camm, age 36, his son Bradley Camm, age 7, and his daughter, Jill Camm, age 5, deceased in the garage of his residence."

After noting another established fact, that Dr. Tracy

> THE "FRESH EYES" CLAIMED THAT CAMM LEFT THE GYM WITHOUT THE OTHER BASKETBALL PLAYERS NOTICING HIM GONE, MADE A BUSINESS CALL WHILE WAITING TO AMBUSH HIS FAMILY, SHOT AND KILLED HIS WIFE AND KIDS, AND THEN RETURNED UNNOTICED.

Corey-Handy had determined Jill had been killed by a gunshot wound to the head, he had moved on to Jill's non-lethal injuries and his assertions were anything but incontrovertible. He'd claimed he had interviewed a "medical expert" but it obviously hadn't been Dr. Corey-Handy. His new expert "came to the conclusion that the trauma to Jill Camm's vaginal area is consistent with a sexual device and/or a penis."

That was an explosive allegation by the new expert as the allegation didn't comport with the findings of the original medical examiner, as their findings differed as to the cause and location of Jill's injuries in two distinct, critical ways. In her report, Dr. Corey-Handy had stated that Jill's injuries were "non-specific…blunt trauma of the external genitalia (hymen intact)." "Non-specific…blunt trauma" doesn't equate to injuries from a "sexual device and/or a penis."

Even taking into consideration Dr. Corey-Handy's trial testimony that Jill's genital injuries *could have been* the result of molestation (or a straddle fall), what medical expert would make the allegation Jill had been raped, and on what evidence had he or she based that opinion?

While I didn't know anything about their new "expert," I wasn't going to accept, carte blanche, the person's allegation of rape, due in large part to the fact that the original blood expert and crime scene reconstructionist, the lead detective, and the original prosecutor had all been radically wrong in their assertions.

Gilbert's next allegation wasn't unexpected in light of the rape allegation. He had learned "there were sexual devices taken from the David Camm residence during the investigation," and, further, he had been "advised by Detective Sam Sarkisian that there were numerous sexual devices found in the master bedroom at the David Camm residence." There was no doubt Henderson wanted that graphic information disseminated to the public since Gilbert had made the exact claim *twice* in the same paragraph. Left unsaid, I thought, was the fact consenting adults do utilize such devices.

Most importantly, though, was what had not been alleged, as there was no assertion that any of Jill's DNA had been found on any of those devices.

The next claim was a new one, as Gilbert also said Sarkisian had told him, "there was a cover found on David Camm's bed in the master bedroom, that contained the sperm of David Camm and body fluids of Jill Camm." That could be very incriminating, but the devil is always in the details. The fact Camm's sperm had been found on the bed clothing he shared with his wife wasn't surprising, particularly since there had been sexual devices in the bedroom.

Several questions sprang forth from that assertion. What kind of body fluids from Jill? Were they vaginal fluids? Were they mixed with Camm's sperm? The fact that kids played in bed with their parents, or grandparents for that matter, wasn't incriminating.

It was clear they were trying to tie Jill's genitalia injuries directly to her father, but, unless I was missing something, they still only had thin inferential evidence at best. If they'd had more, the affidavit would not only have charged Camm with the three murders but also with sexual molestation of his daughter.

The next paragraph related the facts Gilbert had learned from the original medical examiner's report that both Kim and Brad had been shot to death, Kim in the head and Brad by a wound through the spinal cord.

Gilbert's next claim was, at least to me, another new one. Forensic evidence had shown that "protein matter from Jill Camm, was found embedded into the weave of the shirt" of Camm. The fact the matter had supposedly been embedded in the weave of the shirt meant it had gotten there through high velocity impact, i.e., a gunshot, and the observation was obviously important to their case.

The state's purported bloodstain experts were in the next paragraph, with Gilbert claiming Camm's shirt had stains resulting from "high force impact spatter." There was no mention, of course, of the conflicting opinions of the other experts.

Catching me totally by surprise, however, was the next assertion. Prosecutor Henderson and Gilbert had resurrected the disproven 7:19 p.m. phone call from Camm's house, falsely portraying the 6:19 p.m. call as having occurred an hour later, in an attempt to put him in his house planning the murders of his family rather than at the gym playing ball.

I was trying to absorb their making such a false claim, since during the first trial, a GT&E[55] billing representative testified that the correct time of the phone call had been, in fact, 6:19 p.m. The Indiana Court of Appeals had articulated that very same time. Why would Henderson have allowed the fictitious assertion to be made? Why would Gilbert have signed his name to that bogus claim? If they hadn't known the call had really been at 6:19 p.m., then each had been ignorant of an essential fact in the case. If they had known, I was forced to draw an even worse conclusion.

It was obvious they hadn't considered the impact that 7:19 p.m. call made on their entire theory of Camm's having left the gym, unnoticed for several minutes, driving home to murder his family, driving back to the gym, and sneaking back in, with no one the wiser. In fact, their purported sequence of events was as follows:

- Camm had been at the gym at 6:59 p.m.;
- He had left unnoticed around 7:15 p.m., while playing five-on-five, full-court basketball;
- It had taken four to five minutes to drive home;
- He had made a call to a customer at 7:19 p.m.;
- He had then waited until around 7:35 p.m. to ambush his family;
- Camm had engaged Kim in a violent struggle, inflicting 22 bruises and injuries on her without having any injuries or scratches on himself;
- He had shot and killed his wife and children;
- He had re-arranged, cleaned, and manipulated the crime scene; and
- Camm had then driven back to the gym.

---

[55] GT&E is now Verizon.

The entire time elapsed would therefore have been from around 7:14 p.m. to 7:45 p.m., or 30 plus minutes, with no one having missed him, including those with whom he was actively playing basketball. And, oh yeah, after murdering his wife and kids, he had acted normal, and no one saw any blood on his shirt.

If one could somehow or another believe the timing made sense, did it make any sense a guy lying in wait to murder his family would make a business call?

All of it was just plain nutty and strongly suggested, once again, the "fresh eyes" hadn't known the facts of the case. Or worse, they hadn't cared about the facts.

That the bogus 7:19 p.m. claim was contained in their affidavit, however, caused me to further question each and every aspect of all of their other allegations, including their next one, wherein Gilbert had related a claim made by the original investigator, Sean Clemons. According to Clemons, "…during the collection of standards[56] at the Floyd County Hospital, David Camm made the statement to me and Detective Darrell Gibson that 'this is what they do to you when you kill your wife and kids.'"

Had that really been a confession? Or had it been an exasperated husband and father making a sarcastic statement? More importantly, that comment had been made *before* Camm had been arrested. Why hadn't it been included in the original probable cause affidavit if Clemons had thought it was, in fact, a confession? We needed to know more, including Detective Gibson's take on the comment.

The murder weapon was next discussed, as was a .380 gun supposedly owned by Camm. Gilbert said he had been "advised that during the time that David Camm was considering joining the Floyd County Sheriff's Department Reserves—between May 2000 and September 2000—he told Floyd County Chief Deputy Frank Loop[57] that he possessed a .380 caliber handgun. Further information was provided to [Gilbert] that .380 caliber handgun casings were found at the homicide scene at the Camm residence on the night of the homicides. All three victims were killed with a .380 caliber handgun. Also, during the investigation there was no .380 caliber handgun found at the David Camm residence."

I was unaware as to how this point had been argued during Camm's first trial, but he'd told both Detectives Neal and Gibson during his first interview he'd had no hand guns. It would have been a big lie if it could be proven

---

[56] Standards meant body standards, or DNA obtained from a cheek swabbing, blood from a blood draw, and also hair standards obtained from combings from the head and pubic region.

[57] Loop was later elected Sheriff of Floyd County in 2014 and reelected in 2018.

otherwise, but the fact remained there had been no other evidence he owned a .380 or any handgun. Still, an independent source had claimed David Camm was lying.

And then the final short paragraph and the last new evidence from Gilbert: "During my investigation, I received information from a confidential informant that advised me . . . David Camm told him that Camm had shot and killed his wife and two children."

So, David Camm had supposedly confessed to killing his wife and children to a confidential informant. That person hadn't been identified, but I knew it wasn't a deep mystery as to *if not who but what he was*. Camm had been incarcerated for over four years, first for almost two years in the Floyd County Jail awaiting trial, and then for the last two and a half years at the Indiana State Prison in Michigan City. That informant, no doubt, was another inmate.

In summary, Henderson had based a large part of his new case against Camm on the previously disproven time of the murders; another inflammatory allegation of sexual abuse of Jill, which had not been alleged by the original Medical Examiner nor tied to Camm; and the credibility of an unknown jail/prison inmate.

All of that didn't speak well, in my view, of Prosecutor Keith Henderson or his "fresh eyes" team led by Gary Gilbert. If a prosecutor and investigator have to resort to untruths, innuendo and speculation, they don't have much of a case. That didn't equate, however, to not having much of a chance to secure a conviction. Stan Faith had already secured three guilty verdicts without any purported confession by Camm.

While I was reviewing Gilbert's affidavit, Kitty called and said we needed to meet the next day. She wanted to introduce me to Sam Lockhart and Donnie, David's brother.

CHAPTER 9

"Meet Sam Lockhart"

Kitty, Stacy, and I were in the law office conference room an hour before David's brother, Donnie, and his uncle, Sam Lockhart, were due to arrive for our 9:00 a.m. appointment.

"You know, guys," I began, "I'm still in the process of mentally working my way through this." When a quizzical Stacy asked my meaning, I continued, "I'm trying as hard as I can, but I still can't wrap my mind around the ISP's investigations. I don't know all that much about Faith, but I do know a lot about the ISP, and I've seen nothing but great work from them in the past. I can't comprehend, though, how and why they did what they did in this case. Their investigations, at least what I've seen so far, doesn't even rise to the level of poor."

Stacy was silent, but Kitty responded, "Well, 'it is what it is,' as you would say, Dunner" was her quick answer. She continued, "Apparently, Faith didn't think much of the ISP either. After Clemons had gotten the times wrong on the first affidavit, Faith used his own investigators on follow-up stuff and had even refused to allow Clemons to sit at the prosecution table at Dave's trial."[58]

> "ALL WE WANT IS JUSTICE. IF I THOUGHT THAT DAVID WAS GUILTY, I'D BE THE FIRST TO FLIP THE SWITCH."

"Yeah, I saw where Faith had his investigators trying to get the ballers to say they saw David with the gray sweatshirt and also to claim he might have been able to leave the games without being seen by them."

"The ISP labs were still used extensively, though," Stacy added. "The lab in Evansville did the firearms testing, fingerprint comparisons and all of the blood swabs and DNA testing and, all in all, it appears they did a very good job, with the exception of not catching the unknown male DNA in the collar of the BACKBONE sweatshirt."

Stacy continued, saying Lynn Scamahorn, the lead analyst, had examined the sweatshirt and found DNA from blood on the front had come back as female DNA. It wasn't Kim's blood, and it remained unidentified.

---

[58] The lead investigator on most major crimes, at least in the State of Indiana, sits with the prosecution team at the same trial table.

Mike McDaniel had done what any good defense attorney would do, Stacy said, as he had solicited and gotten good advice from his two forensic experts, Bart Epstein and Terry Laber. Mike had then sent the garment to a private but certified DNA laboratory, Orchid Cellmark, which also did work for many law enforcement departments. That lab had found skin cells, which had probably been sloughed off the person's neck, on the inside collar of the shirt.[59] They were, she said, identified as being from an unknown male, and they still hadn't been identified.

"I assume they ran it through CODIS," I asked, referring to the FBI's repository of DNA profiles.[60]

Stacy said McDaniel had Stan Faith check the unknown DNA profile to those known profiles in CODIS, but there hadn't been any match. Kitty quickly added she had already been on Henderson to have the DNA profile run through CODIS to see if someone had entered the unknown DNA in the last three years, or since October 2001, when the profile had been first run. To date, Kitty said, Henderson hadn't gotten back to her on that request.

"Who was the witness who said he saw the gray sweatshirt in David's garage?" I asked. A neighbor, I was told, whose testimony had been very generic in its description of the garment, and no one had corroborated him. David, I was further educated, had been adamant he'd never had a gray sweatshirt, even more adamant that he'd never had anything with the name BACKBONE, and hadn't a clue as to the identity of that person.

"What about the original PC affidavit?" I asked. "I assume Mike tore Clemons apart on the stand?"

Both Kitty and Stacy answered in unison that McDaniel had shredded Clemons' original allegations and had also damaged Stites over his wrong deductions.

"So, you're telling me what? There was no evidence, other than their bloodstain guys?"

"That," Stacy replied, "was the extent of their evidence, such as it was."

I continued, "And then Faith got the jury to believe that the 11 other men who were with David at the time his family was murdered weren't to be believed?" Both Kitty and Stacy nodded their heads. "How was that possible?" I asked.

Their response was the same as they had presented to the Court of Appeals in their brief and upon which the Court had reversed the conviction. Faith, they said, had marched several women in front of the jury to tell of their

---

[59] The ISP did not attempt to collect any scrapings from the same area.

[60] CODIS, the acronym for the Combined DNA Index System, is maintained by the FBI and contains DNA profiles from convicted felons and missing persons, although many states now submit DNA profiles from all arrestees.

affairs or flirtations with David. And then the judge had allowed Faith to claim, with zero evidence, that David had molested Jill.

"Stir in the motive of murder for life insurance money," Kitty said, "and by the time McDaniel put on his defense, the jury absolutely hated David."

"The prejudicial effect was so thick it overwhelmed common sense," added Stacy.

"The inadmissibility of the affairs was the reason for the reversal, I know," I responded, "but didn't the jury see that the original affidavit was totally bogus?"

Kitty again said McDaniel absolutely tore apart the original PC affidavit,[61] adding the basketball players had also testified, and testified honestly, but Faith had gotten them to admit they couldn't remember if they had their eyes on David literally every second of every game or had looked at the clock to verify the times certain things happened.

"I never saw such minutia asked of any player in any interview," I said, "until well after the arrest. So, in essence, the State of Indiana benefited from their own poor and incomplete interviews because during their trial testimony, the ball players were asked questions designed to make them appear as having poor memories?"

"That was true," Kitty responded, "as the ball players didn't change their stories of seeing David at the games, never saw him leave the gym and, of course, never saw him return. They just hadn't been asked the minor details surrounding the games until much later, and when they were asked, they didn't recall who scored the most points, who guarded who in which game or the score of each of the games. Faith had used those unimportant facts to convince the jury the ball players couldn't be trusted on their recollections that David had always been present during the games."

"I know character assassination was essential for David's convictions," I said, "but it's incomprehensible to me as to how the jurors could accept the story that David left the gym, was unnoticed by *anyone*, was gone for probably 30 minutes if not longer, returned to the game with blood on his shirt, which was also unnoticed, of course, and acted completely normal."

It was Stacy's turn. "He not only supposedly got back into his truck but didn't transfer anything, including blood. No trace evidence was found in

---

[61] David's original defense attorney for a few days, George Gesenhues, just after David's arrest, had also vigorously litigated the validity of the probable cause affidavit, particularly questioning the credentials of the blood expert/crime scene re-constructionist, whose qualifications were unknown at the time.

the truck." [62] She then addressed the overall scenario. "Dunner, when I first read the trial transcript, I was in shock at what all the judge allowed Faith to do. You cannot comprehend how totally prejudiced the jury was against David. Yes, what you describe is a totally impossible scenario, but we can't realistically envision the degree of vitriol that permeated Dave's trial."

"It's still beyond astounding," I replied. "But how about the new evidence?" I asked. "Have you gotten any discovery? What's Henderson saying about his informant?"

Kitty responded that Henderson wasn't yet giving up the identity of the informant, but we all agreed it was someone who had crossed paths with David in jail or prison. For David to confess to another inmate didn't make a lot of sense for a man who had been fighting hammer and tong for a new trial. He'd not only betray himself, but his many family supporters. Still, if David was the self-centered monster the state had painted, any "concern" for his family wouldn't be genuine. Nonetheless, we'd have to do a full background investigation on that inmate, including getting his DOC records, deposing him, and definitely interviewing those around him.

Henderson, per Kitty, was also mum on the identity of the new expert who was claiming trauma to Jill's vagina with a penis or some kind of device, adding that had been a completely new revelation, which, to date, didn't have any evidence backing it. "Remember," Kitty said, "that all experts aren't the same, and all experts aren't necessarily experts."

As for the protein matter in David's shirt, that term had originated from the examination of Terry Laber, one of the defense blood/forensic experts who didn't think much of it, other than it was located in the same area as were the eight tiny spots deemed by Rob Stites and Rod Englert as having been blowback. [63] "Laber," she said, "didn't use the term embedded, and the source of that meant someone else was characterizing it that way in order to give it greater significance."

As for Jill's body fluids on Kim and Dave's bed clothing, both Kitty and Stacy opined that the affidavit allegation had probably been designed to slime David as much as possible. Still, that allegation could be answered through the discovery of ISP lab reports on just what kind of body fluids had been found. We'd also want to determine if David and Kim had been sexually intimate in the days leading to the murders.

As for the sexual devices, Stacy said Gilbert was correct that those had

---

[62] It is a core belief in law enforcement that a perpetrator can't leave the scene of a crime without taking at least a tiny part of the scene with him in the form of trace evidence.

[63] Blowback is interchangeable with the term high velocity impact spray, or HVIS.

been located in the master bedroom, but that he had failed to mention most had been kept in a top drawer in Kim's dresser. That revelation possibly added a new twist. Did Henderson or Gilbert think Kim had been involved in or knew of the purported molestation of her daughter by her husband? Were they also going to drag Kim through their mud as well as David?

Both Kitty and Stacy had been stunned when Gilbert had claimed the call from the Camm residence had occurred at 7:19 p.m. rather than 6:19 p.m. It didn't make any sense to either one that Henderson would attempt to re-litigate a fact that had been firmly established and publicly discussed in the first trial.

"So much so," Kitty said, "that it garnered a lot of negative press coverage for Faith, which he later blamed on him losing the 2002 election to Henderson." She then laughed. "Faith got what was coming to him, but we got Henderson. Life ain't fair."

"Ironic," I said. "Henderson is now pushing the same wrong timing of the call that helped elect him."

We stopped for a few minutes to refill our coffee mugs. Walking from the conference room down the spartan hallway to the cluttered break room allowed us to not only stretch our legs but to also search for the proper adjectives to describe the inability of Henderson to accept Dave's innocence.

Back around the dark, oval walnut table, we talked life insurance monies. Kitty said Kim had been an astute accountant who had worked in Louisville for Aegon, a very large, multinational insurance company. At home, Kim had been in charge of the family's finances. When David had left the ISP, six months prior to the murders, he'd lost most of his life insurance coverage, and it had been Kim who'd arranged, with David's brother Dan Camm, to secure $350,000 of new coverage on David. She, on the other hand, had gotten most of her life insurance through her job and had only increased her own coverage $18,000.

Kitty continued, "Dan was residing in Florida at the time and helped his brother and sister-in-law obtain their coverage through a friend and business associate. Stan Faith made a big deal of that arrangement, claiming Kim didn't know of the deal arranged by Dave and Dan. It was a bogus allegation as the insurance broker and Dan both testified at trial Kim was fully aware of the life insurance amounts. Kim, in fact, was the financial brains in the family."

As for the insurance on the children, it had been minimal, with Dave's being unaware Frank and Janice Renn, Kim's parents, had purchased small life insurance policies on their two grandchildren.

"What was their financial status?" I asked. Kitty responded that in the year prior to the murders, Kim had made over $70,000 in salary and bonuses.

David, she said, was on track to make twice as much working for his Uncle Sam as he had with the ISP.

"Together," she continued, "they were going to make over $135,000." In the Louisville metropolitan area in the year 2000, that had been an excellent income.

"The family certainly didn't want for money," Kitty concluded, adding they had rental income and had been sending their children to a private Christian school. "The State will argue that greed was a motive, but it's just another false claim. The family was better off financially than ever before."

I then asked about the .380 of David's he had supposedly told a deputy he'd owned. "David didn't have any handguns," Kitty responded. "The only thing he had were shoulder weapons for hunting, and the search of his residence revealed only a rifle and shotguns. He did have lots of revolver and semi-automatic handgun ammunition, accumulated over years from firearms trainings as a trooper and being on the ISP's Emergency Response Team (ERT)."[64] David hadn't known, she continued, why the deputy had said what he said, but he'd been adamant he hadn't owned any handguns and hadn't wanted any.

It was then Sam Lockhart and Donnie Camm came in the front door and walked towards the conference room. Sam was about 6'2", gray-haired, and in his late 50s. Donnie was several inches shorter than Sam, had dark hair, and looked to be in his mid-40s. Kitty stood. "Meet Sam Lockhart and Donnie Camm," she said. I also stood and first shook Sam's hand and then Donnie's.

We then sat around the shiny oval table while Kitty took the lead. "Dunner has already briefed himself on much of the case. He knows a lot but wants to know a lot more, right?" She looked at me.

I took my cue. "I've just scratched the surface, but I'll be reviewing every aspect of the investigation to see what was done, what was missed, and what leads should have been and still need to be followed. I can't help but believe all that information will only help David's defense. Those leads will also include any that may help us identify the person or persons responsible for killing Kim, Brad, and Jill," I said.

I continued by telling each that I wanted to interview not only them but others in their family. "Sam, Donnie, you both know of possible issues or leads that haven't made it to the ISP reports or trial testimony. I'd like your input."

They all nodded, and then, responding to my pregnant pause, Kitty asked what else I was thinking. My response was aimed at Sam and Donnie: "And, I'm also going to search high and low to discover whatever piece of evidence

---

[64] The ISP ERT is the same as a SWAT unit.

or indicia I can find that points to David's guilt. There's still a small piece of me that simply can't comprehend the ISP built a bogus murder case on one of their own while the real murderer is running around free."

Kitty heard my spiel before and gave her perfunctory "Sure," as Stacy merely nodded. Donnie Camm agreed, but Sam Lockhart practically stared a hole through me. It took him a few seconds before he responded, deliberately and coldly, "You do whatever you have to do, and I hope and pray that the real killer is found. David and our family have gone through hell the last four years, and justice has been denied for him and for Kim, Brad, and Jill. All we want is justice for all of them and for the real killer to be found. By the way, if I thought that David was guilty, I'd be the first to flip the switch."

"Who owns David's house now?" I asked, quickly moving on. "It'll help me to walk through it, especially the garage, and to get a decent firsthand perspective of the entire crime scene." Sam said that wouldn't be a problem, as a friend of a family member had bought the house, and consent could be obtained. Once he got the person's permission, he'd give me a call to arrange a date.

"Also, can you get me access to the church gym?"

Sam responded that although his brother Leland was no longer the pastor, after having retired, Sam knew the current pastor and could get me into the gym.

"Also, I want to speak with David, particularly about what Kim and the kids did, not only on September 28 but in the days and weeks leading up to it." Timelines helped immensely in giving clarity to the events surrounding a crime, but also in providing leads. Such leads included Kim's interactions with others, possibly including where and how she may have crossed paths with the real killer. Such an interaction could be minor, significant, or even unnoticed by the victim.

Kitty quickly interjected that timeline would be crucial for the bond hearing we were going to have in front of Judge Aylsworth. "That bond pleading will be filed soon," she said.

Kitty added, "In addition to her other roles, Stacy is in charge of collating all the DNA and blood evidence, particularly since she possesses her undergraduate degree in chemistry.[65] She is going to review all the other forensic evidence to see what analyses, tests, and/or additional scrutiny need to be accomplished."

I added that when I had conducted my overall review, I would also compile a list of items I thought should be tested as well.

---

[65] Stacy, I would soon find, possessed an encyclopedic knowledge of all things forensic in the case.

In regard to forensic evidence, Sam interjected his opinion on the bloodstain pattern experts. Rob Stites, he said, had been overshadowed and forgotten after his mentor, Rodney Englert, had testified. Englert had been an excellent witness who had literally acted professorial when he gave the jury his bloodstain tutorial. He had been allowed by the judge to stand in front of the jury box, to get close to the jury, and to point to his props, educating his new students on the difference between bloodstains that had been transferred by contact, low velocity dripping and/or high velocity spatter or whatever. It was elementary, Sam said, but the jurors had been captivated by the man.[66]

Even though there had been the "Battle of the Experts," as the appellate court had noted, Sam warned all of us that it had been very obvious Rod Englert was most favored by the jurors. He had been absolutely critical to the prosecutor's case: Englert had no doubt, none whatsoever, of his own expert opinion. The eight tiny stains, bearing Jill's DNA, on David's lower left hem of his T-shirt had come from blowback; thus, Camm had to have been within four feet of Jill when she had been shot.

It was clear, Stacy added, the defense would have to counter with our own defense blood witnesses in addition to Terry Laber, who had testified as most forensic scientists would testify in that he would not categorically claim the stains on the shirt were positively transfer but rather his experiments, training, and experience strongly supported that opinion. "Englert," she said, "is well-known as an expert whose opinions aren't as limited as others." Stacy added she already had several good leads on other reputable bloodstain people and was in the process of contacting them.

The subject of the unknown DNA on the BACKBONE sweatshirt was again discussed, with Sam stating, "When I was interviewed by Detective Gilbert, I told him I had a copy of the DNA profile obtained by Orchid Cellmark. I even offered him a copy of the profile, but he didn't take it." Both Kitty and Stacy reassured Sam and Donnie they would press the unknown DNA profile with Henderson.

Sam then added he not only had told Detective Gilbert the real time of the 7:19 p.m. phone call was 6:19 p.m. but had also tried to give him a physical copy of the phone records but had again been rebuffed by Gilbert.

It was a sobering moment for all of us as there was now no doubt the prosecutor and his new investigators weren't incompetent but rather still knowingly and intentionally rehashing the same old disproven allegations.

---

[66] After Sam's trial testimony, he was allowed, along with other witnesses who had already testified, to attend the remaining portion of the trial. Normally, the trial judge excludes witnesses from hearing the testimony of other witnesses, but both the defense and prosecution waived the imposition of the exclusion of witnesses if they had already testified.

Returning to the moment, and continuing with the team organization, Kitty added she would be the one who primarily dealt with Henderson and his office, including pursuing all discovery. When the identity of witnesses was established, depositions would then be arranged. She also had been in touch with others in the Indiana defense bar in an effort to find and speak with a good counterpart in Warrick County who would educate her and Stacy on the more subjective aspects of trying a case in Judge Alysworth's courtroom.

Kitty then said she and I would interview the ball players and Tom Jolly. They, after all, were the witnesses who had been with David when his family was slain, and their credibility would be key to getting an acquittal for David. Unlike the first probable cause affidavit in October 2000, the basketball players hadn't been considered, much less mentioned, in the most recent one. That wouldn't be the case when Kitty and Stacy argued for David's release.

As for that bond, after the Indiana Supreme Court had upheld the appellate ruling, Kitty had immediately filed a motion for the release of David, or in the alternative, a motion for bail. Normally, the judge who would have handled those pleadings would have been the same judge who oversaw the trial. In David's case, however, Judge Richard Striegel had retired after David's trial, and to no one's surprise in Floyd County, Susan Orth had been appointed to serve the remainder of his term. Orth had been Stan Faith's Chief Deputy Prosecutor and had served as the second chair in David's trial. Orth, however, had to recuse herself due to her conflict, and Judge Terrence Cody had assumed temporary control of David's case.

By the date of the most-recently scheduled bond hearing, however, Henderson had filed his amended probable cause affidavit, and Cody had then denied bail. Judge Aylsworth, as the new judge, would make the final determination on bail. The chances of bail weren't good, but the effort needed to be made.

It was then Kitty asked two questions she and Stacy had previously discussed but would remain unanswered until the second trial began. First, should the next jury be told of David's past convictions? That wasn't as easy a question to answer, even though one would think a jury shouldn't be told; after all, that was a basic tenet of defense attorneys, to start with a clean slate. Nonetheless, at least some on the jury would know of the convictions, while others would be curious as to why it had taken several years for the case to come to trial.[67]

The second important question was whether David should testify. He had testified in the first trial, and it hadn't gone well. Stan Faith, in his sneering

---

[67] It would eventually take almost five and a half years from the time of the murders until the commencement of the second trial.

cross-examination, had been successful in getting David to become angry over being repeatedly accused and demeaned. Still, most jurors wanted to hear from the accused, and many would think, despite any instructions from the judge to the contrary, the defendant was hiding something if he didn't testify.

"Well, we've got plenty of time to decide," Kitty said, "but I wanted to toss it out there for all of you to think about."

All of us began gathering our notes, and I then excused myself, allowing Kitty to speak privately with Sam and Donnie. After all, she and Stacy needed to be paid for their work.[68]

---

[68] The expense of defending David during his first trial, including the cost of defense attorney Mike McDaniel, came almost entirely from family sources, although second chair Patrick Biggs was the Floyd County Public Defender, and his salary was paid by the taxpayers. David had been forced to sell not only all of his personal property, including the vintage Corvette and Mustang he was restoring, but his welding machines, compressors, high-pressure cleaning equipment, John Deere tractor and the house itself, leaving him penniless. The liquidation of the house and personal property wasn't enough, though, as Sam and other family members also reached into their own pockets. For his appeal, the family also bore the brunt of that cost, although I later learned the source of that funding, as well as the forthcoming defense expenses, would be incurred mostly by Sam. While I understood blood is thicker than water, I also thought Sam must have been completely convinced of his nephew's innocence, in that he and the family had spent, I estimated, several hundred thousand dollars. Unfortunately for them, the expenses would continue to skyrocket, both in terms of money and personal attacks.

CHAPTER 10
The Crime Scene & Church Gym

Early the morning after our meeting, Sam called and said he had gotten permission for us to access David's former home as well as the church gym. We agreed to meet at 9:00 a.m. on Saturday, December 4. After those two visits, Kitty arranged for me to meet David at the Floyd County Jail; it would be the first of dozens.

Photographs Of The House

After Sam's call, I had returned to viewing the crime scene photographs, having been surprised at the relatively small number of pictures taken of the interior and exterior of the garage and house. The three bedrooms of Kim and David, Bradley, and Jill, in addition to having limited photographs, were also from limited perspectives. The rest of the of the house had even fewer photos.

Granted, the primary crime scene had been the garage, but that didn't mean the perpetrator(s) hadn't been in the house at some time or another. Was there something out of kilter? Something taken and therefore missing? While it appeared, at least to me, to have been a sexual assault, burglary wasn't out of the range of possibilities. A photo might catch something of importance and when shown to David or another family member, might prompt a good lead. The lack of photos, however, indicated a lack of interest in the house.

> "ON WHAT EVIDENCE DID THEY BASE THAT STORY?"
> "NOTHING. THEY JUST MADE IT UP"

In fact, normal crime scene protocol is to secure an abundance of photographs early in the process and prior to any disruption occurring during a search. That's true not only of the overall scene, but also of any *possible* individual item that could *potentially* be evidence. A second rule-of-thumb, and as a means of reiterating their importance, is there is no such thing as too many photographs.

Although there was a crime scene video that had been taken in the garage, it was quite dark and of very poor quality. It did show Kim and Brad on the garage floor, but it failed to capture, most critically, Jill sitting in the back seat of the Bronco. Whoever took the video had done so without proper lighting and hadn't even bothered to point the camera into the vehicle.

One unlikely source, I learned, had secured literally hundreds of photographs: Robert Stites, the debunked bloodstain expert and crime scene reconstructionist. Stites had arrived from Portland, Oregon, two days after the murders and had been picked up at the Louisville airport by a Faith investigator. He'd begun securing photographs that afternoon, a full two days after the crime scene technicians had taken their limited number, after searches had compromised the original scenes and, of course, without any victims at the scene. Still, they'd added some context the ISP photos hadn't provided.[69]

Two drawings of the garage/driveway and the house had been made by ISP Master Trooper James A. Bube. Normally, a rough crime scene sketch is made prior to the collection of evidence and before the removal of bodies. However, Bube had begun his process the morning after the garage had been processed, after evidence had been collected, and after the bodies had been removed. Rather than rely on his own observations, he had referred to photographs of the bodies and the one shell casing found on the floor to make his garage sketch.[70]

As for the "nail polish scrape," which Bube had noted as being near Kim's body, I couldn't find any photograph of it. According to Bube's later recollection, the nail polish had been pointed out to him by someone at the scene.[71]

Two photos were of David's UDI truck—neat, clean, and professional-looking—parked in front of the right garage bay. The truck had borne the names of *Brad & Jill Camm* under each window. If the man had been intent on killing his children, he had sure gone to great lengths to portray himself as a loving father, I thought.

---

[69] Stites had been granted permission, again two days after the murders, to photograph the victims who were still at the Kentucky Medical Examiner. And photograph he did, that day and the next, securing dozens of photos of the three victims and even inserting a plastic rod into the skull holes and bullet path in Kim's head and placing a protractor adjacent to her face. Knowing it was Faith who directed the ISP to give Stites unfettered access to everything, it wasn't surprising he was also examining, positioning, and photographing the bodies of the victims.

[70] We later were told by Bube that his diagrams were "an off and on project" and they took 14 months for him to complete.

[71] In fact, no photograph was ever discovered of the nail polish nor did it appear in the video.

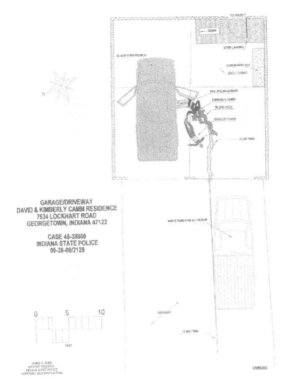

*Diagram of garage with locations of Kimberly and Bradley Camm,
the Bronco of Kim's and the white Ford pickup truck of David's,
completed by ISP Master Trooper James A. Bube.*

Bube's house diagram allowed me to visualize the movements of David as he had run from the garage, up its steps, across the porch/breezeway, and into the kitchen where he'd called the ISP Post from the phone on the wall.

As I studied the house photos and diagrams as well as the photo and contents of the detached garage, another thought was the Camm family, although doing well financially, certainly hadn't lived extravagantly, as the house had only around 1500 square feet of living space, rather simple furnishings, and an unfinished basement. Additionally, the Bronco of Kim's, several years old, certainly hadn't screamed wealth or privilege. The family had been middle-class, and someone targeting Kim and/or the kids hadn't done so based on any outward display of affluence.

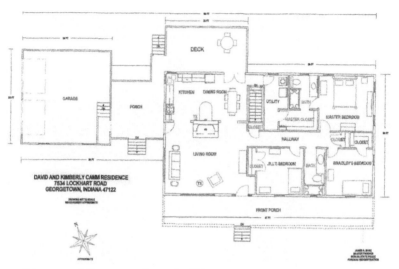

Diagram of Camm residence by ISP Master Trooper James A. Bube.

I returned to the photos and saw the exterior of the open three-bay detached garage, although I found none taken from inside. In the right bay I saw a utility trailer, which contained a large commercial power washer and a mid-60's Ford Mustang that was undergoing body and engine repair. To the left of the Mustang I saw an older Corvette, also having body and mechanical work done, and in the left bay a John Deere tractor with a belly mower. I saw the garage floor had been populated with an air compressor, welding machine, various tools, radiators, brake parts, batteries, wiring harnesses, and other car parts. Clearly, David Camm enjoyed working on cars, both as a mechanic and body man, and mowed his own yard, which I estimated to be almost an acre.

One photograph in the rear of the house was very unique. It had been taken by someone in the Camm backyard and was of a woman, not in uniform, reaching into an exposed septic tank.[72] On bended knee, reaching with a stick into the black muck was, according to an ISP report, Deputy Floyd County Coroner Becky Balmer. It appeared the object in her reach was a condom. That wouldn't mean much, not if David Camm had used condoms. It could be incredibly pertinent if he hadn't.

I deviated from acquainting myself with the house and attempted to find why the septic tank had been opened in the first place and then what had happened to the condom, whether it had been examined, and what had been the results of the exam.

---

[72] In much of rural America, household wastewater is disposed through a ground filtration septic system utilizing a design approved by the local health department.

As to the first question, Rob Stites, upon examining the clean-out pipe for the septic, had thought he'd seen blood on the cap. It later turned out it hadn't been blood, but nonetheless, thinking that David had hidden the murder weapon into the pipe/tank, Clemons had secured another search warrant. The ISP had first used a remote camera to look into the pipe but hadn't found anything. A backhoe had been brought in next to scrape the dirt and grass from the concrete lid and then to lift the lid, exposing the black muck and the condom.[73]

No gun had been found. But as for the condom? Granted, if it had been in the tank for a lengthy period, any DNA would be degraded and useless. However, if it had just been recently flushed from the house, as it appeared it might have been, there was a chance any ejaculate or DNA contained therein could have been preserved and a DNA profile achieved.[74]

Also, if the perpetrator had sexually assaulted Kim, and then flushed the condom down the toilet, that meant the existence of such an assault wouldn't necessarily have been caught during Kim's autopsy.

Nonetheless, after spending hours searching through the ISP custody records and lab reports, I found no mention whatsoever of any condom having been placed into ISP evidence custody and, obviously, no lab report. Still, I'd ask Camm if he and his wife had ever utilized condoms.

Floyd County Deputy Coroner Becky Balmer retrieving a condom from the septic tank located behind the Camm residence on October 1, 2000.

---

[73] The septic search occurred on October 1, 2000, three days after the murders and at the same time David was being interrogated and then arrested.

[74] Additionally, other evidence, such as size, manufacturer, and lubricant can possibly be determined which could possibly be matched to unused condoms found in a perpetrator's possession.

I then turned my search to photographs of the church gym. I didn't find any—not of the gym, the alarm, the other exits, or the church exterior or parking lot. The basketball gym, such a key aspect of the prosecution's theory, I thought, should have many photographs. Many, that is, if photographs would buttress their assertion that David had snuck away from other basketball players.

The Crime Scene

On a drab December day, I drove the 85 miles from Bloomington to rural Georgetown and met Sam at his nephew's former home. It appeared, at least to me, not to have changed at all as it was still sitting innocently atop the same small grassy knoll with dense woods behind it.

I met Sam in front of the open garage, which was essentially barren and bore no resemblance to a place where a terrorized mother had struggled and fought tenaciously in a desperate and futile attempt to save the lives of her terrified children. The fact that so much carnage had taken place in such a small area would be incomprehensible to many. I took numerous photos, including some of the steps to the breezeway from the pedestrian door, then of the breezeway and the rear deck.

Before Faith had changed the timing of the murders, it had been established the Bronco had been seen entering Lockhart Road shortly after 7:30 p.m. How, then, I asked Sam, was it initially explained that Kim and the kids were still in the garage, over an hour and a half later, even with the seatbelt still on Jill? That was easy, Sam explained. The explanation was Kim and the kids hadn't just arrived home when they were murdered, but rather had been leaving the house after Kim had discovered that Jill had been molested.

"On what evidence did they base that story?" I asked.

"Nothing," Sam replied. "They just made it up."

"But Brad was returning from swim practice. Did he change there, or did he wear his suit home?"

"He was still wearing his trunks," Sam responded.

"How, then, did they explain that Brad was in the car and didn't change out of his trunks for almost two hours?"

"No problem," answered Sam. "They did what they always did if they couldn't explain something. They just ignored it. Of course, when they changed the time of the murders, when Dave snuck out of the gym, the trunks still on Brad fit with their story of Dave ambushing them just after they arrived home from swim practice."

"It just gets crazier, Sam," I said, speaking the obvious.

"We've lived crazy for over four years. But, hey, speaking of really, really, crazy stuff," Sam continued. "Do you know about the garage door blood?" I said I had seen photographs of a garage door, which had been removed and disassembled, but I hadn't yet had time to delve into the specifics. "Well, the world-class blood expert, Rob Stites, claimed there was blood blowback on the inside of the right overhead door. That's the reason he ordered the ISP to remove it, take it apart, and have it tested. It wasn't blood, though. The spots were oil-based."

"Oil but not blood!" I no longer was amazed at any of the declarations by Stites and told Sam as much.

"It gets better" was his response. "As Sean Clemons later told me, Stites could visualize the outline of the shooter on the door. He actually told me that he could visualize Dave's outline. I said that both he and his expert were crazy."

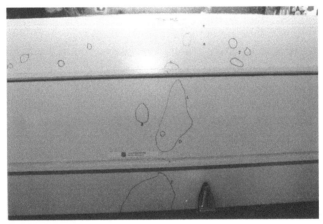

More of Rob Stites' handiwork: the spots which are circled were those he believed to be blood spatter; in fact, they were oil-based and not from blood.

"That's *beyond* crazy," I replied. I then opined, "Wait a minute. If Stites believed there was blowback on the door, that meant he thought it came from Kim, since she was the only one shot who was outside the Bronco, That means he thought the stains on Dave's shirt also came from Kim."

"That's right," said Sam, "so he got that doubly wrong. Not only that, but Stites commandeered the crime scene four nights after the murders as he was spraying luminol in the Bronco, garage, and house, all in an effort to track blood.[75] Everyone knew there was blood, and lots of it in the Bronco, so what

---

[75] Luminol is a chemical mixture sprayed in darkened conditions in areas thought to contain blood as the chemical reacts with the blood to create a short-term luminescence, thus identifying the location and, at times, the possible tracking of blood; false-positives often occur, however, and laboratory testing is needed to confirm the blood if it isn't destroyed by the luminol.

he did wasn't necessary. He did find what he thought was blood on the carpet in the house, but whatever it might have been wasn't followed up by the State Police."

"And in the process, he also destroyed any miniscule droplets of blood whose DNA might have been identified in a lab," I responded. "So, nothing was ever gained by the luminol?" Sam said there wasn't but that it did allow Stites to take center stage once again and for him and Englert to bill Floyd County even more.

As to how much Englert and Stites had charged, Sam's reply was stunning: "Over two hundred thousand dollars." He added that Englert had billed $300 per hour and his protégé slightly less.[76] Floyd County had spent hundreds of thousands of dollars, not only in "expert" fees, but on an expensive nine-week trial, based upon the deductions of a man, now known not to be anything close to an expert, who had been sent by the man who was purportedly one of the greatest bloodstain experts in the world.

I spent the next hour going from room to room on the upper level, in the unfinished basement, and back on the deck and breezeway, taking numerous photos along the way. After taking more photos outside, I spent a lengthy period of time talking with Sam about his recollections of the days leading up to the evening of the murders and of the following days, as I wanted the timeline to be as specific as possible.

As we were beginning to leave the house, I noticed a really neat two-story playhouse and play equipment across the gravel road and asked if it was on his father's property. Sam said it had been dedicated by his father on the Saturday before the killings. "Dad,"[77] he said, "loved children and that was as happy as I'd seen him since Mom had died. He was shattered over the murders, though, and died within days of the guilty verdicts. Dad was old, but when he was told of Dave's convictions, he simply gave up. Anyway, we later sold the property."[78]

"Perhaps you don't know," Sam continued, "but Jill suffered a straddle injury that day. As she always did, she was running and jumping but lost control, fell, and hurt herself. Dave and her aunt Debbie consoled her and she was soon back up, active as ever."

Sam asked if I wanted any photos of the playhouse dedication. I said I'd very much like to get those. He reached into the front seat of his car and produced several photographs, including one of his aged but obviously

[76] Englert's hourly rate later increased to $400 and his total billing to well over $300,000.

[77] Amos Lockhart had nine children with Daisy, who had died in late 1999, and in 2000 had 35 grandchildren and numerous great-grandchildren.

[78] Much of the proceeds of that sale went to pay for David's defense.

very happy father sitting in front of the yellow and blue playhouse, cane in hand and surrounded by eight of his grandchildren and great-children, all enthusiastic, including Brad and Jill.

Another photo was of the cousins sitting on the stairs to the second floor of the playhouse, with Jill looking as though she had just played a joke on all the world while her brother was smiling ear to ear. If there was turmoil or fear in their lives, these photos didn't divulge it. In two other pictures, David was seen planting, and then watering, a purple mum near the stairs.

"It must have been a fun family event," I asked. It was, Sam responded, adding that although he and Jeff Lockhart had provided much of the labor and material, the entire family had pitched in, with Kim and Dave contributing not only time and labor but $500 towards the construction costs.

Sam then gave me the thank-you he had received from Jill for the playhouse. It damn near brought tears to my eyes, as did the thank-you from Brad.

Jill's thank-you note to Sam, her great-uncle, when the playhouse had been dedicated on September 23, 2000, five days before the murders.

From the soft tone of his voice, it was clear to me that Sam had envisioned, if only for a moment, a time when murder, mayhem, and injustice didn't rule his life. He quickly turned from the past and said, "Well, let's go to the church."

The Church Gym

It took right at five minutes for us to drive the three-and-a-half miles to the Georgetown Community Church (GCC). Once there, Sam explained his brother Leland and his wife Vonda had founded the church in the basement of their home over twenty years prior and, due to vigorous membership growth, had moved it first to a local elementary school, then to a small church in front of the Family Life Center (FLC), which had been built in 1999.

An aerial photo, taken by me on September 28, 2005, of the
Georgetown Community Church and Family Life Center (white roof);
north is on the top of the photo, and south is on the bottom.
At top right is the entrance/exit road used by David Camm

Upon arriving through the drive northeast of the church, the same one David had used that evening, Sam pointed out where he and the other ball players had parked that evening, near the double-door entry. As we walked through that door, waiting for us was the new pastor. He was quite gracious and gave us complete access to the facility, permitting me also to take photos.

As we were walking in the gym, Sam said the FLC was built, after a decision by the church elders, as an outreach to attract more families. Services were held on Sundays as well as Wednesday evenings, and, of course, the gym was large enough to allow, and indeed encourage, the children to play basketball, tag, jump rope, or whatever activity they desired.

On Wednesday evenings, Sam added, Kim, as the volunteer church treasurer, would bring the kids, and all would break bread with other members and their children. The kids would enjoy crafts and learning as the adults had their service, with the exception of Kim, who would be in the office, writing checks and balancing the church's financial books. All told, the three would spend about two hours each Wednesday, including the night before they were murdered.

I walked to the farthest end of the gym, from the front door, and saw the altar and chairs stacked against the wall. From that vantage point, I took a photo of the very well-lit gym as Sam recalled that he had arrived around 7:15 p.m., after the first game had started.

While the five-on-five, full-court game was being played on the opposite end of the court, Sam had been shooting baskets near the entrance when Tom Jolly had arrived after 8:00 p.m.[79] Shortly after Tom's arrival, Sam said

---

[79] Tom Jolly's recollection had been that he'd arrived after dusk around 8:15-8:20 p.m.

the ongoing game had ended, and he'd replaced Dave who had then sat out one game, speaking with Tom. The two of them had been standing near the entrance to the kitchen.[80]

Trying to envision how David escaped the notice of the ten others, for at least 20 minutes if not more, while he was still playing basketball with those very same players, was an impossibility.

And then, if David had left during the time he and Jolly had been talking along the baseline, that meant Jolly was an abject liar as were the ball players who had seen him speaking with Jolly during the time he had sat out. And, of course, if they had lied about seeing David, that also meant they had lied to cover for his murders of his wife and kids. And that implied a huge conspiracy. What were the odds of one person, much less ten or 11 people, including those who hadn't even known David, lying to cover his murderous acts?

A photo of the church gym, taken by me in December, 2004,
looking southeast with the entrance and alarm
on the far right, adjacent to the door.

While I was thinking, Sam said, "You know there was another person in here that night?"

"What are you talking about?"

"Tony Ferguson's grandfather."

When asked to explain, Sam did. Tony, at age 18, was the youngest of the 11 ball players and didn't have a driver's license. His grandfather, with whom he had been living, had driven him to the games and had stayed along the sidelines. When asked why I hadn't seen his name as an alibi witness, Sam's response was succinct: "Because he died within a year of the murders and was dead prior to the ISP ever knowing of him or much less thinking to interview him."

---

[80] The white table in the photo hadn't been present at that location on September 28, 2000.

It wasn't the first time, nor would it be the last, that I had to shake my head.

I then walked the distance of the full-court and snapped a photo of the alarm adjacent to the entry doors whose records had provided definitive times as to when David had arrived and left the gym.

The alarm had been disengaged by Jeff Lockhart at
6:59 p.m. and re-engaged at 9:22 p.m.; at both times,
David Camm had been present.

I made the comment that it astounded me that the ISP hadn't looked at the gym or alarm, at least sometime within the first few days. Sam responded, "Oh, several were in here the next day." I asked him to explain. "During the first few days of the investigation," he said, "my brother-in-law, Mike Suttle,[81] opened the gym and kitchen and served hot coffee, orange juice, donuts, and rolls to the detectives and troopers. That stopped, of course, when Dave was arrested."

"And no one ever thought to take any photos? Amazing," I replied. "Okay, Sam, before I leave, let me ask one more thing. Do you know if there was any video retrieved from the golf course next door?" Sam said he wasn't aware of any and, further, that the course had been closed for some time. "I noticed a security camera on the wall facing the parking lot. Chances are very slim that any video was taken that evening or that any still exists. Still, I'll follow up with that."

Changing gears, I said, "Well, time to see David. How's he doing?"

---

[81] Mike is the husband of one of Sam's sisters, Gloria, and the two were also GCC church members.

"He knows you're coming," Sam replied, "and wants to meet you, but understand he's still not all that trusting of others."

"Understood. That's to be expected."

CHAPTER 11

"I'm Dave Camm"

Kitty had arranged, through Floyd County Jail Commander Danny Emily, for me to meet with David in the attorney-client room in the aged and over-crowded jail.[82] During my first visit, and with dozens of others I would make with David and other inmates at the jail, Danny and all the other officers, including every Correctional Officer (CO) and staff associated with the jail, were always organized and professional.[83]

I arrived well after lunch for a reason: I had learned earlier in my career, when visiting jails and prisons, not to arrive during meals or counts as no visitation would normally be allowed and, if the count didn't jibe, the wait could be long.[84]

After I spoke with the duty officer, I was told I was expected and Camm would soon be available. Rather than sit in one of the straight-back plastic chairs in the spartan lobby, I meandered through the public notices posted throughout, including the dos and don'ts of visitation, recalling my prior visits to offenders at the Indiana State Prison in Michigan City.[85]

---

[82] In Indiana as with most states, County Sheriffs are responsible for their county jails and appoint a Jail Commander to oversee the incarceration of inmates, including bookings, feedings, medical visits, administration of prescriptions, transportation to/from court and prison, visitations, religious services, commissary, work release, and practically everything associated with each and every inmate. A Jail Commander is faced with a limited budget as he/she must feed and care for each inmate in a healthy, fair, and equitable manner while often hearing a cacophony of complaints from the public that jails are too costly and that inmates are too well-fed and cared for. He/she, in my opinion has one of the most difficult and thankless jobs in the entire criminal justice system.

[83] The proper term for those officers who oversee security within a jail or prison is Correctional Officer.

[84] Counts are when COs conduct a physical counting of each and every inmate to ensure all are still somewhere in the facility and/or their whereabouts are known.

[85] My observations were that most visitors were wives, girlfriends, mothers and/or grandmothers, many with minor children. The visitation room was large, open, and crowded; all sat on plastic chairs with hands above the very low tables as the duty CO, perched on an elevated landing, observed all interactions. Off to the side of the room was an area for photographs where an offender, with his loved ones, could pose in front of a nature scene, which provided the delusion of fresh air and freedom.

The City-County Building in New Albany, which contains the offices of Floyd County officials, including the prosecutor, courtrooms, and judges' chambers. On the left is the two-story jail.

After a few minutes, I heard the unmistakable sound of steel on steel as the unlocking of the impenetrable door was followed by "Mr. Dunn?" I turned around and heard the officer behind the glass. "Through the door and to your right," he said, "and then on your left."

I walked the short distance from the lobby to the attorney-client room. Only after the entry door clanged shut and locked did the other steel door clang and unlock.

I opened the door.

Standing there was, according to practically all civilized people in the metro-Louisville area, a very despised and evil man.

I was somewhat taken aback by David's appearance, for, unlike the smiling, trim and uniformed trooper I had seen in a photo provided by Sam, David was at least 40 pounds heavier and his complexion much whiter—almost pasty—than when he had been booked into the same facility over four years before. The initial demeanor he displayed was the same I'd seen in most

> "EVERYTHING I SAID THEY TWISTED TO FIT WITH ME BEING THE MURDERER. ALL I WANTED— ALL I EVER WANTED—WAS FOR MY CLOSE FRIENDS TO HELP ME."

inmates, convicts, and offenders in my other jail and prison visits. The term utilized for those people is *institutionalized*. He also looked as though he were a beaten man—a very, very beaten man—who had conformed to the instructions of those surrounding and watching him. Nonetheless, he extended his right hand and softly said, "I'm Dave Camm."

I extended my right hand, and we then shook each other's hands as I introduced myself, then asked what he preferred being called. "David or Dave is fine," he responded.

"Then Dave it is," I replied. "I'm called Dunner. Sit down and let me address some elementary things," I said. "I'm sure Kitty and Stacy have already gone over many of the questions I'll ask, but bear with me as we'll do it again." I then spent the next several minutes telling him of my background, my prior associations with the ISP, what I would do to attempt to find additional evidence in his case and to hopefully allow that evidence to lead us to the one who killed his wife and children. I also added my caveat that if any evidence went against him, well, then, "It is what it is, Dave."

"That's fine by me," he responded, expecting, I was sure, for me to then ask if he was innocent. I didn't.

"How's it going in here?" I inquired. Better than the state prison was the answer, as he said he was allowed in general population, or "Gen Pop" as it was commonly known, so he could play cards, read the paper, and converse with other inmates about sports, especially Indiana University basketball. He was also allowed outside time each day to exercise where he mostly shot a few hoops. We then spoke for a few minutes about the state of Hoosier basketball, both lamenting the firing of legendary coach Bob Knight four years earlier at Indiana University.

As a former police officer, and by definition a potential target, he had, against his own preference, been placed in the Protective Custody Unit (PCU) at the Indiana State Prison in Michigan City.[86] Only by being a range officer within the PCU had he been allowed out of his cell more than the other offenders, socializing with the CO's and his fellow offenders.[87] Those offenders, of course, were other convicted murderers, violent offenders, pedophiles, and, of course, informants.

And that was the perfect segue into the obvious question: "Any idea on the identity of the guy who claimed you confessed?"

"I didn't confess," Dave said, "and no, I have no idea on who it might have been, but whoever it is, is lying. I didn't confess because I didn't kill my wife or my kids."

"You know, Dave, that anyone in here with you now, and certainly anyone with a pending case, is a potential witness against you?"

"Yeah, I know. I also know I can't control what anyone says about me."

"Sure," I responded, "but try and keep your comments to others about

---

[86] The Indiana State Prison is no longer the sole maximum security prison in Indiana, but it still houses violent offenders as well as Death Row inmates, since it is the scene of all executions in Indiana. The three primary determinations as to which facility an offender is placed are determined primarily on the crime(s) for which one is convicted, the length of the sentence(s), and a psychological evaluation of each offender.

[87] A Range officer is essentially a trustee of the CO; he delivers mail, helps feed other offenders, and runs errands for the CO. For those efforts, the pay is pennies on the hour.

sports or anything other than your case. But let's move on. One thing I want to do is to construct a definitive timeline for you, Kim, and the kids, as to the events in the days leading up to the murders. Among other things, it may allow us to get an insight into how and when Kim was targeted," I said, adding, "And I do think Kim was probably the one who was the target, probably a target of a sexual attack. In that regard, did you and she use condoms?" I asked.

"No," was Dave's response, "and I know why you're asking." He further stated that he and Kim never used condoms, and he didn't have any idea as to how they had gotten into the septic tank, other than someone, someone he didn't know, had flushed them from his house. He then emphasized that Kim never had any affair at any time with anyone: "That wasn't Kim."

"Well, we won't be getting any forensic answers because the condoms no longer exist," I added, "but the fact they did exist is important."

And then, referring to the latest allegation of his and his daughter's DNA being found on his and his wife's bed clothes, I had to ask when he and Kim had last been intimate. It was the Sunday before, he said, adding that it was after he and Kim had seen a movie in Louisville as his mother-in-law looked after Brad and Jill.[88]

His recollection sparked a memory. Dave said as he and Kim had left their house to drop off the kids, they had told them that Daddy and Mommy were 'going on a date,' and Jill had replied, "You can't have a date, you're married!" A small smile crept onto Dave's face as the memory was obviously a fond one.

Anyway, that was how his DNA had gotten on the bed clothes, he said. As for Jill's DNA, his only thought was that it had come from her playing on the bed with him and Kim. "We were a family and we played with our kids on our bed. I played with my kids, and now that's a crime," he said as his words tailed off.

"No, it's not, but we have to have a truthful response to all of their allegations. How about your telling the Sheriff's Deputy you had a .380?"

"No. I never told him that. I didn't have any handguns, and I didn't want any handguns. When I left the State Police, I didn't see a need to have any guns, other than my shoulder weapons, since I was still going to hunt. We did speak about the possibility of me becoming an Auxiliary Officer,[89] but I never said I had any handgun, much less a .380. I don't know where he came

---

[88] Kim's parents were Janice and Frank Renn.

[89] Voluntary and unpaid Auxiliary Officers supplement the ranks of numerous Indiana law enforcement agencies, particularly in those counties where funding for law enforcement is limited.

up with that claim, but it's not true. Besides, if I were going to own a .380, it would have been a Baretta."

"Okay" was my response. "Let's go on to their other new allegation of Clemons claiming you confessed to him at the hospital?"

"Yeah, 'This is what they do to you when you kill your wife and kids.' I said that," said Dave. "No doubt about it. I also said it sarcastically and mockingly and at a time when I knew their investigation was off the rails." He had been asked by Clemons to provide body standards and, after talking with Sam, had driven to the hospital where they had a lengthy wait. Even after Clemons and Gibson had arrived, they still had to wait for the nurse to arrive.

He had then felt humiliated when asked to provide pubic hair combings to the nurse with whom he, as a trooper, had often interacted at the hospital.[90] "So, yeah, I was angry. And I had every right to be," he finished, with his voice rising. "By the way, did Gilbert also include my other comment?"

"What do you mean?" I asked.

"After I made that sarcastic comment, I added, 'My wife is looking down from heaven, shaking her head because I have to do this.'" As Dave knew, it wasn't in Gilbert's affidavit.

Dave then added, "You know, everything I said they twisted to fit with me being the murderer. First, I called my friends at the State Police rather than 9-1-1 because, they said, 'I wanted to control the investigation.' I really controlled it, didn't I? I got 195 years in prison because 'I controlled their investigation.' All I wanted—all I ever wanted—was for my close friends to help me. Just to help."

"And it wasn't only Clemons," Dave added, his voice getting stronger, "but it was Jim Biddle, Sam Sarkisian, and others who twisted my words or read something totally different into what I was saying."

I asked him to slow down, and he did, as he began explaining, first about Biddle. "It all began late Saturday afternoon after Sam and I left the hospital and went to my grandfather's house," he said, referring to Amos' house across the road from his home. "I sat there for around an hour, looking at what they were doing in my house, and things only got worse."

Sam's wife, Carol, he said, had first noticed a woman sitting in his easy chair in the living room. David had recognized her as Jacque Vaught, Faith's lead investigator. She'd just sat there, he said, nonchalantly for several minutes, talking with someone else. "She wasn't involved in any search but was relaxing in my chair," he said.

---

[90] As a road trooper, he would take intoxicated drivers to the hospital for a Blood Alcohol Content (BAC) draw.

During that same time, he added, he'd learned in a phone call that Mark Seabrook,[91] the funeral director, had determined, much to Dave's distress, the conditions of the bodies of Kim, Brad, and Jill would not be suitable for public viewing.

"But it kept getting worse, if that was possible, as several of my former co-workers and friends, both in and out of uniform, walked by without speaking to me. They didn't even look at me," he said. In fact, he continued, within hours he had gone from a grieving friend to what he knew was a suspect.

Around dusk, Dave said he and Sam had walked across the road to the evidence tape barricade to look at his lawn, which was littered with cigarette butts, plastic bottles, and other trash. "I became really pissed. I tried to control my temper, but it was getting extremely difficult," he said.

Darrell Gibson walked over, and Dave had told him he needed to retrieve burial clothing and photographs of Kim, Brad, and Jill from the house to facilitate the funeral arrangements. Darrell, he said, had told him that he couldn't enter the house. "Sam could see that I was beginning to lose it, so he stepped in front of me," Dave said, "and he then asked Gibson to speak with whoever was in charge." Gibson had left, and Jim Biddle had returned.

"Biddle came out of the house to speak with us, and Sam explained our need to retrieve clothes and photos from the home for the funeral," Dave continued, "but Biddle flatly refused, saying he needed to protect the crime scene. 'Protect the crime scene?' I thought.

Dave continued, "I looked at the trash and saw people just sitting and milling around in my house. Then I completely lost it when Biddle said, 'David, I know how you feel.' I took a step forward and bumped my chest into his, yelling, 'You have no fucking idea how I feel!'"[92]

The story continued, as Dave said Sam had immediately put his hand on his shoulder and pulled him back as another good friend of his, Barry Brown,[93] had also stepped between Dave and Biddle. As he'd turned to leave, Dave had then seen an overflowing cardboard box of trash sitting on the lawn, which, he said, he'd kicked and then yelled at Biddle to get out of his yard.

"Were you able to finally get the pictures and clothes?" I asked.

---

[91] Mark Seabrook had, for decades, served Southern Indiana as a well-known and highly respected funeral director. His compassion, understanding, generosity, and public service were well known within the community. Leland Lockhart, Dave's uncle, often conducted funeral services at Seabrook's for decedents/families who had no church home. Seabrook died in 2021.

[92] Biddle denied making the comment but later said if it had been anyone other than David Camm who'd bumped him, he would have arrested that person for battery, claiming he'd given Dave special consideration by not taking him to jail.

[93] Barry Brown and Dave had been on ERT together.

"Yes, but only after Biddle got permission from Stan Faith, and that took another day," he answered. His sister Julie was the one who'd had to go through one of Faith's investigators who had kept bringing the wrong clothes out and spreading them on the hood of a car. It had been so frustrating, Dave said, that Julie had finally said she'd go to the store and buy new clothes.

"Oh, and Kim's jewelry box was also brought from the house," Dave recalled. "Two of Kim's necklaces and a pair of expensive diamond earrings I bought for her were missing. Julie told the investigator, but the bottom line was they were never found. Not that I expected them to look for them."

"That maybe puts a different take on the person or persons who did this," I replied. "Although I still believe that Kim was the target of a sexual offender, that doesn't mean the person or people who did this didn't steal her jewelry. Do you know if anyone at least tried to track the jewelry?"

"If they did, they never told us. But it didn't matter to them since they already had their guy" was Dave's response, adding the obvious that burglary and robbery had been dismissed by the ISP as possible motives.

After Dave told me where he had bought the earrings, I made a note to get a copy of the bill of sale for them and then to subpoena the local pawn shops to see if the earrings had been hocked in the aftermath of the murders. The odds were low, but every now and then the blind squirrel finds a nut.

Continuing with the Biddle-related story, Dave said after a very packed and highly emotional Sunday service at the GCC,[94] the day after the bumping incident, had been when he'd called and apologized to Biddle for his outburst the day before. He further said he'd also cried when talking with Biddle, telling him it hurt so much that his old buddies, ones he had known for so long and had loved as brothers, had ignored him and refused to speak with him. Biddle's response had been to reassure him that they were "exhausting every lead, every bit of evidence" and further the "evidence techs are just being so meticulous."

"Of course, they weren't being so 'meticulous.' That wasn't true, nor were a lot of things he told me, but regardless, I told Biddle I'd do anything, including taking a polygraph test. Nothing made a difference, though."

"Did they ever follow through on the polygraph?"

"No. And I volunteered after I was arrested. They didn't want to screw up their case with me passing the lie detector."

He had also known, he said, the call to Biddle had been taped, as had been a later call to Sam Sarkisian, as were all calls from the public to the ISP Post, but said, "I didn't care and I didn't have anything to hide."

---

[94] Media trucks and reporters had flooded the parking lot of the GCC, and afterward David had been interviewed in a very emotionally-charged atmosphere.

After the Biddle call, he had then called Sarkisian, as he'd pleaded with him for some kind of information as to how the investigation was going. "They later said that was me, once again, trying to manipulate the investigation," Dave said. "Once again, I did a great job, huh?"

In the call, Sarkisian had told him only there were "ten guys working around the clock," and, further, they had "that expert from Oregon," referring to Rob Stites.

He said he had practically pleaded with his good friend Sam to tell him, "I know Dave that you didn't do this." All he got, said Dave, had been lip service in return.

The one trooper who did express overt concern for Dave had been Shelly Romero after he'd told her on Saturday afternoon that he couldn't retrieve any clothes, including his own, from the house. Shelly had offered to take him shopping the next day for a suit, but on Sunday afternoon called him and said she had been ordered by Sam Sarkisian not to help him.[95]

By then, he had known it was only a matter of time before, as he told his sister Julie, things would "get ugly." When she had asked what he meant, Dave said he didn't kill his family and "kept repeating it."

"She couldn't understand what I was saying, asking me how the ISP could believe it was me who killed my family when I was playing basketball. I finally told her that I didn't know *how* they were thinking, but I did know *what* they were thinking."

I had to stand up to collect my thoughts. Listening to Dave's recollection of the events was beyond emotional, and not only was he recalling them but apparently reliving them as well.

We returned to the timeline, spending over an hour on the days and hours leading up to the murders. I made voluminous notes.[96]

"Okay, now what're your thoughts on to the identity of BACKBONE on that gray sweatshirt?" I asked. He didn't know, but he was convinced that gray nondescript sweatshirt was similar if not identical to ones he had worn while in the Indiana Department of Corrections (DOC). As such, over the years, he had asked several offenders at both the Reception and Diagnostic Center (RDC) as well as at the Indiana State Prison, the two facilities where he had spent time, if anyone had known anyone with that nickname. No one had, he said, as I told him that we'd get a request to the IDOC to see if they

---

[95] Per Clemons, he had been the one who'd made the decision, and Sarkisian had been the one who'd made the call. The reason? Clemons thought she might be involved in a "potential hostage situation" if David thought he was going to be arrested.

[96] After I'd scrutinized all the ISP reports and interviews and his daily work sheets, reviewed his phone and bank records, and interviewed his family members, I later returned with much more information, and together we constructed the detailed timeline.

had any such nicknames in any of their databases, particularly those who tracked prison gangs.

"Any other ideas as to who did it?"

"No. I have no idea." He then explained, however, that early on he had told of three people, when asked by several detectives and troopers if he had *any* idea whatsoever as to *anyone* who had it in for him or his family. One was the irate neighbor whom Camm had arrested for cultivating marijuana and had soon been eliminated as a suspect. The other two were co-employees who hadn't gotten along with him, and they, too, had been eliminated. "It's not that I thought they did it," he said, "but I was searching my brain for anyone who could possibly have wanted to harm me or my family."

As I began to collect my several pages of notes, I said we'd meet soon and that I'd have continuing questions for him. "Whatever you need" was his quick and direct answer.

We stood and shook hands, and I left with what would become my farewell message each time we met: "We're getting there, Dave." What I didn't tell him was that I had been wrong in my initial assessment of him. He wasn't, as I had first thought, a beaten man, for that implied a defeated man. David Camm was far from a beaten or defeated man as he was clearly ready for another fight.

CHAPTER 12
Evidence Techs & More Searches

Prior to listening to and watching the arrest interrogation of Dave, it was important to comprehend the full extent of what the ISP had *at the time* they had arrested their former colleague. Of course, Stites' deductions hadn't been accurate, but oftentimes prosecutors hold back other evidence and rely only on enough probable cause to support an arrest. I didn't think that was the case with Dave, though, as I suspected Faith hadn't had much of anything else. Anyway, having a good handle on the original case was important.

If there had been a narrative, authored by the lead detective or anyone within the ISP, which laid out the totality of their evidence, I didn't find it. It took several days of reviewing the reports of dozens of detectives and troopers who'd had some degree of input into the evidence collection to finally evaluate their case.[97] In order to do so, I divided the investigation into forensics and detective interviews and began with the work conducted by the evidence technicians.

> NINETEEN INDIVIDUALS, INCLUDING SEVERAL WITH NO POLICE EXPERIENCE, HAD SEIZED EVIDENCE AT A TRIPLE HOMICIDE CRIME SCENE.

As to what forensic evidence had been tested and the results from those tests, that was an easy question to answer. Nothing had been analyzed or tested by anyone prior to Dave's arrest, with the exception being Stites, and his credibility was in tatters. In fact, the ISP labs, which, overall, had excellent and well-deserved reputations, hadn't even *received* any evidence when Dave had been placed behind bars.

Photographing & Processing The Crime Scene

Regarding the techs, Sam Sarkisian of the Sellersburg Post had been the first of four ISP evidence technicians to arrive at the crime scene, getting to the Camm residence around 9:50 p.m. He had soon been followed by Sergeants Jeff Franklin and James Niemeyer, the most senior ISP tech. Niemeyer had initially thought, since the ISP had been in physical and investigative control of the scene, they would also be in charge of collecting the evidence. Not so, according to Sarkisian, who had told him Stan Faith had made the decision

---

[97] In addition to the ISP reports, I also reviewed selected depositions and trial testimony.

to have two New Albany Police Department (NAPD) techs, Sergeants Kyle Brewer and Paul Jefferson, in charge. They were the ones, he'd said, who were going to "process the scene."

As it had turned out, the NAPD had not been in charge after all, since, according to Niemeyer, the NAPD techs finally told him they'd been there only to observe and help if needed.

With the ISP supposedly back in charge of the scene, and according to their own protocol,[98] there should have been an ISP scene supervisor. That hadn't happened, even with the arrival of other techs. For Niemeyer's part, the administrative supervisor of the other techs,[99] he'd believed Sarkisian, as the local district tech, had been in charge of the scene. With respect to his having told Sarkisian what to do, Niemeyer said, "...you don't as a supervisor look at him and tell him, 'well, you need to do this or that...'"

For his part, Sarkisian said there had been no protocol for determining who was in charge when multiple technicians responded to a crime scene.

Prior to searching the garage and house, however, a decision had been made by Niemeyer to secure search warrants from a judge. Although Dave had granted verbal permission to search whatever they wanted, it was a sound decision by Niemeyer because a suspect could later claim he hadn't given authority, and the results of the search could be legally challenged. And, yes, Dave had been a suspect, as he should have been. "Everyone is a suspect until they're not" is a good rule-of-thumb to follow. A suspect, that is, until solid evidence eliminates them.

Trooper Josh Banet had returned with the multiple warrants around 1:05 a.m. In addition to the house search warrant, others had been issued for Dave's pickup truck, Sam's Chevrolet Tahoe, and an older Oldsmobile, owned by Kim and Dave, which had been parked in front of the detached garage.

Niemeyer immediately had begun videotaping the interior of the garage, but his report listed the time as 12:05 a.m. and not 1:05 a.m. Niemeyer, living about 60 miles west of New Albany, had lived in a different time zone and cited that time. Further complicating the time issue, it wasn't uncommon for ISP reports to list times other than local time on their reports, as they often used "State Time," meaning the time in Indianapolis, the location of ISP Headquarters. State Time could be, or may not be, the same time as the time where an investigation is being conducted.

Still, Niemeyer's video had been shot without adequate light as the garage had been dark without overhead lights and no supplemental light had been

---

[98] The third step in the ISP Seven Step Crime Scene Protocol was "...to decide who's going to be the case officer...in charge of the case..."

[99] Niemeyer "did evaluations (on the other technicians and) their payroll."

available.[100] The poor video images of Kim and Brad, as well as the blood flow, had failed to adequately capture the vivid detail of the carnage.

Niemeyer also hadn't attempted to video any aspect of the interior of the Bronco. We'd later learned he hadn't wanted to disturb any evidence prior to the Bronco being processed, which contradicted the intended purpose of capturing the scene accurately, as it had been observed by first responders.[101]

Fifteen minutes after the searches began, Deputy Coroner Becky Balmer had arrived at the scene, almost four hours after the house had been cleared by the responding officers. She had been struck by the fact that "inside the garage there was [sic] probably ten police officers," in addition to the bodies of Kim and Brad on the floor and Jill in the Bronco. Ten officers just standing in the middle of a crime scene within a few feet of three bodies is not exactly good protocol.

Photos of the victims, the garage, and the Bronco, as well as of the interior of the house were limited in number and not taken from all perspectives. The house photos, for example, consisted of very few photographs of an entire room, mostly from one angle and with very little, if any, overlapping. There had been many photos taken of the master bedroom and laundry, two respective rooms which respectively became the focuses of scrutiny after Jill's autopsy and because of Stites' opinion of a clean-up. That meant the photos had probably been taken well after the murders and not contemporaneously with the initial search.

As for the ISP photos, under the orders of Stan Faith, contrary to ISP protocol, and according to Sarkisian's report, "All photo film was collected and in the custody of Robert Stites." [102] Stites' importance had once again been underscored and trumped protocol.

Some photos, however, had added to the confusion. According to Dave, Kim had always kept her purse in the front passenger seat of the Bronco. Yet, it had finally been collected from the *kitchen*. Weirder still, it had been found

---

[100] The first five technicians on the scene apparently hadn't had portable lighting.

[101] Franklin, also in the garage with Niemeyer, said he hadn't paid much attention to Jill. "Other than just a brief peek in the window, that was the only contact I had with Jill."

[102] Rather than having the ISP developing the film, Sarkisian took all the rolls to a local 24-hour kiosk. When they were retrieved by the ISP, the photographs had been co-mingled with one another. Since the identifier lists included by the techs had also been lost, the identity of who took each photograph remains unknown. Niemeyer, like most technicians, had placed with his exposed rolls a small piece of paper on which he had written his name, the ISP district number, case number, date and time taken, and the location and item photographed. The identifier list had then been placed into the negative holder after the ISP had developed and returned the film to him. That list allowed Niemeyer to refresh his memory about the photos and to readily identify those which needed to be duplicated. Because of Faith's orders, techs were often unsure if they or another tech had taken a photo.

inside a purple gym bag, which had also housed a plastic backpack. Those two items, however, were pictured only on the floor of the garage, meaning they had been found and taken from the car. There was no report that detailed how the purse had gotten from the car, into the house, and into a gym bag, along with the plastic backpack. [103]

A photo of a partially bloody shoeprint on the garage floor, taken by Franklin, hadn't been depicted in Bube's sketch. Where was it? No one knew, as there had been no indication as to its location, directionality, or size.[104]

Beyond who had been in control, and who had documented what, the extent of the search had also been a point of confusion, as during the first hours at the scene only the garage had been a focal point while the house had been relegated to an apparent afterthought. Niemeyer had thought it was Sarkisian who had taken "the house," but Sarkisian's "search" consisted of his doing what he had described as a "walk-through."

In fact, Sarkisian had acknowledged he didn't recall being in the master bedroom, but, he'd noted, "I did walk by it. I do know I looked in it." Sarkisian, in fact, had concluded there had been no need to search the house since he "… didn't see anything…didn't see any ransacking, didn't see any drawers pulled out, didn't see anything turned over, disruption, didn't see any missing property, obviously, televisions missing, anything like that missing."

Sarkisian had concluded the house was unimportant based on his not seeing any forced entry of doors or windows. He apparently hadn't been aware, as Dave had told Neal and Gibson, that the Camm family didn't lock the doors of their home.

Regardless, and because of Sarkisian's conclusions, no one had searched or processed the house for fingerprints or sought to determine from Dave or other family members whether money, jewelry, or other valuables may have been stolen.

Around 6:40 a.m. early Friday morning, Clemons had noted in his report the evidence techs had completed their photography and videotaping of the

---

[103] Much later, we learned Sergeant Gregory Oeth and ISP Evansville Regional Laboratory Manager, First Sergeant Joseph Vetter, had each taken responsibility for searching the Bronco. Oeth had removed items from the Bronco while Vetter kept an electronic inventory of the items on his laptop computer. That inventory, kept contemporaneously with the removal of items from the Bronco, would have answered questions about Kim's purse, the gym bag, and backpack. Yet no inventory of the Bronco made it from the crime scene as Vetter later said his computer crashed; thus, the electronic copy of the inventory had been lost prior to his printing it or backing it up.

[104] Looking at the configuration on the soles of the shoes of Dave indicated that it had, quite probably, been his shoe which had dipped slightly into Kim's blood trail as he gave Brad CPR on the garage floor.

inside of the house. That was a problematic assertion because the tech who actually had videoed the interior of the house, Gregory Oeth, hadn't done so until about 12 hours *after* Clemons had returned early Friday. Additionally, and as noted, many of the photos had also been taken well after Clemons' assertion that both video and photos had been completed.

Compounding the confusion was the fact it had been Sarkisian, rather than Oeth or Vetter, the two responsible for searching Kim's car, who'd seized Kim's Nokia cell phone from the Bronco. Its location? Under the driver's seat of the Bronco. The location could have lent credence to the idea that Kim and her assailant had fought over the phone, but if any photographs had been taken of it, either under the seat, or anywhere, none are known to exist. Perhaps more critically, the phone had never been processed for fingerprints.[105]

Of the existing photographs taken in the garage by Niemeyer, Sarkisian, Oeth, Franklin, Brewer, and/or whomever, Kim is shown lying on her back with her feet lying slightly under the open passenger side door. Her dark blue, long-sleeved sweater is still on her upper body, though her lower abdomen isn't covered.

Kim's sweater and the surrounding area resulted in Franklin's having seized so much hair that it caused him to comment he hadn't ever collected as much from any other body. Kim, according to Dave and others, had been a meticulously neat person and wouldn't have allowed herself to be seen in such a manner. Had she lost her hair in the violent struggle with her murderer who, in addition to inflicting all those injuries, had pulled her hair?

Kim's shoes on top of the Bronco had gone unexplained, but there were other strange aspects as well. There had been no photos of her socks, nor were any found by a tech. She had also been wearing black panties. Black panties. Not one of the male troopers or investigators had thought of any possible significance of a professional woman, probably the victim of a sexual assault, wearing black panties under white pants. However, that unlikelihood did make a distinct impression on Shelly Romero who'd stood outside the garage and studied the scene. She'd quickly realized no businesswoman would dress herself in such a manner, particularly since she had been wearing a white bra.

Romero had also been able to discern, as she wrote in her report, that Kim's "...underwear wasn't on right (partially pulled down or folded over...)." She'd wondered whether Kim had changed underwear. If so, what

---

[105] The phone and its later questionable handling by a detective not associated with the investigation resulted in many unanswered questions.

had happened to the underwear she had originally worn? And why were the black panties either "pulled down" or "folded over?"

The possible ramifications of that observation were obvious as well as horrific. To change from the panties she had been wearing, had Kim been forced to go to her bedroom? Had she been assaulted there with condoms flushed down the toilet? If she had been there, where had the kids been? The evidence, of course, pointed to their not leaving the back seat, as Jill had still been strapped in her seatbelt. If that were so, then perhaps another person had been present, guarding the imprisoned children.

Had Kim also been forced to give her worn panties to the perpetrator and then made to wear the black ones? That wouldn't be strange, at least not to some sexual offenders, as they and other criminals on occasion took souvenirs of their conquests.

Since the other ISP detectives and techs had already dismissed the possibility that Kim had been the target of a sexual attack, along with Sarkisian's dismissal of any importance in the house, Romero's information hadn't been pursued.

The photographs of Brad as he lay on the floor did serve as possible clues in the investigation, even if they had gone unnoticed by the techs. Photos showed him lying where his dad had placed him, on his back with his head towards the rear of the car, his arms extended from his body. Seen underneath Brad was a gray garment and what turned out to be the gray Hanes, XL sweatshirt, the BACKBONE sweatshirt.

It was understandable the sweatshirt hadn't been noticed early on, in the dimly-lit garage, but after the portable lights had finally brightly illuminated the garage, that garment still hadn't been noticed by any of the techs and, in fact, had only first been noticed when it had been found in the same body bag as Brad at the medical examiner's office. Niemeyer's explanation as to what had happened to the garment had been that it had "gotten away" from them.

For his part, NAPD tech Brewer had been in the garage with a unique piece of equipment in the form of an electrostatic dust lifter, designed to lift dust and other particulate matter from a surface. A smooth surface, such as finished concrete or a laminated floor, walked upon by victims or perpetrators, could possibly lift a shoe print or a footprint.[106] Thus, if a suspect's shoe were eventually collected, a possible match might be made with that of the shoe impression obtained on the electrically-charged plastic film used to lift the

---

[106] The theory of trace evidence, of course, is that tiny and even unseen material or items are often transferred to/from interacting objects, including perpetrators.

impression.[107]

Brewer had seen numerous shoe and foot impressions throughout the garage. He had also clearly seen the impression of a bare footprint, located at the rear of the right side of the Bronco. In fact, he had carefully and successfully lifted an impression and sat the fragile film aside. Further scrutiny could have revealed whether it had belonged to Kim, Nelson, or possibly someone else. The delicate lift, however, had been destroyed at the scene when another officer, whose identity Brewer could not recall, had sat on it.

Niemeyer had also attempted to identify shoe prints in the garage but had given up after several troopers had told him the prints were theirs. Still, no lifts had been obtained from the area underneath the Bronco,[108] nor had any ever been obtained from the interior of the house, which had laminated wood flooring throughout.

Brewer had pointed out to the ISP techs what he'd thought was polish on the floor, between Kim's outstretched legs, thinking it the same color as her painted toenails. Matching a scraping from the floor to the polish could have supported Kim's engaging in a violent struggle with her murderer. No one, however, had pursued recovering any of the scrapings.

Other items had piqued the interest of the techs, though. Sergeant Jefferson had noticed a green jacket, lying on a large cardboard box on the south side of the garage. Oddly, the jacket had been wet, even though it had been found in the interior of the garage. The jacket had been the subject of much scrutiny, as had been another wet area, this one found on the floor of the right bay, just in front of the steps leading to the house. Jefferson had thought the area was potentially significant, had told the ISP techs of his observation, and had assumed the ISP took photographs of the area; in fact, no one had taken any photos nor retrieved any scraping.

As far as the green jacket, it later had been discounted when it was believed one of the responders had spilled a drink on it.

The phenomena all had seen and noted had been the enormous flow of blood from Kim's head and from which Stites had made several erroneous deductions. That blood flow from Kim's head, in fact, had traveled to the end of the garage bay and onto the asphalt driveway. No one had taken any action about that evidence other than trooper Romero, who, seeing the flow

---

[107] While certainly not as precise as a DNA profile match, most shoes have a very specific tread pattern, as well as having individual characteristics, such as a nick in the tread here or a gouge in the rubber there. Matching a lift to a shoe isn't 100% conclusive, but it can still be excellent circumstantial evidence.

[108] If the perpetrator had been waiting in the darkened garage, it was possible he/she had left footprints where the Bronco had later been parked.

still moving and thinking it might be important for later consideration, had placed a pebble at the end of the flow on the driveway, which by that time, had reached the left side of David's truck. Eventually, the flow had grown to over 30 feet in length, further illustrating the enormity of the blood lost from Kim's head wound.

As to what had caused the obvious damming of the blood flow in the garage, the item had a straight edge and was approximately 18" wide or wider, but no one knew, because it, too, had not been measured. The object causing the obstruction had not been found, meaning the perpetrator had taken it with him/her.

A spent Federal .380 shell casing with FC 380 AUTO stamped on its base had been found on the garage floor by Franklin. He'd concluded it most likely had been the round that killed Kim since no other casings had been found outside the Bronco.

Unspent ammunition had been found in the basement of the house in a metal gun cabinet. Also found had been Dave's shoulder weapons, which were not a surprise, since he had been an avid deer hunter.[109] In the same cabinet had been several boxes of shotgun and handgun ammunition. It was Oeth who'd examined all of the .380 rounds to see if any were Federal or if any had extractor marks;[110] none had. As Dave had told Neal and Gibson, he hadn't owned any handguns and none had been found in the gun cabinet or anywhere else, for that matter.

One tech had photographed and then conducted a search of the exterior and interior of Dave's truck, collecting a total of five items: three swabbings from the center of the hood and the driver's side front fender; a fingerprint, obtained from the driver's front fender; and an ink pen, taken from the middle of the front bench seat. The tech had also closely examined the interior to discern if any blood was inside but had found nothing.

The searches of Sam's Tahoe and the Oldsmobile had yielded no collectible evidence.

Back inside the house, in the kids' bathroom off the main hallway, several people had noticed the shower curtain had a reddish-brown stain, one resembling blood. Niemeyer had been alerted to the stain and thought

---

[109] An eight-point buck's head had hung on a wall across from the cabinet.

[110] As a round is discharged in a semi-automatic weapon, extractor marks are left on the shell casing when it is ejected; those marks may then connect the casings to the weapon that extracted them.

he had done a presumptive field test for blood. Since he thought the test was negative, he'd neither documented his examination nor the results of his test.

As to why he hadn't documented his findings, Niemeyer had responded, "It's the way I did things…and as far as documenting everything you do, it's just an impossible task…"

What had turned out to be truly impossible was testing the shower curtain for blood at a later date. Though there was no record of its being seized and no one had claimed any knowledge of its whereabouts, the shower curtain had simply disappeared into the hands of an unknown person.[111]

As for fingerprinting in the garage, Niemeyer had dusted only a few areas, and they were on the Bronco's exterior. He'd lifted four latent prints, including one on the driver's door, three by the passenger door, and one full, left palmprint on the passenger doorpost.[112] He'd stopped his fingerprinting efforts with the outside of the Bronco, not attempting to lift any inside, apparently not considering the possibility the murderer had been in the car.[113]

Also completely ignored had been the phone in the kitchen where David had placed the phone call screaming for help. In fact, Brewer had seen "blood all over the phone." Securing a blood sample from the phone could have identified the source of the blood on David's hands and helped with reconstructing David's movements, such as touching the bodies of Jill and Kim as well as Brad. That hadn't happened, however, but calls had been made from that phone the next day by detectives in their de facto kitchen headquarters, indicating it had been cleaned by someone, most probably one of the detectives.

---

[111] When the family was given custody of the house over a week later, the shower curtain was missing.

[112] Finger and palmprints were later taken from Dave, but they did not match the unknown prints from the Bronco exterior.

[113] One couldn't assume the murderer had just been waiting in the garage, although that was a possibility. Had he/she gotten in the Bronco some distance from the house, possibly portraying himself as a stranded traveler?

*An aerial view, taken by the ISP, of the Camm residence,
looking south, on the morning of September 29, 2000;
David's white UDI truck is parked in front of the
attached garage; gravel Lockhart Road runs from the
left (east) where it intersects with Alonzo Smith Road
and to the right (west) where it dead-ends; and
Amos Lockhart's house is on the upper left with
the children's playhouse barely visible behind some trees.*

Greg Balmer,[114] the Floyd County Coroner who'd arrived at the scene near dawn,[115] began transporting the bodies to the Kentucky Medical Examiner's office in Louisville. Kim and Brad had been transported first; an hour or so later, Jill's body had followed. Sarkisian, Franklin, and Detective David Makowsky had been designated to attend the autopsies, make notes, take photographs, and secure fingerprints.

It had been Sarkisian's duty to secure fingerprints and palmprints of each of the three victims. Thus, any prints discovered in or on the Bronco or elsewhere could have been eliminated if matched to one of them. Inexplicably, though, Sarkisian obtained prints from just a few fingers of each victim and, as such,

---

[114] Coroner Greg Balmer was the husband of his deputy, Becky Balmer; Balmer and her husband routinely alternated between being elected Floyd County Coroner and appointing their spouse as Chief Deputy.

[115] There was even confusion over the time the coroner had arrived—i.e., Biddle's report reflected, "At approximately 0615 hours, I requested the Floyd County Coroner return to the crime scene to remove the bodies." Sarkisian's stated, "The Floyd County Coroner's Office arrived at the crime scene...at approximately 0430 hrs," and per the crime scene log, Coroner Balmer had arrived at 5:45 a.m.

numerous fingerprints on the Bronco were never identified.[116]

After Jill had been removed, Niemeyer entered the car and collected two .380 shell casings, which had also borne the same markings as the one found on the garage floor; one had been found under the front passenger seat, and the other had been located in a crease of the backseat.

Three corresponding .380 projectiles had been found under the lower trim of the windshield, which had been shattered into a spider web; on the floor behind the driver's seat; and in the cargo space at the back of the vehicle. The projectile in the windshield trim had logically been determined to have been made by Kim's fatal round, which had struck her in the left side of her head, exited her right side, and traveled through the open Bronco passenger door and then into the windshield.

The projectile behind Jill in the cargo bay had clearly been the one to kill her, and the one on the floor, by elimination, had been the one to kill Brad.

Jacque Vaught had been the first of the prosecutor investigators to arrive at the crime scene at 1:28 a.m. Friday morning; within a day, five other investigators had joined her.[117] They had also collected evidence, but their work product was questionable, as everything they collected was stored at either a separate storage facility or a safe in the prosecutor's office. Worse still, some of their collected evidence had apparently never been physically provided to the ISP, nor did the ISP know of its collection.

Why would such people have even been allowed at the scene of a triple homicide? According to Sarkisian, the ISP "really didn't have a choice in the matter." Clemons had gone a step further in explaining the presence of the Faith's sleuths by saying the ISP had a "reliance upon the...prosecutor" that his investigators had known what they were doing.

Niemeyer, however, had been more vocal. According to him, the prosecutor's investigators "wanted anything and everything that they saw ... they wanted [it] collected...They were excited. When they would discover something, they were thrilled to death and they voiced it very loudly...*I had no control over them.*"[118]

Anger had finally overcome a frustrated Niemeyer, who, of Faith's investigators, said he "felt like throwing a real screaming fit." As a result, he had refused to seize some garage window curtains one of them had ordered

---

[116] It was such an aberration, in fact, ISP fingerprint examiner Jon Singleton of the Evansville Lab had opined they "were the worst post-mortem prints I've ever seen"—not exactly a great endorsement from a fellow officer.

[117] The others were Tony Toran, Jeff Winstead, Steve Mennemeyer, John Wilcox, and Emily Fessel.

[118] Emphasis mine.

him to collect. He even had tried to escape from the scene but had been told by Sergeant Vetter that "Stan Faith called. *It's his case.*[119] Quit complaining and start collecting." Niemeyer had collected the curtains. After all, it had been Stan Faith's case.

When later asked of his thoughts of Faith's investigators at the scene, Sarkisian had a divergent take than Niemeyer, stating that he'd been "indifferent," adding, "They didn't interfere with me."

The Genesis Of The Molestation Motive

Shortly after taping his "interpreted" gunshots interview with Debbie Ter Vree on Friday afternoon, Clemons had been telephoned by Sarkisian, who'd been present at Jill's autopsy, telling Clemons about the medical examiner's assertion that Jill had possibly been molested.

Per Clemons' report, Sarkisian had told him, "It appeared as though Jill's vagina had been penetrated." Clemons, upon hanging up with Sarkisian, had immediately contacted Faith and secured another search warrant from Judge Striegel, claiming during "the initial search of [Camm's house], sexual paraphernalia was found in plain view," and "the female child victim has indicia of sexual molestation."

Clemons' characterization of "indicia of sexual molestation," of course, had differed radically from the medical examiner's later written report, which reflected the injuries were to Jill's external genitalia, not her vagina, and, further, that the injury had been a result of "non-specific, blunt force trauma."

Regardless, the injury to Jill and the existence of the devices had been enough to convince Clemons that Dave had molested his daughter, and he'd strongly alluded to the alleged molestation in his murder affidavit two days later.

I had found nothing, no evidence or allegation—nothing whatsoever—in any ISP investigative or laboratory report, which had either linked Dave to Jill's genital injuries or indicated that he had mistreated his daughter in any manner.

As part of her own investigation, Deputy Coroner Balmer had contacted the family doctor, the local hospital emergency room, and others to search for any evidence or indication that either Jill or Brad had been abused in any manner. She had found none, and as for the perineal irritation noted on Jill during a pre-school doctor's visit a month before, the doctor and Balmer had thought nothing of it since such rashes are very common on little girls.

---

[119] Emphasis added.

114

More Searches

Regardless, and building on the new "discovery" in his new sworn statement, Clemons had claimed there was "indicia of child pornography, sexual paraphernalia and video tapes" in the house. He hadn't specifically described those items, however, and in fact, if there had been "indicia of child pornography," the ISP would have been duty bound to have collected it when first discovered.

The new search had begun late Friday after the warrant had been issued, again by Judge Striegel. Items seized were six "sexual devices" as listed on ISP evidence sheets. Those items were what most consenting adults would classify as toys or marital aids, and, in fact, the term "sexual toys" had been used by Clemons in his original report when describing them. Not found during their search had been any "indicia of child pornography" or video tapes containing sexual images or pornography.

Detective Delmar Gross, the detective who'd conducted the search of Jill's "neat and clean" bedroom, noted the evidence techs had used a "light device" on Jill's bed and bed clothing in an attempt to find blood or seminal fluid. Nothing had been found or taken from the room.

Even Lieutenant Biddle had gotten in on still more searches. On Saturday, September 30, he'd gathered four detectives to conduct another search of the house, the same residence that had been discounted the first night by Sarkisian. All Biddle had seized, though, were insurance policies for both Dave and Kim as well as retirement fund applications for each.

One of Faith's legs of his three-legged motive stool had been Dave's killing Kim for her life insurance proceeds. That Biddle had seen fit, apparently immediately on the commencement of the third search, to seize those papers without direction from Faith or one of Faith's investigators seemed unlikely. Their collection had further solidified Faith as having been in charge of the investigation.

The various reports and custody sheets had revealed a total of 19 people had been involved in the collection process. Nineteen different people had seized evidence of some kind or another, with several of those being Stan Faith's own politically-appointed investigators.

Anyone with a passing knowledge of crime-scene searches would conclude the processing of the crime scene had been chaotic, confusing, and without consistent professional supervision. The fact that 19 individuals, including several with no police experience, had collected evidence at a triple homicide crime scene is, most would agree, appalling.

The total lack of adequate control and coordination had resulted in negligent taking and/or handling of photographs and video, some evidence not being collected, and other evidence being incorrectly handled, mislabeled, lost for years, and even being lost entirely.

Incredibly, though, no one has ever been held accountable. In fact, First Sergeant Joe Vetter, the Evansville Laboratory Manager, later shared his own assessment of how the searches and seizures were handled: "Everything I observed," he said, "was in accordance to our operating policies."

CHAPTER 13

The Good, Bad, & Ugly Initial Investigation

The reports of the evidence techs dealt almost entirely with their own areas and little, if any, with any investigation, per se. As such, I turned my attention to the efforts of the detectives and troopers. The organized investigation had begun when Sergeant Clemons and Lieutenant Biddle, while awaiting the arrival of the search warrants late Thursday evening, were devising an investigative plan. Very early in that process, several troopers and detectives had been assigned to canvas the neighborhood.

In regards to those neighborhood investigations, they're elementary but can be incredibly rewarding. And neighborhoods don't just relate to neighbors, but also to identifying and locating UPS and FedEx drivers, mail carriers, and others who may have been in the area and seen something. Sightings don't have to be suspicious, per se, and interviews may only yield

> STITES "DOESN'T KNOW WHAT HE'S DOING…GET HOLD OF FAITH AND STOP IT!"
>
> "HE'S GOING TO DO IT. FAITH WANTS THIS DONE…HE'S GOING TO DO IT!"

seemingly small leads. Those leads, however, may spawn significant results.

Neighbors

Trooper David Barclay had been assigned to block Lockhart Road at Alonzo Smith Road to maintain a log of entries for authorized persons and to restrict entries for all others. While there, several neighbors had volunteered information to him; one was John Galloway, who lived at the corner of that intersection. Galloway, an avid fan of *Jeopardy*, which had begun airing at 7:30 p.m., had seen Debbie Ter Vree's car, minutes before the program started, turn onto Lockhart Road. Shortly thereafter, Galloway had seen, also through his front window, the black Bronco, which he had known was Kim's car, turn onto the same gravel road. He'd estimated the time as around 7:35 p.m.

Galloway's stepson, 16-year-old Brandon Beaven, had also spoken with Barclay. That day Brandon had skipped high school to work on his car, which had been parked in his driveway that paralleled Lockhart Road.

Around 2:10 p.m. Brandon had been lying on his back under his car when he'd seen a black Cadillac, with gold trim and tinted windows, one he hadn't seen before, enter Lockhart Road. Brandon had also seen outlines of the driver and a passenger in the front seat, although he couldn't describe them because of the tinted windows. After about three minutes, the Cadillac had returned to the intersection, exited and turned right, or south, onto Alonzo Smith Road. The Caddy had then accelerated and left the area at a high rate of speed.

Aerial photo taken by me in February, 2005, of the gravel Lockhart Road (bottom to top of photo), which intersects with Alonzo Smith Road (bottom left of photo) where the Galloway/Beaven family lived. The Camm home is the second on the right side of Lockhart Road with the detached garage (white roof) to the right of the house. The Camm/Ter Vree driveway extends into the woods to the Ter Vree home. At the top of the photo is the dead-end of the road.

Literally within minutes, the neighborhood investigation had produced solid information. Kim's vehicle had been seen turning on to Lockhart Road at a time that comported with her leaving swimming practice around 7:00 p.m. It also had verified the time Dave estimated she would be home. Equally as important, it was yet another piece of evidence that had failed to support the original claim the murders had occurred after 9:15 p.m.

As for the Cadillac, had someone else seen it? Had it just been a lost driver and passenger? Two people just cruising through the neighborhood on a Thursday afternoon? Or two people reconnoitering a neighborhood and house? No attempts to determine either the driver or occupants had been pursued in any ISP report I had found.

Barclay had then spoken with two other neighbors who had resided nearby on Alonzo Smith Road, but neither of those two had seen anything of note or unusual that day. Barclay, assigned to a relatively routine but important aspect of the case, nonetheless had done a superb job in documenting the results of his contacts.

Trooper Mary Hagar, who'd arrived at the scene within a minute or so of Clemons, was another diligent officer who'd contacted several individuals. She'd questioned, listened, and then documented her results.

The unpleasant task of breaking the horrible news of the murders to Bob and Debbie Ter Vree had also gone to Hager, who had been the first to attempt to interview them. Bob had shared with her that the time he'd arrived home, around 7:00 p.m., he hadn't seen Kim's vehicle or anything else unusual around the Camm house.

Debbie had been in no condition to have been interviewed in depth at that time, but she had confirmed the approximate time she'd entered the driveway with Hannah, on their way home from an eye doctor's appointment. About 7:30 p.m., when Hannah had asked Debbie to allow her out of the car to play with her cousins and best friends, Brad and Jill, her mom had told her she couldn't because they hadn't yet arrived home from Brad's swim practice.

It was Hager who'd also spoken with Nelson Lockhart who'd provided her with his chronological narrative of the evening, from first seeing Dave around 5:30 p.m. and then hearing him banging and screaming his way into Papaw's back door. As Nelson would do every time he told the story, he'd gotten very emotional, particularly when describing how he'd found and touched Jill, who had been "clammy" and without a pulse.

Nelson, as had Dave in his first interview with Mickey Neal and Darrell Gibson, had provided Hager with information about the old man who, along with his son, had been living through the woods, just north of Bob and Debbie's house. The older man had been shooting a gun dangerously close to the Ter Vree house and had been setting fires in the woods. That man's son, who, as Dave had said, was in his 50's, had just recently been released from prison after a lengthy drug sentence. Clearly, Nelson had thought, the man and his son should at least be interviewed as possible witnesses.

Hagar had then interviewed Amos, the patriarch of the Lockhart family. "Papaw" was hard-of-hearing and, as a result, had to have his television set turned up loud. So it was earlier that evening as he had watched *The Andy Griffith Show* and other shows with Nelson. Neither had seen anything or heard any sounds from David's home.

Dave's cousin and Sam's son, Phillip, had been interviewed next by Hager, who'd told her that he had gotten to the gym to play basketball around 7:00 p.m. and that Dave had already been there. During the games, he'd remembered Dave's saying Kim and the kids were at the Hazelwood (Middle School) pool and would be home around 7:30 p.m. After he and Dave had left the games together, around 9:20 p.m., he'd driven home just in time to have Sam, who'd been on the phone with Nelson, yell at him to jump in the car and go with him to David's house. Upon arrival, he, too, had been stunned by what he saw.

Hager had also documented the results of her interviews with three more neighbors and her unsuccessful attempt at interviewing yet another neighbor. Hager had not only performed her duties in a thorough manner, but she had also been efficient: the last paragraph of her report revealed she had met with Clemons and relayed her "information to him." I had to stop. Clemons had thus *known* Dave had left the gym at or around 9:20 p.m. Why, then, did he claim Dave had departed "on or around 9:00 p.m.?"

Schwan's Deliveryman

Detective Charley Scarber[120] had also been conducting interviews of other neighbors, and in the process, had determined a Schwan's deliveryman had been present in the neighborhood earlier that evening, information which Dave had already provided to Gibson and Neal.

Scarber, on his own initiative, had then contacted the Post to have them locate the Schwan's supervisor to identify the driver, later determined to be Robert Steier. Scarber had alerted Clemons to his findings, who had then told Sergeant Myron Wilkerson[121] to surveil Steier's home until he could be interviewed. Wilkerson had arrived at Steier's home at 2:15 a.m. where he had maintained visual contact of the darkened house for almost three hours.

Darrell Gibson, after his interview with Dave, had met with Clemons at the Camm house; from there the two had driven to the residence of Steier, arriving around 5:00 a.m. Steier, who had worked long hours for Schwans, had been cooperative and responsive, answering every question posed to him. He had been on his current route for eight months, and he had contacted the Camm family, along with other customers on Lockhart Road, every other Thursday.

---

[120] He had later re-interviewed Nelson who'd echoed his concerns about the neighbors living near the Ter Vree family.

[121] Wilkerson was the primary drug detective at the Post and was not part of the cadre of other detectives.

Steier had confirmed he had been at the Camm household around 6:40 p.m. and, while making his two-product sale in the kitchen, hadn't seen or heard anyone else, thus believing Dave was the only one home at the time. He had also recalled Dave's telling him that he was getting ready to leave to play basketball at his church. After completing the order, Steier had left the Camm house about 6:45 p.m. and had continued on his route until returning to the Schwan's garage to park his truck between 9:00–9:30 p.m.

Due to Scarber's diligence, Schwan's had provided computerized records of Steier's sales which verified the identity of his customers who'd made purchases that evening, including those by Dave and others in the hours before and after he had left the Camm house. Those records, along with other corroborating evidence, had eliminated Steier as a suspect.

I had to ask the obvious question: why had one man, with numerous alibi witnesses corroborating one another, been eliminated as a suspect while another, with many alibi witnesses also corroborating one another, been arrested?

Other Interviews

The original investigative plan, I'd discovered, had been to have detectives David Makowsky and Delmar Gross interview the basketball players that first evening. Very quickly, however, they'd been re-directed to find and interview Tom Schmidt who, it had been determined, had been in the neighborhood earlier in the day, working on an exterior project at the residence of Tim Baumgartle, who had lived a few hundred feet past the Camm house.

Schmidt had been located, and though he hadn't noticed anything unusual, he had recalled two vehicles driving on the road: a gray and maroon van and what he'd thought was a black Lincoln or New Yorker. The owners of those two vehicles had been subsequently identified and interviewed, but neither had provided any additional information. The interviews of the remaining basketball players, of course, had been pushed back until two days later when they had been conducted over the telephone by Prewitt.

Makowsky had later joined Scarber to begin the interviews of swim parents who'd been with Kim from 6:00 p.m. to 7:00 p.m.

The first to be contacted at 2:20 a.m., or a little over seven hours after she'd last seen Kim and the kids when they were leaving practice, had been Debra Aven. She'd known it had taken Kim between 20 and 25 minutes to drive from the pool to her home, once again substantiating the information provided by Dave, Debbie Ter Vree, and John Galloway.

Aven had later added the fact that Jill had been sitting on the bleachers, watching a volleyball game in the adjacent gym, as Brad practiced. Other parents had also later recalled Jill as being very active, even running up and down the bleachers.

Annette Berger, another swim parent, had recalled Kim was wearing light pants, a blue sweater and brown shoes. Kim, she said, had talked about her home in Georgetown and how the location had been somewhat inconvenient to her children's activities. Kim had then added, in a tragically ironic comment, that though they lived in a rural area they had been "close to family and felt safe...the kids could just go outside and play."

Gross, in addition to detectives Makowsky and Scarber, had interviewed the teachers of Brad and Jill as well as others at the Graceland Church School. Both children had been described as well-behaved, excellent students. As for Jill, none of the adult females who had interaction with her, including her teacher and after-hours caregiver, had recalled anything of any nature which would have indicated that Jill was having any emotional or physical issue.

Mickey Neal was another detective who had done an effective job, as he had found and interviewed several members of Kim's card-playing group who had met just one week prior to the murders. Kim had said nothing to any of the women about any children or family issues but rather two of those friends had recalled Kim's saying her family had been considering moving closer to New Albany.

Brad And Jill's Grandparents

Neal had also conducted the first interview with Frank Renn, Kim's father; Kim's mother Janice had been too emotionally distraught to answer questions. Frank, however, had provided Neal a thorough account of the activities of Kim, Brad, and Jill during the late afternoon hours just prior to their murders.

Per Neal's report: "Renn indicated that his wife had picked up Bradley Camm at Graceland School around 3:45 PM on September 28, 2000. She then took Bradley to his allergy doctor...whereupon Bradley got his weekly allergy shot. She then took Bradley to her home, and Jill was picked up at school by Kimberly...[who]...took Jill to her dance lessons...while Bradley stayed with Janice Renn. Kimberly and Jill Camm returned to the Renn home around 5:30 PM. They stayed until around 5:45 PM at which time Kimberly took both Jill and Bradley to Bradley's swim practice which was to begin at 6:00 PM."

According to Neal, he had also learned Janice said Bradley had changed into his swim trunks and sweatpants while at her house, and, further, "Jill had changed into her dance leotard prior to leaving with her mother, and then had changed back into her school clothes prior to leaving to go to swim practice."

Dance Class

Neal had also interviewed Margie Blair, owner and instructor of the dance studio where Jill had practiced with other little ones, literally within three hours of her death. Blair and the other instructor, per Neal's report, had said they "had not observed anything to suggest that Jill was not feeling well, or that there were any type of problems." Kim had also been present and, per Blair, there'd been no indication she'd had any problems.

In fact, according to Blair, she'd remembered that "Jill had led the dance class out of the dance room into the waiting room, in a 'choo-choo train line,' and she seemed very happy and in good spirits."

Neal, obviously, had secured critical information about Jill. While there may or may not be any emotional manifestations of molestation in a five-year old's behavior, the fact Jill hadn't had any physical issues while wearing a tight leotard when dancing, or later playing at the volleyball game, should have been significant to those thinking her genital injuries were recent and due to her father. Significant as well as exculpatory, because, per those interviewed, Dave hadn't had contact with his daughter since early morning.

The big question to those claiming Dave had molested his daughter, of course, was how could Jill be that physically active when she had, according to the autopsy report, "petechial hemorrhage and submucosal contusions…on the external genitalia…[including] at around three o'clock…seven o'clock… [and] around nine o'clock" and had other "superficial abrasions?" As noted, a skintight leotard would have created significant friction and thus, serious pain, yet Jill hadn't complained of any issue as she had been very active throughout the day.

There had been no other conclusion for me as to the timing of Jill's genitalia injuries; they had to have occurred after she had left swimming practice with her mother and brother.

The "Funnel"

As for Clemons, he had stayed at the scene because his role, he'd later said, was to assimilate every aspect of the developing investigation, later describing himself as the "funnel" for the case. Anyone who had conducted any investigation would report to him of the results of their interviews and findings. As such, he was the person who would have known more than anyone else and therefore have been able to direct the investigation in the most efficient manner.

As the many troopers, detectives, and technicians had responded to Lockhart Road that first night, so had the extended family of Kim, Brad, and

Jill, who had assembled in Papaw's house. Sometime in the early morning hours, Clemons had walked across the gravel road and met with the family. "We will solve this," he had assured them. Nelson, the career police officer, had wanted more information, though. Were search dogs and a helicopter coming? What was being done? Clemons' response had been a generic "daylight is our friend," meaning the investigation would really take off in the morning.[122]

On Saturday, the day after he got the call from Sarkisian regarding Jill's genital injuries, per Clemons' report, a meeting had been held at 10:00 a.m. at the Post. After that meeting, of course, Dave had been treated as a pariah by most of law enforcement personnel with whom he had contact. He, they now were convinced, had molested his little girl.

It was also on Saturday when several troopers, as well as a Department of Natural Resources (DNC) canine and his handler, had also been assigned to scour the exterior of the Camm property, the woods behind the house, and the woods behind Amos' house. Despite several hours of searching, nothing had been found—no gun and nothing of evidentiary value.

This is a photo taken from the poor quality video of the interior of the Camm residence on September 29, 2000, with several ISP detectives sitting/standing around the kitchen table.

---

[122] Clemons had then taken Nelson aside and privately told him something else. Nelson vividly—and emotionally—recalled that comment years later. Clemons had conveyed to Nelson that when the very bloody crime scene was turned over to the family, they would be the ones responsible for cleaning it since it was not the responsibility of the ISP. Nelson couldn't believe the cold, hard insensitivity of what he had heard. For the first time since the nightmare had begun earlier that evening, he'd completely broken down.

The Blood Expert

The next day, on Sunday morning, October 1,[123] Stites had returned to the medical examiner and secured additional measurements from Kim's body. From there, he had arrived, shortly after 10:00 a.m., at the Post and begun holding court with a retinue of followers, including techs Sarkisian, Jefferson, Brewer, and Niemeyer. Joining them were two of the prosecutor investigators, Vaught and Mark Henderson.

True to Faith's orders, complete access to every piece of evidence had been provided to him, and Niemeyer had fetched, from the evidence locker, any item Stites had demanded.[124]

Before he had begun the examinations, however, Stites had been given critical information. He had been told that the clothing he was to examine belonged to "*the suspect*." Stites later thought someone, he believed Stan Faith, had told him the shirt belonged to the "*shooter*."

Stites, therefore, knew he had been going to examine the shirt belonging to the *suspect and the shooter*. Indeed, throughout his many pages of notes, Stites had referred to articles of clothing as belonging to the "suspect," including the first garment he had scrutinized, Dave's T-shirt.

Suspect and shooter had an enormous effect on the investigation, which, within 24 hours of the murders, had shifted radically from one of finding the perpetrator to one of building a case against their suspect.

Using his large, hand-held magnifying glass, Stites had eyed Dave's T-shirt and then had begun testing some small areas, probably blood, with phenolphthalein, a chemical used for presumptive blood testing. After the presumptive test, and convinced he had been dealing with blood, Stites had then begun marking, with his indelible ink pen, an area which he had determined was critical. Critical, he had concluded, because it contained blowback, or high velocity impact spray (HVIS). According to his notes, within as little as 15 minutes of arriving at the Post, he had determined tiny spots on the lower left hem of the shirt were high velocity impact spray (HVIS).[125]

More importantly, though, Stites' conclusion could only mean one thing, he had educated the group: the person wearing the shirt had been present when the blood was blown on it with such ferocity it had to have come from

---

[123]   Stites wrote the date as 9-31-00.

[124]   Stites later instructed Niemeyer to return to the crime scene and secure photographs of the garage floor and deck.

[125]   Piecing together Stites' notes and other reports, I realized it took as little as 15 minutes or as much as two hours for Stites to reach his conclusion. Why, then, as Sam had told me, had it taken Englert so much time for his experiments and examinations that he had charged Floyd County hundreds of thousands of dollars?

a gunshot wound. According to Niemeyer, Stites had said the person wearing the shirt, whom he had known to be the "suspect and shooter," had to have been within six feet of the victim's wound. That assertion would solidify Niemeyer's opinion of Stites as anything but an expert as he knew four feet was the maximum distance blowback would travel, not six feet.

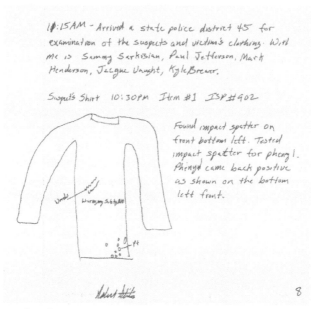

Stites' handwritten notes of his discovery of high-velocity impact spray on Dave's T-shirt; note the long sleeves and term "suspect's shirt."

Niemeyer had then forcefully spoken with Sarkisian and told him Stites' comment was "a bunch of bullshit, the son-of-a-bitch doesn't know what he's doing; you need to get hold of Faith and stop it." Sarkisian's response had been Faith wanted Stites to examine the clothing, and "he's going to do it. Faith wants this done [so] he's going to do it!"

Niemeyer, chastised by his supervisors for not following Stites' orders and Faith's investigators, had also watched Stites handle every piece of clothing without changing gloves, thus possibly cross-contaminating the evidence. It had been infuriating to him, but he could do nothing.

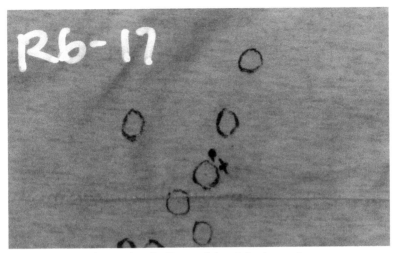

*Photo taken by Stites of the eight tiny stains,
including one which had been tested (+) with
phenolphthalein for the presence of blood.*

Stites, however, hadn't been finished, for he'd continued to examine the remainder of Dave's clothing and shoes, finding blood on one shoe and one sock but nothing on his shorts. That didn't make a lot of sense, for there were four stains on the hem of the shirt which had supposedly been HVIS. Did the blood spray magically stop at the very bottom of the shirt with nothing projected on the shorts? That didn't seem very likely.

Stites' conclusion of HVIS on the shirt, nonetheless, had been the forensic evidence needed to arrest Dave. On Sunday afternoon, shortly after Stites had educated Clemons, Faith, and Susan Orth, the three had constructed their probable cause affidavit.

That affidavit had given Clemons "probable cause to believe that David R. Camm has committed murder, in Floyd County, State of Indiana." That same affidavit had also been replete with erroneous deductions and conclusions of Stites, supposedly eminent bloodstain expert and crime scene reconstructionist. Even so and in spite of those bogus assertions, less than two years later Faith would repeatedly refer to him as "Professor Stites" in Dave's first trial.

CHAPTER 14

"Your Blood People Are Wrong"

I called Kitty, to whom I had sent updates on a regular, if not daily basis, and told her I was almost finished with my review of the initial investigation and said after I watched Dave's arrest interrogation, I'd finish reviewing the ISP reports. I'd then articulate what they hadn't done and, in my assessment, should have done, as well as put together my initial list of what investigation I'd conduct.[126] She was good with all of that.

"By the way," I asked, "has Henderson gotten back with you on the CODIS search for the BACKBONE DNA?"

"Not yet, but he says it's coming. I'll give him time until I won't" was Kitty's response.

"Well, after seeing how diligent and exhaustive the

STITES, OVER THE PHONE, HAD DESCRIBED THOSE STAINS TO ENGLERT WHO HADN'T SEEN THE T-SHIRT; PER STITES, ENGLERT THEN, WITHOUT SEEING OR EXAMINING THE SHIRT, CONCURRED THAT THE STAINS WERE HIGH VELOCITY.

original investigation wasn't," I said, "let's hope Henderson's not like the guys from the first time around."

"Let's not get our hopes up," she said, and then we hung up.

I turned to Dave's arrest interrogation, first reviewing the reports that led to his going to the Post late Sunday afternoon, October 1. I found that Dave, standing with other family members on his grandfather's lawn, had readily agreed to accompany Neal and Gibson to the Post, as they'd asked him to provide major case prints and to follow up on some additional questions. Based upon Dave's previous conversations with Sarkisian, Biddle and others, as well as his being shunned by other friends/officers and his comments to his sister, he had to have known it was only a matter of time before he was arrested.

While Neal and Gibson had driven Dave to the Post late that afternoon, Clemons, Faith, and Orth were still writing the PC affidavit. Thus, nothing he'd later said impacted his arrest, as the decision to charge him had been sealed earlier that day.

---

[126] It's a given that not every successful investigator is going to conduct his/her investigation in an identical manner to another, equally-experienced gumshoe. Assuredly, approaches and methods differ, especially with interview techniques.

I had already listened to the tape of Dave's interrogation during my three-hour drives to/from New Albany, but when I watched the video, I felt even sadder. The grief Dave had been experiencing was palpable; the incomprehension as to why he'd been accused was real; and perhaps the saddest of all were that the wrong allegations against him had come from, as I would later describe Stites, a forensic quack; and then from a lead detective who, in my opinion, had been incompetent at best.

After arriving at the Post, Dave had allowed himself to be printed. That wasn't strange or indicative of any forthcoming arrest, however, inasmuch as prints are often taken of those with normal or routine access to items of evidence, e.g., the Bronco.

What Dave had been told next, however, was a lie, told to him by Neal, his one-time shift mate. He'd claimed Stan Faith, the prosecutor, had decreed that beginning with Dave, all witnesses were to be given their Miranda rights. As a former police officer who had advised hundreds of arrestees of their rights, Dave had known that wasn't true. Witnesses aren't given Miranda rights. Suspects who are to be interrogated and then arrested, however, are advised of their rights. Dave, however, readily acknowledged his rights and signed the consent form.

Neal had begun by asking Dave to repeat the sequence of events that had taken place on the night of the murders, beginning with finding Kim, Brad, and Jill. Dave had related the story, as he had done before to Clemons and Biddle and earlier to Neal and Gibson.

Repeating a story is normal procedure for several reasons. People do recall details, even significant details, after being repeatedly interviewed. Also, of course, those who have lied occasionally forget the substance of their lies and sometimes contradict themselves. Dave's most recent recollections, though, had been consistent with his previous ones.

Their questioning had continued past the chronology of events into his and the family's personal lives. No, he didn't own a handgun. Yes, they were doing well financially. Yes, he was home nights and weekends. Yes, he played basketball later than normal that night. Yes, Kim's schedule was packed with work and with taking care of the kids. Yes, he had an appointment book that would articulate when, where, and with whom he had been on the day of the murders.

What had he done when he'd found his family? Dave had known that Kim, sprawled on the garage floor, was dead. As for Jill? He said he wished he had done more for her, although he didn't articulate what he could have done. Brad, though, had been different. Dave had thought he could possibly help Brad, so that's why he had pulled his son from the car and attempted CPR.

And the shift from an interview to the beginning of the interrogation had come. Interrogations, unlike interviews that solicit information, are confrontational and seek admissions and/or confessions. Interrogations are conducted, however, only if the police have hard evidence, irrefutable evidence, that incriminates the suspect and can be used to bludgeon the suspect over and over. In this case, the hammer had been forged by Rob Stites.

The shift from solicitation to the beginning of confrontation hadn't been smooth or slick but rather obvious as the questioning turned to the family's sleeping habits. Sleeping habits.

Dave had told them Brad often crawled into bed with Kim and him and thought he had done so the night before the murders. And then Dave had had enough. "I ain't stupid, Darrell," he'd told Gibson. He'd then erupted. "This is amazing...dumbfounding...my nightmare continues...you guys really think I'm a suspect...disgusting...You all ought to be ashamed of yourselves. You're wrong...you're wrong!"

He had been trying to control his emotions and hadn't totally lost himself, but I could tell it had been difficult. "I'm going to do this one time. I'm going to sit here and I'm going to look both of you dead in the eye, man-to-man, and I'm going to tell you, and you can believe this in your heart and soul or you cannot. I leave this choice to you. I did not do this. I did not do this, Darrell! Mickey! I did not do this!"

It had been time for Neal to unleash the "hard" evidence they had, their hammer, their money shot. "We took your clothing, and it's been analyzed. There's high velocity blood spatter on your shirt, David, and other articles of your clothing."

That, of course, hadn't been true, as Stites' opinion of HVIS had only been on Dave's shirt, so Neal had added the false assertion—the bluff—about the other clothes.[127] Nonetheless, Dave had quickly responded, "Mickey, I picked up Brad and had blood all over me."

Neal had quickly shut that down. "This is not transfer. There's two different kinds..."

"They are wrong! Then they're wrong! Mickey, you guys better find somebody else to do those tests! Mickey, they're wrong!"

Neal had quickly shifted away from the blood evidence. "What about your sweatshirt?"

Dave had seemed perplexed. "I didn't have a sweatshirt on."

Neal, though, had lied again, claiming they had "talked to all the people you played basketball with and [they] said you had a sweatshirt."

"What kind of sweatshirt? I didn't have a sweatshirt" had been Dave's

---

[127] Lies by law enforcement to suspects, as well as witnesses, are allowed as the U.S. Supreme Court has ruled such is legally permissible during a police interrogation.

answer again, further stating that "…all's I had on was a gray T-shirt. That's it."

"I'm just going by what these people told us over there," Neal had lied again.

Dave's pleadings had become stronger. "It's not right. It's not right. It's not right. It's not right, guys. You're not right. You're wrong. You're wrong, wrong, wrong! You're wrong, Darrell. You're wrong! This is not right! You're getting off the track, something's not right here! Now fix it!"

Ignoring his desperate pleas, they had asked if he had been in the laundry room. Had he gone in there when he went into the house to make the call? Dave had taken a moment to think and then told them he had not been there.

Neal would have none of it and kept to the script of a good interrogator, albeit the most critical questions had been scripted by Stites, as he'd told Dave, "I'm going by what I've been told by technicians. And they've got a mop… You tried to clean some of the blood up."

"This is ridiculous! No, no, no, no, no, no, no, no, no, no! I didn't clean up shit, guys…I didn't try to clean up shit…somebody may have, but it wasn't me! That person is your suspect! I am not that person, and I am not your suspect!"

Neal had persisted, countering, "We're going a lot on the facts left at the scene." What he hadn't said, of course, were those "facts" were deductions made by Stites.

Nonetheless, Neal had then quickly shifted the focus of the questions to the wet green jacket found in the garage. It had had blood on it, he said. Dave had responded that his shirt and shoes had blood on them, as had his hands, and he'd told them, as for the green jacket, "I didn't wipe anything up. I didn't touch anything. I didn't do it."

Another pivot as they had said they knew the location of the gun. That had clearly surprised and pleased Dave, as he'd asked hopefully, "Can you share that with me?" They'd said they believed it to be in the septic system and then they'd quickly moved on.

It had been Gibson's turn and, bluffing also, he'd asked why anyone would have seen Dave on his deck and throwing something off it? Dave had told them he hadn't been on the deck.

They'd quickly returned to their Holy Grail of evidence, the HVIS on Dave's shirt, claiming they were only "dealing with facts [and] not dealing with rumor or innuendo."

Dave hadn't had any of it. "Your blood people are wrong."

Neal had been so convinced of Stites' abilities and pedigree, though, that he'd decided to educate Dave. "This is a man who does this for a living. It's a scientific study, there's blood on your shirt, there's blood on your shirt that is high velocity blood splatter. It's scientific documentation. The only way that comes on is from blowback or blowout from a gunshot wound. They're minute particles that travel at extremely high speeds that come in contact with a surface and stick to it."

"And that is supposed to be on my T-shirt that I played ball in?" Dave had asked. He'd again insisted they find another expert.

And what was to be the Mother of All Lies, although Neal didn't know it at the time, occurred when he'd claimed to Dave, "That's not my expertise and I rely on this man. He's renowned for his expertise. *This is not something he just started to do yesterday.*"[128]

Dave had continued to deny any involvement in the death of his family, regardless of what Neal said this "renowned expert" had concluded.

Interjected throughout Dave's repeated and emphatic denials was Neal's question: "Who did it?" If it hadn't been Dave, then who had it been? An exasperated Dave had told them he didn't know who was responsible as he was relying on his friends to find the murderer.

Gibson had then thrown a curve ball, asking if Dave had gotten home and discovered that Kim was responsible for killing his kids. "You're way off base" had been Dave's quick response.

Neal had then asked if Dave had gotten home and gotten into an argument with Kim. "No, no, no!"

And then, out of the blue, Neal had said they knew about Jill. "We know for a fact she had been sexually molested."

A perplexed Dave had responded, "I don't know anything about that so how could you know anything about that?" Neal said it had been determined at her autopsy.

"Well, then, Mickey, whoever did it, if she's been molested, whoever the son-of-a-bitch was that killed them did it to her!" Dave had been yelling, as he said it must have happened the night they were killed.

And then came the pleading and the begging, as Dave had beseeched his friends to understand both him and his family: "You guys are wrong here… you're wrong! Mickey! I did not do this! I did not do this! Darrell…I didn't do it! This is my family! ... My life was perfect! My life had never been so good at home, at work, with the kids, everything. It could not have been any more perfect. I'm telling you. We didn't fight. We didn't argue. We paid our bills. Everything was perfect. It was perfect. My wife loved me through thick and thin, literally, and I the same for her. My children…I worshipped those children. I worshipped the ground they walked on. And she took care of my babies. And guys, I'm telling you, I did not do this!"

---

[128] Emphasis mine.

Neal had kept on point. "As far as the things we observed on Jill...there were samples that had been taken...is there any way, shape, or form, that you would have a reason where things would be co-mingled...?"

A clearly distraught father had sadly asked, "Did somebody rape her? Did they rape my little girl?"

Neal's response had been direct: "She had been sexually molested." That was too much as Dave had leaned back, held his head in his hands, and, no doubt, I thought, tried not to go insane.

After several moments, he had finally been able to utter some words, telling his former brothers-in-blue, "There is somebody out there. There is some perverted motherfucker out there that's done this to my family. You need to find out who they are."

Neal's response had been to say the murders were just as hard on him and Gibson as they were on Dave.

But then it had quickly been back to the lies, with Dave's being told that "people" in the neighborhood had heard what they thought was gunfire between 9:20-9:25 p.m. when he was already home. Dave had said he had left the gym close to 9:25 p.m. Not so, they'd said.

Another pivot as they'd asked about insurance. Dave had responded that Kim had taken care of all of that with his brother, Danny, adding that he thought Kim had been left with the same amount she had before. Since he had left the ISP, he had needed new insurance, so they'd bought some more coverage, but he wasn't sure how much.

It was at this point that Gibson had been left alone with Dave as Neal had abruptly left the interview room. Dave had told Gibson that if they arrested him, they would be putting an innocent man in jail and the guy who did it would walk away. He'd then asked Gibson, point blank, if they were going to take him to jail and lock him up. Another lie came forth as Gibson had said he didn't know.

I stopped the video for a moment. It was clear, at least to me, that Darrell Gibson wanted to be anywhere else in the world other than lying to his friend and former comrade-in-arms.

As for Neal, he had left the interview room to speak with Stan Faith, now at the Post and monitoring the interrogation via camera, to become more comfortable with David's impending arrest. As the one calling all the shots, Faith had confirmed the arrest warrant was being signed, and David was absolutely going to be arrested for the murders of his wife and children.

Neal had then verbally braced blood expert Rob Stites, still hanging around the Post to see Dave arrested. Neal had told him, in no uncertain terms, that the arrest was based upon his expert opinion the blood on the shirt was blowback. When Neal had pointedly demanded to know how certain Stites was, Stites had sputtered he was "pretty certain" and then gave a percentage of around 90%.

Neal had responded by telling him, "I don't want to hear 90%. I want to hear 100%."

Stites had then excused himself and made a phone call to his mentor Englert. Stites had brought his boss up-to-date on everything he had been doing, as well as telling him, "Stan knows everything as well as the investigators." Everything, of course, had included his findings of blood blowback on the shirt. Stites had described those HVIS stains to Englert and then, over the phone, *without Englert actually seeing the evidence,*[129] said Englert had concurred the stains were high velocity impact spatter. Englert had also told him, Stites later said, that he had been doing a "good job."

Stites had terminated the conversation with Englert and returned to Neal. He'd proclaimed he was now "100% sure."[130]

Returning to the interview room, Neal hadn't talked about his conversations with Faith or Stites. Instead he'd brought with him a CPR mannequin. He'd told David to show him how he had given Brad CPR. He'd said he couldn't understand, if David had truly given Brad CPR, why there wasn't more blood on him.[131]

After a mannequin had been placed on the floor, the video showed Dave beginning an attempt to demonstrate doing CPR, in the cramped interview room, which had been jammed with three chairs and a desk. He had gotten on his knees and tried to begin the process, pinching the nose and beginning to chest compressions. But it had been no good, and finally Dave had blurted out, "If something happened and that came out of his mouth and nose and gets on my shirt, then that's what makes me go to jail, that's okay. I mean, 'cause I did the right thing...I don't have a problem with that at all. If that's what I have to live with the rest of my life because I gave my son CPR, so be it. I wouldn't change anything again. I wish you could believe me. As God is my

---

[129] Emphasis mine.

[130] Stites had later recalled, "Well, during the *examination*, when I saw the high-velocity impact spatter on the shirt, I called Rod Englert and described to him the high-velocity impact stain pattern that I'd found and described to him, and he said that it was high-velocity impact spatter." Per Neal, the telephone conversation between Stites and Englert had occurred during the *interrogation*, which resulted in the 100% confirmation statement by Stites. Thus, there had possibly been two separate phone conversations between Englert and Stites on October 1, 2000. Englert later denied giving an opinion validating the spatter opinion at any time over the telephone.

[131] Neal's comment wasn't based upon the evidence inasmuch as there had been blood on David's shoes and shoestrings and lots of blood on his T-shirt.

witness, I'm telling you the truth. It happened exactly as I said. I didn't do this and there's somebody out there that did."

Neal had sat on the desk, looking down at his former colleague, on the floor, and responded, in earnest I thought, to his wish that they could believe him: "I wish I could, too, Dave."

Any shred of composure Dave had was gone as he'd literally blubbered, "I feel like Jesus. I'm being persecuted. I'm being persecuted by those who are supposed to…Jesus came to save us, that's why He was here. And all the people had to do was listen. They're the ones who persecuted Him, and all they had to do was open themselves up and listen to His message. I didn't do this. I didn't do this. I didn't do it. I didn't do it. I didn't do it, Mickey. I didn't do it."

His sobbing had persisted. Through tears he'd choked, "You just keep persecuting me. And if it's because I gave my son CPR, then so be it. Because it doesn't make any sense any other way. There's no way you can explain it because I wasn't there. I wasn't there. I did exactly what I told you I did. That's it. That's all."

"My wife and I never fought…we never argued…our children were perfect little angels…my life has totally changed in the last two years and especially in the last six months…my wife loved me, and she would stick with me through anything…she gave me two beautiful kids…I didn't do it."

Finally, he'd just hung his head, bent over the mannequin, and wept uncontrollably. The interrogation had been over. After the video had ceased, Dave had been arrested, his mugshot taken, and then he'd been transported to the Floyd County Jail where he'd been booked and placed in a 24/7 lighted cell on suicide watch.

Meanwhile, back at the Camm house, Biddle had strolled across the gravel road and spoken with Nelson. The retired 35-year police lieutenant had been told by Biddle that his nephew had been arrested for the murder of his wife and kids. When Nelson had told him he didn't believe it and, further, from that point onward, he would be "guarded" with his comments and recommend the rest of the family be the same, Biddle had unleashed his coup-de-grace, telling Nelson that "high velocity blood spatter had been found" on Dave's clothing. Nelson, however, had flatly refused to believe it and told Biddle he was wrong.

And the reaction of others who had viewed the emotion-packed video? They had keyed in on Dave's description of his family life as being "perfect" and ridiculed it mercilessly. His life hadn't been perfect, they'd sneered: he'd been a skirt-chasing molester who'd killed for sex, money, and freedom. In fact, Sean Clemons had deduced Dave was a sociopath who was only trying to manipulate others with his lies.

As for the specifics of those lies? Well, no one had been able to articulate any individual lie, corroborated by other witnesses or evidence, Dave had told anyone during any of his interactions, interviews, and/or interrogation other than Clemons, who knew of a really big one. Dave, Clemons had deduced, lied when he had said he was innocent.

CHAPTER 15
"We Couldn't Come Up With Any Other Motive"

After David's arrest, investigators, fewer in number than before his incarceration, had continued their efforts—not on finding the perpetrator but on building the murder case against Dave. Constructing a case against Dave, however, had met some unexpected obstacles.

According to Prosecutor Faith, having Detective Makowsky and others interview numerous UDI clients and prospective customers Dave contacted on the day of the murders could possibly shed light on the demeanor and behavior of the father and husband on the very same day he had been planning the cold-blooded murders of his children and wife.

Twisting The Truth

What the interviewers had found, however, was a guy who had been punctual, arriving at or near the scheduled appointment, "very pleasant…extremely nice and outgoing…businesslike…

> "I DON'T THINK HE COULD HURT THOSE KIDS. I JUST DON'T. HE LOVED THOSE KIDS AND HE LOVED KIM."
>
> "NOT THE DAVID WE KNOW."

good at what he is doing" and "a nice young man." When Dave had spoken of his children, which had been with at least two customers, it had been with fatherly pride, telling them his son was a good swimmer and both his son and daughter attended Graceland School.

If Faith had also thought Kim's co-workers could provide clues as to dark secrets in the Camm home, that, too, was not to be. Jean Hall, a former supervisor of Kim's at Aegon in Louisville,[132] had described her as a "super employee" who, when they met for lunch on the day prior to her death, had "looked nice…[and] had her usual laughing smile." During the four years Hall had known her, Kim had never said anything about any personal problems with Dave or any issues with others. Other employees had echoed Hall's description of Kim as cheerful, positive, and always a good employee.

Rudy Gernert, the head of Aegon in Louisville, hadn't interacted with Kim on a regular basis, but had known her as an excellent employee who'd been highly respected by others. Gernert had also told detectives something else, however, which had raised Faith's antenna, as he'd recalled speaking with

---

[132] Aegon is an international insurance, pensions, and asset firm.

Dave on the morning after the murders.[133] After Dave had broken the horrific news to Gernert, he had further told him to lock Kim's office and to save her emails and voicemails, thinking there could be something, anything, to aid in the investigation.[134]

Gernert had recalled he had told Dave a person from Human Resources (HR) would contact him regarding Kim's life insurance. That person had done as Gernert instructed and later called Dave, telling him she knew that three funerals would be expensive and that he would need help financially. Dave had thanked her and told her he hadn't wanted to talk about it.

No one at Aegon had claimed that Dave ever asked or much less pressed anyone for any payment of any insurance policy or even inquired as to the amounts of Kim's policies. The people at Aegon had been simply saddened, sympathetic, and trying to help, but Dave hadn't wanted to talk. The innocent content of those phone calls, however, would be radically twisted by Faith as he had later claimed Dave, the greedy and remorseless husband and father, literally within hours of the murders, had eagerly been trying to get his hooks on Kim's life insurance proceeds.

There had been no proof Dave had killed his wife for her life insurance coverage, but that hadn't prohibited Faith from *creating* greed as a motive. And that's exactly what he had done, just as he had when he'd argued Dave had murdered for the freedom to chase women. Motives can simply be argued and are bludgeons used by prosecutors; they also, of course, can be designed to inflame a jury.

No Gun & No Drugs

As he had been overcoming the issue of motive, another still lingering concern facing Faith and the ISP was the whereabouts of the murder weapon. Since Dave, at least in their initial theory, only had mere minutes to dispose of the gun, it had to be within a short distance of or in the house itself. Yet several searches by more than a dozen troopers and detectives around the house, another search in the basement, and water searches of two small nearby ponds, all in addition to the septic tank search, had yielded nothing. The whereabouts of the gun had remained a mystery.

A search of Dave's ISP personnel file had revealed his possessing a .380 semi-automatic as a backup weapon, but he had sold that weapon seven years

---

[133] Early in the morning of September 29, Julie, Dave's sister, had told Dave she was calling Aegon and alerting them to Kim's death. Dave had told her that he should be the one to tell them, so his sister handed him the phone.

[134] Kim, in fact, had been attempting to rearrange normal dental appointments for each child; a voicemail message had been left on her phone late in the afternoon of September 28 to confirm the new appointments.

before at a gun shop frequented by law enforcement officers. A check with the ATF had found the gun, still in the possession of the individual who had purchased it.

Knowing they were searching for a .380, Sam had volunteered to Detective Charley Scarber he had such a gun and allowed the ISP to take the weapon and to test fire it. It had been returned to Sam when no match had been made with the three rounds fired from the murder weapon.

Still, if they couldn't find the weapon, perhaps they might find how Dave had come into possession of it. As such, the ISP contacted drivers who had been stopped in the waning weeks of Dave's career as a road trooper. Had any been asked about guns in their possession? Could one of them be the source of the gun? While some had said they had been asked if they had a gun in their possession, not an unusual question of a driver by an officer stopping a vehicle, no one had said anything about any untoward conduct on the part of Dave.

Also telling of the nature of the inquiries to the motorists had been questions about drugs, for it meant the ISP was searching for an additional motive—e.g., had Dave been addicted to or selling drugs and, in the process, shaking down drivers? That road also met a dead end.

Prove You Didn't Do It

But Faith made hay in another manner. In the first few days, recall that Dave had been questioned time and again as to whom he thought might have been responsible. During the first hours of his incarceration, he had again thought long and hard, as would anyone whose family had been viciously murdered, as to the possible murderer. Finally, Dave had reached out to Darrell Gibson and asked to speak with him. When they met, Dave had provided him with a list of names of a few people whom he thought could possibly, even remotely, have had it in for him or his family.

After he gave that short list to Gibson, however, the list, too, became an instrument to batter Dave, as Faith had claimed he was only trying to shove the blame from himself onto innocent people. Once again, Dave had been trying to manipulate the investigation. Manipulation, in fact, had become a key component of the Camm case.

There had been a secondary commodity which had arisen from the question, "If it wasn't you, Dave, then who was it?" Rather than the long-held standard of "proof beyond a reasonable doubt" to convict, his case instead morphed into "prove you didn't do it." That mentality had been pervasive throughout the community, for practically no one had believed Kim and the kids could have been murdered in a random attack. After all, murders didn't just happen without a reason, and Faith had provided the public with three highly incendiary motives.

Fiscally Sound

Subpoenaing the family's bank records had also been accomplished. Rather than revealing any need for money, lavish spending, or greed on the part of Dave, the records revealed a fiscally conservative family spending well within their income, saving money, and having an overall excellent financial condition, exactly as Dave had described to Neal and Gibson.

Records for the cellular and home telephone numbers associated with Dave and his UDI phone had also been subpoenaed. Dave's UDI phone had confirmed the appointment times from his business diary and his own recollections. Nothing discovered could have helped in the prosecution against him. On the contrary, the records had substantiated Dave's whereabouts and his contacts with clients.

Who Placed The Call?

Equally as important, Kim's cell phone records had added an important clue, at least when she was probably still alive. At 7:50 p.m., or 15 minutes after the Bronco had been seen heading onto Lockhart Road, an outgoing call had been placed from her cell phone to a woman living in the Camm's New Albany rental house. That woman and Kim had been engaged in phone tag during the day.

The last call had gone unanswered and then was terminated after just 13 seconds. *How* had the call happened? Had Kim grabbed her phone in desperation, hit a number she had previously called but then had her phone torn from her grasp and then thrown into the car, bouncing around? Was that why it had been found under the driver's seat?

Family Interviews

Others interviewed included Dave's former wife, whom he had married just out of high school. When asked about his relationship with Whitney, she'd told Clemons how "very proud" David was of their teenage daughter. During their marriage, she'd said, David had been mostly quiet and, in answering Clemons' direct question, emphasized he'd "never physically or mentally abused [them]."

Meanwhile, Mickey Neal had still been involved, conducting a follow-up interview with Janice and Frank Renn, Kim's parents and the grieving grandparents of Brad and Jill.[135] If one of the goals had been to find evidence

---

[135] Brad and Jill had been their only grandchildren.

supporting Faith's molestation motive, the exact opposite had occurred.

Janice, as the grandmother who had been integral and very active in the daily lives of her daughter and grandkids, had often retrieved the kids from school and daycare, fed them snacks, and helped prepare them for dance class and swimming. As a doting and loving grandmother, she had been the one who had assisted Jill into her dance leotard just hours prior to her murder.

Neal had made an effort to get Janice and Frank to first accept the allegation that Dave had molested Jill, mischaracterizing her injuries as "irritated around her vagina." Janice had corrected him, telling him the minor irritation she had previously seen wasn't around her vagina but rather the "front part" of the genitals. In fact, Janice had said she'd previously put Vaseline on the chapping and Jill had been fine; she had further told Neal, "But something like what I saw is not uncommon for a little girl, I mean, she had had it before…I didn't think a thing about it."[136]

Janice had continued, "The bottom line is I can't believe that he was capable of doing that. I guess he did. I don't think it was him at the time. Not the David I know. I don't think he could hurt those kids. He loved those kids and he loved Kim. Now he might, you know, have…I don't know. I can't believe he ever did something like that unless something just snapped and I don't think…"

Frank, in the background, had quickly added, "Not the David we know."

Janice had continued, "And that's what I don't understand on Jill. If this happened to Jill, I don't think he could have done it because, I guess, I'm telling myself, 'If he did this, if he killed them, it was in a moment of…' I don't think he could hurt those kids, I just don't."

Neal had been blunt, however, and in the process, had also divulged a lot about the mindset of Faith at the time. "*We couldn't come up with any other motive.*[137] Motive is a big thing for us, we have to, you know, people just don't do something without having a reason. And a reason is motive and *we couldn't come up with any other thing…*"

Neal had sounded, at least to me, that he was not only trying to convince the Renns, but also himself, that Dave had molested Jill. Nonetheless, both Janice and Frank Renn hadn't believed the allegation—at least at that time— their son-in-law had molested their granddaughter.

Neal, in an effort to move past the possibility someone else had been responsible, had told the Renns, "…the prosecutor talked about *the big one-armed hairy stranger.*[138] That's possible, but I mean, even they had to have

---

[136] Clearly, what Janice witnessed and the injuries seen by the medical examiner had not been the same as Jill had suffered a "laceration" on one area of the exterior genitalia.

[137] Emphasis mine.

[138] Emphasis mine.

some kind of reason…these are all possibilities and I'm not say…we wanted to make sure there was no possibility that that existed."

He had continued, "I will tell you, it is kind of *like the prosecutor said, that the first person we always look at stronger than anybody is two people, number one is the husband or spouse and the first person on the scene.*[139] And because, just because of the opportunity and here you have the spouse and the first person being there, being David. So we had to look at him very close. Because getting back to, I didn't feel like that he, you know, in the back of my mind, I thought, *'No, there must be somebody, somebody else out there. But nobody else, we just couldn't put it on anybody else.*[140]

So, because the ISP couldn't think of any other rationale for the murders or readily identify another person responsible, they by default eliminated the possibility of an unknown person committing the crime for an unknown reason. They obviously eliminated the fact random murders without motives do exist, or at least they exist until the person is known and the reason(s) for the crime explained.

Since Dave had been the surviving family member who'd found his family murdered, of course he should have been a suspect, but being the sole survivor who'd discovered the murders doesn't automatically equate to proof, per se.[141]

As he'd continued speaking with the Renns, Neal had dismissed Dave's past promiscuity as a murder motive, either for Dave himself or for anyone else, such as a jealous woman or angry husband. For his part, however, Faith hadn't dismissed that issue, as the mere existence of the prior affairs had been enough for him to claim Dave had killed for his freedom from being a husband and father.

As he finalized his points with the Renns, Neal had said, "Everything we do continues to point back in to Dave, uh, so, you know, and there again, I'm, a couple of us have talked about. I'm not sure at what point in time I would ever be 100% sure. I don't think, I really don't think you ever can be 100% sure unless, you had, unless you were there."

Neal had finally concluded, "But, you know, I'm getting more up there every day. We started out with a little bit more information and, I, obviously, wouldn't have arrested him it if, you know, if we weren't beyond a reasonable doubt."

---

[139] Emphasis mine.

[140] Italic emphasis mine; the audio isn't clear as to whether Neal said "pin" or "put."

[141] Biddle's theory at the time of the murders had been "a heat of the moment type crime and that [Dave] killed his kids to cover the crime." That "heat of the moment" theory obviously didn't mesh with the later theory Dave had planned the murders and snuck away from the gym.

Listening to Neal's tutorial wasn't convincing to me, and I doubt if he had been convinced at the time. The Renns, who certainly hadn't thought Dave capable of harming their daughter or precious grandchildren, would, over time come to a radically different conclusion.

CHAPTER 16
The Stench Of Molestation

I was still assimilating what investigation had and hadn't been conducted, particularly after Dave's arrest, and while I was primarily confined to the investigational aspects of the case, I also wanted to know the mindsets of those involved, including the prosecutors, during that first week.

In addition to the ISP reports, depositions, and trial testimony, another tool of insight, of course, was the media. *The Tribune*, the local Floyd County newspaper published in New Albany, had run stories on a regular basis and, indeed, would do so for the lifetime of the criminal cases against Dave.[142]

Marvin Jenkins, the long-time Sellersburg ISP Post Public Information Officer (PIO), had been the first one quoted in the local paper the day after Dave's arrest as saying Dave had "surrendered last night to the state police at the Sellersburg Post where he once worked…"[143]

Dave, of course, hadn't surrendered, but had been arrested while vigorously proclaiming his innocence. The implication of the word "surrender" is that Dave, faced with and knowing he couldn't escape the overwhelming evidence, had decided to simply give up.

> HOW MANY TIMES DID A PERSON, FALSELY ACCUSED OF MOLESTATION, HAVE TO SCREAM PUBLICLY HE WASN'T GUILTY? 100 TIMES? 1,000 TIMES? A MILLION TIMES? IT WOULDN'T MATTER.

That, one might conclude, was a sneaky way of manipulating the narrative.

And speaking of manipulating the narrative, in that same article, Stan Faith had said that he'd file documents with the court that day that would detail the evidence against Camm. Metropolitan Louisville, no doubt, had anxiously awaited those details, and the next day *The Tribune* hadn't disappointed, as their bold headline screamed, **"Evidence Points to Camm."**[144] "Bloody T-shirt among evidence that implicates Camm" was the sub-heading.

In that article, and in addition to the conclusions of Stites, there had also

---

[142] *The Tribune* of Floyd County later merged with *The Evening News* of Clark County and became *The News & Tribune*, serving both counties.

[143] Associated Press, *The Tribune*, "Camm is arrested for the murder of wife, kids," October 2, 2000.

[144] Ali, Amany, *The Tribune*, "Evidence Points to Camm," October 3, 2000.

been the soon-to-be ever-present vile and repugnant aspect in the article: "The affidavit also states that Camm's daughter 'had a recent tear in the vaginal area consistent with sexual intercourse.' According to Floyd County Coroner Greg Balmer, the molesting of the five-year old girl likely occurred recently. He said additional tests may determine more precisely when the molestation occurred."

If Jill had been molested hadn't been the question, nor had the term "non-specific blunt force trauma" been mentioned in the press or anywhere, for that matter. Rather, Jill had suffered, no doubt—no doubt at all—having been molested, and sexual intercourse had been how the molestation had occurred. After all, the County Coroner had confirmed it publicly. And, of course, her father, who had been arrested for her murder and that of her brother and mother, was the culprit. What else did the community need to know? When a child is molested, especially by her father, the first question asked by many is "Why bother with a trial?"

I recalled the lunch my wife and I had with New Albany friends after Camm had been convicted when we had been told, unequivocally, "David Camm is a rotten son-of-a-bitch who murdered his family because he tried to hide the fact he molested his little girl."

The stench of a molestation claim would never—in fact could never—be overcome by anyone, much less a man incarcerated under a 24/7 suicide watch with no voice. As with the murders, the burden of the molestation allegation had shifted to Dave, as it was up to him, once again, to "prove [he] didn't do it."

I wondered how many times a person, falsely accused of molestation, had to scream publicly he wasn't guilty. 100 times? 1,000 times? A million times? It wouldn't matter, as that unleashed and foulest stench could never be put back into the bottle.

As for Dave's initial hearing on that Monday, it had been short and limited in scope with Judge Striegel entering not guilty pleas for him. Appearing on his behalf, however, had been his new, albeit temporary, defense attorney George Gesenhues, Jr.,[145] who had asked the judge to allow a visit by Dave to Graceland Church where the bodies of Kim, Brad, and Jill had been taken while awaiting the funeral service the next day.

Judge Striegel had approved the request, and later that evening, after visitation hours were over, Sheriff Hubbard and funeral director Mark

---

[145] A major issue facing the family had been to find someone to represent Dave, and it hadn't been easy for Sam, who had taken on the role of Dave's point-man on the outside. As he'd later told me, Sam, stunned as were the rest of the family at the news of Dave's arrest, had spent sleepless and soul-searching nights, asking his wife Carol, as well as himself, if it were possible his nephew had actually committed the heinous acts. While he wouldn't dismiss the horrendous possibility, he still hadn't believed Dave capable of doing so.

Seabrook had secreted Dave from the jail into an SUV, onto the back roads, and then literally across a creek and a field, into the rear of the church and then to the sanctuary where Dave had spent several emotional minutes in front of the two caskets,[146] first standing, and then kneeling, in his orange suit, handcuffed and shackled.

At the bond hearing the next day, and since the burden was on the defense, Gesenhues had been the first to present his case. Reading the transcript and based upon the very limited amount of information he possessed, one had to be impressed with the legal and common-sense acumen espoused by Gesenhues, whose sole discovery had been the probable cause affidavit.

Two sheets of paper was all he had, but Gesenhues was an astute attorney, and he had quickly focused on the meat of the allegations, such as they were. In that regard, he'd accurately stated the "only physical evidence has to do with a T-shirt…having 'high velocity blood mist which occurs in the presence of gunshot…[and the assertion that]…Robert Stites [is] a crime scene reconstructionist."

The mere assertion, Gesenhues had argued, of Stites being a crime scene reconstructionist did not, in and of itself, mean Stites was credible. As Gesenhues had asked, "Who is this person [Stites] and what are his qualifications?" Both of those most pertinent questions should, of course, have already been asked by Faith, Clemons, Biddle, and every other person associated with the case. Yet they hadn't asked either question as they had taken it on face value he was the expert he had claimed to be. No one, in fact, had attempted to confirm, through any source, the man's experience, qualifications, or background.

Gesenhues had then argued the claim that Jill's injuries were "consistent with intercourse" had no legal bearing on any probable cause that Dave had murdered his family. On the contrary, he argued, it was a "red herring,"[147] as were the allegations of manipulation of the crime scene. Neither allegation had created any probable cause, since there was no nexus, or connection, between the assertions and Dave.

Additionally, Gesenhues had argued Clemons' claim that a witness heard sounds between 9:15–9:30 p.m., which Clemons had interpreted as gunshots, wasn't a specific allegation but rather designed to create an inference;

---

[146] Brad and Jill had been placed in the same casket.

[147] A red herring, in legal circles, is an assertion that's misleading or a fallacy designed to direct the attention away from real issues; prosecutors often argue defense attorneys engage in this strategy when, with the Camm case, the prosecutors routinely defaulted to the strategy.

therefore, those sounds, whatever they were, didn't constitute evidence Dave was responsible for the crimes.

When asked if he had any other arguments or witnesses, Dave's counsel had put Sam on the stand to testify as to his nephew's strong connections to family and community. It was obvious it was difficult for Sam, but he responded firmly and with conviction, saying, "Our family is more than just a niece or nephew here or there. We are one family. Dave is more like a son to me and I treat his children, and treated his children, like my grandchildren. And I would be the first one to say if Dave Camm would have done this, he needs to be in that jail."

Sam had continued, "He loved his children so much…the thought of him harming those children is so foreign to me, knowing Dave Camm the way I do, so foreign for me, I can't even imagine that."

When asked, Sam had provided insight into the thoughts and feelings of Dave's in-laws, Frank and Janice Renn, "They are a well-known family in this area and they are a loving family. They loved their grandchildren. I was the one that had to go and notify them that their grandchildren were murdered because I know them…I had to go see them. That broke their heart. But what's breaking their heart now is that Dave has been accused of this murder. And their background and experience with Dave, [they] told me yesterday at the church, at the visitation crying on my shoulder, 'Sam, do what you can for Dave. We know he didn't do it.'"

Faith's Chief Deputy Orth, equally as aggressive as her boss, had begun her cross-examination of Sam, asking him about the basketball games, players, and the timing of events. Sam had given estimations, but he had also always pointed out those times could be verified by getting the telephone records associated with many of those events. Continuing with his story of getting home from the games, he'd said he got the call from Nelson and raced to the Camm house with his son. When he had begun describing what he saw, his voice and composure had broken.

Orth had moved to another line of questioning, asking Sam of his recollection of Kim and Dave separating in the mid-1990's. That, obviously, was a clue Faith had already decided they were going to pursue affairs as a motive to murder. After spending several minutes on an obviously irrelevant topic, Orth had moved on.

The Chief Deputy Prosecutor had summarized the State's objection to the bail request, claiming the probable cause affidavit needed to be viewed in totality. Speaking first of the allegation of Jill's injuries, Orth had said that though the assertion was "sensational" the "tear in the vagina…it's a fact. It's a fact in this case."

Next, Orth had doubled down on the other allegations, reasserting the specific claims in the affidavit. She said Dave had left the ball games at approximately 9:00 p.m.; a witness heard sounds like three gunshots; the crime scene had been manipulated by a cleaning solution; the cleaning solution had been thrown over the back deck, leaving a trail along the way; and blood spatter had been found on Dave's shirt. In reiterating her list, she had clearly been trying to strengthen the tenuous inferences in the affidavit, as though repeating them would make them more believable.

Orth had then thrown down her trump card: "I don't know of any other human beings we've had that have been shot in the presence of Mr. Camm. I don't have that information, but that's what is in the charging information, Your Honor." She then claimed that Dave was a flight risk "times three."

When given the chance to respond to Orth, Gesenhues, more than prescient, had asked about Stites. "Who is…Stites? What are his qualifications…what exactly did he conclude?" He'd also complained about the lack of a report from Stites, adding the fact that "We don't have access to that document, and we can't cross examine it and we can't evaluate it." He'd asked that the report of the expert be supplied within 24 hours.

Orth had responded, telling the court, "[The] report has not been typed." She'd then said she would provide it to the defense within the next few days. In fact, I learned, Stites had never provided nor much less had ever written a report. Thinking it through, no report means, of course, there would be nothing to provide to the defense in discovery.

After the arguments, it had been the judge's turn. "Mr. Gesenhues has brought up some points about the expert. Will he stand up to cross examination? Will he be even shown to be an expert? Those things we don't know yet, but I have to assume, because that's my job at this point, that what is in the probable cause affidavit can be proven. And that they, taken as a whole, do have relevance among each of the statements and do as a whole lead to a conclusion that there should have been an arrest made in this case. And this point that's where I'm at." The judge had then officially denied Dave bail.

Nearing the conclusion of the proceedings, Judge Striegel had brought up the funeral of Kim, Brad, and Jill, which was scheduled to start within an hour or so.[148] Gesenhues, in response, had told the judge that Dave was not making a request to attend the funerals.

---

[148] Dave told me he had wrestled with the idea of attending since he had returned to the jail the previous night from visiting his family at Graceland Church, where the funerals were to be held. He said he had told Gesenhues he wouldn't attend for several reasons, including the fact he didn't want to be seen by Brad and Jill's little friends and classmates clothed in an orange jail suit while handcuffed and in leg irons. It would be too much for them as well as too much for himself, he said.

The hearing had terminated and Orth, who had been to the Camm house on several occasions during the searches, had spoken to the huge assemblage of reporters. Evidence was still being uncovered, Orth had said, adding that she was "very confident in the investigation and the way the evidence has unfolded…"[149]

Another person had the same amount of confidence in the case. He was Nicholas Stein, former Floyd County Prosecutor and one-time mentor of Faith who had been an assistant prosecutor under him. Stein, now in private practice, had opined, "I know the investigation is pretty thorough and we don't want to interfere with it. I have faith in the Floyd County Prosecutor's Office and the Indiana State Police."[150]

Stein, who didn't say how he knew the investigation was thorough, had given those comments after he had been retained by Frank and Janice Renn as their spokesperson. Within days of his comments, Stein had filed a motion with the court to freeze Kim's assets, including her life insurance proceeds, which denied Dave access to them. As a result, Dave had been left with limited financial assets.

Other Anecdotes

I later spoke with a friend who had been intimately involved in the criminal justice system in Floyd County for years.[151] What I was told, my friend insisted, sounded implausible but was true. Before Dave's trial, my friend knew there were attorneys who practiced in Floyd and Clark counties who had been personally contacted by Judge Striegel. The judge, my friend contended, had asked a friend of his, as well as other attorneys, as to whether the judge should allow or deny the testimony of the women regarding Dave's affairs.

The attorney had told the judge, in no uncertain terms, according to my friend, that he should not allow any testimony of adulterous affairs as there was no relevance or connection to the crimes for which Dave had been charged. On the contrary, the attorney told the judge, it was character assassination, pure and simple. The others who had been contacted by the judge also supposedly told him the same thing. If true, the judge didn't listen, and the story is beyond shocking.

---

[149] Ali, Amany, "Camm denied bond; family laid to rest," *The Tribune*, October 4, 2000.

[150] Ali, Amany, "Family of murdered comments via lawyer," *The Tribune*, October 5, 2000.

[151] That friend will remain anonymous.

*Judge Striegel's December 12, 2001, denial on the motion filed by
Mike McDaniel to exclude testimony regarding affairs of David Camm.*

Also shocking were stories told to me by Sam. On more than one occasion, Sam's prospective clients had been contacted by his salespeople and told a competitor had cautioned them against using Sam's business, for "their money will go to helping a killer get off."

Lifetime friends of Sam, he told me, had also ignored and refused to speak with him, including one of his very best friends. A few of the friends of his wife were gracious in person to her but others vilified her and Sam for their audacity of supporting Dave.

The GCC was split as to whether they did or didn't believe David was guilty. Leland, in an attempt to defuse the situation, retired as church pastor, but the split was so great and so many congregants were lost, the demise of the church became reality, and it was eventually sold.[152]

---

[152] I later spoke with Leland and his wife, Vonda, and came away from the interview very saddened. It was obvious to me Leland had sacrificed his love of the ministry for his love of his church.

As Sam had told me, it was clear practically everyone believed Dave was guilty. If you thought otherwise, you were siding with a murderer and molester. For me, I knew being on the defense team wouldn't be easy, but I could not have remotely imagined just how surreal and dreadful that involvement would become.

[Note: As I had told Kitty, after my review of the ISP original investigation, I provided her and Stacy with a list of the things the ISP investigators did do, didn't do, and should or could have done in my assessment, while adding a brief chart as to the sum total of their "evidence" prior to concluding Dave had been the murderer of his family. It is included in Appendix A.]

SECTION II
The "Fresh Eyes"

CHAPTER 17
"A New Set Of Eyes"

During his November 15, 2004, press conference, when Henderson had announced the re-filing of charges against Dave, he had emphasized a "team of Indiana State Police troopers have been interviewing witnesses…[as] the case had to be looked at '*with a new set of eyes.*'"[153] The implication was, of course, that the new investigators had reached a fair and independent conclusion and recommendation, three months after the reversals of the murders, as to whether Henderson should prosecute Dave.

Detective Gary Gilbert, the new lead detective heading those "fresh eyes," a term Kitty, Stacy, and I used in a mocking manner, had said one of his mandates was to have "*…no preconceived notions.*"[154] Belying that notion had been Gilbert's affidavit, which had already repeated the refuted 7:19 p.m. time of Dave's phone call.

> GILBERT HAD SWORN THAT JILL'S INJURIES HAD BEEN "CONSISTENT WITH A SEXUAL DEVICE AND/OR A PENIS."
>
> HE HAD OMITTED THE WORDS "OR ANY OBJECT THAT TYPE OF SIZE AND SHAPE."

Nonetheless, as I organized my own investigative efforts, Kitty called and said she had received the first batch of the fresh eyes' discovery. I was soon in her office going through the reports of the two detectives. Gilbert, we'd learned, was from the Evansville ISP Post, and his assistant was Mike Black, another veteran ISP officer, assigned to the Versailles Post. Their information would force delay of much of what I had planned to do, as our first priority was always providing Dave with the best defense possible. Part and parcel of that defense was quickly reacting to the ongoing investigation, which meant

---

[153] Emphasis mine; Ali, Amany, "Prosecutor: Camm to be retried," *The Tribune*, November 17, 2004.

[154] Emphasis added.

rigorously vetting their information and conclusions, as we weren't going to let false assertions go unanswered.

Finding the source of their informant to whom Dave had purportedly confessed, as well as to the specifics of what that informant had claimed he'd been told, was critically important, as was the source of their new medical expert who had also come to the "conclusion that the trauma to Jill Camm's vaginal area is consistent with a sexual device and/or a penis."

While those two areas were vitally important, we didn't skip over other aspects of their new investigation. As we got into the lead detective's report, what struck Kitty, Stacy, and me was *the amount of time Gilbert hadn't spent on the investigation*, as many of the results of his Camm-related interviews and investigation had been co-mingled with his other investigations and several days of all kinds of training such as CPR, Meth Labs, and EOD and bomb sweeps for three days of a judicial convention.

Additionally, Black had also been involved in other investigations and training and wasn't full-time. In short, despite what Henderson had implied, there certainly wasn't an ongoing *full-time* Camm investigation.[155]

The three of us would gather again and compare notes after we had reviewed their initial investigation. After spending several days digesting their reports, what we found was as follows:

Although Dave's case had been reversed on August 10, 2004, it had taken twenty-eight days for Gilbert and Black to finally meet with Henderson. If the prosecutor had been eager to secure an impartial and fair review of the case, the lapse of four weeks defied that premise, as it wasn't until September 8 that the new team first met. That gathering began at 10:00 a.m. but didn't include those from the prior investigation until Sarkisian and Clemons had arrived at 11:00 p.m.

Clemons "wasn't happy" when told he wouldn't be involved in the second investigation, but Sarkisian had been promoted to District Investigative Commander (DIC) and was expected to provide administrative assistance to the two newly assigned detectives.

Running the BACKBONE DNA profile through CODIS was on the top of our forensic to-do list and should have been on the ISP's, particularly since Gilbert had noted early in his first report that new "laboratory analysis submissions" were included in his duties. Gilbert's involvement with the DNA profile would take only minutes, as all he needed to do was ask the ISP Laboratory DNA analyst to electronically contact CODIS and run the

---

[155] In order to rebut the prosecution's assertion that the "fresh eyes" were devoting an enormous effort to re-investigate the case, I'd eventually chart the amount of time spent by lead detective Gilbert.

numbered profile through their database to determine if any matches existed. From the time of the request to the answer could be less than an hour, as either there was or wasn't a match; if there was, the identity of the person who had the same DNA would be quickly provided.

Unfortunately, not only had Gilbert not run the DNA profile through CODIS, but he and the ISP hadn't accomplished anything forensically other than for him to begin "reviewing the numerous laboratory submissions," and that had been less than a month prior to Dave's being recharged. At the time Gilbert signed his affidavit, however, no laboratory requests had been made by the new team and, of course, no results had been obtained. It was a carbon copy repeat of the first investigation.

In fact, it wasn't until the day after the new charges had been filed when a meeting was held with several present, including Gilbert, Black, Henderson, and Lynn Scamahorn, the ISP DNA Analyst who had discovered the unknown female DNA on the sweatshirt. At that meeting, they began discussing "any new laboratory submissions that may need to be made and who would perform the analysis," but there had been no specific reference to the BACKBONE sweatshirt. It was an amazing admission of omission in a case since much was made in the public pronouncement of investigators taking a brand new look at the case.

As to Gilbert's and Black's interviews, however, another bizarre fact was that one of their first ones was of Stan Faith, and not for the reason one might think. Faith, out of office for two years and an attorney in private practice, had been told by an acquaintance of his that Whitney, Dave's oldest daughter, had confided to a friend that she had been molested by her father. Rather than contact the ISP or Henderson's office with that information, Faith took it upon himself to reach out to the friend of Whitney and personally interview that friend. In fact, Faith was doing Henderson a favor, for he later said if it had any merit, he'd tell Henderson, and if it didn't, he wouldn't waste his time.[156]

When interviewed by Faith, the friend of Whitney had disavowed the claim, stating the comment was about Jill purportedly being molested. Whitney, though, had later been interviewed by the two detectives, and she, too, adamantly denied the false story. More importantly, however, Faith had still been actively involved as an investigator in the case. What other interviews he conducted without telling Henderson or the detectives is anyone's guess.

Two other interviews were of a father and son. The father, 82 years of age

---

[156] During my tenure with the FBI, we memorialized everything we did in regard to an investigation, including interviews that bore no positive results. It was important to do so to preclude others from running down the same negative lead; also, if a person had claimed no knowledge or involvement and was later found, through other investigation, not to be truthful, that original false exculpatory could be critical.

and a former member of the Georgetown Town Board, *thought* Dave could have disposed of the murder weapon by dropping it into an uncapped pipe leading to a wet well, which was a short distance from the church gym. The gentleman had no specific information, but rather had been *speculating* Dave *could have* disposed of the gun in that manner.

After spending a significant amount of time lining up the necessary equipment and personnel needed to search the sanitary sewer lines from the church to the wet well, Gilbert and Black had then met with the new pastor of the church. After the pastor had given them the necessary permission to search their sewer lines, a camera had been placed in the line and well, but no gun had been discovered.

Sam, his sister Debbie Ter Vree, and Dave's brother Donnie had not been proactively contacted by the new detectives but rather had requested to be interviewed. Sam, of course, had emphasized the need to have the BACKBONE DNA profile checked through CODIS and warned of the faulty 7:19 p.m. phone call. However, Gilbert and Black had refused to take copies of the DNA profile or the phone records offered by Sam, each of which had been in his hands.

Donnie Camm had also told the two detectives of the critical difference of an hour between the phone records and the actual time of the call. He, too, had emphasized the need for them to focus on the DNA from the BACKBONE sweatshirt.

The bottom line was the BACKBONE DNA profile document and the telephone records regarding the 6:19 p.m. phone call hadn't received the same scrutiny as afforded the *speculation* of an elderly man who had *thought* a sewer line *might contain* or *could possibly contain* the gun.

Understandably, Dave's uncle had also opined as to the "quality" of the first investigation, citing, among other items, Stites' bogus claim of blood on the garage door. As an adjunct, he had told the two of the need to understand bloodstain evidence was an "opinion, and opinions vary."

As for Debbie Ter Vree, she had told the two detectives of the missing jewelry from Kim's room; the fact Clemons had twisted her words about "gunshots"; and of arriving home around 7:32 p.m. on the night of the murders and seeing both garage doors down and seeing neither Dave nor Kim's vehicle. She had also provided her intense thoughts of the prosecutor's bloodstain experts. As with the prior investigators, the fresh team had never followed up on the fact that Kim's jewelry had been missing from the home and had accepted, without question, the conclusions of their blood experts.

As for the BACKBONE sweatshirt, the two detectives had startled Debbie with their fantastic revelation. Gilbert had been told by Clemons that Debbie's daughter, eight-year-old Hannah, had known the identity of BACKBONE.

Yes, shockingly, little Hannah supposedly had the answer to the most significant question in the entire case, and Clemons had known it for years.

In the aftermath of the murders, Clemons had told Gilbert they'd tried to interview the little girl at her school but had been prevented from doing so by school officials. Even though the sweatshirt was such a potentially critical piece of evidence, they hadn't persisted in their interview efforts because, according to Gilbert's report, "the line of thinking was that the situation was too volatile with the Lockhart family for the interview to take place."

And what had been so volatile? According to Clemons' information, Hannah had known BACKBONE was none other than...Bradley Camm! Brad, age 7, weighing 69 pounds and 4'6½" tall, had worn the men's extra-large sweatshirt emblazoned BACKBONE.

And what had Debbie's reaction been when confronted with this information? Strangely, in Gilbert's report of Debbie's interview, there is no mention of his even asking her about the name BACKBONE nor her reaction. In the recorded statement, however, Ter Vree's response to that confrontation by Gilbert was an incredibly strident and very vehement mocking of the claim, practically shouting, "I am shocked right now! I don't believe what I just heard!" So much for Clemons' blockbuster information.

Clemons had also assisted Black with a "general overview" of the original investigation, not further articulated in Black's report. The report stated, "the main topic of our discussion was a specific phone call that was made from the Camm residence on the night in question." According to Clemons, the Verizon witness who had testified the call was actually 6:19 p.m., rather than 7:19 p.m., *theorized about an error in the actual local time of the call.*"[157]

Gilbert's report on the timing of the call reflected he had "assigned Mike Black to look into the *time glitch* that came up in court during the first trial." According to Gilbert's report, the phone company witness who had testified at trial "said the time may not have been associated with Louisville time, and was *possibly 6:19 p.m.*"[158]

Reading the reports was startling. Years after the time of the call had been definitively established as 6:19 p.m. and not 7:19 p.m., the "fresh team" was still trying to pound the square peg into the round hole.[159] Not only that, but, for information in their new affidavit, they were relying on Sean Clemons, the guy who had gotten so many assertions wrong in his original charging document.

---

[157] Emphasis mine.

[158] Emphases mine.

[159] The telephone company billing expert had left no doubt—none whatsoever—that the time of the call was 6:19 p.m.

As to probing the minds of the original investigators other than Clemons, in his report Gilbert noted the following regarding his meeting with Sam Sarkisian: "I asked Sarkisian if there was anything he has thought of that needed to be explored concerning the case. Sarkisian said that 'nothing came to mind at the present time.'" That comment hadn't surprised me.

As for Darrell Gibson, one of the two detectives who'd conducted the in-depth interviews of Dave, Gilbert and Black had also contacted him, but spent little time probing his mind for any leads that needed to be followed, as they were mostly concerned about finding Gibson's taped interview of Dave in the Floyd County Jail after his arrest, for it had been lost. Gilbert couldn't find it in any of the 30 boxes of Camm documents left in the prosecutor's office. Only after leaving the very short interview of Gibson had Gilbert, however, searching again, found Gibson's report co-mingled with those of Clemons.

Did Gilbert and Black interview the 11 men who had interacted with Dave at the gym? No. Gilbert had only written a synopsis for Henderson, based upon their previous interviews and testimony, rather than formulating his own questions and personal assessments of those witnesses after speaking and interacting with them.

One player, Scott Schrank, had been the exception, however. Schrank's brother was a friend of Henderson's, and he'd been the single player who had been proactively contacted by Gilbert. After Schrank had left the gym, around 8:40 p.m., one of the other players had called Schrank and said he didn't notice him leaving.[160] The apparent implication was if one player didn't see Schrank leave, then the remaining 10 others at the gym could also have missed seeing Dave leave, and, by extension, not have known of his absence, not have noticed him missing for 25–30 minutes, and not have seen him return from his absence after having coldly murdered his family.

Tammy Megenity had been another interviewee of the detectives. She had been initially contacted by Clemons, in the days after the murders, but there had been no follow-up. Gilbert had apparently been unaware the 44-year-old woman, who was the three-day-a-week caregiver of Amos Lockhart, had spoken with Faith and his investigators without Clemons or the ISP present. At the time she had provided Faith with a paper penned by Dave's aunt, Phyllis Rhodes.

Phyllis had written to Dave while he was incarcerated in the months after the murders. Upset with the false stories being told about her family, her nephew, and the case, Phyllis had posed several questions to Dave to which he responded in his own writing. Phyllis had then collated the questions and

---

[160] Recall ten players, including Dave, were still playing five on five at the time Schrank had left the gym.

answers and left a copy at her father's house for her brothers and sisters to read.

Unbeknownst to the family, Megenity had taken the copy and given it to her father, who in turn had given it to Stan Faith to scrutinize. Dave's responses weren't incriminating, nor were they contradictory in nature to anything he had previously said, but on the contrary, he had vociferously voiced his innocence.

I paused what I was doing and began my own background on Megenity. It didn't take long, for in 1989, she, along with six others, had been arrested for her role in a Floyd County cocaine distribution ring. Four of the male defendants had been found guilty with two sentenced to 20 years, one to 11 years, and one to three years. All apparently had been free from prison at the time of the Camm murders.

Megenity, given a 15-year sentence, had served less than six months in the DOC and was then released. Her father, I had learned, had been a strong campaign worker for Faith, and one had to wonder if she had perhaps benefitted from that fact.

The most significant question, however, was why hadn't anyone, including Clemons and Gilbert, followed an obvious lead of questioning Megenity on her former co-defendants? Had any visited her at Amos' house? Even if they hadn't, had she seen anything while she often sat outside the house with Amos? A strange vehicle? Any person? The answer, unfortunately, was that she had never been asked any of those questions.

Instead of directing those questions to her, Gilbert's primary focus had been on a whispered conversation Megenity had heard one night at church after the murders. According to Megenity, Mike Suttle, husband of Gloria, one of Dave's aunts, had walked past Debbie Ter Vree and, Megenity said, "I heard him whisper, 'We found it.'"

Since she had been unaware of any lost items, including car keys, Megenity's translation had been that the murder weapon had been found by the family. Unfortunately for Gilbert, Megenity hadn't heard any other whispers as to the location of the gun. The takeaway, of course, had been that the entire family had been complicit in a giant conspiracy to protect Dave.

The ISP batch of discovery had also answered the question as to the identity of their new expert who had come to the "conclusion that the trauma to Jill Camm's vaginal area is consistent with a sexual device and/or a penis." Dr. Betty Spivak was employed at the Kentucky Medical Examiner's office in Louisville, and while she wasn't a pathologist, she did consult on child abuse cases. She had been contacted on two occasions by Gilbert and Black in the company of Wayne Kessinger, a retired Louisville Metropolitan Police Department (LMPD) officer who had been hired by Henderson as one of his own investigators. Kessinger, we would later learn, would be a critical piece of Henderson's inside circle.

According to Black's report, though, after describing Jill's genitalia injuries, Spivak had asked and answered her own question: "Does that mean she was sexually abused? I don't think I can tell you that." Those words, of course, hadn't made it to Gilbert's affidavit.

In his report, Gilbert also recited the injuries as having been described by Spivak, including petechia,[161] located on the external genitalia. Petechia, according to Spivak, "go away in two or three days." That obviously meant the injuries had been recent.

When Spivak had been asked directly by Gilbert if the injuries "… could've been [caused by] a penis or dildo…Dr. Spivek [sic] said it could be one of those suggestions *or any object that type of size and shape* that is not sharp.[162] She said this would've caused pain to Jill and she probably cried. She probably experienced pain while urinating."

Gilbert, in his affidavit, had sworn that, according to Spivak, Jill's injuries had been "consistent with a sexual device and/or a penis." He, of course, had omitted Spivak's words: "or any object that type of size and shape…"

Also not mentioned by Gilbert in the affidavit were the conclusions the injuries had been recent and would have caused Jill to cry and have pain while urinating. None of the people who had been in close contact with Jill during the final day of her life, including teachers, dance instructors, volleyball spectators, her grandmother, or her mother, had ever reacted to any pain or issue Jill experienced. The obvious conclusion had been that Jill's genitalia injuries had occurred after her dance practice and after her enthusiastic and incessant running during the volleyball game.

Was it so impractical, I then thought, that her genitalia injuries occurred after arriving home and were the result of someone jamming something, perhaps the muzzle of a gun, a "blunt force instrument," between the legs of that restrained and screaming little girl before he/she viciously shot her in the head at point blank range? Could anyone be that depraved or that much in a rage?

Regardless, Gilbert's explosive words in his affidavit, the result of selective editing of Spivak's observations and opinions, had continued with the public character assassination of Dave, as it focused on sex, more sex, molestation, innuendo and, once again, the false allegation of the 7:19 p.m. telephone call.

Recalling Henderson's press conference, though, there had been another motive behind the wording of the affidavit. At the time he had announced Dave

---

[161]   Petechia are the small, red dots that appear on the surface of the skin, the result of capillaries being ruptured.

[162]   Emphasis mine.

would be retried, there had been an unexpected admission, as "Henderson said the original PC affidavit is 'defective' and that a judge could have likely given a bond based on it."[163] He'd probably thought it was a safe bet the new affidavit, certainly with the word "penis" in it, would overcome any judge's tendency to grant bond.

As for the informant to whom Dave had "confessed"? I wasn't Carnak the Magnificent, but I had spent lots of time with many people who were veterans of the criminal justice system. The guy was exactly what we had thought he'd be.

[163] Ali, Amany. "Prosecutor: Camm to be retried," *The Tribune*, November 17, 2004.

CHAPTER 18

"I've Never Told On Anyone"

The batch of discovery had also provided the name and story of Gilbert's "confidential informant" who had advised Gilbert "that David Camm told him that Camm had shot and killed his wife and two children." As we'd suspected, that person had been incarcerated with Dave. Within two days after Dave's convictions had been overturned, the informant had written a letter to his attorney to offer his services to the prosecutor.

Informants, often derided as snitches or narcs, are certainly legal, and the courts routinely allow their testimony, but they bring with them all kinds of issues, not the least of which is credibility. *Why* does a person turn on associates, friends, or even family? To avoid more serious charges? To avoid charges entirely? To get a reduced sentence? To get time off an already imposed sentence?

Those are all understandable reasons, of course, as to why someone might give information to investigators. They're also reasons informants would fabricate stories they think are beneficial to investigations, and in the process, beneficial to themselves. Indeed, since an informant is one who has violated the trust of others, who's to say that deceit won't extend to an investigator, the prosecutor, and to the witness stand?[164]

> HENDERSON NOW HAD TWO WITNESSES TO WHOM DAVE HAD 'CONFESSED,' EVEN IF THE CONFESSIONS CONTRADICTED THE EVIDENCE AND/OR WEREN'T LOGICAL.

James B. Hatton

Finding James B. Hatton's background was relatively easy, as he was a career criminal who had most recently been convicted for attempted manufacture of methamphetamine and an escape from the Bartholomew County Jail.[165] As his prior records vividly reflected, he was also a burglar and

---

[164] In my career, of all of the many informants I managed, or at least attempted to manage, it was imperative to secure information from other independent sources corroborating as many details provided by the source as possible. Even when they provided detailed, excellent, and corroborated information, however, I never fully trusted any of them.

[165] The county seat of Bartholomew County is Columbus, Indiana.

thief as well as a liar and cheat. More importantly for him, though, he had previously provided the State of Indiana with information he had purportedly obtained from two other inmates, both charged with murder.

Writing to his attorney as a conduit to Henderson, Hatton had claimed the following: "David Camm…murdered his wife, son and daughter. He shot all three (3)…the reason he killed them was because his wife was going to let it be known that she was going to file for divorce. He also said that the reason he moved the bodies was because when he shot them blood splattered on him and that he had to cover up the spatter so he done [sic] this by moving the bodies. He told me other things but I'll tell them later."

So, Dave murdered his family due to an impending divorce? That made no sense. And he covered up the spatter by moving *bodies*? That wasn't accurate as Dave had moved only Brad. And the reason he'd moved the "bodies" had been to cover up the blood spatter? Did that make any sense at all?

Hatton had continued, "He told me other things but I'll tell them later. Please make this known to the proper person's [sic]. I have plenty I can tell them." Probable translation: once I get some more information from whatever source, I'll have a better story to sell.

And then Hatton had cut to the chase as he had asked his attorney, "With my [sic] now being able to now provide new information to a state agency, *do you think I can achieve my goal of* house arrest, probation, substance abuse treatment, and *time served?*"[166] And then, just in case his attorney didn't get the point of it all, Hatton had emphasized, "Again, concerning the new information I can now offer, please see this is passed on."

Hatton's attorney had done as he'd asked as Henderson soon had a copy of the letter in his possession, and then Gilbert and Black, on September 20, 2004, had interviewed the serial informant in Bloomington, Indiana. Why Bloomington? That's where he had been incarcerated pending his testimony as a prosecution witness in a murder trial. During the first part of his debriefing, the two detectives had gotten some background on him, as Hatton had joked he'd "had a little vacation" the previous year, thanks to his escape from the Bartholomew County Jail.

Then they had gotten down to business regarding Camm's confession. Hatton had said it had begun when Hatton had asked Dave, "How'd you get caught?" followed by "Damn, man, as a state trooper, you should be smart enough to get away with some shit like that."

That simple question and declaration, according to Hatton, had allowed Dave to laugh and to respond, "I thought I was." Dave, then, in an apparent need to spill the entire story of how he'd murdered his wife and children to a

---

[166] Emphasis mine.

man he didn't know and with whom he had spent little time, had told Hatton the following (italics added):

- He claimed he'd *shot his wife in the car while it was parked outside the garage*; and

- *Removed his wife from the car and carried her into the garage* where he'd

- *Performed CPR on his wife* who was on the floor because

- "One of his reasoning [sic] for *putting his wife on the garage floor* was his excuse would be better to perform to try and to resuscitate her," adding,

- He moved his wife to help mask the blood splatter.

I know what you're thinking. At this point, the detectives could have stood up and told Hatton he was a full of bullshit as they walked out the door. Keep in mind, though, he was in Bloomington to testify in the trial of another person charged with murder. If Hatton had been deemed the liar he was by the ISP, that certainly could have impacted the ongoing trial. As such, Hatton had continued with his story, knowing that somehow or another, blood spatter had been involved in the crime:

- Camm had said he picked up the *bodies* to disarrange the blood; he'd then

- Said he "*moved 'em,*" adding Camm's words were, "I picked *them* up"; claiming also

- Camm had said he unbuckled one of the kids and "picked *her* up" as well as saying,

- "I want to say that he said he had to *take 'em* out of [the] car seat."

Camm had only mentioned the gun's being a pistol, said Hatton, who had also said even if Camm told him the make or caliber, it wouldn't have meant anything to him.

And the motive for Dave murdering his family? Per Hatton, "…the reason he killed his family was because his wife had found out about some extra-curricular activities he was having during their marriage, and his wife was going to file for divorce and he didn't want his name tainted…[because] *he didn't want to look bad in front of his peers.*"[167]

Camm, Hatton had claimed, had said there was no one else involved in the murders other than himself.

---

[167] Emphasis mine.

The reason why Hatton had been willing to provide the information? Because "when it was told to him, it didn't mean much," but since the court overturned the verdicts, Hatton had been outraged, and he was coming forward because "...the children should be afforded the opportunity to live a life."

Conveniently not mentioned, of course, had been the child advocate's goal of getting his sentence—a 20-year sentence—modified to "time served." That sentence had been handed down in 2003, meaning Hatton was still, under Indiana law, looking at serving at least eight more years in prison. According to the magnanimous benefactor of truth, the information he'd given was the truth, and he'd "given it all freely."

Neither Gilbert's nor Black's report reflected anyone's countering Hatton on any of his bogus assertions, including the well-known and established fact that Kim, of course, had been shot outside the car and inside the garage rather than, per Hatton, inside the car, which was outside the garage.

Also completely ludicrous was the reason Hatton had claimed Dave had removed Kim, which was "to mask the blood from his wife." What on Earth did that mean? Why no follow-up question? And it wasn't Kim, of course, but Brad who had been placed on the floor for Dave to perform CPR. Hatton hadn't even gotten that elementary fact correct.

And the motive, according to Hatton, had been Dave's not wanting his name "tainted" over divorce. Seriously? Fifty percent of all married couples divorce, including thousands of police officers each year. Not wanting "to look bad in front of his peers" didn't comport with any kind of reality, particularly since other officers at the Sellersburg Post had failed marriages.

Within days of the interview, Gilbert had contacted Hatton's attorney and asked if his client would take a polygraph. The attorney "didn't have a problem with it as long as there is not going to be charges filed against Hatton in the event he is found to be less than truthful."

Per Gilbert's report, "I didn't think that was an issue since he is already serving time." So apparently, you can lie if you're a convicted felon serving time with no repercussions except to be used as a witness for the prosecution in future trials?

The polygraph wouldn't be an issue, though, as the attorney soon called Gilbert and said Hatton wouldn't take the polygraph because "he had put himself in quite a bit of jeopardy already by speaking to us and asked for nothing in return...and [he was not going to] put himself in danger any further."

Normally, at least in cases where I considered using a polygraph, it was only used if the witness couldn't be corroborated by other evidence and his/her information couldn't already be comported with the known facts of the case. Clearly, Hatton's information was fraudulent, and anyone with any modicum of knowledge of the case wouldn't have wasted time polygraphing him.

In spite of the polygraph refusal, Henderson had apparently been satisfied with Hatton's wildly inaccurate account of the murders, for just a few weeks later, the prosecutor personally visited his star witness in the company of Gilbert in the Bartholomew County Jail.

First, though, Gilbert had asked if Hatton remembered anything else that Camm had told him. Sure, responded the man with a now sharper memory. After he had shot and killed his family, Camm had wiped his hands on and then placed the gun in his shirt. Hatton didn't know that location, but he did recall, for the first time, Camm's saying he "should have gotten his druggie neighbor to have helped him with the murders."

In his original story, Hatton had said Dave hadn't talked about the gun, but now he remembered Dave's saying he wiped his hands on a shirt he used to get rid of the gun. He also remembered Dave's being so close with a neighbor, and so trusted that neighbor—a druggie—that he should have enlisted the person to help him murder his family.

Gilbert had been looking for more, however, so Hatton had been "asked if he knew of any other inmates that Camm may have given information to regarding the murders." The cooperative Hatton had provided the first names of three other offenders who might contrive, uh, *provide*, their recollections of their interactions with Camm.

Regardless, Henderson had apparently been convinced of Hatton's value—so much so, that immediately afterwards, he and Gilbert, per Gilbert's report, had "traveled back to New Albany…[and] Henderson held a news conference…[and] advised that a new Probable Cause Affidavit would be filed" against Camm.

After Henderson's presser, the two had then moved quickly to the prosecutor's office where "discussion focused on the wording of the Probable Cause Affidavit." Of course, the wording in the affidavit didn't mention the "confidential informant" had given information that contradicted key known crime scene facts.

Jeremy "Joker" Bullock

And if one inmate witness was good, others would be better. Gilbert had soon contacted Doug Ayers, the supervisor for investigations at the State Prison in Michigan City. In addition to wanting to know about the three men whose names Hatton had provided, equally as important, Gilbert asked Ayers, "…if there may be other [DOC] inmates that David Camm may have confided in while at the Michigan City Prison."

The answer provided by the seasoned prison investigator, however, had been blunt: "there would be unreliable information being given by inmates once they learn that the investigative unit is trying to gather statements made by Camm...especially if the inmate thinks he can make a deal or better himself." Gilbert apparently, though, didn't ask Ayers to do any research on Hatton to see if he might have fallen into that "unreliable" category.

Nonetheless, within days of his inquiry, Gilbert had spoken with Mike Rains,[168] an investigator at the Pendleton Reformatory, where one of the three men named by Hatton had transferred. That one guy, per Rains, was a "certified nut." The other two hadn't panned out either.

Not to despair, however, for as if on cue, the next day, December 7, 2004, Wayne Kessinger received a telephone call from the mother of an individual who had been incarcerated with Dave at Michigan City.[169] Maybe the word had gotten out to other inmates after all.

Kessinger's memo revealed Jeremy Bullock, the mother's son, had been convicted of murder and had spent the last ten years in prison, most recently in the PCU at Michigan City, for "giving out information on other inmates." While incarcerated, she said, Jeremy had used drugs and "done things in prison" but wanted to straighten out his life so "...he could come home." So, the young man who had repeatedly snitched on others, now wanted to walk on a straight and narrow path.

During a recent visit to Jeremy, Mom said she and Jeremy had seen Camm and his sister who "were laughing and cutting up about him getting out of prison on a technicality." Seeing that, Jeremy had said, "he was paying for his crime and so should Camm." Unlike Hatton's explicit motive, getting his sentence cut to time served, Bullock's motive of revenge was a little less direct, I thought.

Mrs. Bullock continued, stating her son had previously spoken to Camm about the murders of his wife and children. According to Mrs. Bullock, "Jeremy told Camm that shooting someone in the face shows no respect to that person, referring to Camms [sic] wife and daughter and [then] shooting his son in the chest was like, 'I love you but I gotta kill you anyway.' *Camm responded with some type of explanation or continued talking about the Murders.*"[170] That last sentence wasn't exactly detailed or specific.

Regardless, Jeremy had instructed his mother to contact the prosecutor's office and said that he was "willing to put himself in jeopardy..." by talking to

---

[168] Rains had been a long-time employee of the DOC and had a very good reputation as an investigator.

[169] Gilbert had noted the date was December 7, but Kessinger, in his memo, stated the date he'd received the call was December 8.

[170] Emphasis mine.

the prosecutor. Why, when asked, was it important to share his information? Jeremy's response had been nothing short of totally altruistic: "Mom, you want another child to die?" Ah, both he and Hatton were sacrificing their own safety for the sake of children everywhere.

But just who was Jeremy Bullock? The reports didn't reflect much on the man, but a visit to Johnson County, where he had been convicted, revealed him to be serving a 40-year sentence for the pre-meditated murder of his drug dealer, committed when Jeremy was 16 years old. After he and two friends had lured the man to a remote location, Jeremy had shot the man point blank numerous times with a .45 caliber pistol, which he had recently stolen from his grandfather's home. The three had then stolen the dealer's drugs and money.

Upon being told of Bullock's information, Henderson had been excited, so much so that he'd told Gilbert to arrange air transportation via the ISP plane to Michigan City where Bullock could be interviewed in more detail. Once there, and per Gilbert's report, Bullock had asserted, "he has never told on anyone." That a convict had blatantly lied, especially within the first minutes of an interview, is normally considered a clue by most investigators.

Bullock had continued, saying he had seen the news magazine, *48 Hours,* as had several in the unit. When he later spoke with Camm, Dave had made his admission, telling Bullock the day of the ball games "was the best opportunity for him because it was a regularly scheduled game, and so many people would be there." He said he'd "left and went home, and then came back…[and] played like hell the last two games so everybody would know he was there."

If that was a logical explanation, it escaped me. Again, how had Dave removed himself as one of the five members of a team without anyone seeing him gone? So, both teams hadn't comprehended the shift to a five-on-four ball game? And what did "playing like hell the last two games" have anything to do with his supposedly leaving without anyone missing him? It made no sense whatsoever.

As for the gun, and unlike Hatton, Bullock had been well versed in weapons, so much so that he knew the murder weapon had been a *hammerless* .380 handgun.[171] And where had Camm disposed of the gun? Camm had simply said, "They can't drag riverbeds." Hmmm. So, Dave even had enough time to travel to a river, throw in the gun, and return to the games? The only glitch in that scenario was the only river near Georgetown is the Ohio River, a 16-mile trip from the Camm residence to the river and back to the gym, extending

---

[171]   Emphasis mine.

at least 15+ more minutes to the time he had been gone from the gym in his magic disappearance act.[172]

The motive, per Bullock, was "the marriage was over." He'd added that if Dave and his wife had gotten divorced, his in-laws, who'd "had money," would help her "clean him out." That Frank and Janice Renn had been flush with money would have been news to them.

Gilbert had been energized about the information and, after leaving the prison, had immediately called Ed Wessel,[173] the ISP firearms expert who'd confirmed the Lorcin .380 murder weapon had, indeed, been hammerless.

Of course, all of Bullock's information had been generic and could have been, and probably was, gleaned from public record sources, including *48 Hours*.

Regardless, Henderson now had two witnesses to whom Dave had "confessed," even if the confessions contradicted the evidence and/or weren't logical. Once other prison/jailhouse snitches knew of the potential prizes to be awarded, I wasn't taking any bets on the number who would be lining up to testify.

To underscore that thought, I recalled one prison inmate I once had interviewed who was amazingly honest, in at least one aspect: "We're all in here doing time and 90% of us are manipulative assholes."

---

[172] There are *creeks* nearby the Camm residence, but none on the way to the gym and none so deep they can't be searched for guns; in fact, most of the creeks are less than 1'-2' deep.

[173] Wessel, as with almost all of the ISP lab personnel, including Jon Singleton and Lynn Scamahorn, testified within the limits of the science of their forensic expertise.

CHAPTER 19

The Defense Doesn't Rest

After reading through Henderson's first stack of discovery documents, I called Kitty who confirmed she and Stacy had also finished their review. The next day we met, bright and early. Stacy spoke first, not from any degree of surprise but rather disappointment. "There obviously were no fresh eyes. You have to wonder if they even remotely considered the possibility Dave didn't do it."

"Their new investigation, such as it was, could be summed up with their question of Sarkisian if anything needed to be explored," I continued, "and when he said he didn't think of anything, well, that told them all they needed to do was to place their own rubber stamp on it and label it 'fresh eyes.'"

"IF THESE GUYS ARE LYING, THEN THERE'S NO WITNESS EVER WHO SHOULD BE BELIEVED. THEY'RE JUST GOOD, HARD-WORKING, HONEST PEOPLE, AND FAITH SULLIED THEIR CHARACTERS JUST AS HE ANNIHILATED DAVE'S."

"And all the while, still not have the courage to run the unknown DNA," Kitty added.

Not that I needed to, but I had to say, "This isn't the State Police I once knew."

Kitty then wrapped up all our thoughts by concluding, "We're all disappointed, but think about Dave. His family was murdered, he's lost everything, he's spent over four years in prison, and other than his family and us, everyone thinks he's the murderer who molested his precious daughter. He also thought, or at least hoped, as did his family, that Henderson was going to be different than Faith, but he's nothing more than just a retread. It never was about fresh eyes but a fabricated rehash of the first investigation. That, and two lying prison snitches."

Kitty then pivoted and said, "We're staying focused on what we have to do. Dunner, you and I are going to talk with the basketball players beginning in two days. Sam is contacting most of them and giving them directions to his small apartment in Floyds Knobs.[174] We'll do our interviews there, allowing

---

[174] Floyds Knobs is located a few miles northwest of New Albany; the apartment was located behind his residence.

two hours for each person. I also want us to speak with James Benson."[175]

We had learned of Benson about the same time we'd received the first package of discovery from Henderson. Benson was a former member of the GCC. The ISP had just interviewed him, and Benson, according to a woman who'd phoned the lead into the prosecutor's office, was a man who'd supposedly seen Dave leave the gym on the night of the murders.

For her part, Stacy was continuing her diligent review of all the laboratory reports and beginning to compile her list of questions for the impending depositions. She was also continuing her research on more bloodstain experts to contact and potentially ask to examine the bloody evidence.

As Kitty had reminded us, the trial was scheduled to begin in early August, meaning we had only seven months to prepare for as many as 150 witnesses; much time would be spent researching their stories and prepping for their depositions; additionally, we'd want to do our own backgrounds on each.

The "Mistaken Or Lying" Basketball Players

Two days later, we began our interviews of all ten players, in addition to Tom Jolly, one of the two spectators that evening. We had over 35 collections of their stories through ISP reports, transcripts from Faith's investigators, and trial testimonies, but we didn't know each person individually. Were they, as Stan Faith had proclaimed, all "mistaken or lying?" Would the next jury believe them, unlike the first?

In total, we spent almost 14 hours over two days speaking with 11 hard-working, blue-collar guys who loved to play basketball. All had agreed to have their photos taken, which we'd later put in a collage for our bond-hearing PowerPoint presentation.

Martin and Jeff Dickey were very close brothers who, in turn, were brothers of a New Albany Police officer. They had never played at the church gym before, but they had played with Dave and other ISP officers at the Silver Creek High School gym.[176] The two had been the first to arrive around 6:45 p.m., and since the church gym had been locked, they'd waited until others arrived.

Within minutes, players had begun parking their vehicles in the adjacent lot, including Dave, followed by his cousin, Jeff Lockhart. Jeff, with the key and the alarm code, had unlocked the door and disengaged the alarm, and several players had poured into the gym. It had been 6:59 p.m.

Among the other players arriving almost simultaneously had been Jeremy Little, Mark Werncke, Tony Ferguson, and Phillip Lockhart, making a total

---

[175] Pseudonym.

[176] The gym was located in Sellersburg, Indiana, a short distance from the ISP Post.

of eight players. Jeremy and Tony were carpet cleaners; Mark was a self-employed contractor who, five years before, had built Kim and Dave's house; and Phillip, Sam and Carol's son, was a student at Purdue University who had arrived from West Lafayette less than an hour prior to the games.

Eric Minzenberger, Sam's son-in-law, had arrived a minute or two after 7:00 p.m. Within moments of his arrival, the tenth player, Scott Schrank, a friend of Jeff Lockhart, had walked into the gym. Scott had been unsure if he was going to make it or not that evening, not deciding until literally minutes before he'd left home.

If part of Dave's master plan had been somehow or another to get lost in a crowd of ball players so that no one would miss him as he snuck out of the gym for 20–25 minutes, that plan wasn't a good one, since neither he, nor anyone else for that matter, had known how many would play that night. Since only ten had initially showed up, all ten would be playing. If anyone had disappeared from the floor, the other nine would obviously have immediately noticed.

After a few minutes of limbering up and shooting some baskets, the 10 had begun their five-on-five games. By everyone's recollection, the first game had begun around 7:10–7:15 p.m. Sam, the oldest and the 11th player, had arrived after the first game started, or around 7:15–7:20 p.m. While the others played, he'd dribbled and shot baskets when his end of the floor was empty.

Most of the players hadn't remembered who they'd guarded, except the two tallest players, Werncke and Jeff Lockhart, who had been on opposite teams. The Dickey brothers always played on the same team, so they knew they hadn't guarded one another. None recalled the scores of the games or how many points they'd scored, but all said the energy and intensity of the games had been good, and they had gotten a sweaty workout running the length of the floor. All agreed two of the most intense had been the brothers Dickey. Martin, almost 40 at the time, had been stout and muscular, but surprisingly to some, he was quite agile and athletic and could stroke the ball.

With the exceptions of Jeremy Little and Tony Ferguson, each of whom hadn't recalled Dave sitting out a game, all of the others did recall his being replaced by Sam at some time. Most hadn't remembered the approximate time, but three had. Sam had still been on the sidelines when Tom Jolly had walked in the door around 8:15–8:20 p.m., or almost simultaneously with the finish of a game. It was at that time Dave had volunteered to sit with Sam replacing him.

After the other nine players drank some water, rested, and hit the restroom, play had begun again. During that game, Dave had been on the sideline talking with Tom. Some of the players had known Tom by name, and some had never seen him before. All, except Jeremy and Tony, had nonetheless recalled seeing him talking with Dave. Phillip had recalled occasionally making fun of Dave for resting rather than running as he'd said he was going to do.

For his part, Tom said he'd been working outside on his small mini-farm about four miles from the church. As a former church elder who was a driving force behind building the gym, he had wanted to see if it were being utilized, so he'd driven the short distance from his home. Shortly after he had arrived, the ongoing game had ended, Dave had walked over to him, and they had talked of Tom's two sons, one of whom had been close with Dave.

"I didn't see Dave before 8:20 p.m. and I can't say where he was or wasn't before then or after 9:00 o'clock," Tom said, "but I saw and spoke with him that night and knew he was in that gym from 8:20 p.m. until I left right at 9:00 p.m., and no, I won't lie for anybody."

Tom Jolly, Church Elder who spoke at length with
David Camm the one game Camm sat out.

After that game ended around 8:40–8:45 p.m., Scott Schrank had decided he was through for the evening. Dave, who by then had been jogging along the sideline, had replaced him, and, after a short break for the others, another five-on-five game had begun. The 10 ballers had played until right at 9:00 p.m. when Sam and Mark had announced they were leaving.

Even though 9:00 p.m. had signaled the end of most game nights, the eight remaining guys, Martin, his brother Jeff, Jeremy, Tony, Eric, Phillip, Jeff Lockhart, and Dave, had decided to play one last game of four-on-four. By the time they'd finished, their estimates of the time ranged from 9:15–9:25 p.m. The alarm, of course, had reflected the time as being 9:22 p.m. when it had been engaged, corroborating the recollections of all eight players.

All had exited the gym, with Jeff Lockhart setting the alarm and locking the door. Phillip and Dave had walked to their two pickup trucks and as they'd driven out of the northeast driveway of the church, had acted like two NASCAR drivers and raced one another for a short bit to the intersection of Oakes Road. Meanwhile, other players had begun contacting their wives or girlfriends, with their phone records all reflecting the times of the contacts as being within minutes of 9:22 p.m.

In summary, there were some inconsistencies with two players not recalling Dave's being on the sideline with Tom. Eight others had seen him, of course. Did that make the two players liars? Or for that matter, did that make the eight other players and Tom Jolly liars?

Two things the players had in common, other than being fervent ballers. They didn't like being portrayed as mistaken, liars, or idiots. Each of them, they had insisted, had provided their best recollection as to what occurred that night. All of their stories to us, in fact, were the ones they had provided previously to the ISP, Faith's investigators, and under oath at the first trial.

Secondly, as with Tom, all were adamant they wouldn't lie for anyone, including for Dave Camm. In fact, some hadn't known Dave or had only known him slightly. One of those said he hadn't particularly cared for Dave,[177] but he'd also said *he wouldn't lie for or lie against him.*[178] He had only told the truth as to what he'd recalled.

Most critically for Dave's defense was the fact that no one had ever seen Dave leave at any time and certainly no one had ever seen him return to the gym.

After the last alibi witness left, Kitty commented, "If these guys are lying, then there's no witness ever who should be believed. They're just good, hard-working, honest people, and Faith sullied their characters just as he annihilated Dave's."

I responded, "In all the trials in which my cases had been prosecuted, a standard line in opening arguments for the prosecutor was to caution the jurors not to be concerned if multiple witnesses to the same event tell somewhat different stories, as recollections are always somewhat different and minor inconsistencies are to be expected. Faith turned that axiom on its head, claiming minor differences meant the players were lying or mistaken and couldn't be trusted."

Both of us had been astounded that the prior jurors could have agreed with Faith that Dave could have left the gym, but Kitty had put it in perspective: "Faith had managed to get them to hate Dave. The prejudice overwhelmed common sense; even the Court of Appeals had recognized that."

Even though the first jury had, inconceivably, convicted Dave in spite of the testimony of the players, we nonetheless were both very encouraged by the men and their interviews. Having 11 eyewitnesses who had been with Dave at the time his family had been slaughtered was an airtight defense.

---

[177] He had known of Dave and Kim separating in 1995.

[178] Emphasis mine.

Airtight, that is, if Henderson would be forced to play fair and by the rules and not allowed to engage in character assassination by the new judge.

Another Eyewitness

The next day, we spoke with James Benson, who, as a member of the church, also had usage of the gym building on Thursday nights. Pastor Leland Lockhart, Jeff's father, along with the church board, had granted Benson permission to lead his Narcotics Anonymous (NA) meetings in one of the second-floor classrooms, and he had done so for the six months prior to September 28.

He had been sober for 15 years, clean and free from alcohol as well as drugs, Benson told us, and wanted to help others beat addiction. His groups were small, normally fewer than 10 members, with some appearing only because they had been ordered to do so by a judge. On the night of the murders only he and two others had appeared for their 7:30–8:30 p.m. meeting.

When he'd arrived early, around 7:00 p.m., Benson had seen Dave, whom he'd known slightly from church, standing next to his truck. Shortly after the door had been unlocked, Benson had followed the ball players into the gym and then walked up the nearby stairs to the classroom. The other two NA members had arrived shortly before 7:30 p.m.

Their meeting had lasted an hour and adjourned at 8:30 p.m., with the two attendees leaving promptly. A few minutes later, around 8:40 p.m., Benson had walked down the steps and practically run into Dave on the gym floor. Benson had also recognized Tom Jolly nearby on the sidelines.

Benson was emphatic that he'd never told anyone he'd seen Camm leave the gym; to the contrary, he'd seen Dave only on two occasions, the first when he was getting ready to enter the gym around 7:00 p.m. and the second when Dave was on the gym floor around 8:40 p.m.

And then Benson told us, before the first Camm trial, that he had been contacted, on the phone, by an investigator from the office of Stan Faith but never interviewed in person. Thus, the fact he was known to have been in the company of Dave at the gym the night of the murders wasn't divulged by Faith to Mike McDaniel, nor was there any documentation of any interview of him.

Per my request, Benson said he would reach out to the two other NA members and tell them I wanted to speak with them.

After the interview Kitty and I looked at one another. "There were three more people in the gym that night," I said. "In addition to Tom Jolly and Tony Ferguson's grandfather, who was also on the sideline, there were three more, making a total of five people the ISP didn't even know of prior to arresting Dave.

"Incompetence on steroids," she responded. "And they probably won't ever make an effort to interview the other two who were with Benson. The only reason they interviewed Benson was they thought he would impeach the ball players and help their theory."

Kitty and I returned to Bloomington as she continued formulating her list of persons to depose. I soon left again for New Albany, intent upon pursuing our own leads, independent of those of the State.

For his part, Benson, true to his word, had gotten consent for me from each of the other two attendees, Rhonda Turley and Ed Howard,[179] to contact them. I first called upon Turley, who was very cooperative and accommodating, but unfortunately didn't know Dave. She would not have recognized him as one of the players and had never been interviewed by any police officer.

Ed Howard, however, was having second thoughts about meeting or speaking with me, refusing to meet in person or to speak at length over the phone. Later efforts to get him to answer his phone or respond to messages left at his residence were unsuccessful.

---

[179] The names of the other two attendees are pseudonyms.

CHAPTER 20
The Getaway Car?

Sources of Information

Since private attorneys and investigators aren't privy to official records, I had earlier applied to and was approved, as a licensed private investigator, to access a vast database gleaned from public records and collated into an organized format—all for a significant fee, of course. That database had contained literally millions of names; phone numbers, both listed and unlisted; historical residential and email addresses; probable relatives; tax records and real estate holdings; employment history; civil cases; dates of birth; and, yes, even Social Security Numbers.

I also had paid to access a State of Indiana database, which allowed the query of personal driver's licenses, vehicular registrations, and lien holders on vehicles. The amount of information obtainable, literally at my fingertips, was amazing. Once again, all for a fee.

In those databases, I routinely checked the names of every person we were going to interview or depose. Included in that list, of course, were all the neighbors who had lived in the year 2000 within a mile perimeter of the Camm home. And, yeah, I had also secured background on all the basketball players as well.

I spent many hours at the New Albany-Floyd County library, searching the local newspaper microfiche records for articles and criminal bookings on burglaries, robberies, and sexual assaults in the months leading up to the murders,[180] as well as stories of unsolved crimes around

THE LOCATION WHERE SHE HAD SEEN THE PARKED CAR, JUST PRIOR TO KIM'S ARRIVAL HOME, WOULD HAVE ALLOWED THE MURDERER TO HAVE WALKED, UNNOTICED AND HIDDEN, TO THE CAMM GARAGE.

the time of the murders. There is, after all, a reason for the term recidivist. We'd winnow the list of names, eliminating those who had been incarcerated at the time of the murders.

We were also going to subpoena the Indiana DOC, seeking the identity

---

[180] The defense had no access to official police records; online criminal and civil records had been limited in number in 2005.

of offenders released to Floyd and nearby counties on parole or probation for offenses that might have been similar to the Camm crimes such as home invasions, burglaries, robberies, and sexual assaults. Theoretically, those convicted of sex-related offenses would be in a registry, but there was no guarantee every sex offender had registered him/herself. One such offender had, however, and he'd lived within a mile of the Camm home in September 2000. And no, he hadn't been interviewed by the ISP.

During the time I had spent in and around New Albany, and in order to minimize costs,[181] I had accepted the offer of Sam and Carol to stay in their small, detached apartment. The location also allowed me to set up my mobile office and to memorialize some of my interviews.[182]

I also planned to interview Frank and Janice Renn as Kitty awaited approval from their attorney. Janice, after all, probably knew more of Kim's schedules and interactions than anyone and would be invaluable in helping construct the timeline and victimology.[183] Unfortunately, we were rebuffed in our efforts.

Camm/Lockhart family members who could help with the timeline/victimology were also interviewed. Among those were Dave's parents, Don and Susie Camm; his older sister Julie; brothers, Donnie and Dan; Leland and Vonda Lockhart; Bob and Debbie Ter Vree; and several others.

The Parked Car

As part of my neighborhood investigation, Sam told me his father and mother had purchased, in the 1960's, the acreage on which all of the homes on Lockhart Road had eventually been built and thus, he had historical knowledge of many of the neighbors.[184] He also told me Nelson had spoken to a few of those neighbors in the days after the ISP had stopped their whodunit investigation, with one neighbor in particular, whose information was possibly significant. She had been the first I had contacted.

Ms. Lillian Todd,[185] a middle-aged lady, had never been interviewed by the ISP. She had specifically recalled the night of the murders as being Thursday because that's when their family routinely went to a local tavern, ate dinner,

---

[181] Judge Aylsworth had approved my costs and investigative time being borne by Floyd County; thus, I wasn't saving myself any money but Floyd County.

[182] Jennifer True transcribed most of my interviews.

[183] I had several brief interactions with them over the years, and they were always kind and polite.

[184] In addition to Dave and his family as well as Sam's parents, Leland and Vonda Lockhart formerly resided on Lockhart Road in a home where their first church service was held.

[185] Pseudonym.

and sang karaoke. That night, she had allowed her daughter to drive their car to the restaurant.

They had left home around 7:05 p.m. and within moments of leaving, and as they were driving south on Alonzo Smith Road, Todd had noticed a car which was parked just south of Lockhart Road, on the west side, and off the pavement. Lillian had made a cautionary comment to her daughter as she didn't want her to hit the parked car, which was barely off the road.

The car, which Todd had thought was blue or possibly dark blue in color, was facing south. The rear of the vehicle, which was facing towards them, had looked somewhat like a hatchback.

Todd hadn't seen anyone in or near the car, nor did she see anything wrong with it, such as a flat tire or damage to the vehicle. She'd described it as being a smaller boxy-like model, possibly a station wagon. The car, she'd estimated, was a 1980's model.

Later that evening, while at the tavern, Lillian and her family had heard a cacophony of sirens, causing her to call a family member who lived nearby and said he had heard, on his police scanner, that a murder had occurred on Lockhart Road.

When Todd returned home that evening, toward the multitude of police cars, the vehicle she had previously seen parked off the road was gone. She had even asked her husband about it, who had told her that he had not seen the vehicle when he'd driven past the location at approximately 8:15 p.m.

At no other time had Todd seen any other cars parked at that same location, either before or since the murders, nor had she ever seen that car at any location since September 28, 2000.

I drove to the location as described and saw there was no clear line of sight to it from any nearby house. Was that by design or accident? The more significant question was whether the location offered decent access to the Camm house.

The house nearest the parking spot was the Murphy residence.[186] Neither the husband nor wife, they told me, in the years they had lived there, including 2000, had ever noticed any vehicle at any time parked off the road.

The Murphys allowed me access to their property, and I walked from the side of Alonzo Smith, through a wooded and bushy area, along a fence line adjacent to a hay field, to the rear of Amos Lockhart's residence, taking photos along the way. If that had been the path of the killer(s), it provided him/her with exceptional concealment and took but minutes to navigate.

---

[186] Pseudonym.

The top of the vertical black line (on right) is where Ms. Todd sighted the parked car; the straight line/path extends to the rear of the Amos Lockhart property, then veers north (horizontal line) towards the Camm home, depicting the possible walking path of the killer; aerial photo taken by me in 2005.

No vehicle matching Todd's description had been noted in any ISP report, and it didn't exactly comport with the description of the black Cadillac seen by Brandon Beavin. Were the two vehicles related in any manner? Had the driver of the Cadillac in the afternoon returned that evening and parked alongside Alonzo Smith?

Several thoughts came to mind. The first, obviously, was that neither car was connected to the murders as the Cadillac could have simply and mistakenly driven onto Lockhart Road, discovered it to be a dead-end, and driven out.[187] The parked vehicle spotted by the neighbor could have experienced an issue, unseen by Todd, and been parked only briefly.

Another possibility was the two vehicles were connected in some manner or another; i.e., many people, including criminals, have access to more than one vehicle. In the afternoon, the killer visited with the Cadillac and in the evening returned and parked a different car alongside the road, allowing him/her to walk to the Camm house without being seen on the dead-end road.

The last possibility was that both vehicles were one and the same. How could that be? As I found, over decades of interviews, when it came to some details, eyewitnesses often were wrong. That didn't mean, in the case of Todd, she didn't see a parked car at the location she'd described. I was confident of her observation and of the date and time she'd seen the vehicle, particularly since she had connected other events to her sighting: e.g., karaoke night, the

---

[187] There was a Dead-End sign near the intersection of Alonzo Smith and Lockhart, however.

time they normally left, the route they normally took, and hearing the sirens.[188]

I called Kitty and, thanks to Nelson, told her the lead had promise, but even though it was possibly relevant, there wasn't much we could do with it at the time. Kitty told me she had a call in with Henderson about getting more discovery, as well as demanding that he run the unknown sweatshirt DNA profile through CODIS, for he had still failed to do so.

We also agreed if CODIS and a DOC check for the name BACKBONE were negative, a subpoena would be issued to the sweatshirt manufacturer, Hanes, in order to attempt to determine the date of manufacture and any possible uniqueness about it that might aid in tracking it to the point of sale. The odds of success were infinitesimal, but it was worth pursuing.

More Neighborhood Interviews

After my walk in the woods, it took only a few minutes to drive to the residence of William Robertson, who had lived a short distance from the Camm house and had been released early from prison the year before the murders. Knocking on the door didn't provide a response, so I left my business card with a note.

A congenial Robertson later called. Yes, he had been living with his father and wife at the time of the murders. He had been very fortunate, he said, because his former prosecutor, Stan Faith, who had secured his conviction, had agreed to a sentence reduction, allowing him early release.

Since shortly after he had regained his freedom, he had been working as a paralegal for a New Albany attorney who'd suggested he not speak with me. That attorney, somewhat surprisingly, was also Stan Faith.

So, Faith had convicted the man, had argued for a lengthy prison sentence, had seen him receive a lengthy sentence, had helped Robertson secure a modification for his sentence, and had then hired him as a paralegal. And Faith was now giving him advice. That was some kind of strange, I thought. Regardless, Robertson said he was taking the advice but also said he might change his mind in the future. And no, as I had expected, he hadn't ever been interviewed by the ISP.

I interviewed several neighbors with some shutting the door in my face. No leads were generated until I spoke with the young man and his mother

---

[188] A vivid example of an eyewitness getting a description wrong was of a bank teller who had been robbed at gunpoint. The woman had described the robber as a "black man with the worst complexion" she had ever seen. A viewing the videotape of the event revealed the robber had been wearing a dark colored ski mask and he had been white. All of that, of course, didn't equate to the teller not being victimized or a robbery not occurring.

living in the woods adjacent to the hay field, who told me their home had been burglarized just months prior to the murders.

The same neighbors told of yet another neighbor, about a quarter of a mile away, who had two expensive AKC pedigree dogs shot to death within a year of the murders, but didn't think any suspects had been identified. Had that dog-killer returned to the area? Had the burglar visited the Camm home?

The young man had also been working all day in the hay field adjacent to Amos' property. Although he had been surprised no one from law enforcement had spoken to him, he hadn't seen anything of note during the day or evening. Of course, by the time I had spoken with him, almost five years had elapsed since the murders.

I then tracked down a man with a portable sawmill who had been in the area on the day of the murders, but he had been working quite a distance away from Alonzo Smith Road and had seen nothing. The nearby neighbor who had been arrested for cultivating marijuana by Dave was courteous, but he and his wife had refused to speak with me.

Next, I contacted Tammy Megenity, the caregiver of Amos and the former convict who had overheard the whispered conversation at church she'd assumed had been about the murder weapon, and the interview had been what I expected it to be. After I had identified myself and the purpose of my contact, her first words had been "I believe he did it!" followed very quickly by "He molested his daughter!"

I had finally been able to utter a few words, telling Megenity I wasn't trying to convince her of anything, but only to get her recollections as one who was in the neighborhood near the time of the murders. She had been cooperative but hadn't provided any information, and, no, she no longer had any idea as to the activities or whereabouts of her former druggie friends whom she hadn't seen for years.

I drove back to New Albany and briefed Dave on our progress, also running the names of Megenity's drug associates by him and the names of those arrested and booked in the months prior to the murders and getting his thoughts on the local burglaries. There was a possibility the perpetrator(s) had police contact with Dave in some fashion or another, but he didn't recognize any names.

Aerial Photographs

I next told Dave that I was a strong proponent of aerial photographs. They provided greater clarity and relationships between pertinent locations as well as giving me a better view of individual sites.[189] In addition to the list I had compiled, Dave added some additional sites to my list. I subsequently contracted with a USAF reservist pilot who had built his own two-man helicopter. That contraption wasn't just small; it was tiny.

On a below-freezing winter day, as the pilot flew his little blue bird, I used his telephoto camera, as we spent several hours hovering over Southern Indiana and the metropolitan Louisville area. I took hundreds of photos, including of the Camm residence, their neighborhood, the GCC church and gym, their route to the house and church, Kim's normal routes of travel to/ from her Louisville work, her parents' home, the locations of dance and swimming practice, and practically everything in between.[190]

Once developed, those photos did, indeed, help us to better understand the different geographical sites. Kitty and Stacy would later use them as demonstrative aids and introduce several others as exhibits at trial.

Kim's Earrings

One of the first subpoenas I served was for records from the local jewelry store where Dave had purchased the set of missing diamond earrings he'd given to Kim for Christmas of 1998. The jeweler described the diamonds in detail and provided a copy of the receipt; the two diamonds, each over half a carat, had been mounted in a four-prong gold setting.[191] The total cost had been $2,678.55 and no, no one from law enforcement had contacted him.

Even though they would probably be impossible to locate, I wrote several subpoenas, finalized by Kitty, which I later served upon several local pawn shops, all to no avail, in an effort to see if the earrings had been pawned.

"Beware The Innocent Man"

I also spoke with Mike McDaniel, Dave's first attorney and his wife Debbie, primarily to gain their thoughts on the blood experts. Both told me of their overwhelming conclusion Dave was innocent. "Beware the innocent man," Mike had lamented, "he will ravage you."[192]

He then turned towards the nine-week trial, telling me it had been sordid, as he was "lucky to have made the record" he had as Judge Striegel had done "his best to shape the evidence…anything the State wanted, he would let them," including, of course, facilitating salacious testimony. As for Faith,

---

[189] Google Earth, of course, had still been in its infancy.

[190] The time of the year was good inasmuch as foliage hadn't hid structures.

[191] His records hadn't reflected if the gold was white or yellow.

[192] At the time, I had merely noted Mike's words. I didn't comprehend just how devastating they would prove to be.

"there was nothing too rotten, underhanded or sneaky," Mike said. "They were willing to do anything to get a conviction."

Debbie added, "During the trial, it was awful. I got several phone calls threatening both Mike and me. One guy kept calling, threatening to kill Mike, while an older guy called twice, asking me, 'How is McDaniel going to feel when he gets home and finds his wife dead?'" In response, she said, Mike still carried his .45 pistol on him at all times.

> AS FOR FAITH, "THERE WAS NOTHING TOO ROTTEN, UNDERHANDED OR SNEAKY."
>
> "DON'T UNDERESTIMATE ENGLERT. HE GAVE THE JURY AN ANSWER TO EVERY QUESTION THEY HAD."

Debbie also said Mike had suffered serious heart issues during the trial as he had tried to overcome both a prosecutor and judge intent on "obstructing justice to get a conviction." It had damn near killed him, she said, as she also said she had originally argued against her husband even taking the case.

"Whatever you do," Mike interjected, "don't underestimate Englert." The jury, he said, had been enthralled by the self-described expert and crime scene reconstructionist. "He gave them an answer to every question they had."

On the other hand, Terry Labor, the Minnesota forensic expert, had testified as to his own opinions, deductions, and conclusions rather than to absolute certainties. "He was the true scientist," Mike concluded, "but he wasn't Englert, who knew it all. In my final argument, I used Englert's own word to describe himself. Pseudo. He testified, no kidding, that he was a pseudo scientist, and I agreed, telling the jury he was pseudo, false, counterfeit, pretended, and spurious."

But Englert, Mike concluded, had been the "linchpin" in the case, as he had enabled the jury to disregard all the alibi witnesses, become enraged with Dave's extramarital affairs, and buy the motives of molestation and financial gain.

As for the affairs testimony, by the end of the State's case, Mike concluded, "The jury absolutely hated Dave. You could read their glares, particularly the women. Pat Biggs and I were hoping for a hung jury but…."

As it happened, over two years later, on the day Dave's case had been reversed, Mike recalled he had been in the same courtroom where Striegel was sitting as a guest judge. Upon hearing of the appellate decision, Mike had told Striegel, "You motherfucker, you almost killed me with your motherfucking rulings. I'm ashamed of you."

Striegel then shocked Mike, telling him Faith had assured him, in private, he would connect the affairs to the murders. "It was a clear violation of an ex parte contact by Faith," Mike said, as he became outraged and yelled again at Striegel, so much so a Deputy Sheriff had to intercede between the two.

Debbie and Mike McDaniel in their New Albany office; the two were a dynamic defense team for decades with Mike the accomplished litigator and Debbie his office administrator, investigator and paralegal.

As a personal aside, Mike added that he, as a teenager, had played baseball and basketball with Tom Jolly.[193] Tom, he knew, was a rock solid guy whose word was also rock solid.

Mike and Frank Renn had also been childhood friends, and as kids, Mike had been present when Frank had gotten shot in the eye with a BB pellet. During the trial, he and Frank had been on the elevator together when Frank said Faith, unlike before the trial when he'd kept him abreast of developments, "had frozen him out."

George Nichols II Medical Examiner

Mike also recalled he had enlisted the aid of a private pathologist he knew well and respected highly. Dr. George Nichols II had created the office of the Chief Kentucky Medical Examiner and had been its head for 20 years but had since gone into private practice.[194]

I subsequently interviewed Nichols, a veteran of over 10,000 autopsies.

---

[193] Mike had been an excellent all-around athlete, playing football in college and also boxing, in his youth in Louisville, with another kid named Cassius Clay, who later changed his name to Muhammad Ali.

[194] During his tenure, he had conducted over 10,000 autopsies; supervised 40,000 additional autopsies; supervised the exhumation and examination of President Zachary Taylor; and hired and trained his successor, Dr. Corey-Handy.

Unsurprisingly, he was a man much like McDaniel: direct, blunt, and brutally honest. Dr. Nichols' review of the autopsy reports had him agreeing with the opinions and conclusions rendered by Dr. Corey-Handy and Dr. Hunsaker; he had also examined the crime scene photos and added a few observations of his own:

- "I've never seen shoes taken off of a woman and placed on top of a car before…there's something weird about whoever did this";

- Kim "had strange marks on her feet which I had never seen before… not with a shooting…maybe a beating";

- Kim's numerous injuries meant she had "probably crawled around on her knees" and/or had possibly been on her back supporting herself with her elbows;

- Jill had no internal genitalia injuries, and those injuries had nothing "to do with sex at all" but rather had been struck by something, a "knee, elbow [or] a fist" and the injury was most probably intentional; and

- "Whoever thought something was added to the blood flow was a 'stupid fuck' since blood serum separation was obvious to anyone who ever 'paid any attention to a crime scene.'"

Dr. Nichols also knew of Rod Stites' mentor, Rodney Englert, and his involvement in the 1985 death investigation of James Cooley. Dr. Nichols began to explain the circumstances surrounding that death, but while I hadn't known Englert was involved, I absolutely recognized the case. Cooley's death had occurred in Hobart, Indiana, a city adjacent to Gary, Indiana, where I had been assigned to the FBI. Englert's opinion as to the manner of Cooley's death had created, to say the least, a huge controversy between the county prosecutor and a local police department.

It was time to further educate myself on Rodney Englert.

CHAPTER 21

THE Blood Expert

Rodney Englert was a Deputy Sheriff with the Multnomah, Oregon, County Sheriff's Department on April 6, 1985, the same day 52-year-old James Cooley of Hobart, Indiana, was found by his wife in their home, beaten to death in a small photo darkroom of their basement. Cooley, everyone agreed, had died a very violent and bloody death, for he had been struck on his head 32 times with a claw hammer, which was found on the floor adjacent to his left foot.

"Ten of the 32 head wounds were 'very deep,' according to an autopsy by Dr. Young Kim, a coroner's pathologist [and] all the wounds formed a 'parallel' path stretching almost from ear to ear over the top of the head."[195] As would be expected, Cooley's head was very bloody, as were the ceiling and walls nearby, the result of the repeated bloody hammer blows, which flung, or cast, blood from the tool.

As part of their investigation, Hobart detectives had found a partial palmprint on the hammer that didn't match Cooley's or his wife's. Mrs. Cooley had been interviewed, provided details as to her whereabouts during the time of the murder, and

> "IT IS MY OPINION WITH ABSOLUTE CERTAINTY THAT THE [32 HEAD] WOUNDS ARE SELF-INFLICTED"

passed a polygraph examination. Meanwhile, Lake County, Indiana, Coroner Dr. Daniel Thomas ruled the manner of death a homicide.[196]

Two Hobart detectives, who had previously attended a homicide school where Englert had spoken, were impressed with him, and as a result, Englert had been asked for his assistance in the case.[197]

The blood and reconstruction expert, referred to by some investigators at THE Blood Expert,[198] had been provided 19 different 8" x 10" color photographs of the crime scene. After reviewing those photos, Englert had

---

[195] O'Brien, John, "Murder or Suicide?" *The Chicago Tribune*, October 15, 1985.

[196] Ibid.

[197] Ibid.

[198] Englert enjoyed a sterling reputation among many criminal investigators and had been recognized by many as the best interpreter of bloodstains at crime scenes, thus, THE Blood Expert.

written in the first paragraph of his report, dated August 10, 1985,[199] "My conclusions are based upon several observations in the photographs." Later in that same report, however, he'd stated, "My opinion is based upon all the reports and photographs…" Regardless of his basis of his opinion, among other assertions of Englert are as follows (emphases are mine):

- "James Cooley's hands are bloody and…the hammer…was also bloody. If Mr. Cooley was unconscious when the blows were being delivered, *it is impossible for him to have received blood inside his hands and on the outside of his right hand*…[that] blood appears to be transfer blood from the bloody hammer to his hands and cast off blood from the blows to his head";

- "It is *very unlikely Mr. Cooley would have remained in one position while* receiving the blows while *either in a conscious or unconscious* state";

- Of a bloody chisel on the floor, "It is very possible that Mr. Cooley also held this chisel with his bloody hand";

- "…a bloody piece of cloth in coagulated blood…was probably used by Mr. Cooley to act as a towel after some of the blows were delivered";

- "The blood smeared as *he manipulated the hammer* and positioned it repeatedly to deliver approximately 32 blows to his head"; and

- "There is *no evidence whatsoever* to indicate that someone other than James Cooley delivered the blows."

Englert's conclusion: "It is my opinion with *absolute certainty*[200] that the wounds on Mr. James Cooley are self-inflicted."

So, while Cooley had been committing suicide by striking himself 32 times on the head with the claw end of a hammer, including 10 "very deep" blows, he had taken the time to handle a chisel, for some reason or another, and then, after he'd hammered his head a few times, began to cushion the blows by using a piece of cloth. At least that's how I read the report.

Englert had also claimed the blows to Cooley's head were "superficial with the exception of two." I didn't know where he had obtained that information, but he'd used it to then segue into an opinion he'd received from an Oregon medical examiner that "superficial wounds would not necessarily cause James Cooley to pass out."

---

[199] I was provided a copy of Englert's cover letter and three-page report by a friend.
[200] Emphasis mine.

Regardless, all medical examiners, I knew, testified only when their opinions were based upon "reasonable medical certainty." They didn't opine on their findings with "absolute certainty" as did Englert, who was obviously not a medical examiner.

As a result of Englert's analysis, the Hobart police had agreed Cooley was a man very determined to kill himself and closed their case, listing his death as a suicide.

The Lake County Coroner, Dr. Thomas, however, had been incredulous as to Englert's findings, contending Cooley had been hit from behind and, contrary to Englert's "absolute certainty," said it would have been "humanly impossible" for Cooley to commit suicide in such a manner. He had publicly called upon the police department to re-open their closed case. The police chief, however, had refused to do so.[201]

Lake County Prosecutor Jack Crawford had interceded in the matter and issued his own findings, based "primarily on the medical evidence…[which] established that the amount, location and severity of the hammer blows are inconsistent with a finding of suicide."[202]

Crawford had then asked the ISP to conduct their own death investigation; after several months, the Lowell Post of the ISP had reached "the same conclusion [homicide] as Thomas." Still, they could find no suspects.[203]

It was astounding to discover Englert's involvement in a case in which the ISP had concluded he was dead wrong; astounding to me, at least, as I doubted if Clemons, Sarkisian, or Biddle had even known of Englert's role in the Cooley case. If they had, they apparently hadn't questioned his purported expertise.[204]

Discussions with Kitty and Stacy, as well as others, had revealed Englert had become a favorite expert of Stan Faith after he'd met Englert at a District Attorney's conference in California. Faith had soon contacted Englert to assist him on a death investigation, later ruled as a suicide, thanks in part to Englert's opinion.

Faith had also used Englert on another death case, one in which the defendant claimed self-defense. Englert had refuted that claim with his opinions, and the defendant had been convicted of murder. It was therefore easy to understand why Faith had called his buddy within a day of the Camm murders.

---

[201] O'Brien, John, "Murder or Suicide?" *The Chicago Tribune*, October 15, 1985.

[202] O'Brien, John, "Beating Death Ruled Homicide After Year," *The Chicago Tribune*, April 3, 1986.

[203] Ibid.

[204] As of 2022, the Cooley murder case is an open ISP murder case.

Stacy and I, though, spoke with others who didn't think much of Englert and his expensive opinions. One had been present during Englert's field work, and that person's impression was that "...he's a lot of ego and blown up and just a lot more than what...he thinks he's a lot more than what he really is." Further, that person described Englert as "grandiose" and not "real professional."

An internet search for more stories on Englert found his involvement in a Florida murder case. Englert, a prosecution witness, didn't impress the defendant's attorney, Anthony Natale, who was quoted as saying Englert's performance was one of "all form and no substance." Natale added, "If Englert told me my name, I'd call my mother for confirmation." [205] Natale wasn't complaining, though, since his client had been found not guilty.

Within months of the Florida trial, Englert had again served as the paid blood expert for the prosecution in a Utah murder case. On trial had been a surviving husband and father, accused of killing his mentally unbalanced and suicidal wife and their three children. After the man had been acquitted, some jurors were blunt about Englert's testimony, with one commenting he had been "too much of a showman [and]...It bugged us how he kept playing to the jury."[206] Another juror's take: "The personal feelings among the jurors about Mr. Englert was 'Give me a break.' He was too confident of himself. He said he was '110 percent sure' of his findings."[207]

More recently, Kitty told me of Englert's involvement in the case of Julia Rea, an Illinois mother whose 10-year old son, Joel, had been killed in 1997 while in the same house as her mother. Rea claimed she'd been awakened by her son's scream and run to his bedroom. There she had found a male, slight of build, struggling with Joel. She'd begun fighting the man who had soon overpowered her and fled, leaving her with cuts. Her son, however, had later died of stab wounds.

After the murder, Rea had relocated to Bloomington, Indiana, and enrolled at Indiana University where she was living when charged with her son's murder. Kitty had begun representing Rea, who had insisted she was innocent.

Extradited to Illinois, Rea had been convicted of murder in 2002 based upon, among other evidence, the opinion of Englert who'd claimed blood on Rea's clothing was cast-off blood, meaning it had landed on her as she'd stabbed her son.

Not long after Rea's conviction, Tommy Lynn Sells, a transient, had been apprehended in Texas and had provided detailed information about

---

[205] Fidel, Steve, "Experts Find Their Credibility on Trial," *Deseret News*, June 13, 1993

[206] Fidel, Steve, "Jury Members Say Tears Flowed as They Viewed Evidence," *Deseret News*, July 15,1993.

[207] Ibid.

several murders. The self-confessed serial killer had admitted to killing Joel, providing very specific aspects of the crime, further admitting the lad had been a totally random target.[208]

But to what had Englert testified in Dave's first trial? His trial transcript was hundreds of pages in length as he had been in front of the jury for over two days. After the obligatory introductory questions, Faith, in an obvious attempt to blunt Englert's suicide deduction in the Cooley case, had classified that case as "cutting edge."

Faith had then implored the mostly self-taught blood expert to begin his tutorial to the jury. Englert had educated those in the box on low, medium, and high-velocity blood and their staining properties, with the expert stating he had come to his conclusions on Dave's case after he had spent 250 hours on examining the crime scene,[209] reconstructing the crime,[210] reading autopsy reports, poring over police reports, viewing police and his own photographs, and analyzing Dave's clothing and other evidence at the ISP laboratory in Evansville.

Englert had concluded that, yes, the eight tiny dots in the lower left portion of Dave's T-shirt, designated as area 30,[211] were the result of HVIS. Englert, as had been expected, had firmly supported his protégé Stites.

His explanation had rested on several factors, Englert testified, including massive amounts of blowback on the overhead rollbar and ceiling liner of the Bronco as well as some on the console between the front seats and the back of the front passenger seat, directly in front of where Jill had been sitting.

With all that blowback, eight tiny dots of that massive amount of HVIS had landed on the front bottom of Dave's shirt, four on the hem itself, while he had been shooting his daughter. How, many were asking, was it that only eight stains had reached his shirt? Englert explained something had blocked the blowback from hitting other parts of the front of the shirt. That something had probably been Jill's hair, through which the return mist was blocked, he'd said.

The most important question I had was how Dave had gotten HVIS on the lower left of his shirt when the shooter, at least in my mind, had been outside

---

[208] Amazingly, even with Sells' confession, Rea, whose conviction had been overturned on another issue, had been re-tried in 2006 and acquitted. She had later been exonerated by the State of Illinois and provided financial compensation for her false conviction and incarceration.

[209] He had traveled from Oregon to Indiana for a period of several days in January 2001.

[210] Englert had used Faith's own investigators to mimic Dave, as the shooter, and Kim outside the Bronco, with numerous photographs taken of the staged events.

[211] Lynn Scamahorn, the ISP DNA analyst, had designated certain areas of the T-shirt with numbers; some of those tiny bloodstains had been cut from the shirt.

the vehicle leaning into the car with an extended arm to shoot Jill and then Brad. The blowback, it seemed, would have had to exit the car and then make a right turn, as the door jamb would possibly have obstructed the left side of his shirt.

Englert's answer as to the position and location of the shooter when Jill was shot had been a stunning and convoluted answer: *"[The shooter] was between Jill Camm and the backseat* of the Bronco, the right front passenger seat, which would be between the back of that seat…The *shooter's feet could have been outside on his knees.* I doubt that it was standing up, but *coming in on knees and or sort of a squashed or squatted position."*[212]

That didn't make a lot of sense, and, reading the transcript, I realized that clearly Mike had also been confused and had tried to get Englert to clarify his response. "So, the shooter could have been outside on their knees, right?"

"No, I didn't say outside. I said feet hanging outside…"

"Pardon me," McDaniel had asked.

"…that's possible positions or squatted inside of the vehicle," Englert had said.

"With both feet inside?"

"Possible," Englert had replied, adding, "I doubt that would be possible, though."

If that explanation had made any sense at all to the jurors, it sure didn't to me.

Englert hadn't stopped with the eight tiny dots on area 30, though, for his highly-trained eye had found more damning evidence against Dave, HVIS that his junior protégé Stites hadn't found. The shirt also had blood in area 23, located on the right side of the shirt, Englert had said, although he had claimed it could have been on the front, "depending on how it hangs on the wearer." That stain, Englert had contended, contained both HVIS and a smear transfer, he'd further explained, "…that has come in contact with something in that vehicle that *created the obliteration of the lower portion, didn't obliterate it, it didn't take it out, but it artifacted it to change it to where it was wet enough in that moment in time, uh, seconds, to create, uh, a disruption* of it."[213]

So, a massive amount of blowback had literally sprayed from the ceiling liner to the console to the back of the front seat and had only landed on the extreme lower left front and then the right side of the shirt, leaving the entire remainder of the front of the shirt intact? And the blood had "artifacted" the shirt? What the hell did that mean? I had known of no such term.

The rear of Dave's shirt also had blood on it, with Englert's stating the blood, designated as area 40, was contact stain, probably coming from the

---

[212] Emphases mine.

[213] Emphasis mine.

garment's touching the back of the front passenger seat. That made sense, since Dave said he had gone through the two front seats and into the rear compartment to retrieve Brad. That he would have touched the back of the left side of the passenger seat was understandable.

What wasn't understandable, and what Englert's testimony underscored, is the shirt had been bloody enough to have drawn the attention of the other ball players when Dave returned from sneaking out of the gym. No baller, of course, had ever seen any blood on Dave or any of his clothing.

As for Dave's shoes and socks, Englert also had more answers. One of Dave's socks,[214] he testified, had "projected" blood from Kim,[215] meaning it had landed there as "a result of some *bleeding at a high energy event*[216] that got onto something that transferred it, projected it, through the medium of the shoelace onto the sock."

Dave's left shoe had blood on it, but his right one hadn't; in fact, his shoestrings on the left shoe had blood on them as well. That wasn't surprising as Brad's body had been in-between the car and the blood trail from Kim's head wound. That Dave would have gotten his loose shoestrings and at least one shoe in the blood and serum flow was explainable. Recall, after all, a bloody shoe print, probably from one of Dave's shoes, had been found somewhere on the garage floor.

Englert, however, had not only deduced projected blood on the sock, but also on the left shoe. In addition to that finding, he'd found "on the outside portion of [the] shoe...projected blood, and some of those stains are very, very small, like high velocity mist..."

THE blood expert had also been active in the recreation of the crime, as he had been able to discern what no one else had contemplated previously. Kim's "pants had been removed, I mean, from *intuitive inference* at that scene, you, the way her legs are and, uh, *the pants had been removed from her and placed next to her head to where it's been manipulated* to the point that her hair was wound around and entwined with, had to be removed from that button."[217]

"Intuitive inference?" Was that the same as "interpreted gunshots?" There was another problem, as no photograph had depicted such an intertwining of Kim's hair with a button, and no report of any officer documented it either. Nonetheless, Englert had claimed an unnamed officer had told him that he/she had seen the hair/button intertwining, and from that he'd based his deduction.

On cross-examination, Mike had asked Englert if he was certified in blood

---

[214] When the ISP obtained his clothing, they hadn't labeled the socks as left or right.
[215] DNA revealed the blood to be Kim's.
[216] Emphasis mine.
[217] Emphasis mine.

spatter identification, referring to previous testimony of his in other trials. Englert had replied, "I think that I said that I had a pseudo certification, meaning qualification…and I, I correct [sic] myself on that, it's more qualified and recognized other than certification…I think I said pseudo certification as far as recognition."

It was simply a "matter of semantics" that he used the term certified rather than qualified, but Englert still didn't understand the term pseudo until Mike handed him a Black's Law Dictionary and had Englert read the definition of pseudo: "Uh, pseudo is false, counterfeit, pretended, spurious."

Englert, though, had his own definition of pseudo, which meant, he said, "sort of like it or likeness or akin to…"

As for his opinions in the Cooley hammer case, Englert had doubled-down on cross-examination and then some, once again claiming the 32 blows to the man's head by the claw hammer were "superficial."

Mike had asked if Cooley's skull had been fractured in two places, to which Englert had responded, "There was a fracture, but no penetration of skull by the claws from the hammer." I tried to follow the logic of that inference. Did he mean there would be no incapacitation of a person with a skull fracture if there was no penetration of the skull? That made no sense.

Englert then, as he often had during his testimony, wanted to talk of other cases to validate his findings in the Camm case. He had referred to two other, unnamed cases where victims hit themselves in the head with a hammer. He then, incredibly, made the following statement: "I don't know if it was total thirty-two, the number is innocuous, that doesn't mean anything, but they did hit themselves in the head, uh, with a hammer."

"The number doesn't mean anything?"

"No, sir, it does not, if you hit yourself in the head ten times or thirty-two times, you still hit yourself in the head."

Mike had then brought up another case of Englert's where he had opined a headboard on a bed had stains that were "consistent with high velocity," which, after testing, had turned out not to be blood at all. Mike had then connected that story with Stites and his similar description of blood/oil stains on the overhead garage door. The point of Mike's comparison was clear: protégé and mentor had apparently been alike in many ways.

As to Mike's deposition of Englert in Dave's case, Englert's scrutiny of the BACKBONE sweatshirt had also been lacking, for Englert had said he hadn't seen any blood on that garment. In fact, several bloodstains should have been readily apparent to a blood expert who had made a living examining bloodstains. One of those stains, in fact, on the left sleeve, had contained the DNA of Kim. On the stand, Englert had claimed he had "misspoke[n]" in his deposition and acknowledged the sweatshirt did have bloodstains after all.

During his examination of the Bronco, Englert had been able to find an item on the front passenger floorboard that had been overlooked by the evidence techs: a torn fingernail which had matched to Kim, making it even more probable she had fought ferociously with her attacker.

As to the debris found on Kim's side at the scene, Englert said that had been deposited on her when her body was moved, post-mortem, dismissing the possibility she may have been on the floor prior to her death.[218]

And then Mike had zeroed in on the phone calls, made on the day of Dave's arrest, between Stites and Englert. In his deposition with Mike, Stites had said, "Well, during [the] examination, when I saw the high velocity impact spatter on the shirt, I called Rod Englert and described to him the high velocity impact stain pattern that I'd found, and described it to him, and *he said that it was high velocity impact spatter*.[219] And then, of course, I relayed that information to Stan."

Mike had then asked, "Would you comment on the truthfulness or accuracy of Mr. Stites' statement there, Mr. Englert?"

Englert responded of the man he had been training, "That's inaccurate. It's making it sound like, just taking that out of context. I wouldn't do that, and that would be against everything that we stand for to make a statement over the phone regarding that…*that didn't happen the way it read there.*"[220]

And then, amazingly, Englert had accused Mike: "You didn't really interview him in depth when you asked that question." Stites' statement, Englert had then complained, was "under summarized."

It was interesting to visualize Englert squirming on the stand and making allegations a seasoned professional, as purportedly was Englert, should not make, in my opinion, while testifying: e.g., "You didn't really interview him in depth…" That was clutching a weak straw.

Most importantly, though, had been the importance of Stites' sworn testimony that he'd secured his boss' concurrence the stains were blood spatter *before* he had "of course…relayed that information to Stan." The affidavit in which Stites made his claims now had the backing of Rod Englert, purportedly one of the world's finest bloodstain experts.

While Englert had been on the stand, Mike had also wanted to know if he thought there could have been another person present when Dave had slaughtered his family. Englert had been quite confident: "There is no evidence

---

[218] Recall Dr. Nichols opined Kim had "probably crawled around on her knees" and had possibly been on her back supporting herself, thus explaining many of her injuries and the debris on her and her clothing.

[219] Emphasis mine.

[220] Emphasis mine.

to indicate more than one person committed this crime. I could find nothing to indicate that someone else was involved, nothing."

After reading Englert's testimony, I concluded this blood guy was in the same "expert" category as his protégé Stites, but Kitty was getting an entirely different assessment about the man who had his own definitions/uses of pseudo, artifacted, innocuous, superficial, certification, qualification, and under summarized. She had spoken, she said, with an attorney who had been in attendance during most of Englert's testimony, and contrary to my take on the man, the attorney had found Englert to be "compelling" to the jury who had been, he said, "mesmerized" by his testimony.

Clearly, Rod Englert was a lot more persuasive a witness than he appeared in the documents I had been reading.

CHAPTER 22

Camm Family Insights

Just who was the person of David Camm? In his final argument at trial, through a vivid and horrific picture Stan Faith had painted, Dave had become not just a man who'd lied and cheated, but a "bully… [who will]…make himself contrite, whatever the situation demands…" and nothing less than "one who destroy[ed] not only his family but ultimately himself in an orgy of annihilation."

But it had gotten even worse, as Dave had been described by Faith as a father who had betrayed the trust of his little girl by his "perversity," as he'd killed Jill in a "wild rage of hate" and had then "left Brad to die in the cold darkness of that horrible garage."

Kim had been spared of the horror he'd visited upon his children, Faith said, because Dave had probably surprised her and shot her as she was reaching into the car. He then was so devious, crafty, and heartless, that he had "manipulated" her clothing and the crime scene to make it seem like Kim had been a victim of a would-be rapist.

What I had learned to date of Dave didn't remotely jibe with Faith's depiction of him. Still, to help with building our timeline for the family, I needed to interview

> "WHEN I TOLD MICKEY AND DARRELL MY LIFE WAS PERFECT, I MEANT IT. IT WAS PERFECT."

family members, review documents and records, and determine not only their whereabouts but also see just what kind of man Dave had been in the months and weeks leading to the murders.

The family's financial records substantiated the fact Kim had been solidly in charge of that family aspect, as checks from their several bank accounts had her signature almost solely as the payee, including monthly premium payments to life insurance companies. The argument, therefore, Faith had used in the first trial that Kim had been unaware of insurance coverage was as bogus as was his argument Kim had been controlled by her dominating husband.

Those checks and credit statements also enabled us to track the family's expenditures and some movements or whereabouts. Almost every other Thursday, there had been payments to Schwann's, normally in amounts not exceeding $30. Those checks had Kim's signature but on occasion also Dave's.

From March until September 24, 15 checks had been signed by Kim and made payable to Karem's, which, I had known, had been the best butcher shop in New Albany for decades. During one of my jail visits with Dave, he'd told me Karem's was owned by Greg Karem, the husband of Debbie, who was Kim's younger sister. Their mother, Janice, had worked part-time at the store as well. One check, for $25.00, had been personally payable to Debbie on the Sunday before the murders, a birthday present from her sister.

Most of the Karem checks as well as the Kroger checks had been written on Sundays, as Kim had been in a routine with her grocery shopping; routines can and do attract the attention of others, including bad people.

I drifted off for a few moments and recalled that, in my most recent conversation with Dave, he'd told me while Kim and Jill had been shopping at Karem's and nearby Kroger's that same Sunday, he'd been watching a NASCAR race with Brad. His son's favorite driver had been the Rainbow Warrior Jeff Gordon,[221] while Dave, he told me, had been a Rusty Wallace fan. That race saw Jeff finish 9th and Rusty 8th, and Dave had recalled that he had ribbed his son.

Talk about cars had prompted me to ask Dave about the photo of the old Mustang and Corvette in his detached garage. That simple question had allowed Dave to return to fonder times, and it was good, very good, to hear him talk of his family:

"I had been working on the '73 Corvette for a year when Kim bought me a 1966 Mustang with money from her Aegon bonus.[222] The car needed a lot of work, wasn't running, and had to be towed from Louisville.

"After Brad saw the Mustang, though, he took an intense interest in it, and it quickly morphed into *his* Mustang. We then began talking about *his* Mustang and [how] when he turned 16, the car would be fully restored, and he'd drive his car and I'd drive my Corvette around Floyd County."

"Pretty neat memories, Dave."

"Yeah, and we'd look at Hot Rod magazines together, watch television shows specializing in old cars, and just have great conversations about the car," Dave had recalled. "From the wheels it would have, to its color, to how fast or loud it should be, Brad knew exactly what he wanted. He wanted it to be fast, but not too fast. He wanted it to be loud, but not overly loud. And it had to have a round, white shifter knob. He put a lot of thought into that car."

"I also saw a photo of you with Jill's T-ball team for that summer."

"That was a great summer. After I had left the State Police, I had a pretty normal schedule, allowing me to volunteer for the kids' activities. Jill was on

---

[221] Brad had a life-size cut-out of Jeff Gordon in his bedroom.

[222] Checks on their account verified the time and amount of the purchase.

a five to six-year-old T-ball team from school, and I was one of the assistant coaches. We all knew Jill would do well, and she did, as she was a natural athlete and was always tenacious, even on the bench where she cheered and yelled for her teammates. As much as she loved to compete, she loved to win even more."

"Kim was also involved, occasionally helping with the practices, but she wasn't in the team photo," continued Dave, adding, "but that's who she was, though. She did a lot of the work but never sought recognition."

"Let me tell you a funny story," Dave continued, as the jail confines couldn't constrain his memories. "During one game, one of Jilly-Jill's little teammates took a huge swing at the ball but lost control of the bat. I was a few feet behind the little guy and didn't have enough time to duck. That bat hit me squarely in my forehead."

"Ouch!"

"Oh, yeah, it hurt and took eight stitches to close the cut. But before I left for the hospital, I had to repeatedly tell the little guy we'd both be okay, but I don't think he was all that sure."

"Those are memories you won't ever lose, Dave."

"It was a really great summer. Kim and I went out on more dates with one another, we had lots of family outings, I was making much more money with UDI, didn't miss the State Police at all, my stress level was way down, and I had fewer migraine headaches. When I told Mickey and Darrell my life was perfect, I meant it. It was perfect."

There wasn't much I could say at the time, so I just nodded.

I returned to the financial records. Several of the Camm checks had been made payable to Graceland, the church in New Albany, which also had its own elementary, middle and high schools as well as after-school daycare. The cost of weekly summer daycare for the Camm family was $95, and on August 4th, Kim had issued them a check for $2,798 for the cost of the first semester of school for each child.

When Kitty said the Camm family had been doing well financially, she had been spot-on. They had been working hard; earning very good money; and investing in real estate, retirement accounts, and most importantly, their kids.

One of Kim's checks had been written to a fellow church member who, per Dave, had been helping Kim re-decorate the house. That lady, fellow church member Jan Poyser, had painted and hung wallpaper in the master bedroom.

As a church official, Poyser told me, she had often interacted with Kim,[223] whom she'd described as "warm, caring, sweet and a wonderful mother,"

---

[223] Recall that Kim had been the church treasurer.

further explaining the kids had always been clean, well-dressed, and obedient with excellent manners. It had been obvious to all, she'd said, the kids had been raised very well.

On Wednesdays, Poyser had been the second and third grade teacher, and Brad, one of her students, a "delightful little boy," had been conscientious, polite, and the last student to be disruptive or to cause problems. By the age of seven, he had even memorized the 66 books of the Bible. That impressive feat had fascinated me, not only because the little guy had done so, but because he had *wanted* to do so.

Bradley made this poster, entitled, "Best Family Rules," in his church class, and it was proudly placed on the refrigerator door in the Camm home. # 7, "don't scream to loud," is unintentionally hilarious.

The last night she saw Brad, however, he had been upset because he had forgotten to return a paper he'd taken home and his parents had signed. Poyser comforted him and told him to just bring it the next week, which he'd quickly promised to do. "He always wanted to please others," she said.

As for Dave possibly molesting his little girl, Poyser emphatically stated, "I don't see that at all," further explaining Dave would often come in the church and pick up his kids on Sundays, Monday nights from church council meetings, and Wednesday evening dinners and activities. She then described Dave as a "loving father who had a loving relationship" with his children. There was "no way" molestation occurred, she said, further emphasizing Kim, the very protective and loving mother, would never have allowed her children to be harmed by anyone.

I specifically asked Poyser if she had seen any indication of Kim's leaving Dave. She responded first by stating Kim had been the same person, in the three weeks prior to the murders, as she had always been. She then asked me, "Who's going to be painting your bedroom if you're going to leave your husband? That doesn't make sense." And no, she added, the ISP had never spoken with her.

Another active church member was Steve Bobo who had known the Camm family well. He spoke of visiting the family, in their home, to solicit a financial pledge for the building of the FLC. While there, he had made a comment to Dave as to how it was good an ISP officer could afford such a nice home. The quick response from Dave had been to compliment his wife, saying their home wouldn't have been nearly as nice without Kim and the income she earned.

The night prior to her murder, Kim had visited with Bobo and his wife during the church dinner. They'd had their newborn granddaughter with them, and Kim had made a comment about the possibility of Dave and her having another child. After Dave's arrest, Bobo had thought about her comment a lot, stating Kim certainly wouldn't have made it if there had been any trouble in their marriage.

Karla Farnsley, a cousin of Dave's and a good friend of Kim's, had dropped by the Camm home the night before the murders. Kim had graciously offered her home to host a baby shower for Farnsley, and she was dropping off the invitations to Kim, who'd been busy at the time bathing Brad and Jill. While waiting for Kim in the living room, she and Dave had spoken, and he'd seemed relaxed and normal.

After a few minutes, Kim had come out of the bathroom, and the two women had talked. Brad had soon followed his mother, still partially wet, while Farnsley could hear Jill laughing and splashing in the tub.

After Kim and Farnsley had spoken about planning the baby shower, Kim then had told Farnsley she hadn't been satisfied with their family dentist, had wanted to switch to another, and then Kim had asked about Karla's dentist. Farnsley had provided his name and telephone number.[224] During her entire visit, Kim had seemed a busy, normal, engaged mother who had been eager to host the baby shower. If Kim had been going to leave Dave, Karla asked, why would she plan to host an event at her house just weeks in the future?

Farnsley was surprised that no one from the ISP had ever contacted her, particularly after she had been told that some of those baby shower invitations had been found in Kim's purse.

---

[224] One of the voice mails on Kim's work telephone, left late in the afternoon on the day of her murder, had been from the new dentist's office.

Debbie Ter Vree, Dave's youngest aunt and neighbor, had also provided great insight into Kim. The two had been very close, and Kim had not been, as Faith had proclaimed in the first trial, a subservient and quiet wife who had acquiesced to everything Dave wanted. Far from it, Debbie said, Kim had been an intelligent, resourceful, hard-working wife and mother who was, as with most working mothers, a great multi-tasker and whose primary focus was on her children. That she was murdered while fighting for the lives of her children hadn't surprised Debbie.

Daughter Hannah Ter Vree had played with her cousins Brad and Jill practically every day and routinely eaten with the Camm family as had Brad and Jill with the Ter Vree family. Ter Vree was confident there had been no issues with the children and was emphatic Dave would never have harmed his children in any manner.

Bob, Debbie's husband, recalled the dedication of the playhouse across Lockhart Road on the Saturday before the murders, telling me it had been a wonderful family event, with a pitch-in dinner, volleyball, kids playing, and Jill running and playing all over the place. Bob, a golfer, also recalled that Dave had given Jill a golf club and that she'd made several good ball strikes.

Then, laughing out loud, Bob recalled having stood in line in front of the desserts and then feeling a punch on his leg. Looking down, he'd seen Jill, a smile from ear to ear, with a balled-up fist, demanding, "I want some cake!" Bob, smiling, told me that was 100% Jill.

Two Saturdays before the murders, Dave told me he had bought four Indiana University (IU) hats for the family, and they'd gone to the Indiana-Kentucky football game in Lexington, Kentucky. They had sat and cheered for IU in the midst of Kentucky fans, and a woman behind them commented that Dave had the "perfect" family. It was, he told me, one of the best compliments anyone could have made.

Leland Lockhart, Dave's uncle, also provided his observations of Dave's so-called "strange behavior" after the murders. Leland had rushed to the scene after getting a call from Nelson, immediately gone to his nephew, and put his arm around him but it had been like "putting my arm around a post." At other times, Leland said he had been a "walking zombie" and then, two days later, his nephew had been "very angry" as Dave watched the ISP trashing his lawn while not allowing him to retrieve burial clothing for his family from his home.

Three days after the murders, Leland said he had preached the "toughest sermon" he'd ever preached, entitled, "We Can't Know God's Mind, But We Know His Heart." Everyone in the service had been very emotional, including, of course, Dave. Afterwards, Dave had hugged and thanked him, telling Leland he'd found comfort and solace in his words, knew of the love of his family and friends, and knew that God's love was with them.

After the service, a still very emotional Dave had spoken outside to the gathered press, which had assembled en masse. Dave had said he "wanted [his] babies back." He'd then issued an impassioned plea that whoever was responsible should give themselves up. For Leland, Dave's words were "raw emotion," but for the ISP and others, his demeanor and crying were fake. It was a "Susan Smith" moment, some had claimed.[225]

I also learned Kim had taken Brad and Jill to a community pool throughout the summer where Brad had shown a very strong aptitude for swimming. He had previously tried baseball and basketball, but those sports hadn't held his interest. Swimming had, however, and he'd rapidly improved, so much so that Phillip told Dave of a friend who was a swim coach in New Albany. Dave had quickly contacted him and signed his son up for the team, with Brad doing really well in the first weeks of practice. Both father and son had been looking forward to Brad's first meet on Saturday, September 30.

Based upon Brad's enthusiastic embrace of swimming, Kim and Dave had spoken of possibly buying a home with a swimming pool. As such, Donnie, Dave's brother, had told me Dave, Kim, and the kids had visited him and his daughters, Lauren and Cara, in New Albany a short time prior to the murders. His daughters, almost the exact same ages as Brad and Jill, had also been classmates with them. All had walked around Donnie's New Albany neighborhood, looking at new homes under construction. Donnie recalled, "It was a tossup as to which kid was more excited about the possibility the cousins would be neighbors."

Sam had provided all the business documents related to Dave's schedule, customer contacts and contracts, messages, and customer feedback. Dave's whereabouts in the days before the murders had been pretty much spelled out, hour by hour, and the reviews from customers had variously described him as "friendly, professional, courteous," and one had even noted Dave as "one of the nicest guys we ever met."

One could understand why Faith and the ISP hadn't wanted to delve into the real Dave Camm's background, for to do so would have revealed Kim as

---

[225] Susan Smith was the South Carolina mother of two sons, ages 3 years and 14 months. After drowning both of her sons at a lake, she had claimed they had been carjacked by a black man. Her emotional pleas, for several days on national television, had caused many to believe she was faking her story, which, in fact, she was. She later confessed, and her children were found drowned, still strapped in their car seats. The police in the Smith investigation, however, meticulously followed the leads, and it was through hard evidence, and not behavior analysis speculation, which convicted her.

an industrious worker and loving mother and wife who, although reserved, had been a woman of her own mind.

Dave also hadn't been the monster Faith and the ISP had created but a hard-working husband, loving father, and family member who was dependable and well-liked. Also importantly, he and Kim had been as close as ever. In the months leading up to the murders, when he had described his life as "perfect," Dave, I was convinced, had only been telling the truth.

CHAPTER 23

Bond? Seriously?

In preparation for Dave's bond hearing and later trial, Kitty and Stacy had communicated with other defense attorneys in an effort to determine the identity of a counterpart in Warrick County who would educate them on Judge Aylsworth, the culture of the county, and other tangibles and non-tangibles they needed to know to try the case effectively. The overwhelming recommendation was Anthony Long. Anthony, with almost 35 years of law practice, had been the county prosecutor for 16 years, knew the judge well, was involved in many official county roles, and knew practically every person in the county.

Prior to the bond hearing on January 26th, the three of us met with Anthony, and he was as advertised. Lawyerly and knowledgeable, one could see his personality and demeanor had served him well in the courtroom. After sharing his views on Aylsworth, among which was that he was a low-key guy who expected courtroom counsel to be knowledgeable and mannerly, he also told us he had Mark

> "MY ASSESSMENT ABSOLUTELY IS THAT DAVE CAMM IS INNOCENT."
>
> "THAT'S A PRETTY BROAD STATEMENT, WOULDN'T YOU SAY?"
>
> "NO."

Mabrey, a former police officer, do his investigative work. Mark, he said, would be the best person to secure the backgrounds of potential jurors. After jury selection, Anthony would not be involved in the case.[226]

As for trying to get bond for Dave, and since visual information is markedly better than mere oral presentation, we had developed a 56-slide PowerPoint Presentation which articulated the errors, misrepresentations, and outright falsehoods used by Clemons and Faith in the original affidavit. Complementing that, we had also articulated more disinformation, falsehoods, and omissions from Gilbert's and Henderson's affidavit.

Walking in for that hearing, in the relatively new Warrick County Courthouse, we found the courtroom almost full, including several members present from the Camm, Lockhart, and Renn families. There were also several

---

[226] Henderson and Owen would be assisted by the Warrick County prosecutor in jury selection.

reporters from the Louisville news media, including one who would turn out to be a stereotypical newsie.[227]

Regardless, Kitty would take the first part of the argument, and Stacy would finalize and summarize our points. First, Kitty asked the judge to take judicial notice of the appellate decision. She then moved to introduce the first PC affidavit. Henderson objected as to its relevancy, claiming the defense was only "trying to rehash everything" as he wanted the judge not to waste time and to focus only on the pending affidavit.

Kitty responded the defense was just trying to show "the weakness of the case" with the additional and repeated mischaracterizations of the evidence as well as Clemons being "inept." Judge Aylsworth admitted, "I know far less than anyone else involved in the case at this point [and] I will probably err on the admission rather than the exclusion of the evidence." That was good news, for the judge was receptive to being educated.

In her opening statement, Kitty was direct and to the point: "We believe that there is no probable cause to even hold David Camm on these counts… [and]…there has to be a probable cause determination" to hold him in custody. She then schooled the judge as to the areas that exposed the State's weak case: 1) alibi witnesses, 2) exculpatory forensic evidence, 3) evidence of David Camm's actual innocence, and 4) the law of the case.

After telling Judge Aylsworth of the details of the basketball games, she had each of the 10 men, all present, who had played with Dave to stand and be recognized by the court. She then had Tom Jolly stand. After their introductions, Kitty provided a summary of each one's testimony, dryly noting that "even today, we have some…players that have never been interviewed [in person] by a police officer."

Kitty then offered as exhibits—and Henderson didn't object to—the introduction of the ISP's DNA findings and a copy of Jill's autopsy report.

Next on Kitty's target was the amended affidavit filed by Gilbert in November 2004, although Henderson had surprised us just before the hearing by amending that affidavit, omitting the allegations from the prison informant.[228] It was now an amended amended affidavit.

Henderson had downplayed the removal of the information of James Hatton, still not publicly identified, the day before, to Channel 32 WLKY

---

[227] He tried, in my opinion, to come across as knowledgeable, fair, and empathic in person but, once on air, would put his own spin on the day's events, oftentimes completely ignoring salient points made by Stacy and Kitty. He was either ignorant or stupid, but didn't care as long as he was in front of the camera and could hear himself speak with great authority.

[228] Recall the first affidavit of Gilbert had only the allegations of James B. Hatton and not Jeremy Bullock.

reporter Abby Miller: "There's more than ample probable cause without that and I think for the purposes of the hearing tomorrow, which is a bond hearing, I don't think it's applicable." Translation: If the CI weren't part of their probable cause he couldn't be intensely cross-examined and his story fall apart on the stand in front of the Judge.[229]

Kitty then vividly demonstrated the weakness of the State's case, first by articulating the original allegations which Henderson had dropped: 1) the manipulation of the crime scene, 2) the existence of a witness hearing three gunshots, and the 3) 9:00 p.m. ending of the games.

Next, she correctly talked of the mischaracterization of Jill's injury as one to her vagina rather her labia, the omission of other possible causes of Jill's injuries, the blatant attempt to imply the sexual devices found in Kim's dresser drawer were used on Jill, the omission of the revelation Jill's DNA found on the bedspread was likely saliva, and the blatant intentional misrepresentation of the 6:19 p.m. call as occurring an hour later. Kitty also gave more insight into Dave's purported confession to Clemons and Gibson, from which Gilbert had conveniently omitted the words, "my wife is looking down from heaven shaking her head."

Judge Aylsworth was then told of the complete omission of the BACKBONE sweatshirt, which had unknown female DNA in several locations and, of course, unknown male DNA in the collar. Kitty then spoke of the unidentified fingerprints on the passenger door jamb, the location of which was "consistent with the shooting of the children" in the car.

The appellate court comment, "We are left with a definite possibility that the jury might have found Camm not guilty if it had not been exposed to a substantial amount of improperly admitted and unfairly prejudicial evidence," was very compelling, Kitty noted. "Not only is there not probable cause... [but] the evidence is weak, and the presumption is not strong."

Kitty then called Jeff Lockhart to the stand, and Jeff articulated his previous testimony that Dave had been in the gym at all times. On cross, Henderson engaged in the same tactic as had Faith in the first trial. No, not every exact minute had he seen Dave; no, he hadn't known the exact length of an individual game.

Sam was up next. "Dave played every game up until I went in for him," he said, and then identified, as had Jeff Lockhart, a photo of the interior of the gym where he had seen Dave and Tom speaking with one another during the one game Dave had sat out.

---

[229] We later learned Henderson, Kessinger, and Gilbert had traveled to Columbus, Indiana, just two days prior to the hearing to meet with Hatton and warn him his name would be known publicly. Per Gilbert, it was for "his own safety." Henderson had obviously later changed his mind about using Hatton.

And then Kitty asked Sam if he was still helping in Dave's defense. Sam's response made us all proud to be on the defense team. "Dave Camm's innocent. He didn't kill his family. I was with Dave that evening, your Honor, I was with him at the gym that evening from, I got there a little after seven 'till a little before nine. Dave Camm was at that gym. And Kim and her kids were killed someplace between 7:30 and 8:00 that evening. So I know Dave wasn't there."

Sam was speaking from the heart, as he continued, "And I'm involved in this not only for Dave, but I'm involved in it because somebody killed my family…and I'm not going to quit 'til we find out who did that. And I will spend every penny I've got and every minute of time I've got in order to do that. Yes, I've been active and I'm going to remain active."

Sam's profound comments led to Tom Jolly's taking the stand. He pointed out to the judge the same location as had Jeff and Sam before him as to where he and Dave had spoken for 10–15 minutes while Dave had sat out one game, Next, Tom said he had then seen Dave go to the sideline and warm up for re-entry into the next game.

"Absolutely not!" was Tom's response if he had ever seen Dave leave the gym. Dave had been there the entire time Tom had been there, from 8:10 or 8:15 p.m. until he left around 9:05 p.m. And no, Tom said, no police officer had ever interviewed him on what he had seen at the gym that evening.

Henderson then began his cross-examination of Tom, almost sneering, "What did you see in the neighborhood that night…did you see BACKBONE?" It was an obvious attempt to denigrate the existence of anyone else who could have murdered Kim, Brad, and Jill.

I was the next witness. From years of experience, I spoke briefly as to how a large investigation should be organized and managed. Having interviewed all of the ball players, I also testified as to the little initial weight given to them by the ISP and then summarized the testimony of all that none had seen Dave leave the gym at any time after he entered, no one had seen him missing from the gym, no one had seen any blood on him or his clothing, and all those remaining had said Dave left the gym no earlier than 9:15 p.m.

To help me finally be paid for my work, Kitty first asked me how many investigators had testified in Dave's first trial. Fifteen, I responded, plus the prosecutor's investigators, all the while Dave's defense had but one, Debbie McDaniel, and now me. The disparity in numbers was obvious and hopefully compelling to the judge.

As to why I had gotten involved without any assurance of pay, my response was "I'm here for the defense, but I'm also here to seek and secure the truth, and that's never changed regardless of working with the defense or not. My assessment absolutely is that Dave Camm is innocent."

On cross, Henderson first asked, "That's a pretty broad statement, wouldn't you say?"

"No."

Henderson then took me to task for making such a conclusion in the two plus months I had been on the case. My response was succinct: "I made that conclusion based upon interviews of these witnesses…[the] conclusion based upon what they've said previously, based upon…my assessment of their veracity, and the impossibility that Dave Camm could have left that gym without anyone noticing and moving…according to the State Police, five minutes and 30 seconds one way, 11 minutes [total travel time] and then shooting and killing his family. So, yeah, that's my assessment."

"And you're willing to work for free because you believe that he's innocent?"

"If it comes to that, yes, sir."

Henderson knew when to stop, and he did.

After my testimony, Stacy then took over and introduced an internal memo from Verizon. "On February 11, 2002, as a result of an inquiry of the defense attorney in the Dave Camm court case, Verizon discovered a flaw in the process that records the time of some long distance calls made through…Georgetown [and numerous other towns]…[with] the *origination time for some calls [were] shown as one hour later than the calls were actually made*."[230]

Stacy then called a Verizon billing manager, David Eschweiler, who correctly testified the Louisville area was on daylight savings time (DST) but the rest of Indiana did not recognize the same time zone. Prior to the implementation in April 2000, of the small part of Indiana on DST, Verizon employees, unaware the computer had been correct, had adjusted the computer to account for the change. Thus, all the bills in the affected part of Southern Indiana had origination times one hour later than the calls had actually been made, including the 7:19 p.m. call from Dave's house on September 28th. The correct time of the call had been 6:19 p.m.

Eschweiler then made an astounding comment, telling the court that in the first trial, "I believe there was confusion brought into this process." He then testified he had spoken to an investigator a month before, telling him the same thing about the one-hour difference in the billing versus the actual time of the call.

"How do you feel about your conversation with that investigator?"

"Again, disappointed."

"Do you think he listened to you?"

"No."

---

[230] Emphasis added.

Stacy then exhibited the amended amended PC affidavit to Eschweiler, which asserted the call from Dave's house had been made at 7:19 p.m. "Did you tell the detective that it was not made at 7:19 but it was made at 6:19?"

"I clearly told him that."

Henderson then mischaracterized Eschweiler's testimony as "tired of being in Boonville, New Albany, and being questioned, you're just tired..."

"I did not say I was tired..."

After several minutes of trying to get Eschweiler to admit he was the one who had been wrong and not the billing records, Henderson finally gave up.

Stacy then introduced a table showing the differences in the assertions in the original probable cause affidavit and the evidence introduced in the first trial, contradicting those assertions, all to show the State's "rush to judgment." She went through each one and concluded, "The only thing you're left with... is the subjective opinion of Robert Stites...and that is a contradicted opinion."

On a roll, Stacy summed up the case for bond: "the state doesn't have probable cause...[the] case is weak...[and] we ask you to release Dave on his own recognizance or at least set a bond."

Henderson's exhibits were the first trial transcript, Dave's first bond hearing, and the subsequent hearings during which bond had been denied. He then introduced the order of conviction and sentencing order and the other order committing Dave to the Department of Corrections. He methodically went through each verdict of guilty and introduced those verdict forms.

I didn't get it. Henderson was asking the judge not to issue a bond on the merits of their case but on the fact that Dave had been convicted before, despite that fact that his conviction had come from an unfair and prejudiced trial. Translation: we won before because the prosecutor cheated, and now we're offering the scorecard from that trial as evidence that you should deny bail.

After all the arguments, the judge had very few questions, the first of which was "What is your assessment with regard to Mr. Camm as a pre-trial flight risk...?

WOW! No one at the defense table said or did anything, but all of us were stunned by the judge's first question. Could bond really be a possibility?

Henderson, of course, said because Dave was facing another 195-year sentence, he'd be a flight risk. Kitty responded with law and said if the State's case were weak, the court should set a bond. She also referred to Dave's strong ties to the community, the 20 or more family members present, as well as others who would do whatever to support him and to ensure he would comply with the court's orders.

The judge was then told Dave didn't have a prior criminal history, didn't have a passport, and had never been named on any protective order.

But then the judge shifted course, now wanting to set a trial date. Kitty responded that setting a date would be difficult because Henderson hadn't responded to her request for all of their discovery made weeks before. Included in that was the demand to have the DNA profile on the sweatshirt run through CODIS. Henderson responded that he'd comply and then said he wanted a trial date of March or April, a date which was unreasonable inasmuch as dozens of depositions couldn't be finished by then.

Before Kitty could interject, Henderson then wanted the judge to know he was offended by the characterization of the allegations in the State's PC affidavits as intentional misrepresentations: "I take exception to anything under my watch...that I've intentionally misrepresented. There's been nothing...and I take exception to that in a large way."

The offended prosecutor then impugned the mere possibility there was any evidence of a "quote, unquote, 'this real killer,'" practically laughing at the suggestion. I was reminded of Faith's repudiation of the possibility of someone other than Dave being the killer, when he referred to the mythical person as "the big one-armed hairy stranger."

Regardless, the sooner the better to start the trial for Henderson, with his further stating he didn't anticipate any forensic or lab issues in complying with the need for discovery.

Judge Aylsworth finally decided on August 8th and then announced, "A bond amount in the amount of $20,000 cash shall be established for Mr. Camm effective this date." He then added all the other caveats such as travel restrictions, employment limitations, home detention, and the need for electronic monitoring. We all caught our breath as there was an audible stir in the courtroom gallery.

When asked if he had any problems in complying with any of the aspect of bond, Dave responded, "I don't have any problem, your Honor."

Henderson was quick on his feet, demanding the judge issue an immediate protective order forbidding Dave to have any contact with the Renn or Karem family. That demand hadn't been based upon any evidence, but there was no objection, and the order was quickly approved.

After the judge approved funds to pay for our own investigation, Stacy articulated the need to fund the defense's efforts for our own laboratory analysis and to secure opinions from other experts, noting the State, in the first trial, had spent $612,000 just on private labs and experts, a total of 14 in all.

In response, Henderson had the president of the Floyd County Council, Ted Heavrin,[231] tell the court of the dire financial status of Floyd County,

---

[231] Heavrin was also the Chief Deputy of the Floyd County Sheriff's Department.

which was in part due to the high cost of the first trial. The judge was polite but didn't budge on approving the funding needed to defend Dave.

A quick private meeting with Dave occurred after the judge's gavel terminated the hearing. He was excited, pleased, and very thankful. Nonetheless, it would take a day to process him out of the system, get him outfitted with an ankle bracelet, and have Sam secure the $20,000. Dave wouldn't be released until the next day, but the next night, for the first time in four and a half years, he'd be sleeping in a bed that wasn't behind steel bars.

Outside the courtroom, Dave's father Don was almost in shock as he was barely able to utter softly that he was "completely overwhelmed."[232] Donnie, Dave's older brother and never at a loss for words, was more confident: "We felt like all along it was the right thing and I think the judge agreed that the prosecution's case had no merit and that's why he set the bond so low. We can't wait to go down and get him."[233]

Obviously, Henderson wasn't pleased. The next day, the prosecutor, still smarting from being told his case was very weak, sent Gilbert to Warrick County where he obtained confirmation that Judge Aylsworth had worked for Anthony Long as a Deputy Prosecutor several years previously. On February 2, Henderson sent Gilbert back to Warrick County where he filed a motion for a Change of Venue of Judge.[234]

Speaking with Carried Harned of WAVE-TV on the day of that filing, Henderson fumed there was at least an appearance of "bias or prejudice" due to the Judge's decision to give Dave a $20,000 bond and $75,000 for forensic experts and our own investigation. He was also piqued the judge had given us permission to have Anthony Long for local assistance.

Others besides Henderson weren't happy. WLKY-TV's Julia Harding was on the streets of New Albany the same afternoon and received comments from the public ranging from "I think he's guilty," to "a lot of people are upset and hate him," to "he's guilty until proven himself innocent."

Not one person in Floyd County, of course, said the following: "David Camm got railroaded by a fake expert and was screwed by a very shoddy investigation. I feel sorry for this husband and father who couldn't properly grieve for the loss of his wife and children and am outraged he, an innocent man, has spent four and a half years in prison. We need to have real accountability on the part of the State Police and prosecutor."

Within a few days of Henderson's filing, the Judge held a hearing and

---

[232] Kyle Lowry, *$20,000 Bond Set for David Camm*, New Albany Tribune, January 27, 2005.

[233] Ibid.

[234] Henderson could have filed his motion via email, but letting the judge know of an ISP detective's personal visit to the court was intentional, I believed.

refused to grant Henderson's motion to change judges. As it would turn out, we weren't through with the issue of venue, for within the next few weeks, an earthshattering development would occur that would launch the entire Camm case into an utterly surreal orbit.

SECTION III
"Charles Who?"

CHAPTER 24
"Who Is It?"

The day after the hearing, while Sam was busy arranging for the $20,000 bail and Dave had been outfitted for his ankle bracelet, Kitty and Stacy focused on researching, vetting, and then speaking with new experts in the fields of bloodstain interpretation, gunshot residue, ballistics, and metal shavings.[235]

Meanwhile, I was still completing the timelines and speaking with those who had interacted with the Camm family prior to the murders. One such person was an ISP chaplain who knew well the entire family. My attempt to arrange an interview went nowhere as he was brusque and rude and refused even to entertain the possibility of meeting.

> "THE FUCKING WHODUNIT IS SOLVED, BUT THEY WON'T ACCEPT IT. THEY'VE GOT THEIR MINDS MADE UP. IT'LL ALWAYS BE DAVE."

Incarceration & Indiana State Prison

I was also getting ready to travel to the Indiana State Prison, but first, I needed to speak with Dave. Now a somewhat free man, he was still in Sam and Carol's basement when I met with him; perhaps it was more comfortable for him to be in a closed confinement, but I didn't ask.

My goal was to get as much information from Dave as possible about his interactions with staff and offenders at the PCU. I'd soon travel to Michigan

---

[235] The existence of gunshot residue, aka GSR, is a forensic field which can be quite subjective, as the significance of GSR is usually in the eye of the beholder. Once thought to be definitive as to determining a shooter with the old paraffin test on the hands, it is anything but, as GSR can be transferred from a victim by touch and then transferred onto one's clothing or pockets. Dave had fewer than five GSR particles in his pocket, which also had traces of metal shavings, the result of wearing the shorts while grinding metal and doing body work on cars he was restoring, rather than the shavings from the ejection of ammo rounds from a semi-automatic weapon. GSR and minute shavings can survive multiple washings and literally hang around for months or years.

City[236] to speak with several people to determine their knowledge of and comments made by Hatton and Bullock and others, as there was little chance those two were going to be the only ones to fabricate stories. Once the word had spread about the investigators using imprisoned felons as informants, we had to be prepared for an onslaught of new "witnesses."

We quickly got down to business. Dave told me one of the first guys he had encountered in the PCU was Charles Gilroy.[237] Charles had been serving his second bit in the DOC for a burglary-related conviction[238] and had been in PCU not because he had stiffed anyone on a debt or was a molester or a snitch, but rather because a CO mandated it after Charles and an offender had gotten into a fight; the other guy had been convicted of murder.

Although Charles had endured a tough childhood and had only gotten to the 8th grade, Dave said Charles was a well-spoken and intelligent person who had greatly respected an uncle of his, a former police officer. Unlike many offenders, Charles didn't dislike the police, knew Dave had been a trooper, and told Dave if he had any issue from anyone because of his law enforcement background, he'd help take care of the problem.

Charles had been one of the first to warn Dave about snitches, referring to those guys as "dick-riders" or guys who had kissed ass frequently and without apparent reason. They had a reason, though, and that was to get close to others and ultimately get information they would be able to use later for their own benefit.

Charles was also direct and had asked Dave if he had killed his family. "I told him and all others who asked I was innocent," said Dave, matter-of-factly.

Dave also had become friends with other inmates. When I expressed some degree of curiosity, Dave said it was impossible to have been an imprisoned hermit. There had to be human interaction, he said, if not just to exist in an environment as harmoniously as possible, but also to maintain one's sanity. A select few of those had become friends, Dave said, "but that didn't mean I condoned any of their crimes."

Mike Stamper was one of those friends. Together with Dave, their responsibility had been preparing food trays for the four units in the PCU; they in turn had provided the trays to the four porters who had distributed the

---

[236] The driving distance from Bloomington to Michigan City, just south of Lake Michigan, was about 220 miles and took over four hours to drive.

[237] The names of the offenders as well as the Correctional Officers have been changed.

[238] The ISP had its own internal jargon, most of which was used throughout the DOC; Dave said he had learned quickly the meanings of kite, bit, slam, chomo, the bitch, and other terms.

food to A, B, C, and D blocks, which housed as many as 15 offenders each.

The four porters had been convicted of multiple murders, drug peddling, bank robbery, or child molesting. Mike would be honest with me, Dave said, as would three of the other four porters, including one with whom he had exercised and lifted weights on a daily basis. The last guy was problematic, as Dave reminded me one of the criteria needed for membership in the PCU was informing on others, oftentimes falsely.

Another guy, Dave said, was John Carter who had once gotten upset with Dave after Dave had left his breakfast at Carter's cell, without his knowledge, which had allowed the food to get cold. That would be a trivial issue for most, but a significant one in prison. As a result, Dave thought he might still carry a grudge.[239]

Dave gave me additional input on several other guys, known to Dave by their nicknames. "Friar Tuck" had been a straight-shooter who, once he knew I was Dave's defense investigator, would be helpful if at all possible. "Bam-Bam," a self-proclaimed mass-murderer, had, for years, been running up debts in the PCU and couldn't be trusted. "Westside," from Indianapolis, had been a decent guy and a tattoo artist; tattooing was forbidden in prison, but everyone knew the practice had still existed.

Everyone in the unit, after the airing of the *48 Hours* episode "Murder on Lockhart Road,"[240] in 2002, had known about his case with some then calling him a child molester or chomo. After one guy did so, Dave had threatened to fight him, but the guy had stopped jawing. For anyone who asked, Dave said he had repeatedly maintained his innocence and never said anything whatsoever which could have implied, much less vocalized, that he'd killed his family.

Unlike Hatton, whom he didn't remember, Dave had recalled Jeremy Bullock, nicknamed "Joker." He'd been in the PCU for repeatedly stiffing other inmates for loans for commissary and money and was a well-known snitch. He had once claimed, two years before, he had terminal cancer and was gone from the PCU for over three weeks, Dave said, supposedly for treatment in an outside hospital. Most of the guys had thought he was testifying somewhere, a claim Joker had later denied.

Staff and Correctional Officers (CO) had also interacted with Dave on a daily basis. He first told of the "Cat Lady," a CO Dave had seen practically every day. She'd been professional but also fair and compassionate, as she had often brought toys and other items for several cats owned by a few of the inmates. Dave said she would be honest and open with me.

---

[239] I'd later speak with John, on three occasions in fact, and contrary to harboring any ill will towards Dave, what he told me was insightful and helpful, although he wasn't a snitch.

[240] CBS Television, October 2002.

Another officer who'd been friendly was CO Cox who had told Dave, when she'd heard about his case being overturned, that it was one of the best things she had experienced in her eight years as a CO. Ms. Jackson, the "Shakedown Lady," and Ms. G were three other friendly but professional COs who would provide their honest thoughts and assessments.

Dave also gave me the names of two other officers who hadn't been as friendly or supportive with him, although he stated it wasn't over any disciplinary issues or write-ups since he'd had none. "They thought I was getting special treatment since I had been placed in PCU," Dave offered, "but it wasn't special to me. I wanted to be in Gen Pop, since there was a lot more freedom there."

With each succeeding time I spent with him, Dave opened up a little more, and I often listened rather than ask questions. Talking about prison staff and offenders allowed him to segue into his first nights at the Reception and Diagnostic Center (RDC), located west of Indianapolis in Plainfield. It was the initial stop for practically all those recently sentenced. There, all had to be psychologically assessed, tested, and ultimately assigned to their next prison.

Dave, though, had actually gone to RDC *before* he was sentenced, as practically everyone had wanted him out of Floyd County as soon as possible after his trial. After his assessment, he had returned to New Albany for sentencing and then had gone to his permanent home. "Before I had left the county, though, Randy Hubbard drove me to Georgetown. My grandfather, Amos, had survived the trial, but he had died days later. I know my conviction finally killed him. Randy took me to the funeral home where I told Papaw goodbye. I'll always be grateful to Randy for that kindness."[241]

Once he got to the RDC, he said, "I had never before been in a prison. I had been in jail for 18 months and was accustomed to following orders, but prison was very different. I was first taken to a room where I stripped and then was subjected to a full body search, including cavity searches. Jokes are made of cavity searches, Dunner, but they're anything but funny."

Dave had then taken the mandatory shower followed by a powdering with some type of disinfectant and had been given a haircut that was the next thing to a complete shaving. "I was almost bald," he recalled. After having been issued his prison clothing, he then had seen a doctor and dentist and had been given an appointment to see a psychologist.

"It was really surreal," he said, "From the RDC, I could see, a short distance away, the Indiana Law Enforcement Academy (ILEA)." It was where, 13 years

---

[241] Randy Hubbard was the Floyd County Sheriff from 1999–2007 and before that, the New Albany Chief of Police who was good friends with Dave and helped him decide on a law enforcement career. Hubbard died in 2013.

before, he had spent 18 weeks learning to be a trooper. "It was a bitter irony," he said softly. "I thought over and over and over, 'How has this happened to me? What happened to my life? I don't belong in prison.'"

I said nothing.

"Anyway," he said, "back in the academy, we had been taught we were 'Indiana's Finest.'" I had known that all cities and counties, save for the largest ones, had sent their police recruits to the ILEA,[242] and all had intermingled with one another. The ISP had also used the same facilities, but had separated their recruits from others. As opposed to the khaki brown uniforms worn by other recruits, future troopers wore the traditional blue ISP uniform they would eventually wear when they had graduated.

Dave had fiercely believed in the "Indiana's Finest" motto, he said. "While I knew we weren't any smarter than other police officers, my instructors and my pride told me we were the crème de la crème in Indiana. If you didn't believe it, all you had to do was ask any one of us."

That pride, he concluded, was maybe the most significant reason he had been arrested. "The ISP not only wouldn't but couldn't admit to being wrong. Once they concluded it was me, they couldn't accept the possibility it wasn't me. To admit that would be to admit they weren't 'Indiana's Finest.'"

I couldn't argue with his reasoning. I did have to ask, though, about his session with the prison psychologist. "Did you tell him you were innocent?"

"Sure, although it was a her. And she listened to me for several minutes. Did she believe me? I don't know. She was kind, though, and listened. If I was in her position, I probably wouldn't have believed me. Not because I'm not innocent, but because she had to screen hundreds of offenders a year. Would you believe *any* of them?"

"Before a few months ago? Probably not."

I soon left, but for the next few weeks, I spoke with Dave on several other occasions, and began drafting subpoena requests for Kitty and Stacy and doing my due diligence on those I'd interview at the ISP.

Not reluctant to respond in kind to Henderson's public spinning of his narrative of the case, Kitty had always been worth a good quote to the media. The judge had, however, had enough, and had issued a media gag order for both sides on February 7.

Stacy, meanwhile, had been compiling her ever-growing list of evidence that needed to be forensically tested, including running the unknown BACKBONE DNA through CODIS. Due to Henderson's unwillingness to comply with his own commitment to have that done, Kitty and Stacy had filed

---

[242] Marion County, for example, trained their own sheriff's deputies as did the City of Indianapolis their own officers.

a motion with the court on February 23, requesting the judge order Henderson to act. Two days later, on February 25, it had been reported in *The Tribune*, "Camm's Lawyers Seek DNA Tests on Evidence."[243] What happened next was not a coincidence.

"What The Hell Are You Talking About?"

Louisville's WAVE-TV's reporter Carrie Harned telephoned Kitty the afternoon of February 25, wanting comment on the fact the unknown DNA profile from the sweatshirt had been identified. Kitty's immediate reaction was "What the hell are you talking about?" She then quickly demanded of Harned, "Who told you that?"

Harned stammered and stuttered, Kitty said, finally admitting she had gotten the information from "Keith." She then apologized, thinking Kitty must have already known about the match. "No!" was Kitty's response as she demanded, "*WHO IS IT?*" Overhearing the demand, Stacy raced into Kitty's office and listened to the conversation.

Harned gave the name as Charles Boney with Kitty asking, "Charles Who?"

"Charles Boney." She pronounced his last name as Bo-Nay. "Does David know him?" Kitty responded that his name had never been mentioned by anyone with the defense.

After hanging up, Kitty immediately called Henderson who, for once, took her call and claimed that he had been going to call her with the news but, geez, he had gotten really busy. For months, Henderson had been repeatedly asked to run the DNA and had finally been forced to do so through the threat of a court order, but yet the first person he had told of the results outside his office was his favorite reporter,[244] knowing full well Carrie Harned would call Kitty for a quote.

Henderson, in fact, had finally admitted to Kitty that Boney's DNA had been matched almost two weeks before, on February 14. He then assured her that Boney, although convicted of armed robbery in Bloomington, had been very cooperative during his interview, and there was nothing to suggest he had anything to do with the murders.

According to Henderson, Boney said he had donated his BACKBONE sweatshirt to a charity weeks before the murders and, after that, he hadn't been responsible for the sweatshirt's whereabouts. An astounded Kitty described

---

[243] Associated Press, *Camm's Lawyers Seek DNA Tests on Evidence*, The Tribune, February 25, 2005.

[244] Just how much Henderson had favored Harned would be reinforced within the next few days.

Henderson's attitude towards Boney as "smug and completely nonchalant."

Demanding that Henderson immediately provide the CODIS report, the transcript of Boney's interview, and any and all other information they had regarding him, Henderson had calmly assured Kitty she would get that discovery to her as soon as it was available.[245]

Kitty then called and gave me what little information she had on the guy. I said I'd find as much on him as possible and would then get to her office. Next, Kitty called Sam at work and asked him to get Dave on the phone immediately. Dave's name was paged and he picked up an extension in the UDI workshop and was blown away. "Charles Who?"

"Charles Bo-Nay."

Dave said he *didn't know* Boney, *didn't know of* him and had never crossed paths *with* him to his recollection. His most important question, of course, was when would charges be filed against the man who had murdered his family? When told of Henderson's lack of interest in Boney, Dave was profoundly disappointed.

Kitty, though, told Sam and Dave to spread the word amongst the family to see if anyone knew or had ever heard anything about Boney. They first began by telling everyone at UDI. Dave's father, when told by his son of the incredible news, repeatedly proclaimed, "Thank you, God!" Dave next called his mom, who cried uncontrollably. Brother Donnie and sister Julie were called, and each were besides themselves with joy.

Boney's Background

Through an internet search, we soon determined Boney had been arrested in Bloomington for armed robbery and criminal confinement in 1992, had been given a 20-year sentence, and had apparently been released early from an Indiana prison, just three months before September 28.

The internet also revealed Boney had previously been convicted of several robberies in the late 1980's. Sometimes wearing a mask, Boney had physically assaulted numerous Indiana University (IU) coeds, in Bloomington at night and had robbed them of a unique item; unusual, that is, for most robbers. He had forcibly removed from each coed one shoe. The man had attacked women and robbed them for a shoe on their foot. *The man had robbed women for shoes*. The puzzle parts from the crime scene were beginning to make sense.

Armed with all that knowledge, Kitty contacted a good friend with the Bloomington Police Department (BPD) in an effort to get copies of all of Boney's arrest files. Unfortunately, since it was late Friday afternoon, it

---

[245] It would be almost four months before such discovery was provided to us.

would be Monday at the earliest before they could provide them. It was beyond frustrating that it would take three days before we'd find out more about Boney's past crimes and any statements he might have made to victims, witnesses, and/or the police.

I went back to the internet and, through my database, found some incredible information. Boney had been living with his mother when Dave's family had been murdered. And his mother had lived within 200 feet of the residence of Leland and Vonda Lockhart!

Not only that, but his residence had been a short walking distance to the local Kroger's supermarket where Kim had grocery shopped and also to Karem's meats![246] Karem's had been where Kim had often stopped, shopped, and spoken with both her sister and mother.[247] Had Kim been seen by Boney at one time or another at either of those places? Had he been attracted to her? Had he possibly spoken with her or the children? Had he stalked her and followed her home? We needed to know much more about him, and that included what kind of car he had been driving on the day of the murders.

Kitty's Reaction

I hurried into Kitty's office and told her and Stacy what I had found. That generated even more excitement, and I wasn't surprised when Kitty told us of something I had never heard any defense attorney do. Kitty explained, based upon Henderson's lack of charging Boney, coupled with Boney's property and DNA being found at the crime scene, and Boney's violent past— including thefts for shoes—that she was going to request Judge Aylsworth issue an arrest warrant for him.

Well, okay, an arrest warrant. That was a new one from a defense attorney: a defense attorney asking a judge to arrest someone. I had to admit Kitty was, to say the least, taking the proverbial bull by the horns. It took but minutes to put together a two-page affidavit, which had much more probable cause than did any of Dave's charging affidavits.

Well, since we're going to ask for Boney's arrest, I said we should also request a search warrant for his residence, thinking he might have kept souvenirs from the Camm house, such as Kim's earrings or more of Kim's personal belongings. Why not? The "fresh eyes" probably hadn't searched his residence.

Realistically, of course, none of us thought there was any chance of either warrant being issued or much less executed, but they were nonetheless faxed

---

[246] As noted previously, Karem's had been owned by Kim's sister Debbie and her husband Greg Karem.

[247] Both had worked at Karem's.

to the Judge's Boonville chambers and the Floyd County Prosecutor's office. Kitty then notified the news media of her actions and provided them with copies of the arrest warrant request.

What were we to do next? We finally decided to go to a nearby restaurant to eat dinner, more fully digest the events of the day, and determine strategy and tactics.

Compelling Stuff

Still thinking the "fresh eyes" might at least see a glimmer of light, we decided I should call Gilbert and alert him to the fact Boney had lived so close to Dave's uncle and aunt's home and to businesses where Kim routinely shopped. Maybe, just maybe, that information could possibly shake their tree.

Not having Gilbert's direct number, I placed a call to the Evansville ISP Post and asked for Detective Gilbert to call me immediately. Within a few minutes the lead detective was on the line, and I explained the location of Boney's residence and how he might have seen and targeted Kim.

Gilbert, though, wasn't interested in my information and dismissed any significance of it. He then told me his reasoning, and I listened, catching myself shaking my head. I thought of responding but didn't, as it was apparent to me the detective was unable to comprehend the incredible significance of everything associated with Charles Boney. I terminated the conversation and walked back to Kitty and Stacy, still shaking my head.

"So?" asked Kitty.

With a grim face, I told them, "Gilbert said, the bloodstains were, and these are his words, 'compelling.' He said Boney's DNA doesn't mean anything. The fucking whodunit is solved but they won't accept it. They've got their minds made up. It'll always be Dave."

CHAPTER 25

A Glimpse Into BACKBONE

My First Contact

The news about Charles Boney spread like wildfire in the Camm and Lockhart families, with their friends, co-workers, and literally every friend and acquaintance. Did anyone know Boney or anything about him?

Within a day of Boney's identity being revealed, Donnie Camm, divorced for several years, had received a telephone call from a former girlfriend who had said a relative of hers worked with Boney's wife in Louisville. Donnie quickly called me. The place of employment was the Greenlight Lounge, an adult entertainment bar, not far from Churchill Downs. He then gave me the telephone number of Charlynn Boney, also known as Amber.

I quickly called Kitty. My initial hesitancy in contacting Amber and having her contact her husband to contact me was based on my wanting as much information as possible on Boney before approaching him. We, of course, didn't have the Bloomington police reports on Boney's previous crimes and subsequent interviews, and the specifics

> HENDERSON HAD TOLD [BONEY] NOTHING HAD BEEN TAKEN FROM THE VICTIM, "NO PURSE OR ANYTHING LIKE THAT." THE PROSECUTOR HAD ALSO TOLD HIM, "THERE'S NO PHYSICAL EVIDENCE THAT PUTS [HIM] AT THE SCENE."

in those cases would certainly help in crafting appropriate questions for the man. Still, after thinking it over, I recommended to Kitty we should do what we could to get as much information as we could on Boney, arrange an interview as soon as possible, and then attempt to get a story from him. She concurred, so I then called Amber.[248]

After I identified myself, Amber was cordial and helpful. She said she'd give my message to Darnell, as she referred to her soon-to-be ex-husband. She also gave me an idea as to the personality of Boney, as she said she was pretty sure he'd speak with me.

---

[248] First, though, I ran her name through my databases and found her age, former and current addresses, names of probable family members, and employment.

Sure enough, within minutes Charles Darnell Boney called. He had a pleasant demeanor and spoke with measured calm, telling me he had found himself in an "awkward situation." I'd describe it something radically different than awkward, but I let him continue as he quickly acceded to my request to meet personally. He wanted our meeting to be at a "neutral place," and we settled for two days in the future, on Monday, February 28, at the Floyd County Public Defender's office at 10:30 a.m.

Rather than my trying to convince Boney to meet, it was clear he was the one trying to convince me he was a very agreeable and friendly guy, even telling me I could "have him all day." And then, laying it on even more, he told me he was "sympathetic" towards Dave, volunteering, "David Camm has been through a lot and he has my respect." It was but the first of many solicitous comments uttered by a still-talking Boney, even though we had already agreed to meet.

Boney next volunteered he was a former Indiana University (IU) student and referred to himself as the "Shoe Bandit." He also admitted he had committed "an armed robbery," as in *one* armed robbery, not multiple ones.

As for the sweatshirt, he said it was "undoubtedly mine" but that, "in all honesty, I first found out about it on February 17th," when he had first been approached by the police. The "in all honesty" comment, I would find, would preface many other of Boney's comments to me and others.

Nonetheless, he said when he got out of prison, he had put the unwashed sweatshirt in a bag and placed it at a Salvation Army drop box. One of the investigators had told him the sweatshirt also had unknown female DNA on it, but he told them he had "no idea" as to the identity of that person.

Regardless, Boney said he had been "blown away" when told by the investigators he was being interviewed, not about delinquent child support as he had first thought, but about the Camm murders. He had followed the developments of the Camm murder case but "didn't have a belief one way or the other if Camm was guilty." If true, Boney, I thought, was possibly the only person in the Louisville metro area who didn't have an opinion on Dave's guilt or innocence.

Boney then added he was a "fair man" and knew what it was like to have been accused of a crime, and, as he was being accused of murder, he "was in the same position as Camm."

Three more times Boney referenced Dave, and each time it was to sympathize with him.

Continuing, Boney told me, "I'm going to play it like this. There's a murderer still out there, and it's not me or David Camm."

As such, Boney couldn't stop with his comments about Dave, telling me all he wanted was for Dave to be "not guilty and go home." Did he know

Dave? No, he didn't know any of the Camm family or the Lockhart family, but he did want David to know it "truly was not me" who killed his family. In fact, the murders "was something that just didn't seem like me." *Seem* like me? That wasn't a denial.

Boney then provided me with his direct telephone number and told me he didn't mind if I gave the number to David or "Mr. Lockhart," further telling me, "It's okay if David Camm feels compelled to call me, if he would like to speak with me or else meet me at the Public Defender's office." Boney then took it a step further, saying he would like to meet David, "face to face and tell him, as I look him in the eye, that I wasn't involved."

Boney next assured he wasn't a calculating person or even a criminal any more, as he had totally changed. He had grown from his "ignorant" past into a man who was working three jobs for a total of "82–88 hours a week." He was making so much money, he insisted, "I don't have to rob" even though in his past, robbing had been "easy money." So much so, he claimed, he had gotten as much as $1,500 from just one armed robbery.

And then, Boney said Henderson had told him nothing had been taken from the victim,[249] "no purse or anything like that." Henderson had also told him, "There's no physical evidence that puts [him] at the scene."

Boney then connected the dots of his and Henderson's logic. Because nothing was taken from the crime scene, he couldn't be the murderer since, as he put it, "my MO is theft." He repeated Henderson's reassurance: "There's basically no physical evidence that puts me at the scene."

BACKBONE had been so named, he said, because he was a "standup guy." Mr. Standup then offered his thoughts to me on what had happened to the sweatshirt. Boney had a "hunch" his unwashed sweatshirt had been taken by a female at the Salvation Army, and once she was identified, she could lead investigators to the others involved. Then, as he put it, "both David and I will be clear."

After both he and Camm were vindicated, Boney said WAVE-TV and the newspapers would all have to apologize to each of them: "All I want to hear is, 'we're sorry Mr. Camm, we're sorry, Mr. Boney.'"

As for Carrie Harned, Boney said he had given her the exclusive story and also his word that he wouldn't meet with any other press or media reporters until Tuesday. When I asked what Henderson thought of his speaking with the press, Boney said the prosecutor had told him, "It's your call." He also claimed Henderson had "admired him" and even told him, "More power to you."

If those comments were accurate, then Henderson was going overboard in

---

[249] Singular.

helping Boney facilitate a media narrative that would help to eliminate him as a suspect and to preserve the case against Dave. "So much for pursuing the truth," I thought.

Referring to the investigators, Boney also called them "fresh eyes." Boney contacted them every day, he said, and told them of his daily activities and whereabouts. "If they saw me packing up, they would think that David didn't do it."

Those comments were strange as well as contradictory, for Boney had previously told me he wanted Dave to be vindicated, yet he was concerned the police might change their mind on Dave's guilt. Perhaps Boney was now thinking if the investigators thought Dave didn't do it, their only other option would be to believe Boney was, in fact, the killer.

When I asked Boney where he was the night of the killings, he recalled the Camms' killings because they were a "landmark" event. As such, he was able to remember "four sets of people who knew where I was," although he declined to provide me with any names.

Everything he told the police, he insisted, "checks out," although, he said, that did not yet include his alibis. Did that mean the "fresh eyes" hadn't interviewed his alibi witnesses? That didn't seem possible, as any rookie investigator, when told by a suspect of where he was at the time of the crime, would have been on that lead like white on rice. But these were the "fresh eyes" guys, and we had already known they had regurgitated falsehoods and hadn't pursued obvious leads.

Additionally, how did Boney know if his alibi witnesses hadn't yet been checked? Did the investigators or his alibi witnesses tell him that? If it was true that they hadn't been interviewed, then everything hadn't "checked out" as he'd claimed.

Still, the innocent guy said, "there are some other things in the works that will put me somewhere else at the time of the murders." Another interesting comment. He didn't say, "I was someplace else at the time of the murders," but rather "will *put* me…" Was he making a story up along the way? When I asked him if he was talking about more alibi witnesses, Boney didn't answer the question but rather said, "I'm known to be a criminal." If that made any sense, I didn't get it.

Boney then volunteered he wanted to determine the weather the evening of the murders and if it had been hot or cold. When I asked why, he said he had more theories. First, "If it was cold outside then why would I have taken a sweatshirt to the scene, take it off, and then leave it at the scene?" And if it was hot, "there would be no reason to have a sweatshirt."

And then Boney, who claimed he had been doing a "little research" on high velocity blood splatter,[250] asked me, "If a person had killed the three victims, then why would that person have taken off a sweatshirt, particularly if there was no high velocity blood splatter on the shirt but female DNA?" Boney was certainly trying to distance himself from the sweatshirt but in a manner that also encompassed what he thought was hard forensic science.

It was also interesting Boney had begun talking in the third-person format, *"that person,"* after saying "why would *I have taken.*"

Henderson, said BACKBONE, had brought up the possibility that he had worked for Sam and that he and Camm were "in cahoots" with one another and that possibly Camm had him get rid of the gun. Boney responded to that question: "If I was involved, why didn't David Camm kill me?"

Another aspect of what Boney said caught my attention. For the second time, Boney claimed Henderson had interacted with him: i.e., Henderson first told him nothing was taken and then asked him if he worked for Sam, going so far as to suggest he had gotten rid of the gun for David. Prosecutors, or at least prosecutors who don't want to be witnesses and no longer prosecutors, don't question suspects. That Henderson had interacted so much with Boney was unusual, but, more so, at least according to Boney, he was acting as an investigator, asking questions and getting answers.

What Boney told me next was truly astounding, for, if true, he claimed the "fresh eyes" guys had asked him if he "wanted police protection." Why? Because they thought someone in the Camm family could murder him. So, they were treating him as a victim? That was more than shocking. Regardless, Boney had declined the protection, though, because he wasn't afraid of them. After all, he was BACKBONE.

I was not at all surprised by his next comment: "This is God's way of testing me, [and] God will see me through this." I'd figured he'd say at least something similar, since he, too, had begun to paint himself as the victim in the case.

Once again claiming that everything he had told the investigators had "checked out," Boney added, in what was a very prophetic comment, "If you lie about anything, then your credibility is shot."

When I asked him if he had ever been to the Camm house, Boney didn't say no, but rather asked me what kind of house they had. After I told him its location, he then said there was no reason for him to go to or through Georgetown.

Boney, an African-American, then volunteered his current and former wives were both white and further said there were a "lot of Caucasians in

---

[250] Boney referred to splatter rather than spatter.

my family and people in the Lanesville and Georgetown area do not consort with blacks." It was the first time race was mentioned in our conversation. Interestingly, Boney was using it as a means of conveying the idea that he came from a family with whites but yet also using it as a means of an alibi, i.e., he wouldn't go to the place of the crime where blacks didn't live.

After almost an hour of conversation, we confirmed our meeting time and place for Monday with Boney asserting he would answer all of my questions. After all, he said, the "bottom line" was he was in the "hot seat." The man in the "hot seat," though, was still a free man as Henderson and the "fresh eyes" guys had obviously accepted his story.

CHAPTER 26
Showtime

All of us were continuing to search every available source to find as much on Charles Darnell Boney as we could, but it was extremely frustrating to have to be reactive rather than proactive and wait for the next shoe to drop. On Sunday, we learned WAVE-TV would begin airing Carrie Harned's exclusive story that evening.

None of us knew how Boney would react to being publicly identified in the Camm case, but I had a feeling it could possibly cause him to hesitate or even step away

> "HE HAS A TEMPER. WHEN HE GETS MAD, HE GETS A LITTLE MADDER AND HE GETS VIOLENT."

from our interview. As such, I called him, mostly to re-establish a connection with him, but also to see if he was okay in moving our interview from 10:30 a.m. to 9:00 a.m. He was more than accommodating, saying, "I will make it more convenient for you."

WAVE-TV was reveling in their huge scoop—so much so, that they would string out bits and pieces over several days and during their mid-day, afternoon, and evening newscasts. Of great import was Harned's claim that first evening: "State investigators recently questioned him for more than 22 hours and found no loopholes." The reporter, obviously after having been briefed by Henderson, was doing his bidding, unintentionally or otherwise, to help shape the public narrative of the Boney revelation.

In his media interview, Boney was comfortably seated with his left arm extended on a table and clad in a long-sleeve shirt and blue jeans. The epitome of coolness and confidence, he readily addressed the linkage of the sweatshirt to him: "It was a big surprise to me…Once I seen [sic] the shirt, photographs specifically of that sweatshirt, I owned up to it. It was mine. I knew that it was mine."[251]

Harned said, of Boney's claiming he had taken his BACKBONE sweatshirt to the Salvation Army, "Sources close to the prosecution say his stories check out." Once again, the public was reassured they need not be concerned about Boney. His story had been confirmed, and there were no discrepancies.

Intentionally or not, Harned then covered for the lack of months-long interest given to the sweatshirt by Henderson and his "fresh eyes" team by

---

[251] Harned, Carrie, *Charles Boney*, WAVE-TV 3, February 27, 2005.

saying the unidentified sweatshirt had "left both the prosecution and defense attorneys dumbfounded." [252] That wasn't at all accurate, as Kitty had pressed Henderson hard for months, and Sam had pleaded with Gilbert to run the DNA through CODIS, all to no avail. Everyone on the defense side knew it could be critically important while Henderson and Gilbert had been content to do nothing.

When Harned asked Boney about his strong-armed robberies for shoes, Boney again referred to himself as the "Shoe Bandit." [253] It was obvious, at least to me, the moniker was kind of a badge for Boney. She then asked the bandit if he had a shoe fetish. He said he didn't.

When asked as to why he attacked women and stole a shoe, Boney responded, "That was a fraternity prank. It was stupid, it was, I can't even put into words what it was. It was back in 1989." [254]

Harned shifted to the murders: "There are issues with shoes that are unexplained in the Camm case from the crime scene where your sweatshirt is. How do you respond to that?"

"That's the first I've heard about it," claimed Boney.

"Does that worry you?"

Boney's quick response: "Not at all, only that I wasn't there." [255]

Okay, so Boney claimed ignorance of the shoes at the crime scene, but more importantly, he *didn't ask her to explain the shoes at the crime scene*. A normal response would have been "What about shoes at the crime scene? What do you mean?" That he didn't ask for more information could only mean one thing.

Harned then spoke of his alibis, with Boney saying he was "covered," further adding, "There were three sets of people that I remember seeing that day. But, they've all been interviewed, and they all have a testament regarding my whereabouts and they are my alibis." That was strange. He had told me he had four sets of alibi witnesses, not three. Had he found one since he had taped the television interview?

Then, Boney made shocking comments about his earlier crimes: "[And] in regards to my choice of victims, I didn't really put a lot of thought into it, but when I was young, 22 and 23 years old, committing crimes with a gun, uh foolish, uh, I thought to myself, 'another man, for example, would put up a fight, he would play hero. A woman, they'll just hand over the money.' That

---

[252] Ibid.
[253] Ibid.
[254] Ibid.
[255] Ibid.

was my thinking pattern."[256]

Incredible. Boney had answered the question as to why he attacked Kim. She'd just hand over whatever he demanded while a man would "play hero" and "put up a fight." That whoever murdered Kim and the children had been an abject coward was obvious to anyone, but now Boney was confirming it for everybody.

Implicit in that same explanation, of course, was Boney's admitting to planning his crimes. Planning could have taken hours or moments, but planning crimes didn't always equate to carrying them out efficiently.

Harned also had found an EPO,[257] taken out against Boney by his estranged yet publicly unnamed wife, Amber. In it, his wife said Boney had physically harmed her on several occasions, including using a "stun gun on her several times."[258]

Harned's brief interview of Amber, with only her hands being shown, revealed an obviously abused woman: "He has a temper. When he gets mad, he gets a little madder and he gets a little violent, but other than that...."[259] One translation: "Other than beating the hell out of me and using a stun gun on me, well, he hasn't killed me. At least not yet."

And then, no doubt covering for the source of her singular information, Harned was quoted as saying, "Keith Henderson is under a gag order and can't discuss the new evidence."[260] Nice attempt, Ms. Harned, but you admitted to Kitty it was Henderson who gave you the inside scoop.

Still, it was probably a wise strategy on the part of Henderson, since: 1) with a gag order in effect, Henderson had no other way to break the news to the public without a willing media toady; and 2) he had Harned help him tailor his narrative of an unfortunate Boney whose only sin was his charitable gift, all in an effort to downplay the impact of the DNA's being publicly revealed.

Regardless, and even without the detailed results of the police reports or the 22 hours of interviews, what we knew heading into my interview with Boney was 1) he had planned his crimes; 2) he was a strong-arm robber who had routinely attacked women for their shoes; 3) he later had used a gun to rob and then hold multiple women hostage; 5) he also had angrily beaten his wife, threatened her life, and used a stun gun on her; 6) his clothing and DNA had been found at the scene of a triple homicide; 7) he was an abject coward

---

[256] Ibid.

[257] Emergency Protective Order, mostly used in domestic-related cases where physical abuse has occurred or is being threatened.

[258] Ibid.

[259] Ibid.

[260] Ibid.

who had enjoyed his witty banter with the press and others, including me; 8) several key questions associated with the crime scene had been answered; but far worse, 9) he was an effective con artist who had convinced the "fresh eyes" and Henderson of his non-involvement because they hadn't found any "loopholes" in his story. In fact, his story had "checked out."

What little shred of common sense, if any, left with Henderson and the "fresh eyes" was gone.

CHAPTER 27
The Real Charles Boney

As I drove to New Albany early Monday morning, I went over my mental checklist. I knew Boney wanted to spin his story in the manner of a helpful guy who was only trying to overcome his criminal past. That meant having to listen to him, at least initially, waxing poetically all about himself. And it was clear, in his first attempted indoctrination of me, Charles Boney was *all* about himself.

I knew the probability of getting Boney to confess, at least directly, to committing the murders was non-existent, but I did have a plan, and I would build to that plan by letting him talk and then talk some more. I was sure he'd lie to me, for I was equally sure that was the nature of the man; he was a pathological liar who wouldn't be able to help himself. Boney was the kind of guy who would cut his own throat with his own words but still think he was the smartest person around.

> I WAS SURE HE'D LIE TO ME, FOR I WAS EQUALLY SURE THAT WAS THE NATURE OF THE MAN; HE WAS A PATHOLOGICAL LIAR WHO WOULDN'T BE ABLE TO HELP HIMSELF. HE WOULD CUT HIS OWN THROAT WITH HIS OWN WORDS.

During the trip, I spoke with an impatient and frustrated Kitty who was trying to get copies of reports of Boney's prior arrests and interviews before the promised afternoon delivery time. Once she had those reports, she'd call me.

A Friend of Boney's Is With Him

I disconnected the call and then got lucky, finding a coveted parking spot near the courthouse. Just prior to my departing my vehicle, Boney called. He wanted to change the location to a jury room. No problem, I countered, and he gave me the room number.

After clearing the entry security check-point, I entered the nearby elevator, rode to the third floor, and walked into the walnut-paneled jury room. I was surprised, but not by a head-shaven Charles Darnell Boney wearing a Creed T-shirt and sitting comfortably in a chair at the large table. There was another man to his left: ISP detective Gary Gilbert.

When I looked at Boney, he explained he felt "more comfortable" with Gilbert present. Boney also had a tape recorder, telling me he was taping our interview on behalf of Gilbert. I then shook his hand and said, "No problem."

Charles Boney on February 28, 2005.

Boney was a very thick and muscular man who weighed at least 275 pounds, if not more. He had clearly been a weight-lifter who wanted to exhibit his physique, as he was wearing a short-sleeve T-shirt when the weather was in the 30's. I placed my business card near the Coke in front of him and officially re-introduced myself.

After sitting up my video and separate audio recorder, I began asking him questions on background. Such questions were essential, but they were also non-threatening and would give me a foundational basis for Boney's responses to more pointed questions; for instance, "What's your date of birth" is normally answered directly and without any hesitation or evasion while more threatening questions, "Did you possess a gun?" oftentimes bring round-a-bout responses, deflection, and/or evasion.

Boney, breathing somewhat shallowly and rapidly, I thought, as well as looking all-too-comfortable for a man to be quizzed about being a murderer, began by telling me he had lived in New Albany with his mother since the mid-1970's.

After graduating from high school in 1987, Boney then attended Indiana University (IU) and, after less than a year on campus, joined the National Guard in Bloomington, subsequently training as a field artillery specialist. Throughout my questions, Boney often looked away from me, often staring at my notepad, at least when he wasn't appearing to think rather deeply before answering my questions. He was being careful, even when responding to non-threatening questions.

His Crimes

I asked about his first arrests, and his response was direct: "I became a felon January the 19th, 1989. I had been penned by the newspapers. Um, they called me the 'Shoe Bandit,' during the course of what some believed was a fraternity prank and others had their doubts. I have been accused of maybe just having a shoe fetish or something of that nature. You know, I have tried to defend myself on that, but bottom line is anything that I have ever done, I have never had a jury trial. I just went to court and told the truth. The judge asked me, you know…"

True to the preview he had given me two days before, it would be the first of many long-winded explanations proffered by Boney in an attempt to deflect from the heart of the question. Boney was a guy who thought the more he spoke, the more people would believe him, and if he deflected from having a "shoe fetish," no one would pursue the topic.

"Why would you remove the shoes from young ladies?"[261]

"Like I said, it was a fraternity prank."

"Which fraternity was that?"

"I would rather keep them out, but if it's, if it's something…"

"Well, it is significant, yeah, because that goes right to your credibility as to whether or not it was or wasn't. Would you agree?"

"Yeah, yeah, but keep in mind I wasn't a part of this fraternity at the time, I was simply trying to pledge. But it was [name of fraternity]." So, he had committed several crimes/pranks as a member of a fraternity he hadn't really been a part of? No doubt, he had engaged in the same kind of word games with the "fresh eyes," but had they, at some time or another, confronted him on those contradictions and lies during their 22 hours with him?

For me, it was difficult not to tell Boney, "You know you're just slinging total bullshit here, Charles." I didn't, as I wanted his story in his words.

"Yeah, but let me ask you very directly, do you have a shoe fetish?" Boney said he didn't. I then asked if he had undergone any counseling for his problem, whatever it might be.

The self-described "Shoe Bandit" then launched into another lengthy ramble about his sentence, probation, good time, and community service, all without answering the counseling question. When I pressed, he admitted he had to "undergo sessions with a psychologist, but it was such a bizarre thing," all the while not addressing the issue of why he was counseled. He was quick to add, however, that he had never re-engaged in such activity since

---

[261] In Gilbert's report of my Boney interview, rather than acknowledge the victims were women, he wrote, "He removed shoes from *people* 4 (four) times."

"something like that, once you, you know, get caught for anything, it's like, that was a deterrent."

His convictions were so deterring, in fact, he had lasted almost two years before he was arrested for check deception in Bloomington and had his probation violated, resulting in his doing "all the time that [he] had on the shelf," including a year in jail and six months in the DOC. The six months was "to get a taste of prison [which was] sort of like a shock thing."

After serving his time, Boney had returned to Bloomington "for the sole purpose of seeing [his] son" and his ex-wife. It was then, "there was an apartment complex with an office [which] had a young lady in there that was counting out cash and there was an older woman in there that was counting out cash and I had seen it and at the time I was packing. I had a .38 revolver, 5 shot and had no intentions of using it, in fact, the, uh, the, uh, weapon was not loaded."

Notice the segue from "the sole purpose of seeing my son" to being accidently drawn to "counting out cash" and then to "the weapon was not loaded" while racing through the events of the actual armed robbery? Boney was very practiced in minimization and deflection. That didn't equate to his being convincing, though, as he had only stumbled by chance upon an older woman, a "good" victim for him, while coincidentally carrying an unloaded gun. It had only been then, with all of those variables coming together, that he had robbed her.

I moved on to his armed robbery of three coeds in a condominium near the IU campus. As to be expected, Boney prefaced his comments in an attempt to lessen the impact of his crimes. "Well, at the time I was indigent and I was just a very foolish and ignorant person back then. I, I wish I could go back and stop that kid from making that mistake. I wish that I could do that, but the bottom line is that I did make that mistake."

He kept going: "That was something that I felt like I needed. I was going through a period of inadequacy, uh, trying to get over the stigma of prison, and things of that nature, and bottom line is, as a grown man today, and, you know, almost 36 years old, I had a problem with just blaming any, anything and anyone, except for myself. I didn't know how to get down to the heart of it. So, bottom line is, that's the difference between me today and me back then."

Then it was time for the highly intelligent Boney to demonstrate just how smart he was, as he further explained why he did what he did: "But I was looking for reasons to fulfill some of my, I think Sigmond Freud said it best. There was an id, ego, and super ego. The id is your primitive side and I believe that I was more 'idish,' if I may say that."

I directed the conversation back to his armed robbery of the three young coeds, with Boney describing the run-up to the event: "[It was] an apartment complex, um, quite honestly, where I did not know the victims and I went to that apartment complex. At the time, I didn't have a vehicle or anything and I was walking. I remember seeing an individual look out their door, look at me funny, and then close the door and then I went up to that building and I went in because the door was, like, semi-cracked but it was shut. I remember showing the weapon to the inhabitants of the house."

Again, that Boney had prefaced his knowledge of the victims with "quite honestly" told me he was anything but honest. Also, while he may not have *known* his victims, he had seen them and been attracted to them; after all, they were women and not men, again the best victims for Boney.

That Boney was walking to his crimes was also intriguing, since no vehicle had been seen immediately around the Camm residence by Bob Ter Vree, nor later his wife, Debbie, just minutes before the arrival of Kim and the children; yet, a vehicle had been spotted by a neighbor parked several hundred feet from the house about 30 minutes prior to the time the family returned and within walking distance.

Once again, though, notice Boney had separated himself from the nature of the crime by claiming he had only been "showing [his] weapon" to the "inhabitants," not three, no doubt, terrified young women who were looking at the business end of a gun and possible death.

Boney couldn't stop, however, as he had to convince me, and also Gilbert, the crime wasn't all that bad. "My intentions were to foolishly take them to an ATM and just withdraw some money and then, of course, just go about my business because I have never hurt anyone. You know, I have never shot anyone or strangled, stabbed, nothing, you know. I mean I was just desperate. I was looking for that next high. You know, I was, I was just, I mean, I actually feel really good right now, being on tape, and just kind of talking about it even after all these years."

"It's sort of like a catharsis," suggested Doctor Dunn.

"Yeah, it is a release, it definitely is. It is a release just to be able to feel good about airing your dirty laundry." And then a smirk appeared on his face. "That's why I am not afraid of the news and that's why I wasn't afraid to meet with you because this, in a way is like, um, it is like extended therapy. You know, it's like a reminder, hey, don't ever do those types of things again."

One aspect of Boney's comment was accurate, I was sure: "I was looking for that next high." That high, I was confident, didn't come from drugs, as he had made sure to emphasize repeatedly, even twice prefacing his first reference to drugs with "honestly." Boney's addiction was the crime of confronting young women victims with a gun, controlling their movements, and thoroughly terrorizing them throughout. *That* was his addiction.

Let's get back to the women you petrified, Charles. "So, what happened with these three coeds?"

Boney responded that he had "attempted to take them to an ATM," but the Bloomington Police "threw down on me," meaning arrested him at gunpoint, as he quickly left behind his violence and launched into *why* he was caught, saying a neighbor had seen him inside the condo. He didn't stop there, however, as he claimed the guy was probably like a "voyeur or peeper."

"And then you had the three girls with you? The three co-eds?"

"Yes."

"Okay, and you had them under, like, gunpoint?"

"Yes, but I wasn't really like, like sticking it in their back, or anything like that, I had it in a downward position, and keep in mind that it wasn't loaded."

We'd have the police reports within hours to see if Boney's characterization of the armed robberies was anything remotely comparable to the truth. I was betting it wasn't.

After his arrest, Boney said Michael Hunt,[262] his previous public defender, had asked him about having "graduated [from shoes] to armed robbery." Because of that graduation, Hunt had told him, Boney was looking at a lengthy prison sentence.

Boney said he had then told his counsel he didn't want a plea agreement, but he had wanted to "get this thing going" since "maybe prison would help" him.

He continued, "On the day of court, and this is public record as well, I remember saying, and it's true, it's a fact, the judge asks me, 'what am I going to do with you, Charles?' And I looked at her and said, 'to give me anything less than the maximum sentence would depreciate the seriousness of the crime, so therefore, I guess you will just have to give me the maximum sentence.' I'm sure people thought that I was on crack that day."

Prison Life & Silly Stuff

Boney was on a roll, however, as he'd claimed he "was going to work [his] way out" of prison and had done just that, as he was a "Master Tutor" who "was responsible for over 40 men getting their GED" and had "over 10,000 hours of tutoring in prison."[263]

---

[262] Michael Hunt has been the decades-long Public Defender in Monroe County and enjoys the well-deserved respect of all members of the bar in that county.

[263] 10,000 hours of tutoring equates to five full years at 40 hours per week; that Boney was in prison seven years [he was incarcerated in the jail, not prison, for almost a year] and was fully engaged as a tutor for five of those years was highly, highly unlikely.

The man also had earned college credits, had engaged in a "series of different religious studies [and had gotten] credit for anger management [and] worked as a lay advocate, getting cases overturned" as he "jumped right into the law" and got "sentence modifications and sentence reductions."

Law Professor Boney then compared himself to Malcolm X, saying they were "very, very similar" persons, but instead of choosing Islam, Boney proclaimed, "The Father in Heaven that I serve is of the Trinity: God the Father, Son, and Holy Ghost, as a Christian."

Boney had also made friends with one specific role model in prison who taught him "how to survive in prison [and] how to do good time." And how had he done that? "[My mentor told me] don't join gangs, don't be in all these little cliques, here's how you do time, he told me the rules. No homosexuals, don't fall weak to another man. Don't borrow from anyone unless you pay them with great interest. If you have something to say, let it be the truth and tell it like it is."

Mr. Tell It Like It Is then said he'd had "only three write-ups" in prison, for "busting a lightbulb" and "putting extra food on [other inmates] plates, silly stuff." Uh, but, uh, geez, he then snuck in the fact "there was fighting between me and another individual [as] you're always going to hold your ground. That's just part of prison life."

The need to con me was overwhelmed by the need to brag of his prison bona fides, as Boney then went into a more complete description of himself in prison: "You know, it's like, I'm not a perfect person, and I didn't live a completely honest life in prison either. You know, I smoked weed a couple of times, I made homemade hooch, that was against the rules."

His bragging not complete, Boney continued, "We made money the wrong way, you know, we sold drugs and things like that to survive. So I wasn't perfect, you know, I did a lot of stuff. I'll never say oh, 'I was a great guy.' It's just that *I never let the people in charge know what I was doing. They seen [sic] me as a guy helping everybody, but with prison life, you have to survive as well.*"[264]

The compulsion was too great, and Mr. Silly Stuff couldn't stop. "Bottom line is, we hate child molesters, we hate rapists, we hate sexual predators, and we don't like individuals that do things to the elderly, things like that. So we have a police among our little community. So when those people come to prison they get

> "I NEVER LET THE PEOPLE IN CHARGE KNOW WHAT I WAS DOING."

---

[264] Emphasis mine.

dealt with. That's on tape, I'm just admitting it. I was involved in some of that."

When I asked him to explain, Boney, with a smirk, continued: "In other words we don't want, I mean, you know, I'm a father, and if there's an individual that accused of being a child molester and its proven, we know, just doing time is not enough, they got to go through a little bit more. That's just what it's about."

Release From Prison

Boney claimed, in addition to having written sentence modification requests for other inmates, he had repeatedly done so for himself, all unsuccessfully, until early June 2000, when he again petitioned his sentencing judge for a modification. The judge, Elizabeth Mann, surprisingly had him transported from the Miami Correctional Facility in Peru, Indiana, to her courtroom. It was there she had released him over two years early from his 20-year sentence, on June 21, 2000. It was, Boney said, only after his mother and grandmother had prayed for his release that a "miracle" had occurred, and he had once again become a free man.

Almost immediately after his release, his mother had driven him from Bloomington to her home in New Albany. Upon reaching New Albany, taking many of his prison clothes with him, he'd found several other boxes of his clothes had already been delivered to his home.

Within days, Boney said, he'd gone to work as an entry-level employee at Anderson Wood in Louisville, a wood-working factory specializing in the manufacture of various types of mill work, including handrails for staircases.

BACKBONE Name & Sweatshirt

As for his BACKBONE sweatshirt, Boney said there were actually two of them, with the second one, unlike the first with only his nickname, having his DOC number also written on the front of the collar.

I asked why the name BACKBONE. Boney's response was direct, as well as practiced, I thought. "I fit the epitome of what a BACKBONE should have, a person who's not spineless, a person that stands up. He helps people."

Boney had to educate me on his clothes along with other prison possessions. "You gotta understand something. When you're in prison, all you have is what's [got] your name on it, a book, a magazine, anything. You become very possessive of that. That's yours. And you just don't throw it away."

Boney then said he'd gotten rid of the two BACKBONE sweatshirts, sweatpants, pants, shoes, and new prison underwear by dropping them in a Salvation Army drop box because he "didn't want to have anything that reminded [him] specifically of prison."

But then the lesson got confusing and contradictory, as Boney said, *"I just simply gave [them] away, because [they] meant a lot to me."*[265]

However, Boney continued, "I kept the state boots. They were brown in nature and I polished them to a high shine so I kept them. I was proud of them. It took me six or seven months to get to a good shine. It was a military shine."

Amazingly, Boney then smiled, looked directly at my newly shined brown shoes and commented, "Like, you have on some nice shoes." The Shoe Bandit, whose boots, cherished for years, were a prized prison possession, was fixated on my shoes. If it hadn't been on video tape, few would have believed me.

I moved to the unidentified female DNA on the sweatshirt. Boney said he'd never "let a female specifically wear [his] prison clothes," and therefore, any blood or DNA had to have gotten there after he had given them away.

Boney then theorized on how that female DNA had gotten on his garment. A woman obviously had control of the sweatshirt, he said, asking, "Is that female responsible for these murders? And if not specifically, could she be identified such that who she gave those to, or loaned them to, or passed them on to, could be identified?"

Boney obviously knew the chances of tracking the garment from the drop box to the store to a woman to the purported murderer was almost impossible. Still, the guy who liked to "play it" could have been giving clues as to who had been with him when the Camm family was murdered.

When I said I was a skeptic as to his sweatshirt donation, Boney quickly retorted, "I understand what your point is but you have to understand from where I'm sitting." He then theorized that the real murderer saw "my garments with my DOC number, a guy who just got out of prison, 'let me use these and I'll leave these here.'"

Still, if that were the case, I asked, why didn't the real killer leave the better-identified sweatshirt with his DOC number on it? Boney, though, was already onto his next theory: "If it was cold that day, a person would wear a sweatshirt. Why would he take the sweatshirt off and commit murders and leave it at the, you know, the scene of the crime?"

I didn't play along. "It could be a sexual assault."

"Was, was anyone sexually assaulted at that crime scene?"

"Well, could well be. Sure," I countered.

Boney didn't ask who might have been sexually assaulted. He didn't have to.

Returning to the sweatshirt, I inquired, "The BACKBONE sweatshirt, that was not a state secret, that was publicized and well-publicized at that time. Were you aware there was a BACKBONE sweatshirt found out there?"

---

[265] Emphasis mine.

"First and foremost, I had not heard my name BACKBONE on a sweatshirt or anything [that] would be related to the case. That's the truth."

Tattoos

Noticing a tattoo on his upper left arm, I asked Boney if he'd mind showing me his tats. He replied, "I have a [singular] tattoo that says BACKBONE on it, as he lifted his left sleeve to fully expose a skeleton, explaining, "The character is a skeleton because my name's Bone, you know, so Bones like the skeleton. He's holding a money bag and he has a weapon in his hand. It's a .45, because I'm in prison for armed robbery." It didn't escape me this was the same guy who had voluntarily gone to prison to be rehabilitated but had proudly gotten a tat showing everyone he had been an armed robber.

Gang members also had their own tattoos, Boney volunteered, but "I'm not going to say any gang specifically, but they have tattoos that identify who they represent."

Camm Family, Crime Scene, & Guns

I had allowed Boney to spin his stories and, in the process, lie repeatedly, but it was time to ask some very specific questions related to him as well as the crime scene.

No, he said, he had not been in the Camm garage or house. No, he had never met Kim, Brad, or Jill Camm. Yes, he knew Danny Camm, David's youngest brother, for he had graduated from high school with him, but no, he didn't know any other members of the Camm family, nor had he ever associated with any of the Lockhart family.

Boney denied ever being at the Georgetown Community Church, playing basketball there, knowing anyone who attended there, or having been at any Alcoholics or Narcotics Anonymous meetings there. In fact, he said, "I have never played basketball with David Camm."

Turning to his previous assertion he couldn't have been responsible for the Camm murders because he was a thief and armed robber, I asked, "To your understanding there was nothing taken from the Camm residence."

"I was informed of that. That is correct."[266]

"Well, that may not be accurate, okay? There may have been some items that were stolen. If that's the case, then, that would possibly include you as a suspect because of your previous MO. Would you agree or disagree with that?"

---

[266] In Gilbert's three-page report of my interview with Boney in his presence, he wrote, "Dunn tells Boney that there were items removed from the crime scene." Boney had been told otherwise by Henderson, and my question was based upon that knowledge.

Boney stuttered, "I'm gonna, I see where you're going with it."

"I'm not trying to fool you. I'm just telling you straight up."

"Well, bottom line is, it's been brought to my attention that things such as wedding rings, credit cards, cash, things of that nature, stuff that is [sic] just readily available to take was still there. And that why [sic] they looked more at him because it didn't seem or appear to be a robbery."

The ISP's quick and erroneous conclusion that nothing had been stolen from the Camm residence, reinforced by Henderson, was now being used as a defense shield by the very guy who had stolen Kim's earrings and then killed her and the children.

"Would there be any way, shape, manner, or form that any of your DNA would be at the crime scene, other than on the sweatshirt?"

Rather than a resounding, "NO," Boney's response was "I understand exactly what you're saying and the only way that my DNA would be at the crime scene is if I were there, and I was not there, so therefore, no, my DNA would not show up at the crime scene."

"Would there be any way, shape, manner, or form that any of your fingerprints would be on or near that crime scene?"

"My fingerprints would not appear at that crime scene because, first and foremost, once again, I would have had to have been there in order for my fingerprints to appear at the crime scene."

"Okay, so the answer, once again, it's no, right?"

"That's correct."

"From the time you got out of prison until now, have you ever been in possession of any weapon, any gun?" Uh, yeah, he said, his brother-in-law had a gun when he had lived with Boney and Amber, but Boney had never had possession of it.

Let me try the question again, "Have *you* ever had possession of any gun since you got out of prison?"

"No. There's, there's no need for me to have possession of any weapon."

"Have you ever committed any crimes since you've been out of prison?"

He had, he said, because he had struck his wife. "Well, during the course of being accused of adultery, we got in a heated argument, she grabbed her stun gun and I twisted it towards her and I stunned her with it." He added that his wife was an abject liar, and it was "preposterous" that he had ever threatened her with a gun.

"Alright, so if anybody, including your estranged wife or anybody else would claim that you would have been in possession of a gun upon your, from the time that you were released from prison until as we sit here today, they would be lying?"

"Absolutely, because I know what I have had, and have not had, in my possession."

"Ok, and so a gun's not one of them."

"That is correct."

"Have you ever had in your possession a .380 semi-automatic?"

"No, I have never."

"Have you ever had a Lorcin handgun in your possession?"[267]

"No, I have not."

Boney's Car In September 2000

Boney had said previously he had driven to the Salvation Army drop box, and I asked him about his car. He had been, he said, purchasing a 1986 two-door, midnight blue Cadillac Deville, on verbal contract from his uncle in Evansville, and it was the same car he had been driving in September 2000.

"Okay, if someone saw a car strikingly similar to this car in the Camm neighborhood right before the murders, it wouldn't be this car?"

"First and foremost, I've never been there with that car." Boney added that he "had no idea" how to get to the Camm home and had only seen the house on television. He then claimed he had never been to Georgetown outside the years he went to Floyd Central High School as a high school wrestler at New Albany High School or to attend other sporting events.

His Cadillac, which he'd possessed for a year-and-a-half, had never been lent by him to anyone else, and it had been junked in 2003 at a Louisville scrap yard, he said, not far from his home on the near east side of Louisville.

Boney's 1986 Cadillac.

---

[267] In Gilbert's report, he wrote, "To my disbelief, Dunn informed Boney that the murder weapon was a Lorcin .380." Why Gilbert would be amazed at that question is unknown to me.

Boney's Girlfriend

I asked several questions about pawn shops and got the names of two that Boney had frequented in the past but none, he insisted, to sell any item, jewelry or otherwise.

When I asked about his income in 2000, he repeated he'd been working at Anderson Wood, "making well over $300 a week, working 45 hours a week, when I wasn't ditching work to be with my girl at the time."

"Who was your girl at the time?"

"Mala Singh."[268]

Boney then volunteered, "these gentlemen," as he looked at Gilbert,[269] were trying to find Mala, whom he had met at a restaurant in the west end of Louisville. She had lived with him and his mother just after his prison release because, as he said, "My mother knew that after me being in prison, I would need a woman so she allowed me to have a live-in girlfriend." He'd last seen Mala, he claimed, in 2001.

I made a mental note that Boney had needed his mother's permission to have a girlfriend spend the night with him. Was he still a "Momma's Boy," at 31 years of age and a veteran of over nine years in prison?

Regardless, Boney said that Mala was from Trinidad, a place he couldn't go because he was, as he put it, "under investigation."

Alibi Witnesses

Boney then claimed he was keeping a log of everything he did and making "several calls a day, including [to] the prosecutor's office. Everyone knows where I am at all times."

Boney even claimed he had "people follow [him] to work, people that [he'd] appointed to follow" him and, further, he kept a running timeline of his whereabouts every day, with people "watching [him] all the time." Now, *that* was cooperation on steroids, as Boney was having himself followed.

"Was anybody watching your back on September 28, 2000, when the Camm family was murdered?"

"I have three or four sets of individuals," the very cooperative Boney replied, then asking the detective sitting next to him, "These individuals, I,

---

[268] In Gilbert's report, he wrote, "Boney was asked about the women he was with between June and September of 2000. Boney said that he was with Mala Singh and Karen Angel. He described Angel as a pen pal who lived in Indianapolis." At the time of my interview, Boney didn't mention any Karen Angel nor any other woman he was dating in the summer of 2000. Wherever Gilbert had gotten that information, it wasn't in my interview with Boney. We later discovered the probable source of that information.

[269] He also referred to the two detectives as Gary and Wayne.

Gary, what do you think, is this information I should give? I don't have any reason to hide it."

Gary Gilbert said it was up to him.

Boney then confessed to being on Lockhart Road around 2:00 p.m. that afternoon surveilling the Camm residence for his home invasion later that evening. Well, okay, he didn't directly confess to that, but, well, here's the beginning of his answer relative to his alibi witnesses, "Uh, at approximately two o'clock that day, 2:00 p.m., specifically, I was with Marshal King, he's a veterinarian at the Beechwood Animal Clinic."

Kim and the children weren't murdered until after 7:35 p.m., yet Boney began his alibi day at 2:00 p.m., or five and a half hours before the murders. Why? It was simple, as he knew his vehicle had been seen entering Lockhart Road at the same time. Why else would he begin an alibi over five hours before the crimes had been committed?

When I asked how he could recall the specific time and date, Boney responded he was able to do so because, as "Mr. Wayne Kessinger said, I remember the Camm murders because it was a landmark, it was something that you just remember, you always remember stuff like that."

"So," Boney continued, "I went back and I recalled the day that I had first heard about them, and that would have been that Friday, and I asked myself, 'okay what was I doing that day,' and I went back and I thought about and I thought about and it took me a little bit."

It made sense to me that a person would recall what they were doing at the time of a significant event: e.g., the JFK assassination or 9-11. But as for the murders of a mother and her children who weren't close or even known? It didn't compute that anyone would ask themselves what they were doing unless they or loved ones were affected. Or if they needed alibi witnesses. Regardless, Boney's substantiated—or not—whereabouts at the time of the murders, rather than how he came up with his alibis, would be the proof of the pudding.

Returning to his claim of being with a veterinarian, I asked what kind of animal he took to the pet doctor. Boney wasn't on a mission of mercy for a pet, but rather, "I had a request for him." I quickly asked what he meant. "He's going to say that he remembers me asking him for a loan or to cosign for me in order to improve my credit."

In a nutshell, Boney had "ditched work" and had been with his girlfriend while he had asked a man to lend him money to pay his bills so he would have better credit.

The vet, however, couldn't help Boney, but he had referred him to a reverend at a local church. That pastor wasn't good, for Boney "didn't have a really good relationship" with him. Dr. King had next referred him to a different minister, and Boney went to that second reverend's residence, arriving, he said, between 5:00 p.m. to 6:00 p.m.

Follow Boney's logic, if you can, of his visit to the pastor: "I asked him if it was possible to get a loan through the church and he told me that he would have to ask his elders and he asked me, 'are you working?' I said, 'yes, sir.' He says, 'what day are your paydays?' I said 'Friday.' He said, 'well, you know, tomorrow's Friday.' You know, because this is the 28th, so he's like 'well, tomorrow's Friday.'"

"[The minister then] said, 'Aren't you getting paid tomorrow?' I was like, 'yes, sir,' I said, 'but I have to pay my uncle you know, towards the Cadillac and I'll be short and there's things I need to take care of.'"

I interjected, "But your uncle was in Evansville, though, right? How were you going to pay him that night?"

"Money order. I mean, when that man says, 'I want my money,' he wants his money or he would come and get the car. It's that simple. I even sent him money Western Union."

"Okay, but this particular evening how did you pay him?"

Boney's response was beyond perplexing. "I didn't, I wouldn't have paid him that particular evening because Friday hadn't come yet."

"Okay, so he didn't get any money that evening?"

"No, because Friday, Friday is payday. Stay with me."

Boney's lies were getting so convoluted, even he couldn't follow them. I got back to the minister and the man searching for good credit told me that both the minister and his wife, "both of them can recall [my asking for a loan]."

Unfortunately, Boney said, he was turned down by each, but Mala was able to borrow some money from her uncle, also her employer, and Boney said he sent his uncle a money order the next day.

"Where did you get that money order?"

The man with the incredible detailed memory of the events of September 28, 2000, answered, "I have no idea. You're asking me a question I couldn't possibly remember." He quickly added, "I'd have to really just think."

I returned to Boney's alibi witnesses, and asked, after the minister, the next person he visited. Boney said he was "positive" he went to his sister's former husband's home in Louisville with Mala, around 6:30 p.m. That guy and his wife would be the best alibi witnesses, he said, behind Mala who was his "second perfect alibi."

Told that 6:30 p.m. wasn't really an alibi, Boney easily altered his memory. "So, I'm thinking that I would have been there realistically at around 7, 7:15, 7:30. I wouldn't have stayed more than an hour."

What was the reason he visited his former brother-in-law? He wanted to introduce him and his wife to Mala, of Indian descent, because she, he said, was a "woman of color. It's a joke, because I've had nothing but white women. That's why I remember that night so well."

"I'm skeptical here because you had met Mala, you said, immediately after you got out of prison. But it took you three months before you introduced her to [them]?"

"I mean, this man wasn't an everyday part of my life. We visited him that day. And my hope was also to ask him if he could help me out. That was my whole purpose of being over there."

After he was again refused a loan, they left, with Boney driving Mala to see her boss and uncle, a guy named Joe. According to Boney, he and Mala got there "realistically, prior to like eight or nine o'clock."

It was clear Boney didn't really want to talk about Mala, in spite of her being his "second perfect alibi," and I tried to get further information about her, but he claimed he didn't know where she was and had been instructed by the investigators not to try and find her because it would appear he was trying to "orchestrate" a story.

Boney was compelled to again emphasize the veterinarian. "I know I was at the veterinarian's place, Marshall King's, at about two. It was day time."

I was convinced Boney had, through his reiteration of his story for the afternoon of September 28, confirmed it was his dark blue, almost black Cadillac seen by Brandon Beaven on Lockhart Road.

Stan Faith

In preparation for my interview, we had discovered Boney, on probation since his sentence reduction in June 2000, had failed to check in with his probation officer for almost two years. He had been subsequently arrested in Louisville, after Amber had taken out her EPO, and taken to Monroe County where an attorney had filed an appearance on his behalf. That attorney? Stan Faith. Yeah, that's right, Stan Faith, David Camm's first prosecutor.

In his argument to the judge not to revoke Boney's probation, Faith had made a passionate pitch for his client, a sales manager at a rental store, "He was employed all this time and *he really is a good citizen*.[270] He just didn't return to the system. And well, he missed by two days an appointment and it scared him. And he thought he would be revoked for the rest of the time and he just didn't use his head, your Honor. He panicked. And so he stayed out for two years and every day that went by it got worse. Do you see what I am

---

[270] Emphasis mine.

saying? So, he could have remedied it in two days and he didn't. Everything has been paid. And *he's got a very nice mother.*"[271]

I asked the "good citizen" with the "very nice mother" why Faith, who practiced law 90 miles from Bloomington, had been his attorney. Faith and Boney's mother, he said, "just knew each other" and "she campaigned for him." His original lawyer had been Nick Stein and he "would have went [sic] with him, but he's no longer doing defense."

So, the guy who viciously murdered Kim, Brad, and Jill, had hired Dave's original prosecutor as a defense counsel, but only after he couldn't use Nick Stein, Faith's mentor, who was the attorney representing Dave's in-laws in a civil suit against him. It was beyond weird.

"Did your nickname ever come up with Stan Faith?"

"No. I don't talk about prison stuff anymore."[272]

Wives & Women

After Mala, Boney's next girlfriend was Amber, whom he had met at a strip club and later married in a ceremony at the Louisville Zoo. Amber, he said, "makes anywhere from $350 to $500 a night." She was making so much money, Boney said, that he didn't have to work because "she just wanted a house husband and we eventually got married."

While discussing his estranged wife, Boney had to stop, however, and let me know he was a real ladies' man, "I don't have an ego about it, you know, but I do have a past with multiple females, bottom line, if you're not happy, keep moving; bottom line is, I've always had my fair share of women." Most guys would have stopped there, but Boney had to add, "You know, that's why I don't have rape cases." The meaning behind that comment was clear. Kim had been sexually attacked, but it couldn't have been Boney because he was really smooth with women.

"Charles, how about violence toward women? Is there an issue there?

"Well, I mean, I hit my wife. I did hit her." And then, of course, from the serial evader: "But see, the thing is no matter what she did to me, and I promised her that I wouldn't bad mouth her."

After giving himself a few seconds to compose his extended answer, Boney continued, "Am I violent? Do I have a temper? Somebody could say something about my mother and I'd say hey, my mom fights better than I do, and I could laugh and walk away."

---

[271] Emphasis mine.

[272] In Gilbert's report, he wrote, "Dunn asked Boney if there was any connection between him and Stan Faith. Boney said that there was no connection."

Wanting to get his response about Amber's EPO, I found Boney's response predictable, as he blamed his wife. "If she's honest enough to talk about the hot grease, [she] had it right over the bed getting ready to throw it on me. I covered for her because she would have been arrested [by the police who responded]. I wanted to protect her." Chivalry, I just discovered, was an important trait of Boney's.

"How about any other women other than Amber with whom you've been violent?"

Boney responded that he and his first wife had engaged in "pushing and shoving."

When I delved into his first wife and his financially supporting his child, Boney said he didn't see either but claimed he was paying accumulated child support.[273]

I again pressed him on the whereabouts of Mala. He only knew where she had once lived, he said, which had been in an apartment complex in the west end of Louisville. He did claim, though, she had been pregnant with another man's child when he ended the relationship.

Other Background

Knowing, of course, Boney would lie about his own character and behavior, I felt it was important to get as much detail as possible from him about his prior addresses and employment. I'd then get an assessment *of* him as well as possibly some good stories *about* him from neighbors, co-workers, employers, and others.

Boney gave me the names of several previous employers, including three automobile dealerships. He did well, he said, selling used cars but didn't last as a new car salesman because, as he put it, he "wasn't good at their market" and "was going hungry." He also worked, he said, as a door-to-door salesman and at a rent-to-own store.

I moved on to his three present jobs where he supposedly worked the equivalent of two full-time jobs a week. He didn't divulge where those jobs were, but he did say he'd shared that information with Carrie Harned and the prosecutor because they were "people that [he] trust[ed]."

The man who was good with the ladies was currently living with a woman, whom he refused to identify, and her two sons, ages seven and thirteen. He had told the "fresh eyes" her name because "anyone that wants to speak with them on the prosecution's side" he had no problem with, but he had to "protect" them from the defense.

---

[273] Boney's child support was in arrears $23,000+ in 2004.

The Leadup To & The Confession

Boney did opine as to the type of person who was responsible for the murders, when he claimed that "anyone who could kill a kid is a dirty rotten motherfucker [and] it doesn't have to be my kids, it could be anybody's kids, I would become a violent person."

And then, rather than answering my question about motive, Boney launched into another pompous screed. "I did stuff while I was in prison. I took a guy's TV, took their commissary. I wouldn't let a child molester have anything."

Boney then radically shifted and asked me if I knew whether there was possibly more than just his "DNA and the DNA of an unknown female on the sweatshirt."

This was the time to maneuver into my most critical question: "There's a lot, [and] the contentions that the defense has had is that for years this DNA was not run through any database to determine whose identity that DNA belonged. There is a multitude of physical evidence that was found at that crime scene, which hasn't been either tested, or tested to see if there is any matches or database. There are certainly fingerprints, there is blood found at the scene that hasn't been identified yet and that's the reason I asked you, and I ask you again, if any of that belongs to you, then that would put you at the scene, would you agree?"

"That's, that is correct. If, if something of mine was there at the scene that means that I would have been there."

Boney then tried to deflect the question towards his being cooperative. I stopped him. "So, and let me ask you this, in the next extension Charles, would be, if you were at the scene, then you would have been the individual committing that crime then?"

"IF ANY OF THAT (UNIDENTIFIED DNA, BLOOD, FINGERPRINTS) BELONGS TO YOU, THAT WOULD PUT YOU AT THE SCENE?"

"THAT IS CORRECT. IF SOMETHING OF MINE WAS AT THE SCENE, THAT MEANS I WOULD HAVE BEEN THERE."

"AND IF YOU WERE AT THE SCENE, THEN YOU WOULD HAVE BEEN THE ONE COMMITTING THAT CRIME?"

"THAT WOULD BE PRETTY OBVIOUS."

"That would be pretty obvious."

Thank you, Charles, I thought, for being unequivocal. Now, let's hope and pray some additional DNA or your fingerprints will be found at the scene, for then your "obvious" comment will be a confession.[274]

Impersonating A Police Officer

Prior to the interview, Donnie Camm had received information from his original source that Boney had claimed, while in the Green Light, to be a police officer. Thus, my question, "Have you ever presented to anybody that you've been a police officer?"

"In, uh, joking, or for real, serious?"

"Yeah. Anytime?"

After he told me, "That's against the law," I asked again and again, with Boney finally admitting, "Only in jest, I mean," as Boney claimed Amber had thought he might be a cop, and he'd simply played along. When I asked if he had ever shown a badge to anyone, the answer was "I have never had a badge," rather than simply "I have never *shown* a badge to anyone." A badge in the hands of a violent guy like Charles Boney could have devastating results.

Polygraph Examination

I asked Boney if he'd take a polygraph test administered by an expert examiner, not for the purpose of confirming his deception, but to gauge his answer. It was predictable. He'd take one, he said, only if his answers were "reviewed as we go along" by the prosecutor's examiner. It'd take months before I understood the true meaning of his response.

He's Strong

Charles decided he needed to vent some more about being a victim. "I can't stop somebody from coming to do anything to me and I am not going to worry about it because once again, I wasn't there. I didn't do the killings. If it's proven that someone of my caliber has done something like this at that point and time, and keep in mind, I think that I have said this once before, if I knew for a fact that I was guilty and that all this is coming at me, the media, questions and answers, and all of this kind of stuff, my mom, how people would feel about me, how they see me, I would have either killed myself or done something destructive by now."

"If I knew for a fact that I was guilty" was decidedly not a denial of his murdering Kim, Brad, and Jill. But still, was he admitting he had gotten

---

[274] Gilbert had summarized my interview of Boney in his ISP report, but there was nothing in his report regarding my question of Boney's DNA and/or fingerprints being at the crime scene or his "obvious" answer.

into such a frenzy he didn't remember? I doubted that, in the same manner I doubted he would kill himself, as there was no way the most important person in the world to Charles—himself—would ever commit suicide.

Boney kept on: "Honestly, the heat is on. I have never felt this pressure before. Never. Instead of being angry, or crazy, or delirious, I have become aggressively strong, and now this is my chance to face retribution from the past. This is a challenge because really, really, honestly, it's not even about whether Charles Boney did this or not, it is about Charles Boney's past. Could his past have done this? Cause they are not talking about Charles Boney today, they are talking about Charles Boney 1989, 1992."

I asked, "Could Charles Boney have done this in '89 or '92?"

"If Charles Boney could have done it back then, then I think the Charles Boney back then would have done it. You know, I have a conscience. I can't kill people and shit like that."

I couldn't let all of his nonsense ride. "You know, my response to that would be, and clearly you don't want to be a recidivist? Right? You don't want to go back to prison, [and] a cynical response would be that, that's the reason that the victims were all killed because they were witnesses and therefore they wouldn't be able to identify a person to help put that person back in prison."

Rather than deny he murdered anyone, Boney rationalized, "I see your point. The bottom line is, what, what you're really saying is that in every case where I have been exposed there was someone that could talk about it. And in, in, of course, this case, there was no one to point the finger at Charles Boney. That is your point. But keep in mind, my point is really simple. I know what I am capable of, and I know what I have done, and I have been honest with you guys."

The man admitted the victims couldn't "point the finger at" him because they were dead, but Boney, as he constantly did, engaged in victimization. "You guys are hoping that you find something with me so that you can exonerate this man. You got to admit that."

Rather than deny the obvious, I responded, "Absolutely. Because it was either you or someone that had your sweatshirt." I asked if Boney agreed with those two possibilities.

Not responding, but rather evading, deflecting and then moving on to his narrative, Boney's response was, again, to ask as to the reason why the perpetrator had a sweatshirt. Clearly, he had been obsessing about the sweatshirt, so much so, that he had asked, in effect, if his story about it had been believable.

The victim wasn't through, though, as Boney had to brag one more time about having spent 22 hours with the "fresh eyes." He had been honest with them and me, summarizing the interviews as follows: "If you tell lies and everybody had lied, but in something like this, one lie ruins all of my credibility. Because all I have is my credibility right now."

To emphasize his honestly, Boney summarized the reason for meeting with me: "I didn't have anything to hide."

I quickly responded, "That's the reason you got the name BACKBONE. You are a stand-up guy." Yeah, I know. But I couldn't help myself.

Boney quickly smiled and said, "All I can do is tell you that if I put my word on something, that it has to be golden."

Before terminating the interview, I asked Charles if he would let his mother know I wished to speak with her, and he replied that he'd tell her. I also told him I'd follow up on his story and then get back in touch with him. He willingly agreed to a second interview.

We both then stood, shook hands, and gathered our recording instruments, with Boney and Gilbert leaving through one door and me through another.

After I had returned to my car, I sat for several minutes, making notes and thinking. I had interviewed hundreds and hundreds of criminals, many of whom I called "fuck-withs." They loved to fuck with me and other investigators by engaging in their own riddles and occasionally inserting a double entendre, although the riddle and other word meanings were known only to them. After all, they were smarter than anyone else. Boney was a consummate "fuck-with" guy. If he thought he had won the day, that was great, but he had given me a boatload of excellent information.

During my time with him, I had gotten the names of Boney's alibi witnesses; his previous girlfriend; his second wife; where he was living at the time of the murders; his employments; and his other background, such as having a first wife and child. And a confession. He had confessed, but only if additional forensic evidence would be found putting him at the crime scene.

We would thoroughly investigate and interview all of those people, with the first ones being those whom I firmly believed would contradict his alibis and assertions. I'd then re-interview Boney, hitting him with all of his lies as we'd use his own words to make a hard case of murder against him.

We shouldn't have had to do all that because Charles Boney should have been behind bars, already charged with the murders of Kim, Brad, and Jill. The "fresh eyes," though, weren't even attempting to make a case against Boney. Not only were they not vigorously investigating him, interviewing his friends, co-workers, and others, but they had given Boney his talking points and, literally within an hour, they would, incredibly, go public with their own vigorous defense of him.

CHAPTER 28
The "Staged" Sweatshirt

Orchestrating The Case

While I was finishing my first personal interview of Boney, Keith Henderson was fresh off a conference call with Judge Aylsworth. The judge had given him permission to respond publicly to Kitty's filings asking for Boney's arrest and a warrant to search Mrs. Boney's house. Those requests, according to Henderson, were "frivolous and without merit and an attempt by defense council to try the case in the media."[275] That was rich, I thought, coming from a man who had given the inside scoop on Boney to a newsie, in violation of the judge's order, and in a very blatant attempt to frame his story and, in fact, to try the case in the media.

After leaving my interview with Boney, Gilbert was getting ready to join Henderson's press conference, and I was departing the courthouse, trying to weave myself through the cacophony of scrambling reporters, cameramen, and media trucks with their elevated antenna.

Salvation Army

After I reached my car, intent on driving directly to the Salvation Army headquarters in New Albany, I called Kitty. No, she said, she still hadn't received the police reports. She then asked, "What's your assessment of the guy, Dunner?"

> "IT'S BEEN A METICULOUS, THOUGHTFUL INVESTIGATION THAT CONTINUES TO UNFOLD."

"He's the guy who murdered Kim, Brad, and Jill. No doubt about it. Everything fits. The shoes. The sweatshirt. The gun. The violence. And his personality, Kitty. The best word I can use to describe Charles Boney is psychopath."

I further told Kitty that Boney lied with ease; lied when he didn't have to; was always engaged in trying to convince me of his honesty; tried to manipulate me into thinking he was the victim; often evaded and deflected questions; and, clearly, while trying to come off as a caring and sensitive person, was anything but genuine. In fact, I said, "he doesn't have a conscience

---

[275] Lowry, Kyle, DNA Links Ex-Convict to Murder Scene, Attorneys Say, *The Tribune*, March 1, 2005.

or any remorse for his actions, and all the while he's trying to convince me of being repentant for his previous crimes, he couldn't help but brag about his prison exploits. All in all, Kitty, he's a true psychopath."[276]

I told her of his alibi witnesses, even the one covering the time Brandon Beaven had seen the dark Cadillac enter and leave Lockhart Road. "Boney cut his own throat," I said, "and after we get more against him, I'll reinterview him and hit him with everything we have. We'll make the case the 'fresh eyes' doesn't want to make."

"And," I said, "I also got him to admit that if anything else of his— DNA, fingerprints, whatever— would be found at the crime scene, then, in his words, it would be 'obvious' he was the murderer. Stacy's forensic list, hopefully, will find matches of Boney's fingerprints or more of his DNA. If so, we'll have a confession."

Kitty said she would call once she got the reports and also told me that Sam was going to attend Henderson's press conference. Meanwhile, I started driving towards the local Salvation Army headquarters. Within ten minutes, I was sitting at the desk of the business administrator. They had, she said, two drop boxes located at the Grantline Road store, the same place described by Boney, which had been there for over ten years. The boxes were unattended, but clothing and other donated items were removed on a regular basis, taken inside the store, and sorted. The good garments were sized and placed on the racks for sale. The torn or dirty garments were either thrown away or else bundled and sold in large lots.

The administrator further told me there was no way anyone at the Salvation Army could verify the donation of a specific garment since they didn't keep copies of donation receipts. Furthermore, their sales receipts for clothing were non-specific, they had no video surveillance of the donation bins, and people could—and did—steal from those bins. Boney probably knew or surmised all of that information, but still, contrary to the official narrative, his story didn't "check out." At best, it was only his word he had dropped his sweatshirt in the donation bin.

Misleading The Public

Meanwhile, in his office prior to the beginning of his press conference, Henderson spoke on videotape to one reporter of the ongoing investigation: "It's been a meticulous, thoughtful investigation that continues to unfold."[277]

---

[276] Depending on one's source, psychopath, sociopath, and anti-social personality disorder (ASPD) have been used to describe such personalities. I, of course, was not a clinical psychologist attempting to diagnose Boney, but a criminal investigator; as such, Boney was, and is, in my viewpoint, a psychopath.

[277] WLKY-TV News, February 28, 2005.

For the first time, I thought, the prosecutor didn't look confident when making an assertion, which, by any investigative standard of most cops, wasn't anywhere close to meticulous or thoughtful.

A few minutes later, Henderson was standing behind a podium in a courthouse press room crowded with dozens of media types. Behind him was his trusted sidekick Steve Owen; next to him was Detective Gilbert; and then Prosecutor Investigator Wayne Kessinger, who had apparently supplanted ISP Detective Mike Black in the "fresh eyes" pecking order.

One news moderator said Henderson reported, "the DNA on the sweatshirt was just discovered weeks ago and since then prosecutors have questioned Charles Boney extensively. They say he has an alibi for the night of the killings and has no known connection to David Camm."[278] "They say he has an alibi" wasn't the same as "his alibi witnesses confirm." Did that mean they hadn't yet contacted his alibi witnesses? That would be the epitome of investigative dereliction if true.

As I later listened to Henderson, he reinforced his belief in Dave's guilt. "Either David Camm acted alone, or David Camm acted in concert. There is one piece of evidence that links Charles Boney to this crime scene and that's this sweatshirt that's been *staged at that scene*.[279] It hasn't changed my position on who…is culpable in this case and that is David Camm."[280]

The sweatshirt was *"staged?"* That meant they really bought Boney's fabricated story. Still, who said it was staged, and how did they come to that determination? Was it "staged" in the same manner Rob Stites had claimed the crime scene had been "manipulated" with bleach, water, and a mop?

Chief Deputy Owen had stepped to the microphone and immediately "ripped the defense theory [that Boney was the murderer] up one side and down the other," according to James Zambroski.[281] Waving his hands in the air, Owen had asked, "Mr. Boney's going to come out of jail, go to somebody's house in Georgetown, brutally murder three people and then say 'Oh, I think I'll take off my sweatshirt that I got from DOC and lay it down here by the boy.' Does that make sense to anyone? Because it doesn't make sense to me."[282]

That criminals left something of theirs at a crime scene, whether it be fingerprints, blood, DNA, footprint, a personal item or whatever, was an axiom in law enforcement and the primary reason why evidence technicians

[278] Ibid.
[279] Emphasis mine.
[280] Zambroski, James, WAVE-TV News, February 28, 2005.
[281] Ibid.
[282] Ibid.

existed. Owen's denigrating that possibility came off, in my opinion, as his being naïve at best, especially for a seasoned prosecutor. Even so, he was vigorously defending Boney, knowing full well of his past violent crimes.

The animated Owen had then suggested their preferred scenario: "It does make sense that somebody who killed those people thought 'Hey, I got a sweatshirt that don't [sic] belong to me and I know that don't belong to me,' and roll that sweatshirt up and lay it by his boy's side. Now, that makes sense."[283]

Owen wasn't finished, though, as it was time to blast Kitty, referring to her asking the court for an arrest warrant for Boney. "It's a tactic. It's Ms. Liell's job to get David Camm off. Not to seek truth or justice."

To make his point that Kitty didn't give a damn about "truth or justice," Owen, vigorously shaking his head back and forth, pounded the podium with his finger.[284] I had no doubt Steve Owen really disliked Kitty, especially since she and Stacy had forced his and Henderson's hand on running the DNA profile. Previously, convicting Dave was going to be a lot easier for them, but the introduction of Charles Boney into the picture had complicated their plans.

Also being reported by the press was the prosecutor's claim that "Kim's family told them it wasn't unusual for Kim to shop at thrift stores."[285] So, their narrative was now Kim had purchased the sweatshirt, which her husband later used to "stage" the crime scene, and in the process set up Charles Boney? That was, at least, the fourth theory of how Dave killed his family.[286]

After the press conference, it was inevitable Faith would find a way to put in his two cents, and he had: "the sweatshirt was never thought to be an integral part of the crime scene" and "may have been planted as a way to distract attention away from Camm."[287]

How did Faith know to react so quickly to the discovery of the DNA's owner? According to the former prosecutor, "because the man's identity was given to him in confidence by Henderson."[288] Faith had also told the same

---

[283] Ibid.

[284] WHAS-TV News, Louisville, 2.28.05.

[285] Ibid.

[286] The first three theories were 1) Dave had killed the family after arriving home sometime after 9:00 p.m., 2) Dave had killed his family after calling a client at 7:19 p.m. while in the house, and 3) Dave had killed his family at some time or another, and in all three scenarios the sweatshirt had meant nothing. Recall, also, that the "fresh eyes" had returned to the 7:19 p.m. phone call theory in Gilbert's murder affidavit.

[287] Ibid.

[288] Hershberg, Ben Zion, Camm Case: Match on DNA, February 28, *The Courier Journal*, 2005.

reporter, "he [Henderson] does not believe the man is a suspect." Once again, the preferred talking points had been distributed by Henderson, not only to the sycophant press, but also to his predecessor. The bitter election opponents were on the same scheme team.

There, however, was another shocking consistency in both Faith's and Henderson's respective cases against Dave: when evidence was screaming to be heard, the choices had been to ignore it completely, dismiss it as irrelevant, or claim it had been "planted," "manipulated," or "staged." In short, don't confuse me with facts that contradict the Gospel of My Case.[289]

Doubling down on the State's blood experts, Faith had claimed, "The... most accurate scientific knowledge we have in the year 2005 says he [Camm] is the shooter. I think the prosecution's case is the same as it ever was and I think the jury will convict him based upon the high impact splatter like they did the other time."[290] It wasn't surprising that Faith had chosen to totally ignore the appellate opinion, which absolutely refuted his assertion.

After returning to Sam's apartment, I walked over to his house and spoke with both him and Dave. I told them of my interview with Boney and my assessment of him. We all knew the man who viciously murdered Kim, Brad, and Jill was walking the streets a free man. It was devastating but sadly not surprising to any of us, given the entrenched mindset of Henderson and his team.

I then asked Dave if Kim had ever bought any second-hand clothing. "No. No way" was his response. "Kim always bought Brad and Jill new clothes, mostly from Target. She never shopped at the Salvation Army, Goodwill, or any thrift stores for the kids, me, or herself."

Sam said he had also spoken to Debbie Ter Vree, Kim's closest female friend, and she, too, had categorically denied Kim had ever purchased any second-hand clothing. Their clothing may not have been expensive, but it was always new, reported Debbie. Whatever the source, if any, of the prosecutor's assertion Kim had shopped at thrift stores, it wasn't accurate.

Within a few minutes, we got a telephone call from Kitty. What she would tell us about Charles Boney was beyond belief.

---

[289] Another more common term is Confirmation Bias, the rigid embrace of one's existing or preferred theory and the inability to comprehend or accept new information, even in light of new facts and new evidence, which contradict that theory.

[290] Ibid.

CHAPTER 29
Boney's "Perfect World"

Kitty had received a voluminous amount of information, much of it incredibly specific, on Boney's previous crimes, victims, arrests, interrogations, admissions, and court proceedings. The extensive amount of critical material was also presumably in the hands of Henderson and his investigators, and the fact they had refused to use it against the man was incomprehensible.

Attacks For Shoes

Boney's shoe crimes, Kitty said, had begun on October 12, 1988, when a young Indiana University (IU) coed had been attacked at night shortly after leaving her car, parked near the IU campus. She had been violently tackled and forced to the ground by Boney, who had been wearing a sweatshirt, gloves, and mask.

"BONEY'S BEEN CONVICTED OF 11 FELONIES, ALMOST ALL OF THEM VIOLENT. I HAD 11 EYEWITNESSES WITH ME...AND INSTEAD OF BELIEVING THOSE 11 GUYS, THE 'FRESH EYES' BELIEVE AN 11-TIME CONVICTED VIOLENT FELON WHO ASSAULTED WOMEN AT NIGHT FOR THEIR SHOES."

He had ripped the left shoe off the terrified young woman and run away, but in the process had left one of his gloves at the scene

"So much for Steve Owen saying there was no possibility Boney had left his sweatshirt at the crime scene," Sam dryly noted.

Approximately seven weeks later, Kitty continued, during the evening of December 4, Boney had attacked one of two coeds walking together. Again, he had been wearing a sweatshirt and mask. The victim had resisted, and for her efforts, had been punched in the face by Boney, who'd made away with one of her shoes.

The nighttime attacks had persisted as Boney had assaulted another woman shortly before Christmas. This time, he had been wearing his sweatshirt, but instead of a mask, he had clown makeup on his face. Boney had grabbed the victim's left shoe but only after the young lady had suffered abrasions to her knee and ankle, and an injury to her wrist.

"Boney tackling and hitting his victims explains Kim's 22 bruises, cuts and scrapes to her elbows, knees, and chin," said Dave, adding, "The coward could only attack women at night."

Kitty continued, saying Boney's next crime had been a carbon copy of his prior crimes, as he had grabbed and tackled another young woman for her shoe, once again in front of a friend. The startled coed had recalled his wearing something red and white on his face.

Boney had apparently been in a frenzy that night, for one victim wasn't enough, as later that evening, he had attacked once more. This time, though, his intended victim had fought back, as had one of her friends, striking Boney in the face. Boney had run off and then, several feet away, turned around, stopped, and stood with a Superman pose.

The Bloomington Police Department (BPD) had flooded the area and, within minutes of his last robbery, had sighted Boney and begun chasing him near the IU School of Law, ultimately arresting him as he had tried to lose them in the woods behind the complex. It wasn't lost on anyone that he had sought concealment in the woods.

Indiana University School of Law, Bloomington campus.

All of Boney's physical attacks on women had occurred at night; all victims had been in or near cars; all victims or intended victims had been women; and, in all cases, their shoes had been Boney's primary target. His crimes, quite obviously, had a distinct and very unique pattern.

Kitty then said that Boney, true to form, couldn't shut up in his post-arrest interrogation. He had told Sergeant Mike Diekhoff,[291] the investigative detective, he had only assaulted women who had "nice legs." He claimed he had a "thing for ladies' legs and feet."

"Get this, guys," Kitty continued, "he said he never had attacked a woman wearing a dress. All of his victims wore pants." Kim, of course, had been wearing pants when she had been attacked.

---

[291] Michael Diekhoff is currently the Chief of Police for the BPD.

"What did he say about the shoes?" asked Dave.

Boney, Kitty responded, said stealing shoes had been his "hobby" as he bragged he "creeped around and scared" some of his victims before he had attacked them.

"A 300-pound guy, creeping around in the darkness, viciously tackling 100-pound coeds. What a gutless guy," observed Sam.

"Are you ready for the sweatshirt bit?" Kitty asked.

"Well, he wore one at each of the robberies," I said.

"Yeah, but there's more to it," Kitty replied. "Boney said the sweatshirt was, and I quote, 'his escape plan.' He had taken off his sweatshirt after his attacks and had put it in a backpack he took with him so any witnesses would describe him as wearing a sweatshirt. That not only explains the sweatshirt at the scene but it also explains…"

"The backpack. The damming of the blood flow," Sam quickly said.

"Exactly," said Kitty. "Boney probably took his backpack to the garage, and it was sitting on the floor. After he shot Kim in the head, he turned his attention to the kids. Kim's huge head wound, meanwhile, caused a massive flow of blood, which was stopped by the backpack. The delineation in the blood was the edge of his backpack."

"So many questions finally answered," Dave said in a soft voice.

Kitty kept on, telling us Boney had also made a startling admission, telling the officers he enjoyed getting away with his crimes and, further, as Kitty read from the report, "If you can't get caught or no one catches you, you just keep doing it."

"Well, you can't argue with his logic" was my answer. "Not only that, but he had about 18,000 female victims who fit his victim profile on the IU campus. He was in his perfect world."

After his arrest, Kitty said, the BPD had searched his apartment and had found a white mask, one ladies blue leather shoe, another sweatshirt, a pink handbag containing a pair of blue pantyhose, a pair of natural pantyhose, and an advertisement for pantyhose. Kitty summarized, "I think most people, except the 'fresh eyes,' would agree the man was obsessed with women's legs and feet and the hose and shoes that covered them."

In response to my question if Boney had claimed the shoe thefts were part of a fraternity prank, Kitty said he hadn't used that as an excuse for his compulsion.

Boney also, Kitty continued, told the police some of the information of his prior crimes the police had released to the newspaper was wrong.

"He thinks he's smarter than everybody else," Sam observed.

"With the 'fresh eyes,'" I said, "he's got a point."

Dave then asked, "How many more women did he victimize since he murdered my family?" Sam and I just shook our heads, as the rush to judgement to arrest Dave had facilitated the very violent attacker of women to roam the streets for over four years, searching for more prey, while an innocent husband and father sat in jail instead.

Kitty then said Boney had been charged with three Class C Felony Robbery counts and one count of Class C Felony Attempted Robbery.[292] After the initial court proceedings, he pleaded guilty to all charges and had served a few months in the county jail.

Probation Violation

A few months after his release from jail, Kitty continued, Charles Boney had begun writing checks on a bank account with little or no funds. With some of those checks, he had purchased clothing from the J.C. Penny store in the local mall, then had sent his wife to the store to exchange the clothing for a cash refund. During his interview by a BPD officer, Boney had explained he "needed the money." After pleading guilty to theft, Boney, still on probation for his robbery convictions, had been ordered to serve two years in the Indiana Department of Corrections (DOC).

Armed Robbery

Kitty continued with her summations, telling us Boney had been released from the DOC on September 1, 1992, and had returned to Bloomington. One month later, he had walked into an apartment complex where two female rental agents were counting cash receipts. This time he had a gun, a .38 snub nose revolver. I interrupted Kitty, "I'm assuming it was loaded?"

"Of course it was loaded," Kitty responded, "and he put that loaded gun to the back of one of the victims, demanding money." While one employee had been gathering all the cash, the other had been ordered, at gunpoint, to sit on the floor, with the muzzle of the gun pointing at her head.

During the almost 15 minutes Boney had been in the office, said Kitty, he had been unmasked, hadn't worn any gloves, and had touched various items in the office. "So much for the sophisticated and highly intelligent armed robber," Sam opined.

The two victims had then been taken at gunpoint, Kitty said, to the vehicle owned by the manager, but she and the other woman had refused to get in the car. Boney, according to Kitty, had apparently been frustrated with that act of defiance and had driven the vehicle away from the scene by himself.

---

[292] There was no explanation for why he wasn't charged in all five attacks.

"Any bets on what was going to happen with the two if they got in the car?" I asked.

Our consensus was the two women's refusal to go with Boney had probably saved their lives.

Home Invasion/Armed Robbery/Criminal Confinement

One week after his first armed robbery, Boney had struck again, with Kitty again describing the crime. Five IU coeds, she said, had lived in a two-story condominium townhouse near the IU football stadium. Boney, unmasked and ungloved, had a red bag with him as he had calmly walked into their unlocked residence and brandished the .38 revolver to the three coeds present. He later admitted he had stolen it from his mother. Kitty noted, "Yes, it too was loaded, Dunner."

Demanding cash, Boney got little from all three women, after having marched them to their various bedrooms on both floors of the condo. The longer he stayed, the more frustrated he had gotten, the victims later said. Once he had grabbed the hair of one of the girls, had jammed the gun to the back of her head, and had threatened to "blow [her] fucking brains out."

"Kim had a lot of hair on her sweater," Dave said. "It makes sense Boney did the same thing to Kim as he did to that college student."

Kitty continued, saying that during their ordeal, Boney had threatened to shoot all three victims if anyone yelled or screamed. While in the bedroom of one of the women, he had seen a photograph of her father, a uniformed ISP trooper. In a fit of anger, he had slammed the photo down and had told the terrified women he "hated cops."

While in the bedrooms, Boney had also opened one jewelry box and rummaged through it, seeking valuables, but had found nothing of value. At gunpoint, he then had told another victim to open her jewelry box, from which he promptly grabbed an item.

"What with the items found in the search of his home, his rummaging through the jewelry boxes and his prized shoes, there's no doubt Boney had been in your house, Dave, looking for more souvenirs. It's hard telling how long he was in there," I said.

Sam then interjected, "If Kim had been forced by Boney into the house, that meant someone had to have been watching the kids who were still sitting in the back seat. That would also explain Kim wearing the black panties."

"And it also validates Brandon Beaven's seeing a passenger in Boney's car," I added. "Maybe it was the female with the unidentified blood on the sweatshirt. Maybe it was Boney's girlfriend, Mala Singh."

Kitty acknowledged all the comments and then continued, saying Boney had been upset he had gotten very little cash from women he called "rich bitches." He had told them he was going to take them to an ATM, and each would have to withdraw money. Under threat of being shot, he had paraded them out of the residence and to the vehicle belonging to one of the victims. Forcing them all into the car, he had held his gun at the head of the driver and had again threatened to kill each one if they screamed.

Very fortunately, however, a neighbor had witnessed the ongoing robbery through an open window and had called 911. Several BPD units had arrived and surrounded the vehicle, guns drawn, before Boney had a chance to escape with his hostages.

As had Officer Matt Morris, Sergeant George Connolly had his weapon pointed at Boney, as he had yelled instructions for him to lay his gun down, but Boney had been slow to do so. Finally, though, Boney had complied, and the three totally unnerved women had scrambled from the car.

Each of the three victims had later told officers they had been convinced they were going to be raped and then killed by Boney, whose demeanor, they said, had initially been calm, but had become frenzied and panic-stricken at the end.

Each victim had also seen, in the presence of Boney throughout the robbery, as had the officers at the time of his arrest, a gym bag which had "miscellaneous clothing, mask, Halloween mask, gloves, and identification."

During his arrest interrogation, Boney had admitted to the first robbery of the apartment office and the theft of the manager's car. He also had confessed he'd committed the first robbery, as well as the home invasion, because he had needed money and had been refused loans.

"It's interesting Boney's current alibi stories also concerned loans," I said, adding, "but it wasn't about money. It's about his power over women. Boney gets off on terrorizing women. Remember, he said he 'enjoyed' committing his crimes."

Kitty then said Boney had claimed his last robbery was one of randomness, as he had simply been walking through the condo complex and had only decided on the target residence when one of the women had looked at him.

Additionally, Kitty said, Boney had a mask in his red bag that night but said he didn't have enough time to put it on before he had opened the door and pointed his weapon at the victims. And yes, added Kitty, he'd known it was a violation of his parole to have a gun in his possession.

I couldn't help but be sarcastic. "That's hard to believe, as this morning, Boney said his prior crimes were a deterrent to his committing additional crimes."

The ever-prescient Boney, however, Kitty said, had told the interrogating officers of a mistake in a newspaper article describing the first robbery. "His press clippings meant a lot," said Sam, adding, "and he's doing the same thing right now, only this time Henderson and Owen might as well be his media agents."

"Did he take a plea?" I asked. He had, said Kitty, and it was as he had described to me. He had pleaded to one count of armed robbery, two counts of armed robbery with a weapon, and three counts of criminal confinement. His sentences could have been stacked, or run consecutively, but they were all combined, and his total sentence had been 20 years, with parole possible after just ten years.

"And he manipulated the judge and got out over two years early," said Dave, adding, "Kim, Brad, and Jill would still be alive…"

"The system has repeatedly failed you, Kim, and the kids," said Sam, "and it's doing it again."

"Do you guys remember what Henderson said earlier today about the evidence against Boney?" I asked rhetorically. "He said, quote, the evidence is not there, unquote. How can they be this blind?"[293]

"The 'fresh eyes' are willfully blind," said Sam, adding, "It's disgusting."

"Kitty," asked Dave, "Boney has been convicted of how many felonies?"

"Uh, let's see. Eleven. Eleven felonies with 10 of them being violent."

"So," Dave concluded, "Charles Boney has been convicted of 11 felonies, almost all of them violent ones. I had 11 eyewitnesses with me the night my family was murdered, and instead of believing those 11 guys, the 'fresh eyes' believe a 11-time convicted violent felon who assaulted women at night for their shoes. This can't be happening. It shouldn't be happening."

---

[293] Carrie Harned reported on WAVE-TV on February 28, 2005, from Henderson's press conference wherein he stated, "We know that the defense has maintained that this is the killer. That I should dismiss the charges against David Camm. That I should file triple homicide charges against Charles Boney. The evidence is not there."

CHAPTER 30
Alibi Witnesses, Wives & A Confession

The Alibis That Weren't

That Boney was an abject liar wasn't a question but an established fact. For instance, contrast his claim to me, of his prior armed robberies, that his gun hadn't been loaded and, further, that he'd only held it down to the actual event: he had jammed a loaded .38 to the back of a woman's head and threatened to "blow [her] fucking brains out." I think that constituted a really big lie, and my eyes weren't even fresh.

The most critical question, though, was whether Boney had lied about his alibi witnesses. That went to the very core of his defense: he couldn't have been murdering people because he was with his girlfriend, Mala Singh, speaking with several people in search of a monetary loan to make a car payment. If his alibis didn't confirm his story, well then, as he had told me, all he had was his "credibility."

> "HE WAS LIVING IN INDIANA. HE WAS TALKING ABOUT A ROBBERY AND HE WANTED ME TO BE THE DRIVER. ALL I HAD TO DO WAS WATCH AND DRIVE. HE WOULD HAVE EVERYTHING SET UP."
>
> "WHAT KIND OF CAR WAS HE DRIVING?"
>
> "A CADILLAC."

Mala Alibi

I began with the "second perfect" witness, per BACKBONE, who was Mala. I'd already gotten on my database, and her Louisville addresses coincided with her place of employment, a deep-fried fast-food take-out restaurant on West Broadway in Louisville, and two apartment houses on the fringes of downtown. All references were dated, however, and it appeared as she was living in Trinidad, as Boney had claimed.

Still, the best lead on Mala was her uncle and former employer, so I found a number for him, called him, and we met at his restaurant. Eddie Jansen,[294] who had obviously taken a strong liking to his many fried foods, was cooperative albeit cautious of what he said.

---

[294] Pseudonym.

Yes, Jansen said, Mala, his niece, had worked for two short periods of time for him. He told me he'd get her employment records—get them, he said, if he could find them.

Jansen vaguely recalled Charles Boney as having been Mala's boyfriend, although he couldn't put a time on that relationship. He had never personally met or spoken with Boney and had seen him only on one occasion, with Mala, near a bank on the southwest side of Louisville.

Mala occasionally had borrowed money from him, Jansen said, but only in $5.00 or $10.00 increments, and she never had borrowed anywhere near $100 and certainly had not borrowed any money to pay for a loan on a car.

Mala's brother, Seamus,[295] had been living in Louisville for several years, and Jansen provided me with his employment address, which was another restaurant. Jansen added that he was confident that Mala had been residing in Trinidad with her mother for some time.

Waiting until after the lunch crowd, I found Seamus working in the hot and steamy confines of a greasy kitchen restaurant in the southern end of Louisville. He appeared somewhat rattled when I told him the reason for my contact, although he agreed to speak with me, and I subsequently recorded his interview.

Yes, he was Mala's brother, and yes, Seamus added, she was living in Trinidad with their mother. His sister, whom he described as "wild," had, over short periods of time, numerous boyfriends and encouraged her toddler daughter to call each one "Daddy," which offended Seamus. One of those boyfriends had been Darnell Boney, whom Seamus had later recognized from Boney's television interviews.

Seamus recalled that Mala and Darnell had gone together for about three months, during the summertime, and while Darnell had been driving a Cadillac. When he had first met Boney, Seamus described him as a guy who had first come off as being "cool."

On one occasion, though, Seamus and his wife were in the Louisville apartment of his sister and mother when Boney was present. After a few minutes, Boney had approached him and asked for his help, all the while Mala listened. The nature of the request had frightened him, Seamus said, because he didn't want to go to prison. He then explained, "He was talking about a robbery, and he wanted me to be the driver."

"What kind of robbery?" I asked.

"It was either robbing a bank or a Kroger store over in Indiana. He was living in Indiana. All I had to do was watch and drive. He said he would have everything set up. He sounded pretty confident in what he was doing."

---

[295] Pseudonym.

"Darnell asked you to be the driver. What kind of car was he driving at the time?"

"I know it was a big Cadillac."

Seamus explained he had let Boney continue to talk, without interrupting him or telling him he wouldn't have any part of it, because he had just wanted to leave the apartment with his wife, which he soon had.

I asked Mala's brother if his sister may have helped Boney with his robbery. His response wasn't surprising. "To me, it looked like she was down with whatever her boyfriend asked her to do."

After breaking up with Boney, Mala had married a man, name unknown to Seamus, and the two of them had moved to Alaska. After about a year in Alaska, Mala had called Seamus, but he had refused to help her buy an airplane ticket from Alaska to Trinidad. As a result, she had become angry with him, had cursed at him, and the two hadn't spoken since.

Seamus said he hadn't been contacted by any police officer or investigator.

Prior to leaving him, Seamus agreed to allow me to secure a swabbing of the inside of each cheek, as I told him we would use it in order to try and identify unknown DNA on a piece of evidence.

On the phone with Kitty after the interview, I explained to her the solid reasons why Mala was very possibly the silhouette seen in the Cadillac on Lockhart Road and, further, that she could have been the one holding the children in the car while her boyfriend, Boney, was in the house with Kim.

As for our finding and interviewing Mala, I eventually established contact with a private investigator in Trinidad. Unfortunately, things didn't work out. For weeks, we were unable to make contact with her.[296]

Cookout Alibi

Nonetheless, I moved on, being able to trace Boney's former brother-in-law through a background check on his sister, Jacqueline,[297] who had been divorced from him for several years. Her former husband, who had a common name, was living in the near west end of Louisville with his wife.

After identifying myself and the purpose of the contact and providing my business card, which clearly reflected me as a retired FBI Agent and as a private investigator,[298] the couple graciously invited me into their small home. Jack and Naomi Cash[299] had been following the news about Boney

---

[296] It took several weeks for the Trinidad P.I. to respond to me, but I did receive an address where she was purportedly living.

[297] Pseudonym.

[298] I didn't want anyone to get any misperceptions on who I was and the purpose of any contact. This regimen would serve me well in the near future.

[299] Pseudonyms.

and therefore weren't surprised with my visit. They were surprised, however, that I was the first person to ask questions about him, as no one from law enforcement had contacted them.

Each agreed to have their interview taped, with Jack saying he had interacted very little with the Boney family for years, but, on a telephone request of his former mother-in-law, had helped Charles, recently released from prison in 2000, get a job at Anderson Wood. Cash, a former employee who was aware the company had hired former inmates, had made a call and gotten Boney a job.

As for the reason of Boney's prior imprisonment, Jack said he had been told it was because Boney had "roughed up" some older people but had not used a gun when robbing them.

Both Jack and his wife recalled a visit from Boney who had been with his girlfriend, Mala. They had arrived in an older, dark blue Cadillac. The occasion had been for a cookout, but it certainly hadn't occurred on any weekday, they said, as they only times they had entertained was on weekends, most likely a Saturday.

As for Boney's asking either one for a loan, Jack said Boney had never asked him for any money for any reason whatsoever. Naomi's reply was the same: "No, he never, he never came to us and asked for any money."

It was two huge whiffs for Boney on his most "perfect" alibi witnesses.

Afternoon Alibi

I found Marshall King, the long-time veterinarian, at his clinic in New Albany, still working at the age of 81. Dr. King was very gracious and helpful, answering all my questions, first stating he knew Barbara Boney, as she had brought her dog into his clinic, but explaining Charles Boney had never been in his presence. As such, Boney had never attempted to borrow any money from him, and no one, including Boney, had ever asked to borrow from him any sizeable sum of money such as $100.

Dr. King further told me he had never referred anyone, Boney included, to any minister, including Reverend Morton, whom he didn't know.

That credibility of yours, Charles, I thought, is swirling faster around the drain.

Minister Alibi

My interview of Reverend Scott Morton,[300] the now-retired gentleman whom Boney said he had visited, in person, in the presence of his wife, and had asked for a loan to make a car payment to his uncle, was also revealing.

---

[300] Pseudonym.

Of the Boney family, Reverend Morton recalled that he had performed the marriage ceremony for Boney's sister in the 1980's but that was the only time Charles Boney had been in his physical presence. On one occasion, date unrecalled, Boney had telephoned him and inquired as to borrowing money. Boney hadn't told Morton the reason for the request, and Morton, who thought it "audacious" Boney had called out of the blue asking for money, had simply told him to contact some other ministers. In fact, Morton said of the loan request, "That's the end of the story."

The reverend did advise, however, that, contrary to what he had said in his lengthy tale to me, Boney had never been in Morton's home, had never said anything about a car payment, hadn't mentioned his uncle, had never mentioned his place of employment, and had never said anything about a forthcoming paycheck. All the things Boney had told me he had discussed with the reverend had been fabricated.

As for as his wife's being present, the pastor's spouse, since deceased, had been in no physical or mental shape to recall anyone's visiting at the time Boney claimed. Indeed, Morton said of his wife, "she was incapacitated" and had therefore been unable to understand or converse coherently in the year 2000.

As with the Cash couple and Dr. King,[301] no one from law enforcement had spoken with Reverend Morton. And yes, the fact those alibi witnesses had not been interviewed by the "fresh eyes" was, in my opinion, at best, a dereliction of investigative duty. Some might claim it to even be a cover-up by omission. I wouldn't argue.

On another point, at this junction, many people would ask why Charles Boney, looking directly at me, trying to appear sincere and honest, would have concocted several bogus stories about his alibi witnesses. That's a fair question with a simple answer. First, lying is what Boney does. It's natural and easy for him to lie. In fact, lying is an essential part of him, as it constitutes his core personality.

Secondly, and as a practical matter, his mendacity also had purchased Boney time. In fact, when Carrie Harned was reporting there had been "no loopholes" in his story, that had been somewhat true. Since Henderson's team of investigators hadn't attempted to corroborate Boney's alibi stories, "no loopholes" had been found.

Boney's Second Wife

Next on my list was Boney's estranged wife, but before interviewing

---

[301] Dr. King was eventually interviewed by Gary Gilbert and Wayne Kessinger in late March 2005.

Charlynn Boney, I first obtained a copy of the EPO she had obtained from the Louisville Police Department on December 31, 2003.

EPOs were created to provide legal protection for people, almost always women, who had been abused, threatened, and/or stalked. Although state rules differ, in Kentucky, Charlynn had only needed to contact the police and provide a factual basis of the circumstances of her abuse. An officer would then have secured a court-authorized protective order against her husband. If, after the issuance of the EPO, Boney had been caught violating the conditions of the order, he could have been summarily arrested.

The details in the EPO of Charlynn, AKA Amber, weren't surprising. Boney and Amber had been married two years when the EPO had been issued. For over a year leading to that time, Boney had systematically physically and verbally abused, demeaned, and threatened his wife. As with his robbery victims, Boney had repeatedly grabbed her hair with one hand and threatened to shoot her while holding his gun and pointing it at her head with the other. Not satisfied with only using his hands and fists on her, he had also on several occasions used a stun gun on her, all the time threatening to kill her if she ever told anyone.

On December 30, 2003, Amber was in the hospital when she had been telephoned by Boney, whom she described as "having violent mood swings." He had told her he "did not want [her] to die naturally." When she had asked her husband if he was going to kill her, Boney had "laughed," she said. The threatening phone call, overheard by a nurse, had been the catalyst that had caused Amber to seek protection, and the EPO had been issued the next day.

"She Doesn't Know Who I Am!"

As I was preparing to interview Amber, though, I got a phone call from Donnie Camm. An acquaintance of his had a friend, Carl Colvin, who was claiming to have witnessed one of Boney's violent acts against Amber. I called Carl and, although he was somewhat initially reluctant to meet, nonetheless agreed to do so.[302]

Carl was an energetic guy who had a background of managing used car lots, selling cars, and, according to him, "hustling." Carl told me it was about two years prior when he went to a car dealership located in Jeffersonville, Indiana, to speak with a friend of his who had been the manager. While there,

---

[302] Carl explained to me he had lived the "street life" for several years, and those who did so didn't tell on others. After committing himself to Alcoholic Anonymous several years before, however, he had changed his life and was committed to living his life in a positive manner. He no longer followed the code of those in the "street life." In my several dealings with Carl over the years, I always found him to be very forthright and honest.

he had begun talking with Boney, a salesman whom Carl was told had worked there for several months.

After a few minutes, Boney had asked Carl if he had wanted to buy a big-screen television of his. Carl,

> "I'LL SHOOT THAT BITCH! I'LL KILL THAT BITCH! MY CONSCIENCE ALREADY HOLDS THREE MURDERS. ONE MORE IS NOT GOING TO BOTHER ME ANYMORE!"

who had a friend who was looking for such a television, had asked Boney how much he wanted for the 50" model. "$500" had been Boney's answer.[303]

Carl had told Boney that he would be interested so long as there hadn't been anything wrong with the television, including its having been stolen. Boney had assured him it had not been stolen and then had called his wife and told her he was going to sell the television. An argument ensued, and Carl had overheard Boney yelling at his wife, "Fuck you, bitch, I'm coming to get my TV. You can kiss my ass, it's my shit."

Carl had then expressed reluctance to proceed with the deal, but Boney had assured him it was his TV and had not been stolen. The two had then driven together to Boney's home where Carl's friend was to meet them and look at the TV. During the ride, Boney had gotten more and more agitated with his wife, telling Carl, "She doesn't know who I am. I'll shoot that bitch! I'll kill that bitch! I'll leave her where I see her. I can kill her. *My conscience already holds three murders;*[304] one more is not going to bother me anymore."

Carl hadn't thought much of Boney's wild comments because, he said, "Who's going to kill someone over a TV? I just blew it off at the time."

Once they arrived at his house, Boney had walked up to the elevated single family residence by himself. The front door had opened, and Carl had been surprised to see Amber, whom he had known from the Green Light, standing in the doorway. After recognizing Carl, Amber had yelled at Boney that he wasn't taking the TV because Boney still "owed Aaron's for it."[305]

The man and wife had kept arguing as they had turned and gone inside the house, with Carl and his friend, who had just arrived, staying outside until Carl heard Amber scream. He then ran up and into the house and saw Amber on the floor with Boney straddling her. Once Boney saw Carl, he had gotten off his wife. Amber, meanwhile, was holding her throat, yelling to Carl, "He had me by the throat. He was choking me." Boney had denied hurting his

---

[303] At the time, a large-screen television could cost well over $2,000.

[304] Emphasis mine.

[305] Aaron's is a rent-to-own store.

wife who, by that time, was up and, to prevent her husband from taking it, threatening to throw a beer bottle through the TV screen.

By that time, with all the turmoil, Carl said he'd had enough, wasn't going to get involved in a marital fight, and was going to leave, telling Boney he didn't want any part of the TV. Boney had responded, "Well, it ain't stolen. I'm going to pay for it. I just need this cash now. I need the cash." Dismissing Boney's protests, Carl and his buddy had left.

It had been only recently, when he saw Boney on television, that he had equated his comment of having three murders on his conscience with the murders of the Camm family. He viewed those words as a confession. I agreed, although it was clear to me Boney had no conscience.

After Carl left, I called and told Kitty the results of his interview, and she, in turn, told Stacy. I informed Dave and Sam. We all hoped the confession, of which the "fresh eyes" weren't aware, would make an impression on them. Kitty said she'd personally call Henderson and tell him.

As to what would turn out with the results of all of our investigation, Boney's confession to Carl had no impact on Henderson, at least in Dave's case.[306]

Amber Boney

Turning my attention to Amber, I called her, and she agreed to meet with me. Boney's estranged wife was living in a very dated and small rental home in a poorer part of Louisville, which defied Boney's outlandish claim she made as much as $500 per night. Inviting me in, Amber returned to her chair, cuddling with one small dog, Sparkles, as another jumpy and yippy canine, Playboy, ran around the living room, no doubt anxious for his owner's attention.

It was obvious Amber was a hard-working woman whom, she said, had been a bartender for 22 years at the Green Light. It was there she had met Charles Darnell Boney. Boney had first told her he was a police officer, and she had believed him for a short while until he admitted he had been in prison. A felony record, Amber knew, meant he couldn't have been a cop. Thus, one of the first things he had told his future wife had been a lie.

Regardless, she said, Boney had been smart, engaging, and smooth and they had enjoyed one another's company. Soon, he'd shared with her more of his past, telling her he had previously dated Mala, last name unknown, and they had lived with his mother in New Albany. Mala, he had said, had also been working with his mother at the casino boat on the Ohio River.

---

[306] In the trial of Boney, however, his confession to Colvin was an integral piece of evidence they introduced.

After breaking up with Mala, Boney had begun dating a woman, first name Anna,[307] a fellow worker of his at Anderson Wood. When those two had broken up, Boney had quit his job, and soon thereafter Amber and Boney had begun living together in a house of hers on the near east side of downtown Louisville.

At the time they had met, Amber continued, Boney had been driving a two-door, dark-colored Cadillac he had purchased from his uncle who lived in Indiana. Boney had driven that vehicle for several months and had possibly sold it to a friend of his mother's. Amber thought it had later been stolen or else had been sold to a scrap yard in Louisville.

Boney was currently living with a woman, Vivian, whom he had told Amber was his "fiancé," even though Amber and Boney were still married. Several weeks earlier, Amber had told him she wanted a divorce but after initially agreeing to one, her husband had backtracked and said they needed to talk.

During their time together, Boney had held a series of different jobs, ranging from being a laborer at the wood-working factory; a salesman at a rent-to-own store; selling items door-to-door; and selling cars, including a buy-here-pay-here dealership. He eventually had gotten fired from that dealership for creating documents, which, according to Amber had been "forged."

Amber then admitted her husband, in addition to providing false information on car buyer applications, had also used a Social Security number, obtained from a customer at one of his jobs, in order to install a telephone in their home in that customer's name.[308]

It didn't take long after their marriage for the polished and smooth-talking Boney to exhibit anger and violence towards her, Amber said. As to what had triggered that behavior, it was when she'd "stand up to him. He didn't like it." When asked if one of those occasions had been when he'd tried to sell a rental television, Amber confirmed most of the story, and after the two men had departed the day without the TV, she had gotten a "pretty bad beating [and he'd thrown her] on the floor, beat[en] her with his fists and then kicked [her]."

Boney had beaten her on other occasions, Amber said, and had used a stun gun on her "three or four times," although she had "begged him to stop." The location of her having been assaulted with a stun gun by BACKBONE, the standup guy, was her torso because her "friends wouldn't see" the marks the gun had left.

---

[307] Pseudonym.

[308] The victim in that scam turned out to be someone else. Thus, Boney had lied about the identity of the fraud victim.

On one occasion, the guy who had told me he hadn't had a gun in his possession since his release from prison had become incensed with her over something she couldn't recall and had grabbed her and held a gun to her head, threatening to "blow [her] brains out." The gun had been a revolver. Clearly, Boney's first threat had been to threaten to shoot women in the head.

When I asked Amber where Boney had kept his gun, she finally told me it had been stored in the attic access in a closet ceiling in their home. The gun and bullets had been in a small box, which she termed a "robbery kit," which she said also contained a stun gun, black ski mask, plastic gloves, and masking tape. I didn't verbalize my thoughts to Amber, but that "robbery kit" could have also been a "rape kit."

After her husband found out she had discovered his treasure trove, he had threatened her that if she told anyone about the gun, that he would kill her.

At one time, when they needed money, Boney told Amber, "I can rob a bank." She told him to rethink that, and he had said, "You're right. I'd spend the rest of my life in prison." She then said Boney had claimed he had only been joking. When I pressed her, Amber insisted she knew of no places her husband had robbed.

Amber was reluctant to answer my question if Boney had hurt any other people, as she tried to deflect, saying, "He runs his mouth." Repeated efforts didn't get her to say he'd ever admitted or bragged he had hurt or killed others.

Amber did admit, though, Boney had carried grudges and always wanted to "get even" with those who had crossed him. She again insisted, however, he had never admitted to hurting anyone, other than her, and, in their conversations, since he was publicly identified, had denied murdering Kim, Brad, and Jill Camm. He also had denied ever knowing David Camm.

Although her husband didn't talk much about his prison life, he had admitted having been in a prison gang, the name of which she said she couldn't remember.

Boney had few friends, but one guy with whom he was close friends and hung around was Tommy Sandler.[309] Amber, who told me she thought it a "fantasy" her husband would rob a bank, then admitted Tommy had come to her in private and forcefully had told her to "not go back" to Boney because he had been "talking crazy."

I pressed Amber for more details, and she finally said after she took out her EPO,[310] Boney had met with Tommy and had told Tommy he wanted him

---

[309] Pseudonym.

[310] Amber said at the time of her filing the EPO she had been hospitalized due to pneumonia and not from a beating from Boney.

to build "a silencer because he was tired of [Amber] fucking his life up." As she told me the story, tears flowed, and she was only whispering, but I did comprehend her saying her husband was "evil."

But with all of that, Amber, violently abused for over two years by her "evil" husband who had threatened to kill her on multiple occasions, told me she still loved Boney. She refused to accept the possibility her estranged husband had killed the Camm family. After all, she told me, Dave had been "molesting his daughter." When I told her that wasn't accurate, she said, "It's all over the news. I keep up with the news. [If he didn't do it], why was it on the news?"

Prior to my leaving, Amber said if I needed to speak with her again, she'd agree to do so.

Boney's First Wife

Denise Barkley[311] had married Boney in the late 1980's when both had been working at a fast-food restaurant in Bloomington. She described Boney as a "nice, hard-working, intelligent guy who had paid a lot of attention" to her. After a few months, they had begun dating and in November 1989 had been married, shortly after the birth of their son, Damon.

Their wedding occurred, she said, after Boney had been arrested and served time in the local jail for stealing women's shoes. Boney had explained those robberies to her as based on a "fraternity prank." Later, however, Boney had admitted the shoe robberies weren't related to a fraternity but admitted, "he liked women's shoes and it was embarrassing" to him. In fact, she said, Boney had admitted to her that he had a "foot fetish."

Denise said Boney also had created his own fraternity, and it was possible she still had a photograph of Boney wearing a fraternity hat. If she found it, she said, she would provide it.[312]

---

[311] Pseudonym.

[312] She later provided two photographs of her former husband.

Photograph of Boney, circa 1989-90, wearing a hat of a
one-man fraternity he'd created; note the middle Greek
letter could also appear to some as a trident.

On more than one occasion, Denise said she had been awakened at night, in bed, with Boney putting a knee high stocking on her leg and then masturbating over her.

Boney, whom she called Darnell, was a "whole different person" after they had gotten married. Small arguments had quickly become large ones with Boney having grown more and more violent, with his hitting her, throwing her on the floor, pulling her hair, throwing a cake in her face, pouring Kool-Aid over her head, and systematically breaking her dishes. The physical and mental abuse had been routine and had continued for almost two years.

Boney crafted a different public image than his private violent one, though, as he had joined her church and acted as a "wonderful man" in front of others, having his arm around her and telling friends they were in love. Several people had complimented them on their marriage, thinking Boney had been a devoted husband. In reality, he had two personalities, said Denise, the hard-working and loving one seen by outsiders and the lazy and violent one she saw. In fact, she said, her husband had been a real "Doctor Jekyll and Mr. Hyde."

Denise had to stop our interview, for by now she was crying, thinking of all the abuse she had received at the hands of a man who had obviously relished hurting her. Composing herself, she had been able to continue, telling me her husband had graduated to making threats of his taking their child to a place where she "would never be able to find them."

277

Later, Boney had told Denise their one-year-old son had "fallen off the bed [during] a nap" and the red marks on his face were the result of the fall. She didn't think that to be true, but she couldn't prove her husband had hurt their child until later. After having been on a job interview, Denise had

DENISE HAD RETURNED TO THEIR APARTMENT AND HEARD THEIR SON SCREAMING. STANDING OVER THE ONE-YEAR OLD BOY WAS HIS FATHER, DARNELL, WHO WAS REPEATEDLY SLAPPING THE CHILD IN THE FACE WITH HIS OPEN HAND.

returned to their apartment early. She then had heard their son screaming, and after she frantically rushed to the door and opened it, saw Boney standing over their little boy, slapping him repeatedly in the face with an open hand.

So much, I thought, for Mr. Stand-Up who had said he and his prison police force had hated and hurt those who harmed kids.

Denise had finally seen enough. Even though Boney had threatened to kill her on multiple occasions, the incident with their son had caused the abused woman to grab her boy and immediately leave. With the help and love of her parents, she said, she had been able to finally divorce Boney.

During their separation from one another, however, she had been walking to her car from her apartment one night when Boney, dressed in an all-black outfit, jumped out of the bushes and rushed towards her, almost "scaring her to death." Probably practicing, I thought.

At another time during their marriage, Boney had asked Denise to return an item of clothing he had purchased at J.C. Penney, telling her he didn't want it after all. After she did so, she found out he had been writing non-sufficient fund checks on his own bank account. Boney, she said, had then been arrested for check deception and had been incarcerated for a period of time.[313]

After his release from prison, in or around September 1992, Boney had called Denise and announced he was coming to see her, later showing up at her front door. He said he had "really changed" and then tried to persuade her to have sex with him. She had refused but he had persisted, saying no one would believe her if she claimed he had raped her. Denise told him if he didn't leave immediately she'd call the police, further telling me, "I wasn't his punching bag anymore."

A few weeks later, he had again appeared at her doorstep, and again Denise had denied Boney entry to her home. She said, "I gave him money for a bus ticket to New Albany and dropped him off" at the bus station. About

---

[313] The check deception charge had caused his probation to be revoked.

three hours later, he had called her from jail, saying he had been arrested for robbing three women. Denise had been flabbergasted, and when she'd asked him why he had done what he did, Boney had merely said he had been "dumb."

About a year after Boney's release from prison in 2000, he had called Denise wanting to meet with their son, saying he had "done a lot of thinking and felt really bad he hadn't been in their son's life and would really like to know him." Denise had placed strict parameters on any future meeting, however, and after a few weeks, she had never heard from Boney again.

The next time Denise had seen Boney had been when he was on television, talking about giving away his prison sweatshirt. And no, she added, no one from any law enforcement agency had ever contacted her regarding the Camm murders.

In summary, it didn't take me a lot of time to discredit Boney's bogus claim he had been a changed guy or his equally fraudulent assertion of having alibi witnesses on the night of the murders. The guy who tried to come off as smart, polished, and intellectual, was in fact a powder keg who, when angered, could only express himself through violence aimed at those physically weaker than himself, especially women and children.

There was only one conclusion anyone who had any degree of unbiased knowledge about the evidence in the murders of Kim, Brad, and Jill could logically reach: Boney had viciously battered a tenacious mother fighting for the lives of her family, finally grabbing her by her hair and shooting her in the head; he then had turned to the children in the Bronco, and clutching his .380 semi-auto gun, had, at point-blank range, cold-bloodedly shot in the head a totally helpless and terrified little girl, and then had quickly shot to death her big brother who had been desperately scrambling for his life.

Charles Darnell Boney, the man who had insisted that others call him BACKBONE, was one spineless, evil, remorseless, and gutless coward.

CHAPTER 31
About That DNA....

While we had been concentrating on Charles Boney, learning as much as possible about the man, two other questions about him, or rather his DNA, were being raised, and not just by the defense team, but by the press and the public at large. *When* and *Why?*

When had Boney's DNA profile been submitted to CODIS? Since he was incarcerated from 1993 to 2000, when all violent felons in Indiana were mandated to provide their DNA for submission to CODIS, his

> THE ONLY CONCLUSION ONE COULD DRAW WAS EITHER FAITH OR CLEMONS WAS NOT TELLING THE TRUTH ABOUT THE UNIDENTIFIED DNA.

profile should have been on file when Mike McDaniel asked Faith to run the unknown profile in October 2001. Recall, however, at that time, Faith had said there had been no match, well over a year after Boney had left the DOC.

Within days, though, we were able to confirm Boney's DNA had absolutely been in CODIS at the time of the murders. In fact, it had been collected on July 24, 1997. *Why*, then, wasn't his DNA matched at the time Faith had the ISP check on it in 2001?

During his press conference when Boney was defended by Henderson, the prosecutor began the finger-pointing, although he was either ignorant of the facts or else blatantly fabricated his comments, as he told the press, "The DNA evidence was in the defense team's hands during the first trial and they did not seek to have this run through the database."[314] That was simply not true. No way, no how.

In absolving himself of any responsibility, Henderson had also failed to mention Kitty had asked him directly, several times, to run the DNA, and Sam had practically pleaded with Gilbert to accept a copy of the same unknown profile to run through CODIS. Both Henderson and Gilbert had refused, the DNA had not been identified, and Dave had been recharged by Henderson.

After the public disclosure of Boney's DNA, Faith let it be known he

---

[314] Lowry, Kyle, DNA Links Ex-Convict to Murder Scene, Attorneys Say, *The Evening News and Tribune*, March 1, 2005.

had also been told of the match "as a courtesy from Henderson."[315] Some, including me, didn't think it a "courtesy," but rather a continuing effort to ensure they were on the same team and speaking the same language.

As did Henderson and Owen, Faith denigrated Boney's sweatshirt as being in any way significant other than the garment's having been planted at the scene. Dave was still guilty, Faith asserted, based upon the bloodstain evidence. He also defended his one-time BACKBONE client, since "no other evidence puts Boney at the scene."[316]

As for any responsibility he had for the DNA, Faith said, "I thought we'd sent [the DNA] out. Now, I'm told there's no record of us sending it out,"[317] as he then threw others under the bus when he said he had "asked his investigators to run it through [and] evidently, it wasn't, or we didn't get an answer." In a dismissive manner, he then said the sweatshirt had merely "slipped through" because "everybody misses something the first time around. You can go to a crime scene a thousand times and find a thousand new things."[318]

In his opening and closing statements at Dave's trial, though, Mike McDaniels had passionately argued the significance of the sweatshirt, saying it had belonged to the true killer. He had certainly known of its critical significance, and his recollection of events regarding the DNA was a lot clearer than Faith's: he told me he vividly remembered his conversation with Faith three months before the start of the trial. Mike said he had told Faith of the DNA discovery as he physically had given him the DNA profile, telling him,[319] "You need to run this." Faith, in turn, had accepted the document from Mike and had assured him he'd have it checked through CODIS.

About two weeks passed when Faith had seen Mike at the courthouse and, before Mike could speak, Faith had volunteered to him, "I didn't get a hit on that DNA."

As for his role, Sean Clemons contradicted Faith's charge that it was his fault the DNA hadn't been checked. He had been completely unaware of the Cellmark laboratory finding any unknown male DNA profile on the sweatshirt because Faith had never told him the profile existed; never gave him anything to run; thus, he couldn't have run something he didn't have through CODIS.

---

[315] Hershberg, Ben Zion, Camm Case: Match on DNA, *The Courier-Journal*, February 28, 2005.

[316] Sells, George, Mystery DNA From First Camm Trial Identified, *WAVE-TV*, March 1, 2005.

[317] Ibid.

318 Flack, Eric, DNA Evidence Could Have Linked Boney to Camm Years Ago, *WAVE-TV* May11, 2005.

[319] The sweatshirt had remained with the ISP until about five months prior to the start of the trial. Mike had it sent to Cellmark and received the unknown DNA profile in October 2001.

The only conclusion one could draw was either Faith or Clemons was not telling the truth about the unidentified DNA, since both of their assertions were contradicted by the other party. We do know Faith had excluded Clemons from much of the remaining investigation after Dave had been charged, perhaps making Clemons' assertion of his not knowing of the existence of the DNA profile more credible.

Faith's later comments, in my opinion, also pointed directly at him as being responsible: "I knew that Sean had checked out the DNA profiles that we had. I asked him. I said something to the effect, 'I don't want to be ambushed at trial. I want you to check out all the DNA profiles that we have.' And for whatever reason, he didn't check out the one in the sweatshirt that McDaniel found. I don't know that I ever knew why he didn't."[320]

The generic checking "all the DNA profiles" Faith claimed isn't the same as Faith's giving Clemons the specific Cellmark profile from Mike. Additionally, "I don't want to be ambushed at trial" can easily be equated to "If I don't have any exculpatory evidence, I can't divulge it."

A furious Mike McDaniel knew in his own mind who was lying: it was Faith, since throughout the leadup to and the trial itself, the prosecutor had engaged in a pattern of behaviors with the goal of "winning at any cost." Mike, who said Faith had never before lied to him, was confident Faith had done exactly that on a piece of evidence that was critical to his defense of Dave.

The ramifications were obvious and incredibly significant. Even if Faith had still prosecuted Dave, knowing of the identity of the DNA, Mike would have had as defense exhibits 1) Boney's DNA and his clothing found at the crime scene; 2) no doubt, his false exculpatory statements; 3) his numerous prior violent crimes, which shared similar if not identical aspects with the Camm murders;[321] 4) his self-admitted weird sexual fetishes; and 5) his manipulative and remorseless character. All of those would have pointed to Boney as the real killer.

The bottom line, however, in not matching the unknown DNA to Charles Boney when it would have required but a few minutes to query CODIS with the profile was, at best, either an egregious oversight or, at worst, a corrupt and conscious decision. Either way, the only one paying the enormous price had been Dave.

---

[320] Faith's interview with the third defense team, March 20, 2013.

[321] Generally, a person's prior crimes, aka "bad acts," cannot be revealed in a trial for a new crime. Boney's penchant for stealing shoes and his violent behavior—i.e., grabbing women's hair, placing a gun to their head and threatening to "blow [their] fucking brains out"—were criminal patterns of his, however, and should have been admitted if Boney had been charged.

CHAPTER 32

Two New Arrests

The Unidentified Prints

Weeks before Boney had been publicly identified, Stacy had assimilated an exhaustive list of forensic evidence for the ISP to test and/or attempt to match to various databases, and Kitty had promptly given that list to Henderson. Kitty's subsequent calls to Henderson to try to obtain the results of any of those requested tests, attempted matches, or comparisons had not been answered, before or after Boney's identity had been divulged to Kitty by an outsider. It was typical Henderson, as he had talked of providing discovery on a timely basis but hadn't delivered. In fact, it would only get a lot worse.

Nonetheless, in Stacy's list was a request to run unidentified finger and palmprints found on the Bronco. The Automated Fingerprint Identification System [AFIS] was the FBI's digital database containing over 100 million prints of all kinds; it could possibly match the Bronco prints with identified or unidentified prints in the system.[322]

It was on the basis of those unknown prints that I had asked Boney the question, "Would there be any way, shape, manner or form that any of your fingerprints would be on or near that crime scene?"

> "I WENT FROM BEING ON TOP OF THE WORLD TO THE DEPTHS OF HELL."
>
> "IT WAS THE WORST LIE POSSIBLE. IT WAS HENDERSON BEING CRUEL FOR THE SAKE OF BEING CRUEL."

Boney, of course, went on to answer he would have been the one responsible for the murders if anything of his was found at the scene, including his fingerprints. In fact, he had admitted it would be "obvious" he was the murderer if an identifier of his were found.

During the 22 hours Charles Boney had spent with the "fresh eyes," surely, we thought, they would have gotten major case prints from him and compared them to all of the unidentified finger and palmprints. Obtaining good, identifiable prints would have taken but a few minutes and then, for an

---

[322] Some of those prints could have belonged to Kim, Brad, or Jill, but no one knew, due to evidence technician Sam Sarkisian's failure to obtain full sets of their prints at the autopsies.

experienced fingerprint examiner, less than an hour or two to compare and reach a conclusion: they matched, or they didn't.

The time lapse between Boney's presumably providing his prints on or near February 17, when he had been first interviewed, and the investigators' attempting to match any in a database was now approaching two weeks, a relatively long time. Something wasn't right. In fact, we later learned it wasn't until after Kitty's motion to compel discovery that Gilbert had actually obtained, from the Floyd Superior Court, the finger and palmprints, lifted from the Bronco passenger side door jamb, by evidence technician Niemeyer, even though these prints had been introduced in evidence by Mike in Dave's trial three years before.

Henderson, though, had remained silent about literally everything, so we had been kept in the dark. Then, late on Friday night, March 4, 2005, another arrest had been made. Charles Boney, we learned, had finally been arrested and was in custody at the Floyd County Jail, charged with the murders of Kim, Brad, and Jill.

It must have been a significant piece of evidence to cause Henderson to act, since Boney's attributable lies, including his false alibis, weren't a problem for the prosecutor; nor were his past violent crimes; nor was his theft of women's shoes; and, of course, Boney's weird sexual obsession wasn't a motive because there had been no sexual attack of Kim. In fact, Henderson and Owen had publicly defended Boney, with the Chief Deputy's adamantly disparaging the possibility Boney could have left his clothing at the scene while committing the murders.

Only four days after their vigorous defense of Boney, though, Henderson's and Owen's hands had been forced. As it turned out, it was, indeed, a huge hand which did the forcing, both in terms of size and impact. It was the very large left palmprint on the passenger door jamb, just behind the curbside door of the Bronco, which was the location where a right-handed shooter could stabilize himself with his left hand on the door post while his right arm, hand, and gun could be extended into the back seat, allowing him to shoot two totally defenseless children. Charles Boney owned that print.

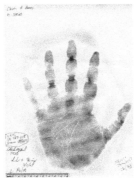

Boney's left palmprint, obtained by ISP evidence technician Charlie McDaniel on March 3, 2005; it was matched by ISP fingerprint examiner Jon Singleton to the palmprint on the Bronco. Both McDaniel and Singleton were professional police officers and let the evidence, rather than any narrative, do the talking.

Boney's prints had first been taken by the Louisville Metropolitan Police Department (LMPD) when he had been detained on February 17, 2005, in Louisville, before agreeing to accompany Gilbert and Kessinger to New Albany where he had been interviewed. Those prints were of poor quality and were useless, however, and it had taken two more weeks for ISP evidence tech Charlie McDaniel to be asked to obtain a much better set of prints. Those had then been used by fingerprint examiner Jon Singleton to compare, and then match, to the Bronco prints.

Boney's arrest, however, created many new questions. What, specifically, had Boney told the detectives? There was no way he had told them the truth, since he was an inveterate liar. What, though, had been the specifics of his lies? How had he "played it" with Gary Gilbert and Wayne Kessinger? No doubt, he had again portrayed himself the victim but with a new plot twist. Whatever his story, we knew we couldn't assume Henderson and his team had been on a quest for the truth, given their past lack of interest in the litany of evidence that had pointed directly and forcibly at Boney.

Based on what we knew Henderson and his team had done, and probably had not done, Kitty and Stacy agreed that I should attempt to speak with Boney. Yes, he was incarcerated, but warning Boney of his rights wasn't incumbent on me since I wasn't a law enforcement officer. As for his having counsel, we were unaware if he was or wasn't represented, thus we wouldn't knowingly be violating any ethical issues. If I did get access, it was up to him to tell me if he were represented and if he wanted to speak with me.

I traveled to New Albany early on Saturday morning, March 5th, and, after hearing of my request, rather than contacting Boney, the jail officer on duty told me to wait until she made a phone call. After several minutes in the visitation room, I was called over to the thick glass and was told Boney wouldn't be *made available to me*. That wasn't the same as telling me Boney wouldn't *talk with me*.

Meanwhile, the multitudes of media people were again assembling outside the front of the adjacent courthouse, eagerly awaiting a Henderson press conference. Sam was among those gathered, and I joined him outside in the very breezy and cold March air.

Rather than hold the gathering inside the courthouse, Henderson spoke in front of the entrance doors. His comments were short. Boney, he said, had been arrested by Detective Gilbert and charged with three counts of murder, possession of a firearm by a felon, and being a habitual felon. Additionally, he had given "lengthy statements" after his arrest. There was no doubt that anyone who knew Boney also knew he had to have talked—and talked a lot.

The murder charges, though, were good, very good, for they had finally arrested the right guy for the crimes. As for the firearms and habitual counts, Henderson should have placed those charges as well against a very violent repeat offender who had been seen by many not only to have carried a handgun but also to have used it repeatedly to rob and threaten others. What the investigators had in the way of evidence in terms of the gun was unknown, however, and Henderson didn't explain any of the charges in detail.

In fact, for the second consecutive press conference, Henderson didn't appear confident in front of the cameras, as he shuffled his feet while pinching his lower lip with his thumb and index finger of his right hand.[323] Indeed, rather than go in detail, as he and Owen had on the Monday before about how Boney couldn't have been involved, he minimized his words and refused to take questions from any of the dozens of people present, retreating quickly into the sanctity of the courthouse.

As the dismissed minions were milling around, Sam and I caught up with several of Dave's other family members. One was Donnie who was being interviewed. He verbalized the concern we were all thinking: "I'm sure [Henderson] is probably going to try to link David and this guy."[324] Indeed, such a linkage had already started in the media, with one headline reading, "New Suspect Has Connection to Camm Family."[325] The connection? As we had known, Boney and Dave's youngest brother Dan had graduated in the same year, 1987, from the 400+ graduates of New Albany High School.

[323] A photo also appeared of Henderson doing so in a news article: Schneider, Grace & Hershberg, Ben Zion, Ex-Con Arrested in Camm Slayings, *The Courier-Journal*, March 6, 2005.

[324] Ibid.

[325] *TheLouisvilleChannel*, March 7, 2005.

Unreported by the media, however, was the fact Sean Clemons had also been in the same graduating class. Boney had proudly told me of that connection earlier.

Even though Henderson was relatively mum, Stan Faith was being quoted repeatedly. After interviewing Faith, one reporter wrote, "He's always believed that Camm didn't act alone." The reporter continued to quote Faith: "'I never had that belief. In fact, it was the general consensus of the people that investigated the crime in 2000 that [Camm] probably didn't act alone. We just didn't have any idea who else. We didn't have any ability to know who else was there.'"[326]

There was zero, nada, absolutely nothing that supported Faith's ludicrous assertion, as none of the investigators or prosecutors had ever suggested another person other than Dave had been involved. There were no ISP reports, no interviews, no inklings, nothing Faith had said in trial, nothing whatsoever or anywhere that even hinted he or the ISP had thought anyone other than Dave had been the one responsible.

In fact, recall that Mickey Neal, when speaking with Kim's parents, had quoted Faith about the "big one-arm hairy stranger" when he had dismissed the idea of another person as preposterous. Regardless, the shift from "Dave Camm did it!" to "Dave Camm did it with Charles Boney!" was yet, again, the manufacturing of a narrative out of thin air.

To another reporter, the verbose Faith had said, "there might be *other evidence*[327] that places Boney in the Camm garage the night of the murders," but, the reporter continued, "he wouldn't be more specific."[328] A close reading of that sentence could mean Boney had admitted to having been in the garage. That, and Faith's continued insistence on Dave's shirt having blood spatter no doubt meant a new narrative was beginning: Boney and Dave had acted together.

That Faith teased the reporter by claiming "other evidence" also told us Henderson, once again, was evading the gag order by feeding a story to a third party who would get the press to report it. And the willing media complied, of course, dutifully printing Henderson's desired narrative through his newest mouthpiece, Stan Faith.

Henderson, we knew, sooner or later had to file his affidavit supporting the arrest of Boney. Since it was the weekend, we were hopeful it would be filed on Monday. Still, it would take two more days before we knew of the bare essentials of their new claims. Regardless, however, the prosecutors now had

---

[326] Ibid.

[327] Emphasis mine.

[328] *The Louisville Channel*, March 7, 2005.

their fourth theory as to the person(s) responsible for the murders and Boney had, for the first time, been included as a culprit, albeit the story was far from finished.

Our Neighborhood Investigations

After I left Sam, I began conducting two neighborhood investigations, one around the home where Amber and Boney had lived in Louisville, and the other where Boney had lived with his mother in New Albany. The more background we had on the ingrained liar, the better, for his lack of credibility and outright falsehoods would be more important than ever to Dave's defense.

As it turned out, Amber and her serial abuser had lived in a small shotgun home on the near east side of Louisville, in the heart of Germantown, and just a few blocks from the Kentucky Medical Examiner's office where the autopsies of Kim, Brad, and Jill had occurred. If I'm being charitable, the residence was in need of some repair; if I'm being truthful, the vacant structure was dilapidated and derelict. I first contacted the neighbor to the west, a very friendly but cautious lady.

She recalled Amber's having moved in a few years before with her niece and great-niece living with her. A year later, Charles Boney had moved in, and Amber's relatives had departed. The overly-friendly neighbor guy had soon told her he was going to work hard on making repairs to the house, including putting up a privacy fence. In fact, in the year he had lived there, he hadn't accomplished anything, and he had even hired a man to cut the often tall and weedy grass.

The neighbors on the other side had moved in after Amber had abandoned the home in early 2004; the house in the rear was vacant, as were several others nearby, and those who inhabited other nearby homes either failed to answer my knock at their door or else refused to speak with me.

As for the other neighborhood, Barbara Boney had lived in her New Albany home for almost 30 years prior to moving to another part of town in 2004. I went to her old neighborhood where those I contacted were friendly, but few people had any direct knowledge of Boney. That made sense, since he had been incarcerated for eight years, or from 1992–2000, and had been essentially gone for the five years prior to 1992.

One older neighbor remembered Barbara Boney as an obnoxious woman who had tried to intimidate him over a parking space; he'd ignored her. Other neighbors didn't have recollections of Charles or, if they did, they kept them private. One man readily spoke to me, though, for he had caught a teenage Charles, on three occasions, peeping in the bedroom window of his young daughter. On each occasion he had called Barbara to tell her, but the last time she'd screamed at him for making up a story about her son.

The rest of the neighborhood interviews weren't fruitful, although I did walk, and Boney walked a lot, the few hundred feet from Boney's old house to Karem's Meats. It took me less than five minutes, and it was easy to envision the hyena eyeing his prey, either as Kim was in the store or in her Bronco. I was convinced Boney had indeed stalked Kim, and Karem's was the most probable site to have begun his deviant strategy of first manipulating, then silently tracking, and finally sexually assaulting her.

The Worst Lie Possible

I returned to Bloomington where we waited for Boney's arrest affidavit to be unsealed, but on Monday, Henderson asked for more time from the judge,[329] which was granted with the approval of a temporary counsel for Boney. Meanwhile, I did background research on the almost ten known Boney employers, taking appreciable time to assimilate the information and to plan my interviews of his co-workers and supervisors. I also drafted several subpoenas, calling for all of his known employment records. Jenn would type, Kitty would sign, and I'd serve each one.

I then met with both Kitty and Stacy. Each of us was hopeful Henderson would finally succumb to the truth and recognize, or I guess the better term was *accept*, Charles Boney was the murderer. The three of us were caught between the faint hope of Henderson's doing the right thing and the harsh reality of thinking it would be impossible for him to do so.

On Wednesday, March 9, while Kitty and I were out to lunch, she got a phone call from Stacy, "What?!" She quickly turned to me. "Henderson called Stacy and said he wanted to drop the charges against Dave. Stacy agreed. She's called Dave and he's free!" It took a moment for each of us to ask if it could really be true. Was Dave finally a free man? Kitty quickly told Stacy we were returning to the office as Kitty called Dave.

Dave was with his dad, Don, at UDI when Kitty called. We heard him on speaker phone, and he was so happy he was crying. Both Dave and his dad kept saying, "Praise God!"

At the time, Sam was in the public defender's office when Janice Glotzbach, the long-time administrative assistant to Pat Biggs, told him, "Sam, you won't believe this! It's just coming across now on my computer that Henderson has dropped the charges against Dave." Sam was incredulous, knowing Henderson, finally faced with a mountain of evidence against Boney, had felt compelled to drop the charges against Dave. "I was so happy," he recalled later, "that Dave was free and Boney was going to finally face justice for killing Kim, Brad, and Jill."

---

[329] The Circuit Court Judge in Boney's case was J. Terrence "Terry" Cody.

Gary M. Dunn

Sam quickly made his way to the Floyd Circuit Court where Boney's first court appearance had just begun. Rather than read the charges Henderson had filed on Saturday, there were amended charges the judge read aloud. Sam's utter joy, sadly, turned to unimaginable dread when he heard the charge of conspiracy against Boney. A conspiracy charge means two or more people conspired or collaborated to commit a crime. That meant Henderson was claiming Boney and Dave together had planned and actually committed an overt act as they sought to murder Kim, Brad, and Jill.[330]

Back at UDI, Ron Reed of Community Corrections showed up and found Dave. "I knew he was there to remove my ankle bracelet," said Dave, "and I was jubilant. Dad and I were almost dancing with joy. We both thought it was finally over and for almost an hour I was on top of the world." Reed, however, had merely wanted to speak with Dave.

At the same time, Kessinger and Gilbert had the arrest warrant and were speeding from Henderson's office with two marked ISP units following them. Upon learning Dave was already speaking to Reed, they raced even faster, leaving one ISP unit behind at a stoplight. Upon skidding to a stop in the UDI lot, Gilbert jumped out of the vehicle and yelled to Dave that he was under arrest as Trooper Manville Nagle, who had emerged from the trail car, placed Dave in cuffs. All Dave could do was to yell to Dave Demuro[331] to call Kitty.

As Dave was being placed in the marked unit, his father Don, who rarely cursed, began demanding, "What the hell is going on here? This is so much bullshit!" Within a few minutes, Sam arrived, but by then the posse and their outlaw had already departed.

"I went from being on the top of the world to the depths of hell," recalled Dave later. "I guess we all should have expected as much from Henderson and the State Police."

"It was the worst lie possible," Sam told me. "And it was Henderson being cruel for the sake of being cruel."

---

[330] This was the fifth theory by the prosecutors as to how Dave killed his family: 1) Dave had killed the family after arriving home sometime after 9:00 p.m.; 2) Dave had killed his family after calling a client at 7:19 p.m. while in the house; 3) Dave had killed his family at some time or another and in all three scenarios the sweatshirt meant nothing; 4) Dave had killed his family, again after the 7:19 p.m. phone call, and had used a sweatshirt to "stage" the crime scene while setting up Charles Boney; and 5) now Dave had an accomplice, Boney, who had supplied the gun, wrapped in the sweatshirt, which had been, after all, more than just an "artifact." It had been a significant piece of evidence.
[331] UDI's longtime CFO and a close personal friend of Sam's.

290

The ISP's New Lies

On the legal front, it took time for Henderson to provide Kitty with Gilbert's affidavit. As with his first one, it was replete with distortions, several lies, a really big lie, and numerous self-serving representations obtained from Boney. Shortly after his release from prison, Boney asserted, he'd "met David Camm in New Albany while playing basketball on 'several occasions.' During one of the meetings, David Camm learned about Charles Boney's criminal background, and asked [him] if he could obtain a 'clean' gun."

As for Dave's playing ball, he had played with many different people, including fellow ISP officers. Was Boney claiming he was among that group? Very doubtful. Still, if Boney were being truthful, he would have given the "fresh eyes" the names of the other players and those people, if interviewed, would have confirmed or refuted his story. There was no identification of other players, much less any confirmation from any one of them, and my bet was those witnesses, if they existed at all, would be in the same category as Boney's alibi witnesses.

The "clean gun" comment was then emphasized in the next paragraph, as Gilbert asserted in September 2000, Boney went to the Camm residence to "deliver the untraceable handgun," delivering "the 380 caliber handgun to Camm wrapped in his gray sweatshirt that he had worn while in the [DOC]."

A "clean" weapon can mean several things but an "untraceable" one? Boney wasn't a CIA operative. He was a street guy and not a very smart one. To think he had obtained a weapon that couldn't be traced, in some manner or another, was as likely as Boney's having a secret agent number. Not only that, but the likelihood of tracing any unrecovered weapon was slim.

"Wrapped in his gray sweatshirt" also covered Boney's ass, for that claim allowed the sweatshirt to pass from Boney to Dave who then "tucked" it under Brad as part of the "staging" of the crime scene.

Imagine, if you will, the accurate scenario in an affidavit only charging BACKBONE: "Boney, known to leave evidence at a crime scene in the past, in the garage and in the heat of the moment had panicked, left his 'escape plan' sweatshirt with his DNA in the collar as well as his left palmprint on the door jamb of the Bronco after he had shot Kim, Brad, and Jill, murdering all three."

Gilbert's bogus affidavit, though, continued that on the night of the murders, the two were at the Camm residence as Kim, Brad, and Jill arrived home, and then, "Boney heard David Camm shoot Kimberly Camm and then fire two more shots at the children. Charles Boney stated that he touched the Bronco as he looked into it and that he was the one that put Kim's shoes on top of the Bronco."

This was getting nutty. Boney *heard* Dave shoot Kim? And then fire two more shots at the children? Obviously, Boney was trying to distance himself from the murders. That Gilbert kept the details of Boney's story from the affidavit, especially Boney's handling and then putting the shoes on top of the Bronco, told us Boney's full story wasn't one Gilbert or Henderson wanted the public to know.

The motive behind Boney's helping Dave, the affidavit claimed, was "for financial gain and that David Camm was to compensate him for his involvement." There was no mention of any dollar amounts.

Normally, in charging a conspiracy, an affiant will detail one or more overt acts in which two or more people engage in an effort to fulfill a criminal plan. Gilbert's affidavit didn't allege the two conspired to kill anyone but rather Boney had only claimed he had sold Dave an "untraceable" weapon.

Of course, also not mentioned were the words of James B. Hatton. The serial informant, who had claimed Dave had confessed in detail to him, had said Dave told him that no one else was involved in the murders. So, which lying liar should people believe?

Other claims of Gilbert's included "Kim and David Camm had marital problems." Yes, they did have issues, five years before the murders, which weren't remotely relevant or connected to the murders. There were no problems leading to September 28, but rather the family had, by all accounts from those close to the family, a great family summer of swimming, baseball, and fun. Regardless, it was an attempt to slime Dave once again over his marriage.

Gilbert then wedged the insurance claim between the false "marital problems" charge and wrote "Danny Camm…was a class mate of Charles D. Boney." No comment as to how close, if at all, Danny and Boney had been. Guilt by association, 13 years before the murders, was enough to establish the link they wanted.

Regarding the insurance, Gilbert wrote that a "$150,000 life insurance policy was taken out in the name of Kim Camm [and] was written by David Camm's brother, Danny Camm." The implication was Kim didn't know of the policy, which was patently untrue. Secondly, it wasn't written by Dan, as Gilbert swore, but by an agent with whom he worked.

And then, the really big lie of Gilbert's was thrown down: "I also learned that Kimberly Camm did not sign the life insurance policy." Robert Barber, the agent who wrote the policy, had testified during the trial he had spoken directly with Kim who had known precisely what was occurring. In fact, he had meticulously gone over each aspect of her application as she had asked Barber salient questions and then had contemporaneously signed the application in front of Dan.

If Gilbert had been interested in providing a more accurate representation of the family's insurance, he'd have noted, after Kim had finished her management of their coverage needs, that she had only increased her total coverage by around $18,000 and not $150,000 as implied. Her primary concern, in fact, had been to replace Dave's lost ISP group life insurance coverage. In fact, Kim had seen fit to obtain $350,000 in new coverage on Dave.[332]

Gilbert's falsification of the events had, for those unaware of the facts, created a motive, albeit one based upon inaccurate implications and false claims.

Gilbert had then included the allegations made by the two confidential informants, including one claim: "the reason for the murders was that Kimberly was leaving him." So, the guy who wanted his freedom to run around, according to Faith and every other crime pundit, didn't actually want that freedom but murdered because his wife was leaving him? Did they not realize they were contradicting themselves?

Gilbert then returned to their two blood experts and the tissue in the weave of Dave's shirt. The claim was that Dave had to have been within four feet of a gunshot wound and Englert's [although he was not identified] expert deduction that Dave was "partially in the back of the vehicle" when Jill had been shot. The lead detective then included the fact that some gunshot residue had been found on Dave's clothing, providing no context whatsoever.

We had learned, of course, that Dave had been taken to New Albany, and then to the Sellersburg Post for his first interview, in a vehicle with two police officers. Those two had just come from completing a nighttime gun shoot and, no doubt, had been inundated with GSR, or gunshot residue.

GSR was notorious for being able to spread and attach itself to people as well as clothing. Dave's clothes had gotten GSR in them while he had embraced one of the officers and/or had been contaminated when riding in a police vehicle.

As for his affidavit on the three-page document, which had been signed by Gilbert, were the words, "I affirm under penalty of perjury…the foregoing representations are true."

The press, of course, didn't question the specifics of Gilbert's claims. In fact, the opposite was true, as one headline announced, "DNA Evidence Could Have Linked Boney to Camm Years Ago."[333] It was a foregone conclusion

---

[332] Dave also lost his ISP health and dental coverage in the spring of 2000; as part of Kim's management of insurance of all kinds, she replaced that insurance with her employer coverage. All four family members, plus Dave's eldest daughter, were on the policies.

[333] Flack, Eric, WAVE-TV, March 11, 2005.

for most, including the press, that Dave and Boney had conspired to kill his family.

The Very Clever Prosecutor

But it got even worse, for on an almost equal magnitude of the outrageous new murder and conspiracy charges made against Dave was the new court where Henderson had filed those charges. After dropping the charges against Dave, which had been pending in Warrick County where jurisdiction had been transferred months before,[334] he had refiled in Floyd County.

In his attempt at justifying his actions, Henderson was quoted, "The facts are inextricably bound, and I intend to try them both [Camm and Boney] together."[335] The man, now on a renewed quest for justice, continued, "We can't try Boney in Warrick County because he has a right to be tried in Floyd County. I have the right as prosecutor to join co-defendants when their cases are as inextricably bound as they are in this case."[336]

Kitty and Stacy knew otherwise. Both were rock solid in their conclusion Henderson's decision violated Dave's right to be tried in Warrick County. The prosecutor could not, they asserted, unilaterally make a decision on jurisdiction that defied and then overruled a previous court order.

In fact, when Dave was brought before Floyd County Circuit Court Judge Terry Cody the day after his arrest, he was represented, but not by Kitty or Stacy as they didn't recognize the legitimacy of the new jurisdiction. David Mosley, who was representing Dave in the civil case involving the life insurance policies, appeared on behalf of Dave.

Another brutal legal fight had been instigated, this time by Henderson, as Kitty summed up her thoughts on the decision by the prosecutor: "Henderson was angry we pushed for the DNA and fingerprints. He was angry Dave got bond. He was angry his case against Dave was compromised. He wanted his own court in his own backyard. He's got it for now, but we're not finished. Not by a long shot."

Indeed, Keith Henderson was taking on two focused and accomplished attorneys. And they, too, were both very angry.

---

[334] In November 2004, Henderson had acknowledged, by agreeing to the change of venue, that Dave couldn't get a fair trial in Floyd County.
[335] Ali, Amany, Prosecutor Drops Old Charges Against Camm, Then Recharges Him in Floyd County, *The Tribune*, March 10, 2005.
[336] Ibid.

CHAPTER 33

A "Mesmerizing" Obsessive Fetish

Everyone knew the case would, sooner or later, be tried, either in Warrick or Floyd County, and everyone knew both sides would still be bound by the rules of discovery. Thus, Henderson would have to release the pertinent details of their investigation, including the multiple hours of interviews and interrogations of Boney.

Henderson, however, was playing hardball. The prosecutor had refused to disclose the details of the original 22 hours of Boney's interview, his subsequent and self-admitted multiple contacts over three weeks with the "fresh eyes" investigators, and however many hours the stand-up guy had been interrogated after his arrest.

> BONEY TOLD HIS FRIEND, OF WOMEN'S FEET, THAT HE LIKED TO "SMELL THEM, LICK THEM, KISS THEM, SUCK THEM."
>
> "HE LOVED PRETTY FEET BUT HATED UGLY FEET."

The only snippets from Boney's story had come from the probable cause affidavit charging him and Dave with conspiracy. That those selected claims were cherry-picked to favor the worst scenario possible weren't up for discussion with anyone who had known of the history of Dave's case.

We didn't wait to be spoon-fed details as I continued a deeper dive into the life of Boney; we were intent upon knowing as much about the person as possible. A search of public records, access to a private database, interviews of his two wives and others who intimately knew Boney, and Charles' own interviews with me and the media all had combined to enable us to see what was obvious to all, or at least anyone who wished to see the truth. Still, there was more to learn.

Mrs. Boney

Boney had moved in 1974 to New Albany, home of several relatives, with his older sister and mother Barbara, from the Detroit, Michigan, area. Years later, Barbara apparently had divorced her husband who had remained in Michigan. Her son had been reared without a father.

I had gained initial insight into Barbara with my interviews of Boney's two wives. Amber had said her brute of a husband had been "just like his mother, a liar and a manipulator," further explaining that after she once had received a savage beating from Darnell, Barbara had rushed to her side, only it wasn't to comfort her or help her seek medical attention which was needed. Instead, Barbara had stayed with her to *prevent* her from going to the hospital.

On another occasion, after she had taken out the EPO on Charles and he had been arrested, Barbara had called Amber, again not out of concern for her daughter-in-law, but to yell at her for having been the cause of her son's arrest.

Denise, Boney's first wife, told me that she, her husband, and their son had visited her mother-in-law in New Albany. During their visit, Barbara had told Denise if her one-year-old grandson "got out of line" that she, Barbara, would "bust his ass." Denise further told me she had never allowed Barbara, whom she had also described as a "prolific liar,"[337] to touch her son in any manner whatsoever.

We would depose Barbara, of course, when venue was restored to Warrick County, but in the meantime, I went to her residence in New Albany. Barbara's house was a small but very neat cottage located in a middle-class section of town.

Within seconds of my ringing the bell, Barbara opened the interior door and, through the closed screen door, asked me what I wanted. I identified myself as I managed to squeeze my business card through the small opening between the door and the jamb.

After glancing at my card, Barbara launched into a tirade. During my 27 years with the FBI and also through a lifetime of interaction with people throughout the world, I had never seen a person turn so quickly from such a neutral demeanor into one who was enraged and screaming inaudible words. Furious would not be an adequate word to describe the woman. I finally heard the term "trespassing," and as she had to pause for air, I simply said, "Thank you. Good day." I did a turnaround and walked to my car.

Boney's First Job Out Of Prison

I next drove across the Ohio River and spoke to a representative in Human Resources (HR) at Anderson Wood, Boney's employer at the time of the murders. Since Judge Aylsworth had dismissed the charges in Warrick County, we had no court jurisdiction from which to subpoena records; thus, I didn't have any legal paperwork with me. Nonetheless, we did want to alert the company there would be a subpoena forthcoming and to preserve any and all employment records, including time cards, for Boney.

---

[337] Denise said Barbara routinely lied about Denise's father, who was employed at Indiana University, but instead of telling people of his true position, Barbara referred to him as the president of the university.

I spoke with an HR representative and received confirmation that Boney's employment had lasted almost a year, or from late June 2000 until May 2001, and further that he had worked third shift, or from 10:30 p.m. until 6:00 a.m. Sunday through Thursday. That meant he wouldn't have been at work at the time of the murders and, thus, probably would have had no work alibi on which to fall back after his alibi witnesses had failed to verify his stories.

The HR employee then asked me why I hadn't been given a copy of the records already provided to the Floyd County prosecutor. I was perplexed, asked what he meant, and was told that Wayne Kessinger had served him with a subpoena a few days before my visit and that the records had quickly been provided to him. That didn't seem right, as both parties in a criminal proceeding in Indiana routinely ran subpoenas by the opposing side before service on the party, and Kitty hadn't been told of any subpoena to Anderson Wood.

The human resources individual did, however, provide me with the names of two other individuals whose records had been subpoenaed by Henderson: Anna Graham[338] and Ernest Nugent.

I thanked the rep and left with more information than I had expected. Graham was probably the woman who had dated Boney after his breakup with Mala. Nugent, however, was a new name to me. Knowing the "fresh eyes" hadn't proactively investigated much, but rather had only reacted to a few leads they had been given, I suspected both names had come from their interviews or interrogation of Boney. Regardless, we needed to learn more about each person.

Before I ran down either of those two people, I called Kitty who confirmed Henderson hadn't told her of any subpoenas he had served. We'd later discover Henderson had issued several other subpoenas without alerting Kitty. In fact, we'd eventually find he had an ongoing investigation, which had yielded very germane information, and which had been kept from us for months.

Ernie Nugent

Victor Ernest Nugent, I found in my database, had been living in New Albany and, in the past, had only lived a block down the same street from the Boney family. After he answered my knock on his door, I told Nugent who I was, provided him with a business card, and then asked if I could speak with him. Small in stature, not quite 60 years old, with a scraggly white beard, Nugent, who went by Ernie, agreed to have my interview with him tape-recorded.

---

[338] Pseudonym.

For twenty minutes or so Nugent answered my questions but downplayed his relationship with Boney, whom he knew was a co-worker at Anderson Wood. Nugent, a machine operator, had only been supplied raw material by Boney, and Nugent had never interacted with him and said he hadn't known the Boney family had lived down the street from him in the past.

I got the impression that Nugent, antsy and jumpy, was expecting to be asked a very specific question, so I cut to the chase: "Did he [Boney] ever ask you to help him secure anything, get something for him?"

His response was quick and direct: "I figure that's what you've been leading up to all along. He asked me if I could get a gun for him." Nugent further told me the request had been made about two months after Boney had begun work, or in the late summer of 2000. The gun Boney had wanted was a semi-automatic, but Nugent only had a .38 revolver, six shot, which, he said, may or may not have been loaded. Regardless, he had sold it to Boney in the parking lot of Anderson Wood for $100, and, no, he had no idea what Boney had done with it.

Nugent claimed he had never seen Boney with any other gun, including a semi-automatic, nor had Boney ever talked about guns after Nugent had sold him the revolver. And, no, Boney had never mentioned the Camm murders, nor had he made any comments about committing any crime.

Whatever credibility Nugent possessed, it was destroyed when I asked, of the gun, "Where did you get it?"

"I found it in the back of a van I bought, back by the spare tire." I pressed Nugent on his claim, but he kept insisting he had only found the gun in a van he had purchased at a used car lot. That, of course, was as likely as scoring a Krugerrand from a nickel gumball machine.

From whom did Nugent get the gun? Was it really a semi-auto? Was he afraid of the person? Regardless, after questioning him two more times on the source of the gun with no change in his story, I pushed no further, waiting until I had more information about Nugent, his friends, and his background before I re-interviewed him.

Before I left, however, I asked Nugent if he had been questioned by any investigator about Boney. No, he said. While they had known of Nugent, the "fresh eyes" hadn't yet contacted him.

The Prison Informant's Mother

I next told Kitty I was going to interview Jeremy Bullock's mother who, after all, could have been a critical impeachment witness. Recall it was she who was the intermediary between her son and Kessinger. If the information she had about her son's supposed interactions with Dave didn't mesh with her son's story to the investigators, then any impact of his testimony would be lessened if not downright contradicted. Additionally, she had already rebutted her son's claim that he hadn't snitched on others.

When she answered the doorbell, Mrs. Bullock was on the phone, but she opened the door, so I gave her my business card and identified myself as a defense investigator on the Camm case. She invited me in as her husband ushered me to a chair while she kept talking on the phone. Within moments, it became apparent she was speaking to her incarcerated son as she looked down at my card and said my name.

She then walked into an adjacent room, phone still in hand, and closed the door, as her husband and I sat at a table in the middle of a room adorned with Indianapolis Colts banners. I went through my introductory spiel with him, telling him of my identity and the reason for being at his house. His comment was simple: "I really don't get into that." Both of us Peyton Manning fans, we talked of football and then of his retirement from being a truck driver.

Several minutes later, and upon her exit from the other room, Mrs. Bullock was demanding to know if I was working "with defense attorney Liell?" I told her I was. She responded by saying she had been on the phone, speaking with Mr. Kessinger of the prosecutor's office, and that she had been told "not to speak" with me.

I told Mrs. Bullock that it was her choice as to whether or not she should speak with me and not the choice of Mr. Kessinger. I then asked her to at least listen to what I had to say, telling her, among other things, that I was there to speak with her based upon a two-and-a-half-page memorandum that Mr. Kessinger had written after speaking with her about information possessed by her son. Her response was that anything he had written in his memo would be accurate, although she admitted that she had never seen the memo.

Mrs. Bullock's phone rang again. It was her son; she related to me that he wanted to speak with me, but she wasn't going to allow that to happen. She then became very animated after I told her she could possibly be a witness, based upon what she had already said. That didn't sit well with her, and she then demanded that I leave her house.

I began gathering my papers, got up out of my seat, and bade my farewell to Mr. Bullock while his wife continued yelling at me to "Get out of my house!"

As with all occupations, some days as a private investigator are better than others.

Boney's Girlfriend Anna

Things got better, however, when I contacted Anna Graham, a hard-working woman with two children who was residing in Louisville. She told me she had worked at Anderson Wood for several months when, on the first

Friday of October 2000, Charles Boney, a very polite and gentlemanly co-worker, had asked her out on a date. She recalled the specific date because that was the same weekend she had attended the funeral of the grandmother of a close friend. A few weeks later, she and Boney had begun living together in her rented home.

If Anna's dates were accurate, that meant Boney had probably stopped dating Mala Singh, and almost certainly had stopped living with her, shortly after the murders. Yet, Boney had told me that he and Mala had dated until 2001. Boney, apparently, hadn't wanted me to know about Anna.

The mother of two young boys continued her story. At work, Anna said, Boney often had asked women, including her, to show him their polished toenails, and many had complied with his request. It was clear to almost every woman at work that Boney had a love for women's painted toes.

Shortly after they had begun living together, Anna discovered that Boney had been a "clean freak" who'd showered two or three times every day. He also had admitted to her that he had been sexually aroused by Anna's feet and also told her that all women's feet, legs, and shoes had been a sexual turn on for him.

In fact, her roommate had been "mesmerized" and "sexually excited" by women's feet for years, even using the term "fetish" to describe his unique need for sexual gratification. Underscoring that compulsion, Boney had admitted that while he was in prison, he had corresponded with several women who had sent him photos of their feet, explaining the photos "kept my mind off doing time." He had kept those cherished photos, along with many other similar ones, which Anna had seen in the trunk of his car.

Other items in Boney's trunk Anna had seen were a backpack, which he had taken literally everywhere with him; lots of receipts and paperwork; and a semi-automatic handgun, which was dark in color. Anna knew the difference between a revolver and a semi-automatic and was certain it had been a semi-auto. She was also certain she had never wanted the gun in her house and had been unwavering in that regard. After she had asked Boney why he needed the weapon, his simple response had been "You never know."

Since Anna knew Boney was a convicted felon, she had warned him he could go back to prison if he were found in the possession of the gun. His response was that he "wasn't planning on going back to prison." He later had claimed he had gotten rid of the weapon.

When I asked her about and then described a "robbery kit," Anna replied that she had never seen Boney in possession of one.

Boney was normally a dependable worker, but, as time passed, Anna said he had missed more and more work. Since Anderson Wood demanded any unscheduled absence have a valid reason, Boney had often provided an excuse from his family doctor, which she had witnessed Boney routinely forging.

Anna recalled she had often laundered Boney's clothes, which included his T-shirts and boxer shorts. Both of those items had his name on them, and both had been prison clothing. Therefore, when she saw him on television, claiming he did not keep any of his DOC clothing, Anna knew he had been lying.

A few months into their relationship, Boney had asked Anna to write a check for repairs to his dark blue Cadillac, telling her he would reimburse her with cash. She'd written the check, and he had quickly paid her back. Still later, he had asked her to write another check, that time for almost $1,000, for additional car repairs, telling her he had been due to get a large sum of money from a program that lent money to ex-convicts. She was stupid enough, she admitted, to have written the check, but Boney had failed to reimburse her.[339]

Despite all the times he had needed money, Anna noted that, sometime in the spring of 2001, Boney had nonetheless come into possession of over $2,000 in cash. He had quickly spent that money on new clothes for himself, moved out of her house, and rented his own apartment. Anna said she had been unaware of the source of that cash.

Darnell, Anna said, had also been very close to his mother, a woman she had met on several occasions. Mrs. Boney, Anna said, was a "whack job" who would constantly tell people, "God bless you" but would then "stab a person in the back." To attempt to retrieve the $1,000 Charles had scammed from her, Anna had also called Mrs. Boney on several occasions, but her efforts had been fruitless, as neither son nor mother had responded.

Boney and Anna often had words with one another, and once Boney had told her he didn't have to "take her bullshit" and that he had beaten his ex-wife, implying he'd do the same to her. Anna had forcibly responded that he wouldn't touch her, as she had a friend next door who was very big and equally as strong as Boney and wouldn't stand for her to be hurt. Boney had backed off on his threats, with Anna describing him as a "wussy" when threatened by those he couldn't intimidate.

Boney had never mentioned the Camm murders, nor had he ever mentioned David Camm, Anna said. When asked if she thought him capable of killing others, particularly children, Anna responded she didn't want to think he could have harmed a child, particularly since he had treated her two kids well.

It was disappointing when Anna told me she and Boney had only purchased cellular phones a few months after they had met and that he didn't have a cell

---

[339] Since she hadn't had enough money in her account to cover the check, Anna had to borrow $1,000 from her mother to cover the check. It was either that or face being arrested.

phone at the time she had first gone out with him. Thus, there was no apparent possibility of our tracking Boney via any cell phone records of his around September 28.[340]

Build Me A Silencer

Based on the silencer information from Amber, I next spoke with Tommy Sandler,[341] who had been a good friend of Boney's for years. It was Sandler, friend or not, who had warned Amber that her husband had wanted Sandler to build a silencer for his gun because of his wife's "fucking his life up." When I knocked on his door, Sandler was very pleasant and invited me in. Throughout our lengthy interview, he and his wife, who also knew Amber and Boney, were cooperative and answered my questions.

Sandler said he had been previously interviewed by Gilbert, albeit not from the lead provided by Amber. After seeing Boney speaking on the television with Carrie Harned, Sandler had alerted his local police department about his concerns over Boney and had, in turn, been contacted by Gilbert after my interview of Boney and prior to his arrest.[342]

A friend of Boney's since middle school, Sandler had re-established contact with Boney in late October 2000.[343] Contrary to Boney's claims of getting rid of all of his prison clothing, Sandler had seen Boney wearing several pieces of prison clothing, including a sweatshirt bearing the inscription BACKBONE. In fact, Boney had exhibited the hand-printed BACKBONE on the sweatshirt collar to Sandler, giving him the "standup" guy shtick.

His friend, whom Sandler knew was a convicted felon, had also proudly displayed a .38 revolver to Sandler and said that he would "never get rid of it" because Amber had a friend who had been threatening him, and Boney "wasn't going to be caught sleeping."

It was that same .38 for which Boney had asked, and then pleaded with, his good friend, who was mechanically inclined, to build him a silencer. Sandler said he had repeatedly refused, but Boney had kept begging for the silencer. His pleas had increased in frequency around the time Boney became

---

[340] Our later contacts/subpoenas to service providers failed to find any cell phones held by Boney in September 2000.

[341] Pseudonym.

[342] Thus, Gilbert was fully aware of very specific and germane lies Boney had spouted to me. As to what lies Boney had told Gilbert and Kessinger previously, I didn't know.

[343] Sandler had first met Boney in junior high school when he had stopped the younger Boney from fighting another boy. Over the years the two had lost contact with one another, but in the late 1980's they had become reacquainted and began running around together. The two then fell out of contact with Sandler unaware Boney had been imprisoned for several years during the 1990's.

more violent with Amber. It was during that time that Amber had told Sandler and his wife that Boney had "tortured" her and held her against her will for several days.

Of course, one had to ask the question of *why* Boney needed a silencer? Was it because of a prior bad experience? The sound of three thundering .380 rounds being fired in a small garage? Were those gunshots so deafening to Boney that he needed to suppress the sound of future gunshots?

Regardless, during that October 2000 renewed acquaintance, the two friends had gone to a topless bar where Boney had first told Sandler of his foot fetish, with Boney further admitting, of women's feet, that he had liked to "smell them, lick them, kiss them, suck them." Boney was such a foot connoisseur, he told Sandler, that he was able to differentiate pretty feet from ugly feet. He loved pretty feet but hated ugly feet.

Boney, in fact, had talked incessantly about his sexual obsession with feet and had been so juiced that Sandler "had to pull his chain to get him to stop." Still, Boney had become so totally enraptured with one stripper that he had paid her $50 for one of her knee-high stockings, which he had repeatedly smelled during their ride home afterwards, telling his friend the smell was still "fresh."

Once, when Sandler had visited Boney in his Louisville house, his foot-obsessed friend had proudly shown him his hiding place, in a wall, for his foot-fetish paraphernalia, which had included the newly-acquired stripper stocking, many issues of foot-fetish magazines, and several other stockings, which Boney said weren't as good as they had been originally, since they were "no longer fresh." Sandler said he hadn't asked Boney the source of those stockings.

I pressed Sandler on other aspects of his relationship with Boney. While incarcerated in 2004, in Bloomington on the probation violation charge, Boney had called and asked Sandler to take care of his car loan. Good friend Sandler and his wife not only kept the loan up-to-date, but also maintained the vehicle, spending over $1,000 over several months.

Once Boney had been released from the Monroe County Jail, he had picked up the car, promised several times to repay Sandler, had failed twice to show for appointments to meet, and then had no longer taken Sandler's phone calls.

Other traits of Boney's, Sandler knew, was that he was "book smart" and the consummate "sales person" who could "sell snow to an Eskimo." He also said the former used car salesman could "read you like a book" and "tell you what you want to hear."

It was obvious Sandler knew Charles Boney as well as anyone. The question I was asking myself: Did the investigators provide Boney with their appropriate clues, enabling him to *tell them exactly what they wanted to hear*?

CHAPTER 34

"A .380 Packs A Helluva Punch"

Unsettled Jurisdiction

Kitty, Stacy, and I routinely met, and during one meeting, they told me again, after their research, that they were convinced that not only had Henderson been legally wrong, but so had Judge Cody in Floyd County, who had begun presiding over the joint murder/conspiracy case. Clearly, they said, jurisdiction had already been established for Dave, and neither the state nor any trial judge could negate his right to be tried in Warrick County. For his part, Judge Aylsworth in Warrick County, having already dismissed the case against Dave, had told the parties to let the Indiana Supreme Court determine which court had proper jurisdiction. My translation of the judge's comments: "I don't want to handle this hot political potato."

To have the case returned to Warrick County, however, Kitty and Stacy first had to appeal to Floyd County Circuit Judge Cody to reverse his decision to maintain control of the case. If he denied the request, which he was almost certainly going to do, then the next step was to file a Writ of Mandamus to the Indiana Supreme Court.[344] Writs of Mandamus are not only very uncommonly filed but rarely do appellate courts grant relief to the relator. Still, Kitty and Stacy were confident of their arguments, and I was more than confident of their acumen and skills.

> "HE SAID HE'S GOT A RAGE THAT ROARS INSIDE OF HIM, THAT HE STARTED SEEING WHITE SPORTS AND THAT HE DON'T REMEMBER NOTHING AFTER IT."

The foundation on which the writ would be based was solid, not only in case law but also statutorily, Kitty and Stacy insisted, and the icing on the cake had been the evidence that Henderson and his Chief Deputy Owen had also given them.

Recall that Henderson, more than irritated over Judge Aylsworth's granting bond to Dave, had already filed a motion for a change of judge after Dave's bond hearing. Henderson had implied in that motion that the judge's

---

[344] From the Indiana Rules of Court, "The Supreme Court has exclusive, original jurisdiction to supervise the exercise of jurisdiction by other courts of the State of Indiana by virtue of Indiana Constitution."

association with Anthony Long, the local attorney and former prosecutor for whom the judge had once worked, had tainted the judge; thus, that association had trumped the evidence presented by Kitty and Stacy, including the appellate court's opinion that the case had been weak.

The prosecutor and his top dog, Owen, were also upset Aylsworth had ordered Dave to be provided with sufficient funds to hire forensic experts and a defense investigator, claiming his order had been "unusual and extraordinary."

At the change of judge hearing, Owen had made the arguments for the State. He had been both animated and, in my view, really whiny, complaining of adverse rulings, including funding for Dave, a trial date which favored Kitty and Stacy's calendars, and, he moaned, "the thing that really kicked it was the bond." And then Owen had made a startling comment when he said the judge's bond ruling wouldn't look good in the local papers if Dave were to be found guilty. When hearing that "argument," Kitty, Stacy, and I had been stunned, as the comment was nothing, we thought, less than attempted intimidation of the judge.

Judge Aylsworth, rather than tell Owen to stuff it, was instead measured and patient, explaining, among other things, that his bond ruling had been, in large part, based on the appellate decision, which the judge found to be the most "direct, blunt or brutal assessment of the evidence presented." What was unsaid by the judge was that Henderson's "best evidence" during the bond hearing was his having entered the order of conviction and sentencing from the first trial, which, of course, hadn't been evidence at all.

Judge Aylsworth had not bought the state's weak arguments and ruled against them, causing, no doubt, Henderson and Owen even more heartburn. Still, I had to wonder if the judge would be more susceptible in the future to rule on behalf of the state, given the extreme flak he had already endured.

So, it was a matter of waiting until after the initial motions were filed and rejected, and then waiting on the direct appeal to the Indiana Supreme Court. It could take weeks or months to decide where Dave would be tried. In the interim, we still had not received any discovery from the State.

We weren't idle, as we were also being aggressive in our own investigation. After meeting with Kitty and Stacy, I took off for Louisville, intent on speaking with one particular co-worker of Amber's who could possibly shed additional light on Mr. and Mrs. Boney. While I believed Amber had been essentially honest with me, I didn't think she had been totally forthcoming. After all, we knew she was still visiting her estranged husband, whom she still loved, in jail.

"I Could Kill You Right Now!"

Toki, the stage name of an adult entertainer, had been friends with Amber for many years, and had been present when I first interviewed Amber. At that time, she had been quite receptive in speaking with me in the future, telling me that she might possibly help her close friend Amber.

Her interview began as did most which dealt with Charles Boney: "Oh, he was a super nice guy. It was like almost too good. He was just so nice," Toki said, smiling, "and he was well-mannered, very much a gentleman, and a smart guy. You could tell he was a smart guy."

Several months after the two had met, Toki recalled, Amber and Boney had married at the Louisville Zoo. For almost a year, Amber had told Toki, the marriage was doing well, albeit Darnell had changed jobs three times, working as a salesman in the latter two jobs.

The beatings of Amber, Toki knew, had begun prior to their one-year anniversary and had increased in frequency and severity thereafter. In December 2003, after a cancer scare, Amber had been diagnosed with severe pneumonia and had been hospitalized. With Amber in the hospital, Toki recalled, Darnell "thought that it was the perfect time to leave and to break it off, and he did."

After being hospitalized for several days, Amber was in need of personal items from her house. Previously, both Amber and Toki had made several telephone calls to both Darnell and his mother to attempt to arrange to secure clean undergarments, hairbrushes, and other personal hygiene items for Amber. All the calls to Darnell had gone unanswered, but his mother, whom Toki described as "really nasty," had told Toki she didn't care what happened to Amber and said she wouldn't forward any message to her son.

Toki had then volunteered to go to Amber's home and retrieve Amber's personal items as well as one of her friend's dogs, which was still in the house. Amber, whom Toki said thought of her two dogs as her children, was afraid Darnell would hurt the animal again, as he had done in the past. He had even, Amber had told Toki, threatened to "snuff" the pet.

Given the key to the back door of Amber's house, Toki had knocked on it with no answer. As she had been inserting the key into the lock, the door suddenly had burst open, and Darnell stood over her with a small dark revolver pointed just inches from her face. He had begun screaming, "What the fuck are you doing here? I could kill you right now! I can tell the cops that you were trying to break into my house." He then had gotten even more excited and had begun waving the gun as he told Toki he hated her while screaming obscenities.

Toki, who had fallen to the ground when she had been confronted with the gun to her head, told me that she had gotten along well with Darnell in the past and couldn't comprehend the drastic change in attitude towards her. She had desperately asked, "Darnell, what are you doing? Stop! It's me, Toki!"

Things had gotten even worse, Toki said, as she lay on the ground as Darnell "just had this look in his eyes" as he had been getting more and more angry, gritting his teeth and staring almost through her.

Finally, Darnell had spoken, but after hearing what she had wanted, had refused to give her anything, including the dog, so Toki had left empty-handed.

Scared but not intimidated, Toki had gone to a nearby police station the next day and reported that Darnell, a convicted felon, had been in possession of a gun. Nothing happened immediately, but that information, coupled with the EPO Amber later filed, had resulted in Darnell's arrest on the Indiana probation violation charge.

Toki acknowledged that Amber had admitted to her that her husband also had a "robbery kit." Amber's best friend said she had told Amber to report it to the police, but she had refused to do so, telling Toki, "He'll kill me if I tell the police."

Although Darnell had told Amber on several occasions that he could get money through committing armed robberies, Amber had insisted to Toki that she hadn't thought he was serious.

Amber also had told Toki of Darnell's infatuation with and worship of Satan. She had seen him standing in front of a mirror with lighted candles and incense while uttering blasphemous chants to God, all the while worshipping Satan. He even had a necklace with a large S emblazoned on it. Most people had thought it stood for Superman, but Darnell had told Amber the S was for Satan, whom he referred to as "his father." Boney even had pictures of Lucifer on the rearview mirrors in his various cars and possessed many issues of satanic magazines.

Amber had visited Darnell in the Floyd County Jail, Toki knew, and, amazingly, Amber had cried when telling Toki that she was still in love with him, even though he had gotten engaged to another woman while Amber and he were still married. Even in spite of all of that, and while she had known of all of his violence and lies, Amber still told Toki that she knew Darnell could not have murdered the two Camm children.

Just prior to the December 2003 incident, Toki and her boyfriend, in trying to help Amber and Darnell, had sold a car to them, with the agreement that Darnell would make the monthly payments on the vehicle. That didn't work out well, as Darnell had failed to make even the first payment.

Contrary to what Boney had told me about an addiction to drugs, Toki said, Amber had earlier confirmed to her that Boney was only a mild drinker and had never taken any drugs of any kind.

After thanking Toki for her time and assistance, I next drove to the Green Light and arrived in mid-afternoon at the establishment, well before the crowd of mostly blue-collar men would be dropping their dollar bills while the entertainers dropped other items.

"I've Done Some Things You Wouldn't Believe"

I was quickly directed to Rob Dennis,[345] the manager who had also manned the door for years. After giving him my routine introduction, I asked about his background. Dennis, free for five years, said he had done ten years in the Kentucky Department of Corrections [KDOC] for numerous burglaries and for having been a Persistent Felony Offender [PFO]. After a few minutes with him, Dennis, I thought, as with a few other convicts I had met, had two good character traits: bluntness and honesty.

Dennis had first met Boney, he told me, shortly after Boney had begun hanging around Amber, who had been the Green Light bartender for almost all of her adult life. Early in their relationship, Dennis had seen Boney sitting at the end of the bar one night, rubbing Amber's feet. Later, Amber had told Dennis that she and Darnell had common interests in that both loved shoes.

When Boney had first frequented the Green Light, he was selling various items such as pocket recorders, children's books, and games. That line of work, Dennis later learned, also had enabled Boney to interact, literally, as a traveling salesman, with people in their own homes.

Dennis also knew that Boney had once driven a Cadillac, because fairly early in his relationship with Amber, Boney and Dennis had been speaking about their cars. Boney said he had previously owned a Cadillac and that Amber had found a used condom in the backseat of the vehicle, causing an argument between the two. A laughing Boney had joked with Dennis, asking him, "Now, Rob, you don't think a man would do anything in his Cadillac, do you?"[346]

Over time, Boney had often appeared at the Green Light, waiting to take Amber home after her shift. During those times, as well as on the occasions when Dennis had also given Boney a ride, Boney had confided in him—probably, Dennis surmised, because he, like Boney, had done prison time.

Boney, who had become a salesman at a car dealership, had bragged to Dennis that he had obtained the key rings of customers and had duplicated keys to their residences, the addresses of which he had obtained from their

---

[345] Pseudonym.

[346] Although Boney's comment about the condom and his Cadillac had only been only a joke, it confirmed he utilized prophylactics at the same time he drove the vehicle.

loan applications. He said he had later "hit" those homes, meaning he had burgled them.

Boney had also, he told Dennis, listened to the conversations of others and often had joined in, learning where the people had worked, where they had lived, and in what other activities they had engaged. After having determined their routines, he said he had broken into their unoccupied homes and stolen whatever he wanted, bragging that he had even stolen a big-screen television from one house, which he had later lied to Amber that it had been a rental.

Boney also had bragged to Dennis that several victims wouldn't even have known that he had been inside their homes. Dennis had responded by telling Boney that he needed to stop the burglaries or else he'd get caught, and he'd really get it stuck to him. Boney had replied that he had been "too smart to get caught."

Dennis, who knew of Boney's armed robbery convictions, had also seen him on several occasions in possession of a handgun, which Boney had kept in the glove box of his car, under the front driver's seat, and, during cold months, in the pocket of his coat. Although having been repeatedly warned by Dennis of the danger of being a convicted felon in possession of a gun, Boney had shrugged off the warning, telling Dennis he had needed the gun "for protection."

Once, when he had driven Amber home, she and Dennis had stopped for gas at a filling station near the Boney residence. Several guys had tried to surround the car, and Dennis had quickly driven off, thinking they had been planning to rob them. Once home, Amber had told Boney of the experience and he'd become enraged, grabbed his gun, and said, "I'll kill those son-of-a-bitches. I'll show them I got heart. I ain't no fucking punk." He had then jumped into his car and driven to the scene, but the men had already left.

Boney, who was very knowledgeable of guns, had also been proud of his ability to handle a weapon and had boasted to Dennis of the time he had spent in prison for armed robbery. Contrary to any claims of his having been remorseful, Boney had been anything but contrite, Dennis opined.

Bigger guns were better guns, according to Boney, Dennis recalled, with the proud armed robber having told him that he "didn't like .25's, no little .32's" but rather liked .38's and .45's.

The best smaller gun, however, Boney had claimed, was a .380 because "it's so little you can hold it in your hand, put it in your pocket, cover it up. A .380, it's got a hell of a punch. It's little, but it packs a hell of a punch."

Over time, Dennis had learned the relationship between Boney and Amber had radically changed as Amber had often confided in Dennis that she had been beaten on many occasions by her husband. She had shown Dennis the many bruises on her body which had been inflicted by Boney through a stun gun, fists, and, on one occasion, a pistol-whipping.

Dennis, who had been very fond of Amber, had spoken to Boney about his abuse of Amber, and Boney had made a surprising admission to him: "He told me that he was sorry that happened, but he thought he took control of that, that it happened with his first wife and that he thought he had control of it, but he didn't. He said he's got a rage that roars inside of him, that he started seeing white spots, and that he don't remember nothing after it."

Boney wasn't finished with his confessional to Dennis, though, as he had told the doorman, "I've done some things you wouldn't even believe, things that you or nobody else could ever conceive that I've done."

Dennis had later spoken with a still-terrified Amber who had tearfully told him she thought she was going to be killed by Boney. Her husband, Amber said, had gotten a "wild look in his eye" and had threatened to kill her if she ever told the police about the abuse. Validating the threat to kill her, he then had warned Amber, "Check my record. I've done it before."

Of his relationship with the police, Boney had bragged to Dennis as to how smart he was and had laughingly said that "cops were stupid." Boney had experienced lots of run-ins with cops, he had said, ever since he had been a kid, and he'd told Dennis that his personality enabled him to "manipulate the system and manipulate the cops."

Dennis had also seen the man with the uncontrollable rage, on one occasion, become violently angry at one of Amber's dogs, a dog which he had previously claimed to really love. Boney had been in his car when the dog had done something Boney hadn't liked. As a result, Boney had gotten furious at the dog, and, as Dennis put it, "I seen [sic] him smack that dog all the way across the seat. He also said he loved Amber, but if he loved her so much, how could he beat her like that? You know, that's the rage he would get."

For his part, Dennis had pleaded with Amber to leave Boney, and, although she finally had, she had told Dennis that she had still been supportive of Boney even after his all of his repeated and horrific beatings of her and even after his arrest in the Camm murders.

Just prior to Boney's appearing on television and explaining how he had gotten rid of his sweatshirt, Dennis had been present when Boney had come into the Green Light to speak with Amber.[347] Dennis had heard Boney's boasting to Amber that he didn't have to worry about going to prison, as he had pointed to his head and claimed, "I got this up here."

---

[347] The time was after Boney had been interviewed for over 22 hours by the "fresh eyes."

Asked if any law enforcement officer had spoken with him about Boney, Dennis told me that none had, and he was surprised, because he had a lot he could tell them about Boney.

My last question of Dennis was if he thought Darnell Boney was a stand-up guy who had deserved the name of BACKBONE.

"No" was the quick answer. "Boney's a piece of shit."

CHAPTER 35
"Bully-Bragger"

Since Boney was revealed to us in late-February, we had accumulated a voluminous amount of information on him such as his numerous places of employment, including the three places he had been employed at the time of his public disclosure. We had begun subpoenaing all of his records prior to Henderson's shifty legal move, but others were needing to be written and served.

A favorite job of BACKBONE had been with restaurants, and in particular, those which served fast food. He had his first job at a burger joint while still in high school, in the New Albany Plaza, which was within walking distance from his home. He had continued with the same chain while in Bloomington as he had attended IU. Not only had he met his first wife at the restaurant; he had discovered it and others were meccas for meeting other women. One had to wonder which had been a priority: making money or securing romantic results.

> "I SAW HIM WRAPPING A FIREARM IN A TOWEL OR SHOP RAG. IT DEFINITELY WASN'T A REVOLVER. IT WAS BIGGER THAN A .25 AUTOMATIC, LIKE A .380 OR .32"

Regardless, not only had we gotten a plethora of information from some records, but we had also engaged in other online searches, as well as legwork on the ground, and had obtained names of Boney's co-workers, much as we had done with Amber. Since Boney had spoken candidly to Amber's co-worker and friend, Rob Dennis, about his knowledge and love of .380 semi-automatics, there had to have been others associated with Boney who had more insights.

The Shoe Bandit, we would find, had been employed at over a dozen different places from 2000-2005, and the resultant interviews with dozens of co-workers had paid dividends, as Boney, ever the braggart, had shot off his mouth to many people. Although he had mostly tried to disguise himself initially—particularly at his restaurant work, where he had presented himself as a true gem of a fellow—his true personality had almost always had exhibited itself.

His Boys Could "Bust A Cap On You"

Anderson Wood hired recently-released convicts, and many of those employees had become excellent workers. One such person had been with them for over five years, after his release from almost 10 years in federal prison for weapons convictions. I had spoken with Wyatt Collins[348] at his home on the far southwest side of Louisville, where he and his wife had invited me in to their home.

Boney and Wyatt had worked together the entire time Boney had been employed at Anderson Wood, or from June 2000, until Boney quit on May 23, 2001. Boney, Wyatt had said, had an "attitude, the way he carried himself, he intimidated most people," further adding, "he played the role of thug, gangster."

When I had asked for more specifics, Wyatt had explained, "He had some conflict with some of the other workers and he'd say, 'Well, you mess with me, I'll call my boys on you.'" In fact, Boney had bragged of his affiliation in a prison gang and of his "boys" who "could bust a cap on" people.

Wyatt had then said that Boney had clearly been an inmate and had not been a convict. I had known of the difference, but I had asked Wyatt to explain anyway. "Convicts stay to themselves, they've not got big mouths. They don't try to bush hog and bully people around. Inmates, on the other hand, they're just a different breed of animal. [Boney] definitely was an inmate, a bully-bragger, an intimidator, that wanted to be in the spotlight."

"He probably had a little better than average intelligence," Wyatt had continued, "who could hold a good conversation with you and who had the potential to really have gone somewhere with his life."[349]

When Wyatt had seen Boney on the news, involved in the Camm case, and contrary to many who knew BACKBONE, it hadn't surprised him that he'd possibly been "involved in a murder, a robbery, or anything." The man, after all, had previously bragged during lunch of his armed robbery exploits, explained Wyatt.

After Boney had been at Anderson for a while, Wyatt had heard that Ernie Nugent had sold Boney a gun. Shortly thereafter, Wyatt, who had grown up in the mountains and who "knew firearms well," had seen that same gun, blue-steel in color, in Boney's possession. He further explained, "I saw him wrapping a firearm in a towel or shop rag. It definitely wasn't a revolver. It was bigger than a .25 automatic, like a .380 or .32."

---

[348] Pseudonym. All co-workers of Boney, with the exception of Nugent, have been given pseudonyms.

[349] Wyatt's observations had caused me to think of the question many had asked of me during my FBI career: why do smart, intelligent people, who could have been successful in many fields, decide to engage in crime? The answer, at least for many criminals, is simple: that's who they are. Their personalities, of course, define themselves and, in turn, determine their actions.

On another later occasion, Wyatt had again seen Boney in possession of a gun, but whether or not it was the same weapon Wyatt hadn't known, since he had only seen the barrel, which had been protruding from a cloth. And where had he see the gun? It was in Boney's red and black backpack when Boney had removed several photographs he had shown to him. The backpack, Wyatt noted, had always been with Boney.

A word of caution had been given Boney, a convicted felon, by Wyatt, about carrying a gun, particularly at work, but BACKBONE had ignored the advice.

Wyatt, who had known that Nugent had also served prison time,[350] had taken him aside after having seen Boney in possession of the gun that Nugent had sold him. "I told him, 'I'm not trying to be up in your business, but don't you know better than to be messing with a firearm?'"

Nugent's response was "I own a whole bunch of guns. I ain't worried about it. I've carried one all my life. "

The convicted felon Nugent, who hadn't been worried about selling a firearm to another convicted felon, according to Wyatt, "carried a gun at all times, [he] even carried one in his pocket on the job," and, based upon the small size, it would have been a ".25 or a .32 or something like that." Nugent, Wyatt had known, had also been upset with the Boney gun sale because his co-worker had stiffed him on the full price of the purchase.

According to Wyatt, another co-worker, Dick Conrad, had also engaged in a gun trade with Nugent. Wyatt hadn't seen the guns involved, but shop talk was pervasive that Dick had exchanged a revolver for another weapon from Nugent, but the make, caliber, and style were unknown to Wyatt.

Wyatt, not to my surprise, hadn't been contacted by the "fresh eyes." If he had been, they'd learned that Charles Boney had been in possession of a semi-automatic gun, either a .380 or a .32, weeks prior to the murders. I was betting on the .380.

Nugent & His Guns

When I spoke to Dick Conrad, he had told me he had been told by Boney, when he had been leaving work on one occasion: "I got to meet with my crew," implying to Conrad that Boney had been a shot-caller in a gang. Conrad, who had been around literally dozens of former convicts at work, said he hadn't believed the self-important braggart.

The guy who had bench-pressed hundreds of pounds of wood, impressing

---

[350] I had spent several hours doing my own background on Nugent and had discovered, among other things, that he had been arrested with another person for armed robbery in Missouri and had served several years in prison.

many of the co-workers, also routinely strutted his stuff around the factory, according to Conrad. On every occasion that Conrad had seen him, Boney had been in possession of a backpack. Something, though, had struck Conrad as "weird" about Boney, however, and, based upon his demeanor, intelligent talk, and the number of former convicts in the factory, he had asked Boney if "he was a cop."

Rather than answer directly, Boney had asked, "Well, do I sound like one?" Conrad had answered that, yes, he had thought Boney had been put in the workplace as a possible undercover policeman. Nothing had become of Conrad's suspicions, however, as Boney had left the question unanswered.

Conrad said that it had been well-known by many at work that Boney had purchased a gun, caliber unknown, from Ernest Nugent and that Boney had not fully paid him for the weapon.

As for Nugent, Conrad said, he had been a decent worker and one who had, on various occasions, in the late summer of 2000, shown Conrad a total of three guns: a .38 revolver, 9 mm semi-automatic, and a .380 semi. Nugent had talked often of buying, trading, and selling guns.

Regarding the .38 revolver[351] of Nugent's, Conrad, in August 2000, had made an even trade with Nugent for a 9 mm of Conrad's. That had occurred near Nugent's parked pickup truck, which had been the vehicle "that he was driving the whole time that [Nugent] had been working there."

Conrad had thought it had been after Labor Day of 2000 when he had seen Nugent in possession of the 9 mm semi, shown to Conrad after Nugent had pulled a brown paper sack from his pickup truck, parked on the street near the factory. The black gun, which Conrad recalled "had been around," had also been, in his recollection, a fairly expensive gun.

On that same occasion, Nugent had also taken, from the same brown sack, a satin-like .380 semi-auto, which "looked like it hadn't been used much" and also looked less expensive than the 9 mm. Conrad, who formerly had a .380, had verbalized to Nugent that .380s were "nice, little guns," but that he, personally, hadn't really liked the weapon.

Other than trading him for the revolver, Conrad had no further gun dealings with Nugent. He had, however, warned Nugent that "he better be careful," as Anderson Wood hadn't allowed guns on their property. Nugent's response was to have put the two guns back into the sack and to have walked away from Conrad. Although he hadn't seen Nugent in possession of a gun in the factory, Conrad had heard from others that it had been routine for Nugent to carry a gun.

---

[351] Another co-worker had claimed that it had been a .357 revolver which Nugent had traded for Conrad's 9 mm.

Two Other Co-Workers

Daryl Houseman, another co-worker of Boney's, had neither seen, nor had he known, of any gun transactions or possessions while he had been employed at Anderson Wood, although, being a Christian, he had tried to evangelize Boney. That had been unsuccessful as Boney had explained to Houseman that, instead of Jesus, he had followed Satan.

One of the supervisors had agreed to speak with me, but only in the presence of the "fresh eyes" investigators.[352] Brit Carpenter, in charge of the night shift where Boney had worked, had summarized Boney quite well: a lazy, strong thug who was a braggart about getting women and an intimidator who had threatened to "beat the shit out of" another smaller employee who had immigrated from a war-torn country. Some of those he had intimidated, in fact, had often been slapped in the backs of their heads by Boney.

Carpenter had known of some kind of a gun transaction between the backpacking Boney and Nugent; afterward, Nugent had constantly whined about Boney's not having paid fully for the gun.

That Boney had tried to impress others, including prior felons at his menial job with his strength, show of weapons, and intimidation was only the latest box to be checked in the Shoe Bandit's personality profile.

---

[352] Both Gilbert and Kessinger had shown up for that interview.

CHAPTER 36

"He's A Jekyll & Hyde"

Knick-Knacks

I had also tracked down many of the companies where Boney had worked, including the ones specializing in selling knick-knacks and cheap items, such as watches, tools, dolls, and children's magazines. Those items had been purchased by the wholesalers in large lots and then resold to self-employed salespeople, many of whom hadn't lasted past their first purchase.[353]

Boney had been one of those self-employed salespeople and, according to interviews with his prior girlfriends and others, had been one of the ones who hadn't made much money on the venture. The last owner

> "DON'T FUCK WITH ME, OLD MAN! I'LL KILL YOU!"

of the company, not surprisingly, had left the Louisville area and hadn't responded to repeated phone calls and a letter I sent to his out-of-state address.

Still, the items Boney had in his possession had been directed at all ages and sexes, and made his job—or cover, for that matter—ideal for someone who had wanted to have legitimacy while ringing the doorbells and reconnoitering the homes of unsuspecting inhabitants.

Rent-To-Own Salesman

Recalling that Boney had tried to sell his rented, large screen television, it hadn't surprised me that he had actually worked for a rent-to-own company. In fact, at the Louisville store, Boney had first gotten to know the manager, Jimmy Paoli, by trying to sell him some children's items.

Boney, I was told, had subsequently become a customer and had purchased a freezer and a refrigerator from the store; he soon had become four payments in arrears but had promised to pay for the arrearage. Sure enough, the Shoe Bandit, who had been financially struggling in his peddling business, brought in a large sum of cash and made good on his entire debt.[354]

BACKBONE, even after having been a risky customer, had then been

---

[353] Still, the company had made money, even more so when it had been discovered one owner had siphoned off and resold the inventory without ever having paid his supplier.

[354] That had been, at least to my tally, the third time Boney had obtained a sizeable sum of cash.

hired by the company and had passed the employee background check, even though they had known he had a criminal record. According to Boney, his run-in with the law involved him, in his younger days, being into drugs and having an altercation with his drug dealer.

On one occasion at the store, an expensive digital camera had gone missing and, after the entire staff had assembled and been told that stealing would have been cause for immediate termination, Boney had privately insisted to Paoli that he hadn't been the thief. In fact, he said, he had wanted to take a polygraph to prove his innocence.

When I asked of his thoughts about Boney's insistence of innocence, Paoli responded: "I thought that was more incriminating to be so excessive about trying to prove you weren't guilty. It almost seemed a no-brainer that he probably was the thief."

Amber had been Boney's wife at the time, and Paoli had recalled that Boney had often denigrated her as being fat and not trusting of him. He also had admitted to having "knocked her around a little bit." Later, after it had been discovered that Amber had placed an EPO on her husband, alleging he had done much more than had just been "knocking her around," Boney had been terminated.

Paoli had summarized Boney: "A true salesman, definitely a bullshit artist, [whom you can] believe 50% of what he says. It's a matter of which 50% you choose to believe." The always smiling and charismatic salesman also, Paoli had said, "had a way of just breaking people down to where they felt comfortable with him."

Asked if he had been surprised of Boney's having been arrested in the Camm family murders, Paoli's response, I thought, was spot-on: "He comes out on a television interview and says he doesn't know David Camm, he's never met David Camm. He sounded as convincing as convincing can be, right in front of the camera, and then, within weeks, 'I met David Camm.' At what point do you say, 'I can't believe anything that comes out of his mouth.' How do I know his story has any truth?"

Customer Boney

On one of Boney's employment applications, he had listed, as a credit reference, another rent-to-own store in Jeffersonville, Indiana. Although he hadn't been employed there, I nonetheless spoke with the manager, Haley Dufrene, who said that Boney had been referred by his mother and had then become a very good customer, having purchased a set of bridal rings for $1,700, a gas range for $700, and a large-screen television for $2,800.

Boney had been very regular with his cash payments for several months but had then abruptly stopped paying. Repeated attempts to collect had been fruitless, and a call to his mother had resulted in her being quite "nasty" with Dufrene.

A Short-Term Job

Another job had been at a roofing company where Boney had been referred by a friend of Amber's. Bob Asher told me Boney's job as a laborer was to provide slate to the actual roofers. It had quickly become apparent, however, that Boney, afraid of heights, was ill-suited for the job. That, and also, he had taken breaks every five minutes, often walking away from the job site.

When Asher had told Boney that he had needed to take fewer breaks and to keep the roofers supplied with material, Boney had, in turn, given Asher four quarters. When asked why, Boney had responded, in a snarky manner, that he had paid Asher for his break time. He was then fired.

Asher, when giving me Boney's employment file, said that Boney had indicated that he had a degree in psychology from Indiana State, adding, "He probably meant Indiana State Prison." [355]

Within a few days, Boney had appeared in Asher's office and had picked up his small payroll check, but only after telling the office manager, "You guys don't know how to run a business."

One of the co-workers of Boney on that sole roofing job was Max Hoffman who told me that another co-worker had referred to Boney as BACKBONE. Hoffman then had also begun referring to him with the same moniker. Those two men were of the very few that I would ultimately interview who had routinely used Boney's nickname.

Employment Lies

In addition to lying about his psychology degree, Boney had claimed, on other applications, that he had been employed with his father. That had been problematic because, at the time, his father had been dead for several years.

In yet another job application, Boney had listed the name of his one son as a dependent child. Two other children, though, had been named as well, but those kids hadn't existed, nor had the name of a dependent woman he had listed as the mother of those children.

Guardsman Boney

Thad Thompson,[356] the First Sergeant at the National Guard in Bloomington

---

[355] Of added note was the fact the owner told me that Henderson's investigators had requested the company provide Boney's employment records. After having been told of the need of a subpoena, they had not bothered to follow up on obtaining the records

[356] Pseudonym.

where Boney had drilled while at IU, had vividly recalled Boney as working in supply and said he "had the strength of two men." Boney, who had been given a General Discharge after his shoe thefts arrest, had nonetheless shown no indications of behavior issues during his two years of drilling.

Fish Cutter Boney

My next visit had been to a seafood restaurant on the Ohio River in Louisville, where I had spoken with five employees and one vendor,[357] all of whom had routine interactions with Boney, whose primary job had been as a fish cutter. Carla Rossini had hired Boney, whom she had described as "bright, intelligent, very polished, smiled a lot, had a great attitude, and was a smooth talker."

The guy with the great attitude had indicated, on their employment application, that he had been employed from April 1997 to May 2004 at McCracken Industries where he had still been working at the time of the application. For over three of those years, of course, Boney had been in the Big House, apparently working hard to make his lies more believable.

Lindsay Sands told me that Boney had always been respectful and unfailingly polite to her. Sands had also been friends with Boney's fiancé, Vivian, who also was a co-worker.[358] According to Vivian, Boney had been "framed" for the murders, with the girlfriend having based that conclusion on him having been "so good" to her and her boys.

Another co-worker, Sandy Wilkins, although thinking Boney had been smart, intelligent, very well-spoken, and glib, said she hadn't trusted him. Why? "He could stand in front of me and tell me, 'You're not sitting there,' and would convince me that I wasn't sitting in front of him."

Marlene Whitcock had yet another take on Boney, having described him as "a con man, full of crap, you didn't know whether or not to believe him." That belief had solidified during his last two weeks of employment when Boney had claimed to have gotten a job at the Board of Health, even showing his photo identification badge to several co-workers. He had said he'd be inspecting restaurants and laughingly had claimed that he "would be easy" on his then-employer.

On one occasion at the restaurant, Boney had a very loud verbal altercation with a delivery driver and had been given a written reprimand by his immediate boss. Another time he had been accused of making unsolicited

---

[357] All pseudonyms.

[358] I had been rebuffed in my attempts to speak with Vivian, as she had not responded to voicemail messages, written requests left at her door, and a contact I had made with one of her relatives.

advances towards one of the female employees after he had left a note, with his telephone number, on her car windshield, telling her she was pretty. That woman had soon left the restaurant, and there had been no other problems with Boney and women.

Everyone said that Boney had loved to talk with anyone and everyone, including the vendors. I soon spoke to one of those guys, Duncan Jones, whom Boney had routinely helped unload his truck. On one occasion, after Boney's supervisor had reprimanded him for talking too much and not working enough, Boney had waited until after she had left, and then Jones said Boney "started getting really kind of weird with [her] all of a sudden."

In fact, recalled Jones, Boney had said that his supervisor "wasn't aware of what [he was] capable of doing." It had been a threat, no doubt, the vendor had recalled, as Boney had gone from jovial and friendly to having been deadly serious and threatening over a minor comment by his boss.

Car Salesman

It wasn't a surprise that I had also found the "natural salesman" had gravitated towards used car sales. In fact, Boney had been employed at three different locations, including a new car dealership in Louisville. We had gotten but little information from them, as their employment file was barebones and had reflected that Boney had left them with less than a month on the job and literally nothing in their file.

Boney's prior peddling of trinkets, though, had gotten him another car sales position at a buy-here-pay-here dealership in Jeffersonville, just down the road from where he had obtained the large-screen television. That dealership had been the same one where, according to Amber, Boney had forged loan applications.

Boney's personality had lent itself to his becoming the number-one salesperson within a very short time after having been hired. Kyle Constantine, his supervisor, told me, "He was very good with both the low and high educated people. He could relate to the whole spectrum, and he could dictate the conversation. He had a gift of gab." So good was Boney, he had a higher closing percentage of sales than the other salesmen.[359]

When I had spoken with Marty Hankins, the area supervisor of the car lot, it had become clear as to why the high-achieving Boney had finally been terminated: BACKBONE had, without authority, promised free repairs, free radios, and other items to prospective customers. That, and the fact he had

---

[359] The buyers at buy-here-pay-here car lots often have credit issues, and as such, interest rates exceeding 20% are the norm. Closing rates, or the number of consummated sales per loan application, were about 30%.

taken a Kentucky license plate off of a trade-in and placed it on his own car—purchased, of course, from his employer—because Boney hadn't bought his own state-required liability insurance. It had taken a few months to be educated, but Hankins knew he and his staff had been "conned" by the Shoe Bandit.

Did Constantine recall anything else about Boney? "He made comments about kissing and rubbing the feet of female employees and customers." And no, even though they had a basketball hoop in the back of the dealership, Boney "was never even interested" in playing the game.

"He's A Jekyll & Hyde"

After he had been terminated, Boney had landed on his feet at a new car dealership just down the street, after he had impressed the owner and new car manager, Mark Richards. Boney, said Richards, was "very outgoing and [thought of] himself as the best thing walking; he had the personality, you couldn't tell the guy, 'No.'" After passing a drug test, Boney had been hired as a probationary salesman.

Ted Mueller, a career car salesman, had been assigned to teach and mentor Boney, but the new hire had been reluctant to educate himself on his product. Mueller had also observed and heard Boney speaking with prospective customers, but it was obvious he hadn't read the sales manuals. In fact, Boney's talk hadn't translated into any action, as he had achieved no car sales in the almost two weeks he had been with the dealership.

During one mentoring meeting, Richards had been present when Mueller again had tried to get Boney to read the material about the vehicles in order to be certified as a salesman. All at once, Boney had erupted and had begun yelling at his mentor, about 25 years older and more than 150 pounds lighter than the 305-pound Boney,[360] who, with a clenched fist, had screamed, "Don't fuck with me, old man! I'll kill you!" Richards, who had described the situation as "very serious," had immediately gotten between the two and separated them.

Richards, who had never heard anyone threaten to kill another person, had told me that Boney's eyes had "been zeroed in on Ted, with the look that *he would kill him*."

After having Boney sit in his office for a few minutes to cool off, Boney had tried to explain his actions to Richards: "The man just pissed me off so bad that I couldn't take it anymore."

---

[360] His weight was listed on one of his job applications near the same time.

Richards had then been direct with Boney, telling him he had to fire him for his uncontrolled anger and that no kind of violence could be tolerated at the business. Boney had understood, Richards had told me; he also gave me his thoughts on the calm, intelligent, and educated man he had hired: "He's a Jekyll and Hyde."

CHAPTER 37

Another Arrest?

While we weren't getting any new discovery from Henderson, our team had regularly provided him with the transcripts and interview memorandums of all my interviews and all the documents we had obtained through subpoenas. We were upholding our part in the discovery process, but equally as important, we wanted Henderson to be in possession of witness information that had pointed a very direct and incriminating finger at Boney as the murderer of the Camm family.

Henderson, as well as Gilbert, who had heard Boney's preaching to me in his presence that all he had was his "credibility," was thus fully aware of all the following:

> SITTING IN THE MURDER TRIAL OF A MAN FALSELY ACCUSED OF THE HEINOUS CRIMES BONEY HAD HIMSELF COMMITTED—THAT WOULD BE THE ULTIMATE POWER TRIP FOR A PSYCHOPATH AND RIGHT DOWN BONEY'S WARPED MENTAL ALLEY.

- Boney's four alibis had all been lies;
- His prison clothing hadn't been given away;
- His gun had, in fact, been loaded during his Bloomington armed robberies;
- Rather than non-violent, he had been a very violent guy who constantly had possession of and an addiction for guns;
- Boney had personally favored .380 semi-automatic pistols, the very weapon used in the murders;
- The Shoe Bandit had desperately pleaded with his good friend to build him a silencer and had planned to use that silencer on his gun to kill his wife;
- He had solicited a man to be a getaway driver in an Indiana robbery;
- He had snuck into and burgled people's houses without their knowledge;
- He had routinely grabbed his female victims by the hair;
- He regularly had threatened to shoot women in the head and to "blow

[their] brains out";

- He had been fueled by uncontrollable rage against women, even seeing white spots;

- He didn't remember his violence; and

- He had been a full-fledged fanatic when it came to his weird and compulsive obsession with women's feet, legs, and shoes.

All of those very specific issues, plus his DNA, clothing and palmprint found at the crime scene, had tied Boney directly to the Camm murders and were contradictory to his litany of mendacious tales, or at least the ones of which we had been told. What he had specifically told the "fresh eyes," we still didn't know, for we hadn't been given any discovery for weeks, including Boney's claims, whatever they may have been.

Additionally, Boney's two confessions, to me and Carl Colvin, that it would be "obvious" he had committed the murders if his fingerprints were found at the scene and that he had three murders on his conscience, put the case against Boney far, far beyond proof beyond a reasonable doubt.

While we didn't think real evidence against Boney would shake Henderson, we hoped it would, sometime in the future, make an impact on a jury that didn't have a hardened bias in the case.

As all this had been developing, I had gone to a local hardware store and had accidently run into an ISP detective with whom I had once closely worked. "Is it true?" he had asked.

I didn't have to ask what was true. "If it's David Camm," I responded, "yes, it's true, and he's innocent."

I was then told it was "hard for us to comprehend" that Camm was innocent and equally as hard to understand that I, of all people, was working with the defense on Camm's case. My response was that we could sit and talk, and I'd tell him of all the reasons why the ISP had gotten it wrong and of all of the evidence of Camm's innocence. My offer, though, wasn't accepted. We had simply said our goodbyes and walked away.

Later, I had been called by a former ISP employee of the Bloomington Post, asking my thoughts on another, totally unrelated matter. After answering a few questions, I, in turn, asked my own question: "What do the guys at the Post think about me and David Camm?"

"It's about 70/30" was the response. "Or maybe 60/40."

"What does that mean?" I asked.

"That 60 to 70 percent of the people think you've gone to the Dark Side."

Although I fully expected the answer, it still hurt. A lot. I took a moment and then asked, "What's the reasoning on why Camm is guilty?"

"They think the State Police can't be wrong. That, and everyone knows he molested his little girl."

Those two conversations were depressing enough, but soon my full attention was diverted to the possibility another arrest might occur in the case.

A story had been leaked to the press about two of my attempted interviews. Jeremy Bullock's mother had claimed—accurately—that I had told her and her husband, among other things, that I had been authorized by a judge (Aylsworth) to be involved in the case and to be paid as a defense investigator for David Camm. Mrs. Bullock, though, had further claimed I had intimidated her with my presence. After my departure, she immediately had called the Marion County Sheriff's Office (MCSO) and made a formal complaint.[361]

The reporter who had written of my contact with Mrs. Bullock also had known of a previously unpublicized complaint filed by Mrs. Boney, accusing me of trespassing on her property. Rather than filing a report with the New Albany Police Department (NAPD), Mrs. Boney had reported my contact with her to the ISP. That was a clue in and of itself.

All in all, I guess tipping off the press was a smart move, because it put us on the defensive. After being surprised by a call from the newspaper reporter, I simply told him, while not identifying any person with whom I had spoken, "we're entitled to speak with witnesses like anyone."[362]

Kitty, though, had accused Henderson of leaking the story and, proclaimed, "We aren't going to be intimidated."[363]

A third allegation against me, a few days later, came from Ernest Nugent, the convicted felon[364] and self-admitted gun seller to felon Charles Boney. Nugent had filed a complaint with the NAPD that I had claimed to be an FBI Agent—which was totally false—and further that I had told him I had been authorized to be paid as the Camm defense investigator by Judge Aylsworth. That last part was accurate.

After not responding to the press for several days, Henderson finally wanted to see justice for the three "victims" and was quoted as saying he planned to "ask the Floyd Circuit Court to appoint a special prosecutor to review the complaints" and, further, that he was "particularly concerned about

---

[361] Did she call the police or did Wayne Kessinger, with whom she had been speaking during my visit, call for her or encourage her to call? I had my own ideas.

[362] Hershberg, Ben Zion, "Camm Defense Team Draws Complaints," *The Courier-Journal*, April 15, 2005.

[363] Ibid.

[364] Recall that he had been convicted of armed robbery with another man.

allegations that Dunn said he's under the authority of the Warrick County court, which no longer has the case."[365]

It was bad enough the negative publicity would possibly cause other witnesses not to speak with me, but the special prosecutor comment by Henderson meant I could possibly be charged with a crime and be arrested. While I knew I hadn't done anything wrong, or anything remotely criminal, I also knew, of course, that a lack of evidence didn't prevent any prosecutor from filing charges. Rather than focusing my attention on Dave's case, I could be forced to defend myself.

During the process, I had begun asking questions of myself: "Why did you get involved? Will you be arrested? Why didn't you keep that great teaching job?"

It had gotten so bad that I started feeling ashamed, which had no logical basis. "Why should you be ashamed of doing the right thing?" I thought, but I was.

And then I couldn't help but think of Dave. My emotional distress was infinitesimal compared to all that he had gone through, causing me to again feel even more ashamed, ashamed of even thinking I had gotten a raw deal.

As bad as it was, it then got even worse, as I received a voicemail from a trooper assigned to the Sellersburg Post, telling me she had been assigned the trespassing case. I returned her call and left a message. We continued playing phone tag until she left a message that I took as nothing less than threatening, implying I would be arrested if I didn't speak with her.

I immediately called Kitty and we soon sat down together and drafted a letter to Henderson, which contained parts of two transcripts from my interviews with Boney and Nugent. In Boney's interview, I had twice asked him to give a heads-up to his mother that I would be contacting her. He confirmed my request each time. Thus, I had acted on good faith that Mrs. Boney would have been expecting me and had no intention of trespassing on her property.

As for Nugent, I had been concise in describing myself and role to him, further providing him with my business card, which clearly reflected I was a retired—not active—FBI Agent. The transcript of my taped interview with him was crystal clear: he had known who I was, and his description of me to the police had been an abject lie.

As for my contact with Mrs. Bullock, I had written a precise articulation of my visit soon after leaving her residence, anticipating the possibility I'd have

---

[365] Hershberg, Ben Zion, "Man Who Sold Gun to Boney Questioned," *The Courier-Journal*, April 21, 2005.

an allegation made against me. We included that in our letter to Henderson, and it was undeniable as to the events that had occurred in her home; if need be, we'd call our own witness: her husband.

Marion County, thankfully, had decided not to pursue any charges against me, and the transcript of Nugent's interview with me had contradicted his false claims, thus gutting any case the NAPD might have considered. That had only left my attempted interview with Mrs. Boney as being potentially problematic.

It was then Kitty reached out to a former mentor, Richard "Rick" Kammen, and told him of the allegations against me. I knew Rick, albeit not well, for he had cross-examined me, as defense counsel, as a government witness on two occasions in federal court. The first had been in a white collar trial and the other in a bank robbery case for which he had been appointed as a federal public defender. In each instance, his demeanor was very professional, and his questions direct and relevant. Clearly, he was an attorney who got to the point.

Rick had been equally as direct in his letter to Henderson and had been anything but subtle:[366]

I have been asked by the Strike Force of the National Association of Criminal Defense Lawyers to write you concerning Mr. Gary Dunn. Additionally, Mr. Dunn has asked me to represent him should the need arise.

Mr. Dunn, a well-respected former FBI Agent, was acting lawfully and properly in the performance of his duties when he attempted to speak with Ms. Boney.

I must advise you that should you persist in frivolous threats to charge Mr. Dunn, we will have no alternative but to meet such an accusation with the strongest possible legal response.

Kammen was in Indianapolis and I was in Bloomington when I read his letter, but if he had been in the room at the time, I would have embraced and thanked him repeatedly, as his missive was some sunshine in otherwise dismal days.[367]

The summation of all we provided Henderson must have worked, for his furor apparently had dissipated after Rick's letter to him, and no special prosecutor had been officially sought nor had one been appointed. Still, I was never told the case was over; thus, charges against me could have been filed at any time.

While I had already been a stickler for dotting every i and crossing every

---

[366] Dated May 6, 2005.

[367] Little did I know at the time, in the future, we would be in the same room on many occasions and for many weeks.

t, I would be even more so with each and every witness I would interview.

In the interim, Kitty and Stacy's motion to have Dave's case dropped in Floyd County had been denied by Judge Cody, and they were writing their appeal, which would be filed directly with the Indiana Supreme Court.

Did Boney Attend Dave's Trial?

The case had many moving parts, however, as I got a call from Janice Glotzbach, the longtime Administrative Assistant for Pat Biggs.[368] Charles Boney, she said, had in the past been in the New Albany-Floyd City-County Building, which contained all the courts, selling children's books, barbeque utensils and other knick-knacks. Although she didn't specifically recollect the exact timeframe, Janice said it was possible Boney had been selling his items during Dave's trial.

Sitting in the gallery watching the murder trial of a man falsely accused of the heinous crimes that Boney had himself committed—*that* would be the ultimate power trip for a psychopath and right down Boney's warped mental alley.

Janice had also given me the name of a friend, and the administrator of a Georgetown nursing home close to the Camm residence, who thought Boney had been in their facility selling other items. I subsequently contacted Joselyn Carter[369] who told me she wasn't positive, but a man she thought was Charles Boney—who had been very talkative and quite well-spoken and who had matched his physical description—had been in her assisted living facility selling candles, photo albums, children's books, and other items.

It had only reinforced the fact that Boney, as a door-to-door salesman would have had a great cover story when reconnoitering houses for later burglaries and/or stalking women for later assaults.

Writ Of Mandamus Ruling

Then, a big surprise came, as the Indiana Supreme Court had already ruled on the Writ of Mandamus. The five justices had been unanimous, as the court had granted the petition and ordered Judge Cody to transfer the pending Floyd County case against Dave back to Judge Aylsworth in Warrick County. Once again, Henderson had been spanked hard.

The legal decision had impacted several areas besides where the case would be tried. First, among many other things, discovery would begin again, particularly regarding Boney; next, dozens of critical depositions would start;

---

[368] Recall that Pat has been the Floyd County Public Defender since 1987 and, with Mike McDaniel, represented Dave in his first trial.

[369] Pseudonym.

thirdly, defensive forensic experts could be employed; and then, of course, a firm trial date meant compacting all of that enormous amount of work into a limited amount of time.

As Kitty and Stacy were drafting subpoenas and making preparations for the depositions, I began my trip to Michigan City, Indiana, located on the south shore of Lake Michigan, where almost two dozen offenders and staff would, hopefully, speak with me. One of those with whom I wanted to speak was the guy who purportedly also wanted to talk with me: Jeremy "Joker" Bullock.

CHAPTER 38

"That's What Keeps Me Going..."

My Past With The Indiana State Prison

"The City," as the State Prison was known inside the DOC, was a 19th-century, stereotypical, slate-colored, stacked-stone, maximum-security structure, complete with ominous guard towers, located just south of Lake Michigan. If not for its lack of a moat, it perhaps could have been mistaken for a middle-ages castle on three sides. As I got closer, it was easy for me to take a ride down Memory Lane, as I recalled my first visit to the facility in 1986.

Sergeant John Novosel, of the Hammond Police Department, and I had driven from Gary, approximately 30 miles away, eastward along Dunes Highway, parallel with Lake Michigan, to our appointment with a young offender.[370]

Some things really stick in one's mind, and that first trip

"REMORSEFUL FOR THE CRIMES YOU COMMITTED?"

"ABSOLUTELY, MAN. EVERY DAY. I'D GIVE MY LIFE RIGHT NOW IF I COULD GIVE THAT MAN BACK HIS. MAN, I AIN'T BULLSHITTING, YOU KNOW?"

with John has always been starkly, and depressingly, crystal clear, as the day itself had been, like many others in Northwest Indiana, a tedious lead color.

The dismal prison structure itself wasn't the first to have caught our attention, however, but rather the numerous rows of simple white gravestones, which were lined neatly on the well-mown grass on the southwest side of the institution. There lay the almost 350 unclaimed inmate bodies, all of whom had finally paid their debts to society.

John and I had gone to the prison to interview an offender as to his knowledge of and involvement in various auto theft rings and chop shops in

---

[370] I had been transferred from the Chicago FBI to the Gary, Indiana, FBI in 1985 where it was a "target-rich" environment. After my arrival, I had found myself working with John, from the Hammond Police Department, who had been assigned to our office, partnering with Lamar Little of the FBI. Those two had been targeting chop shops and stolen car rings. Detective Tim Andrews of the ISP had also routinely been part of that team. When Lamar left for Miami, John and I had inherited one another, and we had stayed as partners for several more years. Almost 40 years later, John and I remain rock solid friends.

The Region,[371] and more specifically, the Black Oak section of Gary, which, at the time, was home to a disproportionately high number of inhabitants who engaged in such felonious activity.[372]

The man with whom we wanted to talk had a record of stealing anything and everything with an attached engine, whether it be a car, truck, motorcycle, ATV, riding lawnmower, go-kart, racecar, or whatever. If it went, "*Vroom*," it was his.

After our very successful visit,[373] the investigator with whom we had arranged our private debriefing, asked if we had wanted a tour of the facility. John and I had both readily agreed.

Almost immediately after stepping outside of his office, we ran into an inmate with a huge smile. The gregarious offender, probably 60–65 years of age, had warmly greeted all of us. He then had told the prison sleuth he had just been discharged from the infirmary, was on his way back to his cell block, and that there had been no hard feelings on the investigative report our host had filed on him.

After we walked a few paces, John and I had been told that William, the offender, had been in the infirmary a few months prior and had received such good care and attention, that he had recently injured himself, a prison violation, to go back. His return ticket to three days of gentle care was by way of a self-inserted five-inch pencil into the glans of his penis.

Our tour had continued to the oldest block in the prison, which dated to 1860. Depressing was not an adequate word to describe the melancholy. That feeling had only grown, as next was the very drab execution room where "Old Sparky" had been sitting.[374] The floor had been covered with green tiles, some of which were curled on the ends, and dissecting the room had been a lengthy rod with floor-length curtains drawn to both ends. On the opposite side of the

---

[371] The Region is a term assigned to Northwest Indiana, and more specifically, at least to long-time residents, the communities just south of Lake Michigan in Lake and Porter counties. People from the area have often been known, affectionately or otherwise, as "Region Rats."

[372] Black Oak is in the southwest area of Gary and had been originally populated by many people from Appalachia who had been drawn to the well-paying jobs in the steel mills and other heavy industry.

[373] Due in some degree to the outcome of that visit, John and I had later instituted an undercover case, code-name Quietus, which had targeted automobile owners who had arranged for their vehicles to be stolen for insurance purposes. The two of us had operated as M & J Towing, and we subsequently had recovered over three dozen "stolen" vehicles; an almost equal number of individuals had been charged; and all had been convicted, of federal fraud, mostly mail fraud charges, which stemmed from their filing insurance claims on the cars they had arranged to have stolen.

[374] The means of execution in Indiana is now lethal injection.

room from the heavy wooden chair with several drooping leather straps had been the area where witnesses would have been seated, chosen from among many who would have applied to see the grisly event.

We next had gone to the license manufacturing facility, which had been churning out motorcycle plates on that day. It was impossible not to notice that practically all the workers had the same blue hat with large, white block letters spelling LIFER printed on the front. The explanation, we had been told, was due to the higher pay in the unit, and, ergo, the inmates with more seniority had gotten first dibs on the jobs.[375]

Anyway, that had been my stroll down Memory Lane as I pulled up to and then past the outside guard shack. After parking in the lot near the administrative building, I checked in, cleared the metal detector, and then waited for the arrival of a staff officer. Kitty had coordinated my visit with Barry Nothstine, a point person for defense attorneys, and had sent him our list of 14 inmates and nine staff officers with whom I wanted to speak.

The Indiana State Prison at Michigan City. In the background is the Administration Building where, for almost ten of his 13 years of incarceration, David Camm had been housed in the Protective Custody Unit.

In preparation for my visit, I had also authored a straightforward memo, which had asked for assistance to "ascertain the truth in regard to the murders of a mother and her children [and] to secure truthful information from you to the best of your ability and recollection."[376]

---

[375] The IDOC no longer manufactures license plates.

[376] Anyone who would agree to speak with me had to acknowledge my identity and the purpose of my contact, and also agree to have our conversation tape recorded.

Soon, I was met by a CO and ushered into an attorney's room directly behind the visitation area and, conveniently, just down the steps from the Protective Custody (PCU). I was told only two of the PCU offenders on my list had refused to meet with me, but Jeremy "Joker" Bullock wasn't one of them. Still, our conversation would occur after I had spoken with the others.

"He Was One Of The Nicest Guys..."

I first met with Diane Cox,[377] a very pleasant CO who had been assigned to the PCU for over three years; she was instrumental in helping me familiarize myself with the unit. She confirmed the inmates in the four cell block area were in the very front of the prison, sitting on top of the visitation and staff building, but separated physically and administratively from the other offenders.

Each block had 15 cells with one offender assigned to each cell, and the blocks weren't normally at capacity. Every offender was afforded up to three hours of recreation a day. The five favorite rec forms on the roof were 1) playing basketball in the fresh air; 2) lifting weights in the fresh air; 3) walking in the fresh air; 4) reading books in the fresh air; and 5) conversing with others, or conversating as some termed it, with others in the fresh air.

Getting to the rec area, and everywhere else outside the unit, required an escort by a CO. At no time was there any interaction allowed with other offenders from Gen Pop.

CO Cox said that Dave had secured the job of porter, or range tender as some called it,[378] and was responsible for cleaning his assigned cell block, delivering meals, carrying messages, and "any and everything that staff asked him or required him to do, without fail, and without controversy. He can't argue, [even though] he may be correct, but it doesn't matter." Cox continued, "I expect them to do their jobs, to do whatever it is that I ask them to do and to respect me and all other staff to the utmost."

I asked, "What kind of porter was Dave? Good? Bad? Indifferent?"

"He was one of the nicest guys that I've ever met and had to deal with under these circumstances," Cox replied. She then added, "He was always pleasant even when he was at his lowest."

"Lowest? What would those times be, Diane?"

Cox explained that she first had learned of the details of Dave's convictions and then had observed him from a distance until she had gotten to know and then speak with him. She continued, "He was always pretty much the same every day. One day, though, he was kind of low and I had asked him what was

---

[377] The names of all the COs and all the offenders are pseudonyms.
[378] The position is akin to that of a trustee.

wrong. It was either his child's birthday or the anniversary day of the day it all took place."

The CO and convict had continued speaking, with Dave telling Cox, "I just think about my kids and what they are missing right now. I visualize them growing up and now they're not here. It's so hard."

Cox said she had tried to encourage Dave to "keep his chin up" but then respected his privacy and had given him space then and on other identical days.

Although Cox told me that, of those whom she supervised, "I'm to treat them no differently, they're all convicts," that didn't equate to her not forming her own judgment about the offenders. Regarding Dave, she offered this: "I had been around him long enough to say, 'Boy, this dude, if he really did commit such a crime, he sure don't fit the character for it.'"

Cox also told me her opinion of Dave's purported confession. Dave, she said, was confident his chances of a successful appeal were very good; therefore, she didn't believe he'd confessed because "nobody would take a stick and hit themselves in the head with it."

In fact, Cox was on duty with another CO when Cox called Dave to her office, telling him it was a phone call from his attorney (Kitty), who had broken the news to him that he had won his appeal.

"Was he excited?"

"He was happy. He started to cry. He tried his best not to cry, but I told him just let it go, just go ahead and cry about it. You know, we all was pretty much in tears at that point and we did a toast with Pepsis."

Dave left the prison soon thereafter, but Cox said she and others on the cell block had followed the news of his still-developing case, and it was "horrible" the DNA on the sweatshirt, something of which Dave had talked about with her and several others, had been overlooked for years.

When Charles Boney had been identified as the owner of that DNA, Cox had made a prediction to other COs and some offenders: "This dude [Boney] is getting ready to sing like the Jackson Five." The singing didn't mean, of course, that Boney was going to croon a true tune.

The next CO with whom I spoke was Daisy Jackson who echoed much of what the other COs and offenders would tell me as to what Dave had said had happened the night of the murders: "Dave explained that he had been playing basketball and when he came home, he found his family dead, and then he made the phone call to his former post. He always contended that he never killed his family."

Dave also told CO Jackson about the BACKBONE sweatshirt found at the scene, which, he said, had "unknown DNA on it and there were prints on the vehicle. He thought that the person who left the DNA and fingerprints was responsible."

I asked if Dave had made any admission to her or anyone, if she knew, that he was responsible for killing his family, and she replied, "No, he has always been consistent. He didn't do it. His story has always been the same."

Several other COs spoke with me, including Ms. G, the Shakedown Lady,"[379] and others who formerly worked in the PCU.[380] All had the same assessment of Dave: he had been relatively quiet, hadn't associated with many others, hadn't conversed all that much, had spent much of his free time in his cell, had liked to play basketball and lift weights on the roof, and always had been respectful to others and done what he had been told to do. Not once in over two years in prison had he any write-up of any kind.

The only times most saw him as anything rather than a mild-mannered guy was on the birthdays of his son and daughter, and the anniversary of the murders, when Dave would have often become withdrawn and, on occasion, had been seen crying in his cell.

One CO did recall, however, when Dave had gotten angry; in fact, he had gotten very angry. Within months of his arrival, orders had been received by the duty COs to shake down his cell. The object of the search was to find and seize family photos in his possession. Several had, in fact, been found of his wife and children and had been taken from him.

The CO said Dave couldn't understand why the photos of Kim, Brad, and Jill had been taken, and he then had gotten extremely upset and yelled at the officers, demanding their return. The CO didn't know the reason and had assured Dave they'd be returned to him, which they ultimately had been.

All of the COs with whom I spoke said Mike Stamper, another porter with whom Dave had associated with practically every day, had been Dave's closest friend in the PCU, and it would have been Mike, if anyone, with whom Dave would have confided.

"We're A Field Of Snakes"

After a day with the COs, I began speaking with offenders. All, at least when first meeting him, were skeptical of Dave because he was a former police officer, and "you just don't start trusting someone like that." Over time, though, most of the inmates, if they hadn't trusted Dave, at least hadn't had a problem interacting with him.

Mike Stamper said, unequivocally, that there was no way Dave would have confessed to anyone. He had gotten to know Dave quite well, as both

---

[379] The officer assigned to searching prisoners after visitations.
[380] I was unable to speak with the CO known as the "Cat Lady."

were porters, and Dave had often spoken of his love for his wife and kids. Dave was, he said, always hopeful he'd eventually be released and find the person or people who had been responsible for the murders of Kim, Brad, and Jill.

Miles Duncan told me that Dave had expressed his wish that it had been him, rather than his wife and children, who had been murdered. Further, "he couldn't understand why they killed his family." Miles was also emphatic that Dave had "adamantly proclaimed his innocence all the way from the first time" Miles had spoken with him.

As to Dave's possibly committing any crime, Marcus Anderson offered his insight: on one occasion, an offender had been transferred out of the PCU rather suddenly, and his commissary, worth as much as $50.00, had been left behind. Marcus had offered Dave a deal: "I said, 'Dave, I'm gonna steal his commissary. You look out for me and make sure the police[381] ain't looking. We'll split it 50/50. The guy will get his money refunded, nobody will be in trouble and we'll make out."

Dave, though, wouldn't do it, with Anderson further telling me, "Nobody would have seen us. Nobody would have been the wiser, but he just couldn't do it. If he can't steal a bag of commissary, how the hell can he kill his whole family?"

Stu Gideon offered additional insight into Dave's time in prison: "I could tell when things was bothering him. He would sit in his cell and have his headphones plugged into the TV and the TV wasn't on. I asked him, 'Dave are you okay in there?' He'd be thinking about his family, there wasn't a doubt in my mind."

During those depressing times, Stu had tried to get his friend to play basketball or just to talk with him, but it didn't register. "I would tell him, I don't know how many times, I said, 'Dave, I can't know what you're going through, but you're not helping yourself and you're not helping the people that are trying to help you. You need to stay focused, you need to stay positive, even if it's just for a little while. You're always thinking about your wife and your kids, maybe it's a good idea right now *not to think* about your wife and your kids.'"

Practically every inmate told me the same thing as had Mike, Stu, Marcus, and Miles, as Dave had but three unwavering goals: 1) to be found innocent; 2) be released from prison; and 3) once free, to find the one or ones who murdered his family. Finding the person or persons responsible, one friend had recalled Dave as saying, "That's what keeps me going."

---

[381] Euphemism for a CO.

Dave wasn't waiting for his release to try to find the murderer, however, as he had asked several of those incarcerated with him if they had ever heard of an inmate nicknamed BACKBONE. One had: an offender from Harrison County, Indiana, just west of Floyd County. A friend of that inmate had claimed to have heard of the nickname but hadn't been able to obtain the man's real name.[382]

I didn't divulge Bullock as the one who had provided Henderson with Dave's supposed confession story, but every offender with whom I spoke, without exception, knew it was "Joker" who had snitched on Dave. In fact, as CO Cox said of the inmates, "They know everything. They know things before we [COs] do. They know how to get things from one cell house to another. You would think that a bird came and got [that information] and flew it in."[383]

Any doubts it had been Bullock who was the snitch had disappeared when Bullock, himself, had proudly proclaimed to other inmates that he, in fact, was going to testify against Dave.

Several told me that Joker, in the past, had claimed he had been diagnosed with liver cancer but that he had refused to have surgery after being taken to the hospital. Years later, though, he wasn't having any medical issues, so everyone thought the cancer claim was to cover, in some manner, for the real activity for which Joker had been out of the PCU, lending credence to their belief he had snitched before.

In fact, it was Bullock who admitted to others that he had met with a prosecutor and three ISP detectives shortly after Dave had left the PCU. Joker had originally claimed that it had been over a new murder case involving him and had told a fellow inmate, "I was panicked." Soon, however, Joker had been in the cell block, joking and telling others, "I'm not worried."

As one inmate told me, "If something can possibly give you a whole lot more prison time, I'm not gonna be joking, and I'm sure not gonna tell anybody I just got done talking to a prosecutor and three detectives."

The justification that Joker had used when telling others of his testifying against Dave was rather simple. Per one offender, "Bullock hates Camm because he's a cop. Bullock said one of his friends was on death row because

---

[382] When I was first told of this lead by Dave several weeks prior to Boney's identification, I exhaustively followed it, unfortunately with no success.

[383] I didn't divulge Bullock's name to anyone, as we didn't want any harm to come to him, nor did we want to be accused of attempting to intimidate him in any manner.

he shot a cop in a defensive manner.[384] Bullock hates Camm for the fact that he's a cop."

Bullock told others that he thought Camm was treated differently from most of the inmates, although he wasn't, said one CO. It was just that Camm wasn't any trouble whatsoever and always did what he was told to do—the others, not so much.

The other motive of Joker's could have been when Dave had confronted him after Bullock had been mouthing off to others that Dave had molested Jill. Dave had gotten in Bullock's face, and Joker then shut up. Later, though, Bullock had said he believed Dave had molested his daughter.

And while I didn't ask about the crime which had put Bullock in prison, several offenders told me what Joker had told them. Duncan said Joker had laughingly told him of shooting his Asian drug dealer inside a car, and "he even imitated how, how the guy was making these real loud moaning sounds as he died. He was bragging. He was boasting."

Another man said Joker often joked about the man he killed, although Joker had used a derogatory term for the murdered guy. Bullock said he "shot the guy with a .45 with black talons and then stabbed him 22 times. . . . He's lying about that. He's just trying to make his murder look more famous than what it is."

As to Joker's prison background, Duncan also knew him from Gen Pop and was aware he had sold and used drugs: "He asked me a few times if I would run some drugs and I told him I wouldn't." Duncan also knew that Joker had run up sizeable debts with several people, had stiffed his lenders, and had been placed in the PCU because of threats having been made against him.

Duncan ran into Joker soon after hearing the murderer had been the one who was informing on Dave. It was then Duncan had told Bullock that he had "heard bad things" about him.

When Bullock had questioned what it was that Duncan had heard, he was told it was about his informing on Camm. Joker had simply responded, "Fuck that cop! I'm going home!"

Duncan, a hardened criminal himself, said the response had disturbed him because "he's potentially putting a person on death row on a lie." He continued, "Even though Dave was a cop, and he wasn't the most favorite inmate in here, it wasn't right."

Gideon also knew of Joker's big lie, explaining how snitches came to be in prison: "It happens all the time. Inmates who aren't even part of a conversation

---

[384] While I wasn't able to corroborate this information, the idea that Bullock, a liar, would lie, wasn't far-fetched.

will take bits and pieces [from what they overhear] and make their own story and peddle it to the cops[385] in return for favoritism of some kind. It could be an assignment to a different cell block, a transfer out of the institution, or a modification in their sentence."

Gideon, as did most of the others in C block, had a television and had seen the *48 Hours* episode on the murders. From that, they concluded that Dave had been falsely convicted. Joker had also watched that same episode, and many thought he had used it to tailor his false story.

Martin McCoy, who readily admitted to me the reason he was in the PCU was because he "got to messing with some heroin and lost 10 grams and couldn't pay for it" also had thoughts of Joker: "The majority of people, 99.9% of the people in the penitentiaries are scum of the fucking earth. That's just what we are. We're a field of snakes up there," as he pointed towards the PCU.

"I wouldn't go that far."

"Well, I live in here with them, so I see it. A lot of people would sell out their own families—their own mothers—to get out of prison." He then explained that he and Joker were talking after seeing the *48 Hours* episode, and they agreed there was a really good chance Dave would get his case overturned. Joker had told Martin that he had written notes while seeing the show because he wanted to remember as many details as he could about the murders of Dave's family, which he would later use.

"I heard him talking to another inmate up there," one convict told me, "about his future, he's gonna get a good attorney and file for a modification of his sentence. After this trial is over and he testifies against Camm and Camm gets convicted, Bullock will put in for a modification. His lawyer will talk to the DA and say, 'hey, look what he did here, help this guy get out of prison.'"

Yet another inmate confirmed that Joker had said that after he had spoken to the prosecutor, and after his testimony against Dave, that he was going to get a modification of his sentence. That verbal assurance had made sense, since no prosecutor would have officially committed to helping a guy like Joker get his sentence reduced, certainly not on the come.

John Carter was the guy Dave had told me who had gotten angry with him over a cold meal and who had held a severe grudge against him. After introducing myself to Carter, I asked him directly what his thoughts were of Dave. "Frankly, me and him didn't really get along." Why, I asked. "He was a porter and he didn't wake me up for breakfast and we had words. He basically apologized [but] we never did hit it off. I think we had a mutual dislike of each other."

---

[385] Cops can also refer to prison investigators.

Carter then became somewhat introspective, when he further said, "A part of my thing might be jealousy towards him." Camm, he said, had good attorneys working on his appeal, and Camm was very hopeful it would be successful. Carter, however, admitted, "I've got no money and I've got nobody out there to help me."

When I asked Carter about Dave's confession, however, the guy who didn't get along with Dave was blunt: "I didn't like the guy, but if anybody on that unit has ever said that he confessed, they're a liar because David never said that to nobody. I was around him for a long time and he never, never confessed to anybody."

Carter also knew the snitch was Joker and offered his reasoning as to why he would tell a bogus story about Dave: "He didn't like Camm and he can't get out of here for years. He's told me several times that he hated the man cause he was a cop."

"I Got A Lot Of Respect For Law Enforcement"

It was time for my last interview and, very quickly, it was readily apparent Jeremy Bullock wasn't pleased with me, as the first words out of his mouth were that his mother didn't know anything about his conversations with Dave.[386]

I explained to Bullock otherwise: Henderson's investigator, Wayne Kessinger, had written in his memo[387] that during a visit between Bullock and his mother, Jeremy had seen Dave being visited by his sister and that both Dave and his sister were joyful Dave's convictions had been overturned. According to the memo, "Jeremy [said] it wasn't right, [that] he was paying for his crime and so should Camm."

I further told Bullock that in the memo his mother said Jeremy had claimed to have spoken with Camm and told Dave that "shooting someone in the face shows no respect to that person, referring to Camm's wife and daughter, and shooting his son in the chest was like, 'I love you but I gotta kill you anyway.'"

I then cut to the chase: "What, exactly, did Dave tell you?"

Bullock admitted that he was "pissed off" the day I had tried to speak with his mother and further contended, "I purposely didn't tell her anything so that she wouldn't have anything to do with the case at all."

---

[386] Bullock initially refused to allow me to give my introductory explanation and to give him a copy of the memo I had prepared for all COs and inmates, all of whom had listened to me prior to speaking with me. I prevailed, however, and he finally took my memo, and I audiotaped my interview.

[387] That had been the only written documentation we had seen from Kessinger.

I again told him the memo detailed otherwise.

Joker had a sudden change of attitude and told me he wasn't angry at me anymore and even further complimented me on being a former FBI Agent. He didn't stop, saying, "I got a lot of respect for law enforcement. We need law enforcement to do their jobs."

Yeah, I thought. I'll now believe what you say.

Bullock, however, then said he only wanted to set the record straight about his mother and wasn't going to talk further. "I'm not gonna get into telling you about what Camm and me talked about, but he made statements to me that made it real clear that he was at the house at the time of the murders."

The man who had planned and assassinated his marijuana dealer again told me, "I really don't want to speak on it at all, man." He then, of course, began to speak on it. "I'm concerned with the safety of the public, man, because I got family out there and I got little kids that I love and if anything happened to any of them, I wouldn't be able to…"

"You think Camm is a threat to society?"

"With the statements he made to me? Yes, very much so. And I'm willing to put myself in harm's way to keep something from happening like what happened before."

Joker was also agitated that "people knew somehow or another that I'm one of the people that was supposed to be testifying against Camm, everybody on the whole unit up there knows." He implied that it was me who had divulged his name, adding, "Within a couple of weeks after I spoke to the investigators, people knew."

Since we hadn't gotten Bullock's name within that two-week period, it would therefore, I said, have been impossible for us to have told anyone of his identity.

I returned to the motive behind Bullock's telling of Dave's supposed confession: "This is not about any personal issue between you and Dave?"

"Oh, absolutely not. Absolutely not. He's not a bad guy to be around. If they put him back up here today, I would speak with him."

While he again wouldn't detail Dave's confession to him, Bullock did let me know that he didn't "want to jeopardize anything without really getting into too many details." That didn't mean, however, that Bullock wasn't a fair man; as he told me, "I pray to the lord that everything comes out positive. That the guilty gets just punishment and the innocent walk free."

While he had been dishonest in the past, Bullock said he had tried to turn his life around. I asked, "How long has it been since you got this epiphany?"

"Just growing up, man. Day to day. I've been in a maximum security prison for 11 years, since I was 16 years old."

"Remorseful for the crimes you committed?"

"Absolutely, man. Every day. There's no way I can ever pay for my crimes. I had no right to take a person's life. There's a lot of things I need to do in this world to make things right. I'd give my life right now if I could give that man back his. Man, I ain't bullshitting, you know?"

Since Bullock was talking more, I asked him what was the deciding factor that caused him to speak with the prosecutor about Dave. "Because he was gonna be loose on the public, man. While he was here, it didn't matter to me because he wasn't going nowhere. He wasn't a danger to anybody in here, you know? And when I found out that his case was being overturned, I said, 'you know, for once in my life I'm gonna have to say something.'"

The only way to explain Bullock's motive was that he was offering to sacrifice his own safety in prison for the overwhelming good of society.

Bullock insisted he had never before snitched on anybody else for any reason but refused to say why he was in the PCU, other than his wanting to get out of Gen Pop and concentrate on his paintings. He further contended, of Dave's confession, "I haven't told nobody nothing. I never spoke with anybody."

Bullock had repeatedly refused to go into detail about the story he had told to the "fresh eyes," but I had obtained from him his lies about 1) his not giving his mother details of the conversation, 2) his not having snitched on anyone before, 3) his not telling anyone of his plan, and 4) his sharing of Dave's story being inspired by his concern for humanity.

I gathered my notes, tape-recorder, and other items and—unlike Bullock, Stamper, Duncan, Gideon and all the other inmates—soon walked freely out the front door, headed for home.

My two days behind bars were far from over, though, as we had received unofficial reports, including several from Dave, incarcerated in the Floyd County Jail, that he had been told of *numerous* other jail inmates who had contacted Henderson's office offering to tell of his confessions to them. Yeah, Dave apparently just couldn't help himself, as he had to confess to anyone, and apparently everyone, behind bars, that he had killed his wife and children.

On my way south, I called Kitty and gave her the results of my interviews, telling her that everyone had refuted Joker's assertion that Dave had confessed. I thought we had two, possibly three, offenders who would be good rebuttal witnesses to Joker, a convict, in my assessment, who wasn't remotely credible.

To my way of thinking, if the jury initially accepted Joker's story, or for that matter, Hatton's tale, they'd have to at least consider the testimony of other convicts who refuted the contentions of the state's informants. At worst, we had agreed, it would be a draw, and everyone's testimony would be tossed, which would be a win for Dave.

I also told Kitty that I had exhibited a photo of Charles Boney to most of my interviewees. Some vaguely recalled his picture, but no one had ever had any interactions with him. Only one inmate had recalled James B. Hatton, and he said Hatton had only been in the PCU for a "couple of weeks" and therefore wouldn't have made friends with anyone.

Kitty was pleased with the results and then told me she and Stacy had begun lining up the dozens of depositions. We also, she said, would soon be getting the results of Boney's interviews and interrogations, which, she confirmed, amounted to over 33 hours of questioning over several days of time. CO Cox had probably been spot-on, as Boney, no doubt, had been singing like the Jackson Five.

Boney's statements, if Gilbert's affidavits regarding the Shoe Bandit's implausible story were indicative, would only help in the argument at Dave's next bond hearing, scheduled for June 29.

CHAPTER 39

"This Is What Makes The Innocence Project"

Kitty and Stacy's incredibly busy and efficient multi-tasking was more than impressive as they had been researching, vetting, and then absorbing the trial testimonies, prior depositions, and reports of all the prosecution's and our past and potential forensic experts; outlining and prepping questions for the depositions of literally dozens of witnesses; and preparing motions, which would, hopefully, narrow the scope of the case. Narrow, in this case, meant restricting the prosecution from throwing their irrelevant mud against the wall to see if any muck would stick with a jury.

Motions & The LWOP

One motion Kitty and Stacy had already filed was a notice of alibi. Even though they had already filed it when venue had first been established in Warrick County, Dave was starting with an essentially new case, and nothing could be taken for granted.[388]

"WHAT'S NEW IS CHARLES BONEY'S SELF-SERVING & SELF-PRESERVING STORIES… HIS TEN FELONY CONVICTIONS FOR SERIOUS BODILY CRIMES AGAINST WOMEN…HIS VIOLENCE… HIS DISTINCT SIGNATURE WHEN HE GOES ON HIS CRIME SPREES."

Some of the things Kitty, Stacy, and I couldn't do, however, included reading and absorbing over 33 hours of interviews and interrogations of Boney. Several weeks had passed since Henderson's ignominious legal defeat, yet he still hadn't provided that crucial discovery.

To ensure Henderson complied with future timely production of evidence, the two distaff attorneys had seen the need to file a motion that all discovery be placed on the record with the court. Judge Aylsworth had, however, already

---

[388] Indiana statute required such a notice to be filed within 20 days of the omnibus date, or the date set by Judge Aylsworth to ensure, essentially, that all procedural and legal issues be discussed and/or addressed as well as discovery shared. The judge hadn't yet set that date, but it would be within several weeks of the trial, which Judge Aylsworth had wanted to begin on August 5, 2005, the same date Boney's trial was to commence. The chances of either trial occurring in August, however, wasn't remotely practical.

denied that request, perhaps because prior to the hearing, Henderson, the ever-compliant prosecutor, at least in front of the judge, had said he would be providing discovery on Boney *after* the bond hearing.

Another motion already filed had been for the immediate reinstatement of bond, which the judge had initially denied, but which would at least be reconsidered on June 29.[389]

To help in the bond argument, the three of us had interacted repeatedly and had produced a 117-slide PowerPoint presentation. Those slides included what we, without having any of the Boney discovery from Henderson, had uncovered about Boney. Any independent viewer, we had concluded, would be distressed with the State's using the violent, duplicitous, and manipulative Boney as their primary tool against Dave.

We had focused on Gilbert's March 9 affidavit and then an amended one of his, which had been filed on April 1, 2005. Gilbert had written in his last filing, "During the course of my investigation, *I noticed*[390] that the defense had conducted testing [of Boney's sweatshirt]."[391] After Boney had been identified and had agreed to be initially interviewed, Gilbert had only noted that he had "denied any involvement in the crime."

Not mentioned were any of Boney's numerous lies and his confession to me in my interview of him—the one Gilbert had attended and the one Boney had given him a tape of—which, of course, had been a nearly three-hour lie-fest.

The many hours of subsequent interrogations of Boney, we knew, had to have been like mine: with Boney's non-answers and/or answers that contained lies, attempts at misdirection, obfuscations, and non-sensical responses; all added, of course, with the victimization inherent from most psychopaths. Gilbert, however, summarized them as follows: "During the interviews, Mr. Boney made various incriminating statements about his involvement in and his assistance to David Camm in the murders of Jill, Brad and Kim Camm."

Gilbert's last paragraph in his April affidavit reflected the March 9 charges of three counts of murder and one of conspiracy, which had been filed because of the "discovery of new facts and evidence…specifically that a co-defendant/

---

[389] There had also been a procedural argument by Stacy that the State had failed in their need to try Dave within 180 days, and as such, Dave should have been released under his own recognizance. The argument was based upon the State, and not Dave, causing the delay. The judge had summarily denied that request.

[390] Emphasis mine.

[391] Gilbert's take on his own investigation had also been shaded, since, rather than his being responsible for searching CODIS for the unknown DNA, it had been Kitty and Stacy who had repeatedly demanded that the ISP run the DNA through CODIS.

co-conspirator acted in concert with Mr. Camm in the commission of this crime."

If anyone could find any specific evidence of a conspiracy in those generalized words—i.e., "various incriminating statements" and "acted in concert"—neither of which had detailed any acts or formed any specific basis for probable cause, that person could also, perhaps, find fly scat in a pepper shaker.

Regardless, Gilbert had apparently believed that *his Boney narrative*, empty of evidence, had equaled probable cause for a charge of conspiracy.

On the morning of June 29th, we had arrived an hour prior to the start of the hearing, and Kitty and Stacy had later exchanged perfunctory greetings with Henderson and Owen. I don't think the dislike and distrust of both teams for the other had been a secret, but all maintained their professional demeanor until Henderson handed Kitty several sheets of paper, which caused her to shake her head, turn to Stacy, and then speak rather loudly, "This is bullshit."

Kitty quickly returned to the defense table where Dave and I had been sitting and told us of Henderson's filings. The first was a notice of aggravating factors, claiming that a crime of violence had been committed against Kim by Dave, in the presence of Brad and Jill, both under the age of 18 years, and that all three were in a "position of care, custody or control" by Dave. Another aggravating factor filed by Henderson was that both Brad and Jill were under the age of 12 years when they had been murdered.

The last aggravating factor filed by Henderson was "the defendant, David Camm, committed a murder by *hiring*[392] another person, Charles Boney, to kill."

Gilbert's affidavits contained no such allegation, and we had known of no evidence supporting that claim. In fact, there had been no evidence that the two had even known one another. The only evidence, as it were, of the two having even known one another, had come from Boney, and we had still not been told exactly what Boney had claimed.

The second notice filed by Henderson was his intent, upon Dave's being convicted, to seek a sentence of Life Without Parole, commonly known as LWOP. Dave's first murder sentences, each of which had been for 65 years, were now being enhanced.

For Henderson, though, it had been a smart move: the chances of Aylsworth's granting bond to a man on whom a sentence of LWOP hung would be appreciably smaller.

That LWOP filing, of course, was vindictive in nature, since Dave had

---

[392] Emphasis mine.

been sentenced to lesser 65-year terms for each murder in his first trial.[393]

The icing on the LWOP cake, I was convinced, was for payback, as the prosecutor, in my opinion, had taken personal offense from his two recent and major legal defeats at the hands of, no less, two defense attorneys. Making it worse, they were two *female* defense attorneys.

Judge Aylsworth, however, had interrupted my thinking as he entered the courtroom, with the bailiff commanding, "All rise." Ever the unfailingly polite man in black, the judge first addressed the documents that Henderson had just filed.

Kitty immediately objected to the filings, with the LWOP being "vindictive," and she also slammed the allegation that Kim had been under the "custody or control" of Dave.

The judge didn't rule on either, but rather allowed for written motions to be filed and then addressed Kitty and Stacy's motion for additional funds. The two had found and employed additional bloodstain and forensic experts to counter the expected testimony of not only Stites and Englert, but other experts for the state, including a pediatrician, an additional forensic pathologist, a microscopist, and other experts.

Kitty told the judge that Dave was indigent, but he still wanted Dave to be sworn under oath. That took but two minutes, and Aylsworth had then approved an additional $75,000 for the hiring of those experts; for the continued retaining of Anthony Long, through jury selection; and for my investigative services.[394]

The "Cherry-Picking" State

It was time for our bond argument. Kitty took the lead and told the court, "The evidence against Dave Camm is not only weak, but weaker than it was when the court determined bond was appropriate the first time, [and] the presumption [of guilt] is not strong, it's not even there." She then argued, for affidavits, particularly those alleging murder, that the State had to put in the "good, the bad, and the ugly," particularly when using information supplied by co-defendants, rather than "cherry-picking" parts and pieces of stories.[395]

Since Henderson's most recent charges had heavily relied on Boney's

---

[393] It could be argued in a future appeal, probably successfully, that Henderson, seeking a more severe sentence in the second trial on the same charges would have the sentence modified. Still, the very negative impact would have been made.

[394] Sam and Dave's family had continued to pay for Kitty and Stacy's services.

[395] A video of Indiana Court of Appeals Judge Edward W. Najam, Jr. was played for the court in which he had emphasized the need for accuracy of information when presenting an affidavit before an independent magistrate.

credibility, according to Indiana law, that required "a showing of reliability or the totality of circumstances corroborating [Boney's] story."[396]

Kitty then answered her own question as to what had changed since Judge Aylsworth had given Dave bond five months prior: "What's new is Charles Boney's self-serving and self-preserving story, his inconsistent statements, his criminal history [of] ten felony convictions for serious bodily crimes against women, his reputation for dishonesty and violence, and his distinct signature when he goes on his crime sprees. [The affidavit] didn't tell you about the forensics, the exculpatory forensics, forensics that actually exonerate Dave Camm."

As our detailed and evidence-based slides rolled with Kitty's narration, our presentation quickly revealed to the judge how Boney had lied repeatedly and had also focused on his confession that it would be "pretty obvious" he had been the murderer if he had been placed at the scene.

As slide after slide shredded Boney's credibility, we also vividly portrayed him to be the "Doctor Jekyll and Mr. Hyde" psychopath he was, often quoting the witnesses I had found and interviewed. Kitty focused on Boney the Salesman: "He always works in sales, and boy is he good at selling his story. He gets his job through his charm and persuasiveness. It doesn't last long [because] nothing lasts long with Boney because his true character, his true violent nature, always comes out."

She then addressed his foot and sexual obsession and the fact Kim's shoes had been removed and placed on top of the Bronco. She then had told of Boney's claim to his friend that he liked to "smell feet, kiss them, suck them…ugly feet made him very angry."

She then connected the murder weapon Boney's love of a .380 as the "best little handgun you can get. It's so little, you can hold it in your hand, put it in your pocket, cover it up, it packs a hell of a punch."

She again quoted Rob Dennis from the Green Light, who said when Boney "gets angry, when he becomes violent, when he gets that rage within, he sees white spots." Again, from Dennis, "He doesn't remember what happens. [Boney] admits that he was violent with his first wife [and said], 'You wouldn't believe the things I've done.'"

Kitty then spoke of the omissions from Gilbert's multiple affidavits, as there had been nothing mentioned about Boney's violence towards women, his many violent felony convictions, his repeated lies, or his car being sighted

---

[396] For his part, Steve Owen, who had previously waved away the possibility Boney had been involved in the murders, now had a different take with the public, as he had told Kyle Lowry of The New Albany Tribune, on June 3, 2002, "Mr. Boney's statement does have credibility."

on Lockhart Road prior to the murders. Neither had there been any inclusion of his confessions to Carl Colvin and me. For Gilbert's affidavits, the term "sanitized" had come to my mind, but "cover-up" seemed more appropriate.

Gilbert's deception that "Kimberly Camm did not sign the life insurance policy but Danny Camm signed her name to it," was untrue, said Kitty, adding, "You notice, conspicuously absent, is absolutely no source for that allegation."

Kitty then attacked the two inmate informants, although they still hadn't been publicly identified. "Indiana Code requires, if you're going to use hearsay informants, you got to show you worked with them in the past, some sort of reliability, or totality of the circumstances corroborating their reliability. They make no attempt to do that in the PC. It's one paragraph, all jumbled together. They don't tell you that they've made these statements that are completely contrary to the evidence."

Kitty then reminded Judge Aylsworth, "Remember the 11 eyewitnesses, that's not in the affidavit. These men are not conniving, psychopathic felons. These men are good, honest, law-abiding. Eleven of them swear that Dave Camm was playing basketball."

Finalizing her argument, Kitty said, "The state's entire case rests on the credibility of Charles Darnell Boney. Which, if any, of his statements are credible? Which, if any, of his statements are reliable? Which, if any, of his statements are believable? A cherry-picked group of phony statements are the only evidence implicating Dave."

On a roll, Kitty continued, "The forensic evidence exonerates Dave. The word of a murderer and professional informants say Dave was involved. Eleven law abiding, upstanding, outstanding, citizens say Dave could not have been involved. Your Honor, you were right in giving Dave bond the first time, and giving Dave Camm bond this time is also the right thing to do. The evidence is weaker than ever, and we request a reasonable bond be set."

About Those Sworn Lies And Omissions...

Kitty then called Gary Gilbert to the stand, and in response to her question of why he, from the Evansville ISP Post, well over 100 miles away from New Albany, had replaced Sean Clemons, Gilbert said he didn't have "any idea" why Clemons had been removed, but he did know that Henderson wanted a "new set of eyes" to look at the case.

And what did the "new eyes" find? When it came to his claim that Dave's brother, Danny, had forged Kim's name, the "fresh eyes" guy had this response: *"Well, if it was written in such a way that it said that, that is not the way that it was meant to be."*[397]

That admission was shocking, as I couldn't believe Gilbert, whose bogus claim had been sworn to under penalty of perjury, had admitted his assertion had no merit. Even more so, a critical part of their motive, murder for profit, had been undercut. Perhaps even worse, Gilbert's demeanor had been almost casual when he had made his confession.

Gilbert, though, then tried to backpedal his revelation by testifying, "There's still an ongoing investigation into that area [of insurance]." Everything regarding the procurement of life insurance on Kim and Dave had been thoroughly examined and disclosed in the first trial. The detective, though, under Kitty's questioning, was then forced to admit that he had only "reviewed some" of the insurance records. So, since *he* hadn't known of the full extent of the insurance coverages, it was "still an ongoing investigation."

As for other Camm family finances, Gilbert, again, said he had only looked through "some" of the family's financial records. The detective, in an attempt to try and salvage the State's motive of murder for profit, had told Kitty, "The way I understood the amounts [of coverage], Kim Camm is worth more dead than she is alive."

Gilbert, in my mind, had quickly returned to his style of proof: If he said or had written something, even without foundational basis, it was evidence.

Kitty quickly jumped on that assertion, as she led Gilbert through the family's solid financial situation, particularly Kim's earnings. Gilbert was then forced to admit that Dave, his life insurance coverage greatly increased by Kim, was also considerably worth more dead than alive.

On the matter of Dave's phone call to Kim's employer the morning after the murders, Gilbert admitted it had been the *second* call, over two hours after the first, when Dave had asked the HR lady, who had called him, to ensure Kim's co-workers knew of the funeral arrangements.

Dave had also asked the lady to protect Kim's voicemails and computer until investigators could seize them. Those very valid points hadn't made it to Gilbert's affidavit, but only his assertion Dave, in the first call, had asked what he "needed to do about the benefits and insurance." Benefits had surely been discussed, but only after the HR lady had asked Dave if *she* could do anything for him.

In the category of downplaying Boney's criminal past, Gilbert admitted that he had omitted nine of his ten violent felony convictions, only writing in

---

[397] Emphasis mine.

the affidavit that he had been released from prison in June 2000 for "*an* armed robbery" conviction.[398]

His recollection of my interview wherein Boney had said it would be "obvious" he had committed the crime if he had been at the scene was problematic for Gilbert, as he said, "I don't recall that specifically."

Kitty then denigrated Gilbert's inclusion of Danny Camm in the affidavit as having attended school with Boney by pointing out that Sean Clemons and Tony Toran, both involved in the original investigation, had also been classmates with BACKBONE. Gilbert, though, had professed ignorance of Toran, not knowing he had been one of Faith's investigators.

Prior to the hearing, we had also been given a stipulated polygraph document, signed by Boney and Steve Owen. That had been totally new information, as the date reflected that Boney had been polygraphed, after his first interview and prior to his second interview, and well before his arrest. Not knowing the results, Kitty had gotten Gilbert to admit the results had been that Boney had been deceptive.

Not only hadn't the deceptive results—that Boney had lied—made it to the affidavit, but recall, also, Owen, knowing full well of Boney's deception, had publicly proclaimed that "It doesn't make sense to me" that Boney had been involved in the murders.

The testimony continued to be brutal for Gilbert, as he admitted he hadn't written anything of Boney's ever-changing stories in his affidavit, which would have impacted on the Shoe Bandit's credibility or, rather, his total lack of credibility.

As for Boney's claiming he had been at the Camm residence and had only "heard" the gunshots, Kitty asked Gilbert how Boney and Dave had even gotten to the house, with the response being, "He followed David Camm to the residence." Kitty sarcastically inquired if Boney had parked in front of the basketball gym and honked his horn. "Uh, no," was the answer, as Gilbert had become more and more flummoxed with Kitty's questions.

When the detective tried to explain Boney's convoluted stories, he finally admitted, "I might be inaccurate on some few time frames here," and then continued, "I can't recall if there was a second meeting that took place." Then, however, Gilbert got his footing and said Boney had followed Dave home, but "[Boney] wasn't sure what vehicle Camm was driving," further testifying, "Kim sees him and looks...surprised," as Boney then "hears a discussion" and "hears a shot" as he "decides to stay back behind his vehicle."

---

[398] As for Boney's probation violation, Gilbert had also testified that Boney had "to drive up to Bloomington." The Shoe Bandit, of course, had been arrested in Louisville and extradited while in custody.

To make it even more incredible, Boney, Gilbert said, had told them the murders had occurred between "four and six." And this was the guy they had pinned their whole new case on? Everyone had known the murders had to have occurred after 7:30 p.m. Charles Boney had been claiming it was between "four and six," and his word had been accepted?

Gilbert next said that Boney heard the word "Daddy" and then two more shots. Boney had heard or said nothing of a violent struggle but had heard Brad's voice from inside the car?

He continued, "David Camm is walking toward him with the gun pointed… and pulls the trigger." After Boney had noticed "an odd facial expression" on Dave, Dave had turned and walked back into the garage and Boney's "going after [him]." Boney then, according to Gilbert, "trips, almost goes down [over the] shoes" but then "puts them on top of the Bronco."

I was really in a surreal world. Boney had hidden behind his vehicle but then had allowed Dave to walk towards him with a pointed gun? Surely, Boney, who prided himself on being an *armed* robber, had his own gun? Why hadn't he shot Dave?

And Kim's shoes had gotten on top of the Bronco, placed there by Boney, but only after he had *tripped* on them? Were we actually in a courtroom? Was Gilbert's testimony truly real?

Nonetheless, the 27-year veteran officer continued his narration from the psychopath. After Dave had gone into the house, "[Boney] puts his hand up against the Bronco, leans inside and sees the children."

So, in the midst of being nearly murdered, Boney had not only picked up Kim's shoes, put them on top of the Bronco, but then had, conveniently, placed his hand on the side of the vehicle, and looked inside to see the children?

Boney's tale, or what we had learned of it, not surprisingly, had placed himself as the victim of Dave.

All in all, there was no adequate term to describe my disbelief in the story Boney had spun, my contempt for Gilbert who had believed and repeated it, or for Henderson for presenting it.

But it got worse for the lead detective, who still had needed to acquaint himself with many aspects of the case, for he had to admit that he didn't know of critical evidence: blood from Kim had been on the BACKBONE sweatshirt, probably from the violent fight, and Dave's T-shirt had none of Kim's blood.

Embarrassingly, Gilbert admitted still more ignorance: he hadn't known of Boney's usage of "escape" sweatshirts in his prior shoe thefts, nor of the Shoe Bandit's attacking only women who wore pants. In fact, the detective admitted, he had only become aware of those aspects of Boney's past crimes just minutes before from our PowerPoint.

Kitty had convincingly destroyed Boney's credibility and had vividly showcased the State's "cherry-picking" of selected bits and pieces of the story. Gary Gilbert, forced to eat many of those sour cherries, had admitted that their only new evidence had been Boney's stories, and then, appropriately enough, his cheeks, after Kitty had finished with him, had each turned a bright crimson.

On cross examination, Henderson first addressed the two prison informants used by Gilbert, whom Kitty also shredded on direct. Gilbert had given more credibility, he had told Kitty, to "an inmate or someone that would actually make communication with the Prosecutor's Office either through their attorney, through their mother, or through their ex-wife, or their wife, and not actually have us try to solicit information."

The other way Gilbert said he judged an informant's credibility was if they had wanted something in return. Neither Bullock nor Hatton had asked for any favors, Gilbert had claimed.

Well, I thought, "If you willingly remain ignorant..." as I recalled that Hatton in his letter to his attorney, which had been provided to the State, had asked, "With my [sic] now being able to now provide new information to a state agency, do you think I can achieve my goal of house arrest, probation, substance abuse treatment, and time served?"

Any chance that Bullock had done something for the good of society was also infinitesimal, particularly in light of his boast to Martin McCoy of his goal of getting a sentence reduction after testifying against Dave.

The fact that Bullock had been a gun fanatic and had known of the various aspects of many different guns hadn't registered with Gilbert who had, he had testified, been amazed that Dave had told Bullock the murder weapon had been a "hammerless" .380.

Had Gilbert even considered how that tidbit came up in their purported conversation? "So, you viciously murdered your wife and kids, eh, Dave?"

"Yeah, and I did so with a hammerless .380. That way, the hammer didn't get caught in my shorts pocket and I was able to remove it quickly and fire three shots; you know, quick draw style."

As for Bullock's prior snitching, Gilbert explained he "was not aware of any [information]" Bullock had previously given on others, with Gilbert's apparently forgetting Bullock's mother had specifically written and spoken of him informing on other inmates. Gilbert also said he hadn't been aware that Bullock had been in the PCU.

The unaware detective had also been amazed that Bullock had "choked up" over the deaths of Brad and Kim when being interviewed by him. A seasoned and manipulative prison snitch such as Bullock had apparently been an anomaly to Gilbert.

Not impacting Gilbert's assessment of credibility had been Hatton's totally wrong description of the crime scene: i.e., his story of Kim, rather than Brad, having been taken from the car; and the murders occurring outside, rather than inside, the garage. Instead, Gilbert had told the judge, "I just had no reason to doubt that he was truthful."

But Hatton had impressed Gilbert when the escape artist had told Dave that he had disrespected his wife and daughter by shooting them in the head, with the veteran detective commenting, "I never thought of that."

Henderson then led Gilbert through four bloodstain "experts" who had given prior opinions on area 30 of Dave's T-shirt. All four, Gilbert said, had concluded they were the result of HVIS, except, in reality, all four hadn't concluded that, as one, a former FBI analyst, hadn't make a definitive conclusion.[399]

Mala's Blood

As to our request to run the unknown female blood on the sweatshirt through CODIS, Gilbert testified that they had gotten DNA from Mala Singh, in Trinidad, and, yes in fact, it had matched to the sweatshirt.[400]

That revelation had enormous possibilities. Did Kim, in her desperate fight for her life, not only get her own blood on Boney's garment, but had Kim also been fighting with Mala Singh? Was a bloody Singh injured in the melee?

The outline of a passenger had been seen in Boney's car the afternoon prior to the attack. Had Singh been, as her brother had told me, "down with whatever her boyfriend asked her to do?" Had it been Mala Singh who had surveilled the Camm home and then helped her boyfriend commit the attacks?

Gilbert then revealed, for the first time, that Singh had been in the country for three days and had been interviewed by him. She recalled, Gilbert said, that Boney, gone during the evening of the murders, had said he "was going to go meet a buddy" that night, and when he had returned, between midnight and 2:00 a.m., he had been "sweating [and] panting" and shown her a revolver. Mala had also said Boney had bruises on his knees.

None of those three aspects—the departure, the "buddy," or the revolver—equated to any nexus to Dave. And "bruising" on his knees? That absolutely equated to Boney's fighting with Kim.

The gun Mala had seen, Gilbert had testified, couldn't have been the murder

---

[399] The other three had been Englert; Tom Bevel, from Oklahoma; and Dean Marks, an ISP blood analyst. Only Englert had previously testified. Interestingly, Gilbert hadn't mentioned Rob Stites. Sometimes, what people don't say can have greater meaning or impact than what they do say. Was this one of those times? Why hadn't Stites been mentioned as one of their experts?

[400] In that regard, we were still awaiting the results of our lab of the cheek swab from her brother's mouth that I had obtained two months prior.

weapon because she said it had been a revolver and not a semi-automatic. It was clear that Gilbert had accepted Mala's story at face value. Again, if that had been the case, why hadn't Boney, in possession of that revolver, shot Dave when Dave had walked towards him after killing his family?

Gilbert, though, kept relating the story given to him by Mala, wherein the next morning, with the murders on the news, Boney, in the affirmative, had answered his mother's question, if he had known "that cop." Why would Boney's mother even ask such a question? That, in and of itself, was weird.

According to Mala, after Boney and his mother had left the house, she, too, had immediately departed and had never seen Boney again.

We had all been making notes of Mala's story, knowing that she'd eventually be deposed at length.

Gilbert was then asked by Henderson if he had believed the story Boney had told him. "His entire story, no. He's not telling us the entire story. The part that he says…I think there's a lot of truth to those informational statements."

What had that meant? Which *part* hadn't Gilbert believed? When, ever, did a testifying detective use the term "informational statements" when talking of an interrogation with a murder suspect?

Finally, of the specific issues of which he didn't agree with Boney, Gilbert said it was the "time lines" he didn't "agree with."

Henderson didn't ask if Gilbert had believed Boney had simply tripped over the shoes and placed them neatly on top of the car, nor did he ask if he believed Boney had been without his own gun that night.

Henderson, however, quickly asked Gilbert if Boney could have "just as easily denied that he was at the scene?"

"Sure" had been the answer.

How could Boney have done that when his sweatshirt, DNA, and palmprint had been located at the scene? Boney couldn't have denied being at the scene, but what he could have done, and obviously did do, was manufacture a story, which had, of necessity, included those three items, all while blaming Dave.

When again asked if he had believed that Boney's "entire story hasn't been told," Gilbert said it hadn't. And then the prosecutor asked, "And is that why you requested and/or agreed that a conspiracy charge should be filed?" Gilbert answered in the affirmative.

What that meant to me, of course, is Boney had not given them any story supporting any conspiracy charge, but rather Gilbert had deduced, or perhaps a better term was contrived, that the two had conspired to commit murder. It was as Dave had said: if they didn't have the evidence, they would then just manufacture it. Again, their preferred narrative had equated to their evidence.

If Two Inmate Snitches Are Good…

Henderson had moved on, quickly again, with Gilbert's having then dropped a new allegation. Yet another inmate had told them Dave had claimed to have heard Brad say, "Daddy." They were now up to three prison/jailhouse informants.

Kitty had experienced enough and quickly objected, noting that she and Stacy had filed a motion to have the State provide any discovery they had been planning on using in the hearing two days before the hearing. They hadn't, of course, even though every piece of information in our PowerPoint had been provided to Henderson by that date. "It's probable cause by ambush," she complained, and she also said it had been a "pattern of ongoing misconduct of refusing to provide discovery."

The judge, however, only noted Kitty's objection, as he had been too busy to rule on her prior motion, received a week before: "I just did not have time to address it." The judge then had kept the bright green light on for Henderson.

That third inmate, whom Gilbert had admitted had been incarcerated for rape and confinement, had also remained unidentified.

On re-direct, Gilbert had dropped another implausible bomb: Boney had claimed, when he had been racing from the crime scene, that he had seen a black Ford, driven by a female, pull into the Camm driveway. That had meant that Boney had known of the belief, by a select few of the initial investigators, that Dave had supposedly had an affair with a female ISP employee.

After Gilbert had left the stand, Stacy handled the second and last witness. Lynn Scamahorn who, for 12 years, had been the DNA Analyst at the ISP Evansville Lab, had been involved in the Camm case since the inception and had run all the requested DNA tests.

Scamahorn had, she testified, originally tested various locations on the sweatshirt based upon what she had observed as staining, and quite possibly, bloodstaining. After circling the 15 suspected areas, she then had the option of conducting a preliminary test, using phenolphthalein. Those presumptive tests, however, could have consumed the entire stain, without leaving any sample for DNA testing, so Scamahorn had been judicious in running initial tests.

Later, three areas, all on the left sleeve of the garment, had been identified as bearing the DNA of Kim, with the area designated as 18 having a mixture of her blood and the DNA, until just recently, of an unknown female. That unknown female had now, of course, been identified as Mala Singh. Mala's DNA, Scamahorn continued, had been found three weeks before by her and was in two additional areas and in yet a third area which contained a mixture of her and Brad's.[401]

Scamahorn had conducted her own tests on the collar of the sweatshirt and had also found DNA matching Boney's. When asked as to how, in February 2005, she and the lab had known to run the-then unknown DNA, Scamahorn replied that it had been after the prosecutor's office had provided them with the Cellmark profile.

Scamahorn had added an important aspect to her comment: *"We were not able to see any of the testing results,"* she testified, from *"the previous prosecutor's office."*[402]

Henderson then requested that he be allowed to "approach the bench," a request which had been granted. His comments were unheard and, unfortunately, the court reporter failed to capture them.[403]

With his cross-examination, Henderson had Scamahorn note that the sweatshirt could have had DNA deposited at various different times and Mala's DNA hadn't necessarily been placed on the garment at the same time as had Kim's or Brad's. In fact, Henderson had added, "[Mala Singh] has told the detectives she has worn the shirt." That translation had been easy: "We're not going to attempt to determine if Mala Singh had been involved in the murders."

"No Matter What He Says, The State Buys It"

After a brief break, Stacy, who had assumed responsibility for the final argument, had quickly emphasized, "the state's case is only as believable as Charles Boney. [We have extensive] exculpatory evidence, exonerating evidence. This is the stuff that gets people off death row. This is what makes the Innocence Project."

Stacy continued hitting the target smack dab in the middle of the huge red round circle: "When you find somebody else's DNA at the scene, the person who's in custody usually goes free, but today that's not happening, because the State wants you to believe Boney's excuses and explanations." What she didn't add, of course, was that the State wouldn't, or couldn't, for whatever reason, finally admit they had been totally wrong about Dave's guilt.

In addition, Stacy made the obligatory legal arguments and then addressed and, with the facts, subsequently shot down the State's two motives for murder.

---

[401] The mixture of Mala and Brad could have occurred after the ISP allowed the sweatshirt to have been bundled into the body bag with Brad.

[402] Emphasis mine.

[403] We would later discover that many such comments were "inaudible," per the court reporter's transcript.

The critical omissions from the affidavit, such as Kim's violent struggle with her attacker and her blood on Boney's sweatshirt, had been inconsistent with Boney's story of wrapping a gun in his garment.

"There's not even a hint to show that Charles Boney is reliable," Stacy continued. "The lead investigator said, 'we don't believe everything he says.' Every omitted fact from that probable cause affidavit shows that Boney is unreliable." She then listed the four items on Indiana's Rules of Evidence that could gauge a person's reliability: 1) inconsistent statements, 2) motive to lie, 3) reputation for dishonesty, and 4) crimes of deceit. Boney had scored a perfect four for four, equaling a total score of zero for credibility.

As for the State's claiming Boney had made admissions that had been "against penal interest," or the fact he had admitted being at the crime scene, Stacy slammed that as well: "They're not [just] self-serving, they're *self-preserving.*"

Stacy had then referred to Boney's comment to me that he knew he had been looking at the death penalty with the possibility of having a "fucking needle in [his] arm." The deduction had been clear: in "confessing" to being one who only provided a gun, and not as murdering, Boney had, indeed, acted not against penal interest, but against a sentence of capital punishment for himself. That had been as self-preserving as possible.

She'd kept hammering Boney and the prison informants as their statements hadn't corroborated one another: e.g., the two snitches had said Dave had acted alone while Boney, of course, had said he had been involved by having only provided Dave with a gun.

The lack of anything—anything—which had corroborated Boney was real and stark, Stacy said. There had been no connection between the two men. No basketball players. No phone records. No witnesses, whatsoever. And, as a result, she said, "There is no probable cause for the conspiracy."

Pleading with the court to comprehend the personality of Charles Boney, Stacy articulated all of his past actions of lies, violence, manipulations, and the sad fact that "No matter what he said, the state buys it. Your Honor, you don't have to buy it and you shouldn't. The State's case is weaker; it's not stronger. The facts, the DNA, the fingerprints, they don't lie. But convicted, violent felons, they do lie."

Henderson, in his rebuttal, was, as I had previously seen, classic Henderson. He slowly rose to his feet, adjusted his tie, looked down at the floor for a few moments, and then, in his superior and smug manner, began, "This is an entirely new case, [and] the State's case is absolutely stronger. We have a better idea of what happened at the scene that night." He then said that, since Boney had been incarcerated and was facing a LWOP sentence, he wasn't someone "in control."

That wasn't true, of course. We had discovered that during his past incarcerations, Boney had manipulated the correctional officers, other inmates, and, of course, the judge who had released him. Being behind bars hadn't prevented Boney, the master manipulator, from controlling the one judge who had mattered most, and that judge had released him early, certainly early enough to murder Kim, Brad, and Jill. That had been the ultimate control and manipulation and had originated from behind bars.

But Henderson kept on, speaking glowingly of the information provided by Bullock, the new informant claiming Dave had heard Brad say, "Daddy," and the "fact" that none of the three informants wanted anything in return for their testimony. That was complete nonsense and Henderson knew it.

The State's blood experts were cited, with Henderson arguing that their opinions "were for the jury to weigh" as was the informants' credibility. Mala Singh was also credible, he argued, since "she volunteered that [the deal between Boney and Camm] was about money" and said that Boney "left to meet someone."

"There's no indication that [Singh] was at the scene," Henderson continued, claiming her DNA had only gotten on the BACKBONE sweatshirt by happenstance and not, of course, during the time she had been in the garage with her boyfriend.

Henderson finished. And, at least to me, it had been yet another shameful exhibition of the State of Indiana's doing all it could to keep an innocent man incarcerated while relying on the words of four convicted felons and a woman who, quite possibly or even probably, had helped Charles Boney murder that same innocent man's wife and young children.

Judge Aylsworth first referred to his original bond decision, stating that he had done "what [he] thought was legally correct and required." He then called Boney a "purported eyewitness [who had] been discovered whose presence at the scene of the killings seem[s] to be corroborated by the physical evidence."

Boney, of course, wasn't just an "eyewitness." To only characterize him as such was to give the psychopath instantaneous credibility. We all knew where the judge was headed.

And then, referring to Boney's story, the judge continued, "I am not sure if it will even be heard by the jury that hears Mr. Camm's case." That, I fervently hoped, would not be the case, as Dave's jury should hear each and every aspect of the case against the real killer.

The judge then, not surprisingly, denied Dave's bond request.

Maybe it was the correct "legal" thing to do. Almost everyone in the system, at least outside the defense, it seemed to me, was supposedly doing the correct legal thing, but no one had given a damn about doing the right thing or the just thing.

Although the defeat stung, Stacy was quick to her feet, as she cited the many reasons why the impending August trial date was impossible, including the lack of discovery, particularly of all of Boney's interviews and interrogations; the failure of the ISP to have forensically tested our requested evidence; the defense's not being allowed to have deposed anyone to date; and the lack of funds to pay for the defense experts.

Of course, since Henderson hadn't provided discovery for months, he said he'd be ready for the August trial, adding, "I wasn't aware we were doing depositions." Henderson was again very smug, I thought, and he was also clever. Neither of those traits, however, equated to his being fair.

Judge Aylsworth then set the trial date for January 9, 2006, allowing for a five-week trial. The omnibus date was set in October and the final pre-trial hearing for November 30th.

After court was dismissed, the parties met in the judge's chambers. When Kitty and Stacy emerged, they joined Dave and me in an attorney's room, guarded outside, of course, by a Warrick County Deputy Sheriff. The judge, Kitty had told us, had sided with the prosecution and had ordered Mala Singh's deposition to be taken on July 5, just six days away.

We weren't in possession of any of Boney's or of Singh's statements, nor had any testing been completed regarding any of her DNA on evidence other than the sweatshirt, nor had her fingerprints been compared to any of the remaining unknown ones from the crime scene. The order by the judge was, per Kitty, akin to "Take your best shot...blindfolded."

The bond defeat, the judge's decision on Singh's deposition, and all the other favorable rulings for the State by Aylsworth didn't portend well for us, and we all knew it. After Dave's comment, "This judge is just like the other two," we all expressed our concern that Judge Aylsworth would continue to favor the State in his rulings.

The next day, Kitty and Stacy filed an emergency motion to compel a comparison of her fingerprints to unknown ones and to delay Singh's deposition. Not surprisingly, both were summarily denied by the judge, as was their request, objected to by Owen, to allow Dave to appear in civilian clothes at Singh's deposition. The trend in the judge's decisions had been, it seemed, all one way.

The next few days would be incredibly busy, as we had to read, view, absorb, and make detailed notes on all of Boney's interviews, interrogations, and his failed polygraph, as well as cram as much as we could from Mala Singh's interviews. Had her story radically changed over time, as had Boney's? Could it have been that Mala, the owner of the unknown female DNA on the sweatshirt, the same sweatshirt which held the DNA of Kim, had also been present with the Shoe Bandit the night of the murders?

SECTION IV
"Make That Connection"

CHAPTER 40
"He's Lying Through His Teeth"

At Least 35 Hours

Although I had already interviewed many of Boney's employers, co-workers, and acquaintances, we still needed to obtain more records from other companies, as well as find out more about Mala Singh. We had already written and served several subpoenas,[404] as we needed to scrutinize each and every document associated with Charles Boney, including those of his hardline telephone, cell phone, job and rental applications, and bank and prison records.

Since we had finally been given Boney's interviews and interrogations, however, reviewing those many hours of tape and transcripts was a priority prior to deposing Mala Singh.[405]

As for those who had engaged with Boney during his initial questioning, we were aware that at least six people had some degree of personal interaction with him: Henderson, Gilbert, Kessinger, Owen, and two polygraph examiners, Douglas Inghram and Robert Ennis. And, as we had only

> "HOW COULD YOU HAVE 11 WITNESSES THAT CAN ALIBI FOR YOU BUT YOU STILL GO TO JAIL? I WOULD HOPE THE JURY WOULDN'T GO FOR IT."

just learned, Boney had been given not just one, but several polygraph tests in between his first and second interviews.

That first interview had taken place three days after Boney had been identified on February 14, 2005, the date of the CODIS hit; thus, the "fresh eyes" had taken three days to conduct their first interview of him. That only

---

[404] Our subpoenas would eventually number over 50.

[405] The length and depth of Boney's interviews and interrogations couldn't be fully digested in the few days prior to Singh's deposition, but, in the interest of continuity, they will be discussed at length.

made sense. Preparing for such a critical interview should have only been done after they had accumulated as much information on the Shoe Bandit as possible.

Indeed, Gilbert and Kessinger, with 57 years of police experience between them, had gathered an extensive amount of knowledge of Boney's personal and violent criminal background prior to sitting down with him on the afternoon of February 17.[406]

After that initial interview, which had lasted several hours, Boney had been tested by the two polygraphers for several more hours. He then had been re-interviewed for at least four more hours beginning in the wee hours of February 18. After 17 hours, if not more,[407] of interaction with Boney, he had been released, but told to maintain contact with the investigators.

Two weeks later, and after his arrest on March 3, a tag-team of three investigators, this time including Myron Wilkerson, had taken turns interrogating Boney for a third, fourth, and fifth time over a period of three days. At least those were the three occasions of which we had been given transcripts. That there were other undocumented contacts and information provided by both Boney to the investigators and vice-versa had been undeniable.

Thus, over a period of two-and-a-half weeks, Boney had interacted with at least seven different individuals for a period of *at least* 35 hours, if not more. The results of those interviews and interrogations are as follows:

Self-Serving First Interview

Gilbert and Kessinger, the leaders of the "fresh eyes," had conducted that first interview. In addition to all of those years of their police experience, including in multiple homicide investigations, the two also had extensive training in interviewing and interrogation techniques.[408] Thus, coupled with their knowledge of the violent felon, not the least of which knowing that his DNA and clothing had been found at the crime scene, they should have been well in command of a man whom they should have known was going to lie repeatedly to them.

Both investigators had a pre-conceived mindset, however. Recall that

---

[406] Kessinger had told Boney, "I knew you wrestled in high school; I knew you played in the band; I knew you was a drum major; I knew you were on student council, got kicked out; I knew what your grades were; I knew you went to IU; I knew you got locked up for robbery and you got locked up for armed robbery; I knew who your wives were; I knew who your girlfriends were; I knew where you lived; I knew your cars [and] I knew which cars; I checked your corrections literature, everything in there…but I could not get your nickname."

[407] Recall that Carrie Harnad had claimed Boney had been interviewed for over 22 hours.

[408] Kessinger, in fact, later had taught interviewing and interrogation at the college level.

Gilbert had refused to entertain the possibility that Dave had not been involved in the murders as he had told me, upon the identification of Boney through the DNA profile, that the blood evidence against Dave was "compelling." One translation of that: "Don't confuse me with any other facts."

But Gilbert wasn't alone in his thinking, as Kessinger had also been, from the start, a firm believer in Rod Englert's blood expertise, later admitting that the blood evidence had been "sufficient to convince me."[409] That had only been reinforced when the former LMPD Major later acknowledged that the role of the "fresh eyes" was to have "look[ed] at the case to make sure the evidence was there in order *to have a second trial [against Dave].*"[410]

Thus, both Gilbert and Kessinger had entered the first interview of Boney with their firm belief that Dave had to have been involved in the murders and the active role, if any, of Boney, had been the only key unanswered question.

With all of that as background, Boney's first interview had been enabled by means of a traffic stop, in Louisville, arranged by Kessinger through his daughter, who was an LMPD sergeant.[411] Boney's vehicle had been pulled to the curb by the two LMPD officers near an apartment he had shared with his newest fiancé, Valerie, and her two children.

Gilbert and Kessinger had then driven to Louisville and spoken with Boney; afterward, Boney had agreed to be driven to New Albany. Once there, Boney had been Mirandized and had begun speaking with the two investigators at 4:07 p.m. The two began their interview by telling Boney that an article of his clothing, containing his DNA, had been found "next to a homicide victim." Rather than ask who the victim was, what piece of clothing, or where it had been found, Boney had responded, "Right."

It was only after a lengthy pause, when Boney had finally asked, "what clothing," that Gilbert had told him it was a sweatshirt. Kessinger had then exhibited to Boney a photo of the BACKBONE sweatshirt, which Boney had readily acknowledged was his. That acknowledgement had pleased Kessinger.

As the interview continued, there were still no questions from Boney on who had been killed or where the murder had occurred. Finally, though, he had inquired, "The only thing that I have questions about is how [the sweatshirt] got there." No question had emerged from the Shoe Bandit, however, as to the actual location of where it had been found.

---

[409] As to the original crime scene, Kessinger also had his own assessment: it had probably been "one of the best processed crime scenes that [he'd] seen."

[410] Emphasis mine.

[411] Two children of Kessinger were officers with the LMPD, and it was his daughter who had first met her father in New Albany to be briefed on Boney; she had then returned to Louisville where she and her partner had engaged in the traffic stop of Boney.

Boney then had launched into several minutes of a self-serving diatribe, first claiming he had gotten rid of all his prison clothing as he articulated a list of items he had when he had been freed from incarceration. He didn't stop for a breath, though, as he had segued into going to court and getting released early. He had been proud of the fact the judge had expressed that Boney had proven himself and "paid [his] price."

Even if Gilbert and Kessinger had wanted to ask a question, Boney had provided little opportunity, as he then had talked of getting a job at Anderson Wood and then, once again, of having gotten rid of his clothes, except his boots, at the Salvation Army drop box in July or August 2000.

Boney, who had previously volunteered to take a polygraph regarding his truthfulness about how he had disposed of his clothing, again asked the two questioners to be polygraphed.

The questioning, though, by design of Boney, had quickly devolved into the only gun of which he had exposure since prison, which was owned by Amber's brother. Boney had then seized upon that opportunity to talk of his 1992 crimes, which had happened only with an "empty weapon."

Gilbert had then given Boney the date of the still-unidentified murders as September 28 but hadn't provided any specifics. And Boney hadn't asked.

After several more minutes had passed with Boney's not inquiring as to what by then had been explained as a triple homicide or where his sweatshirt had been found, Gilbert finally displayed a photo of Brad on the garage floor, although he didn't identify him. Boney's sweatshirt, he had been told, had been lying next to Brad. No, Boney had responded, he had never seen the boy before, and in answering how his sweatshirt had gotten next to him, Boney again spoke of the Salvation Army drop box.

Boney had begun another spiel as he had spoken of the traffic stop in Louisville, saying he had been unaware as to the reason he had been stopped. He then added, "I've not killed anyone. I done things but not murder. I mean, I know you guys want it to be anybody, cause it's obvious on TV, everybody knows about that case."

"What case?"

"The David Camm case. Everybody in this whole nation, if they watch TV, *48 Hours*, whatever, everybody knows about this case. I said over and over again in my mind, whoever would do this, they deserve a lot more than just 180 years."

He then had denied knowing or meeting Dave in any manner, having only seen him on TV. When asked if he had killed any of the Camm family, Boney again asked to take a polygraph, even a stipulated polygraph, because, as he put it, "I don't see how I could fail."

When Boney asked if David Camm had taken a polygraph, Gilbert said he didn't know, but had continued, "I would have offered him one if I would have been the lead investigator." That assertion had made it apparent that Gilbert had faith in polygraphs, but yet, once again, he had shown more ignorance of the history of the case.

Boney was off again, though, as he had begun name-dropping. First, he said, "You know, Stan Faith, he's a friend of our family and I've actually sat down and ate with him, even recently, and then, of course, Sean Clemons, State Police Officer, I went to school with him, we wrestled together and we played football together."

When he had been asked of his knowledge of the Camm case, Boney, interestingly, had said Dave had "11 witnesses," but "the thing about him molesting his daughter makes people hate him." That statement by Boney, I thought, had captured the David Camm murder case as cogently as anyone.

And then a shift in the questions. Who had he been dating in 2000? "Mala Singh, an island girl. She was from Trinidad."

And then, the guy who had just acknowledged that he had been brought in for questioning relative to the Camm family murders was kind enough to ask the two investigators, apparently looking at their recorder, "You got enough tape left?" They did, and he, again, had gone off about Dave, even commenting about his promiscuity, "That's no big deal, that's no reason to convict someone just because they had a bunch of girlfriends."

Boney had then asked the question everyone in the room should have had to answer: "How could you have 11 witnesses that can alibi for you but you still go to jail? I would hope the jury wouldn't go for it. So, in my opinion, for him to have new life, to have a new trial, that's a good thing."

I had to think that Boney, believing he would then have been subjected to a barrage of confrontations on the litany

> "WHAT WE'RE LOOKING FOR IS THE CONNECTION BETWEEN YOU, THE SWEATSHIRT, AND THIS LITTLE BOY."

of his past crimes and violent actions, the similarities to the Camm crimes, and his physical evidence being left at the crime scene, would be not far from finally bursting out with "You guys got it wrong for so long. Here's what really happened." He had, after all, done the same thing with the cops when he had finally been arrested for the shoe thefts.

No barrage of questions came, however, and after an hour of questioning, Boney had shifted to talking about his relationship with Faith and when the two of them had lunch together: "He [Faith] couldn't figure out how the phone company had messed up the times.[412]"

Boney had continued, "[Faith] spoke of some evidence which is irrefutable and other evidence is questionable or circumstantial . . . he was trying to teach me a few things about what it's like to be a lawyer, and [the] sacrifices that he made, sacrifices that he made with his wife and also losing the election. He was talking about some of his personal feelings and some stuff that I won't discuss because that was, you know, just strictly between the two of us. I'm just not one to betray him like that, you know."

Amazingly, it appeared as though Stan Faith had actually taken Boney into his confidence and the ultimate con had conned the prosecutor, not only into talking about the Camm trial, but, essentially, into crying on his shoulder.

It was then time for Boney to have preached his victim sermon: "I come here voluntarily, as a man, but you don't know me, you know my past. Looking at my past, it doesn't matter what kind of person I am today. I work three jobs, all the things that I do right, the way I treat people, I'm not on probation or parole. All that means nothing. All that you guys will look at is: 'he has been in trouble, he's been in jail . . . but we're not going to worry about the good things.'"

Kessinger then told Boney, "What we're looking for is the *connection*,[413] between you, the sweatshirt and this little boy. That's what we're interested in, is the *connection*, how it got there."

Boney said he had understood, and I really think he had. It had registered with him at that time: the *connection*. As if to underscore that point, Kessinger had repeated, "We're interested in the *connection*. How it happened. Did you ever have contact with David Camm?"

Boney said he hadn't, and, furthermore, he hadn't ever played basketball with Dave.

But it had been time to return again to the sweatshirt, as Boney had been "very confident" he had dropped it and another one in the drop box, with his memory now becoming much clearer. "I made sure that the dumpster door was shut. No one was behind me, no one was in the parking lot. I wasn't wanted for anything, so no one was watching me or noticing me specifically. I was wearing regular clothes, [so] I look like a regular civilian." He had then pondered and said he thought it possible that someone had "intercepted" his clothing. "That's my conclusion," he finished.

Boney had recalled, however, in a response to Gilbert's question, that Mala had worn one of his sweatshirts after he had been released from prison

---

[412] Faith had been referring to the 6:19 p.m. phone call.

[413] Emphasis mine; connection will be italicized throughout.

and prior to his donating it. Gilbert liked the idea of the unidentified female DNA belonging to Mala, as he told Boney it would help explain the DNA and further that Mala "has *nothing to do with this* crime.[414] It would be nice if we could get . . . DNA from her so that we could kind of explain an unknown female DNA that has absolutely *nothing to do with this case.*"[415]

Boney then had voluntarily agreed to provide his fingerprints, which, he was told, would be matched to any unknown prints on "the Bronco." Boney, though, hadn't asked anything about the "Bronco." He obviously hadn't needed to ask about any vehicle, for he knew of the Bronco and had seen it many times.

The subject of the polygraph had again been broached, and Boney once more had said he'd take one. He also volunteered he had submitted to a prior prison polygraph, which he said he passed, regarding his knowledge of a shank that had been used in a stabbing. There were no follow-up questions, though.

Gilbert had then broached Boney's prior shoe thefts, and the Shoe Bandit had replied that it had been a fraternity prank involving himself and two others. As to a possible shoe or foot fetish, Boney had laughed off the suggestion, telling the two that his sex life had been normal. Nothing further as to his sexual preferences had been asked, although Boney volunteered he had gotten rid of all his sex-related magazines after he'd left prison.[416]

As to any violence, BACKBONE had said he had only gotten into two arguments with his wife, and both had been, naturally, Amber's fault. The first time had been when she had touched him in anger, and he had reacted by striking her. The last time was when she had confronted him in the bedroom as to his cheating on her. Although claiming only two physical encounters with Amber, Boney then had admitted the police had come to their home on four occasions. That discrepancy wasn't addressed.

And then, out of the blue, Boney had volunteered that his "best friend is an Indiana State Policeman, Wilbur Turner." He continued, "That's my best friend. I just seen him on Sunday at my mother's house. It was her birthday." A short conversation about Turner had then ensued with very few probative questions as to why a guy such as Boney, an 11-time convicted felon, would be friends with a trooper.

Kessinger had re-focused on the sweatshirt and then had inquired, as he exhibited a photo of Boney's garment, "Do you recall any spots like that on

---

[414] Emphasis mine.

[415] Emphasis mine.

[416] Pornography was banned in the Indiana Department of Corrections, but that didn't equate to its non-existence.

there, stains on there? Did you ever wrap anything in that sweatshirt when you got home? Did you ever wrap a weapon in it or anything like that?"

"Wrap a weapon? I didn't have any weapons" was Boney's response.

"Dear God," I thought. It had been Kessinger who had planted the seed of Boney's wrapping his gun in a sweatshirt.

It hadn't stopped there, however, as Kessinger had then asked if Boney, in fact, had known of any guns while

> "DID YOU WRAP A WEAPON IN [YOUR SWEATSHIRT]?"
>
> "[HAVE YOU] POSSESSED A DIRTY GUN? ONE THEY CALL UNTRACEABLE?"

in prison. Boney had responded that he had only heard tales, prompting the next question from Kessinger, "And the ole saying, that you have never possessed a *dirty gun*?"[417]

"No," asked Boney, "what is your definition of dirty gun?"

"You just gave me a definition of dirty in the penitentiary," responded Kessinger.

Kessinger had then asked about another kind of weapon: "How about a "defaced weapon, serial number scraped off? One that they call *untraceable*?"[418] Boney said he hadn't ever possessed such a weapon.

"Untraceable." That term had also come from Kessinger, and Gilbert had used it, along with "wrapped gun," in his affidavit: "Charles Boney went to the David Camm residence . . . to deliver the untraceable handgun."

Gilbert and Kessinger hadn't conducted an interview of Boney, I thought, but rather they had been giving him a script.

After Boney again had denied any involvement in the murders, Gilbert had asked, "Did you *assist*[419] David Camm in any way with these murders?" No, he hadn't, said BACKBONE, who obviously knew, by that time, that he would, more than likely, eventually have to provide the two with some kind of a *connection*.

Gilbert, in wrapping up the interview, had asked if there was "anything else that should be brought to [their] attention."

Boney's response was unique, as he had been somewhat upset because it had taken "four-and-a-half years for someone to come and talk to me about something that was so important." He continued, "I'm a father, too. I would stop at nothing to make sure justice was done."

---

417 Emphasis mine.
418 Emphasis mine.
419 Emphasis mine.

As the lie detector was again discussed, Boney was pleased to tell his interviewers: "The polygraph is my only friend right now. You guys will become my friends when you see I'm telling you guys the truth." That comment would have amazed many, but to me, it had been yet another predictable attempt at Boney trying to con the two cops. As it would soon turn out, though, that hadn't been a difficult job with the two willing subjects.

At 6:05 p.m., Gilbert terminated the questioning. Or at least any questioning or conversation which had been captured on tape.

Polygraph

Steve Owen had next appeared and had personally explained the stipulated polygraph form to Boney, which Boney then had read and signed, the form having been witnessed by Owen. A stipulated polygraph meant the results could be used by either the prosecution or defense in court.

The ISP, however, wasn't going to conduct the polygraph because, as Gilbert said in his bond testimony, "If I ask for a polygraph, the quickest you're going to get one [from the ISP] is probably 30 days." The three had then driven across the Ohio River to Louisville.

After having arrived at the LMPD headquarters, officer Doug Inghram had met Gilbert and Kessinger. Inghram later said that Kessinger had told him that they had been interviewing a man who "was [possibly] *involved with*[420] Mr. Camm in this case, and they were wanting to find out if he was involved." There had been no possibility—none—that Dave hadn't been involved.

Inghram had gone over with Boney the basic background questions, later recalling that he also had asked Boney his whereabouts on the day of the murders. Boney's response was "I can't remember where I was that day." Boney's memory, no doubt, had improved significantly by the time he had told me of his four alibi witnesses for September 28.

At 7:55 p.m., Inghram explained the LMPD polygraph form to Boney, who, in turn, had placed his signature on the document. Three relevant questions had been asked of the Shoe Bandit: 1) Did you shoot anyone at the Camm house? 2) Did you plan or participate with anyone to injure anyone at the Camm house? 3) Were you at the Camm house the night of the shooting?

It took three charts to complete a full test, but Inghram hadn't been comfortable with using the name Camm in the questions, so after the second chart, and before the third chart, he had omitted the Camm name.

Prior to beginning the third chart, however, Inghram had become so sick that he couldn't finish the exam and thus couldn't render an opinion as

---

[420] Emphasis mine.

to whether Boney had been deceptive.[421] He did, however, tell Gilbert and Kessinger, "the charts were not looking favorable for Boney."

Robert Ennis, a retired Jefferson County Police Department (JCPD) polygrapher, had then been called, and the civilian had willingly agreed to volunteer his expertise and time.

When Ennis had arrived, he had been told by Inghram that the test was regarding the Camm case, and of Boney, they had been "trying to either eliminate him or find out what his knowledge was to the case and if there's anything else involved."[422]

The time had been near midnight upon Ennis' arrival, or eight hours after Boney's interview had begun. As part of his pre-polygraph exam of Boney, Ennis has asked if he had any physical or mental issues, and Boney had responded that he had been diagnosed as bi-polar.

As with all polygraphers, Ennis, in his pre-test, had gone over the questions with Boney to ensure he had known there would be no surprise questions. While doing so, Boney had claimed the only knowledge he had of the Camm murders came from "what he saw and heard in the news reports."

The veteran polygrapher had later recalled, of Boney's denial of having been involved in the murders, that "everybody thought he was telling the truth." That revelation, not surprising, had nonetheless caused me mental heartburn.

In addition to other questions, including control questions, Ennis had asked Boney three relevant questions: 1) Did you shoot any of those people in Indiana? 2) Were you there when they were shot? and 3) Did you see who shot them?

After he had spent several hours and had run a complete set of tests that included the three relevant questions, Ennis had reached his conclusion: "I took it back in and told [Gilbert and Kessinger], 'He's deceptive. He's got knowledge of it. He's involved some way or another. He's involved in this case.'"

In Gilbert's report, he wrote that he and Kessinger had been told by Ennis, "the likelihood of Boney being truthful, according to the polygraph data, is less than 1%."

When later asked of the reaction of Gilbert and Kessinger when they had been told Boney had been deceptive, Ennis had responded, "They were

---

[421] Most polygraph examiners do not conclude a person is lying, per se, but rather if they are deceptive or not.

[422] Ennis later explained *his* philosophy, "When I go in to give a polygraph, I don't care what you think. I don't care what the prosecutor thinks, I don't care what the defense thinks. [I'm a] seeker of the truth. I'm not going to let you influence me one way or the other. It's what the charts say and what the test tells me."

surprised." Asked if the investigators had even been shocked, the man with over two decades of administering polygraphs, said they had been.

The two "fresh eyes" guys then had wanted to know if Ennis could run another test. He had responded that he could run a "peak of tension test," which would be to ask a question not known to the public and based upon the caliber of the murder weapon. Seven questions had been asked: "Was the gun used a [caliber of weapon]?" The fifth question was "Was the gun used a .380?"[423]

Boney had willingly agreed to the new test and had claimed on three charts that he didn't know the caliber of the murder weapon when asked if it had been a .380. Ennis later labeled Boney's reactions to the .380 question, not surprisingly, as also deceptive.

After that test, Ennis had told Boney that he had flunked the tests and bluntly him told that he had been involved in the Camm murders. Boney, whom Ennis had described as open and friendly, maintained

GILBERT AND KESSINGER "WERE SURPRISED" AND EVEN "SHOCKED" THAT BONEY HAD FLUNKED THE POLYGRAPH.

his same demeanor even after Ennis told him he had been lying. Still, Boney had remained calm.

After having left Boney in the exam room, Ennis personally had told Gilbert and Kessinger, "He's involved. He's lying through his teeth."

Ennis later said he "would have loved to have gone in there and interrogated Boney," further adding, one of his first questions to Boney would have been, "What did you do with the weapon?"[424] Ennis hadn't been given any opportunity to do so, however, as Boney had soon been en route to Indiana in the company of Gilbert and Kessinger.

Knowing all they had known about Charles Boney's violent criminal history towards women, coupled with his personal property and DNA at the crime scene, sexual obsession with feet and shoes, passion for guns, and then a failed stipulated polygraph, it would have been time, at least in my way of thinking, for any dogged investigator to confront Boney with the enormity of all of the evidence, articulating each and every lie of his and refuting each

---

[423] That a .380 had been the murder weapon had obviously been divulged in the first trial. Still, Boney had claimed not to have known.

[424] Ennis was like all the polygraph examiners I had known, as they all, once they had the hammer of deception over a suspect's head, loved to use that tool, in addition to the facts of the case, to obtain a confession.

with the truth. In fact, a normal investigator would have used the "lying through your teeth," remark repeatedly.

Thus, Gilbert and Kessinger's next sit-down with Boney should have morphed into a full-blown interrogation. That would have been what the vast majority of investigators, at least the ones I had known, would have done, but it didn't happen with BACKBONE. Instead, his tutorial focusing on *the connection* would continue.

CHAPTER 41

"We Got To Make That Connection"

More Lies In The Second Interview

Whether by default or design, Kessinger had taken control of the second interview, with Gilbert having assumed a subservient role. The questioning had begun at 3:13 a.m. on the morning of February 18. Kessinger had told Boney that there had been "some issues" with the polygraph and exclaimed, "we're going to have to try to figure out what happened."

To assist the two investigators and the polygrapher, Boney had previously written down eight questions he thought would have cleared him on the lie detector. Kessinger had decided to go over those eight questions with Boney. The first question was if Boney had possessed a handgun since his release from prison. Boney said he hadn't.

The former Louisville police officer had next read six more questions aloud with Boney's answering no to each one, followed by Kessinger's response:

> BONEY'S CAR COMMENTS WEREN'T JUST WHITE LIES, BUT RATHER *THE FOUNDATIONAL LIES* AND THE BASIS FOR HIS ALIBI WITNESSES, ALL OF WHOM HE HAD SUPPOSEDLY CONTACTED IN AN EFFORT TO OBTAIN A LOAN.

1) Have you ever shot anybody? No. "You know, I might believe that."

2) Did you kill a family of three persons? No. "I might believe that."

3) Have you ever killed children? No. "I might believe that."

4) Have you ever killed a woman? No. "I might believe that."

5) Did you kill the Camm family in Georgetown? No. "I might believe that."

6) Did Camm hire you to kill his family? No. "I might believe that."

The last question had dealt with Boney's disposal of the "sweatshirt in question during the month of July or August." Boney said, again, that he had gotten rid of the sweatshirt at the drop box.

Kessinger next had shown Boney the same picture of Brad on the floor. When asked what he had seen, Boney had responded, "I see a young man that's lost his life." Brad had no visible gunshot wound. Boney didn't have to ask, "What happened to him?"

Not only that, but Boney had said, "lost his life," rather than murdered or dead. Culprits often stay away from such stark words.

How had the sweatshirt gotten there, Kessinger had asked. Boney said he had no idea. Kessinger's response had been "There's a *connection* with these murders . . . and you and possibly David Camm."

The subject had shifted to Boney's car in 2000, with his having spoken of buying his uncle's blue Cadillac. Boney said he had generously and unilaterally bumped the price from $1,000 to $2,000 "out of respect" for his uncle. The payments on the car had been flexible, Boney contended, with his uncle's having told his nephew to "just do the best you can to pay me each week."

"Just do the best" on payments was radically different than what Boney would tell me less than two weeks later: "I mean, when that man says, 'I want my money,' he wants his money or he would come and get the car."

In fact, since my interview with Boney, I had interviewed his infirm uncle in Evansville who had wanted to help his nephew transition from prison. The price on the well-kept car had been $4,500 with Boney's having agreed to pay $300 per month for 15 months, although there had been no weekly payment schedule. Regardless, payments often hadn't occurred, as Boney had been late and/or hadn't paid at all. And there had been no pressure from his uncle.

Boney's car comments weren't just white lies, but rather *the foundational lies* and, indeed, the basis for Boney's alibi witnesses, all of whom he had supposedly contacted in an effort to obtain a loan to make a car payment to his uncle who had been demanding money.

Kessinger had then shifted to the caliber of the murder weapons, asking what type of gun had killed the Camm family. Boney said he "had no idea," although he did say he was thinking .38, since that had been a weapon he had previously used and that caliber was "in [his] head."

Kessinger, though, had then jumped back to his theme: "There's a *connection*. But do I think you killed them? Do I think you were there? You were either there or you know something about this murder and you're not telling us. *The connection between you and David Camm.* . . you're the only one that can tell that."

Boney, however, had again denied knowing Dave, said he had never played ball with Dave, claimed he had no idea who Dave was, and reiterated he had "no connection whatsoever to him or his family." In fact, Boney continued, "if you were to bring him here tonight and say, 'take a look at him, do you know this guy?' he wouldn't know me."

Kessinger's education of Boney had continued: "Do I think you killed the Camm family? Personally, I don't think you did. Do I think you have knowledge? You better believe I do. If you didn't kill them, you're connected to it."

Letting Boney off the biggest hook, as the one who hadn't committed the murders, was a huge step and, no doubt, had been mentally embraced by Boney. Thinking of the comments of Boney's close friend, Tommy Sandler, I knew it was obvious Boney didn't need to read Kessinger "like a book" to know what Kessinger had wanted of him.

The former Louisville homicide cop then told Boney he didn't believe his story about getting rid of the prison clothes. That was explainable, I thought, for in order for Kessinger's theory of the sweatshirt connection, the story of the donation couldn't be true. The itinerary of the sweatshirt had to have been important to Kessinger who had already suggested to Boney that he had provided Dave with a gun wrapped in that sweatshirt.

Next was a pivot to Boney's work at Anderson Wood, as he answered he had worked the month of September 2000, but as to which days, he had said, "I wouldn't know."

And then, the guy who thought the more he spoke the more credible he became, launched into a 1098-word unrestricted diatribe about the events he had experienced in the last 24 hours, including his past life; attempts at turning his life around; credibility; work ethic; financial support of his son; willingness to take a polygraph; and the reasons he hadn't done well on the lie test: he'd been hungry, thirsty, sleepy, and soon to have been up 24 hours. But, he'd lamented, "I can't catch a break . . . once you're in the system . . . "

Curiosity, however, had then finally gotten to Boney, "And when, did you guys, when did the computer link me? And why did it take so long?" That would have been a very legitimate question, I thought, for a guy who had been free for over four years and who had to have wondered if and/or when the proverbial shoe was ever going to drop on him.

Kessinger had sloughed off that question by telling Boney, "We responded as quickly as possible."

Kessinger, though, then had thrown out another olive branch from the same tree: "Do I think you killed them? Man, I don't know? I don't know. I don't want to believe that you did. But you're not helping me. You're not giving me something to hang my hat on."

Just so Boney wouldn't have forgotten, Kessinger had repeated, "We've got to explain that sweatshirt. We've got to explain your DNA on that sweatshirt, we can do that, to a certain extent. There is a *connection*."

Boney had seen an opportunity. "If I had done this, honestly, I wouldn't have been stupid enough to leave that [the sweatshirt] there," he'd claimed, even though he had previously admitted that he had been a "terrible criminal" and who had, indeed, left evidence at a previous shoe theft.

Kessinger had readily agreed, "No, you wouldn't have." That scenario obviously hadn't been in Kessinger's preferred narrative.

A new hypothesis was tossed out by Boney, asking about the weather at the time of the murders and then asking, "Why would I take off my sweatshirt, kill three people, and leave it at the scene?"

Kessinger didn't respond to the perfect opportunity with "Charles, you used a sweatshirt as an 'escape plan' in your prior crimes." Instead, he said, "That's a good question."

Boney again had asked as to why he would have worn a sweatshirt but had been quickly interrupted by Kessinger: "I'm not saying you're wearing it. Why do you got to be wearing it for? You don't necessarily have to be wearing it that night."

Boney, I thought, would have had to have been the most stupid person in Floyd County not to have known that the sweatshirt connection and the gun had been the two main themes which had been repeatedly espoused by Kessinger.

It was time to pull the victim card again, though, as Boney moaned, "I'm the perfect target. Perfect person to have everyone believe, 'Oh, it wasn't Camm. It was Charles.'" He continued, "I'm known for robbery. You told me yourself earlier today nothing was taken. Nothing. Not a wedding ring, not credit cards. I'm using your words."

Kessinger had no prior problems with helping Boney craft a story but had appeared aghast at the suggestion of Boney: "I didn't say any of that stuff. Now, don't get too carried away when you're putting words in my mouth."

Boney thought, and then said, "I'm sorry. It was, uh, the other prosecutor.[425] You don't remember him saying that? There were no credit cards taken, no ring. 'Obviously, you're a thief, you would take something, you would have, you wouldn't have went there and you would have at least came away with something.' That's what he said. So how come there's nothing taken?"

Boney, of course, had later told me the same thing, and I had been stunned when hearing that those words had been given to him. I was again astonished that a prosecutor would have thrown a life ring to a psychopath such as Boney. His story, I thought, was being aided by both the investigators *and* the prosecutors, and both had been involved in questioning/tutoring Boney.

Having kept with his weather hypothesis and the sweatshirt, Boney had asked Kessinger to determine the weather for September 28. Kessinger,

---

[425] The "other" prosecutor verified that both Owen and Henderson were present during the interviews with Boney.

instead, had pivoted back to his theme: "That *connection*…that's what we're looking for. And all we're looking for. Have you heard me say one time in here during this interview that you killed Kim Camm? Bradley Camm? Jill Camm?"

Boney said Kessinger hadn't accused him of murder, and when the investigator asked Boney what it was that Kessinger was interested in, the answer was quick and direct: "The *connection*."

Kessinger quickly concurred: "The *connection*. Tell me how that shirt got there."

Finally, after almost an hour of questioning by Kessinger, Gilbert took his turn, telling Boney that if he, Gilbert, were a juror, he wouldn't have believed Boney's story about the sweatshirt. Boney's response had been to assert that none of his fingerprints or hairs could have been at the scene. He then asked, "Did anyone see me? No. No one seen me. I wasn't there."

Gilbert then made a surprising comment about the sweatshirt and DNA: "This is probably one of the best pieces of forensic evidence you're going to have at a crime scene." Yeah, I dryly thought, that's significantly more than just a subjective opinion that had been "compelling" to you.

The detective then had asked Boney if he had any alibis for September 28. The man who would but days later describe to me, in detail, where he had been on that day, responded, "You're asking me to go back almost five years. I mean, I can't think. Let's say I had a hot date that night. How can I prove that I was really with that person? There's no way that I can honestly go back to September 2000, and say, 'Okay, I did this and I did that.' I can't do that. I don't remember anything back almost five years. I don't have an alibi."

Boney had continued with his inability to recollect what he had done almost five years prior, saying he had only been at work, with Mala, or with his mother. "Those are the only activities. I wasn't doing anything else. I wasn't in any sports, no activities."

By that time, Charles Boney had been significantly educated, but he had still wanted to let Kessinger know that he hadn't been a "punk ass dude that would kill some kids."

Kessinger, again, had reassured Boney, "I don't think we've accused you of killing them kids. I think we said that from the very beginning."

Still, Boney had been leery. "Yeah, but when you say that someone's deceptive, and you can't explain how this got there, and that only you can clear it up. It's the same thing as saying . . . 'you're the only one.'"

Kessinger hadn't used the opportunity to list the repeated lies Boney had told but had once again let him off the hook. "There's a *connection*. You are the missing link. You've been the missing link for four years. You're no longer the missing link, now you're part of that chain. Where do you fit in it? That's what we've got to figure out. You've got us up to a certain point."

The retired Louisville cop again kept drilling Boney on the *connection*: "It took four years to identify you [and] you've got to fill in the blanks. You've got to fill in the gaps. You are a link to this triple homicide."

"I DON'T THINK WE'VE ACCUSED YOU OF KILLING THEM KIDS. I THINK WE SAID THAT FROM THE VERY BEGINNING."

"I STILL DON'T THINK YOU KILLED THEM."

Kessinger had then told Boney that they were sure they had the right man in David Camm: "This case went to trial. A guy got convicted and got 195 years . . . he didn't get convicted just cause the jury [didn't] like the son-of-a-bitch."

The former LMPD Major had been unrelenting on the connection involving Boney, his sweatshirt and Dave. "If you did not kill this family, that little girl, that little boy, and their momma, for God's sakes man, try to help, figure out how that sweatshirt got there. What's the *connection*? How could it have happened?"

Since the journey of the sweatshirt was pivotal to his connection, Kessinger had then asked Boney if he had been "absolutely 100% positive" that his sweatshirt had been placed in the drop box.

Boney said he was certain and then said he had known the two investigators had been "frustrated" and wanted "resolution," but Boney said he would "go to hell and back to prove [his] innocence."

The response from Kessinger had been supportive. "I'd go there and back with you, to help you, if you were innocent. You tell me. You convince me [that] you wasn't involved in that triple homicide, you give me something to work on. I'll go to hell and back with you to prove that, because I still don't think you killed them."

And just in case Boney hadn't been drilled enough, Kessinger had continued, "My only concern, the only question is how that sweatshirt, your DNA, and your nickname . . . how's that sweatshirt get there? Now the issue is, how did it get there? That's the question."

A clearly frustrated Kessinger was upset that Boney hadn't yet provided the connection between him and Camm and again drilled Boney, "we got to make that *connection*." The Shoe Bandit again had said he couldn't recall anything from five years prior, including the date of the Camm family murders. Kessinger told him he'd have to find "something" to "jog [his] memory" if he were not the "perpetrator [or] co-conspirator."

The stand-up guy had then been given a restroom break, and the three had reconvened at 6:27 a.m. The tenor of their conversation had been much different, though, with Kessinger's having asked Boney if he could think of anything that was "important that we failed to touch on" that Boney thought "might assist in trying to verify anything to do with [his] activity or whereabouts" on September 28?

Boney had then given the two investigators a suggestion to check with his mother and also to see if he had "worked that day." And then, at 6:29 a.m., the taped interview had ceased.

Still, after not one but two failed polygraphs and the deduction that Boney was "lying through his teeth," the two investigators had failed to interrogate Boney in a vigorous manner befitting a cold-blooded murderer who had assassinated three people at point-blank range. In fact, the interviews of Boney essentially had come down to "You did have a connection!" and then, "I did not," followed by: "Well, okay, do you have anything else for us?"

Most other seasoned investigators, I thought, would have picked apart Boney's story, piece by significant piece, based upon their knowledge of his violent past; his armed crimes targeting women at night; his sexual obsession for women's feet and shoes; his Cadillac being seen at the scene; and all the other numerous and very specific aspects of his past and his lying stories, such as his gun being unloaded during his armed robberies. They had, literally, the Illustrated Book of Boney, with many chapters, from which they should have literally shredded his story.

Their focus on Dave and, indeed, their hardcore conclusion that Dave had to have been involved, was inescapable, though, and that bias had consumed all of the time the two investigators had spent with Boney. Kessinger, in fact, had demanded of BACKBONE, whom Kessinger had told he believed didn't commit the murders, to know of *the connection among him, the sweatshirt, and Camm an astounding 20 times* during the second interview.

Most investigators would agree that the questioning of a murder suspect is not very stressful when the questions are centered on one central theme: "Confess how your sweatshirt fit in with the other guy who killed his family."

Aftermath Of Boney's Interviews

Regardless, as Boney had waited at the prosecutor's office after the second interview, the tag-team of Gilbert and Kessinger had then interviewed Mrs. Boney on the gambling boat on the Ohio River.[426] Yes, she said, her son had

---

[426] Boney apparently had stayed in the prosecutor's office about another two-and-a-half to three hours after his interview had ceased. There was no indication that Boney, who loved to talk, had engaged anyone else in a conversation, although that would be difficult to comprehend.

donated some of his prison clothes, but she couldn't recall if she had been with him or not.

Mrs. Boney also divulged two things during her interview. First, she said she had known Greg Karem from buying meat at his nearby butcher shop and was aware he was Dave's brother-in-law. The two investigators had been told of the store, the familial relationship, and the Boney family's proclivity for shopping there. They, however, obviously placed no significance in that knowledge then or later, when I also told Gilbert of the closeness of Boney's home to Karem's.

BACKBONE's mother also acknowledged seeing Greg Karem in court during Dave's first trial. That she had seen fit to attend the trial, particularly after working third shift, apparently didn't require any follow-up questions such as "Have you attended any other criminal trials?" or "Why would you attend the Camm trial?"

Regardless, the doting mother, who had rushed to the side of her daughter-in-law, after her son had badly beaten her, in order to prevent her from seeking medical help or calling the police, had been sure of two things: 1) if some of her son's clothing had ended up at the scene of the murders, he had nothing to do with the crime and 2) her son couldn't hurt or, much less, kill anyone.

One thing was certain, however: after Boney had been released early on Friday morning, February 18, Gilbert and Kessinger had taken the next three days off, and it wasn't until the next Tuesday when they had spoken to an employee at the Salvation Army. That person couldn't confirm any part of Boney's story other than there had been a drop box at the location he had described.[427]

That same Tuesday afternoon, Gilbert and Kessinger could have interviewed Boney's Anderson Wood co-workers; checked his work schedule; conducted a neighborhood investigation of Boney's former and current neighbors; or interviewed his wives and girlfriends, including friends of theirs, such as Rob Dennis.

If the "fresh eyes" had done that, they would have learned from Dennis, the doorman at the Green Lounge, that Boney had bragged about a .380: how it could have been hidden in the palm of his hand and how he knew it packed a "helluva punch." Maybe, just maybe, they then could have explained why Boney had been found deceptive on the polygraph regarding his knowledge of a .380.

That afternoon, however, rather than attempting to corroborate or contradict Boney's story, Gilbert had focused on responding to a letter that had been written to Henderson by an elderly reverend who had an intuition that Dave

---

[427] Two other Salvation Army employees had later been interviewed.

had thrown the murder weapon into a lake in Georgetown.[428] Despite Boney's being found "deceptive" by a polygraph examiner, an intuition had been given more priority than a detailed scrutinization of Boney's story.

Boney's Continued Contacts

On Wednesday, February 23, Gilbert had arrived at the prosecutor's office, and, per his report, he had seen that "Boney was in Wayne Kessinger's office. Boney was advised [by Gilbert] to keep a log of his whereabouts each day."

About what had Kessinger and Boney been talking? No one knew, as there had been no report generated by the man who had preached that documentation was critical in criminal investigations.[429]

> IN WHAT OTHER INVESTIGATION, EVER, HAD A MURDER SUSPECT'S ALIBI WITNESSES NOT BEEN DOCUMENTED OR EVEN INTERVIEWED? IT WAS A BIZARRE WORLD IN FLOYD COUNTY.

Through the later-subpoenaed telephone records of Boney's cell phone, we discovered that there had been over two hours of telephone contact between Boney and the "fresh eyes." In fact, each and every day Boney had been free, or from February 19 to March 3, often multiple times a day, he had telephoned the prosecutor's office and/or the ISP Post.

On 29 occasions Boney had called the prosecutor's office and on four times the Sellersburg ISP Post. On 33 total occasions, Boney had spoken with Kessinger, Gilbert, and/or another in law enforcement. In fact, on February 26, the duration of Boney's phone call to the prosecutor's office had been 26 minutes long, and on March 1, his conversation had lasted for 58 minutes! 58 minutes, and still no report of what Boney had said or what he had been told.

We did know, however, of *something* Boney had told the two investigators which hadn't been documented, and it was based upon Boney's having said he couldn't recall where or with whom he'd been on the night of the murders. There was nothing I had found in the transcripts or police reports which reflected Boney's having divulged his alibi witnesses to Gilbert or Kessinger prior to my interview of him.

---

[428] The lake was about a 15-minute drive from/to the Camm residence.

[429] Kessinger had later admitted that articulating the stories told by a suspect was "the most important thing [in an investigation]. *Documentation is the most important thing that you can do.*" He also later said it would be a serious mistake for any police officer not to document his contacts with a murder suspect.

Eleven days later, in fact, Boney had articulated in detail to me his four different alibi stories—but only after he had asked Gilbert if it was permissible for him to do so. At some time or another, BACKBONE had to have told them of his alibi witnesses, but no documentation had existed.

In what other investigation, literally ever, had a murder suspect's alibi witnesses not been documented, and as equally important, not even been interviewed? It was a bizarre world in Floyd County.

Regardless, Kitty, Stacy, and I had spoken repeatedly throughout our review of Boney's first interviews, and the conduct of Gilbert, Kessinger, and the prosecutors, while shocking, had no longer been surprising to any of us. The term "fresh eyes" had been laughable.

As for the next interviews and interrogations of Boney, we had all agreed that they would be conducted in the same manner as had the first two. We had all been wrong. They had been even worse.

CHAPTER 42

"I'm Not Going Down For This"

The Dilemma

Boney's two interviews and two polygraph sessions had lasted, according to Gilbert's reports, from 4:07 p.m. on February 17 to 6:29 a.m. on February 18. That's 14 ½ hours. When Carrie Harned had reported that the investigators "had found no loopholes" in Boney's stories, she had said he had been grilled for over 22 hours.

Knowing what we had discovered, Harned's 22 hours was probably the more accurate figure, with as many as seven or more hours of interviews with Boney possibly having either never been documented or conveniently been lost. In either case, however, there was absolutely no way that he had been "grilled."

> THE INVESTIGATIVE DILEMMA WAS HOW TO GET BONEY TO TELL A STORY LINKING TOGETHER THE FOUR ENTITIES OF BONEY, CAMM, THE SWEATSHIRT AND GUN.

Also in the aftermath of Boney's two interviews and lie detector exams, Keith Henderson had gone much further than Harned in supporting Boney's stories, as he had assured the public, in light of the revelation of the Shoe Bandit's sweatshirt and DNA, "It hasn't changed my position on who . . . is culpable in this case and that is David Camm."[430] Henderson had also claimed in his press conference that only one item of forensic evidence "links Charles Boney to the crime scene" and that the sweatshirt "had been staged at that scene."

Recall that Steve Owen had also validated Boney's own theory of what happened to the sweatshirt after Boney had dropped it in a drop box: "It does make sense that somebody who killed those people thought 'Hey, I got a sweatshirt that don't [sic] belong to me and I know that don't belong to me,' and roll that sweatshirt up and lay it by his boy's side. Now, that makes sense."[431]

What those two had forgotten to tell the public, though, were the results of

---

[430] Zambroski, James, WAVE-TV News, February 28, 2005.
[431] Ibid.

384

Boney's stipulated polygraph exams: Charles Boney had been "lying through his teeth." Most people would think that, indeed, was an *enormous* loophole.

In fact, if Dave hadn't had the vigorous defense of Kitty and Stacy, 1) Charles Boney's DNA wouldn't have been matched, 2) his palmprint would have remained in an evidence folder, 3) Boney would have remained free, and 4) he would never have been charged.

Forced to act after Boney's left palmprint had matched to the one he had left on the Bronco, the two prosecutors, as we had already known, had a major issue on their hands, particularly after proclaiming the sole murderer had been David Camm. They either wouldn't, or couldn't, have admitted that Dave had been innocent. That scenario was not in the cards.

Boney, though, in spite of many hours of questioning, hadn't come through with the *connection*, even after having been thoroughly educated, especially by Kessinger. In fact, Boney hadn't even admitted knowing Dave, which would have been difficult to do since there had been no evidence of any connection between the two.

Thus, upon his arrest, the investigative dilemma was how to get Boney to tell a story linking together the four entities of Boney, Camm, sweatshirt, and gun. If it didn't make a lot of sense, so be it, as the narrative was more important than the evidence: e.g., the stories provided by the first two inmate informants didn't jibe with the physical evidence at the scene on which everyone had previously agreed. Henderson, though, had touted their stories as highly significant, and they had been instrumental in keeping Dave incarcerated at his last bond hearing.

Third Interview: Laying It Out

That had been the lay of the land on the afternoon of Friday, March 4, when Boney had been invited to the prosecutor's office, still not under arrest.[432] After waiving his Miranda Rights at 2:03 p.m., he'd been interviewed by Gilbert and Kessinger.

The first topic broached by Gilbert had been Boney's foot fetishes. He'd told the two that he had gone to a strip club with a good friend and further stated, "I even admitted that to you at the apartment." Boney had been stopped near his apartment by the LMPD, but there had been no documentation from either Gilbert or Kessinger as to anything Boney had told them about what had happened either in or near his apartment.[433]

---

[432] Only later would we know that voluntary visit hadn't been Boney's first visit since his second interview.

[433] Additionally, there had been no interview, at least no documented one, of Boney's girlfriend who had been present.

Early in the third interview, Gilbert had brought up my interview with Boney, with Gilbert upset that Boney had lied to me about his gun being loaded in the two Bloomington armed robberies. The ISP detective had then said, "Mr. Kessinger and I spoke to you about something that I found a discrepancy, pertaining to the firearm, you remember that?"

Boney said he did, and then, echoing Gilbert's exact word, claimed it had only been a "discrepancy" and said, "when questioned again when you guys brought it to my attention, I just spoke out of turn." Yet again, there had been another session with Boney which hadn't made it to print.[434]

Gilbert had responded that the *discrepancy*, which would be a lie to most sane people, concerned him.

Boney's retort had been in reference to their undocumented time together: "I do remember us saying that we all make mistakes and you said, 'just make sure you tell us the truth.'"

Gilbert had moved on, once again asking the Shoe Bandit about the disposal of his prison clothing. Boney had repeated the same story as he had several times previously. Gilbert had then confronted him with his good friend Sandler who had seen him wear a prison sweatshirt. His friend, said Boney, had been mistaken, or even worse, had been "trying to fuck [him] up."

Next on Gilbert's agenda was Boney's lie about having owned a gun since his release from prison. Boney had claimed what he had exhibited to Amber's friend, Toki, when she had tried to get in the house had, in fact, been an attachment to a vacuum sweeper. Gilbert's response had been a mere "Okay."

Gilbert had then asked Boney about the time he had shown Sandler his .38, also when Boney had asked his buddy to build him a silencer to kill Amber. Boney had begun, "I don't remember ever telling . . . I've never told another that I wanted to get rid [of a person]." He then denied ever having talked about a silencer.

Boney then had begun verbally swerving all over his proverbial winding road, as he had spoken of his wonderful treatment of Amber, and how, in spite of his concern for her, that she had often mistreated him.

Apparently finally having enough, Gilbert had then confronted Boney that his palmprint had been matched to the Bronco. "That's impossible" was the quick response, followed by "This cannot be."

It had been time for Gilbert to explain a few things to BACKBONE. "This is the time. This is the place. This is your last stage. This is it! We've been doing everything we can to see if we can eliminate you, and every time we turn around we find something else. We found you in lies and now we're

---

[434] During Gilbert's bond testimony on June 29, 2005, he had responded, when asked if all of Boney's interviews had been tape recorded, "To my understanding, yes."

finding you with both DNA and your fingerprints on the Bronco where three people were murdered. You better tell us what the hell happened now, cause this is it! This is it!"

"This can't be happening" had been the weak response.

"There's extensive evidence on you now, Charles, extensive. And the best thing you can do for yourself is tell us the truth as to what happened. This is the time, this is the place, this is your opportunity to tell us what happened out there. There might be some explanations for what took place, but unless we hear it from you, it's looks extremely grim, extremely grim, evidence wise for you. And there's nothing we're going to be able to do to help you. So you need to tell us what happened out there."

I stopped for a moment, thinking that Gilbert had done what most investigators would have done with Boney: having him tell a story with multiple parts that had been germane to the case and had already been disproven, and then, after the lies had accumulated in sufficient number, most would stop the interview and then recap: "Let's see, Charles, you told me 1,2,3,4,5,6, and all are lies. You're lying." And then, the hardcore interrogation would have begun.

That didn't happen, for after having built and preached a decent case against Boney for murdering Kim, Brad, and Jill, Gilbert culminated his argument: "This is serious business, very serious. So tell me, what is the *connection* between you and David?"

After several more minutes of back and forth, Boney had asked, "How do I know that Camm doesn't have someone affiliated with the fingerprint people?" He then had asked to see the email with the confirmation of the palmprint match to the Bronco and then had read it aloud. Still, Boney had claimed something was awry, as he quoted Gilbert as having previously told him that the "fingerprints probably wouldn't be ready until Monday."[435]

To make a believer out of Boney, Gilbert had then called Singleton who, over the speaker phone, had told Boney the matching of the prints had been easy, as the comparison points had been "far more than we needed."

A photo of the Bronco with Brad and the sweatshirt lying next to him had then been shown, once again, to Boney who had asked, "Where's the sweatshirt?" When it had been pointed out to him, Boney had responded, "That's staged." Those words confirmed that Boney had certainly been listening to Henderson's press conference, just four days prior, where the "staged" sweatshirt had played a prominent role in exonerating the Shoe Bandit.

---

[435] There was nothing in any report, after Boney's second interview, which documented any contact between Gilbert and Boney where the processing of Boney's fingerprints had been discussed.

The two investigators were giving it to Boney, however, with Gilbert's demanding, "Now, we need to know when you were there, why you were there, how long you were there, and what you saw! Your DNA is there, your fingerprints are there. That's more evidence than I have in a [normal] case."

Boney had responded, "I'm not going down for this, there's just no way."

Gilbert had continued pressing: "The evidence is overwhelming. The evidence is overwhelming . . . DNA and fingerprints. Two separate [pieces] of confirming evidence that both are yours. DNA on a sweatshirt by a dead seven-year-old boy and a palmprint on the doorpost of the Bronco where a mom and little girl and little boy have all been murdered. And Charles Boney was there. *What did Charles Boney see?*[436]

The Shoe Bandit had continued to deny, so Kessinger had hit him with an additional blast: "You were deceptive on seven tests, deceptive on seven tests. You haven't told the truth yet in regards to this crime scene."

Kessinger had then given Boney his best spiel: "We were on your side. We were trying to do everything humanly possible to eliminate you, everything possible. We gave you every benefit of the doubt. You are lucky you weren't charged when that sweatshirt was found, but we gave you benefit of the doubt."

Henderson's primary investigator continued, "You were fortunate you weren't charged when those deceptive tests came about, not one, not two, but seven deceptive charts you failed. We still gave you an opportunity to come forward and tell us what's going on, but you kept playing this game . . . until we had the link today, which is that palmprint on the side post of the Bronco. That's the link between you, the sweatshirt and those three dead bodies."

Kessinger had been unrelenting: "You have got a story, a truthful story, I don't want any more bullshit. You've got a story that has to be told. And only you can tell us that story in reference to that sweatshirt and that palmprint at the crime scene to those triple murders. We're pleading with you to tell your side of the story once and for all. We can't do anything for you. We've done everything in our power to eliminate you and [we] can't do it. We have put you there. Now you have got to tell us what happened at that crime scene."

Boney offered some weak denials as Kessinger kept pounding. "Your background. Those feet. Those shoes. You start adding everything, you add your past history of violence with a gun, fetish with feet, fetish with shoes, DNA on the sweatshirt, the sweatshirts you used in the past armed robberies, weapons you've used in past armed robberies, and now a palmprint at the door post."

---

[436] Emphasis mine.

And then Kessinger made his conclusion: "You couldn't ask for more evidence than what's being put on you right now."

"I WANT AN ATTORNEY. CALL STAN FAITH."

In a normal investigative world, Boney would have then been given some hook on which he could have explained how he came to have committed the murders, e.g., "You didn't go there with the intention of hurting anyone, Charles. What happened? Did Kim lose control?"

But the murders of Kim, Brad, and Jill hadn't occurred in any normal world of interrogation, as Kessinger had told Boney what he'd wanted: "The only thing lacking is your story. You have got to tell the story, Charles. You have got to tell us what happened. How did those people get killed? *What's the connection?*

"Anything that I say, you guys are just going to think I'm lying anyway."

Both Kessinger and Gilbert had simultaneously said they just wanted the truth. Kessinger had then said, "the truth will set you free," to which Boney responded in kind.

Kessinger had again pressed, "The truth will set you free, but that truth has to be yours."

Boney finally had given them the answer they had wanted for weeks: "David did this."

Kessinger had demanded, "You tell me how."

"I'll talk in his presence."

"You talk now" had been the response, with Kessinger's telling Boney that he had listened to him for hours and hours and had "run down leads from what [Boney] said."

Boney had used that response to ask his own question, "Did you even bother checking my alibis? All my alibis?"

"Not yet" had been Kessinger's response. He'd added, "I was doing that until I got this call today."

That, of course, had been nonsense, as neither Kessinger, the 30-year detective, nor Gilbert, the 27-year detective, had seen fit to check on the very foundation of Boney's defense that he had been with others during the murders. If they had, they would have had four more lies with which to pound the psychopathic liar.

Boney, though, had clearly been trying to gain time and to manufacture a story to minimize his role, as he told the two of his assessment of their demands of him, "the only thing that you guys have a problem with was whether or not I had a gun in my possession."

Kessinger had responded that three separate polygraphers had determined he had been deceptive.[437] He'd then pleaded with Boney, "Tell your story. This is your opportunity and chance to explain what happened. For God's sake, don't pass up an opportunity like that. How did that happen?"

"Two words . . . David Camm."

"Explain it. Tell me the story," asked Kessinger, who clearly had been in control of the interrogation.

Boney, though, had tried to shut down the questioning. "I want an attorney."

"What do you need an attorney for?" Kessinger had asked.

"I'd like to tell [my story] to my attorney. Are there any public defenders downstairs?"

Kessinger had pressed, "Tell me what happened. I'll get your attorney for you. Tell me what happened."

Boney's response hadn't been a surprise. "Call Stan Faith. Have him come down and I'll talk about it."

Both Kessinger and Gilbert had told Boney that Stan Faith would probably have been a conflict of interest on his part. Kessinger had then implored, "I have not asked anything of you except this time. Please tell us what happened."

"The only thing I can honestly tell you is that I didn't commit the murders."

"I'm not arguing with you," Kessinger had assured Boney. "I want you to tell me what happened."

"All I know," the man whose lies had overwhelmed the room had responded, "is that David Camm was the shooter. That's all I'm going to say until I get an attorney." My translation: "I'm under a lot of pressure right now, and I need some more time to come up with a story that you guys might accept and will still portray me in the best possible light."

Kessinger had then ended the 71-minute interrogation at 3:14 p.m., with the comment "We're going to see if we can get a hold of an attorney for you." Boney was left in the interview room by himself.

Per Gilbert's report, however, just afterwards, and during the time Boney had been held in that interview room, pending transport to the jail, just an elevator ride away, Boney had initiated a request to again speak with the two investigators. That Boney had decided, upon his own accord, and without prodding from either Kessinger and/or Gilbert, to begin talking again was unlikely in my mind.

Nonetheless, after having secured a form for Boney to sign, Boney once again had waived his Miranda Rights. BACKBONE, though, wasn't interested in talking but had made an unusual request, either on his own volition or upon

---

[437] We knew the names of only two polygraphers who had examined the charts. Kessinger had told Boney a third had looked at the charts and had determined him to be deceptive.

a suggestion of one of the two detectives: leave me alone with a pen and a paper. That had been immediately granted, and, for the next four hours, Boney had sat by himself in an interview room. It was story time.

CHAPTER 43

"Perfect Fall Guy"

"I Am Not Responsible For The Murders"

The next interview/interrogation of the Shoe Bandit was the fourth documented one, and had begun at 4:44 p.m. on Friday afternoon, March 4, but the tape hadn't begun rolling until 4:52 p.m. Then Gilbert had said, "I believe you stated that you would rather make notes, write out what took place, and then talk with us about it, or words to that effect. Is that true?"

"That is correct."

"Okay. We're going to stop the tape for Mr. Boney to start on his written statement."

Up until this time, Charles Boney had been subjected

> A CRYSTAL BALL WOULD NOT HAVE BEEN NEEDED TO PREDICT THE PLOT OF BONEY'S STORY.

to a massive amount of pressure, albeit it skewed towards his providing the elusive "connection." Kessinger, in fact, had again accurately described the enormity of evidence against Boney, but then, rather than increase the heat, had decided to allow the man some quiet time to compose his thoughts. Over the course of almost four hours, Boney had composed his story of a tad over four pages.

A crystal ball would not have been needed to predict the plot of Boney's story: he would have incriminated Dave while trying to manufacture a story that Gilbert and Kessinger would accept; all the while, of course, Boney would characterize himself as a victim while minimizing or eliminating his involvement.

At 8:45 p.m., Gilbert and Kessinger had gone back on tape with Boney, with Gilbert's recapping that Boney had waived his rights and further explaining, "Mr. Boney, at your request, you asked to be left alone to kind of write some information pertaining to what the offense [we're looking into], is that correct?" After Boney had answered in the affirmative, Gilbert had continued, "If you don't mind, Mr. Boney, would you mind reading us what you've written up to this point?"

Boney had agreed to do so and then had recited from his statement of almost 900 words.[438] In it, he had covered all the bases he'd wanted to cover, including

---

[438] Boney had read his statement in its entirety, but I will address each section and/or point with selected comments and/or responses of the two investigators.

having immediately given them their needed connection. The following is his statement, including a portion which he had originally scribbled over and which had been later reconstituted by a document examiner.[439]

"I first met David Camm July 2000 at Community Park. We played ball against one another and I lost that game."

That Boney had known to include basketball in his story wasn't a surprise, for he had already expressed his knowledge of Dave's 11 basketball/alibi witnesses. Those men, of course, had repeatedly been maligned and accused of lying. One would therefore have thought that Boney's basketball players would have been given equal scrutiny, e.g., "Give us details of the basketball game, Charles. Why did you only play one game? How many played? Was it five-on-five? Full court? What day of the week? Who were the players? You didn't have a car in July, Charles, how did you get to Community Park? What was David driving? Who else was present during your conversation? How many other times did you play there? Who saw you at the park then or on any occasion?"

None of those questions, however, nor any others pertaining to him and Dave's supposedly playing basketball, had been asked, nor had there been any attempt, we'd later discovered, by the investigators to attempt to run down the regulars who, in fact, had played at Community Park.[440]

Not corroborating one's story had evolved into what I had concluded had been part of the "fresh eyes" way of thinking: If something can't be verified, they were allowed to assume it occurred—or didn't occur—depending on what best fit their story.

Another question had arisen: with the later splashing of Boney's mugshot across the television screens of metro Louisville, wouldn't it have been probable that anyone who had ever played basketball with him anywhere, and particularly with Dave, would have contacted the "fresh eyes?" No one had ever come forward.

Boney's story had continued:

"I remember bragging about how I just got out of prison. And it was, you know, great to have to get fresh air and have a hot summer to enjoy. David Camm told me that he was a former State of Indiana Police Officer and asked me what I had done. I told him very little about my crimes but I did state that it was Armed Robbery. David Camm talked to me about Jesus

---

[439] Spelling and punctuation are as written by Boney.

[440] Kessinger had later said the time that had elapsed between the game and Boney's having told them of the game meant there was "no way" he could corroborate Boney's story. In another comment, Kessinger said, "I personally have not talked to anyone who could confirm or deny either way" that the two had met playing basketball.

and church. Mr. Camm told me that Christ could put me back on track if I put Jesus first. He told me about church gymnasiums and fellowship but I was not that interested. I was more interested in work and my girlfriend at the time. Mr. Camm was sincere, but not too trusting of me as a felon."

Boney had again put together two primary pieces of the story from which he, as with untold others, had been educated in the past four years: Dave had been an ISP officer who had played basketball at his church gym. Boney had also obviously known of the family's strong link to the Georgetown Community Church. So far, the essentials on which the Shoe Bandit had been basing his story had come from public information.

"My second encounter with David Camm was in September of 2000. I met Mr. Camm at Better Way Food Mart on State Street, New Albany. I spoke with him briefly and I asked for a rematch of basketball. He told me that he was up for it but didn't know when. Mr. Camm seemed to be distracted and kept looking at the next building over, which was a Karem's Meat Market."

To me, this was incredibly significant. Boney had tacitly admitted that he had known that Karem's had been a link to Kim. Of course, if nothing of any significance had occurred up to that time, why had Dave seemed to have been "distracted and kept looking . . . [at] Karem's?" Not to matter, though, for Boney had rushed into his next phase.

A photo taken by me in 2005 of Karem's Meats (right side), adjacent to the Better Buy, earlier known as Better Way Food Mart, was just a five-minute walk from the New Albany Residence of Charles Boney.

The next paragraph had been obliterated by Boney, but it had been reconstructed by ISP Document Examiner Diane K. Tolliver:

David Camm asked me to follow him to a secluded area. He wanted to talk to me about something that could help me financially, he said. I followed him from Betterway Foodmart to the parking lot of Target. David Camm and I _____ discussing.

The Target store was located across the nearby and very busy State Street in New Albany and is not in a secluded area but rather has a large, open, and quite visible parking lot. For Boney to have written about it, and then eradicated that part of his story, probably meant that even he had known that aspect wouldn't have passed muster.

"I was not able to admit that I knew David Camm for fear that a triple murder would be placed on my head. I was not able to discuss the connection due to my insight of a possible set-up."

It hadn't taken Boney long to have raced towards his victimhood status, but he couldn't talk with Gilbert and Kessinger about the connection because of a possible set-up? That made absolutely no sense whatsoever.

BACKBONE had continued:

"David Camm couldn't say anything about knowing me or else his case is completely ruined. David Camm has a great chance in court so long as no one uncovers the one person that can land him in jail, Charles Boney."

Absolutely no one had needed any translation of "the one person that can land him in jail, Charles Boney." Boney might as well written: "***HERE I AM, GUYS! I'M YOUR CONNECTION!!***"[441]

"When I discussed the purchasing of a handgun to David Camm, I was in his Bronco. David Camm paid me two hundred fifty dollars for a .380 caliber weapon. <u>I will not tell</u> where I got the weapon but I did sell it to David Camm."

Boney had obviously placed himself in the Bronco to explain his palmprint having been placed on it. But regardless, where did this happen? Presumably, and following Boney's own story, Dave had been adjacent to the meat store owned by his sister-in-law and her husband and, after evangelizing for Jesus Christ in the only other time he had met Boney, had segued into asking Boney about buying a gun.

Additionally, at least in the real world, Dave had driven his UDI truck and had only driven the Bronco with Kim or with his family. It was Kim's car, and she had been the one who had driven it, not Dave.

That Boney had sold a gun to a guy he had known had been a cop, and Boney hated cops, also didn't compute, and his claim that it had been a junk gun, a Lorcin,[442] worth maybe $100 on the street, for $250, was as believable as the story that Dave had trusted a violent felon to sell him a gun at all.

Nonetheless, Boney's having stated that he would "not tell where [he] got

---

[441] Emphasis added.

[442] Even though Boney had claimed not to have known the manufacturer.

the weapon" had perhaps been crucial, I thought. Why wouldn't Boney have simply offered up that person if there had been no risk to Boney, particularly since Boney, a coward, wasn't any kind of stand-up guy? As such, had the person who provided Boney with the gun had involvement in or knowledge of the murders?

His story had continued:

"When I met with David Camm to receive payment for the weapon, a .380 caliber handgun, I didn't have anything to wrap or place the weapon in, so I used my sweatshirt. I had already sent many things to the Salvation Army, so I knew that one of the sweatshirts would surface in the thrift store. David Camm knew my name and where I did time so he could have easily looked into my history."

Where had this meeting occurred? Boney had first written that it had occurred in the Target lot, but he still hadn't identified the location. Regardless, the suggestive interviewing techniques of Kessinger had paid huge dividends: "Did you ever wrap anything in that sweatshirt? Did you ever wrap a weapon in it or anything like that?" Boney had aced that part of Kessinger's test.

Boney still, however, had overstepped his helping hand. Had it made any sense that he'd continue to go with the bogus clothing donation? He had already, at least in his story, told Dave his name and that he had been an armed robber. What had been the need for Boney to have added more? The only thing, I thought, was that he still could not stop talking, ergo, lying.

A portion of Charles Boney's handwritten statement, March 4, 2005.

But it had been time for Boney to summarize the case against him, just in case the two detectives had begun to have other ideas:

"My case is based is on selling an illegal handgun to a person who eventually used it to murder his own family."

And if the guys needed some additional prodding, Boney had been glad to oblige by repeating the canard of molestation:

"He was molesting his daughter,[443] *cheating on his wife and it came crashing down when his family had <u>enough</u>. The truth of his affairs and the secrets of what he was doing to his daughter was about to be told, so he shut them up for good."*

After reinforcing the staunchly-held blood beliefs of Kessinger and Gilbert, Boney had thought it was time to remind them, again, of just how he had been a victim, as had Kim, Brad, and Jill:

"A guy fresh out of prison is a perfect fall guy for the crimes. My fingerprints, my sweatshirt and my past are perfect ingredients to set Charles Boney up. David Camm knew that I couldn't tell anyone or anything or I'd go straight to jail."

Boney, of course, had chosen to have only mentioned, and then to have skipped over his fingerprints, sweatshirt, and violent past, in the line of "nothing to see here folks, just move along."

Still, one of the first questions the investigators should have asked themselves was, if Boney's story had been true, then *why hadn't David Camm told on Charles Boney?* According to Boney, Dave had known his name and that the gun and sweatshirt had come from him. So, then, why hadn't Dave, sentenced to 195 years and serving that time in prison, told someone, a cutout perhaps, who could have then anonymously alerted the ISP that it had been Boney who had killed the Camm family?

Boney, though, had continued with his story:

"The polygraph showed deception on the weapon and the lack of deception as to whether I was there specifically Georgetown, Indiana. I am wrong for providing a weapon, but I am not responsible for the murders. I am wrong for knowing about evidence against David Camm, but that doesn't make me a murderer."

There had been nothing in any report or interview of Boney that I had read where anyone had told him of any *"lack of deception* as to whether I was there." Someone, then, had given him that idea. It wasn't true, of course, but Boney nonetheless had grasped at that and then had inserted it while still having provided the desperately-needed *connection*. His tale, conveniently, also had included the most minimal involvement for himself: he had only wrapped the gun in his sweatshirt, he hadn't used the gun, he had only withheld evidence, and he hadn't been the murderer.

---

[443] When Boney had read from his statement, he had added, "allegedly molesting" his daughter.

"David Camm has blood spatter and brain matter on his sweatshirt,[444] *none was found on the sweatshirt, on my sweatshirt, just my DNA and unknown female DNA that could have belonged to the helper of the Camm murders."*

THE SWEATSHIRT HAD "UNKNOWN FEMALE DNA THAT COULD HAVE BELONGED TO THE HELPER OF THE CAMM MURDERS."

Boney certainly had knowledge about what had purportedly been on Dave's T-shirt; had that come from his own readings during the first trial, or had it come from Gilbert or Kessinger?[445] Regardless, he saw fit to regurgitate the information to assist the two detectives.

Strangely, though, Boney had also added his thought that the unknown female DNA could have been "the helper of the Camm murders." Why had he gone there? I had to consider the possibility that Boney had been engaging in yet another "fuck-with" moment.[446] Had he been telling them, "Hey, you idiots! Don't you know Mala Singh was with me?"

"David Camm never did say what he was going to do with the gun, and as a convict, I didn't ask."

Once again, Boney had distanced himself from the murders while still having given the two detectives their *connection.*

"If David Camm had used me in the actual crime, he would have killed me too! This would have been perfect, former State Trooper comes home and discovers his family slain with a black male wondering [sic] around, so he gets shot and the authorities see Camm *as protecting his household. Why would David Camm let me live to tell on him? He could have killed his wife, the daughter and me, then allow his son to live and keep quiet about it. How could I be thought of as having more significance than his only son. Yet, I was allowed to walk away from the crime scene? No. David Camm knew that he was using me from the second time he had met me.*

Why had Boney written about a hypothetical? It was, of course, his

---

[444] One defense bloodstain interpreter had described a tiny "particle" as being one of the eight tiny dots of contact blood from Dave's shirt-tail contact with the ends of Jill's hair. It had later morphed into "protein matter" in Gilbert's affidavit and had later been described as brain matter. In fact, it had more than likely been derived from the entry gunshot wound to Jill's head. It, as had the other seven tiny dots, been transferred from Jill's hair to Dave's shirttail and then pressed into his shirt when Dave had clutched Brad to his body.

[445] There had been no documentation if Boney had been told of the tiny particle.

[446] Recall that at the time of his statement, Mala Singh's DNA hadn't been matched to the sweatshirt.

affirmation that it hadn't made sense for him to have been present when Dave had murdered his family.

Regardless, think of that scenario, not as a hypothetical, but as reality: that Dave had been intent on killing Boney after Dave had killed his family. That storyline meant that the two had to have arranged to have met one another simultaneously with the arrival of Kim and the kids. That had also meant some kind of coordination, yet there had been nothing whatsoever linking the two together, including phone records.

But even if—*if*—the two had coordinated, that meant that Dave had snuck away from the games, unnoticed by anyone, in order to also kill Boney, and he then would have called the police, blaming the murder of his family on Boney. Thus, there would have been no reason for him to have snuck away from the games in the first place, as both Faith and Henderson had claimed.

The practiced psychopath, though, had returned to his singular role:

The polygraph shows that I was not at the Camm house, but I could not get past the fact that I knew about the weapon.

Again, there had been nothing I had found where Boney had been told that he had only flunked the polygraph on *only* his knowledge of the gun. Boney had, again, twisted the facts for his benefit.

Boney, thanks to the inability or unwillingness of Gilbert and Kessinger to check his alibis, had again felt confident enough to proclaim he had been elsewhere as he had ended his statement:

My alibis are still intact, because during the actual murders I was in the presence of at least six people and I have a time line that begins at 2 p.m. and doesn't end until around 11 p.m. on September 28, 2000.

The Real Confession Of Boney

In short, Boney's summarized "confession," or at least my translation, was this:

"David Camm killed his family because he had molested his daughter and cheated on his wife. I had only accidently run into Camm while playing basketball with a group of others, none of whom have ever come forward, nor have you asked me about any of them, or any details surrounding that game.

When I first spoke with Camm, that cruel, vicious child molester tried to bring Jesus Christ to my attention, which was very offensive to me because I'm a Satan Worshipper.

Camm, an ex-cop, who wasn't trusting of me, and was a very knowledgeable man about guns, had also convinced me, a guy who hated cops, to sell him a junk gun for over twice as much money as it was worth, and only after we met by chance next to Karem's Meats which his sister-in-law owned.

You didn't ask me anything about Karems, but when I did go in there, on several occasions, I never saw or spoke with Kim or her kids, nor was I attracted to her, nor did I follow her home, learning that she lived on Lockhart Road.

When I later delivered that junk gun to Dave, bought from a guy that I, BACKBONE, am terrified of, I had wrapped it in my sweatshirt as the brilliant Kessinger had previously surmised I had done.

My palmprint, somehow or another, had gotten on the Bronco far, far away from the crime scene while it had been driven by Camm, even though he didn't drive that vehicle by himself. Remember, also, that I wasn't anywhere near the crime scene because my alibi witnesses, who you haven't contacted, are still alibiing me, although they're really not.

The fact that Kim's shoes had been placed on top of the Bronco by me wasn't addressed by you guys, and I thank you for steering clear of my having to think of a story that would explain my doing so.

Oh, and I didn't drive my Cadillac down Lockhart Road, surveilling the Camm residence, in the mid-afternoon of September 28.

I do have to add that me being me, a superb intellect who is smarter than any other person in the room, is also fucking with you two when it comes to my knowing who "my helper" was. I know and you don't.

Thank you for allowing me to provide you with your connection."

Signed: Charles Darnell Boney, aka BACKBONE, AKA Shoe Bandit

P.S. Remember, I only sold a gun.

I returned to their interrogation, such as it was, of Boney. After he had read his statement, Boney had made a drawing of the gun he said he had sold to Dave and had then signed and dated the paper.

BACKBONE had then responded to additional questioning, adding to his statement. Yes, after their initial meeting, he had accidently met Camm, two months later, at Better Way. They had talked, for five to ten minutes, Boney had claimed, about playing basketball, jobs in general, Boney's job at Anderson Wood, if Boney had sold drugs, of Boney's armed robberies, how Boney had "supplemented" his income, and if Boney "had weapons."

Also, during that five to ten minutes, Boney said he had told Dave he could get a gun for $500, but Dave had said he'd pay $250 for a gun he knew nothing about—e.g., the manufacturer, model, caliber, or anything. According to Boney, he had told Dave he could get the gun immediately, and they then had agreed to meet in the back parking lot of the nearby Floyd Memorial Hospital at 6:00 p.m. The Target parking lot had been scrubbed from his statement by Boney.

How had he been able to have gotten a gun so quickly? "These are things that I know," Boney had responded, as he had refused to identify the person.

Boney then had a revelation, as he had recalled the date of his gun delivery as having been between September 15 and 20.

He and Dave had met then in the hospital lot, Boney had claimed, with Dave's having driven the Bronco and Boney his midnight blue Cadillac. Boney had walked over to the Bronco, and Dave had even opened the door for him wherein he had given Dave the gun "wrapped in [Boney's] sweatshirt" in exchange for $250 in cash.

When he had exited the Bronco, Boney had said he "didn't have on gloves, so that explains contact with the Bronco."

That had been the last time Boney had seen Dave until he had "seen him later on television" and "knew he did it."

First Gilbert, and then Kessinger, had told Boney they didn't believe all of his story.

Kessinger, in fact, had told Boney, "I don't believe it unless you tell me who sold you the gun. Bits and pieces is not gonna, it's not gonna fly tonight, partner. You got to tell the whole story and you got to lay it on the table tonight cause this, what you're trying to do, is to take care of Charles Boney. *Don't leave yourself hanged and involved in the crime. If you are not the trigger person in this homicide, you better tell everything you know.*"[447]

Boney had then claimed that he had gotten the gun in Louisville but first said he didn't know the person's name, and then had refused to say his name and snitch.

Kessinger had responded that it was a serious case to which Boney had accurately replied that it had been a "capitol murder case." The implication had been the same as when he had told me of the possibility there would be "a needle in [his] arm." Charles Boney absolutely had known he had been facing the death penalty, an incredible incentive to be just a *connection*, rather than the "trigger person."

A light had then apparently flickered in Kessinger's brain, though, as he had told Boney that Dave had "never [driven] the Bronco. That was Kim's car." Kessinger had followed that with "Why don't he drive the company truck?"

Boney had a quick answer: "Who would drive a company vehicle, picking up a dirty weapon?" The term "dirty," of course, had originated with Kessinger in a prior interview.

Kessinger had seen fit not to pursue the issue of the Bronco, as he had gone back to the gun, telling Boney that his refusing to have identified the person who had provided the gun was "an extremely strong deception . . . a big hole in your story." Kessinger, in an attempt to convince BACKBONE to give the

---

[447] Emphasis mine.

name, explained that, with the identity, "The story flows a little smoother, it's more believable."

Boney had only replied that he had gotten the gun for less than $100 in a "crackhead deal."

Kessinger, though, had said the story without the identity of the man who had provided Boney with the gun had not been good enough and had, finally, denigrated the entire time Boney had spent manufacturing his tale: "I could make up a story as good as that [in] three and a half hours."

Boney had replied that he couldn't become a snitch on the gun provider, for, if he had, as he put it, "I've got death for sure coming. I'm not fucking with him." Kessinger kept pushing, but Boney hadn't budged. Clearly Boney could have fabricated a name, but the fact he had been steadfast in not providing a true name possibly did mean the gun supplier had been involved in the murders.

And then, after the tape recorder had "abruptly stopped" and had restarted, Kessinger had continued, telling Boney that he was "concerned" about Boney's claim that, on the second time he and Dave had ever met, Dave had asked Boney about getting him a gun.

Boney's response had been, to him, quite logical: "He took a liking to me when he first met me." The psychopath had then told the two questioners, "It seemed like both of you took a liking to me. So did Mr. Camm."

Kessinger had been questioning. "[Did he] feel comfortable enough that he'd ask you [if] you would sell him a dirty gun? And my question, back to you, is how did you know the gun was clean?"[448]

Boney said he had trusted his sources. So, in a "crackhead" deal, Boney had been confident the gun he had purchased for less than $100 was clean and untraceable?

The gun had been loaded, Boney had known, because his source had told him that. Boney, though, had not ejected the clip to see how many rounds had been in the gun. He had, once again, trusted his "crackhead" source to have provided him with a loaded gun.

Kessinger's assessment of all of Boney's story had been that "the biggest hang-up" on the story was that Boney refused to tell where he had "acquired the gun." That comment was stunning. A thorough investigator, I thought, could have, and indeed should have, driven a semi-truck through the many huge holes in Boney's story. Kessinger had chosen not to.

Gilbert also had followed suit with Kessinger, as he had then told Boney that a car, identical in appearance to Boney's Cadillac, had been seen on

---

[448] Kessinger had used both terms, "clean" and "dirty," during the interrogation. In his bond hearing testimony, Gilbert had testified the term "clean" came from Boney.

Lockhart Road at 2:00 p.m. in the afternoon. Boney had responded, "I don't believe it, because I know where my alibis seen me." That wasn't the same as "I wasn't there."

Gilbert, however, had chosen not to pursue Brandon Beaven's critical sighting of Boney's car. Another golden opportunity had been summarily flushed.

And then, yet another story had come from either Kessinger's own imagination or the undocumented ether of the Kessinger and Boney relationship, when Kessinger had reminded Boney of a prior conversation: "There's a statement that you made way, way back, a statement you made to me [that] an individual, when you came into New Albany: 'I got some business to take care of, I owe somebody a favor, I'll hook up with you after I get into town and do it.' What was that favor? What was that business that you had to do? Sometime in July, August, first of September of 2000?"

Boney had a tough time following. "I have a favor?"

"Uh, huh," Kessinger had responded, further educating Boney, "I got, I have some business to do. I owe somebody. I got to do a favor when I get into town. After I get that done, I'll look you up."

A clearly quizzical Boney had asked, "I'll look you up?"

Kessinger had kept trying. "These favors you're talking about. Where are you coming from? Guy owes you; you owe somebody. Are you a member of any kind of an organization, a club?"

If it hadn't been deadly serious, Boney's answer would have elicited a laugh: "The only thing I've ever belonged to was the Cub Scouts."

Kessinger hadn't stopped. "Did you owe somebody a favor? Somebody take care of you while you were in prison, and you had to do a favor?"

Boney had responded, "I don't know what you're talking about." The subject had then been dropped, but it wouldn't be the last time, however, Kessinger's story of Boney's supposed meeting a friend would be discussed.

Your Story Is A "Crock Of Shit"

The questioning had returned to the source of the gun, with Kessinger's having told Boney that his entire story had been a "crock of shit," but that if he had given them the name of the gun dealer that could possibly "validate [his] story."

How a name would have validated Boney's preposterous "crock of shit" story was beyond me. Still, Boney hadn't budged, as he said if he had identified the person, he "opens up doors of the worst kind of hell."

And then, for many more minutes, Gilbert and Kessinger had engaged in a tag-team match, demanding of Boney that he needed to provide the name of the source of the gun, with Boney, of the man's age, quipping, "He's in-between three and 93 [years of age]" and telling the two that the man was feared throughout Louisville.

Kessinger had tried to further coax the Shoe Bandit: "[Your] story is, it's a good one. But I don't know that we can believe it. It sounds good. *It could fit*,[449] if it could be substantiated."

The 30-year Louisville detective, though, had soon done a 180-degree turn after Boney had still refused to provide the name. "I don't buy your story. I think it's a story of convenience. You asked to be alone in here, and I think the reason you asked to be alone here so you could think up something that would be plausible enough, palatable enough, believable enough, that we would buy it. And you had to think of a way that you could integrate both your sweatshirt and the gun and your DNA and your palmprints all into that crime scene without you being there."

Finally, I thought, Kessinger had been doing what a good interrogator should do. It's time to shove Boney's bullshit story right up his ass. But then, reality had set in, once again, as I continued reading and listening: "I think you were there when David shot his family. I think you were there, I don't know if you helped him. I don't know if you just watched. I don't know if maybe you removed some clothing from somebody, but you were there. *You were there with David Camm.*"[450]

I knew the answer, but I still had to mentally ask: how had it come to be that two very seasoned, and no doubt, experienced detectives, had chosen to embrace the blood spatter opinions of Stites and Englert while ignoring hordes of evidence from various different areas and sources which had explicitly pointed to both Dave's innocence and Boney's guilt?

Returning to the interrogation, although I wouldn't have classified it as such, Kessinger, who had assumed the Alpha Dog role, had educated Boney again: "You tell me where you got the gun and who you got the gun off of, and I can verify and validate your story, I might believe you."

While he had then been engaged in a tirade, denigrating Boney's nickname, Kessinger had landed on the truth. "I don't have anything in that story that you've told me...that has not been known up to this point. You haven't furnished us with that."

Henderson's point man was practically pleading, "We knew the *connection*. We knew there had to be *an additional connection*; we pretty much figured out what we thought happened. But you have got to fill in all the blanks."

There was absolutely no way that Kessinger or Gilbert would have

---

449 Emphasis mine.
450 Emphasis mine.

accepted a story that hadn't included Dave, as they had been trying to find something, anything, to corroborate Boney's story, and he hadn't helped with anything other than what had been publicly known.

Gilbert, though, had taken his turn, also belittling Boney's story: "I think you tried to come up with this story the best you could when you were in here alone, and a lot of the pieces in the jigsaw puzzle are just there because you didn't have enough time to think about it."

Gilbert, however, then had given Boney another out: "*You know the story* and you can fill in those missing jigsaw puzzle parts for us. And frankly *I think we would have a better case with David Camm*[451] as well."

One didn't need a United Nations translator to have determined the meaning of that comment: "You be the witness we need you to be, our case against Camm will be better because of you, and you will benefit accordingly."

After several more minutes of making demands, for the second time that evening, the tape recorder had "stopped abruptly." The tape recorder utilized by the two detectives had a proclivity, it had seemed, to have "stopped abruptly."

Before he had answered another question, Boney had talked, but not about the photograph he had been shown repeatedly of a dead little boy lying on the floor. Instead he had spoken of *his* "fucking nightmare" of having lost his normal life of "taking kids to school, buying groceries, losing my jobs, going to work."

And then, finally, after thanking both Gilbert and Kessinger for having been "patient" with him, Boney had capitulated on giving them the name of the gun dealer: "All right. His name is Larry Gerkin."

Gerkin, nickname Slim, reported Boney, had resided in the West End of Louisville, had sold guns and narcotics, and had agreed to meet Boney after having been called on the phone number Boney had remembered from years before. That number, remembered for the eight years he had been in prison, alas, had since been forgotten by Boney.

The crafty Boney, however, said he had spoken on the phone in code with Slim, as he had referred to a gun as an "extension." They had met at a West End car wash in Louisville where Slim had opened the trunk of his car, which had been described by Boney as something which looked like "you'd do a drive-by in." In the trunk was a gun in a plastic bag, purchased, Boney had recalled, for something less than $100.

Boney had even recalled that Gerkin had a "ball fade" haircut, saggy pants, no gold teeth, and no identifiable jewelry. And, oh yes, he had always worn a "regular mustache."

---

[451] Emphasis mine.

The ever-cautious Boney, although a "terrible criminal," had then been smart enough, after taking possession of the gun, to have removed the gun from the bag and to have wrapped it in his sweatshirt, the same sweatshirt with his prison nickname.

Kessinger had been pleased, as he had then told Boney, since all they had wanted from him was his "story." The veteran cop had admitted to Boney that the "fresh eyes" had taken a "tremendous gamble, a tremendous chance" leaving Boney free.

The man who had investigated dozens of homicides continued, "The defense wanted you arrested immediately, murder warrants issued immediately. We were taking some chances, but we were trying to validate your story."

Borrowing one of Kessinger's own phrases, their investigation and interrogation of Boney had been a "crock of shit," as they hadn't done a modicum of investigation, especially with the bogus alibi witnesses, nor had they spoken with Boney's friends, neighbors, co-workers, or others who would have given them additional evidence, and much more, to convict Boney for three murders.

Regardless, after Boney had provided the name of Larry Gerkin, rather than drill Boney on any other parts of his fabricated story, Gilbert had simply asked, "Charles, besides all the things we've discussed here this evening, before we conclude, is there anything else that you want to add?" Boney had said he hadn't thought of anything. Gilbert then concluded, "I have no further questions."

"No further questions." Amazing.

CHAPTER 44

"The Conspiracy Note"

Boney Gets An Attorney

Unbeknownst to me at the time, of course, in the hours after Boney's written statement, had been the unresolved issue between BACKBONE and his two self-described friends, Kessinger and Gilbert: Dave, in fact, hadn't been incriminated by Boney's totally self-serving story, particularly in view of the overwhelming forensic evidence against Boney. That Boney hadn't provided any details of the murders, nor of even being at the Camm home, was very problematic for their case, as they desperately needed a much better tale for their *connection*.

Recall that, at the time, I had known none of the details of the four interviews/ interrogations of Boney; thus, the Saturday morning after Boney had confessed he had only been a victim, taken in by Dave's evangelizing of Jesus Christ, only to have then been tricked into selling Dave a dirty and untraceable gun, I had ventured forth to the Floyd County Jail in order to try and interview Boney by myself. I had been unsuccessful, as access to Boney had been denied to me.[452]

"IN ORDER TO KEEP HIM FROM GETTING THE DEATH PENALTY, [WILKERSON] THOUGHT [WE] SHOULD ASK MY SON ABOUT SIGNING THE CONSPIRACY NOTE."

On that same Saturday, March 5, Kessinger and Gilbert had gone to Louisville and, with the assistance of Kessinger's LMPD officer son, had secured consent from Boney's fiancé to search their apartment. It had been the second search of the unit in three days, but they had previously left behind a cable bill from mid-2004, which they had then seized as evidence. In addition to basic cable and a premium channel, that bill had reflected that several movies had been purchased by Boney, including *Panty Frenzy 2*, *Pantyhose Passion 1*, and the ever-popular tandem of *Foot Teasers 1 & 2*—all just additional examples of, no doubt, fraternity pranks.

---

[452] Still, and since that time, I've often thought of what might have happened had I been allowed to speak with the Shoe Bandit. As with polygrapher Ennis, who would have jumped at the opportunity to interrogate Boney, I would have given anything to have spent a few hours together with the guy.

Later that same afternoon, Kessinger and Gilbert had checked in with Boney at the jail but hadn't asked him any questions as BACKBONE had secured an attorney, Lisa Harris Thalmann, a friend of Boney's mother. The attorney had met with Boney for an hour earlier in the day, and, upon her advice, he had refused to talk with the two.

The New Interrogator Is Related To Boney

The next day, Sunday, a new player had emerged on the scene. Myron Wilkerson, an ISP sergeant who specialized in drug investigations,[453] had been personally asked by Henderson if he would attempt to get Boney to talk. The thinking behind that request had been that Wilkerson, a black officer, might have a better rapport with Boney. The fact that Wilkerson had also been related to Boney's mother, no doubt, also had an added benefit.

Wilkerson had quickly gone to work and had first contacted Boney's mother at her New Albany home, asking her if she'd agree to visit her son in jail. The purpose of the visit? According to Mrs. Boney, Wilkerson had explained, "In order to *keep him from getting the death penalty*, he thought either my daughter or myself should come down and ask my son about signing the *conspiracy note*."[454]

What was the urgent need to have Boney confess to a conspiracy? Mrs. Boney had quoted Wilkerson, "If he waited too long, Keith Henderson was not going to make any deals. Now was his best time to do this if he wanted to save his life."

Mrs. Boney, who had already been taking medication for the shock involved in her son's arrest, had been too upset to speak with her son but had instead suggested that Wilkerson ask her daughter to speak with her brother.

Charles' older sister, Jacqueline,[455] had then been called by her mother, and the daughter had arrived at her mother's house late that afternoon. Wilkerson had schooled Jacqueline on some of the details of the crime scene, including her brother's palmprint's having been found on Kim's Bronco.

The drug detective, who had also told Jacqueline that Boney had been facing the death penalty, had prevailed in his request, and she had agreed to "go down and talk with Darnell [and] to convince him to sign some papers."

Jacqueline's visit to jail had been quickly approved and she had been

---

[453] Up until then, Wilkerson's only roles in the murder case had been to assist in protecting the crime scene, to have surveilled the home of the Schwan's delivery man until the arrival of the interview team, and to have retrieved and reviewed the dates and times of the telephone numbers from and to Kim's phones.

[454] Emphases mine.

[455] Pseudonym.

granted access to her brother, whom she had told, "If you are involved in it, you need to tell them everything. You need to tell the truth." She had also known her brother had been "facing the death penalty." Clearly, Jacqueline had been trying to help her brother save his life.

During the time brother and sister had met, the two had cried together, with Darnell insisting to Jacqueline that he had not "pull[ed] the trigger" and that he "would never kill kids."

His sister had responded, telling Darnell "It's best to confess. To confess your involvement with David Camm."

Boney's response had been no response, according to Jacqueline's later recollection: "He didn't say anything. He just looked at me. He just stared at me." Her effort didn't result in Darnell's writing any statement.

Much of what had transpired that Sunday had apparently been done without Gilbert's knowledge, as his report reflected that he had been contacted by Wilkerson at 6:30 p.m. Sunday evening. It was then he had been told that Wilkerson had become involved in the case due to Henderson's request. Upon Gilbert's arrival in New Albany from Evansville later that night, he, Kessinger, Wilkerson, and Henderson had conferred, with the drug detective promising the others he would try to convince Boney to confess that he and Dave had conspired with one another.

At this point, I stopped and mentally reviewed the situation. That Henderson had been behind the new approach to Boney, who had already invoked his attorney-client privilege, was a strong indication to me that the prosecutor, late on a Sunday evening, was truly desperate to get Boney to provide a much better story than the one Kessinger had referred to as a "crock of shit." They had badly needed *both* Boney and Camm intimately involved with one another in any future story.

Boney, however, hadn't been in the mood to cooperate with Wilkerson and again had refused to talk that Sunday night, but only after the Shoe Bandit had telephoned his attorney, with Thalmann having advised him, once again, not to give a statement.

Yet another day had passed, and upon Gilbert's arrival on Monday morning in the prosecutor's office, he had been told by Henderson that Boney's counsel had a 9:00 a.m. meeting with Henderson. Afterwards, Thalmann would enter an appearance in court on behalf of her new client.

Boney's attorney, though, had been a no-show for the meeting with the prosecutor. That failure to appear might have been related to what Mrs. Boney had later termed a "confrontation" between Wilkerson and Thalmann. According to Mrs. Boney, the drug detective, after having spoken with Attorney Thalmann, had told Mrs. Boney that she really didn't need the attorney, "that [the attorney] would be more trouble than she would be good" to her son, and "that she [Thalmann] was a black woman going to make a name for herself.'"

Regardless of whatever had caused her to change her mind, Thalmann had then sent a fax to Henderson at 10:43 a.m., telling him that she had met with Boney earlier that morning and was no longer going to be representing him.

With Boney's attorney now safely out of the picture, Wilkerson had once more spoken with Jacqueline and had arranged for her to meet privately in a detective's office with her younger brother.[456]

The siblings had met, with Jacqueline again telling her brother, "It's best for [you] to confess, to confess your involvement with David Camm." She had also reminded Darnell that he had been facing the death penalty. His sober reaction had been "Yeah, I know. I realize what's at hand."

Fifth Interview: "How Can I Prove David Camm Was Affiliated With You?"

With the skids sufficiently greased, Wilkerson, for his third time, had then met with Boney, and that 3:48 p.m. meeting had, indeed, generated results, but only after Wilkerson had thoroughly educated BACKBONE:

"My motive right now is to keep you alive. I've told you off the record,[457] but now I'll tell you on the record, you're going to have a hell of a time getting around with what's already there. Your best scenario is to be a witness. I told you downstairs, no more diversions, okay? The attorney is no longer a diversion. Charles, you're stubborn, you're scared and you're an opportunist. Know what I mean by that Charles? You understand? You need to let go. Do you know David Camm?"

Boney had been ready to talk and he first had replied that he had known David Camm, having met him at Community Park playing basketball, with at least "10 people plus any amount of additional people that were waiting on the sidelines for the next games." Unfortunately, however, Darnell couldn't recall the names of any of the others present.

The next time the two had met was, by chance, at the Better Way Food Mart, "right next to Karem's Meats." Dave, Boney had said, had been driving the black Bronco, but "was hesitant about talking to me . . . looking toward Karem's Meats to see if maybe someone there was watching him."

Still, Boney had insisted, in the ten minutes they had spoken, many

---

[456] Wilkerson had not written anything in any report about having met either Mrs. Boney or Jacqueline prior to his interview with Darnell.

[457] It would be impossible to surmise just how many times Charles Boney had been contacted, interviewed, and/or educated "off the record" over the course of almost three weeks.

different topics had been discussed: playing basketball in the past, future games, other places where they could play, jobs, what Boney had been doing to stay out of trouble, Boney's job at Anderson Wood, Boney's prior crimes, his prison time, how Boney had been surviving, Boney's trade skills, other things Boney had done to make money, Boney's having done drugs, and Boney's thinking Dave had been leading up to a "job offer" or perhaps "use [Dave] as a reference."

All of that had been discussed in ten minutes, all while Dave had been "hesitant about talking."

And then, Dave had asked BACKBONE if he had ever sold any weapons, to which Boney said he had. In fact, he had a good connection, but a gun would cost Dave $500. Dave had countered that he only had $250. Unlike his story to Gilbert and Kessinger, however, this time Boney had added the important aspect of Dave's having wanted an automatic. Perhaps one of those "off-the-record chats" had already paid dividends.

The two of them, Boney had claimed, had then met in the hospital parking lot, and the gun/cash exchange had occurred. Boney had added that he had known for four years that Dave had killed his family, but, he'd added, "Unless [I] was there, [I] wouldn't know for sure, and that's one thing that I can't say."

That Boney had denied being at the crime scene had caused Wilkerson to erupt:

"That's bullshit, Charles! That's why we're here! That's the come to Jesus! That's the saving element! Charles, Don't fuck with me! You had to be there! Scientifically, you was there. You was there when that family was killed, Charles. God damn it, Charles, you're there!"

The tirade had continued:

"Stop playing games with your grave, okay? Do you understand, Charles? You can't afford that at this point in the game. Charles, let me tell you again: you are at that scene. You're no dummy. Let me ask you something, Charles, if David Camm had this opportunity to come clean, what do you think he's going to do? He's going to hang your black ass."

Wilkerson had then invoked the personal connection:

"You know David Camm. You got him the gun. I know he did [kill his family]. You know he did, Charles, cause you was there. I will tell you, man to man, I swear I'm not coming back, Charles. You understand? This is it. When I walk out of here today, I'm going back to what I do best, working dope.

> "I KNOW [DAVID CAMM] DID IT, YOU KNOW HE DID, CHARLES, 'CAUSE YOU WAS THERE. NOW, HOW DO YOU KNOW DAVID CAMM KILLED HIS FAMILY?"

You with me? I'm here because I know your mother, and I met your sister, and we share family members. Now, how do you know David Camm killed his family"?

Boney had denied any other involvement but only had responded that he "gave him the gun." He continued, "I sold it to him. I honestly did not kill anyone."

Wilkerson then had pivoted toward Boney's being a witness to the murders:

"Did you see anybody killed, Charles? Did you see anybody killed, Charles? You need to answer the question. Why are you holding this, Charles? What do you have to gain? What the fuck do you have to gain holding on? You're done. I told you in no uncertain terms: the goal is save one's life, Charles. One's ass is of utmost importance to them, Charles. You have a potential for a death penalty. Did you see David Camm shoot anyone?"

And, just in case Boney had been really thick-headed, Wilkerson had added:

"What's your role, [that] is the million-dollar question. How you became involved is a very important question. These can also be saving factors, Charles."

Given all of that, Boney had reverted to his having "given the investigators three sets of alibis," with his knowing they hadn't been verified. I had to think of the fact that Gilbert and Kessinger still hadn't even attempted to verify Boney's false alibis. That had been tragic, sad, frustrating, and idiotic.

Wilkerson had been unfazed with the alibi response, however, and he had hit his relative with the fact the Cadillac of Boney's had been seen in the area of the Camm house. He also continued with his long-term lecture:

"Don't let [your mother] go to her grave with you on death row. You was in that garage that night, Charles! And even worse, Charles, they can put you in that garage. It's time to put it to rest. Charles, why was you at the Camm residence the night the children were killed and their mother? Why was you there? What was your role?"

Faced with the death penalty or being a witness, Charles Boney had known the game was *Let's Make a Deal*, and he had then chosen Door Number Two. Rather than face the death penalty, he would be their witness: "The reason why I was there was to bring him the gun."

Ah. BACKBONE had finally admitted to being *there*.

To reinforce the witness role, Wilkerson had asked Boney:

"Do you have any reason to hold anything else back now? Let it go now, cause the only other, the worst case scenario, is that you pulled the trigger." There was no translation needed on that comment.

Ever true to his victimhood, Boney had replied, "David Camm's intention was to kill not only his family, but me, too, because when he aimed the gun at me, it jammed. That gave me enough time to get into my car and drive."

Wilkerson had wanted to know what Boney had *seen*, but BACKBONE said he had "only heard the shots." He then had claimed that he had gone to the Camm home, had given Dave the weapon, and then approximately three minutes had passed when Kim and the kids had arrived.

Wilkerson had asked if Dave and Kim had been arguing. Boney had replied, "I don't remember."

When did things go bad, Wilkerson had wanted to know. "When I heard someone say no, and that was his wife. And then [I] heard a pop." Boney had been away from the gunfire, of course, "parked in the driveway."

So, if I had gotten all that right, Boney had delivered the gun to Dave; three minutes had elapsed; Kim and the kids had come home, and there had been an argument; Boney had returned to his car; and, at some time or another, Dave had tried to kill him, but the gun had jammed.

Boney had then added, "I'm already in this now, man, so I can't lie about it."

Wilkerson had reassured, but then cautioned Boney:

"You're a very articulate young man [but] it's going to take more than your statements to close the coffin." That box of death, of course, belonged to Dave.

"It's going to take all of it, and then somebody's got to do some legwork. They've got to be able to say, 'Charles Boney told us this, but this is how we know it's true. Cause, can we listen to this convicted felon? So you see why we can't have no loopholes here?"

Good luck with that legwork, I thought. The "fresh eyes" couldn't have even been bothered to have checked Boney's bogus alibis. It would be highly doubtful they'd attempt to corroborate any of his other lies.

Wilkerson's approach to Boney had been a forceful, blunt, in-your-face, hard interrogation. It could have worked on Boney, except for the fact Wilkerson had also been a staunch member of the "fresh eyes" groupthink:

"How can I prove David Camm was affiliated with you?"

The Shoe Bandit had responded, "If anyone had seen us play basketball and talk together. If anyone [had] seen us at Karem's." And no, they had never gone out to eat. They had never talked on the phone.

Wilkerson had become somewhat frustrated, I thought, as he then had asked Boney how he had wound up at Camm's house in the first place. "I knew how to get there because of him," Boney had replied, further stating, that after the Better Way meeting, he had "followed [Dave] back to his place, so [he]'d know how to get there."

Boney hadn't recalled the vehicle Dave had been in, even though he had previously claimed Dave had been in the Bronco. Recall, though, that

Boney, in his Friday tutorial, had been previously schooled by Kessinger that Dave had driven a "company truck" and not the Bronco. The only problem, of course, had been that he couldn't describe the truck; ergo, Boney hadn't ventured a guess on the color or description of the truck.

Continuing, after the two had arrived, they had stood in the driveway and talked about the price for the gun. It had been then that Boney had then admitted telling a little lie: "I honestly didn't go to [the] hospital. I went and followed him." And then, after claiming to Kessinger and Gilbert that he had gotten the gun "within five minutes," he had done some re-calculating with Wilkerson and said, "So, at that time, I wouldn't have had a weapon yet."

Boney had explained that he had left the meeting with Dave, but that it had taken a few days for Boney to have located a gun from his buddy Gerkin.

Boney had kept talking, though, and when BACKBONE had met Gerkin, he had paid him "less than $100" for a gun in a plastic bag, which Boney had then wrapped in his sweatshirt. But, oh wait, Boney had another recollection: that gun, as were all the guns in Gerkin's trunk, was "freshly oiled, so, once I dumped the weapon into the sweatshirt, that's how oil would have gotten on it."

One of the previous questions/suggestions of Kessinger's had been: "Do you recall any spots like that on [your sweatshirt], stains on there? Did you ever wrap anything in that sweatshirt...did you ever wrap a weapon in it or anything like that?"

I quickly recapped Boney's story: he had purchased the now semi-automatic gun at a busy car wash from a "crackhead" whom he had known for over 15 years, but had forgotten his number, but who had been motoring around in a "drive-by" car, who had "freshly oiled" his guns, which he had displayed and sold out of the trunk of his car. Oh, and he had been deathly afraid of Gerkin–not to be confused with Jerkin'—but now he wasn't.

How had Boney and Camm met, Wilkerson had wanted to know. "Did you go directly to Camm with this handgun?"

Since the two hadn't had each other's phone numbers, there had been no way to contact one another. Thus, Boney had said, "No, we waited, waited for another day. He and I did agree that we would meet on a certain day. That particular day, we would [meet] sometime towards the end of the week, and we didn't know exactly what day it would be, but it ended up being on that Thursday."

So, the buyer and seller had no means of contact or communication, but had been going to meet "sometime," which "ended up [on] Thursday."

And then, Boney had tried but failed to clarify the confusion, saying that he "didn't know exactly how to get back to [Dave's] house, didn't have a number by which to call him, didn't know exactly where he worked, [and] didn't know his cell number."

Wilkerson, no doubt as baffled as was I, then had asked, "how did you get back in touch with him?"

"I knew that, well, the, the one thing that we did say, was like Wednesday or Thursday, and I was like 'where,' and he was like, 'where you going to be,' and I said, 'I can just meet you at the Better Way.' So, I knew that at some point in time, especially with work schedules, and stuff like that, we had picked that day."

What day? Wednesday or Thursday? Was I actually listening to anything that had resembled a cogent conversation?

By now, even Wilkerson had to ask, "That's not good enough. How did you know what time to meet him at the Better Way?"

"Specifically, that's one thing that puzzles me. I don't remember how we chose a time or how we came about meeting on that particular day. I don't remember. I honestly don't remember." Ah. Boney *honestly* doesn't remember.

Wilkerson, an experienced drug detective, had, no doubt, been told a ton of lies in his career, but rather than calling a timeout and telling Boney that he had been lying through his teeth, as had polygrapher Ennis concluded, the distant cousin had then asked Boney if he and Dave had met "on the day of the murders at the Better Way?"

Well, as a matter of fact they had, Boney contended, even though Dave, at least according to Boney, had kept looking at Karem's Meats, as he had done during their first encounter at the same location.

Boney had been asking Wilkerson to believe that Dave had been so concerned about being seen in front of Kim's sister and brother-in-law's store that he had agreed to meet Boney at the same place weeks later. Had that even remotely been plausible?

Not a problem, though, as Boney then had claimed Dave had given him $250 for the gun and had said, "he had another thing for me to do. He wanted me to find him another weapon. So, at that time, I followed him back.

What was the need to have followed Dave back to his house? That question hadn't been asked, as Boney's story had continued. After having arrived at the Camm residence, Boney had waited outside, and then "his family had come home, in the black Bronco, and, uh, I just remember hearing someone saying, 'No.'"

It was beyond stunning to me. Boney had been claiming that Dave, on the night of the murders, had been at the Better Way in New Albany, paying $250 for a gun, and then had driven to his house in some kind of vehicle other than the Bronco with Boney's following him. That had left no time whatsoever for

Dave to have ever been at the church gym, where literally everyone, including Stan Faith, had agreed he had been.

The Shoe Bandit had then kept talking about his presence near the Camm garage, recalling that Kim had asked, "'Who's he,' referring to [Boney]."

Boney then claimed he had heard "a little bit of chatter and then [he'd] heard, 'No.'"

Asked if he had heard the children, Boney said he had "like out, like, out of fear." What did that mean, Wilkerson had wanted to know. Boney had then said, "I didn't hear them say anything." So, he had heard them, but then he hadn't heard them?

And Dave, by the way, had been wearing "workout" clothes, which included "jogging pants." Literally no one, at any time, had ever seen Dave wearing anything other than shorts that night. The pathological liar just couldn't help himself, however, as he added his own imaginary details to his manufactured story.

After he'd heard the first "pop," which Boney had known was a gunshot, he had then heard a second shot. What, Wilkerson had wanted to know, had he heard Bradley say? Boney had quickly answered, "He didn't say anything. It was the sound he made." And the sound? "I recall him saying, 'Daddy.'"

I stopped and recalled that Gilbert had testified in the most recent bond hearing that their third prison informant, imprisoned for convictions of rape and kidnapping, had told them Dave had claimed to have heard Brad say, "Daddy" during the murders. It wasn't much of a stretch for me to believe that aspect of Boney's story had also been given to him, either during the times the tape recorder had "abruptly stopped," during times Boney had been convinced to drop his lawyer, and/or at any other of the hours of meetings with Boney that hadn't been documented in any fashion.

The story had continued from the psychopath: "I heard a third pop," and that was when "David Camm came out and I asked him, in so many words, 'what the fuck?' Cause I was scared. That's when he proceeded to point the weapon at me. He was winded, distressed. He had a real scary look on his face. I seen [sic] the weapon pointed at me, and he pulled it. It jammed."

How had he known the gun had jammed? "Because I'm sure there were more than three projectiles in that weapon." The same weapon that he hadn't bothered to check, at least during his prior story to the "fresh eyes," had now been a gun with multiple "projectiles."

The tale had continued, with Boney's telling the drug detective that Dave hadn't said anything, but rather, "he tried to play it off," even though Boney had known he had shot his wife and children. "Play it off?" How the hell do you "play off" three murders?

Boney had continued. He had almost forgotten that he had left out a piece of information. At the moment Dave had pointed the gun at him, "at that time, I am in the garage. I am in defense mode." There was no explanation as to how he had gone from being outside the garage, unable to see, but only hear of the prelude to the murders and the actual murders, to being inside the garage in "defense mode."

The storyteller had continued, as he had also seen Kim lying on the garage floor, wearing white pants, as Dave had begun running into the house, saying, "You did this."

That Boney had seen fit to remember, in the utter chaos of everything, that Kim was on the floor, still wearing her white pants, was significant, for that meant, of course, that he couldn't have been responsible for the removal of the pants, nor of Kim's having to change into black underwear. There had been no follow-up, though, by the drug detective, who had achieved his primary goal of putting Dave with Boney at the murder scene.

What else had he seen in the garage while Dave had run away? "I took a look at, at each of the victims," even Bradley and Jill in the back seat of the car. Boney had recalled that Jill had been wearing her seatbelt and that Brad had been "doubled over."

So, the story was that Boney had found himself in the garage, after Dave had killed all three, and then Dave had tried to kill Boney. As Dave had run into the house, Boney, rather than run away, had stopped to look at each of the three victims, even recalling how each had looked, rather than running away, scared for his own life. Of course, inherent in looking in the Bronco was the fact he had touched it with his left palm. That explained how his palmprint was on the vehicle.

Also, of course, the man who had bought and sold guns apparently hadn't had one of his own to defend himself against the crazed killer. Boney without a gun had contradicted several of his friends/workers who had repeatedly seen him, a convicted felon, carrying a weapon.

Wilkerson, however, had been mostly pleased, letting his relative know, "You're telling some truths." The drug detective, however, had thought Boney might not have followed Dave home but had driven there with him. That line, though, hadn't been pursued.

Boney, meanwhile, had been off on another direction, telling Wilkerson that he finally had gone back to his own car and had driven it away, for he, once again, had felt "scared."

As Boney had driven away, he had seen, in his rearview mirror, another vehicle turn into Dave's driveway, the event to which Gilbert had testified in the bond hearing. That vehicle, Boney claimed, had been driven by a female and was a "state-issued vehicle, uh, like a Crown Victoria."

"Did it have red lights on it?" Wilkerson had wanted to know. It had no red lights, Boney had said, but it "was possible that it was a police car."

Boney had gone from the utter unbelievable to the complete bizarre, as he had been trying to implicate a female trooper who had been friends with Dave and who had been viewed with suspicion by many of her male counterparts.[458] That Boney had known to include her in the story had meant that he had been educated, yet again, at some time or another, in that non-public aspect of the case. There was no doubt, at least in my mind, the master storyteller was trying to tell them what they had wanted to hear.

Wilkerson, although telling Boney there had been "holes" in his story, had been encouraging of his protégé. "I believe you've told me a lot of truths, Charles." Still, Wilkerson had been "pissed" that Boney hadn't told him of their biggest need, which had been the "agreement between you and David."

Wilkerson had then driven the point home: "Do you want to sit in front [of a jury] and ask them to believe the reason your palm is on that door is because you walked in there to look at these bloody bodies *after the fact* Charles? You're excluding yourself from pulling any triggers. You're making a fatal mistake. If you pulled a trigger, I need to know it. If you killed that family and you were not hired, I need to know it."

Along that same line, recall that at the recent bond hearing, Henderson had filed a motion claiming that Dave had "committed a murder by hiring… Charles Boney…to kill." So far, there had been nothing whatsoever from Boney which had remotely suggested that he had been hired. If Henderson had claimed it happened, though, Wilkerson was trying his best to fill the hole.

The drug detective had kept on that same track: "There was an agreement other than the gun that night, Charles, between you and David."

Boney had insisted there had been nothing more, as his story, as it had been told, didn't include him in any violence, but only in his having sold Dave a gun. A gun which Boney had no idea was going to be used in murdering anyone. As Wilkerson had summarized it, "You just happened to be there on this night, and he lost his cool, and he killed his family."

Finally, a light had dawned on Wilkerson, when he thought, at least for a moment, perhaps Boney alone had slaughtered the Camm family: "If you pulled a trigger, if you played Billy Bad Ass and then you punked out, I need to know it. If you killed that family, and you were not hired, and that is the truth, I need to know it."

---

[458] She had become a suspect because she had expressed support and compassion for Dave in the aftermath of the murders and prior to his arrest.

Boney had reassured his cousin, saying, "I wouldn't have killed that family. No."

The momentary lapse towards the truth had quickly ended. "Well, I'm glad to hear that. I hope that's the truth." That Boney could have acted without Dave's involvement had been dismissed with the wave of a hand, as Wilkerson had asked, "Did you help him clean it up or something," followed by "Make a deal with him to kill his family?"

Boney had responded that he had not conspired with Camm. Wilkerson then wanted to know why, if all he had done was to sell a gun, hadn't he come forward four years earlier? Because, Boney had replied, he had been a felon, who had sold a gun, who had been on probation, and who hadn't wanted to return to prison.

That explanation had been palatable to Wilkerson. After all, Boney couldn't have told him the real reason he hadn't come forward four years earlier: "I had tracked and then had violently tackled and sexually assaulted a mother, Kim, at gunpoint, in her darkened garage, shooting her point-blank in the head; and then I shot her helpless, terrified, and screaming, little five-year old daughter, Jill, in the head; and then finally took aim and shot little seven-year old Brad in the chest while he had been looking at me. Oh, and I really don't give a damn about those three lives because I'm a remorseless psychopath who loves to lie to and manipulate you ignorant cops."

Rather than ram the totality of all of his lies down Boney's throat, Wilkerson, probably unaware Boney had already flunked seven polygraph exams, had then asked if the Shoe Bandit would take a lie detector test. Sure, said the habitual liar. Anytime.

Wilkerson had quickly thought about that and then had reconsidered. "I'd have to check. There are some important factors here. Did David act alone? It's going to be a hard time [because] the first thing they're going to do is jump up and down. 'Uh-huh, he's the one that did it.'"

There had been only one way to construe that comment—anything which could have helped the defense, even the truth, was, of course, verboten.[459]

It had been time for Boney to again make his own self-serving statement, as he had claimed that nothing would have ever made him "kill a mother and two children." He continued, "I would never do that. I don't kill kids. My name is BACKBONE. There is no way I would have killed a fucking kid."

A relentless Wilkerson, though, had kept with the need for Boney to divulge the "agreement," further telling him that he, Wilkerson, had wanted Boney "to win." Still, Boney wouldn't admit to any agreement.

---

[459] There had been another problem, unknown to Wilkerson, however, for the stipulated polygraph which Boney had thoroughly flunked, was between him and the prosecutor. Dave's defense couldn't use it in his defense.

It had been time for a break, however, and one had been taken, allowing Boney to eat dinner and, quite probably, again converse off the record with Wilkerson and/or others, especially after weighing Boney's uncorroborated narrative and finding it light years beyond far-fetched.

The Big Problem

Once back on the record, Wilkerson had told Boney of the dilemma facing the prosecution: "David Camm does have an alibi. He really does, and that's going to be a problem. He has an alibi that

> "DAVID CAMM DOES HAVE AN ALIBI. HE REALLY DOES, AND THAT'S GOING TO BE A PROBLEM. HE HAS AN ALIBI THAT IS NOT MATCHING UP WITH WHAT YOU'RE SAYING."

is not matching up with what you're saying. If you're not careful, you're going to be a better witness for him than against him. Do you understand?"

And then, reinforcing the theme of the "fresh eyes," Wilkerson had cut to the chase: "You either conspired to commit murder or you committed murder. If I were the prosecutor right now, I just got to be honest with you, and I'm going to take two people to trial for a triple murder, I'm going to be more comfortable with yours than his."

The fact that Henderson had been placing all of his chips on Charles Boney, the vicious and cold-blooded murderer of Kim, Brad, and Jill being both the underling and the linchpin with Dave had not only been undeniable but reprehensible.

In an attempt to corroborate something, anything, of Boney's story, including how he and Dave had arranged to meet for the gun transfer, Boney said he hadn't remembered how they had done so, nor had he remembered the vehicle Dave had been driving when he, Boney, had followed Dave home.

Wilkerson had clearly been frustrated, as he had told Boney they had a problem of the change in Boney's story of touching the Bronco in the garage rather than previously when he had met Dave at the hospital parking lot. Boney, though, had responded with his own question: "How do you get high velocity blood splatter and brain matter on you if you're not the shooter?"

"You've done your homework" had been Wilkerson's answer. That he had, Sergeant.

And then, continuing with his own defense, BACKBONE had asked the dope detective, "Does it make sense that I capped two and then gave him the gun, so he can cap one of his own family members? That doesn't make sense."

"None of it makes sense to me" had been Wilkerson's answer. Yeah, I thought, nothing had made sense because of the inability of anyone to consider the possibility Dave hadn't been involved.

Oh, I Forgot…About The Shoes

Asked to go over his story of being in the garage, Boney had obliged, and then, amazingly, had added, "I remember tripping over the shoes, and I remember touching them." He had even recalled they had been brown and "were in [his] path." The incredible then had become totally wacky, as the Shoe Bandit said, "when I tripped over those shoes, I remember picking them up, looking into the backseat . . . so that's when I would have placed them on top."

Rather than drill in on the preposterous shoe story, Wilkerson had asked, "How did you feel when you seen [sic] them kids in there?"

"Petrified" had been the victim Boney's answer, who had also opined that he thought Dave had been going into the house to get another weapon, which had caused BACKBONE to claim he had then "got the hell out of there."

"You've given me nothing to put you with him" had been the disappointed conclusion of Wilkerson, who then had lamented that Boney's story hadn't made any sense at all, but that Boney had been "there when the Camm family was killed."

The well-educated Boney had responded, "And David had high velocity blood spatter on him."

To reinforce his truthfulness, the psychopath had then pleaded with Wilkerson to have understood how it would have been "very difficult for me to sleep, and to function, and to be normal" if he had killed a child.

Okay, I thought, it would be very difficult for this guy to function, a man who had already bragged, "My conscience already holds three murders, [so] one more is not going to bother me anymore."

Boney, now controlling much of the interrogation, had then said, "David Camm and I are both at the crime scene. There's no doubt about that [but] he is the shooter [because of] high velocity blood spatter."

Wilkerson had readily agreed, "That's correct."

"But now, you just don't know what my role was. Did I participate or did I conspire?"

"Exactly right," agreed the dope detective, who probably hadn't even considered that Boney had now taken over the interrogation. To buttress that conclusion, Wilkerson had then asked, "why is he killing them with you sitting out in the driveway?"

"Because," BACKBONE quickly replied, "his goal was to kill them and then to kill me, and to make me look as if I had done it." Dave hadn't, continued Boney, because "the gun jammed." He then had reiterated that he had seen a woman who had "pulled in [Dave's] driveway." Clearly, Boney had wanted to capitalize on that gem.

Wilkerson, though, had been focused on his conspiracy, as he'd lectured, "It's more important to know what conversation did you and Davy have before the fact and during. It's more important to know exactly what role you…what was you promised?"

To underscore his truthfulness, Boney then had admitted to "lying about certain things" in his prior polygraph exams but proclaimed that he would have passed any future ones. Yeah, he actually said that the basis of his future truthfulness would have rested on his past deceptions.

And then Boney had asked Wilkerson if Henderson had been present during his ongoing interrogation.[460] He had been, Wilkerson said, to which Boney told the drug detective to ask the prosecutor if he could take another lie detector exam, promising the drug detective that he, Boney, would pass the question on whether or not he, Boney, had been present at the murders.

Of course Boney had been present. He had committed the murders. Boney, the ever-present manipulator, though, was trying to get a polygraph examiner to test him on whether or not he had just been present at the scene of three murders he had perpetrated.

Wilkerson, though, had wanted to know if everything Boney had told the drug detective had been truthful. He could pass that question, Boney asserted, as he also had told of being "crushed" and a "nervous wreck" when seeing Jill, shot through the head, and dead, still strapped in the backseat of the Bronco.

And then, ever the author willing to write more of his story, Boney had wanted to know what part of his rendition Wilkerson hadn't been "comfortable with."

Among other things, Wilkerson had said that after the gun had jammed, that Boney, with his size and strength, could have "kicked [Dave's] ass and "ended this right there" but had let Dave escape into the house.

Boney reiterated that he had been "scared to death" but then had said instead of running away, he had looked into the Bronco out of "curiosity." Boney had actually said it was "curiosity" that drew him to the Bronco and then led him to kick the shoes, to pick them up, and then to place them on top of the car. *Curiosity* from a man who had claimed he had been fearing for his life.

Wilkerson, still without his much-needed "conspiracy note," had then admitted that he was tired and was ending the questioning.

---

[460] Outside the interrogation room.

Boney had outlasted a veteran interrogator who had been thoroughly hamstrung by the mandate to have included a conspiracy when none had existed. It had then been time to turn Boney, still fresh and ready to answer questions, back to Gilbert and Kessinger. It would be their last chance to turn a "crock of shit" into a conspiracy.

Kitty, Stacy, Sam, and I had all routinely called or emailed one another as we had been going through the interviews, interrogations, and written ISP reports dealing with Boney. By the time we had finished with Wilkerson's failed quest for the "conspiracy note," we had all become enraged, furious, exasperated, and very saddened, as the possibility of any of the "fresh eyes" becoming anything other than programmed robots had been totally eliminated.

CHAPTER 45

"I'm All Storied Out"

Sixth And Last Chance Interview

After taking a respite, I sat down once more in an effort to find Gilbert's sworn but elusive conclusion that Dave and Boney had conspired to commit murder with one another.

After Boney had thoroughly worn out an exasperated Myron Wilkerson, it had taken another 30 minutes until he had sat down once again with Gilbert and Kessinger. If anyone had thought that Boney had been on the edge of finally admitting that he had done more than just sell a gun, that thought should have been dispelled by the fact Boney had refused to take a bathroom break and had refused any "refreshment." He had, it appeared to me, to have been energized by the inability of anyone to convince him to incriminate himself beyond being a gun broker.

Gilbert had summarized, albeit had also minimized, the dilemma of the "fresh eyes" quite well: "Mainly what we're trying to do

> HIS STORY WAS NOW IN THE TWILIGHT ZONE.

here, is kind of follow-up, and see if we can straighten out some of these inconsistencies, that just aren't quite making sense to us." He then had asked Boney to tell them, again, of his first meeting with Dave in July 2000, at the basketball courts at Community Park.

During this telling, Boney had the wherewithal to remember that there had been anywhere from "14 to 16, maybe even 18" players, both white and black, who ranged in age from 16 to 40. Alas, however, BACKBONE still hadn't recalled anyone by name. He had recalled, however, that after the game, Dave had talked to him about Jesus Christ.

Their next chance meeting, two months later, was at the Better Buy, where Boney had repeated his same story, including, of course, that Dave had kept looking towards Karem's Meats. Boney had needed money, he said, because he had "missed a lot of days" at Anderson Wood. Gilbert had asked if he had intentionally missed days, to which Boney said he had, because his work ethic wasn't good. Boney thought the two investigators had known that, because, he said, "By now, you surely have had a chance to talk to them."

Anderson Wood had already provided work records to the "fresh eyes." As such, they should have known that Boney had missed numerous days of work, including the evening of September 28, as had Ernest Nugent, on the same shift as Boney, and the same man who had admitted to having always carried guns and having sold a gun to Boney.

For some—okay, for almost all investigators—those facts would have been a possible clue that needed an intensive follow-up.

Regardless, Boney had said he had followed Dave home after that chance meeting, somewhere around the 15th of September. Yeah, he had previously lied, he said, about the hospital parking lot meeting, and he had also admitted he had lied about not being in Georgetown. After agreeing to a price of $250, and after knowing where to deliver the gun, Boney had been stumped as to when the delivery would occur. "We didn't honestly have, uh, a date, uh."

As for having obtained the gun from the enigmatic Larry Gerkin, Boney, unfortunately, upon viewing a number of photos Kessinger had secured from the LMPD, hadn't recognized any as Gerkin.

Regardless, after Boney had telephoned the man, Boney had recalled the gun dealer had quickly arrived at the car wash on Broadway, though, and, upon the popping of Gerkin's trunk, Boney said he had a "choice of at least twenty, they were all wrapped in plastic bags and all had been oiled. I chose a .380," which Boney had "guessed" was a semi-automatic. BACKBONE had then emphasized that he had then wrapped the gun in his sweatshirt and then had left.

The time he had left Gerkin? That had been problematic for BACKBONE whose memory was crystal clear on his alibi witnesses. "I'm just having problems with the times." Unfortunately, Boney and Camm hadn't communicated with phones because Boney had no cell phone, but he had then remembered the two "establishing a communication that allowed [them] to meet one more time" back at the Better Way.

After Boney had waited at the convenience store for ten minutes, Dave had appeared, and the two had exchanged the money for the gun, although Boney had a "very difficult" time recalling on which side of Dave's car, which he now thought might have been a light-colored Buick, they had made the deal.

And then things had changed again. Rather than the gun transaction occurring the same night, Boney had said it had been within two or three days. Boney had insisted, though, that Dave had then ordered another gun. They would meet when? Uh, Boney hadn't remembered "how [he] set that date," but "to the best of [his] recollection, it would be at that Better Way again."

His story was now in the twilight zone. Dave, who hadn't wanted to be seen, had now agreed to meet Boney two more times adjacent to Karem's Meats, a place where he had looked extremely nervous, to conduct yet another gun transaction?

Neither Gilbert nor Kessinger had halted the unstoppable liar, as Kessinger had asked the time of the next meeting. "Somewhere between 4:00 and 5:00" had been Boney's answer. They had met at that time, but Boney hadn't been able to find another gun for Dave, as Gerkin had apparently already sold the other 19 guns in his trunk.

After the two had met, Boney had said he had then followed Dave back to his house to get the money for another gun, although the amount of money had been "undetermined because [they] hadn't talked exactly about what he wanted."

And the vehicle Dave had driven which Boney had followed for over ten miles from New Albany to Georgetown? "I don't, I don't remember. It was just a regular vehicle."

After a moment's pause, Boney had then remembered that he had followed Dave to also retrieve the BACKBONE sweatshirt. Why hadn't he dumped the gun from the sweatshirt at Better Way? "I knew I was going to his house anyway, so I don't remember that being a topic of conversation."

So, Boney had followed David back to his house to retrieve his sweatshirt, which he could have done while parked at Better Way, but it wasn't a "topic of conversation."

Illogical comments notwithstanding, Boney said he had arrived at Dave's house between 5:00 and 5:30 with Dave going into the house to get the money for Boney. It was at that time the Bronco had arrived, as "Mrs. Camm, she waved at me,"[461] as she passed Boney's Cadillac and parked at the end of the Camm driveway as Boney had stood next to it. She "had a look on her face, like, 'who is that,'" but then had driven into the garage.

Kessinger had asked for more specifics, and Boney had told him that "five, six minutes pass and I remember her saying the word 'No,' like it was out of fear or fright, and that's when I heard the first pop. It was a gunshot."

That "pop," according to Boney, had caused him to "duck behind [his] car," when he heard a second and then a third pop."[462] Before the third pop, though, Boney had said, "All I remember hearing, what I believe was Bradley saying, 'Daddy.'"

So, if one took Boney at his word, the only words he had heard were "No" and "Daddy." There had been no yelling, screaming, or fighting, for if there had been, he surely would have heard all of that, particularly since he, behind his car and well outside the garage, had heard Bradley, from inside the Bronco, which was inside the garage, saying, "Daddy."

---

[461] That Kim had waved at Boney had probably been accurate at some time or another.

[462] It was then the detectives experienced still more issues with their tape recorder, as Gilbert said he had to start with a new recorder.

Additionally, everyone, including Faith, Henderson, and all the investigators had agreed that Kim had fought ferociously with her attacker, since she had sustained 22 bruises, cuts, and contusions, and had probably been tackled onto the concrete garage floor. The tops of her feet had been battered, causing immense pain, no doubt. Had all of that occurred without her screaming? Why hadn't Boney heard the commotion as Dave, in the "fresh eyes" story, had beaten the hell out of her? When, also, had her shoes and pants been removed?

And there was also the minor issue of the timing provided by Boney. It had been between 5:00 and 5:30 when Kim and the kids had arrived? Janice Renn, of course, had all three in her house at 5:30.

But Boney was about to be victimized in his story. He then said, "I seen [sic] David Camm aiming that same weapon at me, 15–20 feet away."

That made no sense at all, as Dave, according to Boney, had shot all three inside the garage, and Boney had described himself as hiding behind his car at the beginning of the Camm driveway, which, I knew, had been about 50 feet away from the garage entrance.

His story had continued, though, with Boney's saying he had remembered Dave "squeezing off the trigger, [but] it didn't fire. It appeared to have jammed, because there was no other pop." Boney had even recalled Dave's having a "distasteful look on his face," as he then had seen "blood coming from [Kim's] head." He continued, "I was in total shock. I remember tripping over something, which was, of course, the shoes."

I had become really confused. Boney had been at least 50 feet away from the garage; then he had been 15–20 feet away from Dave; and finally, he had been in the garage; all the while he had gotten much closer to Dave, the man he had been convinced was going to shoot him. The explanation from BACKBONE? "My intent was to try and get the gun away from him."

Dave, alas, had turned and gone up the garage stairs to the breezeway. Boney, by then, had tripped on the shoes and put them on top of the car. He then had looked into the back of the car to "see if there was still life." Jill had been strapped in her seatbelt, but Boney couldn't recall Brad's position, which had differed from his story to Wilkerson, when he had said Brad had been "doubled over." He also had forgotten his prior assertion, when Dave had approached him, claiming Dave had said, "You did this."

But wait! Boney had remembered a detail he had previously told Wilkerson. As he had raced out of the garage, jumped in his car, and as he was leaving the driveway, he'd "looked in [his] rear-view mirror because [he] seen a car coming upon [him], but then it stopped short of [him] and turned into the same driveway that [he] had just exited."

Lockhart Road was a gravel, *one-lane*, *dead-end* road. If Boney had been claiming to have only seen the car in his rear-view mirror, that meant the car had to have been lurking between the Camm driveway and the dead-end. Still, Boney continued, explaining that the car was similar to a cop car and had been driven by a white female whom he had "thought was a cop." He had continued, "I quickly dismissed it when I seen [sic] they weren't chasing after me."

Boney had been so perceptive, in fact, that after getting caught up in a triple homicide, almost being murdered himself, and then frantically fleeing the scene, that the female in the cop car, had, he specifically remembered, her "hair up."

After he had left the crime scene, Boney had driven around New Albany, picked up Mala, and then had gone to his former brother-in-law's home for a cookout, arriving "about 6:30."

At 6:30 p.m., of course, it had been proven that Dave had been logged on his computer, checking the day's stock prices. Within minutes of that time, the Schwan's man had parked in the driveway and had spent several minutes selling Dave two items, while Kim, Brad, and Jill had still been at swim practice with no less than 20 other witnesses.

There had been no words from the two detectives, however, challenging Boney's bogus time, other than Gilbert's bond hearing comment that he didn't "agree with" some of his "time lines."

As he continued his story to Gilbert and Kessinger, Boney had said he and Mala had spent almost three hours at the cookout. Still sticking with his need to borrow money for a car payment to his uncle, Boney had claimed he had taken Mala to her uncle, from whom she had obtained $150, which had been $50 more than Boney had previously claimed. He then had spent the night in a Louisville apartment of Mala's mother.

The next morning Boney had watched the news. He had said, "I knew the truth, that David Camm had killed his family, with me there as a witness." A benevolent Boney had finally decided to come clean but only after his talk with Wilkerson and because, he had said, "the Camm family needs closure."

Kessinger, who had conducted almost the entire interrogation, said, "Well, you had previously given us a 'crock of shit,' but what you've now provided has been a ton of shit." Okay, he didn't actually say that, but rather, said, "There's one thing wrong. It's just, it's not, all the times are off, the activities are off, [and] the cars are off."

The veteran Louisville detective had then asked how, if Boney had been a target, Dave would have explained shooting four victims with the same gun at his own house. "Maybe he wasn't thinking too clear," Boney had said, then adding, "I would have shot [me] with my gun and would have put [the other] gun in [my] hand."

Kessinger had then asked what Kim had been wearing. "White pants" had been the answer. Of course Boney had known the color of her pants. He had, as he had previously admitted in his first shoe theft interrogation, had a thing for women's pants. He had only attacked women who had worn pants.

Continuing, Boney had then reiterated that he had tripped over Kim's shoes. Kessinger had said her feet had been under the Bronco, and thus her shoes would have also been under the car. Boney, knowledgeable of much of the State's story, had responded that the "bodies ha[d] been moved."

Now it was really getting beyond the pale. So, Dave had moved Kim's body prior to walking outside to confront Boney?

Boney had then gone on the offensive and, referring to the "staged sweatshirt," had asked Kessinger why Dave had laid Brad on Boney's sweatshirt. The exasperated Kessinger had replied, "I don't know. *I'm* asking *you*."

The Shoe Bandit wasn't to be denied, though, as he had claimed, "My sweatshirt was nowhere in that garage, nowhere in that garage."

The two detectives had wanted Boney to sketch the scene, and he had eagerly complied, even putting an X on his location when he had looked into the car. No, he said, he hadn't touched either child, nor had he touched Kim. His DNA, though, could have been on the shoes, since yes, he had picked them up and placed them on top of the Bronco.

"You got a dead body laying [sic] in front of you, you got two dead children in the car, and you're worried about picking up a pair of shoes?"

"I asked myself the same thing. I picked them up and I put them out of the way" had been the Shoe Bandit's nonchalant answer.

Kessinger had continued with "It's not a rational act [not what] an average person would do," as he asked the reason why Boney had done so.

"I don't have any."

And just like that, the shoes had been dropped from any further questioning. The guy who had attacked numerous women for their shoes; paid $50 to a pole dancer for her "fresh" stocking; kept women's panties and pantyhose as souvenirs; bragged he could tell if a woman had pretty legs or not, even if she had worn pants; asked random women to see their toenails; routinely rented movies dealing with feet/shoe sexual obsessions; and had ejaculated over the feet of his wives and girlfriends, had no longer

"YOU DON'T HAVE YOUR TIMES STRAIGHT. THERE'S ABSOLUTELY NO WAY THAT DAVID COULD HAVE MET WITH YOU AT THE STORE, YOU FOLLOW HIM, AND EVERYTHING ELSE WITHIN THE TIME FRAME."

been asked any questions about his sexual compulsion involving women's feet and their shoes.

Kessinger had, in fact, moved on to when Boney had met David. And, once again, Boney, with help from Kessinger, had spun his story: Community Park; basketball; Better Way; the gun solicitation; Larry Gerkin with 20 guns in the back of his car; the purchase of a .380; the wrapping of the gun in Boney's sweatshirt; the return to New Albany; the second gun; and the return to Dave's house; although the first visit to Dave's house hadn't been recapped, as Kessinger, probably as confused as anyone, had asked, "You've only been to his house one time?"

And then, if it hadn't been deadly serious, the following could have been straight from the infamous Abbott and Costello comedy routine of "Who's on First?"

"How did you meet back up at Better Way Food Mart?" asked Kessinger.

"Cause we made a time in which were to meet," responded Boney.

"So why didn't he take you to the house? If you're supposed to deliver the gun at his house, why is he taking you there, and why are you leaving at Better Way at 6:30?"

"Because our first encounter, or not the first, but the second encounter, we had met at Better Way, in order to exchange money and the, and the weapon."

"Well why did he take you to his house on September 15, 2000?"

"So I would know where to bring the other one."

"You hadn't delivered the first one yet."

"The first one was delivered."

"He hadn't ordered the first, the second one yet."

"That's exactly what I'm talking about. In order to deliver the next weapon."

Finally, Kessinger had again admitted, "Okay, we're both confused," as he then said the two had met at Better Value, rather than Better Way. Nonetheless, another attempt had been made:

"Why did he take you to his house?" Kessinger had asked.

"So that I could drop something off there, he chose not to do that," Boney had responded.

"How did he get in touch with you to tell you this?"

"I was already in touch with him before I left his house."

By now, it had been apparent that Kessinger had been totally flummoxed, as he had tried to make sense out of Boney's totally convoluted and nonsensical story, asking why Boney had even gone to Dave's house in the first place, if they had always agreed to meet at Better Way. Boney's response had been priceless: "You're just putting words in my mouth."

Kessinger had responded, "We're just asking you to tell us everything."

Responded the man who had the precise times of all of his alibi witnesses from over four years prior, "I can't remember everything after five years . . . five years, you're not going to remember every little thing."

Every second of September 28 should have been "ingrained" in Boney's mind, responded Kessinger, who had then lamented that Boney's pitiful story had been "a crock of shit so far and *it's been transferred to us.*"[463]

That last part, at least to me, had been clear: their preposterous narrative was that Dave, and only Dave, could have killed his family in spite of 11 alibi witnesses and overwhelming forensic and other evidence against the real killer, who had no contact with Dave whatsoever; thus, they couldn't square their impossible circle.

In an attempt to shame Boney, Kessinger had shown him a photo of Kim, lying on the garage floor, clad in her panties, with the massive pool of blood around her head. That technique would have worked, perhaps, with a person who had possessed a conscience or exhibited remorse, but the guy Kessinger had been dealing with had possessed neither, as Boney's response was simple: "He killed her."

Rather than blow up Boney with the mendacious petard of his own making, Kessinger had asked if Boney had "recall[ed] seeing her standing in that garage beside that Bronco for three to six minutes leading to an altercation with David Camm before [he] heard that first pop?"

"I didn't actually see him shoot her. I just heard the pop." Only then had he seen a "lifeless" body and Dave with a "that silver gun in his hand." He had ducked behind his Cadillac because he had been "petrified" when he had heard Bradley. The third pop had been heard next, as Boney then had seen Dave coming at him, but thankfully the gun had either jammed or had run out of ammo.

Boney had then run after Dave, who had also been running into the house, with no mention of "You did this" by Boney. He might have caught the murderer, Boney had claimed, but he had then "tripped over the shoes."

Why in the world, I had to ask, didn't they ask a simple question? "Uh, Charles, according to your own assertion, you've been involved in buying and selling guns for years. You've used a gun in armed robberies. What make and caliber of gun were you carrying at the time of all of these murders?" That question, of course, hadn't been asked.

Finally, Gilbert, silent for much of the "interrogation," had asked a question: "What time did you arrive at the house the night of September 28?"

"It could have been 5:30, it could have been . . ."

"Could it have been later?"

---

[463] Emphasis added.

"I'm thinking not," replied the man who had reiterated he had been at the cookout at 6:30.

You're Lying, But....

Gilbert, finally, had told their star witness, "You realize that Kim isn't even home until 7:30? She had swim lessons. David was at basketball at 7:00. *We say he left*[464] to be involved in these murders and then got back before the game is concluded." The lead detective had continued, "You don't have your times straight. There's absolutely no way that David could have met with you at the store, you follow him, and everything else within the time frame. *You do know his alibi that he's using, don't you*?"[465]

Boney said he had known of Dave being with the other ball players. Gilbert's response was astounding: "There's only so much time involved there, *theoretically*,[466] that David could be gone and not missed."

I had to stop. Okay, how much time could a person have been gone from a five-on-five game and not be missed? Or how could he have disappeared in the middle of a conversation with Tom Jolly? Would Tom just talk with himself?

For a few moments, though, Gilbert and Kessinger had possibly engaged with reality, when Boney had been asked if he had shot Kim. That had been short-lived, though, as the necessity of including Dave had been paramount, as Gilbert had then asked, "Were you offered a lot of money by David?"

That question meant that Gilbert also had considered the possibility that Boney had acted alone when shooting the family. If so, though, that meant the blood on Dave's shirt hadn't been HVIS, and that, in turn, meant Dave hadn't killed his family. That line of questioning had quickly stopped.

Gilbert had Boney take him through the shooting part of the story once again, but instead of standing *beside* his car as Dave had tried to kill him, Boney had now been *behind* the Cadillac with his "head exposed."

A disbelieving Gilbert, knowing of Dave's experience as a SWAT officer, asked Boney if Dave hadn't tried to clear the jam in the gun. Boney had only said Dave had a "funny face" as he turned and then ran into the house.

Boney, after tripping over the shoes, had looked into the car at the kids, not out of "curiosity," as he had claimed to Wilkerson but because, he'd said, "I'm a father."

When asked if the story he had told was going to be his final story, the answer by the man who knew what answers were needed, had responded,

---

[464] Emphasis mine.

[465] Emphasis mine.

[466] Emphasis mine.

"Bottom line is, you guys wanted to know if David Camm had killed his family. You have evidence that puts him there. You have evidence that puts me there." The meaning had been simple: "You get Dave, and I get to be the victim who had only sold a gun."

Gilbert had already moved on, asking if Boney had touched Kim. No, he said, and yes, her pants had still been on her when he had seen her on the floor. Gilbert had then politely asked if Boney might possibly have removed the pantyhose Kim might have been wearing. Of course not, BACKBONE had replied.

"Why were her pants removed after you left?" asked Gilbert.

"He made it look like it was a lot more than what it was, so it would look good for the police, during the time he tried to clean up, and all that stuff."

Who would have helped Dave clean up? Why, Boney had responded, it had to have been the female who had immediately driven onto the Camm driveway after Boney had left.[467]

Boney had finally become personally offended, as he'd insisted, "I'm not the type of motherfucker that would kill kids and then kill a woman just to get her pantyhose. That's absurd."

No one, of course, had claimed the murders had stemmed from a shoe or pantyhose theft. Boney had tried to frame it that way, rather than admitting that his burglary of the house and/or his sexual assault of Kim had gotten way out of hand as she, unlike most of his other female victims, had not been compliant, but had reacted violently and in defense of her children.

Neither Gilbert nor Kessinger had dared to brace the man who saw "white spots" of anger, though, nor had they confronted him on his out-of-control rage and violence directed at women.

Rather than go face-to-face with the remorseless and pathological liar, Gilbert had then asked, "What if somebody else killed her when you just happen to be there. David killed her, [and] you got her pantyhose?" Of course he hadn't, Boney had said, as he would never take any clothing from a dead person. Additionally, he hadn't touched Jill in any way, nor had he touched Brad.

Gilbert had then raised the possibility that Boney's blood could have been in his palmprint, and, if so, "It's over."

"It's over?" They had enough evidence to bury Boney, and now they had resorted to a bluff, for there had not been any blood in the palmprint. It was incredible. Rather than shove each and every lie down the psychopath's lying

---

[467] The female officer that Boney had been trying to incriminate had been with two other officers for several hours that evening, in two locations, several miles away from the Camm residence.

throat, they had resorted to a bluff, but Boney hadn't bought in, claiming he had never gotten blood on himself or at least not on his hands.

After several minutes of trying to convince him of their blood bluff, Gilbert had

> "ALL THIS IS BULLSHIT YOU'RE TALKING ABOUT."
>
> "YOUR WHOLE STORY IS SCREWED UP. THERE IS NOTHING ABOUT THAT STORY THAT'S BELIEVABLE."

then told Boney, "the story you give today just does not fly. [All of what you said] wasn't before 6:00; it was after 7:30. All this [is] bullshit you're talking about."

Kessinger had then jumped in, saying, "Your whole story is screwed up," as he articulated his disbelief of many parts of Boney's story: Dave's not knowing how to clear a jammed gun, Boney's tripping over the shoes, Boney's putting the shoes on top of the car, Boney's looking into the car, and numerous other aspects, concluding, "There is nothing about that story that's believable. How many times are we going to listen to, concoct, this story that meets your needs?"

A photo of Jill, bloodied and still strapped in the backseat of the Bronco, had then been shown to Boney. The callous and cold-blooded killer, when responding to the question of what she did to deserve to die, had stated, "Ask David Camm."

Kessinger had responded, "When are you going to tell us what actually happened?"

After being told by Boney that both he and Dave had been in the garage, Kessinger had said, "Right now, I don't know where David Camm's at. All I know is Charles Boney is there. That's all I know right now. You're telling me he's there, but I don't know that. You were responsible for a hell of a lot more than supplying him with one weapon. When are you going to tell the story. Let's not go through this bullshit again."

So, Kessinger had admitted that it had been possible that Dave hadn't been at the scene? That, in itself, had been startling. I knew, though, that he, as had Wilkerson and Gilbert before him, couldn't have continued with that line.

Instead, Kessinger's lecture had continued: "Do you think you're that sharp that nobody's going to understand? You're going to outsmart everybody? Let me tell you something: the common sense part of it, you totally overlooked. [Your story] just coincidentally fits every piece of evidence, [but it] doesn't have common sense attached to it. It has appropriateness for you."

Kessinger had continued, "Remember the last time we talked with you. If you're the trigger man, if you're the shooter, don't talk to us anymore. You haven't told me anything differently, just whatever is appropriate. The story you've told is not believable." Finally, Kessinger had confronted Boney with the total implausibility of Dave's not being able to clear a jammed semi-automatic. "[It] didn't mean anything to David Camm if it was jammed. I know that didn't happen."

The shoes had again been briefly addressed, but not from Boney's compulsive sexual obsession, but rather from only touching them. "I know you picked those shoes up."

And then, another break in the interrogation, as the tape had been changed.

A polygraph had been discussed but then had quickly been dismissed, with Kessinger's having told Boney that he'd flunk yet another test. Boney had responded that he'd pass a question on whether he had been the shooter. He then had added, "I didn't conspire to do anything."

Over several minutes, Kessinger had returned to alternately berating and pleading with Boney, trying to convince him, if for no other reason, to tell the truth because of his mother. Nothing had come from the Shoe Bandit, though, until he'd lamented, "My job was an intent to sell a weapon. I successfully sold a weapon, but I became a victim of the whole situation."

It had been Gilbert's turn, as he had referred back to the prior day when Boney's mother and sister had been brought in to help secure the conspiracy note: "Make your Mom proud. She believes in her son. She believes her son is going to help us [but] right now, we can't tell [her] nothing. 'Mrs. Boney, *he's not running with us*.[468] He tried, but he can't bring himself to go all the way.' Your sister wants you to share this with us, too."

An adamant Boney had dug in his heels. "I didn't kill anyone, and I didn't conspire to kill anyone."

"So, there is nothing else you will tell us besides what we've already talked about," Gilbert had asked.

"I'm just trying to figure out what it is, what it is that you're looking for."

Kessinger had then spent the next several minutes telling Boney that a true story should have flowed freely from his lips rather than he and Gilbert having to "pull teeth." His story made no sense, said Kessinger, as the times had been off and common sense had been missing.

Kessinger had finally concluded his lengthy sermon by answering Boney's question of what they had wanted from him: "Camm is going to be there and we're going to make sure that the *persons*[469] accountable for those three will remain [incarcerated]. *I just wish you could say the right words, say the right thing*."[470] That translation had been simple: "Give us the conspiracy. We

---

[468] Emphasis mine.

[469] Emphasis mine.

[470] Emphasis mine.

don't have it now. We need it. Give us the conspiracy between you and David Camm."

The pleas had been as with water off a duck's slick and oily back, as Boney had said, "I'm all storied out."

The veteran Louisville detective had then told Boney that the gunslinger Larry Gerkin hadn't been found, as there had been no police record of him whatsoever. Again, Boney was unfazed. "He's just incredibly lucky."

Gilbert had been keeping hope alive, though. "You're absolutely positive there is a Larry Gerkin?" It had been, I thought, as though a 10-year old had wistfully asked if Santa Claus had been real.

As he had maintained the Larry Gerkin charade, or what Kessinger had referred to as a "figment of somebody's imagination," Boney had then wanted his friends to know, with "honest sincerity," that he wasn't going to worry about what would happen to him, and further, if a future judge would sentence him to death, he'd said, "I won't be mad at you."

And then, incredibly enough, giving Boney another polygraph had been discussed yet again, even though Kessinger had told the psychopath of the results of the original tests: "You were deceptive to all of it." Why such an exam would have even been considered was nuts.

Finally, the two exhausted and frustrated interrogators had finished, with Gilbert concluding, "I have no further questions. It's about 10:56 p.m."

Four minutes later, however, the tape had begun again, with Kessinger having one more question: "It appears that Kim [had] put up a pretty good resistance. She had some injuries to her body. If you were there, standing outside the garage . . . [and] you can only remember one word that you could make out, that female in distress saying, 'No,' right before the pop? You didn't hear any fight, screaming or hollering? You didn't hear any fighting or altercation?"

"No. No, I did not."

"I have no further questions."

With Charles Darnell Boney, I thought, Gilbert, Kessinger, and all the other "fresh eyes" had been dealt, in poker parlance, a "no-brainer." The forensic evidence against Boney had been overwhelming, as his property, DNA, and prints had been found at the murder scene.

Boney's predilection towards violently attacking women at night had been well-established; his vehicle had been seen reconnoitering the area of his attack; he had missed work the night of the murders; Boney had bragged to a friend of his fondness for holding and shooting a .380; he had bragged to another that he had three murders on his conscience; he had confessed that if his prints had been found at the scene that it would have been "obvious" that he had committed the murders; and, if they had bothered to check, none of his alibi witnesses supported his story. In short, they had Boney by his ass. Their case against him had been a slam-dunk.

There had been no "hiring" of Boney by Dave as Henderson had alleged in Judge Aylsworth's court, and nothing, absolutely nothing, had supported any conspiracy between the two as there had been no evidence whatsoever the two had even known one another, much less had associated with one another.

On what, then, had they later based the conspiracy to commit murder charges against both Dave and Boney? Certainly, it had been nothing on what Boney had said, as, in the words of the two investigators who had spent close to 40 hours with him, had concluded that his story had been "a crock of shit . . . unbelievable . . . bullshit . . . screwed up . . . [and lacking] common sense." How, then, had Henderson charged Dave with conspiring with Boney to have murdered Kim, Brad, and Jill?

The only logical conclusion was that Mala Singh might have told the "fresh eyes" something which had been the foundation of Dave's "hiring" Boney. If so, how did she know, and what had she said?

SECTION V
Mala Sings: The Second Connection

CHAPTER 46
Mala Singh's Interviews

Background

After splitting with Boney, Mala Singh had found a new man, had made him her elusive husband,[471] and had traveled with him from Louisville to Alaska; after several months there, the two had gone to her native land of Trinidad. Her husband had subsequently left her on the Caribbean island as he had returned to Alaska. I had known most of that but had been unable to find anyone who would contact and interview her in Trinidad.

With the revelations from the new discovery finally provided by Henderson, however, we had learned the "fresh eyes" had spoken telephonically with Singh after she had been found with

> "DID YOU EVER HAVE THAT SWEATSHIRT ON AT ANY TIME?"
>
> "SIR, I PROBABLY MIGHT HAVE ACCIDENTLY WORN IT."

the assistance of the DEA in Trinidad. It was the same DEA agent who had later obtained her DNA in April 2005, which had matched to the unknown female DNA on the BACKBONE sweatshirt.

The DEA Agent had also arranged for Mala to have spoken telephonically with both Gilbert and Kessinger on April 1, 2005, and Gilbert had documented the results, or at least some of the results, of that interview in a report. Interestingly enough, in the transcript of that taped call, Gilbert had noted that "Wayne Kessinger . . . spoke with you previously . . . right?" Not surprisingly, we couldn't find documentation of Kessinger's prior contact with Mala.

Over the course of the next several weeks, and in an attempt to get her to return to the U.S., Singh's lack of a visa had been resolved and, after another interview on June 7, she had flown into Louisville. On June 28, or just one day

---

[471] According to several sources, Mala had wanted to marry an American, as a marriage to a citizen would be her permanent ticket to live in the U.S.

prior to Dave's most recent bond hearing, Gilbert had written in his report, "I *was advised* that Singh came into the United States *this past weekend.*"[472]

The essence of that statement meant the lead detective hadn't known much, if anything, of Singh's date of return to the U.S. Where had she stayed and with whom? What information had she already given? Indeed, what information, if any, had she *been* given? Why had several days passed before Gilbert had even been made aware of her return? It was clear, at least to me, that Wayne Kessinger had now been Henderson's primary go-to guy with a most critical witness.

Our copy of the June 28th audio-tape interview of Mala was poor, as she had often coughed, cleared her throat, and reverted to her Caribbean accent, making certain parts of the tape difficult if not impossible to comprehend. Added to those issues, part of the interview had been lost, with Gilbert acknowledging, "It looked like the tape recorder stopped. We'll have to keep an eye on it. I don't know why it would do that. It stopped again. It might have been a voice activation. We'll check and see."[473]

Mala's First Interview

According to Gilbert's report, in her interview, by telephone, on April 1, Mala claimed that she "didn't really know him [Boney] that well." Regarding the time she had spent with Boney in the summer of 2000, she had claimed:

- Boney had taken "pictures of [her] toes";
- She had never borrowed any money from her uncle on behalf of Boney;
- She had not been with Boney during any supposed attempts of his to borrow money from other people, including a reverend, a veterinarian, or his former brother-in-law;
- Mala "had no knowledge" of the Camm murders but then recalled that the husband of the family had been a cop who "came home and he saw what happened";
- She "didn't think" she had ever seen Boney with a gun: when asked the question, "Did he have one?" she replied, "Oh, I don't know. I don't remember seeing one";
- Her boyfriend might have mentioned being in prison, but she "really

---

[472] Emphasis mine.
[473] With the ISP, bad video and recording equipment had been the norm.

didn't pay attention";

- Boney hadn't lost his temper with her, Mala had said, but "he was always angry at his mom";
- She had never noticed any scratches or injuries on Boney;
- It had been Boney's devil worshipping that "definitely" had been the cause of her and Boney's splitting with one another; and
- One day, when Boney hadn't been home, she'd decided to leave him and had a girlfriend pick her up from his house.

That Mala had been downplaying her knowledge of Boney and her relationship with him had been obvious; e.g., Boney had bragged to me about his exploits in prison; to think he hadn't done so with a girlfriend he, no doubt, had been trying to impress, wasn't logical.

I continued with the report of Gilbert. Rather than respond directly to his second gun question of whether or not she had seen Boney with one, Mala had answered, "I remember we were out somewhere, I don't remember where, and it was the night time . . . I think we went to . . . maybe [his] friend's . . . we parked the car, he got out of the car, he went and got some type of ammunition and went to the trunk, goes into the building, a condominium in Indiana, and then he came back out, walked to the trunk, came in the front seat . . . and I'm like, 'yeah, I'm ready to go home. I'm not [that] type of girl.'"

That had been a confusing comment, causing Gilbert to assure Mala, who, no doubt, had been stressed during the interview, "I want you to know that neither yourself or any of your family members are in any trouble; that's not what we're try to do here. We're trying to see *if anything Mr. Boney told us is accurate information.*"[474]

Then, however, Gilbert had gotten to the real reason they had contacted Boney's former girlfriend: "what we're trying to do, Mala, is eliminate who the unknown female DNA belongs to [on Boney's sweatshirt], so that would help us to be able to *focus on Mr. Camm and Mr. Boney.*"[475]

And then Kessinger had asked some of his own questions,[476] also zeroing

---

[474] Emphasis mine.

[475] Emphasis mine.

[476] One of Kessinger's questions had been, "Didn't you ride with his mother and her boyfriend and Darnell to go to his uncle's house in Evansville, Indiana, to purchase that blue car?" Mala had responded that she had done so. More importantly, though, there had been no prior documentation with those specifics about Boney's retrieving his vehicle. That confirmed, at least to me, that Kessinger, once again, had obtained information from a witness which he had failed to document. More importantly, perhaps, what information *had he possibly given* Mala?

in on the gray sweatshirt that Boney supposedly had 1) already dispatched to the Salvation Army by the time he had begun dating Mala and/or 2) given it to Dave with the gun wrapped in it.

Kessinger, ever the one to help a person with their answers, had asked, "Did you ever have that sweatshirt on at any time that you're aware of, maybe at nighttime or in the morning or in the evening or at bedtime or anything like that?"

"Sir, I probably might have accidentally worn it."

Probably. Might have. Accidentally. Not exactly a definitive confirmation.

"Correct," Kessinger had confirmed, nonetheless.

Mala had continued, "I don't really care to wear his clothes. Probably, like you said, maybe to fall asleep."

"Sure," Kessinger had confirmed once again.

But then Mala had said, "I don't remember taking it to wear it, no, sir."

Too late, Mala, I thought. You'll now be wearing that sweatshirt whether you did or not.

Gilbert had finally returned to the confusing ammunition comment. Mala had confirmed it had occurred somewhere in Indiana and then, rather than being ignorant of any of his prior crimes as she had claimed, Mala had admitted, "He used to talk about robbing people all the time."

Next, and inexplicably immediately after telling of Boney's proclivity of "robbing people all the time," Mala said, "And he, he mentioned his wife, ex-wife and two kids. I think they were divorced."[477]

But back to the ammo. During the time she had been with Boney, Mala had claimed, they had definitely been at a condominium complex in Indiana and Boney had either put something into the trunk or had taken something out of the trunk and had gone into the condo complex and had spent several minutes there.

Her thoughts about having seen Boney with any injuries had also changed, as Mala thought she just might have remembered that at some time she might have seen a scrape on Boney's knee.

As for knowing anything about the murder of the Camm family, she had "remembered a policeman she thought had been with the county and had been accused," but she "didn't know anything else" about the murders.

And then, as Mala often did, as I would learn, she had gone off onto a story of her own, telling the two detectives she had called a relative in Louisville, as she had been watching the news of the Camm murders and had recalled, "An Indiana cop man, they said he came home . . . and the wife and kids was

---

[477] Boney didn't have two children, but Kim certainly did. Boney's assertion and Mala's comments will be explained soon.

killed. I'm like, 'Oh, my gosh, and they charging him for it!' I was like, I couldn't think, and I was like, I couldn't think!"

Why would Mala have been concerned that Dave had been charged for the murders of his wife and kids if she hadn't thought he had been innocent?

The interview of Gilbert and Kessinger, though, had ended when Mala had agreed to allow the DEA Agent who had been present with her to have taken a cotton swab of the inside of her cheeks to secure her DNA. And yes, she said, she'd agree to return to Louisville, particularly if the cost of her airfare and accommodations would be paid.

Clearly, Gilbert's rendition of Mala's story in the bond hearing, of a panting Boney returning home, after midnight, showing her a revolver, as well as him "helping a buddy," hadn't been spun by her in that first interview.

Second Interview

The second telephone interview had apparently been quite short and had occurred on June 7 and consisted, per Gilbert's report, of Mala's confirming that she'd travel to Louisville. During that call, Mala had said, according to Gilbert, that "she was going through a bad situation with her marriage.

Mala's Evolving Story

Many of Mala's original assertions in her first interview had significantly changed when she had given her taped statement almost three months later, on June 28. Keep in mind that June 28 was a Tuesday, and Mala had been in Louisville since the weekend. Contrary to not knowing Boney "that well," she had known a lot about her boyfriend.

"Might have mentioned" his time in prison had changed to Mala's claiming that Boney had "always talked about jail, he was always proud to talk about his [prison] friends and I think he loves [prison]." In fact, Boney had bragged to her that he had been a Vice-Lord in prison and that "When you go to prison, 'you go to learn, you go to become a professional.'"

It had been obvious that Mala had been well-prepared to dish some really helpful stuff on her former boyfriend.

In addition to loving prison, learning in prison, and being a gang member, Mala had added that Boney had often talked of having methamphetamine in prison, although she claimed she hadn't seen him use meth or any drug during the time she had been with him.

From merely *wanting* to be a Satanist, Mala's new recollection of Boney had been that "he loves the devil, he lives for the devil, he prays to the devil," and further, he had "lit candles at midnight," as the Shoe Bandit had also followed the teachings of a Satan master in California.

As for only simply *liking* feet and toes, Mala's new recollection had been that Boney had kissed her toes, polished her toenails, and further that he had talked about feet all the time and had a foot fetish.

Regarding Boney's having a gun, Mala's new recollection had been that Boney had actually asked her if she knew where he could get a gun.

Oops! Boney's solicitation of Mala to help find a gun had been problematic for the "fresh eyes" since Boney had claimed to Gilbert and Kessinger that Larry Gerkin had been his go-to guy for rods.

Had Boney finally found a gun? Yes, Mala said, and she had gotten emotional when first telling the two detectives, "I don't want to know where he got it from" and "I don't want to know nothing!"

Finally, though, Mala had spun a story, but only with the help of the two veteran detectives, and it had taken over an hour to get it. She had been in the bedroom shared by her and Boney in his mother's house, Mala had claimed, in September 2000, when Boney had returned after midnight with a green or black backpack. In fact, "He had a bag all the time, on his back, and he came in the room, I think I was sleeping, and he woke me up, and he sat down."

Boney had then taken the gun out of his backpack and had shown it to her, telling her, "Look! Look!"

I had to stop. Boney comes home, in the middle of the night and heads directly to Mala's bed, maybe awakens her, since she hadn't known if she had been asleep or not, and then had told her to look at a gun she hadn't seen before? Did that make sense?

I continued listening as Mala had then claimed, "I said, 'Oh, my God.' So, I have to play it cool, so alright, okay." And then Mala had added a significant piece of information, "When I seen [sic] the weapon, I didn't tell anybody." When asked why she hadn't told anyone, her response had been telling: "He would come and blow my brains out."

That had been the answer as to why he had shown Mala the gun. "Blow your brains out" had been the favorite verbal threat of Boney to all of his female victims and one, no doubt in my mind, that he had made to Mala on the night of the murders.

There was a simple explanation as to why she had not been merely shown a gun, but it had been brandished, probably in her face or by Boney tapping her head with it, as he had threatened to "blow [her] fucking brains out."

Mala, who had been "down with whatever [Boney] asked her to do," according to her brother, had been, I was sure in my mind, with BACKBONE throughout the night and had been told she'd be dead should she have entertained any thoughts about telling anyone what had happened. After all, she had already seen Boney shoot Kim in the head. His threat to her had been based on her witnessing, I was confident, his shooting Kim point-blank in the head.

Mala's comment could have been the supreme turning point in getting to the "real truth"[478] as she could have been portrayed as yet another victim, duped by a glib-tongued Boney. There had been so many ways:

"You know, Mala, you were living with Darnell at the time the Camm family died.[479] Your brother said Boney had conned you, and you've said yourself he had been violent and had threatened to kill you. And Mala, a person fitting your description had been seen with Darnell in his Cadillac, on the road in front of the Camm house, just a few hours before the crime. Darnell had *made* you go to Indiana to help him in committing his robbery.

"You had a right to be scared, Mala. Darnell is a scary and very violent person and his DNA and fingerprints are all over the crime scene. But he's in jail now and he won't hurt you. You haven't told us everything, but you need to now. Darnell used you like he had used so many others, but we're here to finally get Darnell away from you forever, but only if you tell us what happened that night."

The Real Connection

Neither Gilbert nor Kessinger, however, had taken that golden opportunity to pressure an obviously very stressed and scared Mala Singh who, I firmly believed, could have told them the exact chronology of events of that fateful and fatal night.

In fact, I was sure the elusive *connection* Gilbert and Kessinger had repeatedly sought from Boney had been sitting in front of them in the person of Mala Singh—only the connection didn't include Dave Camm. There had been no follow-up questioning of her, even of her being threatened by Boney. None whatsoever.

Rather than wanting to know more of the connection between Mala and the murders, Kessinger had instead wanted to know what kind of gun Mala had seen.

"I don't recall" had been her answer.

Kessinger then had wanted to know if Mala had known the "difference between a revolver and another type of weapon," not mentioning a semi-automatic by name. Her answer had been garbled in the tape, but Kessinger had responded, "It had a round cylinder is what you're saying?"

---

[478] Another silly term, yet needed in the Camm case.

[479] Yes, they were viciously murdered, but when soliciting the help of someone involved in a crime, it's not a bad idea to soften such terms.

What color had been the gun? "Maybe black or brown" had been Mala's response. And no, she didn't know if the handle was plastic, wood, or whatever, and she didn't know what a semi-automatic gun looked like. In fact, she had exclaimed, "I don't want to know anything about that [gun]!"

The intent of Mala's claim to have seen Boney with a revolver was clear: it comported with the State's story of having Dave maintain possession of the .380 semi that Boney had claimed to have sold to him. The trade-off for the "fresh eyes" was that they'd have to eat the story that Boney hadn't been armed with his own gun while at Dave's house and thus had been able to shoot Dave when the .380 had supposedly jammed.

Did Mala really know what kind of gun Boney had that night? I don't know, and I don't know if she knew, but Kessinger and Gilbert had their story of its being a revolver and thus, by default, Boney couldn't have been the shooter.

Mala, however, had continued talking, almost incessantly at times, of Boney's prison friends and his "buddies." That had prompted her recall that Boney, prior to leaving the night of the gun incident, had called someone on the phone, telling her, after disconnecting the call, that he was going to meet "his buddy."

And then Mala had dropped a shocker, telling the reason of Boney meeting his buddy, as he had explained to her, *He gave his friend some money.*[480]

Wow! That was a huge fly in the *Dave gave Boney money* for the gun" ointment, as Kessinger had quickly tried to clean up that mess, "Is he giving his friend money or is his friend giving him money?"

"He's giving his friend," an adamant Mala had said.

Kessinger hadn't followed immediately with any money or buddy questions. In fact, there had been no question of *Why* had Boney been giving his friend money" or *Who* was his buddy?"

Instead of pursuing the buddy, Gilbert's next question, though, had been "Do you remember the clothes he had on that night?"

"Maybe his gray or blue sweatshirt," in addition to his boots, had been Mala's response. Whoops again! Maybe a gray sweatshirt? No questions asked if the picture of the gray BACKBONE sweatshirt they had shown Mala earlier had been the one worn by Boney that evening. That wouldn't fit either, since the sweatshirt had to have been wrapped around the .380 left with Dave.

The boots comment, though, had hit home. Kim, of course, had the tops of both feet injured. And there was no doubt in my mind those injuries came

---

[480] Emphasis mine.

from Boney having stomped on them with hard-sole boots.

Mala, though, had dropped another bomb, recalling that Boney had told her that night that he had buried something, saying she didn't know what was buried. She had continued with "I don't know what *they* did."[481] When asked what he had buried, Mala had responded it had possibly been cash, and then added, "Maybe he did something."

So, Mala's story had been that Boney, the night of the murders, had come home, panting, with bruises on his knees, waking her and telling her, "Look! Look!" at his gun and then saying, "You know, Mala, me and my buddy, the guy I gave money to, buried something tonight." And somewhere in the conversation she had been convinced that he was going to "blow [her] brains out."

That scenario should have warranted more than a few follow-up questions, such as "*How* do you know something was buried and *who* was the friend who had been with Boney?" Or, how about, "*What* had he done that night?"

Gilbert's next question, however, had been if there had been an odor to the gun when Boney had shown it to Mala. "I thought he did something" had been her response. Yet another opportunity: "*What* had he done?" No questions on that, though.

Mala, yet again, had taken the opportunity to talk of Boney's being "proud of his jail friends." Clearly, the woman had been fixated on those friends of BACKBONE's.

Rather than thinking one of those "jail friends" had been with Boney, the next questions to Mala, as they still tried to connect Dave to Boney, had been "Did he mention at all him trying to help out friends with money? Did he [Boney] come into some money that night?"

"Yes," Mala had finally answered, no doubt initially pleasing Gilbert and Kessinger. But then, she had added, "and I think that's why he gave it to the friend. When he came back, he said he gave it to his friend instead."

And then Mala had said something strange: "I said, 'friend, whatever,' I don't need no money."

So, had Boney offered or had he given her money? No

> "[BONEY'S] MOTHER ASKED IF HE KNEW THEM. SHE CALLED THEM BY NAME. HE KNEW THE FEMALE AND THE KIDS. HE SHOOK HIS HEAD, 'YES.'"
>
> "HE ACKNOWLEDGED THAT HE KNEW THE VICTIMS?"
>
> "YES! TO HIS MOTHER."

---

[481] Emphasis mine.

question about whether Mala had gotten money from Boney and if so, why?

And then, Mala had claimed that Boney had put down his gun and had taken a shower. As in showering to remove debris and blood from fighting with and shooting Kim had been the easy deduction. But no questions.

Next, Mala had remembered the next morning when the two of them and Boney's mother had been gathered together around the kitchen table. The television news had been reporting on the murders that had occurred the prior evening.

Mala had said that it had been a "cop guy" who had come home and found his wife and kids murdered. Later, the "cop guy" had been "accused," and the police had "claimed" he had done the murders.[482]

Mala had continued with the conversation between Boney and his mother: "*His mother asked if he knew them. **She called them by name. He [Boney] knew that person, the female, the female and the kids.** I can't remember the name. **He knew the female. The female and the kids and he shook his head 'yes.'** *"[483]

Mala had again said that Mrs. Boney had "called them by name," but Mala had been frustrated because she couldn't remember the names.

Kessinger, who had previously cautioned Mala to calm down, had asked the question, "So, he acknowledged that he knew the *victims*?"

Mala had been unequivocal, "Yes, to his mother!" She had continued, "She got upset with him when he said, 'yes' [that he knew the female and kids]. She got upset. She didn't like the fact, she got upset with him over the thing going on in the news."[484]

The shocking claim of Mala, shocking at least to Gilbert and Kessinger, had directly contradicted Boney's prior assertion to the two detectives that he had no knowledge or connection to the family.

Mala had continued, "She got upset with him. She asked him if it was them." Mala had then asked of the two detectives, "From what, the information I've got now. That's [the dead female] his [Boney's] ex-wife? Correct?"[485]

Both Gilbert and Kessinger, rather than pursue that angle, had told her that

---

[482] Those had been interesting words for Mala to have used. Why hadn't she said a cop had killed his wife and kids rather than had been "accused?" Mala, however, had not had the sequence in order since it had been three days later when Dave had been arrested.

[483] Emphasis mine.

[484] As noted, it is not uncommon for people to distance themselves from a crime by refusing to describe the nature of the crimes: e.g., "that thing going on in the news" instead of "the murders that happened."

[485] As noted, the tape had major quality issues, but after listening for an interminable time, the paragraph is my best understanding of Mala's comments.

her deduction had been wrong.

"Okay, well" had been Mala's response, continuing, "his mother asked if he knew them . . . he answered 'yes.' And, she got upset."

That's when Mala had claimed Boney and his mother went to another part of the house, and Mala had also left the kitchen.

Why had Mala thought the woman who had been killed had been Boney's former wife? Boney had shown her a picture of a woman, Mala had said, which she had been told by him was his former wife. The woman had long hair, and there had been at least one kid if not two kids in the photo.

Had Boney obtained a photo of Kim and the kids and claimed to Mala that Kim had been his first wife? If so, that could have been a ruse used by Boney to dupe Mala into going with him to the Camm home, e.g., "Help me retrieve some items my ex-wife has stolen from me." Regardless, there had been no questions by either detective on that possibility.

Mala then said she had then called her friend, Tessa,[486] telling her she needed to leave, as Boney was "crazy" and a "devil-worshipper." She had said, simply, "I've got to go."

Had she told Tessa of Boney and his gun and the fact he had known the murdered mother and two children? "I don't remember mentioning anything, cause I don't know. I don't know. I don't know. I couldn't tell Tessa anything. What am I gonna tell her? Something I don't know?"

Kessinger had wanted to return to Mala's "cop," comment, though, and asked, "She asked him if he knew the cop and Darnell said, 'yes.'"

"Well, apparently, the family," said Mala, adding that Mrs. Boney had gotten upset "because she knew them, too."

Mala had then added that she thought "they *probably* knew the cop, because [Mrs. Boney] was in security [at the casino and probably knew the cop] *somehow or someway.*"[487]

It had been Mala's belief that the mother and son had *"probably, somehow or someway,"* known Dave, not from the conversation at the kitchen table, but from her own conclusion. That wasn't proof of any kind of connection between Dave and Boney.

Mala then had said when, in Alaska, she and her husband had seen a television program,[488] she had asked him, "Why would a cop kill his wife and two kids, you know?" It had been a time, she had said, when "they brought back up the case," adding, "I thought it was all done with."

"All done with" had meant, I thought, that Mala had believed, as had

---

[486] Pseudonym.

[487] Emphasis mine.

[488] Probably *48 Hours*.

Boney, that she had dodged any culpability for any role she may have had with Boney.

Mala, though, had kept talking, again referring to the morning-after discussion between Boney and his mother: "She got mad. She probably asked him if he had anything to do with it."

"She would have asked him that?" Kessinger had asked incredulously.

"Probably, because *they both knew the family*."[489]

"It's very important that you're very exact on this, Mala," Gilbert had added.

"I am serious, to the point she asked him if he knew *them*.[490] That much I do know and I do remember she getting mad."

That Boney and his mother had known the names of Kim and the children had validated our belief that he, and now we knew his mother, had met them at Karem's or another nearby store. Knowing Kim meant that Boney would have manipulated her with his smooth talk as he had others, and Kim had probably believed him to be a gentleman.

Mala's recollection had also meant that Gilbert's attempt to claim, in the bond hearing, that Boney had claimed to have known "that cop" had been misleading at best, for he had known Kim, Brad, and Jill and had probably interacted in some manner with them.

However, there was still another issue that had faced the "fresh eyes" and that hadn't been addressed. How had Mala's DNA gotten on Boney's sweatshirt? Had Mala been in the garage that night? When Kim had fought tenaciously for her life and the lives of her children, had Mala been scratched? Had that been how her blood had gotten on the sweatshirt and mixed with Kim's blood?

However her DNA had been deposited, Gilbert had dismissed the possibility it had occurred that evening when he had asked, "Did you ever wear any of Darnell's clothing?"

"Maybe once," answered Mala.

"Did you ever wear, maybe, any of his clothing as a nightshirt?" Gilbert had asked, as he honed in on the issue at hand, i.e., getting Mala's DNA on the sweatshirt in the desired manner.

"Probably once."

"What would you have remembered wearing?" Gilbert had wanted to know.

"Maybe a sweater, something like that."

Gilbert had continued, as he'd focused on the most important garment

---

[489] Emphasis mine.
[490] Emphasis mine.

in the Boney wardrobe, "A sweater, (inaudible) or some type of sweatshirt? Could it have been one of the gray ones?"

"Probably," Mala had answered, repeating herself, as she now was a much better student than she had been earlier in the interview.[491]

Adding to her validation had been Kessinger, in the background, who had repeatedly confirmed her story of wearing some of Boney's clothes by saying, "Okay, okay."

Gilbert had then told Mala that, in addition to Boney's DNA found at the scene, her DNA had also been there and added, "So, we just want to make sure as to how it would have gotten on there."

Kessinger had also asked, "Do you remember wearing that sweatshirt?" That question, of course, had essentially been a statement, as the question was of her memory, not whether she had worn the sweatshirt.

Mala, well-educated by now, had responded, "I probably wore his sweatshirt . . . while I was sleeping."

And then Gilbert had continued, "Why don't we go ahead and talk about it, cause here's some other questions we want to ask you, too. Were you anywhere close to the Camm residence at all?"

Rather than a resounding, "No!" Mala had responded, "I really don't know where they [were] living." And yes, I believe that had been an evasion, as she had distanced herself even further by claiming ignorance of where the Camm family had lived.

Rather than follow-up with the evidence that would have placed her at the scene, Gilbert's next question had been even easier: "Have you ever been to Georgetown, Indiana?"

"Where is Georgetown, Indiana?" Mala had asked, and Gilbert then had given her general directions.

I stopped the tape again. Clearly, the intent had been to eliminate Mala as having any involvement with Boney either during Boney's daytime surveillance of the Camm home or the nighttime invasion of it.

Gilbert's next question had been "Were you involved in the murders of Kim, Bradley or Jill Camm?" That question had been asked in a non-threatening, quiet voice meant only to check a box, I thought.

"No, sir. I do not know Kim, Bradley or who?" Gilbert had given her the name of Jill. "Or Jill Camm," added Mala, and no, she hadn't known Dave.

As the questioning came to an end, Kessinger had wanted to know what Mala had thought when she had first heard that Gilbert and Kessinger had wanted to speak with her. She immediately defaulted to a call she had received from her brother, Seamus, who had told her of being contacted by the

---

[491] As noted repeatedly, the quality of the tape was poor and, at times, undecipherable.

detectives. She had thought, "That idiot, Darnell, he probably did something."

"I DID *SEE* A WOMAN AND TWO KIDS GETTING KILLED."

Continuing, Mala then had dropped a bomb: "When [Seamus] started telling me, I'm like, you know, I did *see* a woman and two kids getting killed."[492] She quickly tried to overcome that enormous slip of the tongue, not with, "on television," but rather, "Uh, by, when he mentioned it was a cop, I do remember *listening* to the news or something like that."[493]

Neither Gilbert nor Kessinger had stopped Mala and had pressed her on that incredible admission. Rather, she had been allowed to continue with her diatribe. Seamus, she said, had told her that detectives had come looking for her. Mala's response had been "Are you sure it's me?"

The lady from Trinidad had then gone off on a self-vouching rant: "I've been in the U.S. almost ten years. I haven't gotten in trouble. I haven't done anything wrong to get in trouble . . . [and] my name was nowhere dirty, so that could be some good credentials I could fall back on."

Then, of the DEA agents who had at first unsuccessfully attempted to contact her in Trinidad, Mala had continued, "I said, 'sure, let them come.' And they came and that's when I started asking them questions. They said there's unidentified DNA and I said, 'Okay, I have nothing to hide. I know I wasn't there. I didn't do nothing. God is my witness.'"

Mala's words had attempted to distance herself from the crimes and to downplay any knowledge of them. Instead, they had been very incriminating and not just her slip of the tongue: "*I did see a woman and two kids getting killed.*" When told she was being contacted due to unidentified DNA, her response, rather than, "Unidentified? What and where? How does that relate to me?" she had claimed, "I know I wasn't there." Those words indicated to me, and I thought anyone with an open mind, that she had absolutely known of the location of "there."

Additionally, when I had spoken to Mala's brother, Seamus, just days after Boney had been arrested and prior to Gilbert and Kessinger interviewing him, I had asked Seamus why I had wanted to speak with him. His response had been direct: "About Darnell, *for the murders he did.*"[494]

That Seamus hadn't gotten in touch with his sister immediately after I had left had been improbable. There had been no doubt in my mind that he had already alerted Mala to Boney's arrest. Thus, Seamus hadn't just told Mala

492 Emphasis mine.
493 Emphasis mine.
494 Emphasis mine.

that Darnell had "probably" done something, as Seamus had already told me of *"the murders he did."* Seamus had been convinced of his guilt. The real question had been if Mala had admitted to her brother of her knowledge and involvement in those murders. I believe she had done exactly that.

Sadly, the purpose of Mala's interview, it had been easy to see, had not been for Gilbert and Kessinger to discover what she had witnessed, but to mold a story, to comport her story with their pre-conceived need to incriminate Dave, just as had been done with their handling of Boney and their attempts to find the "connection."

In fact, and in reviewing her two interviews, Mala had already provided a plethora of excellent evidence against Boney. Mala had, in fact, done all of the following:

- Contradicted Boney's alibis and loan story;
- Negated Boney's story of the gun-dealing Gerkin;
- Put Boney in possession of a gun just after the murders;
- Placed Boney in possession of a backpack, which probably had been the "dam" blocking Kim's huge blood flow;
- Confirmed he had been involved in a fight and had bruising on his knees;
- Verified Boney's obsession with women's feet;
- Firmly established Boney as a devil-worshipper;
- Given the detectives a lead as to the involvement of another person, the "buddy" Boney had owed money to and with whom he had met that evening;
- Related the story of Boney's burying something after the murders;
- Provided a critical connection of the victims to Boney in that he and his mother had both known Kim and the children; thus
- Confirming the attack on Kim had been planned and methodical;
- Had given them the name, Mrs. Boney, of another with whom Boney had discussed the murders;
- All but confessed that she had been with Boney at the time of the murders; as she admitted, ***"I did see a woman and two kids getting killed"***; and
- Had known her brains would be blown out if she had told anyone of what she had seen.

In fact, rather than take Mala's story at face value and vigorously press her on each and every part of it, the "fresh eyes" had simply modified her story to help with the "connection" between Boney and Dave, particularly with Gilbert's claim that Mala had said Boney had known that "cop." And the "buddy" that Mala clearly had thought had been a former inmate had been twisted to make it seem to have been Dave.

The lady from Trinidad, though, had also been educated by the "fresh eyes." With their suggestion of her wearing the gray sweatshirt, Mala's DNA on it had been brushed aside as something normal. She, therefore, hadn't been involved in the crime and had been summarily dismissed as only a person who had been made aware of the crimes after the fact and whose DNA at the scene had been explained away, much in the same way they had attempted to do earlier with Boney's DNA.

But what about the buddy? I had immediately thought of Ernie Nugent who, we had learned, in addition to admittedly selling Boney at least one gun within days or weeks leading to the murders, had also, as had Boney, missed his night work shift that same Thursday evening.

Nugent, who at one time had resided near the Boney home, had routinely packed a gun at the same job site as Boney, and had, I had discovered, also been arrested as a younger man for the armed robbery of a gas station and had served prison time. He had also lied repeatedly to me and to the "fresh eyes" about the guns he had possessed.

At the time of the murders, and where I had found and interviewed him, Nugent had been living in an apartment complex in New Albany. An apartment complex which could have easily been misconstrued by Mala to have been a condominium complex, in Indiana, where Boney had some kind of transaction involving ammunition.

And Nugent had also been owed money by Boney. Owed money over the sale of a handgun. Had Nugent been the buddy that BACKBONE had met that night? The guy he had given money?

Still, the overall bottom line was there had been no other deduction we could have reasonably made about Mala Singh: she had been "down with" whatever Boney had wanted to do; had been with him throughout the day of September 28, 2000; and had, as she had blurted out, at least witnessed the murders of Kim, Brad, and Jill.

What had been Mala's role? I didn't know for sure, but I did again recall Boney's own "fuck-with" response prior to his arrest when talking about the *"unknown female DNA."* Boney himself had surmised, *"that could have belonged to the helper of the Camm murders."*

If Mala had been there, that didn't mean she'd expected the mayhem, murders, and horror that she had witnessed, thus necessitating Boney's threat to blow her fucking brains out. Mala, to some degree, had probably been yet another victim of Boney's psychopathic personality.

Among other things, I'd find and interview other members of her family, her friend Tessa, and others who had known Mala. Surely, she would have told them something of Darnell and his threats to her.

CHAPTER 47

"If Anybody Gets Laid Out"

On July 4, the day after I had finished reading and studying the tapes and transcripts of Boney's interviews and interrogations, as well as absorbing as much as possible of the interviews of Mala, I had traveled to the Louisville area to interview Mala Singh's brother in preparation for her deposition the next day. He didn't know I was coming, nor did I want him to know.

First, however, I had stopped into the Floyd County Jail where Dave and I had talked. "There's nothing there, Dave. They have nothing connecting you and Boney at all. Nothing. Their star witness is the same guy that murdered your family. The 'fresh eyes' interrogations were them just begging him to conjure up a conspiracy between the two of you."

Dave, who had also been studying the Boney interviews and interrogations, had responded in a matter-of-fact manner, "Boney should be facing the death penalty, but they gave him a pass. It's the same as it's always been, Dunner. Since they didn't have the evidence against me, they just claimed they did, the press reports it, and then the hatred they gin up against me infects the jury."

Continuing, Dave said, "Give them credit. They didn't have the evidence before and were successful,

> BONEY "HAD A CAR AND HE SAID HE HAD A GUN. HE SAYS, 'ALL YOU HAVE TO DO IS DRIVE THE GETAWAY CAR. I'LL CUT YOU A PIECE. I'LL GO IN AND IF ANY BODY GETS LAID OUT, THEY GET LAID OUT.'"
>
> "WHAT'S HE MEAN BY GETTING LAID OUT?"
>
> "WELL, IN SLANG TERMS, YOU GET SHOT. YOU GET SHOT."

and they don't have it now, but somehow or another, with not an ounce of evidence, Boney and I conspired with one another." He then paused a moment, "And Kim, Brad, and Jill still won't get the justice they deserve."

I had tried to remain upbeat with Dave, but it had been difficult. When the entire weight of the criminal justice system is against a person, it's tough enough. But when lies upon lies are built into that same system, it's almost impossible to overcome.

I then had met in Louisville with Nelson Lockhart, whom I wanted to accompany me for the interview of Seamus. Upon arriving at his home, we were told that Seamus had been out with a friend. Seamus' wife, Brittany, and her mother, Ruth,[495] were present, however, and they had agreed to speak with us. Several days prior, they said, Mala had telephonically contacted them, telling her two friends that she had returned to the area, but, to date at least, they hadn't met with her. She had been in an unknown location, they said, placed in "protective custody."

Ruth, with whom Mala had once been close, had been aware that Mala had already been moved from one motel to another after the investigators had discovered Boney had been showing her photo to other jail inmates.

Nonetheless, Mala had been moved, and a woman, possibly the wife of a detective, according to Ruth, had been constantly staying with her.

During one of her phone conversations, Mala had told them that she was going to be a witness who was going to *testify against David Camm.*[496] No, they said, Mala hadn't said as to what she was going to testify. The fact she had been educated as to her role, however, hadn't been surprising to either Nelson or me.

Brittany then had her own recollection of the robbery solicitation of her husband by Boney, which, she said, had occurred in the late summer or early fall of 2000. She, her husband, and their child had gone to visit Seamus' mother and Mala in their apartment. While there, Brittany had walked into the kitchen where Boney had been whispering to her husband. Boney had sternly told her, "The men are talking," as he tried to get her to leave. She hadn't.

Brittany, still present with Mala, had clearly heard Boney's telling Seamus, "I can get us some quick money." Seamus had asked what Boney meant.

Boney had then said, "I know a place we can rob. We can rob a bank in Indiana."

Brittany had continued of Boney, "He proceeds to tell Seamus he [Seamus] can drive the getaway car and that he [Boney] has a gun."

After trying to convince Seamus that it was "easy to get money" in Indiana, Brittany had become convinced that Boney knew exactly what he had been talking about, further adding that Boney had gotten much louder and was "getting into what he's saying, getting excited."

Boney was also a braggart, Brittany recalled, as he had seemed proud in exclaiming, "I've been to jail. I'm not afraid to do hard time. Man, you know how many times I've been to jail? I ain't scared of that."

I asked if Brittany had remembered the name of any specific bank. No, she said, but then she had added, "He said he had a car, and I know he said he had a gun. And, he says, 'All you have to do is drive the getaway car. You

[495] Pseudonyms.
[496] Emphasis mine.

456

don't have to do nothing else. That's all you have to do, you don't have to do nothing else, just drive, and I'll cut you a piece. I'll go in and if anybody gets laid out, they get laid out.'"

"What's he mean by getting 'laid out?'"

Brittany's response had not been vague. "Well, in slang terms, you get shot, you get shot."

Brittany, Seamus, and their child had soon left, but Boney had been angry with Brittany's husband for not taking him up on his offer.

Boney, according to Brittany, had also been teaching Mala how to drive his dark-colored "square" car, and she had further opined that Mala had been "easily influenced [by Boney about] whatever was going on at the moment."

I asked Brittany if she thought it possible Mala had been the one who had driven the car for Boney the night of the Camm murders. She replied that it wouldn't have surprised her because "she followed him everywhere. I don't believe she would hurt anyone, but I do believe she would go [with Boney]."

A few days after that apartment conversation, Brittany had recalled Boney's having been back in the same apartment. She had heard him say that he had been staying with Mala and her mother, rather than with his mother, because "he was going to lay low over here and 'let Indiana cool off.'"

"He's Crazy"

Shortly afterwards, Brittany had been with her mother at one of the extended family's restaurants, and both had seen Boney with Mala. After buying some food, Boney had been upset for some reason, and both had heard Boney angrily exclaim, "I ought to rob this motherfucker."

Still later in 2000, just prior to Halloween, and contrary to Mala's assertion she had already left Boney, Brittany had become aware that Boney had taken Mala, who had been "threatened and terrified" by Boney, for a ride in a cemetery—a cemetery in Indiana—and he had told her he'd kill her, warning, "This is where you'll be if you try to leave me."

Seamus' mother-in-law had also told me that Mala had kept repeating, at the time of the cemetery incident, of Boney, "He's crazy, he's crazy, he's crazy. He could have killed me and nobody would have known where I was."

The gravesite of Kim, Brad, and Jill in New Albany had received a lot of publicity and, in turn, a large number of visitors in the aftermath of their burial at Kraft Cemetery. That Boney would have known of its location—and thought to have driven past it while threatening Mala she'd receive the same fate as had Kim, Brad, and Jill—dovetailed well with other psychopathic aspects of the cowardly killer.

The two women said that at no time, however, had Mala or Boney ever mentioned David Camm or the Camm murders.[497]

Brittany had also given me further insight into Mala: "She's secretive when it comes to things that have happened, Certain things. And she's like, there are certain things she said that are lies cause she does lie. Those lies you can always pick apart, but the things that really happen, I mean, that was the hardest thing about Mala. The things that were done, or any of the bad things, you can just never get that from her."

Both mother and daughter had also confirmed that Mala would speak very good English and then, quite quickly, resort to her Trinidadian accent, at times becoming almost impossible to understand.

Eventually, after Mala and Boney had broken up, Brittany had recalled that Mala's personality had gotten even worse: "It was like her innocence was gone. She was different. And the men she started dating got worse and worse and worse." Brittany had added that a friend had also seen Mala entering a known crack house in Louisville, causing the family to believe she had spiraled into drug addiction.

During our conversations with Brittany and Ruth, Seamus, who had returned home, had drifted in and out of the room, and it had been apparent he hadn't liked the presence of Nelson and me asking our questions. When we had finished our conversation with the two ladies, I had asked to speak with Seamus, but he had been abrupt, said he didn't have any further information, and escorted us to the door.

After we left, I called Kitty and gave her a full accounting of our interview. She responded that Mala's deposition had been scheduled for noon the next day, and we had agreed to meet the next morning in New Albany.

---

[497] Ruth did tell us of her thoughts about the murders, "I never could get over the fact that all these people seen [Dave] playing basketball. Nobody seen him leave but then, 'Bam!' he killed his family. I couldn't understand that. Then I starting watching the media, and it started coming up about the women and different things that women was supposed to be saying about him. So then, they start portraying him as this angry nasty type person. So I'm like, 'Oh, God, he probably did kill his family.'"

CHAPTER 48

"Do I Have To Look At Him?"

Henderson's Deposition Of Mala

Four days prior to our deposition of Mala, Keith Henderson had sat down with her and taken his own, singular, deposition. It had been a smart move on his part, since he'd lock her into her answers, or more likely, the answers he wanted to have heard from her, prior to Kitty's more aggressive questioning.

Reviewing the relatively short question-and-answer document, I realized it had been apparent that Mala had been much better prepared than she had in her prior interview with Gilbert and Kessinger. Her answers to Henderson had mostly been short, concise, and full of "Yes, Sir," and "No, Sir" responses with few self-serving rants or lengthy answers. I had no doubt that she had been well-coached.

Responding to the question if she had remembered anything significant that had occurred in September, Mala hadn't missed a beat: "Yes, one night [Darnell] left and he said he would be back later . . . and he came back after [his mother had left for work]. I was sleeping and he sat on the bed and he woke

> IN SPITE OF HER PRIOR ANSWERS TO GILBERT AND KESSINGER, HENDERSON HAD HIS SINGULAR CONNECTION: BONEY HAD KNOWN THE COP.

me up and he showed me a weapon, description, a revolver and . . . it was a round one, a round one."

She had then continued with a more refined version of Boney's "panting and sweating," as she had "observed a bruise on his knee."

Without being asked, Mala had segued into the next morning: "there was this live coverage on television about a murder and his mother asked him if he knew this person and he acknowledged to her, 'yes.' Voices was [sic] exchanged and her voice raised." Mala then related that she had left the room and started packing her bags, and then, realizing that both Darnell and his mother were gone, Mala had then called Tessa who, within half an hour, had picked her up, and Mala had left.

Thus, Mala had laid the foundation for Henderson's follow-up questions, prompting her to say that Darnell had left the evening to "meet a buddy," and when he had returned, he had shown her the gun. She had quickly moved onto the next morning with her, Darnell, and his mother sitting in the kitchen, watching the television coverage of the murders of the Camm family.

Mala had continued, *"The mother asked him if he knew that person, the cop, and he acknowledged to her, 'yes,'* and she got mad at him."[498] She had made no comment about knowing that both his mother and Boney had known Kim and the children, nor of her comment that Mrs. Boney had gotten upset with her son because she had thought him responsible for their murders.

In spite of her prior answers to Gilbert and Kessinger, Henderson had his singular connection: Boney had *known the cop.*

Mala had then been directed back to the night before and her fear of being shown the gun. She'd then said Boney had "mentioned money, money was exchanged." He, or someone gave him some money or he gave someone some money."

With Mala having used the terms, *description, observed, exchanged,* and *acknowledged,* there had been no doubt in my mind that she had parroted the words an investigator would have used while prepping her for Henderson's deposition. She, as with Boney, had told the preferred story after having been coached.

Continuing, Mala had also told of Boney's always having two sweatshirts, a gray one and a blue one. One he would wear, and one he would keep in his backpack, she'd said. In fact, she had recalled him wearing one of those sweatshirts, and he also had worn his work boots.

The only other important point Henderson had needed to address had been Mala's DNA on the gray sweatshirt: "Would you be surprised that your DNA was on the gray sweatshirt?"

"He could have gotten it from a hair or my sweat or something . . ."

"Because you were intimate with him, were you not?"

"Yes, I was. Yes. Yes."

Twenty-three pages. That's all it had taken for Henderson to have covered the three things he needed to address to make his case against Dave even stronger: 1) Boney had a revolver and not a semi-automatic in his possession after the murders; 2) Boney had known "the cop" whose family had been murdered; and 3) her DNA had gotten on the gray sweatshirt, not from any fight in the Camm garage, but because of her having been intimate with Boney.

Second Deposition Of Mala

The joint deposition had begun in Henderson's office shortly after noon on July 5th. Kitty had first objected to the timing and the mandate of the deposition,

---

498 Emphasis mine.

under the Sixth, Fourteenth, and Fifth Amendments. The objections were noted, but the parade had already begun.

Since it was the prosecutor's deposition, that meant Steve Owen would be the first one asking the questions. That would give Singh yet at least a third opportunity to regurgitate her answers under the tutelage of her friends.

Owen had begun, predictably, by tossing softballs to Mala, asking her simple questions about her background. She had breezed through those, unlike a rare diversion with Henderson, when she had gone off, claiming, "My family wouldn't give me the mental help that I needed."

Initially, when responding to Owen's background questions, Mala had looked directly at the camera, smiled, and slowly articulated her answers. She had even appeared to be having a good time.

When Owen had asked if she had known Dave, who had been present and in his jail clothes, Mala had glanced at Dave but had quickly turned away and said she hadn't known him.

Her story continued, as Darnell had met her at her uncle's store, had later called her and "paid the cab fare [from Louisville to New Albany] and [given her] a bubble bath."

Owen had asked if Mala had seen "something good in him."

Her answer had surprised the Chief Deputy: "I think the feet. He's obsessed with feet. He romanced feet. He like to paint toenails." Did she like that? "I'm the type of girl. Romance me." And, oh, yes, she had, in fact, initially liked Boney.

After describing moving in with Boney and his mother and leaving her mother and one-year-old daughter together, Mala had launched quickly into her story of Boney's returning after midnight with the panting, sweating, gun-wielding, knee-bruising, money-exchanging, and buddy-meeting story.

And then Mala had repeatedly claimed she had kept saying that she'd "prayed for the morning to come."

What had caused such prayers? The money? No. Boney's panting and sweating? No. His unknown buddy? Not hardly. A bruise on his knee? No.

Had her prayers come from the horror of seeing a gun? Mala had been present for her boyfriend's solicitation of her brother to help in an armed robbery and had known of the possibility someone might have gotten "laid out" in the robbery. Also, per her brother, "it looked like she was down with whatever [Boney] asked her to do." So, no. It hadn't been a gun that had caused her to pray.

So *why had* Mala prayed to get away from Boney? The only answer which had come to my mind: she had been with him that evening, and the excitement promised by her devil-worshipping boyfriend had turned into very real evil and abject horror.

Mala's story continued under the soft-spoken Owen's questions—of Boney's mother asking if he had known *the cop* whose family had been murdered. Her boyfriend had nodded his head, yes, and then Mala had left the room. When she had returned, both mother and son had left, and so had she soon thereafter.

The only other point needed to be covered by Owen had been Mala's DNA on the BACKBONE sweatshirt. Well, that had an easy answer, with Mala now claiming she had worn Boney's sweatshirt to bed and, her being anemic, her blood had probably gotten on it because, she had said, "I hemorrhage really bad." Yeah. That's right. Mala had said her menstrual period had been the bloody culprit and source of her DNA.

Since Mala had satisfactorily answered all the State's questions, Owen had then turned the deposition over to Kitty.[499]

Mala's Demeanor Radically Changes

Kitty first had drilled Mala on the need to tell the truth, particularly since she had been under oath. Mala had quickly become uneasy and then, on practically every answer she had thereafter given, had kept her eyes either looking downward or upward and rarely at Kitty. It had been radically different when her eyes had been animated and had directly engaged Owen with her rehearsed answers.

When Kitty asked if Mala had known that her answers could impact whether Dave was found guilty and sentenced to prison for the rest of his life, she had evaded the question, simply saying, "I don't know that man."

Kitty, as she pointed towards Dave, then had told Mala, "I want you to take a good look at him, really look at him, study his face, please look at him, please look at him right now."

Angrily, Mala had responded, "Do I have to look at him?" She'd run her fingers through her long black hair, perhaps mentally trying to rid herself of Kitty's vexatious questions. It hadn't worked.

"Why do you have a problem looking at Dave Camm?"

Her answer had told us much about Mala: "Because it is sick, what I am here for." Oh, so it was about her inconvenience, even though she had smiled and told Owen she'd willingly come back for trial if someone would pay for her transportation and lodging.

A few moments later, Kitty, having had enough of her responses, had told

---

[499] Not every one of Mala's inconsistent claims would be blasted by Kitty, particularly since she'd be called as a prosecution witness at trial, and confronting her there, in front of jurors, had been more important than scoring points in the deposition.

Mala, "It really looks like you have an attitude you didn't have with Mr. Owen . . . what's wrong?"

"Nothing," of course, had been her lying answer.

Kitty had then exhibited a photo of Boney, or at least tried to show Mala his picture. The reaction had been viseral, as the woman had tried to act nonchalantly but had hastily put her entire left hand over her face. She'd then only glimpsed at the photo, looked at Owen, and then shut her eyes completely. It didn't stop as she'd then put both hands over her face and then pulled her hair back with both hands.

"Why don't you like to look at him?"

"He's a devil worshipper. That's it."

Mala's attitude had changed significantly when she had been asked about her husband, Jack.[500] She had smiled, flipped her hair, told of his coming into the restaurant, described him as "cute," said the two of them had exchanged phone numbers, and finished with "that's how we did it."

When describing Mala, the only term I could think of was coquettish. She had believed, I thought, that she had captured Jack with her stunning looks and irresistible charm.

By the time she had met Jack, Mala said, she had been in the U.S. illegally for years. Her quick response as to how she and Jack had married was telling: "He thought I was American [but] there's no reason I'm going to marry someone to get my status. That would just be plain silly. I married out of love."

Mala had then emphatically claimed her mother had never encouraged her to marry an American in order to obtain her status. Status, of course, was a well-known term in any immigrant community and that Mala had seen fit to first use that term had been telling. Additionally, we had been told from more than one source that Mala's attempting to marry to obtain legal status in America had been her primary goal, and she had been pushed to do so by her mother.[501]

After returning from a short recess, Mala had acknowledged that Wayne Kessinger had been involved with her initial and subsequent questioning, travel, transportation from Trinidad, and lodging in New Albany and that he had picked her up at the hotel prior to the depo. It had also been "Mister Wayne" who had encouraged her, during the most recent break in the deposition, to remain "calm."

---

[500] Pseudonym.

[501] When Mala had first been contacted, in Trinidad, she had recalled, two DEA Agents had interviewed her, on tape, about her relationship with Boney. We hadn't received a copy of that tape before the deposition and never have.

That had not been a surprise, since "Mister Wayne," of course, had also been the same man who had worked closely with Boney on the "connection": e.g., the "dirty gun" and "wrap(ping) a weapon" in the sweatshirt. Throughout Mala's deposition, "Mister Wayne" had been present and, no doubt in my mind, had been, at least in Mala's mind, her primary supporter.

Since the break, all of us had also noted that Mala's appearance had changed. Her hair had been pulled back, her demeanor and attitude had worsened, her answers had gotten more and more surly, she had consistently rolled her eyes, and she had been barely audible in many of her answers. Instead of running her fingers through her hair, she had then obsessed with her left earring, twirling and playing with it incessantly.

One of Mala Singh's behavioral responses to a question
from Kitty Liell during her July 5, 2005, deposition.

Body language, along with other behavioral actions of a person, can convey a wholly different answer than what a person is communicating, in spite of her/his words. Mala's non-verbal responses, including her posture, body movements, grooming gestures, yawning, facial expressions, covering of her face, and eye movement/contact/non-contact, had been practically shouting to us: "I don't want to be here! Stop asking your questions!"[502]

Those non-verbal responses had totally belied her verbal responses, which had equated to, "I'm not really concerned about anything."

One of her verbal answers had been that she had not been present when Boney had solicited her brother to help rob a bank in Indiana. Since her brother Seamus and sister-in-law Brittany had been adamant about that

---

[502] A caveat to that, however, is that one's interpretations should only be made in concert and in context with other known facts of a case.

solicitation and Mala's having been present during it, Mala's verbal response, in my assessment, had not comported with her other non-verbal actions: she clearly had been lying.

When the questions had begun to focus on Boney, Mala had admitted that he had an obsession with her feet, as she had also recalled that he had kissed her feet, had put whipped cream on her toes, and then had gotten off sexually. Her toes and feet had to be pretty and clean, though, since Boney hadn't liked any which had not been "clean and nice."

Mala had been given a pair of knee-high stockings to wear by the Shoe Bandit, but only after he kissed and sucked her toes. As for those stockings, Boney had gotten sexually aroused with them and the pantyhose by smelling them and having them rubbed on his legs.

During intercourse with Boney, he had often used a condom, although on one occasion, he had removed it without Mala's knowledge. That might have been the same time she had gotten a surprise gift from the Toe Romancer: sexual herpes.

> SHE HAD NEVER SEEN HIM *WITH A BASKETBALL, PLAY* BASKETBALL, *EXPRESS ANY INTEREST IN BASKETBALL.*

In spite of Boney's claim that he had met Dave at Community Park, playing basketball with 16–18 others present, Mala had claimed that during the three plus months she had been around him, she had never seen him *with* a basketball, *play* basketball, *express any interest in basketball*, or hang out at any park. In fact, she had never seen him with any kind of shoes that would have allowed him to play basketball, as she had only recalled him wearing his prized prison boots.

BACKBONE's girlfriend had no problem denying that she had been with him or had aided him in his efforts—with four different entities—to have secured money to pay his uncle on the loan payment due on the Cadillac. Everyone had known by now, of course, that Boney's alibis for his whereabouts at the time of the murders had been baldface lies, but they had been simply dismissed as unimportant.

Mala had then acknowledged, again, that her former boyfriend "loves the devil." While repeating her story that he had awakened her at midnight, lit a candle, and engaged in a ritual, Mala had yawned. Yes, the man who had two tattoos of the devil on his body; who had blasphemed God with the F word; a guy who had shown her a gun; in fact, a "crazy" and "sick" man, who according to her, would blow her brains out had been boring. So boring, in fact, that she was reduced to yawning when talking about him.

Mala had also admitted that, yes, after he had gotten his uncle's car in mid-August, he had asked her if she had known anyone who would sell him a gun. The woman, now with a much-thicker accent than before, said she hadn't helped her boyfriend find a gun.

Boney had another obsession, Mala had admitted, and then had re-confirmed that had been talking about his buddies from prison. He'd write to them and had often told her that he'd do "anything for them," as he also had "loved jail."

Kitty had asked Mala if Boney had ever threatened her brother, mother, uncle, or any other family member, to which she'd replied, "No, ma'am."

Had Mala been with Boney when the Camm family had been slaughtered? She had been in "his mother's house" when the murders had occurred, and she had been "sleeping." Yes, she'd said she had been sleeping between 7:30 p.m. and 8:00 p.m.

Mala had another memory issue, since she had told Gilbert and Kessinger that she had seen Dave on television, the morning after the murders, while sitting at the kitchen table with Boney and his mother. "That cop," she had claimed, had been in an orange jumpsuit. That had been incredibly problematic, of course, since two more days had elapsed before Dave had been arrested and had been given the distinctive orange jail clothing to wear. Even then, he hadn't been seen in orange by the public until the following day.

I Don't Remember

And then, referring to her interview the week before, Mala's response to Kitty had been startling when she'd been asked if Boney's mother's inquiry to Boney had been *if he had known the murdered family, not simply, "that cop."* Mala insisted that she hadn't been asked that question and further argued, "All I remember saying was that his mother asked him if he knew 'that cop.'"

Kitty had quickly corrected Mala, telling her it had been Kessinger who had suggested the cop comment and that she had agreed with him. Not so, Mala had insisted: "She asked her son if he knew 'that cop.' That's the best of my memory."

Mala had then further insisted that Mrs. Boney hadn't asked her son if he had known the murdered woman or her children, claiming all she remembered was whether Boney had known "that cop."

Kitty hadn't let that false claim rest: "It's your voice, Mala, and you are saying that he said, 'Yes, he knew the victims.' You said he knew the victims."

"No, he did not. This is what the mother asked the son, 'Do you know that cop?' He said, 'Yes.' And then the mother got upset and I got up and I went and took a shower."

Kitty had then drilled Mala on her comment to Gilbert and Kessinger that Boney's mother had asked if "he had anything to do with [the murders]."

"I don't remember saying that. All I knew was that she asked him if he knew that cop and he said, 'yes.'" In fact, she'd added, "I don't even know if any victims were mentioned."

I had to give it to Mala. Hiding behind the claim of "All I remember," and "I don't remember saying that" had been a favorite shield of many politicians and other liars and had worked for many years. Worked, that is, only if those being lied to had accepted those lies.

Nonetheless, there was no doubt in our minds that Mala had been schooled well. In exchange for linking Dave to Boney, we had concluded, she had gotten a get-out-of-jail pass. Had she been told, in explicit terms, what her quid pro quo would be? Even if she had figured it out on her own, the result had been the same: as long as she had kept with "that cop" story, she could return home to Trinidad.

In spite of insisting she hadn't lied as an adult, under Kitty's questioning, Mala had to eat some lies she had told over several interviews: e.g., yes, in fact, she had seen Boney in possession of a gun; and yes, she had been present when the Camm murders had been discussed; and yes, she had, in fact, seen scratches on Boney.

Mala had probably told the truth about Boney's not having a cell phone, but I only believed this because we had failed to establish any such phone though our other interviews and through subpoenas to numerous cell phone service providers. The importance of that, of course, was that Boney could have only called others on his mother's landline, at least when he was at home. Those records didn't reflect any contacts with anyone who could remotely have been considered a "buddy" on the day of or leading up to September 28. None of the numbers associated with Dave, of course, had ever appeared on those records.

Mala had insisted, though, that Boney had not bragged about committing armed robberies: "I don't know about any robberies." How about being present when Boney had solicited her brother, Seamus, to be the driver in an armed robbery in Indiana? "No, Ma'am." Had there been a discussion, with you present, Mala, when Darnell had said he had "a gun, a car, and a plan to commit a robbery in Indiana?"

"I would look at my brother and say, when did, uh, when did, what, this is new to me."

And, as far as someone getting "laid out," Boney "didn't really talk to [Mala] about any robberies." According to Mala, "He just talked to me about my feet."

And her comment about ammunition? Well, she "didn't remember" that comment, either. And the condominiums where they had driven? Uh, they could have been in Kentucky or they could have been in Indiana.

The next topic had been the DNA. When first approached by the DEA agents, Mala said she had been told, "If my DNA don't match, then they won't bother me anymore." That, in and of itself, had been amazing. Ignore the DNA for a moment: the woman who had been with Charles Boney, from just after the time he had been released from prison until the time of the murders, would have simply been dismissed by the "fresh eyes."

But the DNA *had* matched, of course, and now Mala's explanation of how her DNA had gotten on the middle of the BACKBONE sweatshirt had been further explained: Boney had performed oral sex on her, she said, and in the process, gotten her menstrual blood on the sweatshirt.

And no, Mala hadn't known how her blood had become mixed with Bradley's on the sweatshirt.[503] It had, however, been obvious that the stress had been mounting on Mala, and when she had claimed not to have any knowledge of how her DNA had been mixed with Kim's, she had exclaimed that she was an "innocent person."

Kitty had a quick rejoinder, telling Mala there had, indeed, been an innocent person in the room, and "that's Dave Camm."

Mala's response had been cold: "If he was innocent, he wouldn't be in that jumper suit," followed by, "He wouldn't be in [that] suit right now if he didn't have nothing to do with it."

Kitty, though, had a litany of other questions she had posed to Mala, many of which had been based on several photos she had shown her relating to the crime scene. Mala had denied ever seeing the family, ever touching any of the victims, ever being present at the residence or near the car and said no, none of her hair or fingerprints would have been found at or near the crime scene.

When shown photos of each of the victims, Mala's response had been predictable: "Oh, my God! What is she doing to me, God?"

"This is all about Mala?" Kitty had asked.

"This is all about me," a surprisingly honest Mala had answered. In fact, Mala had previously referred to herself as "Beauty," as in "Beauty and the Beast" with Boney having the other lead role. Clearly, Ms. Beauty hadn't liked the pressure.

Kitty had then addressed the aftermath of the murders, with Mala admitting that a week or so after she had left the Boney household, the Toe-Sucker had come to visit her, but no, absolutely not, she had told Kitty, Boney had never taken her on a visit to a graveyard in Indiana. In fact, Mala had insisted, "I don't even know where any graveyards are," and any relative who had claimed that such a trip had been taken had been lying.

---

[503] With Bradley, recall the ISP had placed the sweatshirt in the body bag with him, thus probably resulting in the transfer of his blood to the sweatshirt.

Even though Mala had told Gilbert and Kessinger that she had been deathly afraid that Boney, the devil-worshipper, who was also a "sick" and "crazy" man, could possibly "come and blow [her] brains out," he had never, Mala had contended, threatened her or her family.

And then, Mala had claimed, reminiscent of Boney's claim of his honesty, "There is no reason for me to lie. Everything that I've said [is] my word." I had mentally gagged.

How about taking a polygraph test, Kitty had asked, mockingly. While Mala had been agreeable, Steve Owen had immediately objected, claiming, "That's something that maybe we should talk about and there are documents that need to be signed . . ." With a wave of her hand, Kitty had dismissed the possibility, as she had known there was no way the "fresh eyes" would have allowed such to occur. They had her story, and there was no way they were going to jeopardize what they had.

Those "fresh eyes," caught in so many previous lies and misrepresentations, had once again been engaged, in my view, in helping a critical witness, if not an accomplice, craft her story while neglecting real evidence, all in the never-ending quest to keep Dave incarcerated and ultimately convicted.

In fact, both Mala and Boney had gotten great deals from the prosecutor: Boney wasn't facing the death penalty, and Mala wasn't going to be charged with a crime at all. In return, each had told the story Henderson had wanted. Each, in their own manner, had provided the desperate *connection* Henderson had needed, although he had no evidence of Dave's either hiring the psychopath or of any conspiracy whatsoever between the two.

For Henderson, however, he'd produce whatever narrative he needed to convict Dave, and if the second judge were as compliant as the first—who had allowed the prosecution to speculate, to create false motives, and to assassinate Dave's character—well, so much the better.

After the deposition, Kitty and I joined Dave, still in his jail uniform, as all of us were depressed, but we didn't want to show our feelings to one another. We spoke of our future interviews, depositions, strategy, forensic testing, and whatever else came to mind, all in an attempt to get past yet another proceeding where the cards had been stacked against Dave. No one, at least no one in the system in which we had been dealing, had given a damn about the truth. It had been all about winning at whatever costs, including making a despicable deal with Boney, a proud satanic disciple.

And Henderson's charge of a conspiracy between Dave and Boney to commit murder? That, according to Henderson, Dave had "committed a murder by hiring . . . Charles Boney . . . to kill?" It hadn't been based upon anything Boney had claimed, nor anything from Mala, nor any evidence from anywhere. That charge had simply been manufactured out of thin air.

Left unsaid in our meeting were the questions that would never die: would anyone ever truly listen to the truth? Would evidence finally trump lies? Would sanity ever return to the criminal justice system? Would Dave finally get a fair trial?

When, if ever, would Dave's hell on Earth and his persecution end? When, if ever, would Kim, Brad, and Jill finally get the justice they deserved?

*****

During the eight months I had been part of the defense team, I had seen and experienced some of the worst imaginable aspects of the criminal justice system, but what occurred in the subsequent months and years in Dave's case was even more disgraceful.

Part II will again reveal more shocking aspects of a true but incredibly egregious crime story which absolutely never should have occurred in the United States. Amazingly, however, by coincidence, chance, or as many of us know, Divine Intervention, another revelation materialized that significantly aided in Dave's defense.

Part II will be available in 2023.

Appendix #A
Initial Investigation

Over the years, more than a few people with law enforcement experience have spoken with me about the Camm case and how it was originally investigated by the ISP. Other than those who conducted the investigations or those who weren't knowledgeable of the details of the case, no one has described the ISP's overall efforts as thorough, complete, good, or even adequate. Instead, the descriptions of *"appalling,"* *"embarrassing,"* and *"lousy job"* were used, and those came from retired ISP officers.[504] Assessments by other investigators with knowledge gained, not from media reports, but from true insight into the handling of the investigation, have been just as scathing.

Of course, investigative strategies, methods, and approaches to cases differ, and, assuredly, interview techniques and questions vary among experienced and successful investigators. Indeed, what may work in one case on one day may be an abject failure on another the next day. As Chuck Grelecki, a close FBI colleague of mine often quipped, "Law enforcement is not an exact science."

Likewise, mistakes are made, and omissions do occur in practically every investigation; still, there are traits that most would agree every investigator should employ. The most obvious is to maintain an open mind and not to engage in a rush to judgment. While one's first intuitions and/or deductions may be accurate, it's crucial to let the evidence rather than one's possible bias or hubris chart the path towards a solution to the crime.

In that regard, evidence which doesn't fit with either the pre-conceived and/or desired solution shouldn't be denigrated and/or eliminated. It's not only poor practice, but it also may be in violation of the rules of discovery; for instance, if it is exculpatory in nature, law demands that such be provided to a defendant's counsel.

In larger investigations, especially those involving more than one agency or involving numerous investigators, it is imperative that communication among all investigators is frequent and thorough. While ignorance may be bliss, it can also be fatal.

---

[504] The identities of whom I promised not to divulge.

Documentation, of course, is also fundamental to efficient investigations. There is literally no excuse for an investigator, or anyone assigned a lead in any case, not to report and thoroughly document the results of their inquiries. Every length of chain is dependent upon every other link.

Investigations can become politicized, both with the large P and the small p. In the Camm case, both kinds of politicization occurred: a very political Stan Faith, facing a difficult re-election, had seized the investigation, albeit the ISP had allowed it to happen; and within the confines of the ISP, there had been no apparent freedom of thought or pushback as their quick conclusion Dave had been the culprit had been unchallenged.

All of those mandatory investigative aspects had failed, in whole or in part,[505] and with devastating results, as the ISP "investigation" essentially lasted less than 18 hours:

---

[505] There are, of course, additional aspects to most investigative protocols.

ISP Timeline On The Solution Of The Camm Case

Time	Event
Thursday, September 28	
7:35 p.m.-7:50 p.m. (approximately)	Kim, Brad, and Jill were murdered in the garage of the Camm residence in Georgetown, Indiana, while David Camm was at a church gym playing basketball with 10 others and two spectators present.
9:27 p.m.	David Camm arrived home to find his murdered family, attempted to revive his son Brad, and called the ISP Sellersburg Post.
9:42 p.m.	The first ISP units arrived at murder scene; within minutes Detective Clemons assumed and/or was designated as lead detective.
10:32 p.m.	Prosecutor Stan Faith arrived at the crime scene and assumed control; he made the decision to call bloodstain expert and crime scene re-constructionist Rod Englert to the scene. Rob Stites arrived two days later.
Late Evening	Lt. Biddle made the decision to have all the basketball players interviewed; someone rescinded the decision, and players weren't interviewed until two days later and not in person.
Friday, September 29	
1:05 a.m.	The search of the crime scene began with no evidence technician in charge of coordinating the photographing or collection of evidence and/or in charge of the overall supervision of the crime scene. A total of 19 different investigators from at least four different agencies collected evidence over nine days with no overall inventory compiled.
Near Dawn	The bodies of Kim, Brad, and Jill were transported to the Kentucky Medical Examiner's Office
Approximately 3:00 p.m.	Sarkisian called Clemons from the Medical Examiner's office. From the content of the call, regardless of whose recollection is accurate, Clemons concluded Dave had molested his daughter and, ergo, was the murderer.
Total Time: Less Than 18 Hours to the Solution of the Murders	Neighborhood and other investigation ceased; interviews of remaining basketball players became a formality; few leads, outside of those stemming from their conclusion Dave was the culprit, were pursued; and most importantly, there was no consideration that anyone else could have been responsible for the murders. **The investigation shifted from determining who murdered Kim, Brad, and Jill to building the case against David Camm, including constructing three motives for murder.**

From that singular deduction, the need to be aggressive and exhausting in a search for every lead and piece of evidence was negated: they had their man and it was David Camm. That dramatic shift was solely based upon the contents of a phone call concluding Dave had molested Jill without any evidence that he had engaged in such reprehensible conduct.

That rush to judgment infected everyone associated with the case, from the supervisor who ceased to care about finishing the neighborhood investigation, building a timeline, or personally interviewing basketball players, down to the uniformed officers who refused to personally engage Dave, even in eye contact.

Additionally, to think that the later opinion/conclusion of Stites, the purported blood expert, wasn't impacted when told Dave was the suspect and/or shooter, wasn't realistic, at least not in my mind.

Regardless, my review was designed first to assist Kitty and Stacy in facilitating the impeachment of investigators, especially for Clemons since he was the "funnel" who allegedly was responsible for the thoroughness and efficiency of the investigation. Indeed, Clemons would need to answer any number of questions in his forthcoming deposition as well as at trial.

Secondarily, of course, the list would assist me in interviewing witnesses who may have had some degree of knowledge, either knowingly or otherwise, of the crime and even, perhaps, help in the development of suspects.

Keep in mind, while reading this list, that it was compiled in early 2005, and numerous investigative and forensic measures and/or databases were not yet available and/or in their infancy at that time: e.g., "touch DNA," DNA phenotyping, facial recognition software, and biosensors in fingerprints. Also, home security devices such as video surveillance cameras linked to the internet while being captured on the cloud were still years in the future for most homeowners.

As such, here were *some* of my findings of the initial investigation, many of which were previously detailed and which I provided to Kitty and Stacy:

- The **NEIGHBORHOOD INVESTIGATION** was woefully incomplete:

  ◊ No FedEx, UPS, and/or U.S. Postal Service delivery persons were contacted to see if they witnessed any person, vehicle, or anything else on the day of or the days leading to the murders;

  ◊ In the wake of Dave's arrest, neighbors who hadn't been contacted were deemed no longer important and weren't interviewed;

  ◊ The drug dealer, recently released from prison and living behind the Ter Vree residence, wasn't interviewed, nor was his father;

◊ No attempt was made to identify or find an unidentified, never-before-seen man who was seen by neighbors walking in a nearby dry creek bed just days prior to the murders;

◊ No attempt was made to identify another man, in the same time period, who was seen on Alonzo Smith Road, inquiring about a house for sale when none were for sale; and

◊ There was no attempt to identify more specifically the Cadillac nor the owner or the occupants of that dark-colored vehicle spotted by Brandon Beaven on the afternoon of the murders.

- The **INITIAL INVESTIGATION** lacked the necessary substance and/or was severely compromised:

◊ No videos were checked, nor had any employee been interviewed from the golf course adjacent to the church parking lot to determine if

  – Dave could be seen in the lot between 6:59 p.m. and 9:22 p.m. or if

  – His truck left its original parking location;

◊ The church gym where the basketball players had congregated, which had been critical to the prosecution's case, hadn't been visited by the lead detective and/or prosecutor and/or investigators prior to the first trial; and

  – The ISP wasn't knowledgeable of the existence of the alarm system;

◊ There were no NCIC off-line searches conducted of vehicles or individuals stopped or whose identities and/or license plates had been checked in the vicinity of the Camm house in the days prior to or after the murders;

◊ A detailed timeline of David's movements, initially important to Lt. Biddle, wasn't constructed. One could have further

  – Aided in providing a better evaluation of Dave as a suspect;

  – There was no compact timeline or victimology constructed for Kim, the apparent primary focus of the violent attack, including interviews of all of her co-workers, church friends, and others to determine her movements and interactions in the days and weeks leading to her murder;

◊ Burglary, robbery and/or a sexual assault against Kim were all summarily dismissed, even though there was no sound rationale for dismissing those possibilities;

◊ Kim's expensive earrings weren't in the house, indicating they had been stolen;

  – Yet no attempts were made to locate those, either through pawn shops or jewelry stores;

  – Nor had there been any efforts to determine if anything else, of financial or intrinsic value, had been stolen; because

    •• Criminals of all persuasions often take souvenirs from their victims;

◊ The assertion by Clemons that Dave left the gym around 9:00 p.m., was off by an incredible 22 minutes;

  – Even though none of those interviewed had claimed such, but more importantly,

  – There had been no apparent communication between the "funnel," Clemons, and the other investigators which would have refuted that time;

◊ The 10 other basketball players and two spectators were treated not as critical witnesses, but as afterthoughts and only after Dave was fingered as the sole suspect;

  – Those two spectators were unknown to the ISP and not interviewed prior to Dave's arrest, nor were

  – Three others in the gym building who had attended an NA meeting;

◊ The assertion by Clemons of the three "interpreted gunshots" wasn't based upon any evidence, but it did

  – Fit nicely with his erroneous initial timeline of the murders;

◊ Several conclusions by Stites, the original blood expert and crime scene reconstructionist, critical to the probable cause affidavit, were in fact wildly inaccurate as there had been

  – Nothing added to the blood flow;

  – No evidence of any "manipulation" of the crime scene; and

  – No cleaning solution thrown off the back deck; plus

  – The overhead garage door hadn't any blood on it;

◊ Evidence found at the crime scene, if it couldn't be readily explained, was summarily dismissed as unimportant, "manipulated," or "staged," such as the shoes on top of the Bronco;

◊ The original blood expert Stites had been deemed by evidence technician Niemeyer to be a "son-of-a-bitch [who] doesn't know what he's doing," and he

  – Had implored Sarkisian to "get hold of Faith and stop [him] ," but

  – Stites was given free reign of the crime scene, possibly destroying evidence through needless spraying of luminol and/ or the cross-contamination of evidence.

• The **CRIME SCENE INVESTIGATION & ANALYSIS** was faulty:

◊ A multitude of evidence found at the crime scene was never examined, tested and/or attempted to be matched to any database,

  – Including unknown fingerprints and a palmprint found on the passenger side door post of the Bronco, but

  – It was impossible to exclude the prints of the three victims because a full set of fingerprints and palmprints weren't obtained post-mortem;

◊ The crime scene was repeatedly denigrated and contaminated by individuals who had no evidence collection experience (several of the 19 who seized evidence) and/or who weren't involved in processing a crime scene but rather spectators and/or others;

◊ Evidence had been maintained at three separate agencies:

  – The ISP,

  – The Floyd County Prosecutor's evidence locker, and

  – The New Albany Police Department,

  – Without any one agency in control of an overall inventory;

◊ Perhaps the worst commission of all was the direction of the case, as well as the supervision of the crime scene and the collection of evidence had been summarily seized by Prosecutor Faith and his investigators, causing

  – Crime scene photographs to be comingled, their photographers and dates often unknown, causing

- Those who engaged in photographing not to know if they had, in fact, captured those pictures;

◊ Critical photographs didn't include measurements and/or locations, including

- The half-bloody shoeprint;

- Other photographs weren't taken, including

•• The apparent toenail polish scraping on the garage floor;

◊ The BACKBONE sweatshirt was co-mingled with Brad in a body bag, thus causing cross-contamination;

◊ The original crime scene video was taped in the dark and didn't contain any footage of Jill; and

◊ Evidence such as the condoms and shower curtain were lost.

- The **HOUSE SEARCH** was an afterthought and had occurred after it had been contaminated repeatedly by many officers;

◊ Photographs were taken and a videotape made well after a search of the house had begun;

◊ The house was never even considered to be a part of the crime scene except in relation to the allegation that Jill had been molested; and

◊ Marital aids and insurance policies had been seized to buttress the false motives of molestation and to murder for an insurance payout.

- Any attempts at the **IDENTIFICATION** of other **SUSPECTS** weren't pursued:

◊ Records of recent parolees and those on probation, especially sex offenders, weren't checked, nor, of course, were any interviewed;

◊ No attempts were made to identify and/or interview known burglars or sex offenders;

◊ No known efforts were made to determine the identity of BACKBONE, including checking with the Indiana and/or Kentucky Department of Corrections for that moniker; and

◊ The lead detective had apparently been totally unaware of the unknown DNA which had been discovered on the BACKBONE sweatshirt.

Author Biography Gary M. Dunn

Their Bloody Lies & Persecution of DAVID CAMM

Gary M. Dunn is a retired 27-year FBI Agent who served in Miami, Chicago, Gary, Indiana, and Southern Indiana. Dunner, as he was known throughout the FBI, was an undercover Agent who directed the year-long efforts of a top echelon informant in securing hundreds of hours of incriminating taped and video-recorded evidence resulting in the convictions of dozens of public officials in Chicago and New York City; was an undercover Agent who twice was solicited to murder informants; ran a two-year undercover car theft investigation wherein almost three dozen people were convicted; was the case Agent on a Chicago arson case which was upheld 9-0 by the U.S. Supreme Court; who worked ceaselessly with the Indiana State Police in finding and convicting five Southern Indiana persons who kidnapped, repeatedly sexually tortured, and then brutally murdered a mentally-challenged woman; and who was awarded numerous citations and honors throughout his career for his successful investigations of a broad range of crimes. He is a graduate of Indiana University with a B.S. in Education, holds an MPA from DePaul University, and is also a former Naval Officer, and Associate Professor of Criminal Justice, who continues to guest lecture at Indiana University.

Front Cover Photographs

Clockwise from upper right: the T-shirt worn by David Camm on the night of the murders; enlargement of the lower left front of the T-shirt containing the eight supposed "high velocity blood mist" stains; and the jail booking photo of 36-year old David Camm on October 1, 2000.

Ingram Content Group UK Ltd.
Milton Keynes UK
UKHW041021040523
421223UK00004B/160